HINDU SPIRITUALITY
Postclassical and Modern

D1450802

World Spirituality

An Encyclopedic History of the Religious Quest

1. Asian Archaic Spirituality
2. European Archaic Spirituality
3. African and Oceanic Spirituality
4. South and Meso-American Native Spirituality
5. North American Indian Spirituality
6. Hindu Spirituality: Vedas through Vedanta
7. Hindu Spirituality: Postclassical and Modern
8. Buddhist Spirituality: Indian, Southeast Asian, Tibetan, and Early Chinese
9. Buddhist Spirituality: Ch'an, East Asian, and Contemporary
10. Taoist Spirituality
11. Confucian Spirituality
12. Ancient Near Eastern Spirituality: Zoroastrian, Sumerian, Assyro-Babylonian, Hittite
13. Jewish Spirituality: From the Bible to the Middle Ages
14. Jewish Spirituality: From the Sixteenth-Century Revival to the Present
15. Classical Mediterranean Spirituality: Egyptian, Greek, Roman
16. Christian Spirituality: Origins to the Twelfth Century
17. Christian Spirituality: High Middle Ages and Reformation
18. Christian Spirituality: Post-Reformation and Modern
19. Islamic Spirituality: Foundations
20. Islamic Spirituality: Manifestations
21. Modern Esoteric Spirituality
22. Spirituality and the Secular Quest
23. Encounter of Spiritualities: Past to Present
24. Encounter of Spiritualities: Present to Future
25. Dictionary of World Spirituality

Board of Editors and Advisors

EWERT COUSINS, *General Editor*

A. H. ARMSTRONG
Dalhousie University

R. BALASUBRAMANIAN
University of Madras

BETTINA BÄUMER
Alice Boner Foundation, Varanasi

THOMAS BERRY
Fordham University

JOSEPH EPES BROWN
University of Montana

JOHN CARMAN
Harvard University

JOSEPH DAN
Hebrew University

LOUIS DUPRÉ
Yale University

MIRCEA ELIADE
University of Chicago

ANTOINE FAIVRE
Sorbonne

LANGDON GILKEY
University of Chicago

GARY GOSSEN
State University of New York, Albany

ARTHUR GREEN
Brandeis University

JAMES HEISIG
Nanzan Institute for Religion and Culture, Nagoya

THORKILD JACOBSEN
Harvard University

STEVEN T. KATZ
Cornell University

JEAN LECLERCQ
Gregorian University

MIGUEL LEÓN-PORTILLA
National University of Mexico

CHARLES LONG
Syracuse University

BERNARD MCGINN
University of Chicago

FARHANG MEHR
Boston University

JOHN MEYENDORFF
Fordham University

BITHIKA MUKERJI
Banaras Hindu University

SEYYED HOSSEIN NASR
George Washington University

JACOB NEEDLEMAN
San Francisco State University

HEIKO OBERMAN
University of Tübingen

ALBERT OUTLER
Southern Methodist University

RAIMUNDO PANIKKAR
University of California, Santa Barbara

JAROSLAV PELIKAN
Yale University

JILL RAITT
University of Missouri

DON SALIERS
Emory University

ANNEMARIE SCHIMMEL
Harvard University

KARAN SINGH
New Delhi

VIBHUTI NARAIN SINGH
Varanasi

KRISHNA SIVARAMAN
Concordia University

HUSTON SMITH
Syracuse University

DOUGLAS STEERE
Haverford College

YOSHINORI TAKEUCHI
University of Kyoto

WEI-MING TU
Harvard University

JAN VAN BRAGT
Nanzan Institute for Religion and Culture, Nagoya

FRANK WHALING
University of Edinburgh

Volume 7 of

World Spirituality:
An Encyclopedic History
of the Religious Quest

HINDU SPIRITUALITY

Postclassical and Modern

Edited by
K. R. Sundararajan
and
Bithika Mukerji

A Crossroad Herder Book
The Crossroad Publishing Company
New York

1997
The Crossroad Publishing Company
370 Lexington Avenue, New York, NY 10017

World Spirituality, Volume 7
Hindu Spirituality (v. 2): Postclassical and Modern
K. R. Sundararajan and Bithika Mukerji, editors

Copyright © 1997 by The Crossroad Publishing Company

All rights reserved. No part of this book may be reproduced, stored in a retrieval system, or transmitted, in any form or by any means, electronic, mechanical, photocopying, recording, or otherwise, without the written permission of The Crossroad Publishing Company.

The Trans Indic font used to print portions of this work is available from Linguist's Software, Inc., PO Box 580, Edmonds, WA 98020-0580, tel. (206) 775-1130.

Printed in the United States of America

Library of Congress Cataloging-in-Publication Data

Hindu spirituality.

(World spirituality ; v. 6)
Bibliography: p.
Includes index.
1. Hinduism—Doctrines. 2. Spiritual life (Hinduism).
I. Sivaraman, Krishna. II. Series.
BL1212.72.H55 1988 294.5 88-3714
ISBN 0-8245-0755-X (v. 1)
ISBN 0-8245-0756-8 (v. 2)

Krishna Sivaraman

IT IS MOST APPROPRIATE that this volume be dedicated to the memory of Professor Krishna Sivaraman, who died on October 30, 1991. He was the editor of *Hindu Spirituality I: Vedas Through Vedanta*, which appeared in 1989. Professor Sivaraman had also planned the present volume and had been working extensively on it before he became seriously ill the year before his death. Even during his sickness he was deeply dedicated to the project and looked forward to its completion.

Krishna Sivaraman was eminently qualified to be the editor of these two volumes since he embodied in his own life the person and richness and diversity of the Hindu tradition. Born in southern India, he was formed in the Saivite tradition and the cultural heritage of Tamil Nadu. After studying at Annamalai University and the University of Madras, he moved to Varanasi in northern India, where he studied and taught at Banaras Hindu University, receiving a Ph.D. with a dissertation on Saiva Siddhanta. After some twenty-five years at Banaras Hindu University, he moved to Canada, where he taught for almost two decades at McMaster University. Having spent some time previously studying and teaching in the United States, he became increasingly familiar with the ethos of the West. It was a testimony to his academic achievement that, toward the end of his career, he was granted the first chair of Hindu Studies in Canada, at Concordia University in Montreal.

He had a rare gift for guiding his students and colleagues into the very heart of philosophical and spiritual issues. His ability at interreligious dialogue was so deep and sophisticated that he could help members of another religion see for the first time new depths of their own tradition. All this he accomplished with an authentic warmth and charm conveyed by his friendly smile and his joy in life, which he shared abundantly through his capacity for relating to others on a very personal level. He was himself the embodiment of the spiritual values he taught.

I express the gratitude of Crossroad Publishing Company for the contribution of Krishna Sivaraman and of his collaborators: Bithika Mukerji, Bettina Bäumer, R. Balasubramanian, and K. R. Sundararajan.

Ewert Cousins
General Editor

Contents

Part Four: Contemporary Hindu Spirituality

Part Five: Cultural Expressions of Hindu Spirituality

Part Six:
Hindu Spirituality in Dialogue

Preface to the Series

THE PRESENT VOLUME is part of a series entitled World Spirituality: An Encyclopedic History of the Religious Quest, which seeks to present the spiritual wisdom of the human race in its historical unfolding. Although each of the volumes can be read on its own terms, taken together they provide a comprehensive picture of the spiritual strivings of the human community as a whole—from prehistoric times, through the great religions, to the meeting of traditions at the present.

Drawing upon the highest level of scholarship around the world, the series gathers together and presents in a single collection the richness of the spiritual heritage of the human race. It is designed to reflect the autonomy of each tradition in its historical development, but at the same time to present the entire story of the human spiritual quest. The first five volumes deal with the spiritualities of archaic peoples in Asia, Europe, Africa, Oceania, and North and South America. Most of these have ceased to exist as living traditions, although some perdure among tribal peoples throughout the world. However, the archaic level of spirituality survives within the later traditions as a foundational stratum, preserved in ritual and myth. Individual volumes or combinations of volumes are devoted to the major traditions: Hindu, Buddhist, Taoist, Confucian, Jewish, Christian, and Islamic. Included within the series are the Jain, Sikh, and Zoroastrian traditions. In order to complete the story, the series includes traditions that have not survived but have exercised important influence on living traditions—such as Egyptian, Sumerian, classical Greek and Roman. A volume is devoted to modern esoteric movements and another to modern secular movements.

Having presented the history of the various traditions, the series devotes two volumes to the meeting of spiritualities. The first surveys the meeting of spiritualities from the past to the present, exploring common themes

---

A longer version of this preface may be found in Christian Spirituality: Origins to the Twelfth Century, *the first published volume in the series.*

that can provide the basis for a positive encounter, for example, symbols, rituals, techniques. The second deals with the meeting of spiritualities in the present and future. Finally, the series closes with a dictionary of world spirituality.

Each volume is edited by a specialist or a team of specialists who have gathered a number of contributors to write articles in their fields of specialization. As in this volume, the articles are not brief entries but substantial studies of an area of spirituality within a given tradition. An effort has been made to choose editors and contributors who have a cultural and religious grounding within the tradition studied and at the same time possess the scholarly objectivity to present the material to a larger forum of readers. For several years some five hundred scholars around the world have been working on the project.

In the planning of the project, no attempt was made to arrive at a common definition of spirituality that would be accepted by all in precisely the same way. The term "spirituality," or an equivalent, is not found in a number of the traditions. Yet from the outset, there was a consensus among the editors about what was in general intended by the term. It was left to each tradition to clarify its own understanding of this meaning and to the editors to express this in the introduction to their volumes. As a working hypothesis, the following description was used to launch the project:

> The series focuses on that inner dimension of the person called by certain traditions "the spirit." This spiritual core is the deepest center of the person. It is here that the person is open to the transcendent dimension; it is here that the person experiences ultimate reality. The series explores the discovery of this core, the dynamics of its development, and its journey to the ultimate goal. It deals with prayer, spiritual direction, the various maps of the spiritual journey, and the methods of advancement in the spiritual ascent.

By presenting the ancient spiritual wisdom in an academic perspective, the series can fulfill a number of needs. It can provide readers with a spiritual inventory of the richness of their own traditions, informing them at the same time of the richness of other traditions. It can give structure and order, meaning and direction to the vast amount of information with which we are often overwhelmed in the computer age. By drawing the material into the focus of world spirituality, it can provide a perspective for understanding one's place in the larger process. For it may well be that the meeting of spiritual paths—the assimilation not only of one's own spiritual heritage but of that of the human community as a whole—is the distinctive spiritual journey of our time.

EWERT COUSINS

Introduction

THIS VOLUME FOCUSES on the postclassical period of the Hindu tradition and explores its spiritual dimensions. The topics included here are grouped under the following six headings: The Regional Spiritualities; The Spirituality of the Purāṇas, Āgamas, and Tantra; The Spirituality of Modern Hinduism; Contemporary Hindu Spirituality; Cultural Expressions of Hindu Spirituality; and Hindu Spirituality in Dialogue. Like the first volume, the second volume also draws on the expertise of scholars of the Hindu tradition in India and abroad to explore and highlight the spirituality of the Hindu tradition. The editor has attempted to retain the pluralistic heritage of the Hindu tradition both in terms of the contents of the volume and in terms of the individual style of the authors whose articles are included in the volume. In most cases the editor has let the contributors speak directly to the reader with minimal editorial intervention. The variety of ways in which the writers have sought to communicate in the volume is itself illustrative of the basic tenet of Hindu spirituality, which accommodates plurality and diversity and accepts them as valid ways of describing Reality.

Most of the articles included in this volume were gathered several years ago by Krishna Sivaraman, who had also begun the process of editing the second volume after the first volume of *Hindu Spirituality* was published in 1989. He soon fell ill, however, and after his death in 1991 I was entrusted with the task of completing the work that Sivaraman had begun. Though some articles have been added to the volume at my initiative, by and large the selections included reflect the preference and choice of its first editor. It may appear that Part One is somewhat oriented toward the spirituality of the Tamil area. There are four articles that deal with some aspects of the spirituality of the Tamils. Since this volume is being dedicated to Sivaraman, who came from the Tamil region, I consider this an appropriate way of paying tribute to Professor Sivaraman, who put forth a great deal of effort in planning and giving shape to these two volumes of *Hindu Spirituality.*

The volume includes two articles of V. A. Devasenapathi, contributed especially at the request of Professor Sivaraman. It is my sincere regret that I could not get the book ready for publication earlier. Professor Devasenapathi died in March 1995 in Madras, India. He was eagerly looking forward to the publication of the second volume of *Hindu Spirituality.* Professor Devasenapathi, as a scholar and as a person, was influential in the life of Krishna Sivaraman and was my mentor at the University of Madras since the days I joined the Department of Philosophy as a research student. I believe that the articles included in the volume are the last major ones that Professor Devasenapathi wrote before his death. I feel honored to include these articles of Professor Devasenapathi, and by doing so, to pay tribute to one of the outstanding scholars of Saiva Siddhanta and an exemplary person whose life had truly reflected the best of the Hindu tradition.

The Nature of Hindu Spirituality

In his introduction to the first volume, Sivaraman describes the spiritual journey as a process of "turning around," "turning from what serves one's temporal ends toward a growing insight into reality and a resulting fullness of life variously called life eternal or life divine or more simply life of the spirit." This turning around in the Indian context is achieved through what Sivaraman describes as "worldlessness." Worldlessness is not "life and world negation" but a disposition "to live in the world singly or collectively, not for its own sake, not as a goal in itself worthy of pursuit as a sufficient 'human end,' but as a means or medium to life 'in God,' as a condition of life in the spirit." According to Sivaraman, the traditional Hindu notion of *adhyatma,* meaning literally "pertaining to the *atman,*" plays almost the same pervasive role that the category of "spiritual" does in the West. "*Adhyatma* functions itself as a symbol pointing beyond itself, opening levels of reality which remain undisclosed without a corresponding opening of levels of the human mind beyond the discursive and sense bound." The dynamics of Hindu spirituality includes *brahman,* representing the highest state of existence, universal, transcendent, unconditional, the ultimate source of all existence, and *samsara,* the conditioned state of existence governed by the laws of *karma,* and the *summum bonum.* The ultimate goal of life is liberation or "freedom of the spirit." This ultimate goal in the light of the notion of four ends of human life (*purusartha*) in the Hindu tradition is a journey where "every point on the journey is also an arrival point." "Seeking and finding are a dialectical continuum involving, in existential terms, an inner transformation of life." Thus, Sivaraman points out, spirituality as an outlook is a "matter of winning an orientation or a sense of perspective and wholeness or completeness which the ideal of liberation implies. Living in the presence of the ideal with such a perspective enables one to look in retrospect at 'life in the world' and to see it as continuous with its transformation. This is spirituality and spiritual life." The present volume then explores the various ways of "turning around" in the period that is appropriately described by Sivaraman as the postclassical period.

Sivaraman points out that the division of time into the classical and postclassical periods is more chronological than strictly historical. "What is called later Hinduism stretches back to dim antiquity; some aspects of its culture and cultus are clearly traced even to pre-Vedic Harappa culture." Many of the postclassical expressions of Hindu spirituality, such as the Purāṇas, "are related by a straight line to Brahmanical Hinduism." Even the Tantras, according to the tradition, derive from Vedic texts that are believed to have been lost. For Sivaraman, postclassical Hinduism is deeply rooted in the Vedic tradition. He points out that the "Veda" in the singular "comprises not merely the four Vedas structured as hymns, rites, and doctrines, but all words that speak of 'God,' all utterances that are self-revealed, and, therefore, partaking of the 'word' (*Vāk*)." Hence, the term Hinduism refers to a tradition that marks the Vedas as the significant point of beginning. According to Sivaraman, "It is indeed used to mean both the archaic-classical Hinduism of the Veda and Vedanta and its neoclassical and postclassical transformation inclusive of what has come to be called Renascent Hinduism." It is this "Vedic connection" that provides a sense of unity to the various forms of spiritual expressions that we find in the postclassical period of Hinduism.

Contents of the Volume

Exploring the spiritual core is indeed discovering those areas that open us to the transcendent dimension. Here writers have sought to explicate the spiritual dimensions of a rich area of beliefs and practices, such as the spirituality of ecstatic devotion, the cult of the temple and other popular expressions of piety and devotion, the spiritual dimensions of the purāṇas, āgamas, and Tantra, all coming under the category of postclassical Hinduism. In the postclassical period, the volume begins with "The Regional Spiritualities." It includes articles on spiritual ways in the Kashmir Śaiva tradition, some of the saints of the Maharashtra region, the spirituality of Bengal Vaiṣṇavism, the devotional poetry of Sūrdāsa and Tulasidāsa, the spiritual contributions of two Tamil saints, Māṇikkavācakar and

Nammāḻvār, and of a Tamil classic, *Tirukkuṟaḷ*. The section also includes articles on two women saints, one from the Tamil region, Āṇḍāl, and the other, from the Hindi-speaking region, Mīrā.

In chapter 1, "The Four Spiritual Ways (upāya) in the Kashmir Śaiva Tradition," Bettina Bäumer explores the spirituality of the Kashmir Śaivism traditionally called *Trika* (the trinitarian school). According to Bäumer, in terms of metaphysical formulations, the nondualism of Kashmir Śaivism is different from the nondualism of Advaita Vedānta. "Śaṅkara's Brahman is static and without any internal or external relation, whereas the Unsurpassable (*anuttara*), supreme Lord (*Paramaśiva*) of *Trika* contains everything within." Here, though the reality of manifestations is not denied, there is also an affirmation of a fundamental duality. Unlike Advaita Vedānta, ignorance (*avidya*), which causes suffering and hinders liberation, is not the outcome of illusion or false knowledge, but rather of forgetfulness or incomplete knowledge. Liberating knowledge is a recognition of the forgotten Reality underlying all things and experiences. This knowledge is gained as one moves from the state of waking (*jagrat*), which is characterized by subject–object dichotomy, to the state of dream consciousness (*svapna*), which is the state of unity-in-diversity consciousness; then to the state of deep sleep (*suṣupti*) in which all differentiated consciousness is overcome, and finally to the "fourth state," which is the state of highest mystical consciousness. These four states are called *anu, sakti, sambhava,* and *anupaya,* respectively. The state of *anupaya* is described as one of perfect freedom, which is "natural" and "inborn," and Abhinavagupta, one of the chief exponents of Kashmir Śaivism, describes it in the following manner: "There is no need here of spiritual progress or contemplation, neither of discourses nor discussion, neither of meditation nor of concentration, nor the effort and practice of prayer. Listen: neither reject nor accept (anything), share joyfully in everything, being as you are."

In chapter 2, "The Spiritual Contribution of Maharashtra Saints," S. N. Bhavasar focuses on the life of the following saints: Jnāneśvara, Tukārāma, Ekanātha, and Rāmadāsa. The spiritual contributions of these saints are many. The saints had appeared on the scene when *dharma* had become "weakened" in the current age (*yuga*) of *kali,* and therefore, they had often been considered divine incarnations (*avatāras*) in popular piety, with the task of reestablishing and reenergizing *dharma.* These saints propagated the spiritual path of devotion (*bhakti*) to transform an individual's self-centered life into what Bhavasar describes as the "Life Divine." Instead of the scholastic language of Sanskrit, they spoke and wrote in the common language of the people, using familiar meters, images, and symbols. Thus, all the knowledge confined to Sanskrit was made open to the common people, though most of these saints had a good grounding in Sanskrit. These saints, therefore, without losing respect for the divine language, Sanskrit, with modesty state that they have simply made explicit what was implicit in Sanskrit. They revived the true Vedic tradition by rejecting some of its "degenerated" forms of ritualism and dogmatism. "In short," Bhavasar says, "the Life Divine in terms of body, speech, and mind is the spiritual contribution of Maharashtra saints."

In the chapter on Bengal Vaiṣṇavism, S. C. Chakravarti situates this religious movement in the context of the classical tradition of devotion (*bhakti*) of Rāmānuja, Madhva, and Nimbārka, and points out that the distinctive feature of the Vallabha devotion (Bengal Vaiṣṇavism) is its focus on love and service to Rādha-Kṛṣṇa. For Bengal Vaiṣṇavism, *Bhāgavata Purāṇa* is the crucial text, considered as a commentary by Vyāsa on the *Brahmasūtra* of Badarāyaṇa. The love of *gopis* for Kṛṣṇa, particularly the love of Rādha, is the very spiritual core of this tradition. Rādha is considered as *gopi par excellence* in whom the bliss of love reaches its highest ecstatic state. According to Chakravarti, Bengal Vaiṣṇavism transforms *bhakti* (devotion to God) to *prema* (love of God). The hearing and the reciting of Vaiṣṇava scriptures and the continued repetition of divine names (*japa*) are techniques that create and sustain this supreme form of *bhakti, prema bhakti.* In transforming *bhakti* into *prema,* Bengal Vaiṣṇavism gave a new orientation to the understanding of the relation between God and humanity. Caitanya, by his living example, delineated the path of love, which in itself becomes the fulfillment of its goal. In response to the question, What is the most important means of achieving this goal? he stated: "Recite the name of Hari, repeat the name of Hari, say the name of Hari constantly. In this dark age of Kali, there is no other way, none other, nothing more needs to be done."

Nagendra's contribution on the devotional poetry of Sūrdāsa and Tulasidāsa explores the spiritual dimensions of Hindi poetry. Nagendra points out that the impetus for the *bhakti* movement in India is indigenous. "Besides a number of devotional hymns in the *Ṛgveda,* there is a sizable volume of material available in the *Gītā,* in the *Śāntiparva* of *Mahābhārata* as well as in some of the earlier *Purāṇas.*" Sūrdāsa was one of the greatest poets of the "Kṛṣṇa cult" during the Mogul times, at the time of Akbar and Jahangir. Sūrdāsa's poems contained in his *Sūr-sāgar* deal with the "playful" episodes of Kṛṣṇa, and the Lord's person. According to Nagendra, Sūrdāsa was primarily a poet of love, and in his poems one finds three important forms or models of love, namely, that of parent for child, that of friend for friend, and that of bride for bridegroom, or conjugal love. Though Sūrdāsa was a male, he easily assumed the role of Yaśodha, the mother of Kṛṣṇa, and was able to experience fully and give expression to the love of Yaśodha for her child Kṛṣṇa. The playful episodes of Kṛṣṇa continue in Sūrdāsa's expression of *sākhya-bhakti*, where Kṛṣṇa becomes the devotees' friend. However, it is in the delineation of the conjugal form of devotion that the genius of Sūrdāsa shines forth. Nagendra points out that Sūrdāsa gives expression to *kānta-bhāva*, or the erotic form of divine love, through the medium of the love of Rādha and Kṛṣṇa, which he describes in all its varieties and minute details. Here he highlights *virāha*, pangs of separation that Rādha experiences when she is separated from Kṛṣṇa. While this is the case with Sūrdāsa, the spiritual dimensions of Tulasidāsa are somewhat different. Nagendra points out that Tulasidāsa was not just a lyricist but also one who excelled in epic and narrative poetry. In his *Rāmacaritramānas*, Rāma is not only a hero of the great epic *Rāmāyaṇa*, but an object of devotional sentiment. "From the invocation to the conclusion, the poet seeks the grace of Rāma and announces over and over again that the final object of his poetic performance is the attainment of *bhakti*—complete dedication to Rāma. The narrative ends with an elaborate discourse on the supremacy of the devotional sentiment." In Tulasidāsa, *kānta bhakti*, erotic love, which has characterized many of the poems of Sūrdāsa, is absent. The poet observes perfect decorum in describing the conjugal love between Rāma and his consort Sītā." Nagendra concludes that although there are descriptions of parental love in *Gītāvali*, Tulasidāsa prefers single-mindedly the attitude of servility to the Lord. "Actually, Tulasidāsa is so obsessed with the greatness and glory of the Lord that he cannot even unconsciously assume the role of a parent toward him."

In chapter 5, "Exemplars in the Life of Grace: Māṇikkavācakar and Nammāḻvār," V. A. Devasenapathi focuses on the spiritual dimensions of two great saints from the Tamil region, Māṇikkavācakar, belonging to the Śaiva tradition, and Nammāḻvār, of the Vaiṣṇava tradition. Devasenapathi believes that mystics, whatever tradition they come from, belong to one spiritual community. "Though the denominational name of God as Śiva or Nārāyaṇa may be dear to the devotee, the devotee's reference is to the same overall, overarching Divine Principle that out of compassion and grace chooses to reveal Itself in the form and mode in which the devotee longs to see It." It is in the light of this personal conviction that Devasenapathi analyzes the lives of Māṇikkavācakar and Nammāḻvār and shows how these two have indeed become the exemplars in the life of divine grace, model devotees for others to emulate. They could become such exemplars since they succeeded in "emptying" themselves of their personal ego and letting their being be filled with divine energy and grace. Now the focus is not "egocentric" but "theocentric"—God-centeredness. "Possessing the Lord, the soul has now an inexhaustible wealth, immune to any loss. In this realized state, the soul devotes itself to the worship of the Lord in thought, word, and deed. The redeemed soul glorifies the Lord and serves His creatures."

In "The Personal and Social Dimensions of *Tirukkuṟaḷ* Spirituality," S. Gopalan discusses the contents of a famous Tamil ethical treatise, *Tirukkuṟaḷ,* where the life of goodness is rooted in a profoundly spiritual concept of *aram,* corresponding to *dharma* in the Sanskrit tradition. Gopalan points out that according to *Tirukkuṟaḷ*, *aram* is the principle of transformation that spiritualizes one's personal and social lives. Thus, "the personal is no longer 'individual' and the social is nothing less than a real involvement in the cares and concerns of others without a trace of the egotistic motive." *Tirukkuṟaḷ* acknowledges *vītu* corresponding to *mokṣa* as the ultimate aim of human life. It is achieved not by renouncing *aram* (*dharma*) but by observing *aram* in its most comprehensive sense. According to Gopalan, the stages of householder (*illaṟam*) and renouncer (*turavaṟam*) for Tiruvaḷḷuvar connote not a change of status as in Brahmanical Hinduism, when the person "leaves" one stage of life and moves on to another, but an extension of caring, concern, and love (*anpu*). "In general, *illaṟam* stands for the duties of the individual as a member of a family and *turavaṟam* connotes the responsibilities of a human being as a member of humanity. Tiruvaḷḷuvar's view is that the spiritual ideal can be realized only by the individual who undergoes moral growth, by progressively developing concern for others and ultimately becoming sensitive to the whole of creation."

In the chapter entitled "The Spiritual Quest of Āṇḍāl," Saroja Sundararajan focuses on an analysis of *Tiruppāvai,* considered to be one of the most important devotional compositions by Āṇḍāl, a woman saint highly respected in the Tamil region. Āṇḍāl is the only woman included in the list of the twelve Āḻvārs, who are considered to be model devotees of Viṣṇu. According to Sundararajan, the exploration of spiritual experiences of women saints, such as Āṇḍāl, could "provide insights into new forms in which we can think of the divine being and [its] nature." Sundararajan feels that the theism of *Tiruppāvai* is much closer to what Charles Hartshorne calls neoclassical theism, where one includes contingency, becoming, and variability in divine nature, without, however, diminishing the metaphysical perfections of the divine, such as constancy and necessity. On these lines, Sundararajan reads the theology of *Tiruppāvai* and understands its spirituality. "The basic or underlying theme of *Tiruppāvai,*" according to Sundararajan, "is that the Lord must be thought of as the most adequate fulfillment of every power and faculty in us. . . . If we think of God as one, we should also think of this single or simple essence making itself available to each one in her/his own unique way." "If He is the Infinite knower, He is also the Infinitely knowable—knowable by every form of awareness and sentience." But this does not in the least lessen the distance between God and every other being; "He continues to surpass everything—only He is to be thought of as the self-surpassing surpasser of all."

Braj Sinha, in his essay entitled "Mīrābāī: The Rebel Saint," explicates the spirituality of one of the great saint-poetesses of northern India. She was a princess of Mewār, modern Udaipur, in the state of Rajasthan. Mīrā's early life was beset with several calamities of a personal nature, including losing her husband, father, and father-in-law. Infused with deep spiritual yearnings even during her early childhood, Mīrā had come to dedicate herself to Lord Kṛṣṇa, whom she looked upon as her true Lord and on whom she poured all her loving devotion. Mīrā's devotion to Lord Kṛṣṇa is an epitome of intense emotional relationship, the highest level of conjugal love, which she felt for Lord Kṛṣṇa. In Mīrā's poems Kṛṣṇa appears not as the Supreme Lord of the *Bhagavad Gītā* but as the beloved Dark One for whom she felt pangs of love that verged almost on ecstatic madness of the human spirit seeking to be united with the Divine Lord. Separation from Kṛṣṇa, her beloved lord, made her heart yearn with the greatest urgency for union with Him. Her lyrical outbursts are the cries of an agonized soul experiencing in each moment of separation the intense ecstasy of the joy that the union with the Lord will bring. Thus, her poems are imbued with direct, immediate, and intense emotional fervor that sets her apart from all great saints of medieval northern India, including Kabīr, Sūrdāsa, and Tulasidāsa. Sinha describes Mīrā as a rebel saint because she ignored the patriarchical assumptions of the Indian society of her times. He writes:

> Another difficulty for Mīrā was prejudice against a woman, especially a widowed one who had renounced and rejected caste, class, and family traditions to pursue her spiritual goals in response to the call of Lord Kṛṣṇa. . . . Mīrā defied all categories, transcended all boundaries; with a free spirit, a discerning mind, and an open heart, she sought spiritual inspiration, wisdom, and comfort from all sources available to her. But she never totally committed herself to any earthly being, whether her husband, a Rāṇā of Mewār, or a spiritual mentor. Fully saturated with her love for Lord Kṛṣṇa, completely immersed in her devotion for her only Lord, to whom she was committed in body, mind, and spirit, she was both an enigma and a challenge to the religious teachers and lineages of her time.

Part Two, "The Spirituality of the Purāṇas, Āgamas, and Tantra," begins with a chapter on Purāṇic spirituality. According to Giorgio Bonazzoli, the Purāṇas focus on the "ideal of fullness," which may be described as *bhukti* (enjoyment of this earth and heaven) and *mukti* (release, *mokṣa*). Thus, the Purāṇas cater to the needs of every person throughout the course of one's life. This ideal of *bhukti-mukti* is neither a disembodied spiritualism nor a refined hedonism but rather a "holistic realism." The Purāṇas are "pluralistic" in their attitude since they incorporate different ways of conceiving life, different ways of approaching reality, different degrees of doctrines and morals. "So when a Purāṇa insists on the greatness of Śiva, for instance, even in a quite strong sectarian way or polemically, it does not hurt, really, the devotee of Viṣṇu, who will extend his indulgence toward the Śaivite, and vice versa." Bonazzoli points out that in the Purāṇas, the union between God and the individual self is mainly reached through "internal dispositions." A person not only must focus his or her mind on God but must perform all actions—ritualistic, social, and others—with full attention and with total awareness. Hence, the spirituality of the Purāṇas is a journey inward by which all outward human actions are transformed, a process by which the profane is transformed into the sacred.

In chapter 10, "Mysticism in the Śaivagamas," Hélène Brunner focuses on a study of "Sanskrit" Śaiva Siddhānta (in contrast to Tamil Śaiva Siddhānta), which is based solely on the Āgamas, their commentaries, and the Sanskrit manuals on the Āgamas and their commentaries. According to Brunner, though the Āgamas with their details on rituals may appear to be least "mystical," it is in their understanding that the goal of ritual action is finally liberation (*mokṣa*) itself that we find the mystical dimension of the Āgamic writings. The Āgamas do not deal with rituals (*kriyapāda*) alone, but they include a section on behavior (*caryapāda*), a section on knowledge (*jñānapāda*), and a section on yoga (*yogapāda*). It is the *jñānapāda* and *yogapāda* components of ritual action that provide a mystical dimension. The "liberation is the effect of the rite itself; the intellectual knowledge of the dogmas and of the psycho-somatic structure of the individual is but preliminary to the effective practice of yoga and, above all, to the performance of the rites in which this yoga is integrated." The final goal or the state of liberation, according to the Āgamas, is gaining "Śivahood" (*śivatva*). Brunner describes it as realizing one's identity with Śiva.

> A liberated *ātman* is Śiva; it can unite with Śiva but does not disappear into Him. . . . A liberated soul can "feel" itself to be the equal of Śiva without blending into Him, and without being anymore limited by Him, since it possesses the same infinite power of knowledge and action. Let us concede, too, that one day it can discover that it had always been Śiva without feeling that its previous experiences as well as the world in which it was then plunged, as the other beings still are, were illusory.

In the chapter on Tantric spirituality, Sri Hemendra Chakravarty explicates the spiritual dimensions of Tantric philosophy and practice. With the focus on Śakti, the goal of a Tantric yogi is to realize his/her identification with Śakti, who not only transcends the universe but also is immanent in every entity. The Tantric path consists in attaining a state of equilibrium at every stage of one's spiritual journey, beginning from the gross, physical level, to the subtle, and then to the causal. The fourth level is called "Supreme equilibrium," which is to be attained only after going through the first three levels. This state of "Supreme equilibrium" is described as the unity of Śiva-Śakti, "which encompasses in its cosmic sweep all diversities of time, space and objecthood." The worship of Śakti is an essential feature of the Tantric path. This is possible only after receiving initiation from a teacher. In the initiation process, the teacher connects the student to Śakti by giving a sacred seed *mantra* to the student. According to the Tantric tradition it is the *mātṛkas* (letters) that make the *mantra* powerful and efficacious. *Mātṛkas* are the basic element of all principles, and the human body is said to be made of them. "They lie within the body forming *cakras* [circles, centers in body] in order to create thought-constructs . . . and thus push the *jīvas* to remain in bondage. But as soon as their real nature is realized, they become Śakti, and thereby providers of release or freedom (*mokṣa*)."

In chapter 12, "The Way of the Siddhas," T. N. Ganapathy explores the spiritual path of a group of Tamil Tantrics called Siddhas, the word *siddhar* meaning one who has "fulfilled." These Siddhas are, according to Ganapathy, God-realized beings "alive in the world for the sake of humankind and all living beings." The writings of the Siddhas are highly symbolic. They can be understood and appreciated only by those who have been initiated; to the uninitiated they remain obscure and often obscene. The sexual imagery in the poems of the Siddhas reflects their understanding of woman as the cosmic engery. It is this energy that is present in all human beings in the form of *kuṇḍalini śakti,* and achieving union with this energy is indeed the goal of every practioner of yoga. The yogic method of achieving the goal requires first the realization that the human body is a microcosm of the macrocosm. According to Ganapathy, "Yoga recognizes the underlying unity—nay, *sameness* or *oneness*—between the cosmos and the individual and helps one to extend the ego-boundary and liberate one from a limited attitude, toward a cosmic vision. Once this feeling of oneness is developed, the internal and the external are no longer polarized and one sees the universe as though it were within oneself." The cosmic vision thus gained provides the groundwork for the Siddha philosophy of well-being of all, and this is best seen in the system of Siddha medicine. The Tamil Siddha literature describes liberation as *vettaveḷi,* which stands for an infinite, transcendental awareness. This state cannot be described in words, as it transcends language and the subject–object duality. Hence the best description of it is indeed "silence" (*cumma*).

Parts Three and Four, on modern and contemporary Hindu spirituality, highlight some of the major issues that have shaped the spirituality of Hinduism in modern and contemporary times. Modern Hinduism has sought to emphasize the positive orientation of the tradition toward the world, against the criticism of Hinduism as "world-rejecting." We find also among modern Hindu thinkers a rethinking with respect to the relevance or irrelevance of the traditional Hindu class and caste system (*varṇa* and *jāti*). Another area of focus in modern Hinduism is its reponse to religious pluralism. Here modern Hinduism has highlighted the commonality of the religious quest among the various religious traditions and also the universal relevance of Hindu philosophy and its spiritual paths. The authors of chapters in these parts have sought to give expression to the spiritual dimensions of modern and contemporary Hinduism by dealing with the spirituality of some of the leading Hindu thinkers and philosophers of this era, such as Saint Rāmaliṅgar, Rabindranath Tagore, Rāmakrishna Paramahaṃsā, Vivekānanda, Sivānanda, Aurobindo, Jiddu Krishnamurthi, and Gandhi.

The first article in the section on modern Hinduism, entitled "The Spiritual Vision of Rāmaliṅgar," by V. A. Devasenapathi, focuses on the spiritual dimension of a saint from the Tamil region whose main concern was the promotion and maintenance of communal and religious harmony in India. For Saint Rāmaliṅgar, these goals could be achieved only in a society where individuals' actions are marked by compassion and love. Such actions fulfill two purposes: on the one hand, they ensure social harmony and, on the other hand, they enable the individuals to achieve their spiritual goal. For Rāmaliṅgar, one should act toward all forms of life with compassion and concern, not limiting those actions to humankind alone. "[Rāmaliṅgar] could not bear to see hunger, whether it was human beings or even vegetation thirsting for water." For Rāmaliṅgar, the spirituality of universal love and compassion is based on two theological sources: (1) We all worship one and the same God using different names and forms. "He is Brahṁa, Nārāyaṇa, Hara, Parāśakti, Para Brahman, Arhat, Buddha." (2) The best way to express one's devotion to God is by serving God's creatures. As one of God's creation, Rāmaliṅgar says that human beings should feel their kinship and affinity with every living thing in the world since they are also God's creatures. Hence the practice of nonviolence (*ahiṁsa*) is essential since such nonviolent actions are expressive of compassion and love. Rāmaliṅgar stresses nonviolence and service as the core of one's spiritual life. Rāmaliṅgar gives expression to his spiritual mission in the following prayer: "Oh my Father, listen to my prayer and grant Your Grace. I should express in my action my love for all beings. I should go to the worlds everywhere, to worlds of all kinds and proclaim the Glory of Your

Grace. I should direct the Light of Grace so that the pure Good Path may prevail in (as yet) undeclared exalted places."

In "The Spirituality of Rabindranath Tagore: 'The Religion of an Artist,'" Sitansu Sekhar Chakravarti explores the spiritual dimension of one who has been a poet, a novelist, an educator, and a social reformer. According to Chakravarti, spirituality for Rabindranath Tagore is the dynamic principle that touches every aspect of life and is the guiding principle that "leads human existence from partiality to fullness." Life's journey, for Tagore, achieves its fulfillment through the creative interaction of an artist or a poet, and not through renunciation of the world. He characterizes his spirituality as that of an artist. This implies a change in one's attitude to the world; one should move away from an egoistic appropriation of the world, which results in experience of the world as a source of suffering and happiness, to an artistic experience of the world, where it is the source of unconditional joy (*ānanda*). Tagore writes, "Joy flows through the universe, / The sun and moon drink of it / A full measure. / The light of the joy of goodness / Stays ever effulgent. . . . Why are you all by yourself, confined to / Your own ego?" Integral to the spirituality of Tagore is the Upaniṣadic notion that everything is *Brahman*, and *Brahman* is blissful. Tagore was also influenced by the Vaiṣṇava and Baul traditions, which focused on the indwelling presence of God. Thus, in many of his writings Tagore stresses the need to respond to the call from within, from "the man of the heart." The relationship between the man of the heart and the individual is very intimate. The initmacy is often described as the relationship of the lover and the beloved. It is this inner intimacy that also enables one to experience unity with the external world. According to Chakravarti, it is this unitive experience of the inner and the outer that characterizes the religion of an artist, and this is indeed the very core of the spirituality of Rabindranath Tagore.

In chapter 15, "Śrī Rāmakrishna: At Play in His Mother's Mansion," Walter Neevel explores the spiritual dimensions of a mystic from Bengal who has remained highly influential in the modern and contemporary phases of Hindu self-understanding. Neevel focuses on the "mother–child" relationship as the very core of Rāmakrishna's mystical dimension, where this relationship, instead of becoming "regressive or pathological," remains a source of "creative experiencing," which is "seen most clearly in the spontaneous and joyful play of a young child while her or his mother is close at hand." The notion of Divine Mother is an essential aspect of the spirituality of Rāmakrishna. Rāmakrishna's mystical experiences seem to authenticate both "*Brahman* with attributes" (*saguṇa Brahman*) and "*Brahman* without attributes" (*nirguṇa Brahman*), a point that has divided the followers of different Vedāntic schools. "The eternal, unchanging, formless *Brahman* . . . is real, but so is the dynamic Śakti at play." Rāmakrishna says: "Brahman and Śakti are identical. If you accept the one, you must accept the other. It is like fire and its power to burn. . . . One cannot think of the Absolute without the Relative, or the Relative without the Absolute." According to Neevel, Rāmakrishna's ideal was not *jñāna* but *vijñāna*, or "full knowledge," which realizes the reality of both *Brahman* and Śakti, of both the Eternal (*nitya*) and the Play (*līlā*) aspects of the one that becomes all. It is in the affirmation of nondual *Brahman* and the affirmation of the reality of the manifold world as creative expressions of Śakti that we find Rāmakrishna moving away from the traditional Vedantic formulations. Highlighting the theme of creation as the Play (*līlā*) of the Divine Mother (Śakti), Rāmakrishna seems to invite us all to participate in the divine play with spontaneity and joy as Her children.

In the chapter on the spirituality of Swami Vivekānanda, Anantanand Rambachan explores the spiritual dimensions of one of the most influential interpreters of Hindu tradition in recent times. "Vivekānanda was the first to offer to the Western world a detailed and systematic exposition of some of the central claims of the Hindu tradition." His participation in the 1893 Parliament of the World's Religions constitutes one of the landmarks in the history of modern Hinduism; at this time Hinduism came to assume a mission for the world with a spiritual message of universal relevance and meaning. For Vivekānanda one of the central features of Hindu religion is its emphasis on "the direct experience" of the ultimate Reality. Religion is to be realized, not simply to be heard or repeated like a parrot, and there is a diversity of spiritual paths to direct, personal experience of the ultimate Reality. These are the disciplines of *karma, bhakti, jñāna,* and *raja,* to be practiced according to one's innate nature and temperament. Rambachan points out, however, that there is some ambiguity in Vivekānanda's writings about whether *rājayoga* is the only way to attain the *final* state of realization (*samādhi*), with *karma, bhakti,* and *jñāna* serving as preparatory steps, or whether these disciplines are four independent ways to reach the final state of *samādhi.* On the theme of diversity of religions, Vivekānanda holds the view that all religions are true and meaningful since they are diverse expressions of the same Reality and appropriations of one Ultimate Truth. The goal of all religions, Vivekānanda points out, is a "final unitive experience," which for him is highlighted in the Hindu philosophical school of Advaita Vedānta. Thus, for Swami Vivekānanda, the *advaitic* experience (nondualistic experience) is the final goal toward which all religions are progressing, representing different points along the journey, a "staircase model" by which he is able to advocate tolerance, reject claims of exclusivism, and affirm the relative importance of various religious traditions of the world. The important contribution of Vivekānanda is that in the face of the Christian exclusivism of his times, he affirmed that Hinduism included a variety of independent ways to liberation, and that Hindu spirituality, especially in its Advaitic form, had global significance and relevance.

Focusing on the theme of spirituality, Ravi Ravindra describes Jiddu Krishnamurti, a contemporary Indian thinker, as a "Traveler in a Pathless Land." Chosen by Annie Besant to lead the Theosophical Society, J. Krishnamurti at the age of thirty-four broke with the society and also renounced the messianic role that was assigned to him by Besant. This also meant for Krishnamurti breaking with all forms of organized religion. Describing Truth as a pathless land, Krishnamurti points out that Truth cannot be reached by any path, religion, or sect: "Because I am free, unconditioned, whole, not the part, not the relative, but the whole Truth that is eternal, I desire those who seek to understand me to be free, not to make out a cage which will become a religion, a sect." For him the spiritual dimension is not created by the mind, nor is it an acquisition or an achievement of any sort. "This dimension is manifested precisely when there is no center of ambition in the self which wishes possessions or which struggles for achievement." Krishnamurti calls it the dimension of insight, a special sort of intelligence, that can express itself in thought but is not conditioned by thought or brought about by it. According to him, thought leads to fragmentation and subsequently to fear and sorrow. For Krishnamurti, the moment of insight is *in* time but it is not *of* time. That moment is experienced in the state of "total attention" when the meditative mind is open, whole, and quiet, and this state of mind is reached effortlessly, like an oak tree which naturally unfolds itself from an acorn. This is the state of freedom for Krishnamurti, where one is free from fear, from memory and anticipation, and from time and all things. "True action takes place only in the moment of the awakening of insight. Otherwise action is in fact a reaction to the memory of insight, whether it is one's own insight or someone else's."

In chapter 18, "The Spiritual Descent of the Divine: The Life Story of Swāmi Sivānanda," David Miller explores the spiritual dimensions of Sivānanda by focusing on his life as an excellent example of the process of writing contemporary Hindu hagiography, "the purpose of which is not only to spiritualize an ordinary human life but to universalize that life story, providing a Hindu model of the spiritual life for all those who are 'religious seekers' to emulate whether they live in the East or in the West." Here he examines the biography of Sivānanda by one of his closest disciples

Swāmi Venkatesānanda. The biography, entitled *Gurudev Sivānanda*, portrays Sivānanda as a divine incarnation (*avatāra*) alongside the Buddha and Jesus Christ, with a specific mission to restore *dharma*. His description of the events surrounding the birth of Sivānanda is very similar to the description of the birth of Siddhārtha Gautama. Again, Venkatesānanda's description of the childhood of Sivānanda appears to have been influened by description of the childhood of Kṛṣṇa in the Purāṇas. According to Miller, Venkatesānanda's "purpose was to picture his Gurudeva, Swāmi Sivānanda, as the most recent incarnation of the Divine, a wonder child for the modern age, who, in the tradition of Swāmi Vivekānanda, would restore the *sanātana dharma* to its rightful place in India." It is with similar adoration that Venkatesānanda describes Sivānanda's life as a doctor, which was, according to him, "divinely inspired and divinely directed." This mission of service was continued even after Sivānanda was initiated into an ascetic order. For Venkatesānanda, it is in this combination of an ascetic austerity with dedicated and selfless service "the purpose for which the Divine had incarnated Himself as Swāmi Sivānanda" that we find a model person to emulate so as to live a meaningful life in the modern world.

In chapter 19, "Śrī Aurobindo: The Spirituality of the Future," Sisirkumar Ghose explores the spiritual dimension of Śrī Aurobindo, a contemporary Hindu thinker and mystic. "A constant of human aspiration, spirituality has been glimpsed and voiced in every age by rare souls," writes Ghose, "but not many have defined, described, and developed in taxonomy or hinted at the plentitude of its possibility so constantly and confidently as this Indian sage, who has cast his dreams as a mold for coming things." For Aurobindo, spirituality is the master key of the Indian mind. According to him, "the core of Hinduism is a spiritual, not a social discipline." "Not only did it make spirituality the highest aim of life, but it even tried, as far as that could be done in the past conditions of the human race, to turn the whole life towards spirituality." The final aim of Indian religion, Aurobindo says, is to divinize human nature by drawing the whole human being upward, including one's physical and mental planes. In such a situation, it is not a *sannyāsi* who turns away from the world and is often negligent of his body that is the ideal person, but rather it is a *ṛsi*, who has lived his life fully and has reached the world of supra-intellectual, supramental, spiritual truth. Only such a person, "viewing all things from above and within," can "guide the world humanly as God guides it divinely, because like the Divine he is in the life of the world and yet above it." The integral yoga of Aurobindo maps the spiritual journey as a series of sublimations of consciousness, each with its characteristic power and action, of Higher Mind, the Illumined Mind, Intuition, Overmind, and Supermind. "The passage from the lower to the higher is the aim of yoga," writes Aurobindo, and this is not achieved by the rejection of the "lower" but "by the transformation of the lower, and its elevation to the higher nature."

In chapter 20, "The Spirituality of Ahiṁsā (Nonviolence): Traditional and Gandhian," John Arapura examines the way that the spirituality of *ahiṁsā* in Hinduism reached a state of full bloom in the life, works, and teachings of Mahatma Gandhi. Gandhi's unique brand of spirituality, according to Arapura, is the dynamic relation between truth and *ahiṁsā*. Gandhi writes, "I can say with assurance as a result of all my experiments that a perfect vision of Truth can only follow a complete vision of *Ahiṁsā*." This has to be understood in the light of Gandhi's obverting the proposition "God is Truth" to the form "Truth is God." *Ahiṁsā* is the loving service of all that lives, and it is by this service one reaches the Truth. Arapura points out that *ahiṁsā* in the Indian tradition had great cosmo-ethical implications, but its sociopolitical implications were not fully worked out. Gandhi's contribution consists in highlighting the sociopolitical dimensions of *ahiṁsā*. Gandhi advanced *ahiṁsā* as a mode of battle—Truth's own battle, *satyāgraha*—to right the wrongs in the social and political order in every concrete situation, since for Gandhi "right is Truth." For Gandhi, "right" belongs to the realm of ends as well as the domain of means. The means employed must be right as much as the end itself. According to Arapura, Gandhi's *ahiṁsā* spirituality is of dynamic nature—of righting things in the world through "militant" action. The militancy involved here is stated by Gandhi in the following manner: "Although [the *satyāgrahi*] must love the wrong-doer, he must never submit to his wrong or injustice, but oppose it with all his might, and must patiently and without resentment suffer all hardships to which the wrong-doer may subject him in punishment for his opposition." Such spirituality of *ahiṁsā* (and truth) is for Gandhi the very essence of struggle for independence, which is spirituality at work in the form of service (*sevā*).

Part Five, "Cultural Expressions of Hindu Spirituality," explores the spiritual dimensions of Indian art, Indian classical music, and the Hindu temples and festivals. The chapter entitled "Hindu Temples and Festivals: Spirituality as Communal Participation," by Prema Nandakumar, deals with one of the important aspects of Hindu religious life, namely, temple worship and participation of the Hindus in temple festivities. According to Nandakumar, in the Vedic age people apparently felt that God was omnipresent and therefore we could pray anywhere and worship any visible part of nature as God. The sacrificial post where people kindled fire and worshiped the Gods by placing their offerings in the flames was perhaps the first idea of temple. However, by the time of the Epics, temple worship as a distinct religious activity had taken its roots. The entire paraphernalia associated with a king's court was transformed into temple ritual. The idea of taking the deity out of the sanctum during festival days was born from the manner in which the king left the palace periodically to be seen by his subjects. Each temple came to have a sacred calendar of religious festivities. The temples also became centers of education. Social services such as feeding the poor were done in the temple premises. There were also hospitals in temples, and we find the names of some physicians associated with some of the important temples in South India. Thus, the temple culture synthesized the secular and the sacred, becoming the focus of community life. Hindu temples have also been instrumental in fostering communal harmony, often providing links between deities of various religious sects. For instance, the temple of Sundareśvara (Śiva) in Madurai is closely aligned with that of Aḻakar (Viṣṇu). Again, the goddess Māriamman of Samayavapuram, who is Śiva's creatrix power, is considered a sister of Lord Raṅganātha (Viṣṇu) of Śrīraṅgam. "The Hindu temples have taught us the art of living together harmoniously as also living at peace with oneself. Entering a Hindu temple is, indeed, entering the life of the divine on earth."

Exploring the spiritual dimensions of music are two chapters: Sushil Kumar Saxena's exposition of Hindustani (North Indian) music and R. Venugopal's study of the spirituality of Carnatic (South Indian) music. Describing the function of music as spiritualizing sense activity, Saxena's article explicates the spiritual implications of some of the important concepts in Hindustani music, namely, *svara*, *rāga*, *ālāpa*, *dhruvapad*, *laya*, and *tāla*. Saxena points out that the Sanskrit word for music, *saṅgita*, includes not only vocal or instrumental music but also dance. Both music and dance include *laya* (rhythm), and *laya* includes musical duration measured by means of beats (*mātras*). It also includes *bols*, a *bol* being a letter or a brief tuft of letters having no literal meaning. According to Saxena, Indian music is spiritual, and not simply a mode of entertainment. "If it is granted that the concept of the Absolute as sound is true and that music is a possible way to final Reality, it would follow that a musician has to cultivate sound in all its aspects and infinite variety." Referring to the ancient understanding of *rasa* (aesthetic experience) Saxena points out that a good *ālāpa* may very well generate *rasa*. "In Indian music, . . . *rasa* is not taken as a merely secular experience. The text of some *dhruvapad* songs speaks of it as the locus of *Brahman* Itself" and in fact the various attributes that are used to explain *rasa*-experience are close to the experience of the Absolute (*Brahman*), such as undifferentiatedness, transcendence of distinctions, and self-existence. Referring to rhythm (*tāla*), Saxena points out that it also generates a similar aesthetic experience (*rasa*). Saxena concludes:

> The music of India is no necessary push into the realm of spirit, but its own character *and inner amplitude* are here certainly of help. Any number of songs can be composed in the same *rāga*. Every single segment of beat-measured *laya* admits of countless syllabic arrangements. . . . This vision of infinity in a limited extent makes us revere the art; and insofar as the natural direction of reverence is at the personal, it seems only proper to let music inspire our longing for God.

R. Venugopal explores the spiritual dimensions of Carnatic music. Venugopal points out that the Indian music in general has its roots in ancient Vedic chants. "Of the Vedas, the *Ṛg Veda* supplies the literary text, the *Yajur Veda* represents the ritual; and the *Sāma Veda* gave the musical representation. In the *Sāma Veda* the text of the *Ṛg Veda* is altered to suit a musical way of chanting that originally employed only two notes. Certain vowels with no particular meaning were also introduced for chanting purposes." The evolution of these chants from one to two, to three, to five, to seven notes, and ultimately to countless microtones, Venugopal says, invested Indian music, more particularly the Carnatic music of South India, with a tremendous range of nuances and aesthetic values retaining the basic religious and spiritual core. Around the seventh and eighth centuries of the Common Era, South India saw a great upsurge of devotionalism with the emergence of a number of devotee-poet-singers, namely, the Āḻvārs and the Nāyanmārs, who to a great extent constructed the edifice upon which the later Carnatic music was built. In the late eighteenth and early nineteenth centuries, however, Carnatic music witnessed its golden era with three great composers of Carnatic music, Thyāgarāja, Muthuswāmy Dikshitar, and Shyāmasāstri. According to Venugopal, to some extent North Indian music belonged mostly to royal courts and flourished under their patronage, and South Indian music belonged primarily to temples and gained its momentum from devotees of the Lord who often spurned royal patronage. Venugopal then proceeds to analyze the lyrics of some of the songs of Thyāgarāja in order to bring forth the spiritual dimension of Carnatic music. The lyrics of Thyāgarāja are often in the form of a "dialogue," where he converses with God and solicits divine response. Some of them are also in the form of "exercises" in self-introspection, "discourses" on God's glories, and "philosophical expositions" highlighting the impermanence of human existence and of worldly possessions. According to Venugopal, the songs of Thyāgarāja reflect the spiritual climate of the Vedas and the Upaniṣads and also the implied teachings of the epics and the purāṇas. "To Thyāgarāja one sure method of purging one's mind of all evil and of purifying the mind is through music, remembering God and reciting His glories. To him music was not just a source of sweet sounds; it was verily the path to

God. Thyāgarāja says categorically that those who do not understand music do not qualify for salvation. He goes to the extent of saying that music itself is the form of God." "The greatness of Thyāgarāja seems to lie in the fact that here was a man who lived so close to our times, but still was able to realize and express the ancient spirituality of the Hindus to us in a form we could understand easily and appreciate."

Writing on the spiritual dimension of Indian art, Bettina Bäumer points out that one of the possible approaches to the understanding of the relationship between art and spirituality is the metaphysical idea that God is the greatest artist and the world, his creation, a marvelous picture or piece of art. Bäumer refers to several sources in the Indian tradition, early Vedic, Upaniṣadic, Yogic, and Tantric, that connect art to spirituality. The art activity itself is a means or way of self-integration demanding preparation and a congenial state of mind. With respect of religious art, the artist is instructed to observe fasting and silence before starting to work, and then to concentrate fully on the divinity or other subjects he/she has to create. It is said that the art that is produced out of meditation (*dhyāna*) leads to the ultimate goal of life, liberation (*mokṣa*). Bäumer points out all Hindu, Buddhist, and Jaina art is basically religious, since there is no distinction between secular and religious art. "Even scenes that would be regarded as secular in other civilizations, such as natural beauty or human love, are here part of the spiritual universe." The so-called erotic sculptures on temples owe their inspiration to Tantric spirituality, and later miniature paintings representing love themes equate the lovers to the divine couple, mostly to Rādha and Kṛṣṇa. With the *rasa* theory in place, images representing scenes of war, fighting, killing, love making, etc., gain spiritual meaning; they become sources for purifying human emotions. Thus, in the Hindu world, its sacred art has inspired the devotee as much as its mystics and philosophers.

The final part of the volume, "Hindu Spirituality in Dialogue," includes articles on Sant Kabīr, the spirituality of Indian Christianity, and Sikhism. The theme of this section is to highlight the interaction that has taken place in India between various religious traditions and to draw out the distinct modes of spirituality that have resulted from such interactions. As there are other volumes dealing with the spirituality of various religious traditions, to avoid the possibility of overlapping this section is somewhat brief, and at best a sampling, in the context of India, which has been home to several major religious traditions since the ancient times. We have focused on Sant Kabīr, who in terms of his spirituality has integrated the insights of the Hindu tradition and the Islamic tradition, particularly in its mystical form, Sufism, and has exemplified this integration in his personal life as well as in his teachings. The articles on Indian Christian spirituality and Sikh spirituality highlight the theme of dialogue with Hindu spirituality that is still going on in India and delineate the results of such fruitful interaction.

According to K. Banerjee, the spirituality of Kabīr provides a unique synthesis of *jñāna*, *bhakti*, and yoga in the Hindu tradition and of Sufi mysticism, and all these are directed by Kabīr to his devotion of Rāma. "From Vedānta [Kabīr] assimilated the concepts of *Brahman*, the unconditioned Absolute, *māyā*, *jīva*, and the basic unity of *Brahman* and *Ātman*. The boundless, formless Supreme Being he called '*Nirguṇa* Rāmā,' whom he sought through devotion. Deep personal love for the impersonal Absolute was characteristic of the Sufis. Kabīr applied this Sufi trend to his own loving search for Rāmā, not as an incarnation (*avatāra*) but as *Brahman*, whom he called 'Allah' after the Muslims, and 'the invisible Pure Being' after the *nātha* yogis." The line of spiritual pursuit that Kabīr followed has come to be called *sahaja sādhana*, which involves uninterrupted and impassioned contemplation of God as Infinite Light enthroned within oneself, accompanied by the mental repetition of the *mantra* or sacred name received from one's guru. Kabīr's religious discipline rejects the value of ritualism, and focuses intensely on the theme of love, love especially on the lines of bridal mysticism. In consonance with the Sūfi and Vaiṣṇava traditions, Kabīr speaks of the state of *virāha*, where the lover is separated from the beloved and longs for the union. The state of *virāha* for Kabīr is in a way a welcome state since it compels the mind to remember the Lord all the time and with exclusive concentration. The goal of *sahaja sādhana* is to attain *sahaja siddhi*, which is described also as *Rāmarasa*, where one's body is as it were transmuted, becoming totally egoless. Such a person "need not shun the world, nor seek it. All his acts are inspired and regulated by the Divine Will." Kabīr describes this state in the following verses: "By the grace of the *Sat Guru*, I am away from both heaven and hell; immersed in joy, I live for ever at the Lotus feet of the Lord."

> I have made friends with Him, says Kabīr,
> who is free from the duality of joy and sorrow;
> Now I shall always play with Him as my playmate,
> and will never be separated from Him.

In chapter 26, "Indian Christian Spirituality," J. Valiamangalam identifies different forms of Christian presence in India. According to Thomas Christians, the message of Christianity entered India in the first century of the Common Era through the preaching of St. Thomas, one of the apostles of Jesus. The various Christian denominations have been active in the Indian scene from early times. Valiamangalam points out that in course of time, the Christians have changed their attitude with regard to their missionary work in India. The works and writings of persons like Swami

Vivekānanda, Rabindranath Tagore, Śrī Aurobindo, and Mahatma Gandhi have greatly helped the Christians to appreciate the spiritual wealth of Hindu and other religions of Indian origin. "However, this change toward openness is yet to grow fully in depth and width in order to become the general character of Christian presence in India." In order to do so, Christian spirituality needs to have serious and sincere encounters with Indian spiritual traditions. Valiamangalam points out that, except in Kerala, generally Christianity has been looked upon as a foreign religion. The reason is that the major portions of Thomas Christians in Kerala came from the high castes in the Hindu society. In addition, Thomas Christians retained the native Indian customs in their daily life and actively interacted with the Hindu community in their social religious lives. This was, however, before the Synod of Diamper, which, as it were, transplanted a Syrian or European church to India and placed restrictions on religious interaction with the Hindus. There are, however, attempts in the present time to recover the Christian spirituality of the pre-Diamper period, and the "Christian Ashram" movement reflects the Christian openness to Hindu spirituality. Christianity, in its turn, has greatly influenced Hinduism, particularly the modern Hindu religious movements like Brahmo Samaj, and also persons like Mahatma Gandhi, Śrī Aurobindo, Ramakrishna Paramahamsa, and Swami Vivekānanda. Gandhi stands as one of the prime examples of enrichment through Hindu and Christian interaction. Gandhi's confession, "It was the New Testament which really awakened me to the rightness and value of passive resistance. The *Bhagavad Gītā* deepened the impression," is to the point. Valiamangalam feels that it is this enrichment gained by deepest contact with Hindu spirituality that should mold the spirituality of Indian Christianity. As Upadhyay has stated, "The negative plate of Jesus, developed in a solution of Hinduism, brings out hitherto unknown features of the portrait." It is in the directions given by persons like Abhisiktananda, a Catholic priest, who reflect deeply the spirit of interaction between Christianity and Hinduism and their mutual enrichment, that the future of Indian Christianity seems to lie. The author concludes that a church without rigid institutional formalities is perhaps the best basis for a genuine Indian Christian spirituality or even for a world religious culture.

In the chapter on Sikh spirituality, Nikky-Gurinder Kaur Singh discusses the focus of Sikh spirituality, noting its similarities to other religious traditions of India as well as its unique contribution to the spiritual soil of India. Highlighting the *Weltanshauung* of the Sikh tradition, Nikky Singh points out that, unlike some of the Indian traditions, the Sikh tradition recognizes the importance of the natural world, and of our social contexts. From the theological dimension of Sikhism, the statement *Ikk oan Kar,* with which

Jap begins, expresses the central aspect of the Sikh faith. In the spiritual nexus of Sikhism, the Ultimate is an inner, subjective experience rather than an objective knowledge of God out there. The five *khands,* namely, *Dharam Khand, Gyan Khand, Saram Khand, Karam Khand,* and *Sach Khand,* reinforce the centrality of the Transcendent in one's spiritual journey. *Dharam Khand* is the sphere of duty. Here the Sikh tradition stresses the social and spiritual equality of all. The human body is not an impediment to one's spiritual journey; the body indeed houses the divine reality. The body and the earth are celeberated as the starting point in one's spiritual odyssey. *Gyan Khand* is the second stage of one's spiritual journey; it is the region of knowledge. At this stage one realizes the vastness of creation. In contrast to this vastness one also experiences his/her infinitesimalness. As the result of this, one realizes one's "nothingness," recognizing the transcendent as the sole and entire reality. The third stage of the spiritual journey is *Saram Khand.* It is the region of beauty, where one develops aesthetic sensitivity. From this stage one moves on to *Karam Khand.* This is the region of Grace. It is a stage that is very essential in order to reach the final stage, namely, *Sach Khand,* for without Grace the journey could not even be undertaken. Grace is the benevolent, female aspect of the Transcendent that sustains the seeker throughout his/her spiritual quest. For Guru Nanak *Karam Khand* is the abode of "warriors and heroes of mighty power." For Guru Nanak, the true hero is one "who kills the evil of egoity within." The real might and strength lie in one's conquering his/her own self. Among the heroes and heroines, Guru Nanak mentions only the name of Śita, wife of Rāma. However, he also mentions "Sitas" and such usage in plural, according to Nikky Singh, takes away the distant "goddess" stature of Rāma's wife and makes Śita a model person, one who could easily be emulated by both men and women. Here women become the paradigmatic figures. Hence the spiritual journey involves movement from the stage of aesthetic appreciation to a stage of heroism, since valor is an essential aspect of one's religious life. Finally, one reaches the stage of *Sach Khand,* which is the realm of Truth. "Sikhism fully celebrates the existence of the Transcendent as Truth." This is the realm of *Nirankar,* the Formless One. "The subject does not view the transcendent object; the subject–object duality dissolves and the individual partakes of the infinite. At this point of the spiritual journey, the origin and destination have become one."

I wish to express my gratitude to Ewert Cousins, general editor of the series, for his trust in me and encouragement to complete this volume. I am very thankful to Eleanor Ash of Fordham University for her help in editing this volume. Eleanor did preliminary copyediting, and her insightful comments and suggestions on the contents and structure of the papers included in this volume have been very helpful. Her organizational skills have always remained exceptional, and her positive attitude toward this volume provided me with the needed strength to complete the task. I wish to thank also Sandra L. Goodliff and Lilian Gavett, both of St. Bonaventure University, for their help in getting these articles into electronic form. I wish to thank all the contributors to the volume for their patience, as the completion of this volume has experienced many years of delay. At last we are reaching the end of the tunnel.

K. R. Sundararajan

Scheme of Transliteration

Vowels	a	ā	i	ī	u	ū	ṛ	ṝ	ḷ	e	ai	o	au
anusvāra	ṁ												
visarga	ḥ												

Consonants					
gutturals	k	kh	g	gh	ṅ
palatals	c	ch	j	jh	ñ
cerebrals	ṭ	ṭh	ḍ	ḍh	ṇ
dentals	t	th	d	dh	n
labials	p	ph	b	bh	m
semivowels	y	r	l	v	
sibilants	s as in *sun*				
	ś palatal sibilant pronounced like the soft *s* of Russian				
	ṣ cerebral sibilant as in *shun*				
aspirate	h				
medial	ḻ (in Tamil)				

Part One

THE REGIONAL SPIRITUALITIES

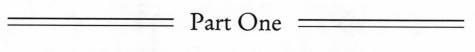

1

The Four Spiritual Ways (upāya) in the Kashmir Śaiva Tradition

BETTINA BÄUMER

Historical Background

THE TERM KASHMIR ŚAIVISM refers to the religion and philosophy accepting Śiva as the supreme Reality and Lord that was prevalent in Kashmir in the medieval period; it is traditionally called *Trika* (*Śāstra*) (the "trinitarian" school). It is also known as *Pratyabhijñā* (the doctrine of "recognition") as well as *Rahasyasampradāya* ("the mystical tradition") or *Svātantryavāda* ("the doctrine of absolute freedom"). These names themselves indicate some essential features of this school that distinguish it from other schools of Śaivism. Based on the Śaiva Āgamas or Tantras, it represents a unique synthesis of spiritual movements and philosophical trends that existed in Kashmir from the eighth century on, and yet it takes its own clear doctrinal position, which is pure *advaita*, or nondualism. Though it rejects the teachings of other systems, such as Buddhism (especially Vijñānavāda), Advaita Vedānta, dualistic Śaiva Siddhānta, the grammarian school, and so on, it integrated elements of each of them in a new vision of reality. Somānanda in his *Śivadṛṣṭi* calls it "a new, easy path,"[1] indicating that it is essentially a spiritual path.

Since most of the revealed texts of the Śaiva Āgamas are dualistic (*dvaita, bheda)*, the Kashmir Śaiva authors reinterpreted them in the light of *advaita*. Among the most authoritative Āgamas are the *Mālinī Vijaya, Svacchanda Tantra, Netra Tantra, Mṛgendra Tantra, Vijñāna Bhairava,* and the *Parātrīśikā,* which is a part of the (now lost) *Rudrayāmala*. One of the basic spiritual texts that represents *Śiva-advaita* belongs to the *Trika* tradition proper: the *Śiva-Sūtras,* which are believed to have been revealed to Vasugupta in the eighth–ninth centuries. Vasugupta is therefore sometimes considered to be the historical founder of the tradition. His disciple Somānanda (ninth century) was the first to give a philosophical basis to the system in his *Śivadṛṣṭi*. The philosophical as well as mystical tradition was further developed by Utpaladeva, disciple of Somānanda (ca. 900–950), who wrote the exposition of the doctrine of recognition, the *Īśvara-Pratyabhijñā-Kārikās* (or *Sūtras*), which have been commented on twice by Abhinavagupta. Utpaladeva also composed the *Siddhitrayi* and the mystical hymn *Śivastotrāvalī*. Another branch of the same school is the *Spanda Śāstra*, the doctrine of "creative vibration," of which the basic text, the *Spanda-Sūtras* (or *Kārikā*) is attributed to Vasugupta (ninth century).

The greatest genius, who developed all the aspects of the tradition—namely, the mystical, aesthetic, philosophical, and Tantric elements—was Abhinavagupta (tenth–eleventh centuries C.E.), disciple of Lakṣmaṇagupta, who was the son and pupil of Utpala, and of several other *gurus*. He wrote commentaries on the *Pratyabhijñā Kārikās*, on Tantras such as the *Pāratrīśikā (Vivaraṇa)*, on poetics such as *Dhvanyāloka Locana*, and on dramaturgy (*Abhinava Bhāratī* on *Nāṭya Śāstra*), as well as independent works such as the voluminous *Tantrāloka* ("the light of the Tantras"), a *Summa* of the Tantric theory and practice; an abridged version of it, the *Tantrasāra;* and mystical hymns (*stotras*) and other works. The universality of his life and work throws light on the spirituality of the school in which the mystical dimension penetrates all aspects of life, art, and thought. It was Abhinavagupta who brought Kashmir Śaivism to its pinnacle of development. Abhinavagupta's disciple Kṣemarāja (tenth–eleventh centuries) was another prolific writer who commented on the *Śiva Sūtras*, on the Tantras such as *Svacchanda, Netra, Vijñāna Bhairava*, on the *Spanda-Sūtras*, and so forth, and also wrote independent works such as the *Pratyabhijñā-Hṛdaya* ("the heart of recognition"). Another important representative of the school was Bhāskara (eleventh century), who wrote a commentary on the *Śiva Sūtras*. Jayaratha (twelfth century) wrote an illuminating commentary on Abhinavagupta's *Tantrāloka*. The creative period of the tradition must have lasted till the twelfth–thirteenth centuries, although there have been later authors such as Śivopadhyāya in the eighteenth century. The Muslim invasion of Kashmir certainly contributed to the disappearance of the school, although it still survives among a few Pandits and yogis in our time. Today, however, there seems to be a revival or reawakening of interest in this mystical and philosophical system, which combines in itself the best elements of the Indian Spirit.

Metaphysical Background

The spiritual and metaphysical dimensions are closely interwoven in the *Trika* school, so that the one can be understood only in the light of the other. For the sake of simplification the system will be presented here as a whole, without reference to the different traditions it contains, such as *Krama*, *Kula*, *Spanda*, and so on, and to the historical developments. As the name *Trika* indicates, there are three basic principles: Śiva (God), Śakti (his Energy), and *nara* or *aṇu* (the created beings, the individual soul). But this explanation of *Trika* is common also to other schools of Śaivism, which are fundamentally dualistic and which accept the principles of *pati* (Lord), *pāśa* (bond), and *paśu* (soul). Hence, the *Trika* school gives other meanings to the term, such as the three levels of reality or stages of manifestation: the supreme (*parā*), the intermediate (*parāparā*), and the lower (*aparā*), which correspond to the stages of nondifference (*abheda*), identity-in-difference (*bhedābheda*), and differentiation (*bheda*). In the realm of spiritual practice it refers to the three ways of access to the Divine, the three *upāyas* (excluding *anupāya;* see below).

This "trinitarian" structure, however, does not exclude but rather presupposes *advaita* (or *advaya*), a nondualistic conception of reality. In spite of many similarities with Śaṅkara's Advaita, there are some fundamental metaphysical differences. Though for both systems the absolute Reality is beyond the realm of thought or imagination (*nirvikalpa*) and is pure Light (*prakāśa*), self-luminous consciousness (*cit*, *saṃvit*), Śaṅkara's *Brahman* is static and without any internal or external relation, whereas the Unsurpassable (*anuttara*), supreme Lord (*Paramaśiva*) of *Trika* contains in Himself the total dynamism of love and self-knowledge which expands into the universe and yet contains everything within it.[2] One way of expressing this dynamic nature of the ultimate reality is the relation between *prakāśa* and *vimarśa;* that is, the pure Light of consciousness (*prakāśa*) is not only contained within itself but is also reflected in an all-embracing, dynamic, and creative act of self-consciousness or reflective awareness (*vimarśa*). Whatever dynamism there is in the realm of consciousness (spirit) or manifestation, it has its root in this relation of "light" and "reflected awareness." *Īśvara Pratyabhijña Kārikā* expresses it thus: "The very nature of manifestation is self-consciousness (*vimarśa*); otherwise the pure light of consciousness (*prakāśa*), even when affected by objects, would be insentient like a crystal" (IPK I, 5, 11).

Abhinavagupta comments that the very essence of self-consciousness is freedom (*svātantrya*), a freedom that can express itself both internally and externally, which is the very nature of manifestation (*avabhāsa*) and which is characterized by a "resting in itself" (*svātmaviśrānti*), independent of anything else. For when the self-awareness (*vimarśa*), "I who am of the nature of light shine myself" (*aham eva prakāśātma prakāśe*), arises, then the pure consciousness (*saṃvit*) realizes itself as the unity of knower, known, and means of knowledge and does not desire anything outside. Abhinavagupta quotes a verse in support: "the fulfilment of the meaning of the projection of awareness relating to 'this' (object) consists in the awareness resting in its very own essence, in the form of 'I am this.'"[3]

In other words, it is the total I-consciousness (*pūrṇāhantā*, *ahaṃbhāva*) that does not exclude but embraces the objective consciousness (*idaṃtā*, objectivity). The object has its existence only in the light of consciousness, but it is not denied its own "objective" existence. It is the analysis of consciousness itself that reveals the nature of the Absolute, and its nature is freedom, a freedom also to manifest.

Though inseparable from *Paramaśiva,* this freedom is also considered his Energy or Śakti. Thus, another way of presenting the theology of *Trika* is the conception of the Śaktis, the divine powers both inherent in *Paramaśiva* and manifesting his activity. Śiva is pure Light (*prakāśa*), whereas Śakti is the creative reflection of this light (*vimarśa*). Unlike the *māyā* of Vedānta, the Śakti of Kashmir Śaivism is a positive force, which in no way diminishes the fundamental nonduality. Śakti, which is essentially one, is ever united to Śiva (their union is called *sāmarasya*, "communion of essence"), and yet there are stages of manifestation that are represented by the different Śaktis. There reality is recognized on the level to which they relate. Thus, corresponding to five levels of consciousness are five Śaktis, of which the first two are inseparable from Śiva: *cit* (consciousness, corresponding to absolute transcendence or *turīyātīta*) and *ānanda* (bliss, corresponding to the "fourth" state, *turya*). The last three represent stages of manifestation. *Icchā śakti* is the first stirring of the will in the womb of absolute consciousness; it corresponds to the level of dreamless sleep (*suṣupti*), of the knower (*pramātṛ*, subject) in the realm of knowledge. *Jñāna śakti* is the power of knowledge, which can be related both within and outside, corresponding to the stage of dream (*svapna*), which is the intermediate stage of speech (*madhyamā*),[4] where thought is in the process of formulating itself in the mind, a stage preceding every external creation. It relates to the means of knowledge (*pramāṇa*). The last Śakti is *kriyā*, the power of activity, manifesting Śiva externally in the universe. It corresponds to the state of waking (*jāgrat*) in which the external world is perceived distinctly (*prameya*, the object; *bheda,* differentiation), and in which the transcendental word (*vāk*) is uttered in gross speech (*vaikharī*).[5]

Although this process of manifestation originates solely in the divine freedom and bliss, it also involves a process of veiling (*āvaraṇa*) the essential nature of the Absolute and of creating the illusion of individual existence apart from divine consciousness.

> These divine energies which are perfectly pure lose their purity gradually. The energy of will or desire (*icchā*) which in the beginning is only acceptance

of the fullness becomes a limited desire; knowledge (*jñāna*) which is nothing but conscious light of the Self appears as a knowledge which distinguishes between subject and object; activity (*kriyā*) which is the simple stirring of the fullness of the absolute I in itself, unfolds itself in dispersed movements and ends in enslaving action."[6]

This is the stage of *aṇu* (literally, the "atom"), the atomized individual, who is limited by the five "coverings" or veils (*kañcuka*): the limitations of activity (*kalā*), of knowledge (*vidyā*), of attachment or desire (*rāga*), of time (*kāla*), and of necessity (*niyati*).

In *Pratyabhijñā* philosophy, ignorance (*avidyā*, *ajñāna*), which causes suffering and hinders liberation, is not an illusion or false knowledge, as in Advaita Vedānta, but rather forgetfulness or incomplete knowledge (see TA I, 22, 26). Liberating knowledge is never something new, unknown, coming from outside, but is necessarily a recognition of the forgotten Reality underlying all things and experiences. The distinction may seem insignificant, but the consequences in the realm of metaphysics and of spiritual practice are far-reaching. The approach of Kashmir Śaivism is essentially positive, using every human experience as a means of liberation or true insight. The similes used by each of the two systems to demonstrate the nature of liberating knowledge clearly indicate this difference. In Advaita Vedānta the false perception of the snake has to be overcome to give place to the right knowledge of the rope. In *Pratyabhijñā* the most common simile is that of a girl in love who has either never seen the beloved but only heard of his qualities, or who has forgotten him because of a long separation. When the object of her love suddenly appears before her, she does not immediately recognize him. It is only when she is told about his identity, or when she recognizes some features from her memory, that she is overwhelmed with the joy of recognition (see IPV I, 1, 1).

The lover is the soul who has forgotten her Lord, though she hears about him in the scripture and in the words of the master. When, because of her longing and spiritual practice, the Lord manifests himself to her, she still needs the help of a *guru* to recognize him as such. So far the simile could also have a dualistic interpretation, but the real content of *Pratyabhijñā* is nondualistic, as Abhinavagupta comments on the simile: "Even when the beloved is close to her sight, yet her heart is not filled with joy. In the same way, though the Lord of all is ever shining in one's own self, this shining does not give fullness to the heart . . . because it is not realized" (IPV IV, 2, 2; KSTS vol. 33, pp. 274–75). But when, through the word of a guru or other means, the heart is attracted to the Divine, one realizes in a moment the fullness of the self and attains liberation in this life (*jīvanmukti*) (ibid.).

The combination of dualistic and nondualistic elements in the simile of "recognition" is not by chance, for the duality of the soul and the Lord is at first not denied. Otherwise the strong spirit of *bhakti* pervading Kashmir Śaivism would have no theological basis. The *advaitic* interpretation, being the ultimately real one, has to correspond to a higher level of consciousness: the realization that the Lord is not somewhere "out there," where the soul has been searching for Him, but that He is the innermost reality of her being. The dualistic approach is thus not negated, but integrated.

This mystical recognition, which is liberating, is certainly knowledge (*jñāna*), but of what kind, asks Jayaratha, the commentator on the *Tantrāloka* (TA I, 156; KSTS vol. 23, p. 192), introducing the following verse of Abhinavagupta:

> Liberation is nothing else but the unfolding (revelation) of one's own real nature (*svarūpa*). The real nature of the Self is nothing but Consciousness.

Jayaratha explains "unfolding" (*prathanam*) as "knowledge of the reality as it is" (*yathātattvam jñānam*) (TA I, 193). Once this knowledge is attained, it cannot be shaken, as Somānanda says in his *Śivadṛṣṭi:*

> Once one gets the unshakable knowledge of the omnipresence of Siva, through the means of right knowledge, scripture or preceptorial instruction,[7] the instruments of knowledge and meditation become perfectly useless. For, once gold is known as such, are the instruments needed to reveal its genuineness? At all times the certainty is due to a firm belief, as in the case of one's parents, etc.[8]

The difference between the states of bondage in *saṃsāra* and of liberation is clearly described by Abhinavagupta in the *Īśvara Pratyabhijñā Vimarsínī* (III, 2, 11–12): The state of *saṃsāra*, which is limited to the three psychological states of waking, dream, and deep sleep, is characterized thus: the I-consciousness (*ahaṃbhāva*) of the worldly beings is merged in "this-consciousness" or objectivity. In other words, the pure I-consciousness is lost in externality. In the state of liberation the opposite is the case, externality being absorbed in I-consciousness, which is the Self of freedom. This is the realm of liberation-in-life (*jīvanmukti*), within which again two stages are distinguished: *turya*, the "fourth" state, in which the body and all external realities "give up their objectivity as it were" (*prameyatām ujjhatīva*); and *turyātīta*, "beyond the fourth," where one realizes in one's own self the divine qualities of all-pervasiveness and eternity. Both these states of *jīvanmukti* are called *samāveśa*, merging in the Divine, entering into the divine consciousness (IPV, p. 231). However, "on the falling off of the body, the supreme Lord remains the only reality (*ekarasaḥ*), then who merges, where and how?" (IPV, p. 232). Even the talk of entering or merging (*samāveśa*) is conditioned by our external existence, because it presupposes a spatial conception of "outside" and "within."

The ultimate theological ground of both veiling or bondage and liberation is God Himself who, in spite of His freedom and self-luminosity, plays the game of hiding Himself and becomes thus the limited individual.[9] In fact, if the source of imperfection or individualization would lie somewhere else, outside the Divine, this would imply an ultimate duality (*dvaita*) and a limitation in the divine freedom. But even the imperfections (*mala*) of the individual are part of the divine nature (TA XIII, 103), and thus it is clear that not much effort is needed to awaken to one's real nature (*svarūpa*). It happens "by the will of the Lord" (see TA IX, 144–47), which is identical with the divine grace or "descent of divine energy" (*śaktipāta*) (see TA XIII). This leads us directly to the spiritual practice which is inseparable from theory,[10] for only he who partakes of the ultimate experience in his own heart, who is of the same spirit (*sahṛdaya*)[11] understands the meaning of the scriptures.

The Four Spiritual Ways (*upāya*)

Spirituality is both a state of being and an activity, static and dynamic; and, as we have seen, in the metaphysics of *Trika* there is place for both. Insofar as the soul is part of the dynamic process of manifestation, its way of return to the source of manifestation will also involve activity and effort. Insofar as it is one with the nondual divine consciousness, it will transcend every kind of activity or effort and it will enjoy the blissful and illuminated, uninterrupted divine state (see TA II, 1). The word *upāya* (from *upa-i-*, "to go near, approach"), meaning path, way of access, method, means of liberation, and the like implies the dynamic approach. It pertains, strictly speaking, only to the three ways that correspond to the three stages of manifestation and the three Śaktis mentioned earlier, implying a movement in the opposite direction: from differentiation to nondifferentiation. The so-called fourth way is in reality no *upāya*. Hence it is called *anupāya*, "non-way," and it would be more correct to speak of "the three spiritual ways and the non-way."[12] The difference lies precisely in the starting point: the three *upāyas*, or rather the soul using them for its ascent (*ārurukṣu*), start from different degrees of limited consciousness, whereas *anupāya* situates itself immediately on the level of divine reality and thus spontaneity.[13]

In his *Tantrāloka*, Abhinavagupta introduces the *upāyas*, which he calls also four ways of knowledge (*jñāna*):

> The Lord reveals himself to some knowing subjects in his fullness, whereas to others in parts (gradually). The revelation of his own nature which is the one reality of all realities (*viśvabhāva-ekabhāvātmā* . . .) is the supreme knowledge

> of the individual souls, what is different from it is the lower (knowledge which is) manifold. (TA I, 140–41)

The "revelation in fullness" refers to *anupāya*, or the highest stage of *śāmbhava*, whereas the partial and gradual revelation relates to the three ways. But Abhinavagupta adds immediately:

> The division in ways (means) and goal (end) is a gross confusion of knowledge, which is due to the power of activity (*kriyāśakti*), the cause of bondage and liberation. (TA I, 145)

In reality, says the commentator, the goal (*upeya*) and the way (*upāya*) are one, Śiva being the goal whose nature is the highest light and who shines everywhere, who is therefore ever attained. "Therefore the ways (means) are perfectly useless, because they are meant to make known what is unknown."[14] Thus the awareness that any means or method is only a relative approach is necessary in order to understand the *upāyas*. For this same reason the *upāyas* are not presented in an ascending order, for that would imply that the individual's standpoint and the effort of the soul to reach the divine are real or more important. On the contrary, the presentation (both in the *Śiva-Sūtra Vimarśinī* and in Abhinavagupta) starts from the highest, the non-way or *anupāya*, and descends step by step through the levels of consciousness. This treatment implies that there is rather a descent of the Divine down to individual human consciousness in order to lead it back to its original nature. The difference of degrees between the *upāyas* is thus due not to spiritual gradation but to the state of consciousness in which one finds oneself when one starts one's spiritual journey. If one is engrossed in one's individuality, subject to the power of activity, and lives on the level of subject–object dichotomy, one must follow *āṇavopāya*, the way of the individual (*aṇu*). It is the level of the waking state (*jāgrat*) with its differentiated perception (*bheda*). If one finds oneself on the level of thought and imagination (*vikalpa*), which is the realm of the power of knowledge (*jñānaśakti*), one must make use of those very means belonging to this intermediate stage of the *śakti* or of *vimarśa*, creative self-reflection. This is called the way of energy, *śāktopāya*. In it the dream-consciousness (*svapna*) prevails representing unity-in-diversity (*bhedābheda*). The one whose mind is purified of all dualistic thought (*vikalpa*) and who has received sufficient grace to be open to the divine I-consciousness can proceed on the divine way, *śāmbhavopāya*. This "method" depends only on the power of the will (*icchāśakti*):

> That which is the first moment of self-consciousness shines clearly and directly in the one realm beyond thought (*nirvikalpa-ekadhāmani*) is known as "will" (i.e., the divine way). (TA I, 146)

Since in this state all differentiated consciousness is overcome (*abheda*), it is related to deep sleep (*suṣupti*), which immediately precedes the transcendental consciousness.

In the *Śiva-Sūtras* as interpreted by Kṣemarāja, the three states of consciousness related to the three *upāyas* are characterized in an extremely concise way: On the level of *śāmbhava* it is said that "the Self is pure consciousness" (*caitanyam ātmā*) (ŚS I, 1), that is, pure subjectivity, which is nondifferent from divine I-consciousness. On the level of *śākta* there is a conscious identification between the mind (thought) and its object: "The mind is itself the *mantra*" (ŚS II, 1), *mantra* being the crystallization of thought (root *man-*) and the manifestation of the divine Śakti.[15] The mind becomes attuned to the power of the *mantra*. "The mind of the devotee intent on intensive awareness of the deity inherent in the *mantra* acquires identity with that deity and thus becomes that *mantra* itself."[16] On the level of the individual consciousness, hence the level of *āṇava*, "the empirical self is mind" (*ātmā cittam*) (ŚS III, 1), that is, in its state of limitation (*saṃkocāvabhāsa*, etc.).[17] In relation to the mind, the three *upāyas* effect the reverse process of the projection (*visarga*) of its three states by the divine Śakti: *āṇava* consists in the resting of the mind in the object (*cittaviśrānti*); *śākta* is characterized as the awakening of the mind (*cittasambodha*); and in *śambhava* occurs the dissolution of the mind and thus of all objectivity (*cittapralaya*) (see TS III, p. 17).

Since, with the exception of the highest mystical consciousness (*anupāya*), it is rare to find a state of mind in an absolutely pure form, there cannot be any watertight distinctions between the *upāyas*. Their division is mainly based on a prevalent state of the soul and the corresponding means of liberation, but they are closely interrelated. Their goal is one and the same, as Jayaratha says:

> Thus though the ways of liberation (*upāya*) are three-fold due to their (different) nature of will (*icchā*), knowledge (*jñāna*) and activity (*kriyā*), yet with regard to liberation (*apavarga*) which consists in becoming one with the goal (*upeya*), there is no difference whatsoever.[18]

Therefore all the four *upāyas* are also called ways of absorption or union with the divine, *samāveśa* (literally, "entering completely," "compenetration," "communion") (TA XXXIV). Abhinavagupta quotes the *Mālinīvijaya Tantra* as the scriptural authority:

> This threefold way has been taught by Parameśvara (the highest Lord) in the ancient text in the explanation of the divine union (*samāveśa*) (TA I, 167):
>
> "The union which takes place in one whose mind is free, by the awakening imparted by the *guru*[19] is called the divine union (*śāmbhava*)." (TA I, 168)

"That communion (with Śiva) which is obtained only by mental reflection on the reality which is beyond the process of enunciation[20] is designated in this tradition as *śākta*." (TA I, 169)

"The union which comes about by means of enunciation (*uccāra*), of physical exercises (*karaṇa*), of meditation (*dhyāna*), of phonemes (*varṇa*) and of concentration on subtle centres (in the body) (*sthānakalpanā*) is rightly called 'individual' (*āṇava*)." (TA I, 170)

We are not betraying the tradition if we present the single *upāyas* in ascending order, because it is easier to understand for the uninitiated, since the *Mālinīvijaya Tantra* also introduces them in the order from *āṇava* to *śāmbhava*.[21]

Āṇava, the Individual Way

The *Spanda Kārikās* describe the state of the limited individual, the starting point of *āṇavopāya*, in the following verse:

When the perturbation of that empirical individual who is incapacitated by his own impurity and is attached to actions disappears, then the highest state appears. (I, 9)[22]

Most beginners on the spiritual path and even yogis find themselves in this predicament of distraction on the different levels of body and mind; therefore, the proper means to overcome it are various kinds of concentration of the body, breath, speech, and mind. Since the individual is affected by impurities (*mala*), this *upāya* is above all a way of purification. All types of external practices and exercises are directed to the purification and transformation of activity. This is also the place for ritual and worship, which initially implies a duality of worshiper and deity.[23] Since it depends on imaginative thought (*vikalpa*) and on external means, it is also called *anyopāya*, that is, "meditation by means of something else" (see TA I, 219; TS V) or *kriyā-upāya*, the way of activity. In all the methods described under *āṇavopāya*, what is important is to interiorize the experience, as for example in the psycho-physical practices of yoga, which concentrate on different centers in the body (*cakra*), on the breath (*prāṇa*, *uccāra*), and so on. Because of their psychic nature, these exercises also procure psychic powers (*siddhi*) and various types of bliss (*ānanda*), besides leading ultimately to union with the Divine.

Thus the various supernormal powers accrue to the Yogī by means of purification of the body, purification of the elements, *prāṇāyāma*, *pratyāhāra*, *dhāraṇa*, *dhyāna* and *samādhi*.[24] All such powers are due to a veil of confusion and not (due) to the highest knowledge of reality. (ŚS III, 6)[25]

But even in the context of *āṇava*, *Trika* gives a meaning to the "limbs" of Yoga beyond the level of external practice, thus differing from the classical Yoga of Patañjali. This interiorization, however, leads the Yogi beyond *āṇava* to *śakta* (see ŚS III, 6). Thus, for example, the simple use of posture (*āsana*) in Patañjali's yoga is given a new meaning, as the *Śiva-Sūtra* says:

> Established in the posture (*āsana*) (the Yogī) is immersed with ease in the ocean (of immortality). (III, 16)

The commentator defines *āsana*: "He sits, i.e., that on which he is established in an everlasting oneness, that is his seat (*āsana*), which is the power of the highest Śakti."[26] The meditation (*dhyāna*) done on such a "seat" also transcends all duality, as the *Netra Tantra* exclaims:

> Neither meditate on something above, nor on the middle nor on something down below . . . neither on something within the body nor should one meditate on something outside. . . . Neither one should close one's eyes nor should one keep the eyes open without blinking. Neither one should meditate on something as a support (an image etc.) nor on a negation of a support . . . nor on the senses nor beings. . . .
>
> Thus leaving aside every support, established in *samādhi*, one should only abide identified with the Highest. . . . (VIII, 41–45)[27]

Samādhi itself has been defined by the same Tantra:

> In this world, whether in oneself or in other creatures, if one maintains the idea of sameness (*samāna-dhī*), i.e., if one experiences in everything the same secondless Śiva as I, that is *samādhi*. (VIII, 18)[28]

Obviously, this state already belongs to a higher level of consciousness, beyond differentiation (*bheda*).

Śākta, the Way of Divine Energy

> When the imaginative thought (*vikalpa*) purifies itself, independently from any other means of liberation, when the activity of the bound soul has ceased, and by the grace of pure knowledge (*śuddhavidyā*) it has attained the nature of the śakti of the highest Lord, then it makes manifest the knowledge of the divine Energy (*śāktam jñānam*, i.e., *śāktopāya*), depending on it as a means. (TS V, beginning; KSTS, p. 35)

Between object and subject, externality and internality, lies the realm of thought and knowledge. Hence this spiritual path is also called *jñānopāya*, and it is related to *pramāṇa*, right perception. The yogi whose body and mind have been purified by practice and who has received grace (*śaktipāta*) can proceed on this way. The *Tantrasāra* describes it as consisting of the means of "creative meditation" (*bhāvanā*), right reflection (*sattarka*), true scripture (*sadāgama*), and instruction by the true master (*sadguru*).

> Due to the power of imaginative thought (*vikalpa*) people consider themselves to be bound, this wrong imagination is the cause of the bondage of *saṃsāra*. One therefore has to cultivate the opposite thought which destroys the thought that is the cause of *saṃsāra* and which leads to the consciousness: "The ultimate reality is of the nature of unbroken pure consciousness transcending all limited realities (*tattva*) up to Śiva . . . this is the life-power by which the whole universe lives and breathes, this am I, therefore I transcend the universe and am also immanent to it." (TS IV, 21)

Abhinavagupta gives here a very clear idea of what happens in *śākta*: far from being a mere intellectual exercise, the wrong conception of reality, which is common to all people, is here to be replaced by a kind of meditative practice (*bhāvanā*) in which one convinces oneself of the true nature of reality. In this transformation of consciousness a conscious effort is still involved. The *Vijñāna Bhairava* gives an example of this kind of autosuggestive meditation:

> One should consider the entire body or the entire world simultaneously without thought-construct (*vikalpa*) as a form of consciousness, then one will experience the emergence of the highest consciousness.[29]

The proper "organ" for this process is the heart (*hṛdayam*), which Kṣemarāja defines as "the light of consciousness, inasmuch as it is the foundation of the entire universe" (ŚS I, 15, p. 59).[30] It is clear that the level of Śakti corresponds to a cosmic expansion of consciousness. But because of the imaginative nature of the spiritual practices in *śākta*, it still belongs to the level of the dream state (*svapna*).

One of the most eminent methods here is the practice of the *mantra* with which the mind of the yogi has to be identified.[31] Of course, *mantras* are used at every level of religious practice, but in *śākta* the process of interiorization proper begins, so that the *mantra* is defined by Kṣemarāja thus: "That by which one deliberates secretly, i.e., ponders inwardly as being non-different from the Highest Lord is *mantra*."[32] Since *mantras* consist of the letters of the alphabet, these are to be meditated upon as a form of Śakti (*mātṛkā*).[33] Many subtle speculations and meditations on the mystical nature of speech and the letters as elements of the *mantra* are involved in this *upāya*.

All other religious practices such as sacrifice, adoration, prayer (*japa*), observances (*vrata*), and yoga are equally spiritualized, as Abhinavagupta says in *Tantrasāra:*

> Sacrifice (*yāga*) is the offering of all things to the highest Lord alone, in order to attain a firm conviction that nothing is separated from him. . . . Prayer (*japa*) is the inner act of consciousness that the highest reality consists of its own being without depending on anything else of the form of external or internal objects. . . . (IV, pp. 25–26)

Thus *śāktopāya* also contains a variety of spiritual practices that all have the aim of purifying consciousness, so that it is prepared to receive the highest grace (see TA XIII). Here the guru plays an important role of mediation.[34] In its highest stage this *upāya* leads directly to the "divine way."

Śāmbhava, the Divine Way

The ascending order means a coming ever closer to the divine consciousness itself. In as much as this "approach" still involves a minimum of effort, subtle though it may be, it belongs to the category of an *upāya* and to the metaphysical realm of the Śakti. *Śāmbhava* is the last of the *upāyas,* which is reduced only to a stirring of the will, to an inner impulse directed toward the Divine. It thus belongs to the realm of *icchāśakti*, the first movement of will in the womb of the supreme Śiva, preceding every act of knowledge (*jñāna*) and activity (*kriyā*). At the same time the soul that finds itself on the level of this *upāya* already shares in the divine nature. Just as in *āṇava* it was identified with the limited individual, in *śākta* with the Śakti, here it is itself on the level of Śiva. Therefore, Abhinavagupta explains the name *śāmbhava* in the following way:

> This penetration (*āveśa*) consists in the identification with the highest nature of Śambhu (Śiva), the Original One who is inseparable from his Śakti, due to the dissolution of the nature of the individual self devoid of freedom. (TA I, 173–74)

And again:

> *Śāmbhava* communion (*samāveśa*) consists in a consciousness free from imaginative thought (*avikalpa*) and independent from creative contemplation (*bhāvanā*) etc., which attains the state of identity with Śiva. (TA I, 178)

Having transcended the realm of objectivity (*prameya*) and mediated knowledge (*pramāṇa*), this state partakes of pure subjectivity (*pramātṛ*), of full I-consciousness (*pūrṇāhantā*). Thus, the inferior *upāyas* have several kinds of support, whereas "the way of Śiva is a way without support, without effort, without taking help of the faculties; it is the way of pure desire, of naked intention; it tends toward Śiva alone, not toward his energy or his attributes."[35] Therefore the *Śiva-Sūtra* says: "The elevation of consciousness is itself Bhairava (the Supreme)" (I, 5).[36] And the commentary adds:

> That is *udyama* (elevation) which is an emergence of awareness in the form of the highest intuition (*pratibhā*) which is a sudden springing up of that I-consciousness of Śiva which expands in the form of the entire universe. . . . That *udyama* may in itself be called Bhairava in as much as it is the means for revealing Bhairava who is one's own essential Self. That *udyama* appears in those who are devoted to Him because of their whole attention being concentrated on that inner Bhairava-principle. (ŚS I, 5)[37]

Whatever *mantra*-practice or meditation on the phonemes or *mātṛkā* has been done on the lower levels, it finds its highest culmination in the divine way in what is called *parāmarśa* (or *varṇa-parāmarśa*): an act of consciousness, literally, seizing or grasping, which also means recollection, embracing all the phonemes (*varṇa*) in one grasp. It is again a reversal of the process of manifestation that takes place in the consciousness of the yogi: Śiva having manifested the whole universe by the enunciation of the phonemes or letters of the Sanskrit alphabet, summed up in the first and last, *a-* and *ha-* which together with the *bindu*, or dot, form the word *aham*, "I." Śiva's *parāmarśa* leads to the unfolding of the whole reality out of supreme I-consciousness, whereas the *parāmarśa*, or "act of recollection," of the yogi brings back all the dispersed elements of the universe consisting of letters into the unified I-consciousness (*aham*). He realizes the ultimate identity of all words and language with the Unsurpassable (*anuttara*), the Supreme Śiva. Abhinavagupta says in his *Tantrasāra* that the letters, belonging to the realm of *māyā*, are, so to say, resurrected to their real life by way of *parāmarśa* (TS III), by which they regain their spiritual meaning. The *mantra aham* symbolizes Śiva (*a*) and Śakti (*ha*) in their nondual union (*adavayam sāmarasyaṁ*) (TA III, 203–4), symbolized by *bindu* (the dot).

> Starting with the Unsurpassable (*anuttara*, *a*) and ending with *ha* which is of the nature of Śakti, this expansion is reabsorbed in the Unsurpassable, having condensed in itself the whole universe. (TA III, 204–5)

This is the way of attaining full I-consciousness (*pūrṇāhantā*).

> "I (*aham*) which has the form of pure luminosity of one's own self," this (realization) is what is called *paramārśa*.[38]

As all consciousness rises and finally rests again in the "I," so all letters and words arise and rest again in *aham*. Thus Utpaladeva describes *aham:*

> The I-concept connotes resting of the light of consciousness within itself. Inasmuch as it excludes all (external) expectancy, it is known as Repose

(within itself) or Composure. It is also absolute freedom, main doership and sovereign power.[39]

This way obviously presupposes a great purity of the mind, which, as Abhinavagupta says, may depend on previous practice (including religious practice done in the earlier lives) or on the free will of the Lord, which is identical with his grace (*śaktipāta*) (see TA I, 185–86). It implies the realization that "everything that exists, all this universe, is reflected in the heaven of consciousness" (TA III, p. 10) and "this reflected universe shines in the light of the highest Lord" (TA III, p. 10).[40] In terms of spiritual practice it means that one should constantly be attentive to this state of consciousness and experience the divine reflection (*pratibimba*) in every activity and perception.

The more subtle and interiorized a spiritual way becomes, the less does one find practical injunctions, because with the awakening of the inner consciousness the freedom also increases. Here the yogi has a share in the divine freedom (*svātantrya*) (see TS III, p. 10). If on the levels of practice and discipline the experience of pure consciousness is mostly limited to certain times or states, such as the time of meditation or *samādhi*, or happens in a moment like a flash of lightning, in the "divine state" this duality and interrupted nature of consciousness are overcome. "Thus to the one (yogi) in whom the universe has been assimilated (to the inner Śiva-consciousness), there is no difference between *samādhi* (absorption, ecstasy) and *vyutthāna* (ordinary consciousness)."[41]

Anupāya, the "Non-way"

Walking on a path leaves a trace, but the flight of the bird in the sky does not leave any trace. Passing from the three *upāyas* to *anupāya* could be compared to leaving the gravity of the earth to soar up in the sky of pure consciousness. There is both continuity and discontinuity between *śāmbhava* and *anupāya*, *anupāya* being the "extreme limit" of *śāmbhava*. Abhinavagupta says:

> Higher even than this (*śāmbhava*) is the supreme knowledge which is free from any mediation and method (*upāyādi-vivarjitam*), it is called unsurpassable (*anuttaram*, another name for *anupāya*) and it rests in the power of bliss (*ānandaśakti*). (TA I, 242)

The very subtle difference between the "divine way" and the "non-way" is explained by him thus:

> (In *śāmbhava* there is still) a conception of a difference between way (method) and goal (*upāya-upeya-kalpanā*), whereas (in the case of *anupāya*) there is not

> even a trace of any difference. For in the non-way, who is to be liberated, how and from what? (TA III, 272–73)

In other words, *anupāya* is a state of identity with the ultimate reality (*anuttara*) in which the question of going on a path, making an effort to reach the goal, being liberated, does not even arise.

We follow Abhinavagupta's argumentation in the second chapter of his *Tantrāloka* dealing with *anupāya*, where he himself puts the question: "What is the meaning of teaching the nature of the non-way?" which is hence inaccessible in the true sense of the word. In his answer he gives two levels of meaning for *an-upāya*: in one the negative particle *an-* is explained as a very reduced means (*alpopāya*),[42] such as a unique instruction by a guru that effects an immediate awakening in the disciple (TA II, 2). This awakening can also be brought about by mere "vision" (*darśana*) of a perfectly realized soul (*siddha*).[43] The specific nature of *anupāya* in this first sense excludes any repetition either of instruction or of practice, because repetition and effort belong to the first three *upāyas*.[44] For any means to be effective at once, without any falling back in a previous and inferior consciousness,[45] the soul must be perfectly pure and ready. It is then "pierced by a powerful descent of grace."[46] And "once it has attained what was to be attained, what is the purpose of the active meditations (*bhāvanā*) which imply useless effort?"[47]

The second and real meaning of *an-upāya* is pure negation of any means or method, as Abhinavagupta says in a verse:

> The net of the ways (*upāya*) cannot reveal Śiva.
> How could the thousand-rayed (sun) be shining in a jar (of water)?
> The one who discerns this in a sublime vision,
> He penetrates instantaneously into the self-luminous Śiva. (TS II, end)

The subtle difference between the two stages of *anupāya* is again related to the last two levels of consciousness: *turya*, the "fourth," in which there is still a remembrance of the psychological states (waking, dream, sleep) and thus also of that which caused the leap into transcendence, whereas *turyātīta* ("transcending the fourth") is the pure state of being beyond any distinction whatsoever, which can therefore be characterized only negatively: "This state is difficult to know. . . ."[48]

> Those who are lifted up into pure consciousness, purified by the supreme goal, they have firmly ascended the unsurpassable path, and are not bound by any means. (TA II, 34)

This state of being is in fact nothing that can be attained, because it ever *is;* it is inborn and natural (*sahaja*) to humans as spiritual beings. Its perfect freedom is therefore identical with the "innate knowledge."[49] This "natural state" is described by Abhinavagupta in his ecstatic Hymns:

> There is no need here of spiritual progress or of contemplation, neither of discourses nor discussion, neither of meditation nor of concentration, nor the effort and practice of prayer. What is then, tell me, the supreme Reality which is absolutely certain? Listen: *neither reject nor accept (anything), share joyfully in everything, being as you are.* (*Anuttarāṣṭikā*, v. 1)

"Being established in oneself" (*svasthaḥ*), without giving up (renouncing) or taking possession of anything, seems to be a perfectly passive state, but in reality it contains the whole potential of spiritual dynamism. In fact, it is this "fourth" state that in-forms and trans-forms all other states of consciousness, giving them life and ultimate reality.[50]

There is no hard and fast rule in the spiritual life, and the Kashmir Śaiva tradition teaches that any means, any starting point can serve as a way to reach the highest goal. Ritual and initiation (*dīkṣā*) are not excluded; they are rather presupposed, though constantly interiorized and spiritualized. What alone matters in all religious or spiritual practice is the transformation of consciousness—or, rather, the recognition of the one, all-pervading light of consciousness in oneself and in everything. Therefore the highest state of bliss of the Śaivite yogi is not isolation (*kaivalya*) but univeral bliss (*jagadānanda*), transforming everything into itself.

> The state which is free from all limitations, radiating everywhere, whose consciousness is unimpeded, nourished by the supreme nectar, where there is properly speaking no "realization" (*bhāvanā*) at all—that state which has been expounded by Śambhunātha, is the universal bliss. (TA V, 50–52)

The spiritual category of freedom (*svātantrya*), which implies both being established in one's self (*sva-*) and a complete unity with the divine freedom (for only the Divine is free), brings this tradition very close to the modern person's search for real freedom. This ideal of freedom, however, also shows clearly that it presupposes a spiritual discipline, which alone can prepare human beings and make them worthy to receive it as grace. Thus, the present-day quest for freedom and spiritual fulfillment that does not exclude but embraces other human values could be deepened in the light of the insights embodied in the Kashmir Śaiva tradition.

Notes

1. See IPK, 1, 16 *Sughaṭa eṣa mārgo navaḥ*. . . .
2. This difference can be explained in the sense that Śaṅkara's Advaita is basically an ascetic spirituality, whereas the Tantras have always combined the two ideals of *bhukti* and *mukti*, enjoyment and liberation.

3. *Idamityasya vicchinna-vimarśasya kṛtārthatā, yā svasvarūpe viśrāntirvimarśaḥ so'hamityayam.* IPV I, 41, vol. 1, p. 199. In K. C. Pandey's translation (Bhāskarī, vol. 3, p. 6) : "The ultimate end of all objective consciousness 'this' is its merging in the Self. The consciousness 'I am that' stands for it."

4. Though sometimes *jñānaśakti* is equated with the "seeing Word," *paśyantī*; see V. Raghavan, *Abhinavagupta*, 37.

5. For these correspondences, see *Tantrāloka* and the scheme given by B. Bäumer, *Abhinavagupta, Wege ins Licht* (Zurich: Benziger, 1992) 53.

6. L. Silburn, "Les trois voies et la non-voie dans le Śivaisme du Cachemire," in *Les voies de la mystique, Hermès* I (Paris, 1981) 142.

7. According to Tantric tradition, the awakening to Reality can be caused by the guru, by reading and pondering the scriptures (*śāstra*), or by oneself (*svataḥ*); see *Kiraṇatantra*, quoted in TA XIII, 162–63, also XIII, 156.

8. *Śivadṛṣti* 7, 5–6, quoted in IPV, KSTS, vol. 22, p. 15. Translated by K. C. Pandey, Bhāskarī, vol. 3, p. 5.

9. Cf. TA XIII, 102ff.; TS XI, p. 118: *parameśvaraḥ svarūpācchādanā-krīḍaya paśuḥ pudgalo'ṇu sampannaḥ*, etc.

10. It is beyond the scope of this article to go into the details of the cosmology and other doctrines of the school. See Pandey, *Abhinavagupta*.

11. This concept, which is well known in the realm of aesthetic experience, obviously belongs also to spirituality. See TA I, 332; III, 209–10.

12. See Silburn, "Les trois voies et la non-voie."

13. See, e.g., TA I, 242–44, etc. We will base our presentation of the *upāyas* mainly on the *Śiva Sūtras* with Kṣemarāja's commentary, and on Abhinavagupta's *Tantrāloka* (and *Tantrāsara*), which derives its inspiration from the *Mālinī Vijaya Tantra*.

14. Jayaratha on I, 145, vol. 1, p. 184.

15. *Śaktiḥ mantravīryasphārarupā*, introduction by Kṣemarāja to ŚS II, I.

16. Kṣemarāja's comment on II, 1, translated by Jaideva Singh, p. 83.

17. Commentary on ŚS III, 1.

18. Commentary on TA I, 166, p. 202. Cf. TA I, 149: *bhedo nātrāpavargaḥ*.

19. *Guruṇā pratibodhataḥ* has also been interpreted in a different way by Abhinavagupta as "due to an intense awakening." Cf. TA I, 172–73.

20. *Uccāra:* this term is difficult to translate, but it does not have the ordinary meaning of "utterance" in *Trika*. It involves a practice of breath-concentration. Cf. TS V.

21. The *Śiva-Sūtra Vimarśinī* and Abhinavagupta proceed from the highest to the lowest.

22. Translated by Jaideva Singh, *Spanda Kārikās*, p. 61.

23. In spite of the condition for performing any ritual that "only Śiva can worship Śiva."

24. Five of the eight parts of yoga; see *Yoga-Sūtra*.

25. Introduction by Kṣemarāja, translation by Jaideva Singh, p. 142 (translation slightly modified).

26. My own translation; cf. Jaideva Singh, p. 163.

27. Quoted in the commentary on ŚS III, 16, translated by Jaideva Singh, p. 164.

28. Quoted in ŚS III, 6, p. 145.

29. Translated by Jaideva Singh, *Śiva Sūtras*, pp. 62–63.

30. *Viśvapratiṣṭhāsthānatvāt citprakāśo hṛdayam.*

31. ŚS II, 1, quoted above: *cittam mantraḥ.*

32. ŚS II, 1, commentary, pp. 82–83: *tadeva mantryate guptam antar-vimṛśyate parameśvararūpam anena, iti kṛtvā mantraḥ.*

33. Cf. ŚS II, 3, p. 89; also ŚS II, 7. Cf. Jaideva Singh, p. 116: "The realization of the mysteries of *Mātṛkā* is most important for the aspirant who is in quest of the source of his being. The *Śāktopaya* deals primarily with *mantra. Mantra* consists of words or letters, in other words, *Mātṛkā*. It is therefore, of utmost importance for the aspirant to understand *Mātṛkā* and her host of *śaktis*."

34. See ŚS II, 6: *gurur upāyaḥ.*

35. Silburn, "Les trois voies et la non-voie," 173.

36. *Udyamo bhairavaḥ;* L. Silburn translates *udyama* as "élan."

37. Jaideva Singh, p. 30.

38. Jayaratha on TA III, 203–4.

39. *Ajaḍapramātṛ-siddhi* 22–23: *prakāśasya ātmaviśrāntirahambhāvaḥ* (ŚS II, 7, commentary, translated by Jaideva Singh, p. 108).

40. *Evaṃyathā etat pratibimbitaṃbhāti tathaiva viśvam parameśvaraprakāśe* (p. 11).

41. ŚS I, 7, introduction by Kṣemarāja, p. 36.

42. See Jayaratha on TA II, 2.

43. Cf. quotation given by Jayaratha in TA II, p. 2.

44. Cf. Jayaratha on TA II, 1 and TA III, 271, *bhūyo-bhūyaḥ samāveśam.*

45. *Avirata.* "Unbroken" is the characteristic of *anupāya* or the *anuttara* state (TA II, 1).

46. *Dṛḍho śaktipāta-āviddha* (TS II).

47. Jayaratha on TA II, 2, p. 3.

48. *Bhargaśikhātantra*, quoted in TA II, 28.

49. Cf. ŚS III, 13: *siddhaḥ svatantrabhāvaḥ*, and the commentary, *svatantrabhāvaḥ sahajajñātva.*

50. Cf. ŚS III, 20: *triṣu caturtham tailavadāsecyam*, and commentary.

Bibliography and Abbreviations

Texts Quoted

IPK *Īśvarapratyabhijñā Kārikā* by Utpaladeva (see IPV)

IPV *Īśvarapratyabhijñā Vimarśinī* by Abhinvagupta
Īśvarapratyabhijñā of Utpaladeva with the Vimarśinī by Abhinavagupta, vols. 1–2, KSTS 22 and 23 (Bombay, 1918, 1921)

KSTS Kashmir Series of Texts and Studies (Srinagar)

MV *Mālinī Vijaya Tantram*, KSTS 37 (Bombay, 1922)

NT *Netra Tantram, with Commentary by Kṣemarāja*, KSTS (Bombay, 1926)

SD *Śivadṛṣṭi of Somānanda, with the Vṛtti by Utpaladeva*, KSTS 54 (Srinagar, 1934)

ŚS *Śiva-Sūtra* (see under translations)

TA *Tantrāloka: The Tantrāloka of Abhinavagupta with commentary by Rājānaka Jayaratha*, KSTS 1–12 (1918–)

TS *Tantrasāra: The Tantrasāra of Abhinavagupta*, KSTS 17 (Bombay, 1918)

Sources

English

Pandey, K. C. Bhāskarī, vol. III, *An English Translation of the Īśvara Pratyabhijñā Vimarśinī*, Lucknow University, Lucknow, 1954.

Singh, Jaideva. *Pratyabhijñāhṛdayam*. 2nd rev. ed. Delhi: Motilal Banarsidass, 1977.

———. *Śiva Sūtras, The Yoga of Supreme Identity*. Delhi: Motilal Banarsidass, 1979.

———. *Spanda Kārikās, The Divine Creative Pulsation*. Delhi: Motilal Banarsidass, 1980.

———. *Vijñānabhairava or Divine Consciousness*. Delhi: Motilal Banarsidass, 1979.

French

Silburn, Lilian. *La Bhakti: La Stavacintāmaṇi de Bhaṭṭanārāyaṇa*. Paris: Ed. de Boccard, 1964.

———. *Hymnes de Abhinavagupta*. Paris: Ed. de Boccard, 1970.

———. *La Mahārthamañjari de Maheśvarānanda*. Paris: Ed. de Boccard, 1968.

———. *Le Paramārthasara*. Paris: Ed. de Boccard, 1957.

———. *Śivasūtra et Vimarśinī de Kṣemarāja*. Paris: Ed. de Boccard, 1980.

———. *Vātūlanātha Sūtra avec le Commentaire d'Anantaśaktipāda*. Paris: Ed. de Boccard, 1959.

———. *Le Vijñāna Bhairava*. Paris: Ed. de Boccard, 1961.

Italian

Gnoli, Raniero. *Abhinavagupta, Essenza dei Tantra (Tantrasara)*. Turin: Ed. Boringhieri, 1960.

———. *Luce delle Sacre Scritture (Tantraloka) di Abhinavagupta*. Turin: UTET, 1972.

Studies

Chatterji, J. C. *Kashmir Shavism*. KSTS. Srinagar, 1962.

Dyczkowski, M. G. *The Doctrine of Vibration*. Albany: State University of New York Press, 1987; Delhi: Motilal Banarsidass, 1989.

Lakshmanjoo, Swami. *Kashmir Shaivism*. Albany: State University of New York Press, 1988.

———. *Self Realization in Kashmir Shaivism*. Albany: State University of New York Press, 1994.

Padoux, A. *Vāc, The Concept of the Word in Selected Hindu Tantras*. Albany: State University of New York Press, 1990.

Pandey, K. C. *Abhinavagupta: An Historical and Philosophical Study*. Varanasi: Chowkhamba Sanskrit Series, 1935.

Raghavan, V. *Abhinavagupta and His Works*. Chowkhamba Orientalia. Varanasi, 1980.

Silburn, L. *Kuṇḍalinī, The Energy of the Depths*. Albany: State University of New York Press, 1988.

Les voies de la mystique ou l'accès au sans-accès. Hermès, Nouvelle Série I. Paris, 1981.

2

The Spiritual Contribution of Maharashtra Saints

S. N. BHAVASAR

THE LIFE OF A SAINT either in Maharashtra or in India as a whole presents before us an open book of spirituality, the living example of the Life Divine, of a common man, for common people, attained by common means of *bhakti* and *bhāva*, expressed in common language, with the help of common words, meters, images, and events in life, in all respects and levels. In Maharashtra, the five great saints who are enumerated as a group representing the whole saintly class are Jnāneśvara, Nāmadeva, Ekanātha, Tukārāma, and Rāmadāsa. Historically, these saints belong to a wide span of time, between the last quarter of the thirteenth century C.E. and the end of the seventeenth century. The tradition they followed is called *bhakti-sampradāya* (The School of Devotion), and the religious faith to which they belonged is known popularly as *bhāgavata-dharma*. Although this is a very old tradition, as a distinct *bhakti* movement its beginnings are around 1000 C.E. Jnāneśvara is regarded as the epochmaker of this movement.

The chronology of these saints is well established and does not pose any serious problems. There are some differences, however, regarding the literary compositions of these saints in terms of critical editing, interpolation, linguistics, and so on. Notwithstanding all such points, the traditional and devotional spirit remains intact. The most debated issue about the saints involves three points: (1) internal inconsistency and self-contradiction in their teachings, showing a lack of rationality and logic; (2) the emphasis of the saints on *mokṣa*, by detachment and renunciation of the world; and (3) questions concerning the validity and actuality of the so-called miracles said to have been performed by these saints.

At the very outset, it must be noted that these and other questions concerning the saints are raised mostly by scholars and critics, not by the devotees. No one doubts the spiritual attainment of these saints and the saintliness of their lives.

The Spiritual Contribution of Maharashtra Saints

We can formulate the spiritual contributions of Maharashtra saints as follows:

1. (Re)establishment of *dharma* and *svadharma* (i.e., collective and individual religious innate faith).
2. Establishment of devotion as the practical base of Life Divine, the spiritual life, and as the simple, safest way to self-realization.
3. God-realization as the *sine qua non* of Life Divine, by way of *bhakti* and *bhāva* (devotion and the highest lofty sentiments, emotion, faith), through complete self-surrender and worship (*saraṇāgati* and *seva*), and by annihilation and merging of personal ego at the feet of the Lord.
4. Self-realization (*atmasākṣātkāra*) as the end of *bhakti*, that is, *bhakti yoga*, qualified by *jñāna*. It is the core of monistic Vedānta, qualified by devotion (*bhakti*), knowledge (*jñāna*), and yoga (*hatha* or *rājayoga*).
5. Identification and unification of individual self with all through God-realization and self-realization.
6. Revival or maintenance of Vedic tradition and culture, by casting away degenerated forms of ritualism and dogmatism, through personal example.
7. Going above and beyond caste and creed, time and clime, even though retaining their external framework, and setting forth a practical solution uniting the internal and external forms of these dimensions of life, using the principle of "unity in diversity" as the main key to achieve the above.
8. Employment of popular languages, meters, images, symbols, and day-to-day popular events and expressions as the mass media for expressing the eternal truth, in a simple, straightforward manner in order to educate common people.
9. Exposing and rejecting the pseudo-elements in society by any means possible.

In short, the Life Divine, in terms of body, speech, and mind, is the spiritual contribution of Maharashtra saints.

The Spiritual Life of a Saint

The spiritual life of a saint is a journey toward self-realization, perfection within and without. This can be described in five stages: (1) preparatory, that is, early life, (2) active or internal life, (3) perfection or self-realization, (4) life after realization, and (5) end of life. The spiritual life is based on "experience," direct perception of God, and the transformation brought into one's life as the result of such experience. It is such a life that becomes a model for others, going beyond the narrow boundaries of the particular society to which the saint belongs and the historical time in which he/she has functioned.

Preparatory Stage: The Four Pillars of Divine Life

Though spirituality in principle is above and beyond any set of rules and regulations, we can trace its course in an individual's life from beginning to end. Spirituality may be seen as something that a saint inherits from his or her family, from one's maternal or paternal sides, or both.

Viveka and *vairāgya* are the two pillars of spirituality. The former is the faculty of discrimination—of what is good or bad, beneficial or malefic, eternal or ephemeral, true or false, and so on. *Vairāgya* is the faculty of detachment, desirelessness, and the tendency to renounce worldly life. These two pillars in turn produce *anutāpa* (Tk 3417, 906),[1] which indicates a kind of disgust, repulsion, frustration, and aversion that would in normal conditions be due to disease, disorder, death, poverty, financial loss, defamation, insult (either personal or of family), natural or accidental, and so on. It acts like oil in a fire caused by *viveka* and *vairāgya*. This is the negative side of spiritual life. Its positive side is characterized by *bhakti* and *bhāva* (Tk 3417, 906), devotion and pure lofty sentiments, including love, faith, and trust in God. Thus, *viveka*, *vairāgya*, *bhakti*, and *bhāva* are the four legs of Divine Life, and the devotional lives of the saints amply support this point.

These four salient features of spiritual life must refer to the three planes of life, physical, lingual (speech), and mental. These three symbolize all the activities that govern one's life. Especially important here is the mental

[1] On the age of *kali*, see Ek 2574–2886; Tk 415, 437–39; Jn 462. References and sources are based on *abhangas* in *Collected Works of all the Saints* (Marathi), ed. R. S. Avate (2nd ed.; 2 vols.; Pune, 1967).

plane, which includes four inner instruments, namely, mind, intellect, ego, and consciousness. These instruments govern the lingual and physical plane, which are the outward activities of life. The spiritual life as a whole is thus oriented toward God-realization and self-realization.

The positive aspect of the lingual plane is accepting *nāmajapa*, *mantras* like "Śrī Rāma Jayarāma, Jayajayarāma," "Jayajayarāma Kṛṣṇahari," "Śrī Rāma," "Śrīhari," "Pāṇḍuranga, Pāṇḍuranga," "Vitthala, Vitthala," "Shivo'ham Shivo'ham," and so on. The selection of a particular *mantra* for recitation depends on one's personal preference, one's psychological bent, and the family's traditional religious orientation. In some cases the *mantra* is taught by the master (guru) while initiating a disciple, or is obtained in a dream. In the Indian context, *mantra* has four planes: the gross (*sthūla*, i.e., articulated speech), the middle (*madhyamā*, i.e., the one that is yet to become audible for others), the mentally perceived (*paśyantī*) but not audible even to oneself, and the transcendental (*parā*), a pure state of consciousness that is the original unmanifest sound. The devotee starts first with the articulated form of speech, the *nāmajapa*, and moves on to the higher planes successively. The four planes of speech correspond to four levels of consciousness: waking, dreaming, deep sleep, and the transcendental (*jāgṛta*, *svapna*, *suṣupti*, and *turīya*, respectively). The *nāmajapa* arrives at a higher state of consciousness when it passes from waking to dreaming, dreaming to deep sleep, and higher. At each level the devotee meets with corresponding experiences; thereby the devotion becomes stabilized and effective in stages. Thus, God-realization and self-realization pass through four stages. Though the waking state is the grossest and lowest, it is also the state to which one returns as the result of God-realization and self-realization. This state is a material state, and, curiously, only when one ascends to the highest state of consciousness (*turīya*) is it possible conversely to arrive at the lowest state. The saints have realized God on this plane. Thus, it becomes possible for one to attain a *jīvanmukta* state or *sadeha-videha* state, that is, a noncorporeal state in a corporeal body. The state of God-realization is the result of intense *bhakti* and *bhāva* (devotion and affection, love). Only by *viveka* and *vairāgya*, which are basically forms of knowledge (*jñāna*), does one attain self-realization, often by the help and grace of one's guru. This state of self-realization is regarded as above the state of God-realization, since differences between I and Thou (*aham* and *tvam*), this and that (*idam* and *tad*), cease because of total identification and union, as expressed in the Upaniṣads, *aham brahmāsmi*, *tat tvam asi*, which signify a state of *brahma-jñāna*.

The Inner Life of the Devotee

This is a state characterized by ups and downs in one's *sādhana* (practice). It involves trials and ordeals, pains and pleasures, light and darkness, sometimes a war within. The life of an ordinary person follows a comparatively straight path with ups and downs in the context of family, society, and country, from birth to death. A life that does not follow such a course is an "abnormal" life, out of place socially. A person with such a deviation is often the subject of contempt, degradation, and disparagement by other members of the community, and may even be considered mentally deranged. Often a devotee whose life-style is different from the "normal" ones must face social criticism and contempt.

The inner life of a devotee demands control of *kāma* and *krodha* (desire and anger), the two formidable enemies of spiritual life. According to the *Gītā*, "When a man broods over the sense objects, attachment to them arises. From attachment arises desire, and desire breeds anger. From anger comes delusion of mind, and from delusion, the loss of memory; from loss of memory, the destruction of discrimination; and from the destruction of discrimination, the man perishes" (II. 62–63). *Kāma* and *krodha* have to be curbed, and this can be done by developing a state of mind of constant awareness and reflection through *viveka* and *vairāgya*. Another way is to cultivate the virtue of nonduality expressed in nonanimosity. The devotee could also develop the positive side of the above virtue expressed in love, affection, equality, and the like. This, however, is not an easy task; mind is not easily made to accept all these changes, as it is deeply rooted in division and duality. The ego peeps in; previous impressions of consciousness crop up; and reason loses hold of the discriminating faculty. This causes internal turmoil, noncooperation between internal faculties, dissension, dispute, fighting, or even warfare. Outside too the devotee must face similar situations (Jn 229; Nd 1281). The devotee's behavior, being very "queer and abnormal," becomes an object of criticism and rebuke. An aggregate effect of all these internal and external factors on a devotee is to induce him or her to move toward God-realization and consequently to self-realization. He or she then finds solace in God, sees in God the mother, the father, the brother, the friend, and even the husband, as well as the very abode of learning, of wealth, of everything. One's very existence, all one's life activities, are only for God, the sole focus of one's life. This overall situation leads the devotee to a higher form of worship, whose whole life becomes a sacrifice. Whatever act the devotee performs is an oblation offered at the feet of the Lord. One surrenders one's person completely, the act of *brahmārpaṇa*, to use the term from the *Gītā*. This is accelerated by *anuṣṭhāna* (repetitive penance), *tapascaryā* (severe austerity), and *upāsana* (deep, intense form of spiritual discipline), in an isolated place, a river confluence, a mountain peak, a cave or a temple. Even this process is often marked by ups and downs, depending on the psycho-physical dispositions of the devotee. Fear and joy, regression and progression, darkness and light, and so on are the devotee's common experiences.

One more facet that may be added to the spiritual discipline of the devotee is *sat-saṅgati*—association or the company of holy people, of those who have reached the goal or are progressing on the path of spiritual realization. Reading the biographies of such holy people and their compositions is a way of staying in contact with these holy people. In addition, *bhajana* (worshiping), *kīrtana* (singing), *nāmajapa* (repeating the holy name), *pravacana* (discoursing), and *harikathā* (listening to divine stories) are aids to intensify one's devotion.

The intensity resulting from union of all these factors elevates the devotee to higher and higher planes, from *jāgṛta* (waking state) to *svapna* (dream state), from *svapna* to *suṣupti* (sleeping state), and from *suṣupti* to *turīya* ("the Fourth state," which is beyond deep sleep state). Then the devotee's *sādhana* takes a reverse direction; from *turīya* to *suṣupti*, to *svapna*, and finally to *jāgṛta*, from the most subtle to the subtle and then to the gross and grossest aspects of one's consciousness (*citta*), thus percolating and pervading all the metaphysical, biophysical, physical planes. A devotee lacking this experience must make a conscious and deliberate effort to experience God in the waking state. When one's *sādhana* arrives at a higher plane, the devotee sees God sometimes in a dream. At a stage higher than this, one experiences God unknowingly, occasionally, and unexpectedly, in an ecstatic state of mind. It is only when his *sādhana* attains the highest height that there flashes the divine light, making God-realization in physical form (*nāmarūpa*) possible. Thus, the devotee is able to see God even in the waking state. The next stage of this process of God-realization, which has so far remained at an individual level, is realization at the cosmic level. While in the earlier stage the devotee experiences his or her identity with God, at the cosmic level, one experiences identity of God with the world. In the former stage one sees God within oneself; in the latter one sees God in the world, everywhere, even in inanimate objects such as trees, stones, and the like (Ek 1107, 1125; Tk 953, 972, 3280).

The crowning factor that accomplishes spiritual fruition is the guru, the teacher, the preceptor, the Master. The acquisition of guru is always held to be an act of divine grace, a blessing, a boon (Tk 339, 983, 1643, 3208, 3276). It is the guru who gives final shape, the final touch to the devotee's *sādhana*, by removing ignorance, expelling darkness, and eradicating the sense of division and duality by dissolving one's ego. The guru also establishes the devotee firmly in faith, devotion, sacrifice, in *viveka* (discrimination) and *vairāgya* (detachment), in the knowledge of oneness of the self, and in the identity of the individual with the world. The guru dissolves the trinity of the knower (subject), known (object), and knowledge (the epistemological process) and brings about unity. This ends with the acquisition of the status of *sat* (existence, the real), *cit* (consciousness), and *ānanda* (divine bliss).

Without the guru, the devotee can reach the state of God-realization, but self-realization is generally not possible without the guru. God-realization occupies a high position, yet it is not the highest, because it essentially involves duality, between God and the devotee. Therefore, it is penultimate to Vedantic monism of unity, oneness, and nonduality, which is possible only through self-realization. That is why self-realization is regarded as higher than God-realization. For self-realization and cosmic self-realization, the guru is the *sine qua non* of spirituality. The plane of duality should pave the way to the plane of knowledge of oneness or unity. This is a state where devotion is qualified by knowledge. Such a monistic state of knowledge is both *nirguṇa* and *saguṇa* (nonqualified and qualified) (Jn 7, 330; Nd 1713; Ek 1130–31; Tk 3276). The *bhakti* cults accept this kind of devotion, which is indeed Sāṅkhya qualified by Vedānta.

Thus God-realization, self-realization, cosmic God-realization, and cosmic self-realization are four aspects, four pillars, of Indian spirituality, the Life Divine. The transcendent, which is monistic, merges into the Absolute, which is beyond Time-Space (*dik-kāla*) (Tk 3350), and beyond description (*anirvacanīya*). In view of the above, the yoga of devotion in *bhakti* cults is seen as devotion (*bhakti*) qualified by knowledge (*jñāna*) and action (*karma*), and founded on *rājayoga*. All the four brethren, Nivṛtti, Jñānadeva, Sopana, and Muktabāi, as well as Ekanātha and Rāmadāsa, are the examples of such "integral yoga"—the *purna-yoga*, if the term is used in its proper sense. In such an integral view, the four separate yogas are essentially the four respective dimensions of life as a whole, enriching one another. Without the guru, the practice of such an integral yoga would be very difficult, if not impossible. Gurus such as Janārdana Swāmi and Gahinātha prove the point beyond doubt. A guru of this kind is *vibhūti* (special manifestations), and hence *Gītā* describes the integral yoga as *vibhūtiyoga* (chap. VIII). The guru, therefore, occupies such a high place that he is often regarded as superior even to God. Indian writers traditionally pay respect to their gurus in the very beginning of their treatises.

In the yogic parlance, the state of perfection is *svarūpa-pratiṣṭhā* ("establishment in one's own nature"), which is the result of complete purification of consciousness, cessation of all ripples in one's consciousness (*citta-suddhi, citta-vṛtti-nirodha*), namely, the recurring cyclic pattern of thoughts and impulses. Such a state results in *samatva*, *sāmya*, *samatā*, equilibrium, equality, equanimity in all respects and on all levels. Therefore, it is above and beyond all dualities (Nd 949, 2082; Tk 983, 3208). One experiences complete freedom, happiness, and bliss. Such a person, though having a physical body, is essentially bodiless—noncorporeal in a corporeal frame. Such a person is called *jīvanmukta*, one who is free from birth and death, a "living-free-person." That one has achieved what is called *brāhmī-stithi* (state of "Brahmanhood") according to the *Gītā*.

The External Life of the Saint

The life of a saint is characterized by complete purification within and without (*antar-bahir-śuddhi*) (Jn 229, 672; Nd 239, 926, 949, 1281). Though initially the saint had gone within to find oneself alone by going away from others and the world, once one finds oneself, one finds also what one had left outside. By realizing *ātman*, the self, one discovers others and the world; one realizes that the *ātman* is everywhere and is everything; still the *ātman* is one without a second. This has indeed been the central teaching of Vedānta, the very essence of Indian culture. Once this metamorphosis takes place, there manifests simultaneously the overall change, within and without. This complete identification and unity bring in total peace, *śānti*. One does not any longer search for God and locate God's presence in the outside world alone. One finds God's presence within one's own self. One also finds oneself in the world, in every thing, in good and bad, in rich and poor, in holy and sinful, in healthy and diseased. This makes the saint free from the sense of duality, from hatred and malice, competition, envy, desire, and anger. Since others are not different from oneself, one does not feel superior to others; consequently, in such a person there is no place for pride, egoism, or infatuation, or any vices of this kind. Naturally the person of that disposition does not seek power, position, or possessions, nor does that person try to command or control others. Neither is there room in such a person for wealth, name, or fame (Jn 459; Tk 439, 1169). And having attained the goal, thus being always happy and peaceful, a saint inspires others to aspire to the same goal. The saint, then, feels pity, sympathy, compassion, affection, and love for others; he or she cultivates forgiveness and tolerance for the shortcomings and weaknesses of others. Being one with others, the saint is able also to identify with their grief and suffering, by extending a helping hand to deal with those situations and ultimately overcome them. One may become so identified that one might actually experience within oneself the pain and sufferings of others.

The saint considers caste and creed, time and clime, to be superficial, external factors in a given socioethical frame of culture, not essential and not natural. The saint is not, however, an active social reformer. He or she realizes that in some form or other such matters would remain in society; though they are changeable, ephemeral, they do have practical utility. So long as ignorance persists they would always be powerful aspects of human life. These factors have to be defeated not through social revolution, which is external, but by an inner transformation of the individual. At the same time the saint realizes quite well that a rigid, dogmatic, ritualistic, or egoistic attitude and behavior on the basis of caste and creed, space and time (*jāti-dharma, yama-niyama* in relation to *dik* and *kāla*) (Jn 195; Ek 165; Tk 808) have nothing in fact to do with spirituality of the Life Divine nor even with natural life cycle. Furthermore, they are artificial and subject to change. They are even harmful and destructive to the human life, individually and communally. As the saint becomes a *udāsīna* (Nd 88; Tk 1000, 1178) (literally, seated above, that is, one who has achieved "high-seated impartiality") he or she does not try to demolish such institutions or revolt against them like a socio-ethico-religious reformer, or unnecessarily provoke public feelings or opinions against them; nor does the saint play with public emotions or sentiments. A saint follows *svadharma*. There is no need for one to adopt renunciation (*sannyāsa*) externally; it is natural, and it is within. Nor does the saint need to abandon spouse, children, parents, family, household responsibilities, or profession. The saint earns what is needed just to maintain the family and does not exploit others. The saint keeps away from addictions. The saint's actions, desires, and earnings (*karma, kāma,* and *artha*) follow the path of *dharma*. The saint respects God, brahmins, gurus, the cow, yogis, *siddha*, *tapasvi*, parents, the elderly, the wise, and those worthy of respect. The saint reads the sacred scriptures, is engaged in singing devotional songs, respects holy names, worships God, meditates, and follows socioethical codes of conduct. The saint uses simple words, simple meters, simple images, simple style, which, however, express the highest truths that are found in the Vedas, and in the Hindu philosophical systems. The saint thus leads a fully spiritual life.

As in life, so also in death. The saint is unmoved by disease and disorder but accepts them with calmness and equanimity. At the end of his or her span of life, the saint leaves the body voluntarily or by the yogic way, fully engrossed in divine experience, uttering divine names. The saint normally knows the time of his or her departure beforehand and sometimes even declares it to others. The saint's death may coincide with an auspicious day or time, a day of religious festival, so that it marks a happy departure and not one of gloom.

The Followers, Teachings, and Writings of the Saint

The passage of the saint from personal life to public life naturally results in the gathering of followers. *Lokasaṅgraha* (collection and integration of people, universal welfare) being his or her vow, a saint develops a following from his or her own family circle (for instance, Nāmadeva's followers included his sons, sons' wives, sisters, and maidservant) and also from those outside the family circle. In some cases the saints had followers who were born in the non-Hindu religious groups and practiced their religion. The writings and the teachings of a saint in general have experience as the basis, either personal or of one's guru, and may reflect the teachings of the Vedas, Upaniṣads, *darśanas*, *purāṇas*, *itihāsas* (histories), epics such as *Rāmāyaṇa* and *Mahābhārata*. Among all these, there are two outstanding literary sources, namely, *Bhagavadgītā* and *Bhāgavata Purāṇa*. Both deal with Kṛṣṇa as a central figure, as an incarnation of Viṣṇu, as a yogi, friend, advisor, leader, and so on. Rāma, Śiva, and Dattātreya also have influenced the writings of the saints. Śiva and Dattātreya are the two sources for the Nātha-cult. Jñāneśvara and others were directly initiated into this cult. All their writings are in Marathi, a few in Hindi and also in Punjabi (in the case of Nāmadeva).

The salient feature of the writings of the saints is their adoption of the language spoken by common people instead of Sanskrit, which was the conventional medium of writing of the learned scholars, from the Vedic age on. Knowledge that had been confined to Sanskrit was made open to common people by the saints, many of whom were, interestingly enough, well grounded in Sanskrit. The writings of the saints have left behind a great cultural heritage for the present and the future.

Biographical Sketches

Jñāneśvara and His Tradition
(1275–1296 C.E.)

Family

The family of Jñāneśvara belonged to the eastern Maharashtra region near Paithana on the bank of the river Godavari. Jñāneśvara's grandfather, Govindapanta, was a brahmin who had no children until the age of fifty-five. At this age a son was born, who was named Vitthalapanta, and right from childhood he remained a *virakta*, "one who was detached." Vitthala-panta wanted to travel around India on a pilgrimage in order to make his worldly life truly accomplished by being in the company of holy people (*sat-sangati*) and gaining proper grounding in divine worship (*upāsana*). Despite opposition from his parents, he left home and completed the pilgrimage. Later he came to Alandi on the riverbank Indrayan (near Pune), a holy place of Lord Śiva. He started spiritual practice along with daily sun worship.

There was a brahmin by the name of Siddhopanta, who happened to see Vitthalapanta. Siddhopanta had a daughter named Rukmiṇi, and he had a dream in which the Lord told him to wed his daughter to Vitthalapanta, who had a similar dream in which he was asked to marry Rukmiṇi. (The names Vitthala and Rukmiṇi are the names of Lord Viṣṇu and His spouse Lakṣmī.) The two were married, but they had no children. Vitthalapanta decided to take *sannyāsa* and requested permission to do so; he received an ambiguous answer. He left the house and came to Benaras, where he met Swāmi Rāmānanda, who initiated him. He was given the name Swāmi Chaitanya. After some time, when the master learned that Vitthalapanta was married before he took *sannyāsa*, he ordered him to abandon *sannyāsa* and return to the life of a householder. Vitthalapanta did so but was boycotted by the community, as it is not permitted for anyone to reenter the householder's life once having taken up *sannyāsa*. According to the injunctions of the Veda and *śāstra*, this was considered a sinful action. Therefore, the couple lived outside the village. Subsequently, Rukmiṇi gave birth to four children: Nivṛtti (1273 C.E.), Jñāneśvara (1275), Sopana (1277), and Muktabāi, the daughter (1279). These children also were boycotted by the community. The parents were very frustrated and moved the family to Nasik, one of the twelve Śaivaite centers of Lord Śiva, whose temple was located on the top of a mountain. Here the father began a great, year-long penance along with his children, getting up at midnight, bathing, circumambulating the sacred mountain, and uttering the sacred *mantras*. Once Nivṛtti became separated from the others while avoiding a tiger on the way. He ended up in a cave, where he met a holy man, Gahininātha, who was one of the great saints of Nātha sects in India. Nivṛtti was only nine years old; however, Gahininātha gave initiation to Nivṛtti and imparted to him the supreme knowledge. This knowledge enabled Nivṛtti to attain self-realization (*atmajñāna*) and a state of spiritual perfection. On the last day before Nivṛtti left the cave, Lord Dattātreya appeared to him in physical form and instructed him to impart the spiritual knowledge that he had gained to his brother Jñāneśvara. Nivṛtti went back home and imparted the supreme knowledge to Jñāneśvara for seven days. Jñāneśvara in turn taught Sopana, who was seven at that time, and Muktabāi, who was just five years old. The parents were fully gratified and happy, and they set out on a pilgrimage, knowing that their children were spiritually accomplished. They went to Badrikedara in the Himalayas, plunged into the holy waters of the Ganges, accepting *jalasamādhi* (the yogic way of dissolving the body in waters).

These children of Vitthalapanta and Rukmiṇi are exceptions in Indian cultural history, in that they achieved spiritual perfection within a few days and at the young ages of ten, nine, seven, and five. Moreover, they had gained a mastery over the Hindu religious lore (*śāstras*) at a very young age. They had in fact become yogis practicing "perfect yoga," which combined *bhakti*, *jñāna*, and *karma* yogas.

Miracles

The trials and ordeals of this family induced them to show some supernatural power in the form of miracles. There are thirteen miracles known to have been performed by them, three of which are the following: (1) They made a he-buffalo recite the Vedas as a way of showing that the same *ātman* resides in animals as well as in human beings. (2) They revived the body of Saccidānandabāba, who had died and was being taken for cremation. His wife was then blessed with the boon of a child. This Bāba afterwards became the scribe for Jñāneśvara's commentary on the *Gītā*, called *Jñāneśvari*, or *bhāvārtha-dīpikā*. (3) They performed the miracle of moving a wall to greet Chaṅgadeva, a yogi considered to be fourteen hundred years old, who, along with his fourteen hundred disciples, came to see them riding on a tiger.

Writings

Jñāneśvara authored the following works:

1. A commentary on the *Gītā* in Marathi, which he completed at the age of sixteen. This was a voluminous work on spirituality, rich in diction, metaphor, and style, studded with the loftiest possible images, sentiments, and thoughts. It was popular among the people both high and low in learning and is considered the Bible of the cult of devotion (*vārakarī* tradition of Maharashtra).

2. *Amṛtānubhava* (literally, nectar in the form of spiritual experience) or an experience of *amṛta* (the nectar), in sixty-five *ovis*. This is a masterly work on secrets of spirituality and is highly metaphysical in nature. It is often regarded as the best of Jñāneśvara's philosophy, expressive of his experiences of divine ecstasy.

3. A commentary in Marathi on *Yogavāsistha*, another encyclopedic work in Sanskrit on yoga, mysticism, metaphysics, and spirituality.

This work is in the form of a dialogue between Lord Rāma and his Guru Vasiṣṭha.

4. *Pavana-Vijaya* (literally, victory over breath), a work on the science of *prāṇa*. This is a small book in Marathi, but is very important in the practical application of yoga.
5. *Pañcīkaraṇa*, a small Vedāntic work on genesis.
6. *Harīpātha*. This work, on the glory of Lord Viṣṇu (Hari), is a book of daily recitation for devotees.
7. The *abhangas*, 903 in number, covering all aspects of life and of divine incarnations such as Kṛṣṇa. There are 356 *abhangas* of Nivṛtti, 49 of Sopana, 42 of Muktabāi, and 46 of Chaṅgadeva.

End of Life

With the permission of Lord Vitthala, Jñāneśvara attained *samādhi* at the age of twenty-one at Alandi, his birthplace, in the presence of Nivṛtti, Sopana, Muktabāi, Chaṅgadeva, Nāmadeva, and many other saintly persons. The Lord made him sit on a platform. He sat in the lotus posture, closed his eyes, and went into *samādhi*. Sopana, just after a month, took *samādhi* at Puntambe, a few miles from Pune and Alandi. Chaṅgadeva took *samādhi* two months after Sopana. After this Nivṛtti and Muktabāi visited holy places, and while they were near Edlabad, a place on the confluence of Tapti and Purna (North Maharashtra), Muktabāi was struck by the lightning during a storm and was seen no more. Nivṛtti, being alone, lost interest in life and took *samādhi* at Tryambakesvara, where he had received enlightenment earlier.

Nāmadeva and His Tradition (1270–1300 C.E.)

Family

Nāmadeva's family originally belonged to East Maharashtra; however, three generations prior to Nāmadeva, his ancestors migrated to Pandharpur, the center of devotion to Lord Vitthala. For many generations, this family had been known for its devotion to God. Nāmadeva's father, Damashetha, was a tailor by profession, belonging to the third order of the Hindu social order, *vaiśya*. His mother, Gonai, had taken a vow so as to give birth to a boy, by the grace of Lord Vitthala. She gave birth to

Nāmadeva on a Sunday in July 1270 C.E., in the month of *Kārtika* in the Hindu calendar, which also happened to be the day of a great festival for Lord Vitthala at Pandharapur.

God-realization

At the early age of five, Nāmadeva had his first religious experience, when he was asked by his father to serve milk at the temple of Lord Vitthala, as an act of worship early in the morning. Thinking that the Lord would physically consume the milk that was offered at the altar, Nāmadeva waited a long time.When the Lord did not consume the milk, Nāmadeva insisted, threatening that he would crack his head at the feet of Lord's icon, if He did not. The Lord, therefore, had to reveal Himself to Nāmadeva in order consume the milk. Nāmadeva returned to his parents and reported on what had happened. His parents, however, thought that he was lying and had drunk the milk himself. Next time his father went secretly to see what was happening, and he witnessed the event of the Lord drinking the milk that was offered by Nāmadeva.

Household Life

At the early age of eleven Nāmadeva was married, but he was not interested in worldly life. Day by day his devotion to Lord Vitthala intensified. His parents were worried about Nāmadeva's lack of interest in family life; they rebuked him and threatened him. He was pressured also by his wife and others to change his way of life, but they did not succeed. Because of his father's old age, Nāmadeva had to assume the responsibility of providing financial support for his family by being engaged in a profession; still his devotion to the Lord proceeded unhindered.

Nāmadeva had developed close friendship with the Lord right from his childhood, and he was proud of this achievement. In order to get rid of his sense of ego, he needed the assistance of a guru proper. It was only when he met Nivṛtti, Jñāneśvara, Sopana, and Muktabāi that his ego was challenged, especially by Muktabāi, who talked about this openly before the gathering of the devotees of an elderly saint by the name of Gorakumbhara. This action by Muktabāi made Nāmadeva very sad and disturbed. The Lord then directed Nāmadeva to go to Viṣoba Khechara for proper religious instruction. Viṣoba Khechara imparted the necessary knowledge and enabled Nāmadeva to get rid of his egoism and to achieve spiritual perfection. Nāmadeva's devotion was now qualified by knowledge. From God-realization he had arrived at self-realization. The Lord thought of testing Nāmadeva. Taking the form of a dog, the Lord took away his milk pot;

Nāmadeva ran after the dog with bread in his hand so that the dog would take milk with bread. Now the Lord was convinced of Nāmadeva's spiritual attainment, of his realization of the unity of the self at all levels.

Life after Realization

Nāmadeva was tested by many others, even by a brahmin, Parasa Bhāgavata from Pandharpur. Later Parasa was convinced of the saintliness of Nāmadeva and became one of his disciples. Nāmadeva went on a pilgrimage throughout India with Jñāneśvara and performed miracles on critical occasions. He was famous for his *bhajanas* and *kīrtanas* (divine songs and discourses). Nāmadeva, after Jñāneśvara's *samādhi*, lived for another fifty-four years. He traveled extensively in India, preaching and spreading the message of devotion. He was associated with Guru Nānak of the Sikh tradition. In the sacred scripture of Sikhism, sixty-two *abhangas* of Nāmadeva find their place. He was very well respected in Punjab, and there is even a Gurudwara in his name known as Baba Nāmdevji. His noted disciple in Punjab was Bahoradāsa.

The family of Nāmadeva were devotees of the Lord Vitthala. This included his four sons, Nara (Nārāyaṇa); Mhada (Mahādeva); Gonda (Govinda); and Vitha (Vitthala); their wives; his daughter, Lodai; and his sister, Limbāi. His maidservant, Janabāi, was herself one of the famous saints.

Writings

Nāmadeva's available *abhangas* number 2,373, dealing with the life and episodes of Lord Kṛṣṇa and of other Hindu deities, and life in the four ages (*yugas*), *satya*, *dvāpara*, *treta*, and *kali*. They include *abhangas* also on contemporary saints. Nāmadeva is said to have been blessed by the Lord and, according to the legend, was asked to compose one hundred million *abhangas*. He is said to have done so; but only 2,373 *abhangas* are available. Others are said to have been buried in the place where he attained *samādhi*. All his family members have composed *abhangas*. At present we have 347 of Janabāi, thirteen of Nara, one of Mhada, nineteen of Gonda, eighty-six of Vitha, one each of Ladai and Limbāi, two of Viṣoba Khechara, nineteen of Parasa Bhāgavata. The Lord Vitthala is said to have been the scribe for Janabāi, the maidservant, who was illiterate.

The End

Except for Nāmadeva's daughter-in-law, Ladai, who was pregnant at the time of departure, all are said to have attained *samādhi* at the step of the entrance door of the Lord Vitthala's temple at Pandharapura. This was in 1350 C.E., on twelfth lunar day of black fortnight of the month of *Aṣāḍha* (July–August).

Ekanātha and His Tradition (1528–1599 C.E.)

Family

Saint Bhanudāsa, the great-grandfather of Ekanātha, was born possibly around 1450 C.E. The family came from Paithana in East Maharashtra. Bhanudāsa was a great soul and also a sun worshiper, although a devotee of Lord Vitthala. In childhood, on one occasion when he was casually scolded by his father, he left home and went to a cave where he worshiped the Sun God (*Sūrya*) for seven days. At the end of that time the Lord Himself, assuming a human form, served him milk, as he had nothing to eat or drink. Ekanātha was later married, but was not interested in family life and worldly pursuits. He was known to be very affectionate, pure, and saintly. He composed many *abhangas*.

Janārdana Swāmi (1479 C.E.)

Janārdana Swāmi, a great yogi and the guru of Ekanātha, came from a Deshapande family (in charge of province in royal court). The Swāmi was well versed in the *śāstras*, polity, and administration and was thus an authority in religious matters, arms, and warfare. After his father's death he assumed the responsibility of supporting his family. He worked for the king and was fully engaged in the discharge of his official duties. One day he had vision of Lord Dattātreya in the form of a great yogi, Narasiṃha Sarasvati. Soon the focus of his life shifted to the observance of penance and austerities, and he began to compose poems on Dattātreya. As dictated by the Lord, he handed over his property and family responsibilties to his brother and left for Devagiri. *Jñānesvari* and *Gurucaritra* became his daily readings. It is said that Lord Dattātreya used to talk to him directly. He had three chief disciples, Ekajanārdana (Ekanātha), Jani-janārdana, and Rami-janārdana. It is said that he ended his life by "dissolving" his body by yogic means.

Ekanātha

Bhanudāsa had a son named Chakrapāṇi who was Ekanātha's grandfather. Ekanātha was the son of Sūryanārāyaṇa and was born in 1528 C.E. at Paithana in East Maharashtra. His parents died just after his birth and he was raised by his grandparents. At the age of six he had his sacred thread ceremony. He then studied the Vedas, *śāstras*, and *purāṇas*. The *Bhāgavata Purāṇa* is said to have made a deep impression on Ekanātha. It created in him a desire for a life centered on devotion to God. Knowing that for a truly spiritual life he needed the guidance of a spiritual master (guru), Ekanātha became restless and was disinterested in day-to-day life. He spent his time in the temple sitting quietly in a meditative mood. One day he heard a heavenly voice that directed him to go Devagiri and seek Janārdana Swāmi. This great soul, the voice assured Ekanātha, would make him fully accomplished. He was then twelve years old. Ekanātha narrated this event to his teacher, who encouraged him to follow his call. One day Ekanātha left his home quietly to be with Janārdana Swāmi. He met Janārdana and served him for one year with full devotion. Once when Swāmi was in *samādhi*, enemy forces invaded the fortress to which Swāmi was the guardian. Ekanātha put on his master's garb of warfare, fought the enemies, and drove them away. Returning from the state of deep meditation (*samādhi*), the master was pleased with Ekanātha's valor and devotion. He imparted to him true and saving knowledge and enabled him to experience Lord Dattātreya in physical form, with three heads and six hands. The Lord blessed Ekanātha, saying that he was indeed a great soul and that he would lead people on a right, divine path. Shortly afterwards, Janārdana initiated him in the performance of great yogic penance, which he did, and attained self-realization through the grace of the guru. The guru told Ekanātha that henceforward he need not serve him, as he was fully accomplished spiritually.

Householder Life

By the age of twenty, Ekanātha had accomplished God-realization and self-realization. Janārdana Swāmi, having been informed that Ekanātha's grandparents were unhappy at their grandson's departure, ordered Ekanātha to accept householder's life. Accordingly Ekanātha went home. He was married to Girijābāi and led the life of a householder happily. He had two sons and a daughter. Once when he was with his guru, Ekanātha visited a person named Chandrabhatta who was noted for his discourses on *Bhāgavata Purāṇa*. Chandrabhatta gave his discourses in Marathi language. The master advised Ekanātha to write a commentary in Marathi on the four famous verses of the *Bhāgavata*. Accordingly, Ekanātha composed one thousand Marathi *ovis* on the same. This was the beginning of his literary life.

Ekanātha is said to have performed several miracles, including the following: (1) At the request of Ekanātha, his departed parents came to partake of the anniversary food prepared for them, when he was disparaged by the invited brahmin guests. (2) He fulfilled the wish of a poor old widow, serving death anniversary food for one thousand brahmins. (3) He made a most unintelligent boy of his village, by laying the palm of his hand on him, complete a series on *Bhavartha Rāmāyaṇa* beginning from the forty-fifth chapter, where Ekanātha had stopped earlier, as he foresaw the end of his life.

There are other episodes from Ekanātha's life that clearly illustrate his compassion and also his concern for the low-caste people in Indian society. Once he is said to have saved the life of a donkey that was dying of thirst in scorching heat in a river bed. He saved the animal with holy water of the Ganges that he had brought with him from Benares after a pilgrimage. He willingly overlooked his high-class status and served food to low-caste people. He also took food in the house of a devotee of God who belonged to a low caste. The most remarkable and unparalleled virtue of Ekanātha was his peaceful, calm, and quiet nature. He never lost his temper even when he was being ill treated by some of the brahmins. One day someone deliberately spat on his body each time when he finished bathing in the river; he patiently returned to the river to bathe again and is said to have done so 108 times that day. Finally, the offender prostrated himself at his feet seeking forgiveness, and became his disciple.

Writings

While Ekanātha's writings are mostly in Marathi, he also wrote in Hindi. He had a good mastery of Hindi which was influenced by Persian and Arabic. His son was a great scholar in Sanskrit and in the *śāstras*. Mukteśvara, his grandson from his daughter's side, was also a great scholar and poet, who composed many devotional works in Marathi. Ekanātha's writings include the following: (1) His *abhangas*, numbering 4,001. (2) A commentary on the eleventh chapter of *Bhāgavata Purāṇa*, a voluminous work in Marathi language. The work deals with the lives of Lord Kṛṣṇa, Rāma, Śiva, and Dattātreya. (3) Ekanātha produced the first critical edition of *Jñāneśvari*, which had been corrupted by additions and diverse readings. This is said to have been done by Ekanātha at the instruction of Jñāneśvara himself in a dream.

End of Life

Ekanātha took *jalasamādhi* (self-immersion in holy waters by the yogic way). A day or two prior to this he had publicly spoken of his end during a discourse he was giving. On the sixth lunar day of *Phalguna* (December), Ekanātha took permission of his followers and entered the waters uttering an *abhanga*.

Tukārāma and His Tradition (1608–1649 C.E.)

Family

Tukārāma belonged to a family of merchants at Dehu, near Pune, a family of devotees of God. Tukārāma was born in 1609, and his parents were Bolhoba and Kanakai. Savaji was his older brother and Kanhoba, the younger one. The older brother was, from childhood, a *virakta* (detached from the worldly life) and led a spiritual life.

Traditional training in profession was given to Tukārāma at an early age, and he became quite proficient in it. Being honest, sincere, and sweet—above all a thorough gentleman—he became very successful in trade. He married at an early age, first to a girl with an asthmatic condition. Soon he was married again to a girl named Jijai, from a rich family in Pune. Despite his family responsibilities, Tukārāma remained a devotee of Lord Vitthala. When he had free time from work, he was engrossed in devotion to Lord Vitthala, which he had cultivated from his childhood.

Just after his marriage, Maharashtra suffered from a great famine, followed by another one a few years later. Tukārāma lost his father, his mother, his first wife, and a son in an epidemic. Business was lost, debt incurred. He faced poverty and hunger. All his domestic animals died. Out of dejection and desperation, Tukārāma threw all his bills and account books into the river and began focusing on his spiritual life.

God-realization

Tukārāma often withdrew from his family and spent time by himself on a mountain nearby, remaining there for days performing penance. He began to read *Jñāneśvari*, *abhangas* of Nāmadeva and Ekanātha, and also other sacred literature, but not the Vedas, which were not to be studied by his social class. *Bhāgavata Purāṇa* was another work of his daily reading. Soon Tukārāma himself began composing *abhangas*. At last he was given a sacred *mantra* in a dream by Bābaji Chaitanya. The *mantra* that he was given was "Rāmakṛṣṇahari," a *mantra* he had recited from his childhood days. At the age of twenty, Tukārāma was blessed with God-realization and self-realization by the grace of his guru.

Life after Realization

Tukārāma underwent many trials and ordeals at the hands of people of all castes and creeds, including his family. He came out on top every time and was considered a saintly and holy person. Occasionally, he performed miracles, including the following noteworthy wonders: (1) Rāmeshvara Bhatta, an acknowledged Vedic scholar learned that Tukārāma, a non-brahmin, a trader, had composed *abhangas* in Marathi that related to Vedic topics and teachings. He ordered Tukārāma to throw all his manuscripts into the river Indrayani at Alandi, five miles from Dehu. Though Tukārāma did so, he was very sad and felt deeply hurt. He remained on the bank of the river without food for thirteen days, meditating on the Lord Vitthala. At last the Lord was pleased, and all the manuscripts came out to the surface of the water. After this event, Rāmeshvara Bhatta became a disciple of Tukārāma. (2) Angada Shah, a Muslim Fakir, having realized Tukārāma's spiritual powers, became his disciple and was initiated. (3) The famous Deva family, devotees of Lord Gaṇeśa at Chinchvada of Poona, invited Tukārāma for food and teased him by saying that he should invite the Lord for food along with him. Tukārāma prayed. The Lord Gaṇeśa accepted the prayers and took food with Tukārāma and the Deva family.

Preaching and the End of Life

Tukārāma had followers from all sections of the community. Among them, Bahinabāi was a great devotee who is said to have been blessed by Tukārāma after his physical departure from the world. The great Maratha King Shivāji was also blessed by him and became one of his disciples. He had met Swāmi Rāmadāsa at Pandharpur.

Tukārāma left voluminous *abhanga* compositions, about 4,092 in number, on all facets of life. He composed in Hindi also. His compositions display simplicity, lucidity, lofty sentiment, and a great concern for the common person's life and feelings. His teaching emphasized the fact that God-realization is possible even for those who are only householders. It is said that he was called by the Lord to come to his heavenly abode. He told this to his wife and asked her to follow him to the river bank of Indrayani. But she did not take it seriously and therefore remained at home. Tukārāma is said to have left this world and to have gone to the Vaikuṇṭha (heavenly abode of the Lord Vitthala) with his physical body. This was said to have happened in 1649.

The Tradition of Rāmadāsa (1608–1681 C.E.)

Family

Rāmadāsa was born at Jamb village at midday sharp on the ninth lunar day of the month of *Chaitra* (April), one of the holiest days for the Hindus, and time of the birth of Lord Rāma. Sūryajipanta and Ranabai were his parents. His father was a worshiper of the sun-god. It is said that he had been blessed by the sun-god, who told him that he would have two sons. He did have two sons—the elder, Gaṅgādhara, and the younger, Nārāyaṇa, who was later known as Samartha Rāmadāsa (Samartha meaning "the Mighty One" and Rāmadāsa, "the servant of Lord Rāma"). Nārāyaṇa was a very naughty boy in childhood but was also exceptionally brilliant and talented. By the age of twelve he was well grounded in many branches of Sanskrit learning, including the Vedas, Sanskrit grammar, and others.

His father, being a holy person, used to initiate people by providing sacred *mantras*. After his death, the elder son, Gaṅgādhara, continued this tradition. Once Nārāyaṇa also requested him to initiate him with a *mantra*, but he was told that he should wait until "he ripened in age and wisdom." Nārāyaṇa's often irresponsible behavior was a source of anxiety for his mother. Once in anger she rebuked him for his lack of maturity and wisdom, saying that he should assume responsibility for the family, "for the world and people." His mother's remarks were very shocking to Nārāyaṇa but proved to be a turning point in his life. He withdrew and stayed alone in a dark room in the house. Later when he was questioned by his mother, he replied, "I am thinking and worrying about the world, life, and the people." Nārāyaṇa took his mother's words literally and began "to worry about the world."

Nārāyaṇa expressed his desire to renounce worldly life, but his mother told him that he should at least "stand before the wedding curtain," meaning that he should get married. (It was customary for the bride and bridegroom to face each other on either side of a curtain; when the curtain was lifted, they were married.) When Nārāyaṇa was twelve years of age his mother arranged his marriage. Nārāyaṇa went through the ceremony until he was facing the curtain with the bride on the other side. However, before the priest could complete the marriage rites, he ran away. Nārāyaṇa obeyed his mother's commandment in a literal sense, but did not complete the ceremony! He went to Takali at Nasik in North Maharashtra, a place at the confluence of two rivers, Godavari and Nandina. There he practiced severe penance, repeating the Vedic *Gāyatrī mantra* from morning to midday, standing in the waters of the river on one leg and living on alms. He was also engaged in discussions with scholars on philosophical issues and matters pertaining to the *śāstras*. In this way he continued to function for twelve years, during which he completed 1.3 billion *japa* of the famous thirteen-syllable *mantra* of Lord Rāma, and three great cycles of *Gāyatrī mantra*. After this he had a vision of Rāma. He also achieved a great mastery over the classical music of India. In these years he gained a deeper understanding of humankind and other forms of life, such as animals, birds, trees, and insects. His writings display this deeper vision. He had thus gained an understanding of life in its totality; he was able to identify himself with all and empathize.

Nārāyaṇa went on a pilgrimage throughout India. After completing this pilgrimage, he decided to meet his mother, whom he had not seen since he had left home several years earlier. He went to his native place and met her, but she had become blind in her old age and was unable to see her son. He put his hands on her eyes, and astonishingly she regained her vision. His mother thought that this miraculous event was some sort of witchcraft and that her son was in a state of demonic possession. But Nārāyaṇa told her of the spiritual disciplines he had followed since leaving home, and he convinced her that the powers he had gained were not the result of demonic worship or demonic possession. She was then happy about the attainments of her son, blessed him, and gave permission to become *sannyāsi*, to formally renounce ties to worldly life.

Nārāyaṇa then set out on his mission; he became "Rāmadāsa," a devotee/follower of Rāma. He had decided to devote his life to the revival of *dharma* and propagation of *svadharma*. He arrived at the river Krishna, near Satara, south of Pune. Realizing that society had become weak in all respects, he thought of inducing strength, awakening people's socioreligious consciousness and self-confidence. Thus, psycho-physical strength and devotion were the basic requirements of the time. He believed that without divine grace, the task would not succeed. He therefore selected three divinities from the Hindu pantheon that symbolized those qualities needed for the transformation of the individual and society: Hanumān, as the symbol of strength and devotion; Lord Rāma, as the symbol of ideal divine political power based on truth and righteousness; and Bhavanī, as the symbol of *śakti*, the divine power, the source, the Mother. He established temples for the worship of these deities and was engaged in reviving and spreading the message of devotion (*bhakti*). He established eleven Hanumān temples himself, and in all thirteen hundred *mathas* in Maharashtra and nearby provinces. Through songs and discourses he imparted knowledge regarding the real nature of the world and the highest goal of human life. He had both male and female disciples, including Hindus, Muslims, and many others.

Among all the saints of Maharashtra, it was Rāmadāsa who was politically most conscious, probably because he had witnessed political degradation and upheavals in his lifetime. His choice of Rāma as the focus of his devotion reflected the condition of his times. It was only an ideal kingdom such as that of Rāma that could bring about needed social changes. Hence the (re)establishment of the "rule of Rāma" was Rāmadāsa's ideal and divine mission. Such a divine configuration Rāmadāsa found in the Maratha King Shivāji, who became his disciple. To have such an ideal condition one needed a good social, religious, and cultural environment, which Rāmadāsa hoped to create in Maharashtra by his "missionary" work.

Writings

Rāmadāsa had left behind a rich literary treasure for us. *Daśaboda* in twenty chapters is his major contribution. Next in importance, though very small, is *Manache Śloka,* that is, an anthology of verses for the mind. He had composed thirteen hundred verses on two chapters of *Rāmāyaṇa*, *Sundarakāṇḍa,* and *Yuddhakāṇḍa*. Under miscellaneous writings were twelve hundred *ovis* in twelve groups with one hundred each, a chapter on *Atmārāma*, a collection of eight verses each called *Karuṇāṣṭaka*, and besides about 250 *abhangas* and other poetic compositions. His writings cover all aspects of life including political matters. The most outstanding feature of his writings, in comparison to those of other saints, is their garb of Indian classical music.

Conclusion

The article may be summed up by quoting a few passages from the concluding paragraph of *Jñānesvari* (XVIII. 93-97), which seem to define sainthood in Indian society.

> Now may the cosmic Godhead be pleased with this lingual sacrifice. Having been pleased, may He grant this kind of gift, in the form of *prasāda* (graceful gesture). And that should cast aside the ill-sight of the wicked and cultivate love for good deeds. Should that (again) bring about mutual friendship in the selves of the living beings. Let the darkness (ignorance) of the malevolent be expelled. Let also the whole world behold the Sun in the form of their own *dharma*. Whosoever of the living class desires anything, he may get it. Let there be abundant showerings of those who have faith in God and who are well wishers of all. Let all the creatures meet such people all the time. . . . All the creatures should be bestowed with happiness in full and become overall perfect.

Bibliography

Sources

Ekanātha. *Bhikshu Gita: The Mendicant's Song: A Story of Converted Miser*. Translated by Justin E. Abbott. Poona: Scottish Mission Industries, 1928.

Jnanadeva (Jñāneśvara). *Experience of Immortality: English rendering of Jnaneshwar's Amritanubhava.* Commentary by Ramesh S. Baleskar. Edited by Sudhakar S. Dikshit. Bombay: Chetana, 1984.

Jnaneshvari (Bhavarthadipika). Translated from Marathi by V. G. Padhan. Edited with an introduction by H. M. Lambert. Albany: State University of New York Press, 1987.

Kripananda, Swami. *Jnaneshwar's Gita: A Rendering of Jnaneshwari.* Introduction by Shankar Gopal Tulpule. Albany: State University of New York Press, 1989.

Mahipati. *Stories of Indian Saints: An English Translation of Mahipat's Marathi Bhakti Vijyaya.* Translated by E. Abbott and Marhar R. Godbole. Poona: N. R. Godbole, 1933–34.

Rāmadāsa. *Dasa Bodha.* English and Marathi Selections. Pune: Gopewatch Foundation, 1992.

———. *Teachings of Sri Samartha Rāmadāsa of Maharashtra: A Rendering into English of His Works Manache Sloka and Atmarama.* Translated with introduction and notes by S. Suryanarana. Cochin: Suryanarayana, 1973.

Says Tuka: Selected Poems of Tukaram. Translated from Marathi with an introduction by Dilip Chitre. New Delhi: Penguin Books, 1991.

Tukārāma. *The Poems of Tukārāma.* Translated with notes by Nelson Fraser and K. E. Marathe. Delhi: Motilal Banarsidass, 1981.

Studies

Callewaert, Winand M., and Mukund Lath. *The Hindi Songs of Namadev.* Leuven: Department Orientalistiek, 1989.

3

Bengal Vaiṣṇavism

SUDHINDRA C. CHAKRAVARTI

THE COMMON BELIEF that religion is one with philosophy in India is nowhere as evident as in Bengal Vaiṣṇavism. Bengal Vaiṣṇavism focuses on the problem of the central meaning of existence and recommends philosophy not merely for the sake of knowledge but also for the encouragement of living in accordance with the highest ideal. The speculative activity of Bengal Vaiṣṇavism is the result of the profound spiritual disquiet that much of India experienced in the medieval period. Who am I? and Why do three kinds of distress afflict me? are the two questions by which Sanātana Gosvāmin, a wise companion and devout follower of Caitanya, is reported to have elicited from his master the substance of Bengali Vaiṣṇavism.

The Teachings of Caitanya

The individual self is different from the body, the senses, the mind, the intellect, and the ego. It is neither a flowing stream of consciousness nor an aggregate of conscious states. It is a self-apperceiving permanent being, an unchanged immutable spirit that in itself does not possess a physical or mental quality. It is not constituted by space, time, or causality and is therefore eternally free and immortal. As it is not an agent—or doer—of moral actions, no moral properties belong to it. It is of the nature of pure existence (*sat*), consciousness (*cit*), and bliss (*ānanda*). It is, however, not fully identical with the Absolute (*Brahman*), as the nondualist Vedānta says; it differs from the impersonal, infinite, and all-pervading consciousness in being personal, finite, and atomic.

The ultimate reality is Lord Kṛṣṇa. The self is both different and nondifferent from Lord Kṛṣṇa, who is the all-inclusive unity of all that is, the halo of whose spiritual person appears as the *Brahman* or the Indeterminate

Absolute of the nondualist Vedānta. The self is one among the innumerable infinitesimal monads into which Lord Kṛṣṇa, as it were, splits Himself through His power of self-fragmentation of *jīva-śakti*, otherwise called *tatastha śakti*, that stands on the border line between His power of illumination and intelligence (*cit-śakti*) and His power of materialization and insentience (*māyā śakti*). The manifold powers that Lord Kṛṣṇa exercises are but different forms of his essential power (*svarūpa śakti*); the relation between his essence (*svarūpa*) and his powers is one of unthinkable difference-in-nondifference. Although the essence (*svarūpa*) of Lord Kṛṣṇa is inherently spirit, it can appear as the insentient material world, and in spite of His being the one infinite spiritual reality in essence, His *svarūpa śakti* (essential power) can split itself into innumerable limited finite selves or spirits.

While His essential power or the power of illumination (*cit śakti*) reveals the true nature of Lord Kṛṣṇa, His power of materialization (*māyā śakti*) reveals Him as the insentient inanimate material world. These two powers are thus opposed to each other as the original and its distorted shadow. Standing between these two powers, the *jīva-śakti* of the Lord, which shares His being, consciousness, and joy in a limited form, reveals itself in a dual capacity as spirit and as non-spirit. In relation to the *māyā śakti*, the individuals who are but manifestations of the *jīva-śakti* are liable to be led astray by *māyā śakti*'s allurements, yet at the same time, sharing the Lord's essence, they can be released from its trap.

The Lord's *māyā śakti* functions in two different forms: one is called *pradhāna*, which causes the appearance of the insentient world; and the other is known as *avidyā*, or nescience, which causes the individual to forget his real nature as the eternal servitor of the Lord. It is under the influence of beginningless *avidyā* that the individual asserts himself as an independent being and attaches exaggerated values and undue importance to the mundane things and finite enjoyments—and experiences the miseries and disappointments they entail. The individual is not a self-existent, independent, and absolute entity but rather is a fragmented manifestation of Lord Kṛṣṇa, a finite spirit eternally dependent on and wholly subservient to the Infinite Spirit. Ignorant of its true nature and its relation with Lord Kṛṣṇa, the self turns away from Him and becomes accustomed to the mundane ways and, because of deluded egoism and forgetfulness of the Lord, becomes subjected to the threefold miseries of the world.

The material world, however, is a derivative of the Lord's essential spiritual power in the aspect of *māyā śakti*. Though prone to veiling and distortion, the material world as such is not unreal. Like its source, *māyā*, it is a real snare to the individual, but it lacks "eternalness" or "everlastingness" either in itself or in its captivation of the individual. The world is not, therefore, merely a hindrance to the spiritual vision of the earthbound individual; it also teaches, as it were, by subjecting the individual repeatedly to frustrations and failure, lessons of the vanity and futility of mundane ways, lessons that make the individual mature, prone to self-knowledge, and receptive to the way of the Divine Spirit.

Thus, even *māyā śakti*, the cause of the material world, serves to wake the deluded individual to the realization of his real status as a fragment of Lord Kṛṣṇa, the Divine Spirit, and as eternally subservient to His will. With the dawn of spiritual enlightenment the individual perceives the error of mistaking spirit as insentient and material, and the error of understanding reality as a plurality of independent particulars instead of an all-inclusive unity integrating as well as transcending all differences. The individual's attention then turns to the nature of the finite spirit, its relation to the Absolute Spirit, its supreme good, and the means of realizing it as the highest end. This results in *bhakti* (devotion), and *bhakti* leads one to *prema* (love), where the way and the goal merge into the state of bliss. By the grace of Kṛṣṇa the love of Kṛṣṇa (*Kṛṣṇa-prema*) is achieved.

This teaching of Caitanya (1486–1533 C.E.), imparted orally to Sanātana, was recorded by his brother, Rūpa Gosvāmī, himself a close follower of Caitanya. A passionate scholar as well as a trained scholiast, Rūpa Gosvāmī has transformed the erotic type of love (*śṛṅgāra-rasa*) into a deeply religious sentiment in his two famous works *Bhakti-rasāmṛta-sindhu* (the sea of the nectar of devotional sentiment) and *Ujjvala-nīlamaṇi* (the bright blue gem). These texts are valued highly in Bengal Vaiṣṇavism, as they provide a new interpretation of devotional worship, that is, that the fulfillment of *bhakti* (devotion) itself lies in ecstatic love for God.

Bengal Vaiṣṇavism has built its system of spiritual philosophy exclusively on the authority of the *Bhāgavata Purāṇa*, which it considers the most reliable source of all supralogical knowledge regarding the three main *tattvas*, principles: *sambandha* (relation), *abhidheya* (subject matter), and *prayojana* (the goal or the highest end), which pertain to the spiritual needs of the individual. In other words, study of the *Bhāgavata Purāṇa* suffices not only for one's spiritual quest but also for its fulfillment. The identification of the ultimate spiritual reality, called *advaya jñānatattva*, with Kṛṣṇa, the promulgation of exclusive devotion to Kṛṣṇa as the most natural function and the highest duty of the individual, and the establishment of *prīti*, or devotional love, for Kṛṣṇa as the *summum bonum* of human life are the central themes of the system.

Śrī Caitanya

The Classical Tradition of *Bhakti*

Rāmānuja, Madhva, and Niṃbārka

Rāmānuja (1017–1137 C.E.), a major figure in one of the earlier schools of Vaiṣṇavism, maintained that *bhakti* is knowledge of *Brahman*, an unfailing recollection of the supreme Lord, a constant meditation on Him which develops into direct perception of Him. Since, according to Rāmānuja, disinterested performance of obligatory rituals removes the obstacles to knowledge, such actions become the means of attaining the constant memory of God. Madhva's (1197–1276) attitude toward the role of *bhakti* and its relation to *karma* (work) and *jñāna* (knowledge) is not substantially different. For both Rāmānuja and Madhva, *bhakti* is not characterized as of sweet love and comradeship between humans and God; it is rather understood as awesome reverence.

Rāmānuja and Madhva were more deeply moved by the grandeur and majesty of God, while Niṃbārka (1056–1165?) was more impressed by God's grace and sweetness. Niṃbārka was the first among the teachers of the Vaiṣṇava schools to emphasize that devotion is love springing forth from God's incomparable sweetness (*mādhurya-pradhāna-bhakti*) rather than reverence at His incomparable greatness (*aiśvarya-pradhāna-bhakti*). According to Niṃbārka, *bhakti* as a concept interchangeable with *jñāna* is not identical with *upāsana* (the meditative state resulting from ritualized behavior), as Rāmānuja claimed, but implies instead a kind of deep love for God. By knowledge Niṃbārka meant the correct knowledge of *Brahman* and the self. In his works he refers to three other means of salvation, viz., devotion and meditation (*upāsana*), self-surrender to God (*prapatti*), and self-surrender to the spiritual preceptor in addition to work (*karma*) and knowledge (*jñāna*).

Vallabha's Account of Bhakti *as a Means of Spiritual Realization*

Vallabha (1473–1531) admitted on the authority of the Vedas that there were three different ways of approaching God, viz., the ways of action (*karma*), knowledge (*jñāna*), and devotion (*bhakti*). Of these, *bhakti* is the best among them, since it is the only means to salvation, and the state of love (*prema*) and service (*seva*) which *bhakti* implies is better than even release. To one who performs Vedic sacrifices, God manifests Himself in the form of rituals, and to one who not only performs the Vedic rites but also obtains the knowledge of *Brahman* as described in the Upanisads He grants "release" or *mokṣa*, in the form of divine joy. So long as such performance is based purely on the rules of the scriptures (*maryādā-mārga*), the attainment of liberation continues to be gradual. Immediate liberation can be attained only through the grace (*puṣṭi*) of God.

From this perspective individuals are grouped into three classes: (1) the common run of people who are always busy with worldly matters and never think of God (*pravāha*); (2) people who follow the Vedic path, who study the scriptures, strive for understanding the real nature of God, and worship Him in accordance with scriptural rules (*maryādā*); and (3) people who worship God out of the pure love engendered only through His grace (*puṣṭi*). Broadly speaking, *bhakti* is of two kinds—*maryādā bhakti* and *puṣṭi bhakti*. The former is enjoined in the scriptures and has to be attained by one's own efforts, while the latter is inspired by natural love for God and cannot be obtained by any means except God's grace. In the former, love for God results from the gradual culture of the nine varieties of devotion: (1) hearing, (2) reciting, (3) remembering, (4) falling at the feet, (5) worship, (6) salutation, (7) service, (8) friendship, and (9) self-dedication; in the latter, it is not the result of the practice of the ninefold devotion in ascending order but the source from which all spiritual activities including the nine varieties of devotion spontaneously spring.

This distinction, as we shall see, corresponds to the distinction made between *vaidhi-bhakti* (devotion in conformity with law) and *rāgānugā-bhakti* (devotion impelled by love) in Bengal Vaiṣṇavism. Vallabha further divided *puṣṭi* into four types: (a) *pravāha-puṣṭi* is the first stage, in which the devotee engages in activities concerning God. It marks the beginning of attraction to God. (b) The second type, called *maryādā-puṣṭi*, implies worship of God with a full awareness of His majesty as described in scriptures and with an aversion to earthly pursuits. (c) The third type, *puṣṭi-puṣṭi*, indicates the stage in which the devotee attains the knowledge of *Brahman* and realizes that everything is *Brahman*. In this stage the devotee is absorbed in ultimate reality and Immutable Spirit (*akṣara Brahman*). (d) The fourth type known as *śuddhapuṣṭi* ("purified grace") indicates the highest stage of *bhakti*, in which *Para Brahman* or *Puruṣottama* is known and realized as the highest reality. The devotee sees everything in Him and loves Him as his sole belonging. This attitude of love is a gift of God. It cannot be obtained by human effort. God favors some individuals by bringing them forth, giving them divine bodies similar to His own, playing with them for all time and by remaining subordinate to them thus allowing them to enjoy the pleasure of His company. Such enjoyment of His chosen people is called *bhajanānanda*, the bliss of devotion, which is not different from *svarūpānanda*, the bliss of God Himself.

Since *svarūpānanda* is decidedly superior even to the bliss of *Brahman*, it is regarded as the highest stage of release as well as the supreme expression of love toward God. The *gopīs* (milkmaids of Vṛndāvana) are eternally favored with the possession of this love, and God Kṛṣṇa is believed to remain obedient to them for all time. They worship God Kṛṣṇa not because He is the great awe-inspiring Lord endowed with incomparable power and majesty but because He is the most beautiful and lovable one, full of the various *rasas* (sentiments), of which *śṛṅgāra* (erotic love) is the most prominent. The *gopīs'* love for God is so intense and all-absorbing that they never feel an urge to satisfy their selfish needs and assert their personal claims. The *Bhāgavata Purāṇa* relates how they gave up all attachments to worldly life and ignored scriptural duties, social customs, public infamy, as well as the prohibitions and punishments of their guardians. Smitten with the marvelous beauty of God Kṛṣṇa, they ran to meet Him in the forest at night disregarding all consequences; and they defied His admonitions to go back and proved the sincerity of their love for Kṛṣṇa. They won the favor of His company, which, however, they soon lost on account of their pride; they wandered in search of Him, regretting and lamenting; and finally regaining His favor they enjoyed the bliss of His company.

According to Vallabha, the expression of devotion is possible only in a feminine mode. The attitude of the *gopīs* is the best illustration of this kind of devotion. Those who want to enjoy the highest kind of divine bliss should follow their model and remember that God Kṛṣṇa is the natural husband of all souls, and all are expected to love Him. Rādhā is the chief of the *gopīs,* and her love for Kṛṣṇa offers the most perfect model of the ardent love felt by a lover for her beloved. *Bhakti*, the means of immediate release, is marked by natural love for God Kṛṣṇa; this love, attainable only through His grace, is capable of establishing a permanent contact with God; only such ardent love as that of Rādhā can sustain the closest contact with Him. Vallabha upheld the conception of *puṣṭi-bhakti* as illustrated by the *rāsa-līlā* (love-play) described in the *Bhāgavata Purāṇa*, taking care to point out that there is no tinge of sensualism in it. He insisted on the total dedication of oneself and one's belongings to the service of God and recommended renunciation of the world only for those rare devotees who are unable to bear the pangs of separation from God. For him, as for the teachers of the other schools of Vaiṣṇavism, freedom from worldly attachments, the effacement of all forms of egoism, and loving self-dedication to the service of Lord constitute the correct spiritual attitude.

This tradition conceives of the ultimate reality as the unity of Kṛṣṇa, the highest beauty, and Rādhā, the supreme love; this unity consists of *rasa-rāja* (the highest manifestation of *rasa*—here, delight) and *mahā-bhāva* (the highest expression of love). In its view, total surrender to the will of God (*pra-*

patti) is not a means among many other means for the highest spiritual realization; it is the goal itself, as shown in the loving attitude of the *gopīs*.

The classical Vaiṣṇavism of Rāmānuja, further developed by the schools of Madhva and Nimbārka, underwent a definitive change with the introduction of Rādhā and Kṛṣṇa as the dual form of God. Vallabha, a contemporary of Caitanya, interpreted *bhakti* in terms of love and service to Rādhā-Kṛṣṇa. The *Bhāgavata Purāṇa* became a crucial text for these later Vaiṣṇavas, who accord it high respect as a commentary by Vyāsa on the *Brahmasūtra*. Rūpa Gosvāmī exegetes the following verse from *Bhāgavata Purāṇa* at length giving it the status of a Upanisadic *mahāvākya*: "Of all (the Incarnations) some are of parts, others are emanations of the Lord; but Kṛṣṇa is God Himself . . ." (I.iii.28).

Kṛṣṇa as the Concrete Personification of Being, Consciousness, and Bliss (*Saccidānanda Vigraha*)

Spirit is the most precious treasure hidden in the mind-body complex of a living individual, and commonly the process of becoming aware of it and uncovering it is gradual. All individuals are not equally awake or alive to their spiritual essence. For some, their consciousness is clouded (*acchādita-cetanā*), and their awareness of their status as spirit is dim. Unable to visualize the ultimate reality, these individuals turn their back on the light of Kṛṣṇa, the supreme spirit, and grope in the darkness of the phenomenal world. These are the individuals bound to *saṃsāra*, the dismal cycle of births and deaths. Their spirits, like the souls of trees and creepers, are in an enshrouded condition. Second, there are some individuals who are like the birds and beasts that can move from place to place, in whom the consciousness of spirit is in a shrunken condition (*saṃkucita-cetanā*). Third, there are some human beings who are atheists with no concern of morality or atheists with moral concern in whom consciousness of spirit remains in a budding condition (*mukulita-cetanā*). Fourth, there are believers in the personality of God, the Supreme Lord; these are the individuals who believe that He has eternal name, form, attributes, entourage, realm, and pastimes, who think that although He is absolutely beyond the range of sense knowledge, He can be known and served by means of *śuddhā-bhakti*, or unalloyed devotion. These individuals are reckoned among theists in whom the consciousness of spirit has partially blossomed (*vikasita-cetanā*).

Finally, there are the devotees of the highest order, in whom the spirits have fully blossomed (*pūrṇa vikasita-cetanā*). It is said in the *Bhāgavata Purāṇa* that such devotees as Svayambhu, Śambhu, Nārada, Kapila, the four Kumāras, Janaka, Bhīṣma, Sukadeva, Prahlāda, Vāli, and Yama are the devotees of the highest order (*mahābhāgavatas*). They visualize the existence of God in every entity and every entity in the divine personality. As they are endowed with genuine love (*bhakti*) for the supreme deity, who is none other than Kṛṣṇa, their spiritual vision finds no obstruction against its penetration into the transcendental realm marked off from the phenomenal world by *virāja*, but proceeds through the relatively superior spiritual planes of *Brahmalōka* (the hallowed belt of Vaikuṇṭha), Vaikuṇṭha, Dvārakā and Mathurā to Vṛndāvana, where Kṛṣṇa, the Lord of all-love, is seen to dance with the milkmaids of Vraja. The individuals whose consciousness rises up to the transcendental plane of Vṛndavana attain the fulfillment of their spiritual quest.

Kṛṣṇa, the supreme deity, is *Saccidananda-Vigraha*, the personification of being, intelligence, and bliss. These three aspects of His *svarūpa-śakti* (intrinsic power) manifest themselves as (1) *sandhini*, the power of upholding His own existence and that of others; (2) *saṃvit*, the power of knowing and making others know; and (3) *hlādinī*, the power of enjoying and making others enjoy bliss. The combination of these powers has its analogue in the equilibrium of the three *guṇas* of *prakṛti* and is technically called *śuddha-sattva* (pure existence) as distinguished from the material *sattva* of *prakṛti*. Kṛṣṇa's body and senses, His dress and belongings, His flute and ornaments, His cows and their calves, His residences and retinues in the transcendental region are all transformations of *śuddha-sattva* with varying preponderance of *sandhini*, *saṃvit* and *hlādinī*. Kṛṣṇa's form is like that of a human body, but unlike the latter it is infinite, all-pervading, eternal, all-perfect, spiritual, perpetually in the prime of youth and enchantingly beautiful.

Of His three residences—Dvārakā, Mathurā, and Vṛndāvana—which are but three aspects of one and the same residence, where He eternally abides with His immortal attendants, Vṛndāvana, or Gokula, is the foremost since it is here that He disports Himself. In Vṛndāvana His retinue consists of the *gopās* and the *gopīs* (the "spiritual" milkmen and the "spiritual" milkmaids), whose love for Him is unsurpassed and unsurpassable. In response to their love, His *mādhurya,* implying loveliness of conduct, quality, beauty, youth, sport, and emotional intimacy of relationship, is fully manifested. The *gopās* and the *gopīs* of Vṛndāvana do not regard Kṛṣṇa as the omnipotent and majestic master whose commands are to be obeyed under compulsion or for fear of His displeasure. Instead Kṛṣṇa shows himself to them through His loving affection and charming features as the object of constant meditation. To some He is the affectionate master who rules not by force but by love, and in rendering Him willing service as faithful servants (*dāsya*) they attain the highest satisfaction and pleasure; to others He is the dear friend (*sakha*); to still others, He is the affectionate child (*vātsalya*); but to the *gopīs,* who have completely surrendered themselves and all their possessions including their prestige and chastity, He is the sweet beloved (*mādhura*), the dearest (*kānta*).

Rādhā as the Personification of *Mahābhāva*

Among the *gopīs,* who apprehend Kṛṣṇa as their dearest lover, there are graduations according to the various degrees to which His *hlādinī śakti* enables them to taste His *mādhurya* (sweetness). One *gopī* with whom Kṛṣṇa loves to sport even though there are other *gopīs* is Rādhā. She is the *gopī par excellence,* in whom the *hlādinī śakti* of Kṛṣṇa is manifested in the highest degree and in whom the bliss of love (*premānanda*) reaches the highest stage of the ecstatic *mahābhāva*, the stage not attainable by any other *gopī*. She represents *hlādinī śakti* itself. The relation between Rādhā and Kṛṣṇa is one of *śakti* (power) and the *śaktimat* (possessor of power), one of difference as well as nondifference, resembling the relation of the flame to the fire or of the scent to the musk. Rādhā is the most favored of Kṛṣṇa's devotees, the highest *parikara,* or servant, as well as the closest of his consorts. The other *gopīs* are her various aspects or emanations. The vision of Rādhā and Kṛṣṇa as a loving pair at Vṛndāvana is the most coveted sight for a devotee.

The unity of Rādhā and Kṛṣṇa is fully displayed in the *gopīs*' relation with Kṛṣṇa, for it is the essence of Rādhā that pervades the other *gopīs*, in order that they may serve Kṛṣṇa most perfectly. Unless the servants of Kṛṣṇa can know His wishes and unless He makes Himself known to them, they cannot serve Him perfectly and truly. In order that they may know His wishes and know Him, Kṛṣṇa becomes His own servant (i.e., Rādhā) in whose heart He always shines as the Master. Rādhā is just this servant Kṛṣṇa, the female or the serving principle, the inseparable and eternal counterpart of Kṛṣṇa Himself. She is the supreme spiritual power called the *hlādinī* or the bliss potency, the source of all powers including the nonspiritual or material power of ignorance or limitation. Truly speaking, every power is of Her essence. She alone is the direct servitor of Kṛṣṇa, while other *gopīs* are her helpmates; she alone possesses the right to stand at the side of Kṛṣṇa, while the other *gopīs* are privileged only to carry out her behests to perfect her service to Kṛṣṇa.

In Vṛndāvana Kṛṣṇa is eternally served by the plants and creepers, beasts and birds and more arduously by the *gopās* and *gopīs* who are allotted their respective functions by Rādhā herself. Since Rādhā and the *gopīs*, who are but emanations of Rādhā, form the direct and subjective constituents of Kṛṣṇa Himself, they can offer direct service to Kṛṣṇa. The individuals bound to the mundane world of *māyā* and even *māyā*, the principle of manifestation and limitation, are constituents of the spiritual power of Kṛṣṇa's *jīva-śakti*; they are located, as stated earlier, on the margin of the spiritual sphere contiguous to the border of the mundane sphere, on the borderline between the essential power (*svarūpa-śakti*) and the outer or external power (*vahiraṅga śakti*), that is, on the demarcating line between Vṛndāvana, the realm of spirit, which is absolutely real, and the realm of *māyā*, which is but a material shadow of the spiritual realm.

Though material and phenomenal in its nature, *māyā* is a constituent part of Rādhā, the highest spiritual power serving Kṛṣṇa, and it also is employed in the service of Kṛṣṇa, for through it Rādhā serves Him not directly but indirectly and from a distance. Unlike the pure spirits of Vṛndāvana, the embodied spirits, the individuals of the phenomenal world, are perpetually exposed to the opposite pulls of Kṛṣṇa's essential power and external power, to alternating inclinations for Vṛndāvana and for the world of *māyā*, and individuals have been given freedom to choose between them. Vṛndāvana, the highest spiritual world to which the other spheres are subordinate, is the true substantive world, and the material world in which the earthbound individuals reside is a perverted reflection, or shadow, of the spiritual world.

Bhakti as Alternative to Ascetic Withdrawal

The path of spiritual progress that the teachers of the Bengal school recommend is neither yoga nor *jñāna* but *bhakti*. While the followers of the way of yoga emphasize the subjective aspect and those of the path of *jñāna* both the subjective and objective aspect, the followers of the path of *bhakti* emphasize the objective aspect of consciousness. According to the yogis, the higher self or the *Paramātman* is the absolute truth which has to be realized by intensifying the powers of the subject. As the subject is ordinarily occupied with extraneous matters, it has to be completely withdrawn from them. The higher soul or the *Paramātman* shines in full glory only when there is no diffusion or dissipation of its energy due to outward attractions. Hence the spiritual discipline of the yogis consists in following a process of withdrawal, or a negative method. The followers of the way of *jñāna* also recommend a withdrawal of consciousness from external objects at the start of their spiritual life, but they do not stop with the negative process of "not this, not this" (*neti neti*). They admit that although the objects they deny or withdraw from in the first instance are appearances, they have a basis in *Brahman*. Their declaration that everything is *Brahman* leaves no doubt that the withdrawal is not the final stage but a step to the highest expansion.

The followers of the path of *bhakti* seek to experience the Absolute as an object of love. Their consciousness is wholly occupied by love for the Absolute Being. They have no consciousness except the consciousness of God. They see the manifestations of God in outside objects as well as in their own hearts and lead a life of God-centeredness. They forget themselves altogether and lose themselves in God, the sole object of their love, whose infinite beauty and supreme attractiveness keep them captivated for all time. As their conciousness flows spontaneously toward the extremely beautiful and captivating Lord, they feel no effort or strain in their devotion. Recognizing that the objects of the world, external or internal, which tempt or allure the senses and the mind are all manifestations of God, the ultimate source of truth, goodness, and beauty, they believe that one can reach God with little or no difficulty by following any of their temptations according to the normal bent of one's senses and the mind only if one persists in following it up to its source.

It is true that spiritual progress and realization of the ultimate spiritual truth are not possible as long as the mind and the senses are attached to mundane objects, which are usually thought to be absolutely unrelated to God; and it is undeniable that *bhakti,* or exclusive attachment to God, implies indifference to or detachment from all else. Yet the followers of the path of *bhakti* do not condemn the senses and the phenomenal objects as hindrances but see them as venue for service of God. This approach precludes unconditional attachment to sense objects. Phenomenal objects and the senses alike are manifestations of God and are not meant for the mere enjoyment of finite beings.

Detachment from the phenomenal objects or renunication of the phenomenal world under the false notion that the world and its objects have no relation to God is disparaged by devotees as false detachment or pseudo-asceticism. They consider the eradication or forcible suppression of all desires and impulses to be detrimental to mental and spiritual life. What is commendable is to follow the phenomenal object to its source with the firm conviction that God alone is the source of all objects that interest and attract us. True detachment or genuine asceticism is the dispassionate attitude toward one's involvement in the world as a consequence of love toward God. It is not the renunciation of objects simply on the ground that they are material or phenomenal. False detachment or pseudo-asceticism is strained, but true detachment is spontaneous. The latter is sounder and more congenial for pursuit of spiritual life. He who has devotion and love toward Kṛṣṇa does not need to *cultivate* indifference to worldly objects or renounce worldly pleasures, since love or attachment to Kṛṣṇa leaves no scope for the love or attachment to any other object but implies *spontaneous* renunciation of all other objects and all other pleasures.

True detachment or genuine asceticism is, therefore, a natural consequence of genuine devotion. Unless there is indifference to the mundane things and worldly enjoyments, the mind can hardly turn to God in devotion; but again, if the mind is not really devoted to God, it can hardly experience true detachment or genuine asceticism. The teachers of the Bengal school of Vaiṣṇavism have identified the path of spiritual progress with the path of genuine *bhakti*, which is not a path of withdrawal but a broad way of self-discovery through self-dedication to God as His servant.

The spiritual discipline involved in *rāgānugā bhakti* consists primarily in meditation on Kṛṣṇa, His attributes and sportive activities. Constant remembrance, loving meditation, and spontaneous self-surrender (*ātmanivedana*) are among its principal characteristics. The teachers of the Bengal school believe that an individual who has natural and instinctive love for his child, friend, and beloved can enter into loving relationship with Kṛṣṇa through *rāgānugā bhakti*. He has to focus on one or the other of these natural relationships and constantly meditate on Kṛṣṇa as the sole object of this loving relation, for the natural feeling of love can be sublimated only by a gradual process of purification. This purification entails constant contemplation of Kṛṣṇa, which intensifies the devotee's love to the degree of absorbing him in Kṛṣṇa. Kṛṣṇa is all love, and He can be realized through some loving relation if it is carefully spiritualized, sublimated, and divinized. No suppression or extinction of natural feelings and emotions is called for, but only divinization or divine transformation of them. Among the four spiritual disciplines of *karma* yoga, *jñāna* and *bhakti*, *bhakti* is the safest and easiest since in it one is required but to follow one's own natural inclination; for this reason, one's spiritual development is smooth, rapid, without strain, and secure.

According to the Bengal school of Vaiṣṇavism, the goal of the spiritual discipline is *prīti*, or devotional love for Kṛṣṇa. In order to realize this state, one could begin with *sādhana bhakti* that includes *rāgānugā bhakti* and *vaidhi bhakti*. However, of the two, *vaidhi bhakti* is inferior to *rāgānugā bhakti*, since in *vaidhi bhakti* the impulse to devotion is not spontaneous but derived from the scriptural injunctions. *Bhāva bhakti*, or devotion resulting from spontaneous inward feeling, is superior even to *rāgānugā bhakti*, since in the latter there is an *effort* to imitate the forms of natural emotional attachment. It is *bhāva bhakti* that matures into a form of *prema bhakti*, or sentiment of love. In fact *sādhana bhakti*, *bhāva bhakti*, and *prema bhakti* are the three successive stages of *uttama bhakti*, which has been defined by the teachers of the Bengal school as the harmonious worship and service of Kṛṣṇa, free from every other desire and unenveloped by knowledge, action, and similar other conditions.

The goal of the spiritual discipline of *bhakti* in this system is usually known by the name of *sādhya-bhakti*, and the conception of *sādhya-bhakti* or *bhakti* as the goal varies in accordance with the degree of spirituality with which the goal is viewed. There is an account of the gradations of *bhakti* in a dialogue between Caitanya and Rāmānanda stated in *Caitanya Caritāmṛta* (*Madhya-līlā*, chap. 8). The latter begins by saying that the performance of caste duties and *āśrama*-duties is a step toward the attainment of *bhakti*, for such performance purifies the mind and makes one a fit recipient of divine grace (57–58). But since *bhakti* means attaching oneself to Kṛṣṇa for His satisfaction alone, Caitanya refuses to regard the performance of such duties as an indispensable prerequisite of *bhakti* and looks for a better account of *bhakti*.

Going one step further, Rāmānanda identifies *sādhya bhakti* with that state of the mind in which the devotee in all activity renounces his interests in favor of Kṛṣṇa (59–60). Asked by Caitanya to give a still better account of *sādhya bhakti*, he described *bhakti* as that state of mind in which one abandons all duties through love of Kṛṣṇa and points out that one cannot reach the path of love without renouncing all thoughts of oneself (61–63). But, as Caitanya considers this description an account of the outer aspect of *bhakti* and further questions, Rāmānanda proceeds by saying that *bhakti* is that state of mind in which devotion is impregnated with knowledge (64–65). Even this account of *bhakti* does not prove satisfactory to Caitanya. Hence Rāmānanda speaks of the next higher stage of *bhakti* called *prema-bhakti*, which means the natural and inalienable attachment of mind to Kṛṣṇa (68–70).

Pleased with the description of *prema-bhakti*, Caitanya requests Rāmānanda to continue and describe the stages of its development. In compliance with Caitanya's request, Rāmānanda speaks of the different types of *prema-bhakti*, arranging them in a hierarchy of superiority. Of the five kinds of *prema-bhakti*, viz. *śānta* or *sādhana bhakti* (peaceful love/devotional service, 69), *dāsya* (love of a servant for his master, 71), *sakhya* (love of a friend, 74) *vātsalya* (filial attitude, 75), and *mādhurya* (woman for her lover, 79), *mādhurya bhakti* is the highest. This *bhakti* is typified by the love of the *gopīs* for Kṛṣṇa (80). Caitanya admits that this *bhakti* is the farthest limit or the supreme height of *sādhya bhakti* but expresses his desire to know whether there is something more (96). Rāmānanda tells him that the love of Rādhā, the chief among the *gopīs*, represents the highest form of *mādhurya bhakti* (98). The loving attitude of the *gopīs* toward Kṛṣṇa progresses continuously through the stages of love to culminate in *mahābhāva,* which is identified with Rādhā, who is at once the source and fulfillment of all love (160). Even here there are stages of development: In the highest stage Rādhā forgets that she is the subject of love and that Kṛṣṇa is the object of her loving devotion; the subject and the object resolve into one experience of love (195). It is this mystical experience which the teachers of the Bengal school of Vaiṣṇavism regard as the culmination of spiritual realization. What is unique about their conception of this ecstatic state is their conviction that when both the lover and the beloved apparently lose their individuality in the sweet flow of love, the distinction between the subject and the object does not completely vanish but remains suspended.

The *sādhya bhakti* is described as *nirguṇa bhakti* (unqualified devotion), which consists in spontaneous and unrestricted attachment to Kṛṣṇa. It is also synonymous with *prema-bhakti*, the supreme state of spiritual realization, which is not the result of a process but an accomplished fact. Like the experience of *mokṣa,* or liberation, which is the *summum bonum* of the Vedāntic school of Śaṅkara, *Kṛṣṇaprema* (love for Kṛṣṇa) eternally *is* (*nitya siddha*) and never comes into being; that is, it is eternal and uncaused. *Prema-bhakti,* being the most perfect experience of love, is transcendent, and it is not possible for an individual to rise to it by his efforts; it can come down to him through Divine Grace only. It is not of the nature of an acquisition but of the nature of an unconditional revelation. *Prema* is an extraordinary experience which does not depend on the functioning of the mind (*citta*) but is only mirrored in the mind when it is perfectly purified. The hearing and the reciting of the Vaiṣṇava scriptures, the continued repetition of the divine name and the like are techniques that help merely to prepare for the emergence of the eternally realized *prema-bhakti*. These preparations do not condition the emergence of *prema*, because it is unconditioned and unconditional.

In transforming *bhakti* (devotion to God) into *prema* (love for God) Bengal Vaiṣṇavism gave a new orientation to the understanding of the relation between God and humanity. Caitanya by his living example delineated the path of love which in itself becomes the fulfillment of its goal. In response to the question, What is the most important means for achieving this goal? he stated:

> Recite the name of Hari (God) repeat the name of Hari
> (God), say the name of Hari constantly. In this
> dark age of Kali, there is no other way, none other,
> nothing more needs to be done.

Bibliography

Sources

Padāvalī. *In Praise of Krishna: Songs from Bengali.* Translated by Edward C. Dimock, Jr., and Denise Levertov. New York: Doubleday, 1967.

Studies

Archer, William G. *The Loves of Krishna in Indian Painting and Poetry.* London: George Allen & Unwin, 1973.

Chakravarti, Sudhindra C. *Philosophical Foundations of Bengali Vaiṣṇavism.* Calcutta: Academic Publishers, 1969.

De, S. K. *Early History of the Vaiṣṇava Faith and Movement in Bengal.* 2nd ed. Calcutta: K. L. Mukhopadhyay, 1961.

Dimock, Edward C. *The Place of Hidden Moon: Erotic Mysticism in the Vaiṣṇava-Sahajiyā Cult of Bengal.* Chicago: University of Chicago Press, 1966.

——, trans. *The Thief of Love: Bengali Tales.* Chicago: Chicago University Press, 1963.

Singer, Milton, ed. *Krishna: Myths, Rites, and Attitudes.* Chicago: University of Chicago Press, 1968.

4

The Devotional Poetry of Sūrdāsa and Tulasidāsa

NAGENDRA

ALTHOUGH AN UNDERCURRENT of devotion (*bhakti*) had been flowing in Indian literature from the time of the Vedas,[1] it gained enormous momentum during the medieval period, when the whole country from the extreme north to the farthest coastal regions in the south and from East Bengal to Gujrat in the west resounded with devotional songs composed by poets of great eminence in almost all the modern vernacular languages. The sentiment of devotion has been defined as intense love for God characterized by supreme bliss. In terms of modern psychology, it can be described as a mixed sentiment composed of the feelings of love and reverence. The base, of course, is love combined with feelings of reverence and submission to a higher power that controls the cosmos.

There are, roughly speaking, four theories prevalent among historians with regard to the origin of the *bhakti* movement in India. According to Grierson it was the result of the impact of Christianity: scholars such as Tara Chand believe that it came to India with the advent of the Arabs to the western coast of India in the sixth and seventh centuries. Ram Chandra Shukla, among others, interprets it as a reaction to atrocities of the Muslim rule in the sociopolitical and religiocultural life of the Hindus. The first two were more or less conjectures emanating from particular beliefs and attitudes, and they are now completely rejected. Many indologists are convinced, on the basis of authentic evidence, that the *bhakti* movement is of indigenous origin, since, besides a number of devotional hymns in the *Ṛgveda*, there is a sizable volume of material available in the *Gītā*, in the Śāntiparva of the *Mahābhārata* as well as in some of the earlier *Purāṇas* to establish its Indian origin beyond doubt.[2] It is, however, historically correct that the *bhakti* movement received its impetus from the sociopolitical conditions prevalent during the medieval period, and the thin stream of devotional poetry that had been flowing for thousands of years was flooded with myriads of songs extremely rich in spiritual content and musical qualities.

Sūrdāsa and Tulasidāsa belong to this galaxy of devotional poets. They flourished during the first half of the Mughal period—in the reign of Akbar and Jahangir—and possibly knew each other directly or indirectly. Sūrdāsa, the blind poet, lived between the last quarter of the fifteenth and the first half of the sixteenth century. Tulasidāsa was his junior contemporary, who most probably lived from 1532 to 1623 C.E. They are easily the most eminent representatives of the devotional school of poetry in Hindi.

Sūrdāsa

Sūrdāsa, a blind poet of Hindi, may be acclaimed as the greatest poet of the Kṛṣṇa cult in Indian literature. Scholars have been divided in their opinions on the issue of his blindness, but now the consensus is that he was not blind from birth but had seen life—maybe a rather colorful life—before he lost his sight.[3] He was, however, a blind singer when he met Vallabhācārya at Parasanli village near Mathura in 1510 C.E. When asked to give a performance before the preceptor, the story goes, he recited the following song:

> I am the crest and crown amongst all sinners,
> While others have sinned for a day or two
> I am a life long sinner.[4]

Vallabhācārya affectionately rebuked him for that attitude of remorse and guilt consciousness which was uncalled for and advised him to sing of the joyful sports of the Lord. Sūrdāsa, however, pleaded ignorance and requested the preceptor to enlighten him on the subject. Vallabhācārya then gave an intensive discourse on the *Bhāgavata* and explained the divine mystery of the Lord's sports—which was revealed to the blind poet in a flash. Sūrdāsa was thus formally initiated and, by his invaluable contribution, earned the title of the "Ship of Pushti-marg—the Cult of the Divine Grace."

The magnum opus of Sūrdāsa is *Sūr Sāgar*. According to a popular legend, this vast collection, literally an ocean of songs, contained more than a hundred thousand verses. The figure is obviously fabulous and indicates only the enormous volume of Sūrdāsa's compositions. Textual criticism has so far not been able to compile more than five thousand songs. The edition of *Sūr Sāgar*, published by the Nagari Pracharini Sabha of Varanasi, contains 4,907 items, and, although there is a sharp controversy about the authenticity of many of them, this volume has been used as a base by most of our scholars. *Sūr Sāgar* has been directly inspired by the *Bhāgavata*

Purāṇa and is divided likewise into twelve cantos. It is, however, not a translation in any sense of the term; actually it was not physically possible for the blind poet to produce a systematic translation of the *Bhāgavata* or any other work. Here also, the tenth canto, which described the divine sports of Kṛṣṇa, particularly His amorous sports, contains the cream. The rest of the volume consists of prayerful songs, several episodes of secondary importance in Kṛṣṇa's life, the life story of Rāma, eulogies of other incarnations and descriptions of festivals, and so on. The songs of prayer are, by and large, written after the style of the saint-poets in which the devotee recounts his own sins and vices on the one hand and the acts of benevolence of the Lord on the other, and appeals for the emancipation of his soul. These songs may not be very colorful, but they are marked with a rare intensity of feeling and remarkable sincerity of expression. The episodes relating to Kṛṣṇa, Rāma, and other incarnations or deities are generally described in a matter-of-fact style, except in cases where the poet's fancy is stirred up by certain situations. Yet in spite of all the difference in their artistic level, all these compositions are devotional songs, being directly or indirectly related to the devotee's interest in the various aspects of the Lord's personality. While the prayerful songs are direct expressions of the supplicant's intimate feelings, the descriptions of different episodes serve as stimulants to the devotional sentiment.

Vallabhācārya was the last among the great Vaiṣṇava philosophers who refuted Śaṅkara's doctrine of *māyā* and interpreted the basic principle of monism on an empirical plane, which was more acceptable to the people at large. For Vallabhācārya, in Śaṅkara's theory, *Brahman*, the Supreme Spirit, was caught in the snares of *māyā*, or illusion, leading to the creation of the universe. The necessary corollary of this theory was that the universe was a mere illusion and life was only a nightmare. Vallabhācārya ruthlessly cut off the snares of *māyā* that had been woven around the Supreme Self. The Supreme Self was a free and pure entity, untainted by *māyā*. He did not require the snares of *māyā* to create the universe. This was done of His own free will, without any motive or purpose, as a mere sport. The Supreme Being engages Himself in creation as a mere sport. The pure, unqualified nature of the Supreme Being's nondual entity is established by the synthesis of opposite qualities or attributes in Him. He is without attributes and is yet possessed of divine qualities. He is Absolute and yet is endowed with a personality. He has infinite forms and is yet one. He is indivisible and free from desire and yet creates the universe for His own pleasure.

According to the tenets of the Vallabha cult, Kṛṣṇa is the Supreme Being. Therefore, the personality of Kṛṣṇa is the repository of these contradictory attributes. Even though a child, He is engaged in amorous sports. He is free and yet is dependent on the devotee. He is absorbed in His own bliss and yet revels in making love. He is self-fulfilled and yet keen on fulfilling the desires of the devotee. Sūrdāsa has invariably this image of Kṛṣṇa before him.

Just as people enjoy sports for their own sake, Kṛṣṇa is engaged in all kinds of sports, heroic as well as amorous, as a matter of course, as a spontaneous expression of the element of bliss in Him. These divine sports of the Lord are eternal, and they are meant to afford bliss to the mortal beings who are struggling against the bonds of destiny. This is the essential meaning of the doctrine of "Divine Sport," which can be revealed to the devotee only through His grace. Thus, the doctrine of "Divine Grace" emerged as a practical mode of devotion. The great preceptor, Vallabhācārya, in his short and exclusive discourse, explained this basic truth to Sūrdāsa through the contents of the *Bhāgavata* (tenth canto), which became a gospel for him. The divine mystery was thus revealed to the blind poet as though in a flash.

There are two profiles of Kṛṣṇa's personality: (1) as the king of Mathura and Dvārakā and (2) as the playful cowherd of Gokula, who became the amorous hero of Vṛndāvan. Vallabha has highlighted the second profile, which is the cynosure of all Beauty and Love. This image has penetrated deep into Sūrdāsa's heart, and his whole psyche is completely wrapt in its splendor. His poetry presents a magnificent gallery of exquisite pen portraits of Kṛṣṇa's physical charms:

> All of a sudden Śyāma was seen going through an alley of Braja
> all alone.
> His crown was waving in the air, a twist in his eyebrows.
> The saffron garment was flowing around his waist.
> He walked sportingly with a smile on his lips.
> He moved a step or two, then looked back, casting around
> amorous glances. (v. 145, p. 136)[5]

Equally enchanting are Sūrdāsa's poems portraying the playfulness of the child Kṛṣṇa.

> Kṛṣṇa is singing to himself in the courtyard.
> He dances on his little feet and exults within.
> With raised arms he bids.
> and cows come both black and white.
> Now he calls Nanda and then goes inside, pouring butter
> into his little mouth with hands small,
> Feeding his shadow in the shining pillar. (v. 27, p. 59)

All the senses of the blind poet were thoroughly intoxicated with the beauty of his beloved deity. An ocean of beauty was surging before his mind's eyes till the last moment of his life.

The ocean of beauty knows no bounds.
Having flooded the mansions of Nanda,
It is flowing over the lanes and alleys of Braja.
However one may try,
It is not possible to describe its splendor even with a thousand tongues.
It is being talked all around—
A celestial sapphire has been born
Out of the unfathomable ocean of Yaśodā's bosom. (v. 6, p. 49)

Sūrdāsa has communicated the all-pervading effect of Kṛṣṇa's charming physique by means of another prolonged metaphor of the ocean:

Just see, my dear, an ocean of beauty is surging before us. (v. 145, p. 136)

In this verse, Kṛṣṇa's dark body has been compared to azure ocean, and the frills of his saffron garment with the surging waves. His eyes are the fish; the earrings present a spectacle of crocodiles; and his long arms are the water serpents. Finally, the Lord's lustrous face, bedecked with drops of perspiration, is compared to the moon, risen out of the ocean.

Master theorists have defined five major forms of devotion according to the devotee's attitude toward the Lord: single-minded devotion to the Lord of the universe, dedication to the service of the Master, parental affection for God envisaged as a child, friendly relation, and conjugal love. In the earlier compositions of Sūrdāsa, there are unmistakable instances of the first form of *bhakti*. It is the initial form of *bhakti* that is the result of a basic human instinct; one feels completely forsaken in the midst of the toils and turmoils of life, surrounded by Nature, red in tooth and claw, and looks for shelter to some unknown power mightier than nature. Sūrdāsa is convinced that:

The name of the Lord is a mighty force
He who takes refuge in Him is never abandoned.
The castle of His grace becomes his shelter:
They all resort to Him, great and small
As with the touch of the mythical store
Iron becomes gold. (v. 15, p. 24)

He has, therefore, expressed his sense of complete reliance on God through an extremely effective symbolic image of the pigeon and the hunter.

Save me this time, my Lord.
A helpless bird, I am sitting on the branch of a tree.
Below stands the hunter ready to dart his arrow.
Hovering above is the falcon whom I am trying to escape.
The pigeon, beset with danger from all sides, who could save it?

> But as soon as it prayed to the Lord, the hunter was bitten by a snake.
> And the arrow, darted off his bow, knocked down the falcon.
> Such is the glory of the merciful Lord. (v. 18, p. 26)

This devotion is single-minded. The poet devotee declares openly that he does not depend on anyone else. He has tried all the gods—they are bankrupts. Therefore, he has come to the Lord of Gokula to seek shelter (v. 20, p. 27).

The attitude of complete surrender is intrinsically connected with a feeling of helplessness born of the consciousness of one's failings, vices, and sins. It is, therefore, accompanied by a sense of remorse. Expressions of such moods are found in a number of Sūrdāsa's earlier songs, for example:

i. Hari, I am the leader of all the sinners.

ii. Mādhava, I am the king of all the sinners.

iii. I am the chief of all sinners.

iv. O Hari, there is no other sinner like me.

v. There is no other sinner like me, my Lord.

vi. My Lord, pray redeem a sinner like me.

Reference to the servile attitude—to the servant–master relationship—is rather rare but not altogether absent in the earlier compositions of the blind poet. Actually, the feelings of submission and surrender are psychologically interrelated. Sūrdāsa refuses to supplicate to gods because they are the slaves of Lord Kṛṣṇa, from whom they derive all their power and glory.

The fact remains, however, that the later three modes of devotion—parental, friendly, and conjugal—were closer to the poet's heart, and his soul was fully immersed in them. The reason is simple. The attitudes of surrender and submission emanate from awe, but parental, friendly, and conjugal relations are based on affection. Sūrdāsa was an extremely sensitive person, and his blindness had made him all the more sentimental. Therefore, when the mystery of Lord's divine sports (*līlā*) was revealed to him by his great preceptor, he shed off the feelings of depression and remorse and engaged himself, heart and soul, in singing of the Lord's sports, which evoked the sentiments of parental, friendly, and conjugal love.

Sūrdāsa was thus primarily a poet of love. In the words of the great Hindi critic Ramchandra Shukla, he had free access to the innermost recesses of the human heart.[6] Love was the life breath of his being on the devotional as well as the poetic plane. As has been indicated above, Vallabhācārya laid the greatest emphasis on three forms of devotion that were essentially based on love, in which the devotee worshiped God as a child, as a friend, and as the beloved. Sūrdāsa excels in the delineation of these three forms of devotion.

The softest strains of love are found in the love of the mother and the father for the child. Sūrdāsa is unrivaled in this field. Until recently, Hindi critics were intrigued to find a sudden upsurge of child-poetry (poetry based on love for the child) in the works of this blind poet. But later researches in devotional poetry in different Indian languages have resolved this mystery. Quite a number of devotional poets in vernacular Indian languages have presented warm portrayals of this sentiment. The Āḻvārs of the Tamil area, especially Periyāḻvār, composed hundreds of verses bubbling with this sentiment, and the mind of Periyāḻvār was so obsessed with this feeling that he evolved a special poetic genre, "Pillai Tamil," to describe the various moods and activities of Kṛṣṇa during the first two years of his infancy. Among other poets who excelled in the delineation of this sentiment, the author of *Kṛṣṇagatha* in Malayalam, Purandaradāsa in Kannada, and Narasi Mehta and Bhalan in Gujarati stand out prominently. In *vātsalya bhakti*, or the parental form of devotion, child Kṛṣṇa is the object, Nanda-Yaśodā, especially Yaśodā, is the subject, and the various moods and sports of Kṛṣṇa are the excitants. But what is the role of the devotee poet here? one may ask. The reply is that he is the real subject and Nanda and Yaśodā are his symbols or spokepersons to communicate his sentiments. There is another way of looking at the problem. In the treatises on *bhakti*, as also in the *Purāṇas*, it is mentioned that Nanda and Yaśodā had practiced penance in their previous births and as a boon asked for an opportunity to offer their devotion and love to child Kṛṣṇa in the capacity of parents. In this way, the devotee poet is spiritually identified with Nanda-Yaśodā. Sūrdāsa was a man, blind and detached from the world, and yet he has portrayed the sentiments of the parents and strangely enough of the mother, with extraordinary warmth and accuracy:

> Yaśodā fondly dreams of the day
> When her child will crawl on his knees and move a step or two.
> When I see his milk teeth—then he will utter a word or two.
> When he will call Nanda as "dad" and me as mother.
> When he will catch my skirt and quarrel over trifles.
> When he will talk with me and dispel all my worries. (*Sūrasāgara*, v. 12, p. 52)

This form of devotion is based primarily on the emotional reactions and responses of the parents toward the activities of the child. Sūrdāsa has given copious descriptions of such emotional situations. Yaśodā gently rocks the cradle and sings all sorts of sweet lullabies to induce Kṛṣṇa to sleep. The child sometimes closes his eyes, then in a moment quivers his lips. Yaśodā watches all these movements of Kṛṣṇa, and her heart is filled with rapture (*Sūrasāgara*, v. 7, p. 50). When Kṛṣṇa dances about in the courtyard, the whole atmosphere resounds with joy (v. 27, p. 59). An interesting incident of Kṛṣṇa's childhood—his insistence on playing with the moon—has been described by a number of poets in different languages. In Sūrdāsa, when Kṛṣṇa does not feel satisfied with any of the alternative offers, the mother presents before him the reflection of the moon in a bowl of water (v. 29, p. 60). In one of the songs of Narsi Mehta, we hear the child Kṛṣṇa making the same demand: "Mother get me the moon: put the stars in my pocket," and the mother here also plays the same trick.

In such contexts the devotee-poet is faced with the subtle problem of reconciling the divine and the human attributes of his object of worship. Although in intense moments the difference is merged to a large extent, he cannot be completely oblivious to the fact that the object of worship is a divine being. Sūrdāsa and his fellow poets have effected this reconciliation beautifully at the psychological as well as the artistic level. When Yaśodā reprimands Kṛṣṇa for eating crystals of earth, he opens wide his mouth, which contains the entire cosmos within (*Sūrasāgara*, v. 14, p. 53). This spectacle thoroughly upsets Yaśodā and she yells in dismay: "Call the pandits, I have to offer alms for the well-being of my son." Similarly, the celestial marks typical of Viṣṇu are seen on the sole of Kṛṣṇa's foot while he is dancing. The parents are naturally confused at the sight and start praying. In both these situations, Kṛṣṇa withdraws his divine attributes instantaneously and reverts to his usual pranks and sports to restore normalcy. Sūrdāsa's Yaśodā is much too simple a mother to entertain any doubts about Kṛṣṇa's identity—he is her son and nothing else (vv. 20–23ff., pp. 56ff.). The question, however, has exercised the minds of other poets, and they have given a fitting answer.

Sūrdāsa's formal mode of devotion was of the friendly type, *sākhya-bhakti*. It means that he worshiped the Lord as a friend—identifying himself with the cowherd boys who were the playmates of Kṛṣṇa. Although there are explicit references to it in the annals of the Vaiṣṇavas, the fact is not quite borne out by the poetry of Sūrdāsa, who obviously revels more in delineating the parental and conjugal forms of devotion. There are hundreds of songs in *Sūr Sāgar* wherein the poet has described in detail the playful activities of Kṛṣṇa in the company of cowherd boys who join him in looking after the cows, milking them, stealing butter from the houses of the milkmaids, in addition to different kinds of games and sports (vv. 33ff., pp. 62ff.). Here the blind poet, who must have been fairly grown up in age by that time, completely forgets his identity and becomes one with the playmates, sharing their sports, mischief, and friendly acts as well as their quarrels.

These playful songs place the devotee on a par with the Lord, accord him a certain spiritual status whereby he can meet the Lord on an equal footing, and also take liberty in moments of complete identification.

It is, however, in the delineation of the conjugal form of devotion—*kāntā bhakti*—that the genius of Sūrdāsa shines in full splendor. His *kāntā bhakti* is different from Mīrābāi's and even from that of the poets of the Caitanya and Rādhā-Vallabha sects. Being a woman, Mīrābāi could more easily and more naturally address her love to Kṛṣṇa directly as His spouse. The attitude of the poets of Caitanya and Rādhā-Vallabha sects was also explicitly more erotic. Vallabhācārya too had given due place to the conjugal form of devotion, but his own preference was possibly for *vātsalya bhakti*, or the parental form of devotion. The emphasis was, however, shifted by his successor Viṭṭhalanātha to *kāntā bhakti*, as is indicated by some of his writings on the subject. Since the later and more creative part of Sūrdāsa's poetic career was spent during the regime of Viṭṭhalanātha, he engaged himself religiously in depicting the erotic aspects of *bhakti*, which had by that time gained prominence in the Kṛṣṇite cult as a whole.[7] Sūrdāsa has given expression to the erotic kind of divine love through the medium of the love of Rādhā and Kṛṣṇa, which he has described in all its varieties and minute details, with all the richness of emotion and rare skill in poetic art (*Sūrasāgara*, vv. 1ff., pp. 146ff.).

This love starts in a natural homely manner in childhood:

> "Who are you, fair one?" asked Śyāma.
> "Where do you live, who's your father?
> Why haven't I seen you here before?
> Why should I come here? I play at my own place.
> I have heard that the son of Nanda goes about stealing butter,
> I am sure, I shall not rob you of anything.
> Come, let us play together."(v. 2, p. 146)

The love of childhood grew with the age into an eternal passion. Rādhā and Kṛṣṇa drank deep at the fountain of love, enjoyed all kinds of amorous sports in the company of cowherd maidens. Sūrdāsa has elaborately described the varying moods of lovers, their subtlest reactions and the joyful atmosphere around. The most significant of Kṛṣṇa's sports is the *rāsalīlā*, group dance of the cowherd maidens, with Rādhā and Kṛṣṇa in the center. All the major poets of the Kṛṣṇa cult have described this dance in colorful language. Actually Sūrdāsa's descriptions of *rāsalīlā* are superb. This festive dance represents the ecstatic moments of love on the physical level and the cosmic dance at the spiritual plane.[8] Here Kṛṣṇa is the Cosmic Spirit; Rādhā is the creative Energy; and the damsels of Braja are the various aspects of nature. This is the usual symbolic device adopted by devotional poets to convert physical activities into spiritual experiences. Sūrdāsa is normally reticent, but when the occasion demands he sheds off all complexes and presents voluptuous scenes of love.

The essence of Vaiṣṇava *bhakti* is *viraha*, or pangs of separation, because it is in separation that love reaches its climax. Rādhā in the Kṛṣṇa cult symbolizes eternal separation or, in terms of *bhakti-śāstra*, the eternal yearning of the human soul for the Supreme Soul. After Kṛṣṇa's departure from Braja, all the village folk, especially the cowherd maidens, are extremely unhappy, but Rādhā's sorrow knows no bounds. She was Kṛṣṇa's sweetheart in the bloom of his youth and was engrossed heart and soul in his love. But after Kṛṣṇa's departure from Braja, she was left all alone, cut off from all social or domestic activities and spent her whole life in separation. In most of the works on Vaiṣṇavism, Rādhā has been portrayed not as Kṛṣṇa's wife but as his beloved, who never met him afterwards. Sūrdāsa has, however, departed from the common tradition. In *Sūr Sāgar*, she is wedded to Kṛṣṇa in the ceremonial way, and very long after in the eve of her life she meets Kṛṣṇa again for a while in a religious fair at Kurukshetra after the battle of the *Mahābhārata*. This short meeting has been designed with a view to highlighting her lifelong dedication and unique sacrifice. Rādhā has thus become a symbol of perennial separation or unfulfilled love.

Sūrdāsa has strung together his songs of separation around an allegory of the black bee. When Uddhava goes to Braja to advise the cowherd maidens to cast off their infatuation and try to realize God through meditation, they react very sharply (*Sūrasāgar*, vv. 50ff., pp. 280ff.). Just then, by accident, a black bee comes there which provides them an opportunity to express their pent-up feelings of anguish and frustration (v. 46, p. 278). The black bee who goes about from flower to flower in search of honey and as such represents fickle-minded love is made the target of their attacks against Uddhava and through him against Kṛṣṇa Himself, who has betrayed them so callously. These expressions of jilted love are whetted by sharp-edged irony, which conveys feelings of utter frustration on the one hand and deep-rooted, unmitigated devotion on the other (vv. 59ff., pp. 284ff.).

But these women, who have such sharp tongues, possess extremely soft hearts within. Very soon the mood of anger vanishes and they are full of humility and remorse for using harsh language. Yet, about their stand, they are clear. Kṛṣṇa is all in all for them; they know no other deity or any Supreme Being. Theirs is the path of love, not of knowledge or yoga, which are alien to them. Their ultimate goal is union with their beloved and not salvation, which has no meaning for them. Hence, Sūrdāsa has raised the question of the dual and nondual character of the Supreme Reality in a simple, homely manner. By conducting an intellectual debate on a purely emotional level, he has elevated sectarian belief into a universal truth. Religion is a matter of faith, and faith is rooted in love. This is the essence of the emotional retorts of the cowherd maidens against the intellectual arguments of Uddhava.

> Uddhava, we don't have a score of hearts.
> The only one we had has gone with Śyāma.
> Who would now worship the Supreme Lord? (v. 95, p. 299)

This is the final solution of the problem presented by the blind poet in unambiguous terms—simple and straight.

Although his knowledge of the *Bhāgavata Purāṇa* and the basic philosophy of the Vallabha cult was fairly complete, Sūrdāsa was not much of a philosopher by temperament. He had a child's heart full of the milk of human kindness and was mind and soul dedicated to the service of the Lord in his material as well as spiritual life. He was a great devotee of his times—"the Ship of the Cult of Divine Grace" and one of the greatest poets of all times—"the Sun among poets." While his devotion lent sanctity and warmth to his poetry, his creative imagination added color and variety to his devotional sentiments.

Tulasidāsa

Tulasidāsa differs from Sūrdāsa in the sense that he was not just a lyricist. While Sūrdāsa wrote either pure or thematic lyrics singing of the divine sports, Tulasidāsa excelled in epic and narrative poetry as well. Actually the difference is not so much in their art forms as in their poetic genius itself. Tulasidāsa's attitude toward life and literature was distinctly more objective. Quite naturally, therefore, he has used the objective forms—the epic and the narrative—besides, of course, the lyric, as vehicles of his devotional poetry.

Rāmacaritamānasa, the poet's magnum opus is an epic. *Kavitāvalī* (in spite of some gaps here and there), *Jānkī Maṅgala*, and *Pārvatī Maṅgala*, as also the other two smaller poems *Barve Rāmāyaṇa* and *Rāmalalā Nahchhoo*, are narrative.

Tulasidāsa's lyrical genius finds expression directly in *Vinaya-Patrikā*, which is a petition to the Lord Rāma for the gift of his *bhakti*. The same theme is present indirectly in *Gītāvalī*, wherein the poet sings with devotional fervor of the life story of Rāma. Then there is a collection of couplets —*Dohāvalī*—which contains verses dealing with didactic and devotional themes. Out of this list, we have to depend primarily on *Rāmacaritamānasa*, *Vinaya-Patrikā*, and a number of couplets in *Dohāvalī* for assessing the nature and quality of Tulasidāsa's devotional sensibility and the level of his spiritual consciousness, although some stray verses in *Kavitāvalī* and many songs of *Gītāvalī* also are quite relevant in this context.

Tulasidāsa's *bhakti* has a sound sociomoral base. For Sūrdāsa, love was the quintessence of devotion and as such constituted the highest value in general life and, in particular, in devotional life.

I have only one resort, one source of strength,
One hope and one belief:
Tulasidāsa is solely dedicated to Rāma—
As the cloud-bird is to the cloud. (*Dohāvalī*)

Tulasidāsa has employed the symbol of the cloud bird (*chātak*) to express his single-minded devotion to Rāma with all its itensity. This single-minded devotion is expressed pointedly in the following couplet:

Shot down by the hunter, the cloud-bird fell
in the Ganges.
But it immediately turned up its beak
To avoid any intake of the sacred water.
Thus even at the last moment of its life,
The cloud-bird kept its pledge. (*Dohāvalī*)

This, however, is not the proper devotional mood of Tulasidāsa. His devotional attitude is best represented by the central theme or the basic sentiment in *Rāmacaritamānasa*.

Before we set out to define the principal sentiment of *Rāmacaritamānasa*, it is essential to answer another question: What is the poetic genre of this work? Is it an epic or a devotional poem? There are substantial reasons to view *Mānasa* as an epic, and in that case its main theme is the life story of Rāma, which is motivated by a high sense of morality and righteousness. Rāma's primary objective is to destroy evil and establish the higher moral values of life. The principal sentiment under these conditions is the undaunted enthusiasm of the hero for the right and the righteous—an enthusiasm supported by humaneness, benevolence, and valor. It is on this account that Ramachandra Shukla has defined "human welfare," or the good of the people, as the basic theme of *Rāmacaritamānasa*. In the *Rāmāyaṇa* of Vālmīki, that indeed is the theme.

But it is difficult to consider the *Rāmacaritamānasa* as an epic in the same sense as the *Rāmāyaṇa* of Vālmīki. *Rāmacaritamānasa* is the work of a devotional poet, of one who regards himself primarily as a devotee rather than a poet.

Altho' in fine language, the work of skilled poet
Of beauty has naught, unless His name bestow it.
Tho' lacking in charm, tho' as poem none worse is,
Yet if Rāma's name studs the poor poet's verses.
Then wise men will listen and honour ascribe it.
And saints like the bee for its sweetness imbibe it.[9]

He has no doubt that

> Fair jewels of love for the Lord here observing,
> All good men its music will praise as deserving,
> Void of all charms tho' my language itself be,
> One charm to the world known is here;
> All men of good mind and of clearest discernment
> Will think upon that and give ear.[10]

And that essential quality is

> Yes, here is the name of the Lord Rāma,
> The gracious, the essence of scripture, most pure, efficacious.[11]

When we look at *Mānasa* as a devotional poem, the position is changed: the main theme here becomes Rāma's name, that is, devotion to Rāma and not his magnanimous character. This magnanimous character of Rāma, to which Vālmīki looked forward so keenly with a view to setting up a model of human conduct, is the cherished ideal of Tulasidāsa as well, but the basic approach has changed. The devotional poet cherishes it not because it sets up an ideal of human life but because it liberates him from the bondage of human life.

> This poem contains the life-story of Rāma.
> Which liberates the soul from the bonds of human life.[12]

Thus, here Rāma is not just the subject or the hero of the drama, the man who struggles against the demonic forces of life and passes through various kinds of psychic conditions. He becomes primarily the object of devotional sentiment. The subject here is the poet and through him the devotee who sings the glory of Rāma not for the elevation of his worldly life but to seek deliverance from it. Quite naturally, the underlying emotion here is devotion, and that determines the nature of the principal sentiment which cannot be anything but *bhakti* or the feeling of devotion. From the invocation verses to the conclusion, the poet seeks the grace of Rāma and announces over and over again that the final object of all his poetic performance is the attainment of *bhakti*—complete dedication to Rāma. The narrative ends with an elaborate discourse on the supremacy of the devotional sentiment.

Under the circumstances, how are we to determine the principal sentiment? On the basis of the mental makeup of the hero or on the basis of the experience of the poet as communicated through the poem? The answer of the literary theorist is clear: on the basis of the experience of the poet, which is undoubtedly *bhakti*, or the feeling of devotion. Therefore, there is no denying the fact that the principal sentiment in *Rāmacaritamānasa* is *bhakti*.

This raises a question. Does not the sublime personality of Rāma or his noble conduct make any contribution to the emotive pattern or the artistic appeal of the work? Tulasidāsa has solved this problem by making his object of devotion an emblem of the noblest ideals and the highest human values. Besides the inherent divine qualities of Godhead, the object of devotion here symbolizes in his personality the finest human virtues—piety, valor, and grace. In this way, Tulasidāsa has given a broad moral basis to the feeling of devotion and linked it to the fundamental values of life. By raising poetry far above the pursuits of mundane life and linking *bhakti* with the higher values of life, Tulasidāsa has brought about a revolution in the field of poetry and *bhakti*. His *bhakti* is not just an emotion; it is a value.

By assigning a broad base to the devotional sentiment, Tulasidāsa has effected a remarkable synthesis between the objective structure of the epic and the subjective art—pattern of devotional poetry, which is unprecedented in world literature. The intensity with which he has championed its cause throughout leaves one with no doubts regarding the supremacy of the devotional sentiment, but it is equally certain that *bhakti* in *Rāmacaritamānasa* is inspired by a zest for the ethical values of life. Explaining the emotive pattern of the above text in technical terms of Indian poetics, we could say that the poet is the subject (*āśraya*) of the devotional sentiment; the object (*ālambana*) is Rāma; and his magnanimous conduct, being an attribute of the object, is the stimulant (*uddipana*). Just as in the erotic sentiment the beauty and graceful behavior of the object add to the intensity of the basic emotion—love—and in the heroic sentiment the nobility of the cause stimulates the underlying emotion of valor, in the same way, in the context of the devotional sentiment, the qualities of piety, energy, beauty, and the noble deeds of the object contribute to the consummation of the aesthetic bliss.

All the aspects of Rāma's life—the sports of his childhood, the sobriety and restraint in his love, his deep sense of reverence for the parents and the preceptor, his sincere affection and gentle behavior toward the younger members of the family and his attendants, the various deeds of chivalry, and unflinching sense of public duty, his commitment toward the weak and the oppressed, and his generous behavior toward the enemy—all these act as stimulants to the poet's devout love in the natural course. They also impart a deep human significance and a broad social basis to the devotional sentiment, which is otherwise primarily a personal experience. The attributes of the object affect the resultant emotion also. Tulasidāsa is a worshiper of the heroic, of the almighty God, who is the savior of humanity. That is why the devotional sentiment that permeates his epic is infused with the ideals of human welfare and is supported by healthy values of life. While the poetic sensibility of Vālmīki, as it passes through the various phases of Rāma's noble life, identifies itself with the hero's greatness, the poet in Tulasidāsa goes a step farther: after a full identification with the greatness of his hero, he ultimately merges his identity into the infinite personality of the hero who is the Supreme Being. Whereas the reader of Vālmīki's *Rāmāyaṇa* enjoys a sense of elevation, the reader of *Rāmacaritamānasa* has the more rarified experience of a complete dissolution of his elevated self. And that explains the difference between the aesthetic sensibility of a sage and a devotee.

In conventional terms, Tulasidāsa's mode of devotion is generally considered to be based on a slave-master relationship:

> Unless one cultivates slave-master relationship with the Lord,
> No one can go across the ocean of this material world.[13]
> Who is as virtuous a master as Rāma?
> And who is as vicious as I am?[14]

His *Vinaya-Patrikā*, which contains most spontaneous outpourings of his devout heart, is composed in the form of a petition from a serf to his lord. All the qualities of a slave—unswerving loyalty, complete dedication, aweful reverence, humility, self-negation—are feelingly described in the prayerful songs of this collection. In several songs, Tulasidāsa spells out his vices—weaknesses of the mind and the flesh—and prays to the Lord for redemption.

> My Lord, the fault is entirely mine,
> You are an abode of virtue and grace.
> Support of the forsaken and the miserable.
> From my dress and speech, I appear to be a saint,
> But my mind is a store-house of sins and vices.
> But glorious is the name of Rāma and that gives me comfort.[15]

This sort of self-effacement is the secret of *bhakti*, and Tulasidāsa has laid great stress on it. To cultivate genuine devotion, purity of mind is an essential condition, and purity of mind is achieved by purging it of self-pride, which is the root cause of all vices.

Tulasidāsa followed the path of *maryādā bhakti*, which is based on a well-defined code of conduct. The guiding principle here is Ethos. The poet-devotee maintains perfect decorum in his expression. He is always conscious of the greatness of his Lord and his own weakness and therefore keeps a respectful distance. In this respect, he differs from Sūrdāsa, who is capable of taking liberties with the Lord in his lighter moods. That is why the theorists on *bhakti* have drawn a clear line of demarcation between the friendly attitude of Sūrdāsa and the servile approach of Tulasidāsa. As discussed above, Tulasidāsa is a firm believer in the socio-moral code of conduct and permits neither his characters nor himself to violate its salutary laws. *Kāntā bhakti*, or the conjugal form of devotion, is conspicuous by its absence in Tulasidāsa, who was a purist by training and temperament. The conjugal love between Rāma and Sītā has a sound ethical base, and the poet observes perfect decorum in all such contexts. The parental form of devotion finds ample expression in several works—in *Rāmacaritamānasa*, *Gītāvalī*, *Kavitāvalī*, and even in the smaller poems. Although at such places Tulasidāsa compares favorably with the master-poet of child psychology, Sūrdāsa, there are two marked differences in their attitudes. While Sūrdāsa in his playful moods completely forgets the divine identity of the child before him, Tulasidāsa is always conscious that the child Rāma is God Himself and that he is indulging in sports in order to afford bliss to his parents, etc., who are in reality his devotees.

Thus, out of the five major forms of *bhakti*, Tulasidāsa has laid emphasis on the first two—viz. (i) single-minded devotion, and (ii) the attitude of servility to the Lord. There are copious descriptions of parental love for Rāma in all of Tulasidāsa's major works and especially in *Gītāvalī*, but I have a feeling that there is more poetry than devotion, more of emotional warmth than spiritual element in such descriptions. Actually, Tulasidāsa is so obsessed with the greatness and glory of the Lord that he cannot even unconsciously assume the role of a parent toward him.

The external forms of devotion did not find favor with Tulasidāsa. In *Vinaya-Patrikā*, one can search out references to most of the ten or eleven conventional forms, but they are there only in conformity with the *bhakti* cult. Here also he differs from Sūrdāsa. Sūrdāsa had a regular assignment in a temple to compose songs for different rituals connected with the Lord's program of the day. But Tulasidāsa had no such commitment and naturally, therefore, he did not take the external modes of worship seriously.

Whereas Mīrābāi had no philosophical background, and Sūrdāsa was initiated into just one particular school of theology—Vallabha's doctrine of Divine Grace—Tulasidāsa had extensive education in scriptures. He had studied intensively the Vedic literature, *Purāṇas*, the great epic *Rāmāyaṇa*, and many other works of philosophy and theology. At several places in *Rāmacaritamānasa*, in the last cantos particularly, in several verses of *Vinaya-Patrikā*, and in many stray couplets of *Dohāvalī*, the poet has assumed the role of a philosopher and entered into long scholastic discussion on the concept of the Supreme Being, individual soul, material universe, Illusory Power (*māyā*) which creates it, and so on. The primary question that exercised the minds of most of the poets of that age was the dual or nondual character of God. Śaṅkara had established the nondual character of *Brahman* on a firm foundation. But it was much too abstract and impersonal to capture the imagination of the people, and therefore the next generation of thinkers made sustained efforts to make Him relevant to human life. This resulted in a series of interpretations of the *Brahma Sūtra* with a view to dilute the hard, nondual character of the Supreme Reality by separating the identity of the subject from the object. Thus, dualism developed as a regular system of religious philosophy, and the negative ideal of salvation or realization of the Supreme Reality through knowledge gave way to the concept of emotional union with a personal god through devotion.

Tulasidāsa had made an intensive study of the available literature on the subject and was fully conversant with the controversies of theologians about the dual and nondual character of the Supreme Self, about the concept of an Absolute God without attributes versus a Personalized God endowed with human qualities, and about the efficacy of devotion against knowledge as means to achieve the goal. He had conducted full-length debates on these fundamental topics in the last canto of *Rāmacaritamānasa*. Such discussions evidence a positive cognizance of the nondual nature of *Brahman* on the intellectual plane. But that does not, the poet philosoher asserts, deny the duality of His character, which assumes divine and human qualities to become an object of devotion for the individual souls. As such, he does not make much of the academic distinction between the *saguṇa* and the *nirguṇa Brahman*, the Personalized and the Absolute God. "The Personalized and the Absolute are just two forms of the Supreme Self."[16]

But on the practical plane it is easier to devote ourselves to the Personal God, because we can develop a natural affinity with Him on account of His human qualities, which are common to us. This is the usual argument in favor of the Personalized concept of Godhood. But Tulasidāsa probes deeper into the problem. Contrary to the common belief, he felt that by personal experience it was easier on the rational plane to accept the concept of an Absolute God and the efficacy of meditating on His Glory and greatness for the elevation of one's soul. The concept of a Personal God, on the other hand, did not fall within the purview of reason, and it could be realized only through complete faith, which again was a difficult proposition and could be acquired only by the grace of God. The concept of devotion to the Personalized God, thus, moved in a circle: it started with a belief in a particular idea of Godhead and ended with a complete faith in His grace. For Mīrābāi and Sūrdāsa, it was not difficult to accept the concept of Personal God as a matter of faith. But Tulasidāsa was a man of keen intellect, which had been whetted by the theological polemics of his times. There are unmistakable evidences of a sharp conflict in his mind, but he struggled hard to resolve the tangle in favor of a concept of Personalized Godhood to which he adhered in all sincerity throughout his life. The vehemence with which Śiva argues in the first canto of *Rāmacaritamānasa* that Rāma is the Supreme Being Himself is nothing but a forceful expression of Tulasidāsa's own conviction, which he had arrived at after a strenuous mental exercise. In this episode, Satī, who represents skepticism, had to die in order to be reborn as Pārvatī, the daughter of the king of mountains, who is a symbol of faith as firm as a rock.

Having once accepted the notion of Personalized Godhood, Tulasidāsa opted for the path of devotion as natural consequence. Here, also, he had to pass through the same process. On the philosophical plane initially, he made no distinction between knowledge and devotion:

> There is no difference between knowledge and devotion,
> Both of them save the soul from the miseries of worldly life.[17]

On the practical plane, however, the path of knowledge is full of hazards:

> To follow the path of knowledge is to tread on
> the edge of a sword.
> Once you get into it, there is no escape for you.[18]

Bhakti also is not very easy that way. It requires perfect purity of mind and depends entirely on the mercy of the Lord. Yet it is a surer way because it cannot be affected by *māyā*. The devotee-poet makes his point with the help of a metaphor. *Māyā* and *bhakti* are both females, and since a woman feels no attraction for another woman, *māyā* does not make any overtures toward *bhakti*. In simple language, it means that while knowledge has some tinge of self-pride, devotion is a state of complete self-effacement. *Bhakti*, therefore, provides a more congenial mood for the attainment of God.

There has been some controversy about Tulasidāsa's religious cult. There are numerous references in his works that are indicative of Rāmānuja's influence on him, and the earlier scholars linked up with the doctrine of "Qualified Nondualism." But references to the original theory of nondualism are no fewer in number. However, on a close examination of the text, one arrives at the conclusion that Tulasidāsa had a "catholic" vision and genuinely believed in the dictum that the Supreme Reality is one, although the sages described it in different ways—*ekam sad viprāh bahudhā vadanti*. Therefore, his own theory of religious philosphy was a harmonious blend of the different theological doctrines handed down from Vedic times, in which all the apparent contradictions are reconciled into a serene attitude of complete dedication to God.

The Spirituality of Bhakti Poetry

Sūrdāsa and Tulasidāsa are the two great luminaries in the firmament of Indian spirituality. They are Vaiṣṇavas, devoted to a Personalized God. Their goal is not the realization of or identification with the Supreme Reality but an emotional union with God. Theirs is an undivided loyalty and single-minded devotion to one God who is for them not an incarnation but the Supreme Being or *Brahman* Himself—Kṛṣṇa in the case of Sūrdāsa, and Rāma in the case of Tulasidāsa. This undivided loyalty, however, does not degenerate into narrow sectarianism. Sūrdāsa has narrated the life-story of Rāma at great length with devout reverence, and Tulasidāsa has written *Kṛṣṇa-Gītāvalī* with the same feeling of devotion, in spite of the fact that according to a popular legend he refused to bow down to Kṛṣṇa unless he appeared before him in the form of Rāma with his bow and arrow. Yet in spite of these general affinities, there are some clear differences in their modes of devotion. Sūrdāsa was formally initiated into the cult of the Divine Grace and Tulasidāsa's devotional attitude was formulated after a systematic study of Hindu theology. These personal circumstances of the two devotee-poets and also their personal makeup were naturally responsible for certain distinctive features in their concept and mode of devotion. Sūrdāsa was a part of an institution, and consequently his *bhakti* was to a certain extent institutionalized, although in his intense moments of devotion and poetic creation his soul soared high in a pure spiritual atmosphere. Tulasidāsa had an intellectual makeup that was nurtured by extensive scholarship and, as such, his approach had become more academic. Sūrdāsa is the worshiper of the "Lord of Sports" and his devotional poetry is studded with colorful imagery and wit which provide relief even in the darkest moments of anguish and agony. Tulasidāsa is a devotee of Rāma, who is an emblem of moral values and decorum. Quite naturally, a tone of high seriousness marks his devotional poetry. His *bhakti* has a sound socio-moral base with a rational background.

In an age of political and economic depression when people had lost all interest in life, these devotee-poets of Hindi, like their counterparts in other languages of India, kindled hope and zest for life by reaffirming faith in a Divine Power that would transport them into a land of bliss where there is no sorrow and suffering.

Notes

1. Nanda Dulare Vājapeyi, *Mahākavi Sūrdāsa* (New Delhi: Rajkamal Prakashan 1985) 23–24.
2. See Ramachandra Shukla, *Sūradāsa* (Varanasi: Nagarapracharani Sabha, 1973) 1–46; see also Vajapeyi, *Mahākavi Sūradāsa*, 23–56.

3. Vajapeyi, *Mahākavi Sūradāsa*, 95.
4. *Chaurāsī Vaiṣṇavan Kī Vārtā*, ed. Dwarkadas Parikh (Mathura: Sahitya Samsthan, 1962) 405.
5. *Sūrasāgara Sāra Satīka*, ed. Dhirendra Verma (Allahabad: Sahitya Bhawan, 1986).
6. Ramachandra Shukla, *Sūradāsa*, 100–101.
7. Ibid., 101.
8. Vajapeyi, *Mahākavi Sūradāsa*, 183.
9. Tulasidāsa. *Rāmacharitamānasa*, trans. A. G. Atkins (Gorakhapur: Gita Press); *The Rāmāyaṇa or Tulasidāsa* (New Delhi: Hindustan Times, 1954), Bālakānda, Champai 10. All citations are from the original text, translated by Atkins.
10. Ibid., Bālakānda, doha 9.
11. Ibid., Champai 25.
12. Ibid., Champai, 31.
13. Uttarakānda, Chand 5.
14. Tulasidāsa, *Vinaya Patrikā*, v. 72.
15. Ibid., v. 159.
16. Bālakānda, Champai 23.
17. Uttarakānda, Champai 110.
18. Ibid., Champai 114.

Bibliography

Sources

Divine Sports of Krishna: Poems of Surdāsa. Translated by A. J. Alston. London: Shanti-Sadan, 1993.

Surdas. *Poems to the Child-God: Structures and Strategies in the Poetry of Surdas.* Translated by Kenneth Bryant. Berkeley: University of California Press, 1978.

Surdas (Poems). Translated by Usha Nilsson. New Delhi: Sahitya Academy, 1982.

Surdas Poetry and Personality. Edited by S. N. Srivastava. Agra: Sur Smarak Mandal, 1978.

Tulasidāsa. *Kavitavali/Tulsidas.* Translsted by F. F. Allchin. London: Allen & Unwin, 1964.

——. *The Petition to Ram: Hindi Devotional Poems of Seventeenth Century.* Translated by F. F. Allchin. London: Allen & Unwin, 1966.

Tulsidas. *Ramacaritmanas: The Holy Lake of Acts of Rama.* Translated by Douglas P. Hill. London: Oxford University Press, 1952.

Studies

Singer, Milton, ed. *Krishna: Myths, Rites, and Attitudes.* Chicago: University of Chicago Press, 1968.

5

Exemplars in the Life of Grace: Māṇikkavācakar and Nammāḻvār

V. A. DEVASENAPATHI

GRACE IS THE SUSTAINING POWER, the ground and goal of all existence, animate and inanimate. Such is the testimony of all those who live in awareness of grace. Of those many, only a few have left testaments that are available to posterity. That God has not left Himself without witnesses of His grace in any country or in any period of time is seen when we read these testaments of life in grace. The language and/or religious tradition of these saint-sages or mystics may vary, but there is an undercurrent of spirituality that is common to all these testaments. The mystics form one great spiritual community. Though the denominational name of God as Śiva or Nārāyaṇa may be dear to the devotee, the devotee's reference is to the same overall, overarching Divine Principle that out of compassion and grace chooses to reveal Itself in the form and mode in which the devotee longs to see It. These forms and modes may vary, but the longing that all devotees harbor is basically the same. They long for perfection, for fullness of life, which comes only by intimate union with the Infinite Being, which is fullness of Perfection. This union is an eternal one, indissoluble by either party. God, for all His omnipotence, cannot annul it, for His own love for souls would not allow this to take place. Neither can souls, even with all their waywardness, break this union, for they are slender vines that cannot for a split second stand in isolation from God. What actually happens in the apparent separation is loss or dimness of *awareness* of this union on the part of the souls. There is expression of joy in awareness and of sorrow in the anguish caused by loss or dimness of such awareness.

In the following pages, we consider two exemplars of life in grace. In outward circumstances, and in the tradition in which they were born, Māṇikkavācakar and Nammāḻvār differ. Māṇikkavācakar was born in a Śaivite family. He was a scholar at a very young age and was appointed chief minister to a Pandiyan king. The power and authority he wielded did not deflect him from his inward search for a guru, preceptor, who would open his inner eyes to behold truth. The suffering and punishment to which he was subjected when he preferred spiritual apprenticeship to completion of the work on which the king had sent him did not make him go back on his spiritual commitment. Released from official duties, he set out to worship in temples in various places and to sing in praise of the Lord. In contrast to Māṇikkavācakar's life, we find Nammāḻvār, wrapped in silence and oblivious to the world until a person worthy of listening to his poetic praise of God and transmitting it to posterity sought him and stood in his presence. Nammāḻvār had no contacts with the external world; he was absorbed in contemplation of the Lord. The places he sings about and the Presiding Deity of those places presented themselves in his inward vision. Nammāḻvār was born in a Vaiṣṇava family devoted to the worship of Viṣṇu. Despite these differences, when we go through the *Tiruvācakam* of Māṇikkavācakar and the *Tiruvāimoḷi* of Nammāḻvār we find the same longing, the same sorrow, and the same joy. The rose that is God smells sweet whatever be the name we give it—Śiva or Nārāyaṇa, or any other. The fragrance that is its grace, likewise, spreads itself in all authentic spiritual life, no matter what its religious background. We invite the readers to two testaments in the following pages.

Māṇikkavācakar

The *Tiruvācakam* of Māṇikkavācakar has been widely acclaimed as a work having a power all its own to move and melt the hearts of all those who recite it or hear it recited. Its appeal is due to its being a spiritual biography, at once individual and universal. Its author is a person with a name and a local habitation (though these are clouded in the mists of antiquity), but like the Lord Whom he adores, worships, and hails as Śiva of the Southern Country and yet as "the Lord of the countries the world over," Māṇikkavācakar is a representative of all humanity. He records in his poems the moods of denial, doubt, despair, anguish, and joy through which souls pass in their longing to find the source of their being and to be in rapturous union with the source. His message is that divine grace, whether we respond to it or fail to do so, is the prop and support of our life. Like a mother—indeed even more than a mother—divine grace brings us up and tends our growth, which is usually accompanied by joy and sorrow. It is not easy to learn the lesson that the so-called pleasures of the world are fleeting and harmful. We are most truly ourselves only when we outgrow a false sense of "I" and "mine" and when we grow to find our joy in the joy of others. Divine grace enables us to acquire a frame that is charged with undying love for God and all His creatures in the place of a body that is the locus of selfishness and sensual enjoyment. Māṇikkavācakar acquired such a love-charged body.

Tiruvadavur, very close to Madurai in Tamilnadu, is said to be the native place of this mystic singer. Hence he is known as "Vadavūrār," one hailing from Tiruvadavur, or more popularly as Māṇikkavācakar, "one whose utterances sparkle like gems." Scholars differ about when he lived: some place him in the third century C.E. and others in the ninth century. Even if the later date is accepted, Māṇikkavācakar's songs have continued to be sung in the Tamil region for over a thousand years. Impressed with his intelligence and scholarly accomplishments, the local king, belonging to the Pandya dynasty, appointed him as his chief minister. Although he discharged his duties efficiently Māṇikkavācakar was inwardly longing for a guru who would guide him in his spiritual pursuits . An opportunity presented itself when the king asked Māṇikkavācakar to go to a place where horse traders had arrived and buy horses for the royal stable. While on his way, Māṇikkavācakar found a venerable teacher, surrounded by disciples, sitting under a tree. He was so captured by the appearance of the guru and his gracious look, that he immediately fell at his feet, surrendering himself, body and soul. He also placed the wealth meant for the purchase of the horses at the feet of the preceptor. The guru gave him initiation and asked him to construct a temple with the wealth that was intended for the purchase of horses. When the king came to know that Māṇikkavācakar had not carried out his mission, he demanded immediate compliance. Māṇikkavācakar reported the matter to his guru. The guru asked Māṇikkavācakar to send word to the king that the horses would be delivered on a certain day. The guru then went away with the other disciples. The separation from the guru was hard to bear for Māṇikkavācakar, and the agony of separation finds frequent and moving expression in many of his songs.

When the horses did not arrive on the appointed day, the king subjected Māṇikkavācakar to imprisonment and punishment. But then came the news that the horses had arrived. Indeed, Lord Śiva Himself is said to have come in the guise of a horse dealer delivering the horses "bought" by Māṇikkavācakar and then disappearing. That night these horses, which were really jackals transformed by Śiva to appear like horses, reverted to their original form, bit and bruised the horses in the royal stable and made good their escape.

The king became furious and once again put Māṇikkavācakar in prison. Immediately, the river Vaigai, which runs past the city, flooded, threatening to destroy the town. In order to prevent flooding, the king ordered that each household in the city should send one person to help build a dam to hold the floodwaters. There was a lonely old woman in Madurai who earned her upkeep by selling rice rolls. She was in despair, being unable to do the work herself or to find a substitute. Śiva appeared as a young laborer and offered to do her job in return for bits and broken pieces of the rice rolls. Given the job, He not only did not perform it but he spent the time sleeping or playfully interfering with the work of others. When the king came to inspect the work, he was furious to see the portion assigned to the young laborer being neglected. He gave a cut with his cane on the back of the laborer, who immediately disappeared, dumping a basketful of earth that he was carrying. The floods were stopped effectively, but the cut was felt by everyone. The king realized that it was indeed Lord Śiva who had assumed the roles of a horse dealer and a common laborer. He felt he had deeply wronged Māṇikkavācakar, a great devotee of Śiva. He offered his kingdom to Māṇikkavācakar and begged him to accept it, but the saint politely declined the offer and took leave of the king.

Māṇikkavācakar went to visit several holy places, finally coming to Chidambaram. It is said that here Śiva appeared before him in the guise of a brahmin and requested him to dictate the songs he had sung. The collection of these songs is called *Tiruvācakam*. After taking these down, Śiva requested the saint to compose a work on the pattern of bridal mysticism. The saint consented and dictated four hundred verses, now known as the *Tirukkovaiyār*. The brahmin took leave of Māṇikkavācakar. The next morning the temple priests found these works in the temple shrine with the inscription that they were taken down by the Lord of Chidambaram to the dictation of Māṇikkavācakar. The temple priests approached the saint and requested that he explain the meaning of the verses. Consenting to do so, he went with them to the temple and, pointing to the sacred image of the Lord as the meaning of the verses, the saint disappeared into it in a blaze of glory.

Such is the traditional account of the life of Māṇikkavācakar. Scholars differ not only about the date of Māṇikkavācakar but also about the authorship of the *Tirukkovaiyār*. Leaving such problems for critical study, we may see how the *Tiruvācakam* helps us to understand spirituality as life in divine grace.

We shall take up one verse in the *Tiruvācakam* as an epitome of the whole work and as a sketch of spiritual evolution, initiated, guided, and crowned by divine grace. Māṇikkavācakar considers it nothing short of a miracle that one so grossly self-centered as himself should be redeemed by divine grace to grow into perfection by having a frame filled with love for God and all His creatures.

> I cannot understand the miracle of the rare Being sought for by the great *Vedas* catching hold of this slave, and confronting me and giving me slap after slap and forcibly feeding sugar to me—me who, leading a life of pretence in this world and performing many fraudulent, was roaming about babbling a lot about past *karma* out of a mouth scarred by the delusion of "I" and "mine." (41.3)[1]

The saint poses the questions "Who am I?" "What is mine?" He recollects that his life history stretches far, far away into the dim past:

> As grass, shrub, worm, tree,
> as full many a kind of beast, bird, snake,
> as stone, man, goblin, demons,
> as mighty giants, ascetics, *devas,*
> in the prevalent world of mobiles and immobiles,
> O noble Lord, I have been born
> in every kind of birth, and am wearied!
> Oh Reality! Your golden feet I saw this day
> and deliverance from birth gained! (1.26–32)

What about the human birth? The saint recalls the ordeals of life in the womb from the first month to the time of delivery (4.13–25). Then follow the ordeals of human life through its various stages: problems of hunger and sleep; emotional tumults caused by sexual attractions; the vanity and vexation of pointless, multitudinous learning; the affliction called wealth; the poison that is poverty—all these things belong to the realm of paltry goals and mean horizons. When, despite all these, the thought of God arises, what a bewildering variety of counterforces is presented, from atheism to meaningless ritualism, religious polemics, and metaphysical illusionism! God plays "hide and seek" with souls to make them grow. He hides Himself to make them search for Him. This divine game of hide and seek may entail anxiety, sorrow, and suffering for the soul. But these are birth pangs that cannot be escaped if there is to be growth from a lower to a higher stage.

> From those who boasted to see Him
> by some rare device,
> by the same device, there itself
> did He hide Himself:
> He looked on dispassionately (at sectarians)
> and took them into His fold out of welling grace:
> yet, He now appeared (to them) as a male . . .
> and presently as a female with a shining forehead,
> and thus hid His true self from them:

> Bidding the five senses stay far behind,
> seeking refuge in inaccessible hills,
> with bodies stripped of all but the bare breath,
> ascetics in contemplation dwell on Him:
> From their vision He securely hid Himself
> From those with the kind of knowledge
> which vacillates between
> "God is, God is not"
> He hid Himself
> And from those who said:
> "Whenever of old we strove to find Him,
> even today when we strive, He hides Himself;
> that Thief we have found now.
> Raise a hue and cry, raise a hue and cry;
> with garlands woven
> Of this morning's (fresh) blossoms,
> fetter His feet:
> surround Him, encircle Him, follow Him,
> don't leave Him, catch hold of Him."
> He, eluding their grasp, completely hid Himself.
> On the One without a peer coming Himself
> and relating His "I alone am" nature,
> that people like me pay heed to it,
> and on His challengingly hailing me
> and assuming lordship over me,
> and in His grace, showing Himself to me
> in the guise of a Brahmin,
> I, with uncloying love melting my bones,
> Wailed with loud lamentation . . .
> I was beside myself
> In this state
> With tasty honey from high limbs of tall trees
> He fashioned my limbs anew. (3.131–57)

Māṇikkavācakar refers earlier in the same song to the change brought about in him by divine grace:

> The Superb One
> Who, like the fragrance of flowers,
> rising high and filling everywhere without omission
> pervades everything,
> that Effulgent Being who, for my sake,
> coming today without any effort on my part
> and abode in me:
> Obeisance to Him. (3.114–20)

Māṇikkavācakar

Nammāḻvār

Māṇikkavācakar explicitly addresses God and goes on to appeal to Him:

> "Oh, You who bring me up . . .
> see that You do not forsake me
> who, while You took me
> in the crook of Your arm of waxing mercy,
> moved away, and flit about here tantalizingly. (6.4)

The Lord creates, maintains, and, in order to give rest to the souls, periodically withdraws from (destroys) the world. So that souls may not develop premature detachment, He clouds their vision. In other words, He makes worldly enjoyment attractive to souls so they may go through it and realize for themselves its evanescent character. Thus, the sole purpose of all the activities of God is the growth of souls to perfection. But what prevents their growth?

Māṇikkavācakar refers to three impurities enveloping the soul and how God removes them:

> He who enslaves one,
> that one may not be tainted by the
> three *malams* (impurities)
> was holding in His hand the three pronged spear;
> the spark-emitting Effulgence of pure hue,
> Who severs the original three *malams*. (2.109–12)

A brief account of the impurities is in order. Śaiva Siddhānta tradition designates the three impurities (or bonds, as they are alternatively described) as *āṇava*, *karma*, and *māyā*. *Āṇava* is that natural taint that affects the soul and promotes a false sense. Under the influence of *āṇava*, however, the thoughts, words, and deeds of the souls are also corrupted. *Karma* is all these three. Insofar as thoughts, words, and deeds arise from a false sense of "I" and "mine," they become an impurity or bond.

Māyā is the primordial stuff or matter out of which all worlds, physical objects, and the sensory and internal faculties of souls are made. These products are meant for giving some enlightenment to souls, partially redeeming them from the darkness of ignorance. But here again, under the influence of *āṇava*, these products are used for one's own selfish enjoyment and they thus become an impurity or bond. In brief, *āṇava* in its nominative aspect prompts a wrong sense of "I" and thus makes *karma* an impurity or bond; *āṇava* in its accusative or possessive aspect, by making the soul claim the fruits of its *karma* and all objects of enjoyment exclusively for itself, also makes *māyā* an impurity or bond.

In the process of growth that God directs, souls learn quickly or slowly in the measure that they respond to divine grace to give up the false sense of

"I" and "mine." Māṇikkavācakar frequently bemoans going the way of the senses in selfish enjoyment. He has a vivid image in one of His verses:

Living (gluttonously) like an elephant
with (not one but) two trunks,
I have not seen the Embryo in my mind;
I have seen misery only. (5.5, 1)

All the senses and the mental faculties are to be used in the enjoyment of the resplendent and fragrant form of the Lord. They are used in sexual and sensual enjoyment. In contrast, their positive and profitable employment as inspired by divine grace is described by Māṇikkavācakar.

Appropriating my thoughts to Your own self;
appropriating this cur's twin eyes
to Your holy blossom feet;
appropriating my prayers too for the same blossom,
and appropriating my speech for precious words
about You, Oh Mountain,
Oh marvelously adroit covetable great sea,
Of Ambrosia,
Who came and, enslaving me, entered into me,
to the delight of my five senses,
You offered Yourself to me. . . . (5.3, 6)

As for *karma* (thought, word, and deed) to be done for the welfare and benefit of other souls, Māṇikkavācakar uses such telling imagery as a poisonous tree, a tree growing wild in a forest and a bottle gourd that had not been emptied and dried, to describe the unredeemed state. To be redeemed is to be like a fine tree putting forth good fruit for the enjoyment of all (in an accessible place).

Shall I, hapless one, droop and droop
and stand like a withered tree? (32.11)

It is infinitely worse to be a tree putting forth poisonous fruits causing death to others. While Māṇikkavācakar despairs that he is such a poisonous tree, divine grace inspires him with the hope that he who plants a tree will never uproot it, even if it should turn out to be poisonous.

If it is a tree grown by one
even though it is highly poisonous
one will not fell it;
I too am just like that, Oh Lord who owns me. (5.10, 6)

Māṇikkavācakar sings in the verse just quoted, "without seeds You will raise crops." Surely such an Omnipotent Being can transmute the nature of a tree. He sings of the Lord as "One Who transforms poison into food" (35.9). Perhaps it is implied that He can transmute our poisonous tendencies into benevolent ones.

> If I, of unthawing mind,
> remain resembling an unperforated gourd,
> Oh my Hope, (how) have you prospered by this? (32.10)

A fresh bottle gourd may be used as a side dish in a dinner. This way it will be of use just for a day. But if its pulp is removed and the bottle gourd is put out to dry, its shell will be of use for a long time as a container to store things, as a bearer of values. Likewise, if the false sense of "I" and "mine" is taken away, this self-negating results in the emergence of the real self, which will minister unto others and not need to be ministered unto. Māṇikkavācakar prays:

> While heaven-bent men of the world
> Keep performing *thavam* (Penance),
> I, bearing in vain
> the burden of this flesh-ridden body,
> have become a wild tree.
> Oh You who abide in *Thirupperunthurai*
> abounding with *Kondrai* trees
> laden with honey-streaming blossoms!
> If I am a sinner,
> Could You therefore say
> that You will not bestow Yourself on me? (34.10)

The expression "a wild tree" refers to a tree growing wild in a forest, being of no use to anyone. Instead, Māṇikkavācakar wants to be like a tree yielding honey-laden flowers and fruits for the delectation of all who go near it. Like *karma*, the products of *māyā* are to be used in worship and for the benefit of others.

Growth in morality and spirituality arises when a person performs his or her duties actuated by love and without caring for rewards for good actions and without seeking to avoid punishment for evil actions. To be indifferent to the fruits of good and bad actions (not indifferent to the distinction between the good and the bad) is to prevent *karma* involving the agent in a succession of births and deaths. *Karma* thus loses the power to give rise to fresh births.

> On my attaining equanimity towards my *karma*
> good or bad—
> so that the never-desiccating seed of birth
> could not sprout again,

> You, my Lord, came forward
> and wiping away my on-coming sorrows,
> showed me Your countless holy forms in
> *Kazhukkundur*. (30.1)

There is consummation of such growth when the soul gives away completely the fruits of its good actions to others, and while scrupulously avoiding the performance of evil deeds takes on itself the punishment and suffering for such deeds by others. In a passage that is rendered in English as "Forsake not my plea," the saint refers to himself as the "hindmost one" (base person) (6.1) to show that in the unredeemed state he is the lowest among the low inasmuch as he pushes himself forward to enjoy pleasures to which he is not entitled and keeps himself in the background trying to avoid punishment for his evil deeds. This is a state of utter depravity; however, by the grace of God, moral and spiritual growth takes place in the following stages: (1) doing good deeds desiring their rewards for oneself; (2) giving the rewards to others; (3) taking on the punishment for the evil deeds of others while not committing such deeds oneself. In the sixth piece referred to above (30.6) the saint begins by referring to himself as a depraved person, saved by the grace of God. He refers to Śiva drinking poison out of compassion for lowly creatures. The picture conjured up is of Śiva holding himself back when there is nectar to be drunk and putting himself forward when there is poison instead. Followers of Śiva have this supreme example before them. The copper of the depraved self is transmuted by divine grace into the gold of the redeemed self, when it is like its Lord and Master. The "I" of the redeemed self operates like sea scouts to save souls from getting drowned in the sea of worldliness, and the "mine" of self appropriates the moral and spiritual liabilities of others to be liquidated by its own suffering. Such redeemed selves neither appropriate for themselves their own legitimate rewards nor misappropriate the rewards that should go to others. *Āṇava* (egoism) and *karma* thus undergo a moral and spiritual change. Nor is *māyā* left out of the picture, since the body and worldly possessions, if any of redeemed souls, are used in service of others.

Is Māṇikkavācakar concerned only with his own redemption? Obviously anyone desiring to help others must have the necessary resources. Invoking God's grace, he endeavors to overcome his own impurities. Experiencing the bliss of redemption, he wishes to share it with others. He pleads with others, cautions them against missing a golden opportunity, which, once missed, may take long to recur.

> Behold! The time has come to go—leaving the unreal—and entering the haven of the feet of our Owner. (45.1)

To be rid of them [bonds]
join the ancient devotees of the King,
and, accepting His will as your will,
set out on the path
leading to the golden feet. (45.3)

Forsake anger and the disease called desire
There is not much time anymore
Prepare yourself to go along
With the large caravan of devotees
to the feet of our Owner.
We will go and enter the City of Bliss
before its ornamented doors are closed. (45.4)

Lest you get affected
by inescapable delusion
and, later, wail in distress,
let us enter the City of Bliss
even while its gem-studded sacred doors are open. (45.8)

Māṇikkavācakar's prayer is that he may learn to do the will of the Lord. He sings:

See that You do not forsake me
who, doing things according to my will,
and, without ardour in Your will, rush
(to my undoing)
When are You to ripen my mind
like plantain fruit,
and appear before me
like fragrance-filled sweet honey dripping
(therefrom)? (6.34)

It is because of our failure to do God's will that we get caught in the cycle of births and deaths. Māṇikkavācakar considers it a wonder that God's grace redeems even self-willed persons and unites them with the company of devotees.

Without failing in His will
and without knowing the technique
of gaining His holy grace,
I am bent on falling into notorious hell
after my death.
We witnessed the mystic event
Of my Father enslaving such a person
and initiating him into His band of devotees. (26.4)

Māṇikkavācakar considers his redemption from bondage to be a miracle wrought by divine grace and his induction into the company of devotees to be a wonder. Why do saints attach great significance to the privilege of being in the company of devotees? Should they not move among the atheists and the agnostics instead, to win them over? We may venture the answer that the company of devotees gives them the spiritual strength necessary to pray and work for the redemption and welfare of the lowly and the lost. Devotees are the powerhouse of God's grace. To be in their company is to draw on this grace for sharing it with others. We may vary the imagery and say that what such a company provides is spiritual inoculation, which gives them the spiritual and moral immunity to minister to the spiritually diseased without becoming infected themselves.

How are we to understand the frequent references to depravity alternating with Māṇikkavācakar's expressions of ecstasy? It may be that when there is a slight lapse in contemplation, the failure is attributed to one's own impurity. It is somewhat like a person mistaking a cloud temporarily hiding the sun or the moon for a defect in his own vision. It may be that the lapses of several previous lives surface in this one, so that even their faint traces may be thrown out. It may be that the saint identifies himself with the fallen so that through his own prayer, petition, and penance, all of them may be saved.

Divine grace is available not only to the one who has received it directly but to all—near (or far) and dear (or even the ill-disposed) to Him. What is said of rain elsewhere is even more applicable to the descent of grace: "Even if there is one good person, rain [that comes down from the skies] falls on all."

> Obeisance to you.
> Oh King Who bestows Your Grace
> that thrice seven generations of Your kin
> may not sink into discordance-ridden hell. (4.118–19)

There is an ancient belief that God supports and gives strength to ascetics, who go around with the sun so as to temper its heat and save living beings from its scorching effect. It may not be fanciful to extend this protective Grace in respect of saints who, redeemed from preoccupation with themselves, live for others so as to save them.

Māṇikkavācakar is aware of the transcendent aspect of God, how it is beyond the reach of the senses, words, and thoughts. Perhaps we may understand the Purāṇic allusion to Śiva being beyond the reach of Brahma trying to see the top of the column of Light and failing to reach it, while Viṣṇu digs deep into the bowels of the earth and beyond and fails to see the base of the column of Light. The Infinite is more minute than the minutest and far greater than the cosmic immensity. In other words, in this transcendent character, He is beyond our reach. "Yet He is immanent in the body and is the purpose of its creation, pervading it and yet beyond grasp like the fragrance arising from a flower" (26.9).

Māṇikkavācakar describes how such a Supreme Being, in His grace, was pleased to reveal Himself:

> Oh my Father Whom the concourse of heaven-dwellers,
> saying : "His colour is not rosy, pale it is not;
> many is He, nay One is He;
> atom is He, nay tinier than atom is He";
> and thus blundering in their thoughts,
> Could not find the way to reach;
> Your colour as it is showing me,
> Your form showing me,
> Your blossom anklet-girt feet,
> the very same, showing me,
> positively preventing this lost soul
> from being born again, You enslaved me;
> Oh my mighty Lord, what shall I say or think? (5.25)

Māṇikkavācakar contrasts himself with Saint Kaṇṇappar, whose love for the Lord is far beyond the love of all other devotees. In lack of love for the Lord, Māṇikkavācakar considers himself far below even those utterly lacking love. Yet the Lord's grace is such that it could include him in Its sweep. References to himself "being like a dog" and "being worse than a dog" may be understood thus. One is like a dog in returning to sensual pleasures, even after prevenient grace has given the soul a foretaste of bliss. This fall is like a "dog returning to its vomit." One is worse than a dog in two highly reprehensible ways: (1) in failure to recognize one's master, whereas a dog does so; (2) in sheer ingratitude, whereas a dog is known for its gratitude. For all the good God does, humans return only ingratitude. Yet God can hug to His bosom ungrateful souls! Does He not wear the cobra as an ornament? The popular belief is that while we feed the cobra with milk, it responds by spurting poison. Māṇikkavācakar is amused by the high divine comedy of his salvation. He rates himself as utterly ungrateful and totally lacking in love. Yet he says that God's grace has redeemed him from bondage and shown him to the World as a devotee.

Māṇikkavācakar sings thus of the happy consummation of the divine comedy of his salvation:

> Who else, indeed, could gain like me the grace
> bestowed on me by the primal Being—
> the Source of everything, my Mother—

Who, severing my bonds of the three *malams*
and making even me a thing of worth—
me who was wandering in the Company of dunces
who did not know the benefit of deliverance—
made this cur ascend the palanquin? (51.9)

Māṇikkavācakar sings of his desire to be withdrawn from the spiritual darkness of preoccupation with false values and to be led to a life of light and love. The Lord granted the fulfillment of this desire. A saint of the nineteenth century, Ramaliṅgam, gives a most appropriate description of Māṇikkavācakar's life:

> Acquiring first a body of love, then a body of grace, you my Lord of Tiruvadavur, attained a body of bliss.

Perhaps after redeeming him from bonds, this is the beauty, the abiding beauty of holiness, grace, and bliss that the Lord conferred on Māṇikkavācakar.

> I was a base cur, thanks to my petty knowledge uninformed by education. I saw my Lord in the hall at *Tillai* (*Cidambaram*) worshipped by everyone. He came as a mighty one and with many persons to witness it, severed my bondage of finitude and conferred abiding beauty on me. (31.4)

Nammāḻvār

Āḻvār is a Tamil word meaning "one who is immersed." The "immersion" in the case of Vaiṣṇava saints to whom the term refers is in the "sea of divine bliss." Changing the imagery, we may speak of them as "God-intoxicated" persons. Vaiṣṇava tradition speaks with great reverence of twelve such God-intoxicated Souls. One of them, Āṇḍāl, was a woman who referred to herself as "one practicing the presence (vision) of the Blue-hued *Kaṇṇa* (Kṛṣṇa)." The twelve saints constitute a select, representative group, drawn from all sections of society. Nammāḻvār, who was given the name Māran by his parents, is considered the most important of the Āḻvārs. The term Nammāḻvār means "our *āḻvār*," indicating the love and respect Vaiṣṇavas have for him. In fact going through his inspired verses, we feel that all those who cherish spiritual values can speak of him as "our *āḻvār*." Such is the universality that his verses enshrine!

Little is known about the life of Nammāḻvār. He was born in Kurugur, near Tirunelveli, in the deep south of India. It is said that he was born in response to the prayer of his parents, who were childless for a long time.

He displayed no signs of a normal child, such as moving his hands and legs, crying or calling for food. His parents placed him near a tamarind tree, and he grew up, sitting in a yogic posture, with closed eyes.

About the time Nammāḻvār was sixteen years of age, a pious brahmin by the name of Madhurakavi from the south was on a pilgrimage. One night when he was in Ayodya (near Delhi), he saw a bright light in the southern direction. He walked in that direction every night till he reached the tamarind tree where Nammāḻvār was seated. He dropped a stone in the vicinity to see if the motionless figure would respond to the loud noise. Nammāḻvār opened his eyes for the first time since his birth. Madhurakavi wished to find out if Nammaḻvār would speak. So he posed a question, "If the little one is born in the womb of the dead one, what will it eat and where will it abide?" The reply was prompt. "It will eat that and abide therein." This reply highlights the fact that the soul, which is an intelligent entity, tenants a physical body and it experiences through that body. Madhurakavi fell at the feet of Nammāḻvār and became his ardent disciple and devotee. The collected works of the Āḻvārs, known as the *Nālāyira Divya Prabandham* ("Four Thousand Sacred Songs") include Madhurakavi's eleven verses in grateful praise of Nammāḻvār, whose name is sweeter to him than even the name of the Lord. Nammāḻvār was absorbed in contemplation of the Lord. He opened his eyes only when he saw in Madhurakavi a kindred soul. He broke his silence only when he found someone who could take his message and spread it.

Nammāḻvār is known as Saṭakopa, a name that means "one who rebuked the wind that covers the intelligence of the soul when it is born in the world." In other words, at the time of his birth Nammāḻvār conquered the forgetfulness of their nature as intelligence that envelops other souls. Another way of recognizing this freedom from postnatal ignorance is expressed by Nammāḻvār himself: "The Lord has rid the intelligence of its delusion and granted it excellence."

Nammāḻvār has left four works: *Tiruviruttam*, *Tiruvāciriyam*, *Tiruvandādi*, and *Tiruvāimoḻi*. These are considered to be the quintessence of the Veda. The *Tiruviruttam* begins with a supplication:

> Oh! Lord of the celestials! In order that we may not hereafter be in a predicament characterized by knowledge rooted in falsehood, by iniquitous conduct and by defilement of body, You were born in any sort of womb to succour souls. Abide with me and graciously listen to my prayer.

The use of the plural and the singular in the petition calls for attention: "That *we* may not be in predicament" and "*my* prayer." Nammāḻvār offers his prayer not only for himself *but on behalf of all souls* in the same plight as himself. Saints do not long for their individual salvation. They feel saved only when others are saved as well. An oral tradition about Rāmānuja, a great Vaiṣṇava teacher who consolidated Vaiṣṇava philosophy is worth recalling in this connection. Rāmānuja's teacher imparted a saving *mantra* to him and bound him to secrecy. Rāmānuja went out, collected all the people in the neighborhood and gave out the *mantra*. The news of its public announcement reached the ears of the teacher, who immediately sent for Rāmānuja and asked him, "Don't you know that violation of secrecy in this matter entails punishment in hell?" "Yes," said Rāmānuja. "Why then did you make it public?" asked the teacher. Rāmānuja replied, "It does not matter if I go to hell so long as others are saved." The teacher was overwhelmed by Rāmānuja's compassion for souls in bondage and forgave the technical lapse.

Whatever its historical authenticity, we notice the heartbeat of true spirituality in this account. Rāmānuja was greatly inspired by the songs of the Āḻvārs. He encouraged writing of commentaries on Nammāḻvār's verses, wherein we find the surge and overflow of such compassion. The first decade of the centum of verses in the *Tiruvāimoḻi* records the ecstasy of Nammāḻvār as he contemplates the infinite auspicious qualities of the Lord. In the second decade of this centum, the saint gives advice to the world in a peremptory call: "Give up (at once) completely (all attachment)" (1.2.1). A commentator raises a number of questions and answers them in order to explain the sudden shift from contemplation to preaching.

(1) Is it because Nammāḻvār has sized up the limits of the object of his contemplation? No, the Lord is beyond all limits—even beyond His own understanding. The joy of contemplation is inexhaustible. So there is no reaching of limits.

(2) Is it because he has become devoid of all desires? No. Nammāḻvār's desire for the Lord far exceeds the size of the firm earth, the seven seas and the expansive sky. His desire is greater than even the object of his contemplation. It excels even the Infinite in this respect.

(3) Is it satiety? No. The joy of contemplation is ever fresh, never stale.

(4) Is it out of a desire to establish himself as a teacher? No. Nammāḻvār is far too modest to cast himself in such a role. He considers himself a devotee of the devotees of the devotees, attenuating his ego in a long chain of devotion to devotees.

Why then does he turn to preaching? The joy of his spiritual contemplation is such a volcanic upsurge that he cannot contain himself. He must share it with others. As he looks around to see whom he may share his joy with, Nammāḻvār notices that the people around him are immersed in sensual pleasures to the same extent that he is immersed in spiritual ecstasy. He could not abide in peace without rescuing them from their decadence. Why should he bother about them, instead of leaving them to wallow in their ways? To leave them in such a plight would not be consistent with the tenor of Vaiṣṇavism. Nanjīyar, a great teacher, used to say often: "If a person is moved to compassion on seeing the misery of others, he is in touch with God. If, on the other hand, he says 'Let them suffer. They deserve to undergo all this suffering,' he is definitely out of touch with God." Human beings are endowed with reason and powers of discrimination. They have the capacity to reject the evil pleasures of the senses and to enjoy the right ones, but this capacity must be awakened. Hence Nammāḻvār endeavors to enlighten them about the eminence of the Lord and the hollow nature of the objects to which they are attached. In detaching themselves from these objects and attaching themselves to the Lord, they are not forging a new relationship: instead they are made to realize their true state of being. In fact, the peremptory call "Give up" is like telling a child who has caught hold of a snake, "Drop it," without mentioning the word "snake." When the snake is dropped, the child is restored to its original safety and security.

Nammāḻvār calls upon his mind to worship the Lord and rise from his fallen state. Who is this Lord? He is the One whose excellence is ever on the rise. It is such that nothing can exceed It. Like the horizon ever moving ahead of the traveler, or like a mountain with peaks soaring in height, It beckons to higher and yet higher peaks or levels of excellence. We have a dynamic conception of reality here, inviting and challenging souls to scale ever-higher heights of perfection. We are reminded of the following lines:

> As a mother bird each fond endearment tries,
> To tempt its new-fledged offspring to the skies.

The Lord's excellence towers above time and is beyond the reach of mind and speech. It is the Lord who rids the mind of delusion and grants it excellence of understanding. Delusion consists in (a) treating the body as a soul, (b) worshiping false gods, or striving after limited and unworthy ideals, and (c) taking oneself as a free person, as "captain of his own soul and master of his own fate," thus failing to recognize the Supreme Ruler who dwells in everyone and in everything and failing to realize that the highest joy consists in service to Him and to all his creatures, and not in the selfish and sensual pleasures. Souls and world are said to be His body. Hence service to them is service to His body.

The Lord who thus interests Himself in curing the sickness in human understanding and restoring its normal health is no petty Lord. He is the

Lord even of the celestials. Nammāḻvār calls upon his mind to worship the resplendent feet of the Lord free from sorrow and to rise from its fallen state. The expression "free from sorrow" could be understood as referring to the sorrow of souls wallowing in the misery of the so-called pleasures of the world and being freed from such sorrow by worshiping the Lord. Worship removes the sorrow of the soul. Rāmānuja, according to oral tradition, raised the matter to a loftier plane. He took the sorrow as referring to the Lord when He sees souls caught in ignorance speeding on the path of perdition. When they respond to His healing touch and recover their understanding, He rejoices even as—nay, much more than—a human parent does when an erring son or daughter returns to the path of righteousness. Here we have a noble conception that the All Highest is yet soft-hearted.

In meditating on twelve out of countless names of the Lord, Nammāḻvār discovers in one name especially the great concern and solicitude the Lord has for the salvation of souls. In meditating on the name *madhusūdana*, Nammāḻvār sings that a veritable destiny encompassed the Lord to confront Him in all the births, of any and every kind, aeon after aeon to grant His grace (II.6.4). The Lord is said to have taken nine incarnations for the redemption of souls. The tenth, according to tradition, will be in the future. The nine are fish, tortoise, boar, man-lion, dwarf, Paraśurāma, Rāma, Balarāma, and Kṛṣṇa. Why should the Lord appear in some subhuman forms? As if in answer to this question Nammāḻvār says, as we saw already, that He was pleased to be born in any sort of womb to redeem souls from their degradation. It is not as if the Lord is bound by *karma;* He is unlike souls caught in a cycle of births. Even as a parent would dive after a child that had fallen into a well to rescue it, the Lord's love makes Him follow the soul as it goes up and down the scale of evolution. No soul will be left in eternal damnation, however "rough it hews its ends." The Lord shapes these rough and ragged ends to perfection with His boundless love and patience.

The Supreme Reality is at once transcendent and immanent. In its transcendent state, its preeminence is beyond the reach of thought and words. Any ascription of characteristics to It would belie Its real nature. In order to bring home this truth to us, a negative approach is suggested: "not this, not this." Yet the human mind is to be helped to intuit this reality. The Supreme Reality is thus described as the plenitude of Infinite auspicious qualities.

> He is not male, not female, nor eunuch
> He cannot be seen: He is not existent nor non-existent,
> He assumes the form in which devotees desire to see him:

He is not of such form,
It is extraordinarily difficult to speak of Him. (II.5.10)

In this verse the masculine particle *allan* forms part of the verb in the phrase "He is not male, not female, nor eunuch." One commentator draws attention to the repeated use of *allan* and refers to another of the Lord's names, *Puruṣottama*. *Puruṣa* is a man. *Puruṣottama* is man *par excellence*. In bridal mysticism the Lord alone is masculine. All souls whatever the sexual characteristics of their physical body are female in relation to Him. The commentator would find validity for a personal conception of God.

Nammāḻvār sings of beholding the Lord to the utter delight of his eyes, rooting out all traces of his past *karma* and giving out garlands of praise for the delight of devotees. The main outcome of his effort is the weaving of garlands of praise. An incidental by-product is the rooting out of *karma*. Nammāḻvār's singing is not prompted by the desire to get rid of *karma*. Adoration of the Lord is the main concern. One is spiritually alive only when one adores the Lord. Then *karma* is automatically destroyed, even as in the cultivation of rice and other crops weeds are thrown out. Changing the imagery, we may say that lighting a candle is the best way to remove darkness. When one loves the Lord, seeking no return, it becomes His concern to remove one's *karma* and to restore one to moral and spiritual health. Love for the Lord constitutes spiritual health. Lack of such love is a spiritual disease. To practice the presence of the Lord is all that devotees seek.

The Lord presents himself before Nammāḻvār and offers him His great heavenly abode. Nammāḻvār politely and yet firmly declines the offer. The Lord pretends to be surprised and stresses the unique value of His offer. It is not a temporary residence from which there will be a return to the world of sorrows and doubtful pleasures. It is His own great abode (*Vaikuntha*). Nammāḻvār is still unmoved. "What then do you want?" the Lord asks. "Place your great lotus like feet on my head" replies the saint. "Why do you desire this?" the Lord asks. "Are you not the Lord Who speedily removed the suffering of an elephant?" Nammāḻvār puts this counterquestion. The Lord, as if vaguely remembering His succor to an elephant caught by a crocodile, asks: "I suppose I did so. But what is its relevance in the present context?" Nammāḻvār says that his need for help is far, far stronger than the need of the elephant. The elephant was caught by one crocodile, whereas, Nammāḻvār says, he is in the vicious grip of five crocodiles, meaning the five senses. Again the elephant was in a small pond, but Nammāḻvār finds himself in a vast ocean of *saṃsāra* (cycle of births and deaths) (VIII.7.2). The elephant was in suffering for a limited period time. Nammāḻvār, on the other hand, has been suffering through ages, for aeon after aeon. The Lord appears to be impressed. Yet He would like to find Nammāḻvār's answer to one apparently innocent question. The Lord asks Nammāḻvār: "What more do you want?" Here is a trap. Does Nammāḻvār want only the Lord and nothing else? Or does he crave for worldly or even other-worldly values? Nammāḻvār's answer is firm. "I, Your servant, want only this: Your feet on my head and nothing else" (II.9.1–3).

Nammāḻvār continues his prayer.

> All that I pray for now and forever is that You give me the hand of wisdom to reach Your Feet without the least delay. Fill my mind with Your Presence without any let-up and bid me to Your eternal service. It does not at all matter to me whether at death I go to the Eternal Abode or to heaven or to hell. Let me instead have the joy of being aware of You, without the least lapse. Let me joyfully worship You by thought, word and deed. Such is the fickleness of the mind that it may stray away even after You have brought me to Your Feet. So please ensure that I never depart from Your Feet. (II.9.4–5)

Throughout the verses, we note that Nammāḻvār prays that, whatever the vicissitudes of life, there should be no lapse in awareness of the Lord. There are two moods, quite different, worth noting here. Both stem from realization of the incomparable Excellence of the Lord. In one, Nammāḻvār sees himself as utterly unworthy to approach the Lord, to be in His presence or even to hear His name:

> "I am a depraved person. I utterly lack any kind of perfection. Even my words of praise would only soil You, as I lack the necessary purity."

A charming anecdote tells how Nammāḻvār, feeling his unworthiness even to hear the name of the Lord with his polluted ears, hid himself behind a dilapidated wall. Someone carrying a heavy load on his head came that way and, laying it down for a brief rest, said "Nāraṇa" (Nārāyaṇa). When Nammāḻvār heard the Lord's name in spite of the precaution he took not to hear it, tears instantly filled his eyes:

> Hearing the name of beloved Nāraṇan
> Tears filled my eyes. I seek Him in wonder
> Through night and day without let-up
> The Lord approaches me, never letting me go. (I.10.8)

The soul may deny the Lord's existence; it may doubt His existence. Or, filled with remorse for its gratitude or with an aching sense of its impurity in sharp contrast to His purity, it may seek to draw away from Him. It may flee Him "down the days down the nights, down the arches of the years." Yet His strong feet follow the fleeing soul with "unhurrying chase and unperturbed pace, deliberate speed, majestic instancy" (Francis Thompson, "The Hound of Heaven").

When Nammāḻvār and other saints attribute all kinds of lapses to themselves, these are not to be taken as autobiographical references. Saints tend to see even the least trace of imperfection in themselves as an enormous blemish, a huge blot on the white radiance of eternity. The dazzling purity and holiness of the Lord overwhelm them with a sense of contrast. Nor do saints feel virtuous or self-righteous. Rather, they identify themselves with the lowly and the lost, the vicious and the wicked. The repentance they express is for, and on behalf of, others, though offered in their own names.

The other mood we referred to above is an optimistic one. Whatever the actuality of our lives, however we debase ourselves and deface the image of God in us, we are really living in inseparable union with Him. We forget this union with Him and try desperately to wrench ourselves free, not realizing that such a divorce would be a betrayal and denial of our real nature. In explaining Nammāḻvār's prayer to the Lord to place His feet on his (Nammāḻvār's) head, one commentator gives the illustration of a jewel fashioned like a socket and cylinder. The socket would be void without the cylinder; equally, the cylinder cannot rest elsewhere than in the socket. Metaphysically, God may not and does not require any support. But God, being not only *sat* (existence) but also *cit* (intelligence) and *ānanda* (joy), longs for the spontaneous response of love from souls.

The Vaiṣṇava conception of Reality expressed by Nammāḻvār is that God is the soul or spirit. In relation to Him, souls and the physical world are His body. Nammāḻvār says that the Lord, hidden like the soul in the body, is all-pervasive: "He is in me, His servant; He is in my body. He is the soul of the universe. He is outside it." The Supreme Being is not of a nature that can be described. Of all the characteristics of the soul, capacity for service and its capacity for knowledge, which is unique to it? According to the Vaiṣṇava tradition, Rāmānuja sent one of his disciples to his own preceptor to obtain clarification on this question. The disciple learned that though the soul is an intelligent entity, its uniqueness consisted in its capacity to serve the Lord. Being a bride of the Lord gave the soul an unrivaled opportunity to attune itself to His will and to offer Him unqualified love and service.

We have one whole work, the *Tiruviruttam*, and a few decades of another, the *Tiruvāimoḻi*, on the pattern of bridal mysticism. Nammāḻvār sometimes sings in the role of a lovesick bride, at other times like a love-intoxicated bride. Sometimes Nammāḻvār assumes the role of the bride's mother (II.4); at other times, he assumes the role of the bride's bosom friend (IV.6). In some passages, we find the bride sending birds as messengers to the Lord. Verses expressing rapture in the joy of union and agony in the woe of separation enable us to understand the intense love Nammāḻvār had for the Lord. We have highly insightful explanations in the commentaries on Nammāḻvār's verses. We may refer to one here. Nammāḻvār, in the role of a lovelorn bride sent a bird as a messenger. "What can I convey through you to my Lord, Who has seen how I suffered when there was the least diminution in the closeness of our union? Tell Him that my soul will no longer abide in my body, as He is away from me and is unaffected by my suffering."

A Tamil scholar raised an objection to Parāsara Bhaṭṭar's commentary on this verse. A message is called for only when the addressee is away. So the appropriate word would be "heard." "Tell my Lord who even after hearing" and not "who has seen." Bhaṭṭar referred the questioner to two Tamil classics that speak of the lover witnessing pallor spreading over those portions of the body of the beloved which are not in close contact with his body. Having himself seen this, he has now only to be reminded of this, so that he could recollect the suffering of the beloved.

Allusions to human relations, as between male and female, should not be taken in an erotic sense. To illustrate the desire for uninterrupted intimacy between the Lord and the soul, of the Infinite and the finite, the only human analogy is love between a lover and the beloved. Thus, sublimation is one mode of approach. Another is to take the references in an esoteric sense. Thus, the lover and the beloved would stand for God and the soul. The birds would represent the preceptors. The wings of the birds are symbolic of knowledge and conduct. Teachers set an example of combining knowledge with conduct. Knowledge that is not matched by appropriate conduct and conduct that is not illumined by correct knowledge are both incomplete. They must coalesce and complement each other for spiritual perfection.

Yet another matter must be borne in mind. Human beings are attracted to sensual pleasures, which are used as bait. Thus drawn to the idea of intimacy, one must be weaned from these before one can relish the joys of spiritual life. Even as a medicinal pill is coated with sugar to tempt a patient to take it, sensual pleasures are held out as bait to force one to take a first step. Aspirants are thus led on to learn for themselves the fleeting nature of worldly pleasures and the permanence of spiritual joy. While worldly pleasures cause satiety, spiritual joy never cloys but grows from strength to strength.

Joys are experienced by the soul in union with God; sorrows, in separation from God. There is also another state in which there is total identification with the Lord. This may be described either as a state of spiritual intoxication or as a state of possession by God. The soul starts singing as if it is the Supreme Soul. Naturally this causes bewilderment to those around. The image used here is of the mother of the bride describing the state of her daughter identifying herself completely with her love:

> I am the One who created the sea-girt world.
> I am the One who is the sea-girt world,
> I am the One who took the sea-girt world
> [as a gift— a Purānic allusion]
> I am the One who pulled out the world
> [a Purānic allusion]
> I am the One who swallowed the world,
> So says my daughter.
> Has the Lord of the sea-girt world taken possession of her?
> How indeed can I explain to the people of the sea-girt world
> What my daughter of the sea-girt world has learnt to say? (V.6.1)

The expression "sea-girt world" is repeated to enable us to get a glimpse of the sweep of the infinite. It is remarkable that the grace of God can enable the soul to identify itself so completely with the Lord. One can see here a contrast to spiritual life being the very locus of all impurity in contrast to the white, spotless radiance of God's purity and holiness. The polar opposite of this state is a feeling of such purity and holiness in oneself because of total identification with the Lord. This extension of grace is an interesting variant of the cosmic vision that Kṛṣṇa grants to Arjuna, as described in the eleventh chapter of the *Bhagavad Gītā*. It is as if the soul offers a cosmic vision to the world. One must go through verses of both types to note the low and high notes of spiritual life.

We may also take note of how Nammāḻvār himself regards his works. It is not Nammāḻvār who sings; it is God who sings through him. God makes Himself as the soul and sings through the soul. Hence, when Nammāḻvār praises the songs he sings, he really praises the Lord, Who uses him as a lutanist would use a lute. The Lord, says Nammāḻvār, knows his unworthiness and yet uses him. In one verse Nammāḻvār says that God makes Nammāḻvār Himself! Nammāḻvār sings: "How can I ever forget my Father, my Lord? He makes Himself me. Faultlessly He sings (through me) His songs. He redeems me—who am a person of incomparable iniquity. He refines my nature. How indeed can I forget Him when I witness His excellence in wandering in quest of me?" In this verse we find both modes: "The Lord makes me Himself" and "The Lord makes Himself me" (VII.9.1).

We may consider two questions here: (1) Why should the Lord, directly or indirectly through His devotees, sing His own praise? (2) Why should the devotees ceaselessly sing His Praise? Is it not enough if we realize His greatness once? Must we go on referring to it again and again? Perhaps there is only one answer to both questions. Awareness or an uninterrupted sense of the presence of God and His infinite, auspicious qualities is as necessary for spiritual life as the heartbeat is necessary for physical life. When His praise is expressed in the form of songs, these songs illumine the souls of the listeners, removing the darkness of ignorance that covers them. It is not empty praise, as in the case of the praise we offer to human beings. Although it will provoke hostility, says Nammāḻvār, "yet I will maintain that I will sing only of the Lord, not of any human being" (III.9.1). What is the use of singing of human beings who rate themselves and their ephemeral wealth highly, even above the Lord? How long will the wealth obtained from them last? Sing instead of the Lord, Whose bounty is inexhaustible and who will grant all that we seek from Him. Praise of the Lord will indeed be true and meaningful, while praise of human beings will only pile up unadulterated lies. If anything, our praise of the Lord will fall far short of His glory, while in the case of humans, praise will be far in excess of their merits (III.9).

Nammāḻvār looks around and finds no one who will use his worldly wealth for good cause. So he calls upon poets to sing only of the Lord and not misuse their poetic talents. As if in anticipation of a question from the poets, "How are we to maintain ourselves and our family if we do not sing the praise of the rich and the worldly great ones?" he answers: "Come you, poets! By the exertion of your body and by the use of your hands, earn your livelihood" (III.9.7). This message is important not only to the poets but to others as well. We must use our hands in some pursuit according to our talents while our thoughts and words praise the Lord. We must earn to give to others who may seek our help and to maintain ourselves without seeking help from others. It is noteworthy that Nammāḻvār emphasizes the value of physical labor for the maintenance of society. He would reserve use of intellectual and spiritual talents for higher ends—or for the highest end, that is, for praising God.

Nammāḻvār stresses manual labor, but he would have us give up attachment both to its fruits and to those who are to be its recipients. Attachments must be to the Lord alone. Three stages may be noted. The first is our usual state of attachment to one's kith and kin and to worldly possessions. When we succeed in giving up our possessive sense, we reach the second stage. There, as a result of overcoming worldly attachments, the self shines with its natural characteristics of knowledge and joy. We must overcome the temptation to stay arrested in this state of self-enjoyment. Self-realization is good insofar as we realize our nature as self, not as body, but this self-enjoyment also has to be conquered. We should also be ready to renounce attachment to our "selves." Nammāḻvār suggests that we pass on to the third and final stage when we realize that we are truly the servants of the Lord, Who is the Self of our "selves," as well as Self of the whole universe. The real "I" is really "He." To take our soul as our real "I" is megalomania. Hence, we must stabilize ourselves by attaching ourselves—or realizing the ever-present but forgotten attachment—to God. To attach ourselves to God is at once to overcome the false sense of "I" and "mine." We come to realize our nature as His servants. Instead of coveting everything as our possession, we realize that everything is His possession. To reach this state is our destiny. The Lord is eager to confer this destiny on us.

All approaches, even the negative one of denying His existence outright or the skeptical one of doubting His existence, ultimately lead to Him. Indeed, it is He who has planned and sanctioned these approaches. The Lord's mercy is such that whatever the deficiency in our understanding and conduct, He is ever ready to redeem and restore us to our natural state of enjoying eternal bliss as His servants. While Nammāḻvār's commitment and devotion to the Lord as Viṣṇu (Nārāyaṇa) are firm, he is open-minded enough to see the manifestation of God as others see Him. Everyone worships God according to his or her understanding. No one can claim that his or her understanding does adequate justice to the infinitude of God. God reveals Himself in whatever measure He is sought and quickens further growth of understanding.

To enable others to have a glimpse of the Lord Whom he sees everywhere, Nammāḻvār presents various pictures. In the language of bridal mysticism, Nammāḻvār sings as the lovelorn bride reminded of the Lord by everything in nature. The dark rain-laden clouds remind him of the blue-hued Lord (IV.4.9). The serpent reminds him of the Lord's serpent couch. Cows taken for grazing remind him of the flock tended by the Lord in His incarnation as Kṛṣṇa (IV.4.5). Kings of the country remind him of the King of Kings. Any temple with a spark of divinity is the Lord's temple (IV.4.8). The Lord Whom he worships appears in such grandeur that he asks in wonder: "Is the effulgence of Your crown really the blossoming of the radiance of Your face? Are the lotus flowers on which You stand really the blooming of the radiance of Your feet? You are verily the Supreme Light Whose nature I am unable to set forth."

Nammāḻvār invites attention to the stories of the Lord's incarnations—the aesthetic grandeur, the moral splendor, and, above all, the boundless compassion of the Lord to be born among defiled humans, not to speak of the Lord's appearance in subhuman forms. All these incarnations are actuated by one supreme purpose: grace. Setting aside His transcendence, the Lord stoops to redeem souls from their fallen state.

We may see God in and through nature, learn about Him through the accounts of His incarnations, behold Him through our physical eyes in the aesthetic excellence of sanctified images in temples, and through our inner eyes, illumined by wisdom. Nammāḻvār sings of other manifestations too.

> You are beauty itself with Lotus eyes!
> You are the blue-dark-hued One!
> You are the Perfection of conduct forcefully dragging
> my soul to Yourself
> You are Time, with its past, present, and future.
> When may I see and obtain You? (III.8.8)

We may note here that Nammāḻvār sings of the Lord's beauty manifested in a form. That beauty is grace charged, even as the black cloud is rain-charged. It is not merely the beauty of form. It is also the beauty of righteous conduct. Like the beauty of holiness, it is the beauty of righteousness. It is not static or statuesque or frozen beauty. It is like a flowing stream, vibrant with movement through all three phases of time—past, present, and future—ever fresh, never stale. Verily, time is the moving image of eternity. While time on the physical and biological planes is associated with mortality, when linked to the spiritual plane, it is transformed into eternity as an image of God. In other words, when we link our lives with the Lord, the mortal becomes the immortal.

In referring to time, Nammāḻvār makes a veiled suggestion. The Lord may say that the aspirants must bide their time for obtaining His Grace. But is not God the Lord of time also? He need not wait to bring to pass anything that is prayed for. He may grant His grace right now.

Nammāḻvār thinks of another aspect of time. This is in relation to the *yuga* conception. There is deterioration as the universe moves through time, from perfection to imperfection. To use a traditional image, the cow of righteousness stands firmly on four legs in the age of truth or perfection. It then stands on three and then two legs as decadence sets in. Finally it stands precariously on just one leg. This era is called *kali yuga*, when there is an almost total eclipse of values. Tradition speaks of such *yugas* starting from perfection and ending up in total iniquity, repeating this pattern over and over again.

Against such a bleak view, Nammāḻvār offers a rosy picture. The Lord's devotees have come to this earth. There can be no dark fate, disease, or damnation if we look up to these torchbearers. Indeed, there can be no dark or iron age, if all of us come together for corporate worship. When hearts are united in prayers, even a curse becomes null and void. It is to promote such worship, at once individual and corporate, that Nammāḻvār has given the world his garlands of verses. It is because of his grace (like the Lord's) that Nammāḷvār has blessed the world with his songs. Not only is the time transformed into eternity when we sing the Lord's praise, either alone or in company, but space, or the earth, also is changed into heaven (V.2.1). Nammāḷvār says that for those who sing praises of the Lord, their entire dwelling place on earth itself becomes *Vaikuntha*, or the abode of the Lord. Recalling Nammāḷvār's act of benediction in giving the world the quintessence of all spiritual wisdom in his songs, Madhurakavi, a grateful beneficiary of Nammāḷvār's grace proclaims, "Behold! Grace is the greatest asset in this world."

All our woes are traceable to our wrong sense of "I" and "mine," with the result that we degrade ourselves in self-importance and sensual pleasures. "What is it that may be rightly called "I"? What is it that may be called 'mine'?" Nammāḷvār sings, "I could not understand my *self*. Hence I remained satisfied that I was of sole importance (or even that I was sole existent!) and that everything was mine. Oh, Lord of celestial! I am indeed You: You are my possession."

It will be noted that there is a redeeming change in the axis of personality and possession. The focus is not egocentric but theocentric now. The Lord lives in the devotee as his or her very soul. Possessing the Lord, the soul has now an inexhaustible wealth, immune to any loss. In this realized state, the soul devotes itself to the worship of the Lord in thought, word, and deed. The redeemed soul glorifies the Lord and serves His creatures.

The Lord envelops matter that sprawls high, wide, deep, and all around. He envelops the soul in a bright light dwelling in a physical body. He envelops the flaming joy of wisdom. Above all, He has enveloped the immortal, infinite longing of Nammāḷvār's soul in His embrace.

Note

1. The citations from the *Tiruvācakam* are from the English translation by G. Vanmikanathan under the title *Pathway to God through Tamil Literature, I—Through the Thiruvaachakam* (New Delhi: Delhi Tamil Sangam Publication, 1971). The numbers in parentheses after the citations refer to the serial number of the poem and the verses (or lines) cited from the text.

Bibliography

Sources

Ayyangar, S. Satuamurthi. *Tiruvāymoḷi English Glossary*. 4 volumes. Bombay: Ananthacharya Indological Institute, 1981.

Ramanujan, A., trans. *Hymns for the Drowning: Poems to Viṣṇu by Nammāḷvār*. Princeton, N.J.: Princeton University Press, 1981.

Studies

Deheja, Vidya. *Slaves of the Lord: The Path of Tamil Saints.* New Delhi: Munshiram Manoharlal, 1988.

Kaylor, R. D. and K. K. A. Venkatachari. *God Far, God Near: An Interpretation of the Thought of Nammāḻvār.* Bombay: Ananthacharya Indological Research Institute, 1981.

Navaratnam, Ratna. *Tiruvachakam: The Hindu Testament.* Bombay: Bharatiya Vidya Bhavan, 1963.

Ramanujachari, R. *The Mysticism of Nammāḻvār.* Indian Philosophical Congress Endowment Lecture for 1969–1970. Madras: Madras University, n.d.

Reddiar, N. Subbu. *Religion and Philosophy of Nālāyira Divya Prabhandam With Special Reference to Nammāḻvār.* Tirupathi: Sri Venkateswara University, 1977.

Varadachari, K. C. *Āḻvārs of South India.* Bombay: Bhartiya Vidya Bhavan, 1966.

Yocum, Glenn E. *Hymns to the Dancing Śiva: A Study of Māṇikkavācakar's Tiruvācakam.* New Delhi: Heritage Publishers, 1982.

6

The Personal and Social Dimensions of *Tirukkuṟaḷ* Spirituality

S. GOPALAN

THE TAMIL CLASSIC *Tirukkuṟaḷ* (also called the *Kuṟaḷ*) probably belonged to the first century B.C.E. Little is known about its author, Tiruvaḷḷuvar (also referred to as Vaḷḷuvar) except that he had an open mind to all worthwhile ideas, whatever their source, and was eager to construct a system of practical ethics that would help the transformation of human life in all its variegated aspects. The work is divided into 133 chapters, and each chapter consists of ten couplets.

This work, considered the greatest ethical treatise written in the Tamil language, reflects the positive affirmation of life on earth that is characteristic of Tamil literature. The distinctive feature of this work is its deep concern for propounding a serious ethic even while taking a lively interest in the secular aspects of human life. An analysis of spirituality as revealed in the Tamil classic must therefore examine its concept of the good and the good life.

This Tamil classic should not be approached from a dichotomy between secular and spiritual. The terms "secularism" and "spiritualism" stand for a spectrum of ideas that show continuity rather than discontinuity. The *Kuṟaḷ* could be considered secular in the sense that it views the human person as the seeker of values. If the Tamil work is regarded as secular in this deeper sense, then the idea of spirituality discernible in it refers to the deeply personal and highly idealistic aspects of person-in-society.

The deeper spiritual significance of the *Tirukkuṟaḷ* can be grasped only through an understanding of the scope of Indian spiritualism. The correlation of ideas in the *Tirukkuṟaḷ* with those of Indian spirituality in general will, rather than relegating the work to a certain locality and a regional culture, magnify its essence and intensify the understanding of its precise makeup and deeper significance. Spiritualism is *not* to be visualized as time-bound and space-centered, having a relative status that can be grasped only by studying it in the setting in and through which it expresses itself. If the idea of spirituality is to be understood ultimately in terms of the deeper reaches of human being *anywhere*, it can be understood *everywhere*, provided we take our bearings carefully.

Spirituality

At least three of the senses in which the term spirituality is understood are important in our context. The first and the most commonly accepted usage pertains to the *incorporeal* aspect of human beings. Whether this incorporeality is to be understood as the mind or, more difficult still, as a soul in addition to, or beneath, or behind, or above the body is a difficult issue to settle.[1] But most religious traditions hold that the distinctiveness of human life consists in something that transcends the corporeal elements, and this, in a broad sense, is the *spiritual* element.

The second meaning follows as a necessary corollary of the first: the refusal to be solely concerned with the physical is indicative of concerns that do not pertain to this world alone. The view of life that such an approach engenders may be considered idealistic-normative inasmuch as the transcendental aspects provide transforming influences to the empirical-positive. Such a *view of life* must result in a *way of life* that is not solely concerned with the secular aspects. The implications of the close-knit relationship between the "this-worldly" (positively oriented, secular) and the "otherworldly" (normatively oriented, spiritual) concerns is obvious: the spiritual can and does provide ultimate seriousness to the secular and securely integrates the personal and the social aspects of human life.

The third sense of the term "spiritual" is its being visualized as the seat of the moral and religious righteousness. The transformation potential that the normative aspects provide for the person-in-the-world cannot but affect and influence the man of the world. That is, the attitudinal changes that such a view of life warrant can be expected to be reflected clearly in the ways of a people. In more concrete terms, this correlation signifies that institutional life derives a meaningful pattern from the idealistic approach to personal life. The various institutions that are directly and immediately concerned with secular matters (such as property, marriage, and the state) and those that have some connection with the religious-moral sphere (such as education and religion) are infused with deeper meaning and lend significance to the personal as well as the interpersonal aspects of person-in-society. In this sense, the genesis of an ethical approach to personal as well as social aspects of life may be located in the "spiritual" approach to life. The secular and the sacred thus are not considered opposed to one another but as being involved in each other, as one is reflected in the other. Indeed, the former is then transformed into the latter, and in this transformation, the this-worldly concerns are reinforced by a keen sense of what is right.

Indian Spirituality

In order to explicate the idea of spirituality as presented in *Tirukkuṟaḷ*, an understanding of the Indian, Sanskritic, Hindu tradition is important. The first aspect of spirituality cited above, incorporeality, is perhaps the most evident and is acknowledged even by critics of the Sanskritic Indian tradition who portray the Indian tradition as overly pessimistic.[2] They recognize that in this tradition the bodily aspects of humans do not constitute the be-all and end-all of life.

The second aspect of spirituality is identifiable in the characterization of Indian thought as otherworldly. Those who interpret the Hindu tradition as representing a dichotomy between the secular and the spiritual see in the value placed on *mokṣa* (liberation from the cycle of rebirth) an otherworldly aspiration. Similarly, the idealization of *sannyāsa* (renunciation) entails withdrawal from the world. The net result of both is that a life-negating rather than a life-affirming attitude is commended to not only the spiritual aspirant but also to all Hindus who are resonant with their culture's values. But another interpretation is possible.[3] Hindu philosophy considers *mokṣa* to be the supreme spiritual value (*paramapuruṣārtha*) no doubt, but it is only as an integral aspect of the *puruṣārtha* scheme that *mokṣa* becomes meaningful. That is, the importance of the other *puruṣārthas*, *dharma* (virtue), *artha* (material wealth), and *kāma* (desire) is paramount, for in the absence of their proper pursuit, attainment of the ultimate state of spiritual perfection is not always possible. In this sense the value of pursuing these secular ends can be vindicated and the reciprocal relationship between the secular and the spiritual values reiterated. The idea is that by bringing in an idealistic approach to secular concerns, one seeks a transformation of outlook which in turn helps the individual to become spiritually oriented. In this sense a characterization of the pursuit of *mokṣa* as otherworldly is a misunderstanding of its precise significance.

Similarly, the *sannyāsāśrama* is not to be understood outside the graduated scheme of the *āśrama* system, since a prolonged and progressive preparation prior to the assumption of the role of ascetic is essential. Apart from the fact that Hindu philosophy suggests not one but four stages—*brahmacārya* (the stage of the student), *grahastha* (the stage of married life, also referred to as the stage of civil life), *vānaprastha* (the forest-going stage), and finally *sannyāsa* (the stage of renunciation), the question to be considered is whether *sannyāsa* is merely a formalized institution or represents a cultural attitude. To deny the latter aspect would amount to missing the kernel and adhering to the shell; on the other hand, to concede the importance of the attitudinal aspect would indicate that the idea of *sannyāsa* represents more than a formal institution[4] in that it provides an inner meaning or orientation that motivates the culture's behavioral patterns.

The third aspect of Hindu spirituality, viz., its providing the fountain-springs for both religious and secular life, has been hinted at above. The insistence on an ethical approach (*dharmic* approach, in the Hindu terminology) in the various social contexts signifies that human personal development cannot be evolved outside interpersonal situations or apart from social situations. This emphasis on *dharma* has an idealistic dimension and accounts for the normative approach to secular and religious behavior. Developing such an approach transforms the individual's attitude to life, for this approach establishes a rigorous standard of conduct in personal life. It also results in the positive and earnest affirmation of this-worldly concerns; every act of the individual pertains to and is evaluated by the concept of social order that one's participation in the world is visualized to bring about. In this respect the spiritual aspects of life are not opposed to but are conjoined to the secular aims of the individual.

Spirituality in *Tirukkuṟaḷ*

In the light of this analysis of the Indian tradition, the idea of spirituality in the Tamil tradition may now be considered as patterned along Indian lines of thinking. Incorporeality is as clear in the Tamil classic as in the Sanskritic Hindu tradition, though there is an important difference. The Tamil work, being temperamentally opposed to a deliberate analysis of the transcendent state, emphasizes the ethical-social aspects of human life. This approach is taken, however, without disregarding the need for attaining a state of spirituality in human life. The transcendent state (which is as difficult to achieve as it is to visualize) is referred to as *vīṭu* (emancipation) in the Tamil ethical tradition and is accepted in *Tirukkuṟaḷ* with an emphasis on the *process of transformation* of human life that the ideal effectuates. But the *Kuṟaḷ* maintains that the transformation is achievable only by following *aṟam* (the principle of morality akin to the Sanskrit concept of *dharma*), which regulates the pursuit of the corporeal aspects of human life. In the terminology of the *Kuṟaḷ*, these are the values of *poruḷ* and *inpam*, respectively standing for the economic pursuit and the desire-propelled aspects of human life.

According such an importance to the corporeal aspects of human life ought not to be taken as countering what was suggested earlier, for the *Kuṟaḷ* does not preach a bare acceptance of secular values but insists on their being pursued strictly according to principles of morality. The prime importance accorded to *aṟam* becomes especially clear when the author of the *Kuṟaḷ* characterizes ascetics as exemplars. As exponents of morality, ascetics demonstrate that spiritual good (*vīṭu)* is achievable in life, and they exhort the acceptance of *aṟam* as a sure way of realizing this good.

Tiruvaḷḷuvar's (the author of *Tirukkuṟaḷ*) emphasis on the efficacy of *aṟam* is significant in two respects. First, it seems to be addressed to those who are intent on the pursuit of *aṟam* (*aṟavor*, in the Tamil terminology) to assure them that the pursuit ultimately brings in its own reward—the state of spiritual realization. Second, the focus on *aṟam* is meant as a clear preamble to the discussion of its significance for the personal as well as the social life of humanity. Tiruvaḷḷuvar asks: "Virtue begets honour as well as riches and so can there be a greater good for mankind than virtue?" (4.1). The assuring tone with which the yields of wealth (*poruḷ*), happiness (*inpam*), and glory (*pukaḻ*) are described when *aṟam* is the inner core of action is indeed noteworthy.

The pervasive nature of *aṟam* is epitomized in these words: "Be spotlessly pure—in heart!" (4.4)[5] for purity of mind is the *sine qua non* of one's happiness within and for ensuring the same in one's dealings with others. This emphasis is evident from Tiruvaḷḷuvar's explanation of the expression "being spotlessly pure in mind": "That is righteousness which is free from these four things: envy, lust, wrath and harsh word" (4.5).

Tiruvaḷḷuvar's insistence on the development of mental purity and his concrete enumeration of the qualities that make for it clearly point to an acceptance of an incorporeal aspect of human life. The inculcation of mental purity is a means to achieving a state of transcendence. This achievement—in the Sanskritic tradition as well as in the Tamil ethical tradition—is more concretely spelled out as the attainment of a state of freedom from the cycle of birth and death.

The Tamil classic visualizes the ultimate ideal of *vīṭu* as encompassing all aspects of life. The author of the *Kuṟaḷ* suggests, as do the majority of Indian philosophers (belonging to the Hindu, Jaina, and the Buddhistic traditions) that if one lives a life of *aṟam* in its comprehensive sense and exemplifies it by developing compassion for fellow humans—nay, all creatures—one's deeds reflect goodness and that person is one who has realized the ultimate human purpose.[6]

The brief reference to the ideal of *vīṭu* provides an easy transition to the second aspect of Indian spirituality as reflected in *Tirukkuṟaḷ*. In the context of the Sanskritic Hindu tradition, this aspect relates to the supreme spiritual ideal of *mokṣa* and the ultimate stage in life, the *sannyāsāśrama.* In the *Tirukkuṟaḷ* the corresponding reference is to the ideal of *vīṭu* and the idea of *tuṟavu.*

Without suggesting that the *Kuṟaḷ*'s ideas are directly modeled on the Sanskritic scheme, it might be proposed that the significance of the former becomes easily and better understood in the light of the latter. The underlying concept of spiritual perfection and the basic means to attain this perfection are quite similar in the two traditions. In both, spirituality is considered to indicate a total transformation of inner life through the pursuit of certain values, though the *Kuṟaḷ*'s emphasis on the moral value *aṟam* makes for a different approach.

The variation in emphasis becomes apparent in the fact that, though the Tamil tradition too accepts four values—*aṟam*, *poruḷ*, *inpam*, and *vīṭu* (roughly corresponding to the four values of *dharma*, *artha*, *kāma*, and *mokṣa* of the Sanskritic tradition)—the *Kuṟaḷ* goes into a detailed discussion of only the first three, with the implicit suggestion that the ideal of spiritual perfection (*vīṭu*) can be realized by living up to the ideals postulated in the three values, which are dealt with separately in the three major divisions of the *Kuṟaḷ*, entitled *Aṟattuppāl*, *Porutpāl*, and *Kāmattuppāl*. The way in which the three values are treated indicates the originality of Tiruvaḷḷuvar. Apart from restructuring the fourfold value scheme in terms of three values while reconceiving them, the author makes yet another important modification in the treatment of the values in his classic. He replaces the integrated pattern of the fourfold scheme by envisaging one key concept, namely, *aṟam* in such a way that the other two values—*poruḷ* and *inpam*—become extensions of *aṟam*.

The concept of *aṟam* is thus seen to hold the key to the philosophy of good life in the *Kuṟaḷ*. The subtlety of the presentation and analysis of *aṟam* in the *Kuṟaḷ* matches indeed the subtlety with which *aṟam* pervades human life, both the personal and the interpersonal aspects. The imperceptible, though not ineffective, presence of *aṟam* in the workaday concerns of human beings is paradoxically responsible for the presence of the warmth of human feelings and the depth of human emotions[7] and for the idealistic motivations of human action.[8] The result is that the very idealizations of the human person are presented not as exhortations to humans to become seriously and strenuously ethical but as gentle suggestions (though characterized by firm conviction) that extending principles at work at the personal level to interpersonal situations constitutes the very essence of one's spiritual life.

The rather deliberate omission of the fourth value in the Tamil classic has not resulted in a qualitatively diluted approach to the concept of spiritual life. The omission is to be understood neither as a disregard of the spiritual dimension of human life nor as a playing down of human metaphysical aspirations. This interpretation is clear from Tiruvaḷḷuvar's visualization of a transcendent state in which the shackles imposed by the individual's own *karma*[9] have been broken for good.

Thus the seriousness of the problem of human existence is clearly expressed in the *Kuṟaḷ* as is the need to seek the solution. The reason for the *Kuṟaḷ*'s emphasis on the ethical-moral is to reiterate the need for the strict observance of *aṟam* in every sphere of life, the personal as well as the social. The importance accorded to *aṟam* does not place it above *vīṭu* as the ultimate value. The interest in secular matters is born out of a deep concern to transform human life in accordance with an ultimate ideal through adopting the appropriate means. The significant solution to the problem of human life suggested in the *Kuṟaḷ* consists in dwelling on this-worldly values such as *poruḷ* and *inpam* while insisting that the principle of *aṟam* be observed scrupulously in realizing them. Implicit in Tiruvaḷḷuvar is the axiom that such an adherence to moral principles ensures both the realization of the supreme spiritual ideal (*vīṭu*) by the individual and the dawning of the social good. The one is not opposed to the other but makes possible its very achievement; consequently, the this-worldly concern also becomes charged with idealism of a unique kind and raises the quality of personal as well as interpersonal life to an incredibly high level.

Likewise, the *Kuṟaḷ*'s teachings reflect the value Indian spirituality places on asceticism through its treatment of *tuṟavu* (asceticism); in the *Kuṟaḷ* asceticism is an *attitude*, not the "abdication" of the field of action. In terms of the *āśrama*-scheme of the Sanskritic Hindu tradition, *tuṟavaṟam* would correspond to *sannyāsāśrama*. There is also a similarity between the ideas of *illaṟam* (the state of domestic life) in the *Kuṟaḷ* and *grahasthāśrama* in the Sanskritic Hindu tradition. This raises the question of whether the *illaṟam-tuṟavaṟam* (domestic-ascetic) scheme is based on the fourfold *āśrama*-scheme. It would seem that the four stages of life recognized by Brahmanical Hinduism were reconceived by Tiruvaḷḷuvar in terms of *illaṟam* and *tuṟavaṟam*.[10] Meenakshisundaram's suggestion that it may not be wrong to consider the *Kuṟaḷ*'s scheme as possibly reflecting the quintessence of the *āśrama*-scheme is significant in our context. He writes:

> The four-fold *āśrama* life has not been followed in full in Tamil land. But the four-fold life is a natural development towards universalism and perfection. There is the life of a *brahmacāri*—the unmarried student receiving education. Next is the state reached by the *brahmacāri* when he marries and leads a family life with all its social responsibilities. The third is the stage of *vānaprastha*, where the husband and wife retire to the forest, seeking perfection. The next

spiritual development in this path is that of the *saṁnyāsin*, the man of the Universe.[11]

It may thus be maintained that the basic idea behind the *āśrama*-scheme—that the ultimate ideal in life can be realized only by a deliberate and a long preparation—is found acceptable to Tiruvaḷḷuvar.

But Tiruvaḷḷuvar does not emphasize the change of status of the person who starts practicing *tuṟavaṟam*. The idea is succinctly argued for by Meenakshisundaram:

> In the Tamil country the four-fold life was looked upon as a two-fold life, of the family man and of the man of the universe, spoken of in terms of *illaṟam* and *tuṟavaṟam*. (The) *brahmacāri* or the student after all belongs to the family. The refusal to divide the non-domestic life into two as *vānaprastha* and *saṁnyāsa* is significant in the Tamilian thought. *Vānaprastha* and *Saṁnyāsa* are clubbed together as *Tuṟavaṟam*. The emphasis here, therefore, cannot be laid on living away from one's wife in *tuṟavaṟam*. The couple, no longer cooperating for the greatness of the family, now cooperate for the perfection of their universal love. Therefore, *tuṟavu* is not renouncing the world. One cannot get away from the world of action. What is important is the change in the attitude towards life, that there is no longer an emphasis on the reality of "my family," "my country," and "other countries." Therefore Tiruvaḷḷuvar emphasises the liquidation of the pride and ignorance involved in one's using the terms, the "I" and the "Mine."[12]

What is perhaps suggested by Tiruvaḷḷuvar is that the spiritual ideal, *vīṭu*, can be attained through two overlapping but distinct attitudes to life. If *vīṭu* is attaining a state free from narrow attachment, a state in which the individual transcends the egotistic feeling, then the intermediate states indicating the gradual progress toward this end can be envisaged. In this sense Tiruvaḷḷuvar may be referring to *illaṟam* and *tuṟavaṟam* as two "stages," but the term "stage" does not connote a definite change of status as in Brahmanic Hinduism,[13] when the person "leaves" one *āśrama* and "enters" another.

This idea of a continuum is derived from Tiruvaḷḷuvar's premise that the ideal of *anpu* (love) exhorted to be practiced in *illaṟam* is the mother of *aruḷ* (benevolence) (76.7), the ideal to be achieved in *tuṟavaṟam*.[14] In general, *illaṟam* stands for the duties of the individual as a member of a family, and *tuṟavaṟam* connotes the responsibilities of the person as a member of humanity. Tiruvaḷḷuvar's view is that the spiritual ideal can be realized only by the individual who undergoes moral growth, by progressively developing concern for others and ultimately becoming sensitive to the whole of creation.

Yet this transition from a familial to a universal context, during which the state of *illaṟam* is replaced with that of *tuṟavaṟam*, should not be construed merely in terms of a shift from a smaller to a larger group, for basically all groups are similar inasmuch as they are hedged in by bounds—biological, social, and cultural. The concern and love that are exemplified even at the level of general humanity may not be of the most spontaneous kind[15] and really unqualified unless the operation of the ego-motive is suspended in a dramatic shift from "I" and "mine" to total equanimity. Such evenness of mind indeed deserves the description of unequivocal love and indicates that a total transformation of human personality has been achieved. Goodness, considered the essence of humanity and spirituality, in its strictest sense, points to the individual having attained the full stature of human perfectibility.

Thus, *tuṟavaṟam* is to be understood not as renunciation in the physical sense of "detaching oneself" from all worldly concerns but as an attitude of non-attachment to the fruits of one's action. It is this attitudinal change that aids in the transformation of personality. In terms of society, social concern predominates in *illaṟam*, although there the ego-motive is still at play; in *tuṟavaṟam* social awareness is not lost or replaced by an attitude of detachment, but is purified of its sloth, of its ego-motives.

The distinction between *illaṟam* and *tuṟavaṟam* drawn in the *Kuṟaḷ* was not merely to indicate that spirituality is intimately related to a progressive expansiveness of social concern but more basically to point to the transformational effect social concern has on human personality. Thus it is that the *Kuṟaḷ* is reflective of the third aspect of Hindu spirituality referred to above, that is, the sanctity placed on the maintenance of social structure.

The approach of the *Kuṟaḷ* to the question of social structure is as idealistic as the approach of the Sanskritic classics and entails two dominant themes: setting ideals to be achieved and exhorting individuals to internalize these ideals in order that they may engender a purposeful society. The first sense of idealism emphasizes the interpersonal nature of social relations and, more specifically, the attitude of give-and-take required of all the individuals who represent the "functioning units" of the social organization; the second sense of idealism underlines the need for a personal transformation in each individual to achieve these ideals.

In the *Tirukkuṟaḷ*'s reflections on society, both elements—the social and the personalistic—are intertwined. They should not be considered as two realms that can be compartmentalized. These two elements of human beings are so inextricably woven together in the texture of human nature that it is only by a dogmatic assertion that either of them may be said to be more predominantly significant than the other.[16] The peculiarity of human nature is such that it projects itself now in the social, now in the metaphysical realm, and each projection itself seems to be all-encompassing. These alternate dimensions of human activity do not point to eternal contradictions in human nature but rather to the fact that the two aspects of human personality are organically related and that through understanding their interrelationship we can meaningfully refer to the personalistic roots of the social and the social ramifications of the personal.

The *Kuṟaḷ*'s emphasis on the social cannot be appreciated fully if the work is considered to be a purely secular text or if it is approached merely as a metaphysical treatise. We get the cue for our understanding of the text from the great concern for social weal expressed in the classic when it delegates social responsibility to every individual. In this reference to individual responsibility the metaphysical aspects of the classic's teachings become evident. But the characteristic feature of the Tamil work is that it emphasizes the social aspect—what in the Indian discussions of the classic is referred to as the this-worldly as against the otherworldly aspects of human life—almost to the point of making the cursory reader of the classic believe that any reflection on the metaphysical nature of the human person is absent from the *Kuṟaḷ*. But by carefully reflecting on the two aspects of the human personality, the *Kuṟaḷ*'s author has indicated the importance of the social aspects of human life as well as the deep metaphysical significance of individual and social living.

We have now come full circle. In explicating the individual and the social dimensions of spirituality as understood in the *Kuṟaḷ*, the stress was earlier laid on understanding the deep and comprehensive significance of the principle of *aṟam*, interpreted as indicative of social concern in the deepest sense of the term. The metaphysical aspiration for attaining spiritual perfection referred to as *vīṭu* was considered to have the purifying effect on the individual. The very functioning of society is a result of the integration of personal as well as social ideals. Social structure itself may be understood as resulting from idealizations about morality. This seems to be the significance of Tiruvaḷḷuvar's view that morality and social organization of it should not be considered to be two distinct processes.[17] What is more significant is that even when Tiruvaḷḷuvar refers to social institutions, he emphasizes the idea of moral goodness (*aṟam*)[18] and conversely, while referring to morality he makes it clear that social institutions are helpful as "sources."[19] Thus, the personal and the interpersonal aspects of the serious pursuit of *aṟam* indicate the two dimensions of spiritual life as visualised in the Tamil classic.

Conclusion

The viewpoint taken in this article can thus be succinctly stated. Starting from the well-accepted view that the term "spirituality" is comprehensive in its significance, the focus was kept on three aspects and an attempt was made to show that they together are indicative of the *personal* and the *social* aspects of spiritualism. The presupposition is that no meaningful concept relating to human life can be analyzed by overlooking either the personal or the social dimensions of human living.

The spiritualistic ideas discernible in the ancient Tamil classic *Tirukkuṟaḷ* are understandable both in terms of the Indian tradition of which it is a part and in terms of the Tamil genius through which it has found *one* specific expression. The *Kuṟaḷ* is concerned with showing that the principle of *aṟam* provides the connecting link between the *personal* and the *social* aspects of human life. The metaphysical implications of morality are explicated fully by Tiruvaḷḷuvar through his emphasis on the need for a scrupulous observance of the moral principle in every transaction in human life, be it in the purely personal or the largely public context. The resultant understanding of spirituality is that the transcendent aspect of the human psyche provides the grist and vital sap for a way of life that emerges naturally from and is a logical sequel to a view of life that is extremely idealistic in its orientation and deeply human in its content and intent. The barrier between personal and social morality is crossed over, for according to such a view, the personal is no longer "individual" and the social is nothing less than a real involvement in the cares and concerns of the others without a trace of the egotistic motive.

Notes

1. Pitirim A. Sorokin's attempt to get at the meaning of the term "spiritual" is contextually significant here. He observes: "The vague term 'spiritual' signifies . . . a man who succeeds—mentally and behaviorally—in identifying his true being . . . not so much with his organism and his unconscious and conscious ego-centered 'mind', but especially with the super-conscious Infinite Manifold, transcending man's ego indescribable by any words and undefinable by any concepts.

"For the partisans of the supraconscious, the total man appears not as a diadic creature, consisting of body and mind, but as a triadic being made up of body, . . . mind . . . and pneuma (or spirit . . .), or of the unconscious, conscious and the supraconscious forms of being. Accordingly, the summit of spirituality is achieved by those who succeed in identifying themselves—in their living, feeling, thinking and acting with the supra-conscious, by making their body and their unconscious and conscious mind a mere instrumentality of immortal self" (*Forms and Techniques of Altruistic and Spiritual Growth* [New York: Kraus Reprint Co., 1971] v).

2. See, e.g., J. Mackenzie, *Hindu Ethics* (London: Humphrey Milford, 1922) 216. It is interesting to find other orientalists arguing equally strongly that such an interpretation of Hindu ethics is wholly unacceptable. See A. B. Keith, *Religion and Philosophy of the Vedas and Upanishads* (London: Humphrey Milford, 1925) 581; and F. Max Muller, *The Six Systems of Indian Philosophy* (London: Longman Green, 1928) 106–8.

3. For a detailed discussion of this issue, see my *Hindu Social Philosophy*, chapters 3 and 8.

4. The term *institution* refers not merely to certain social practices but also to the inner thought patterns that lie as foundational aspects of the social observances themselves. This idea is clearly brought out by Walton H. Hamilton: "Institution is a verbal symbol which for want of a better term describes a cluster of social usages. It connotes a way of thought or action of some prevalence and some permanence, which is embedded in the habits of a group or the customs of a people" ("Institution," in *Encyclopaedia of the Social Sciences*, vol. 8). It seems the stress needs to be laid on the inner aspects of person-in-society, since institutions are frequently the outcome of deliberation and design. This is not to deny that institutions are meeting points of the accidents and design, of reason and unreason, but only to affirm that the subjective, reflective elements in them are crucial to a proper understanding of them.

5. There are striking parallels to this idea in Sanskritic writings, where the "satisfaction of an enlightened conscience" is referred to as one of the sources of *dharma*. See, e.g., *Manu* II.6; *Yājñavalkya* I.3–5 and 7; *Baudhāyana* 1.1.1 and 1.1.3–5; *Vasiṣṭha* I.4–5; and *Mahābhārata* 12.251.3.

6. This is referred to as *vīṭu*. This word is derived from the Tamil word *viṭu*, which means "leave." Even though the term imparts the sense of giving up, in actual popular and literary usage the term has a very positive meaning. *Vīṭu* in Tamil also refers to home; realizing *vīṭu* is like homecoming. Just as in one's own home one is free from constraints, "realizing *vīṭu*" in the religious sense becomes a synonym for the ideal of real freedom.

7. This indicates in brief the treatment of the theme of *inpam* as extension of *aṟam* in the "Kāmattuppāl" part of *Tirukkuṟaḷ*. See my *Social Philosophy of Tirukkural*, chapter 5.

8. The idealization of the economic and political aspects of human life are specifically found in the "Porutpāl" part of *Tirukkuṟaḷ*. See my *Social Philosophy of Tirukkural*, chapter 4.

9. The transcendent state referred to here is visualized as resulting from the transcendence of the birth–death cycle. This idea in *Tirukkuṟaḷ* is not different from the idea of *karma* accepted in the Hindu, Jaina, and Buddhistic traditions. According to the theory of *karma* (referred to as *ul* in the *Kuṟaḷ*) every action (*karma*) brings in its trail a consequence which is also referred to as *karma*. The corollary of the doctrine of *karma* is that the fruits of all the actions done (the consequences) may not be had in one life. All the same, the significance of human life is not construed here as consisting merely in answering one's good and bad deeds, but in attempting to attain a state of ultimate good. The attainment of this state is considered the epitome of spiritual perfection and is regarded as "overcoming" *karma*. Thus, alongside the insistence that one cannot escape from the effects of one's past deeds, there is also the clear suggestion that overcoming the effects of *karma* is possible by a process of transmutation. *Karma*, it is

emphasized, has its sway in strict proportion to the sense of agency and possession with which one acts. If one does good deeds and abstains from evil ones, one surely creates for oneself a good fate, just as by doing the opposite, one is sowing the seeds for an evil destiny. In either case, the individual is caught up in the cycle of birth and death and by getting over the sense of agency the ultimate state of spiritual perfection can be realized. This state of spiritual perfection is referred to as *mokṣa* or *mukti* in the Hindu tradition, *nirvāṇa* in the Jaina and the Buddha tradition, and as *vīṭu* in the Tamil tradition.

10. The two subsections "Illaraviyal" and "Tuṟavaraviyal" under which the chapters under the section "Arattuppāl" in *Tirukkuṟaḷ* are organized are the work of the classical commentator Parimelaḻakar. While the chapter arrangements of the entire work with ten couplets in each chapter could possibly be part of the intention of the author, one cannot be so sure with regard to the two subsections, believed to connote two distinctly different "stages" of life. We find some basis for the distinction in the general tenor of treatment in terms of a mere distribution of emphasis. There is no warrant for acquiescing in the commentator's principle of division and accepting his view that the section "Arattuppāl" deals with two dissimilar life-styles or institutions.

All that can be accepted here is that the distinction between *illaṟam* and *tuṟavaṟam* and especially its significance for a good life become explicable when viewed in the light of the *āśrama*-scheme of Brahmanical Hinduism. But the relation of Vaḷḷuvar's treatment of *aṟam* to the four stages of life accepted in Brahmanical Hinduism is a subject of considerable obscurity, exegetically speaking. Can Vaḷḷuvar's description of the householder as the mainstay of "the three others" be considered a direct reference to the three *āśramas*? It is surprising that not only the brahmanically inclined Parimelaḻakar but also the other commentators of old have, with a consensus, thought so. But it is against the grain of Vaḷḷuvar to introduce numerical expressions without specifying what he means, leaving it to the commentators to fill the gap. What is more, in the present case, the very following couplet specifies "the three"—the forsaken, the poor, and the dead. There is no textual basis here or in any other place in the Tamil classic to support the thesis that Vaḷḷuvar acknowledges the *āśrama*-scheme as the basis of his philosophy of good life.

11. T. P. Meenakshishundaram, "Philosophy of Tiruvalluvar," in *Thirumathi Sornammal Endowment Lectures in Tirukkural*, ed. M. V. Venugopaula Pillai (Madras: University of Madras, 1971).

12. Ibid. The interpretation gets support from the *Kuṟaḷ* couplet (35.6) that reads: "He who cuts off the pride of 'I' and 'mine' enters a world beyond that of the Gods." It is striking that Parimelaḻakar and the other classical commentators here understand the attitude reflected in shedding of the pride of "I" and "mine" as symbolizing the realization of *vīṭu* rather than as expressive of the ascetic ideal.

13. P. V. Kane observes: "We see that Yajnavalkya when about to become a *parivrajaka* (a wandering ascetic) tells his wife Maitreyi that he was going to leave home and that he wanted to divide whatever wealth he had between her and her co-wife Katyayani. This shows that a *parivrājaka* had even then to leave home and wife and give up all belongings" (*History of Dharma-Sastra* [Poona: Bhandarkar Oriental Research Institute, 1941] vol. 2, pt. 2, p. 930). The contrast between the *Kuṟaḷ* concept of *tuṟavu* and that of *sannyāsa* is clear. The latter, as much as the former, implies inner renuncia-

tion. But the renouncer, going away from his kith and kin and worldly possessions, seems to be an integral aspect of asceticism as conceived in the ideal of *sannyāsa*.

14. Our using the expressions "in *illaṟam*" and "in *tuṟavaṟam*" needs to be explained here. It is the predicament of language that forces us to make use of the expressions and give the impression that *illaṟam* and *tuṟavaṟam* are spatial categories and that the passage from the one to the other involves leaving the one and entering the other. All that we mean here is that there is a movement from a less perfect to a more perfect stage. Perhaps Tiruvaḷḷuvar, by making use of the terms *illaṟam* and *tuṟavaṟam*, wants to indicate that the second is the result of the individual consciously growing and maturing ethically and spiritually.

15. Cf. Sorokin, who draws the difficult but significant distinction between the expressions altruistic and spiritual (*Forms and Techniques*, v).

16. The type of understanding of human nature found in *Tirukkuṟaḷ* can be borne out by scores of references. However, in one significant phrase (*vaiyattuḷ vāḻvānku vāḻpavan*, 5.10), the author implies the interwovenness of the two natures in human beings when he describes human life on earth as participating in heaven when it is led in the light of the ultimate ideal.

17. A distinction between the ideal of goodness and institutional morality is not simply read between the lines. Tiruvaḷḷuvar himself uses the term *aṟan* instead of *aṟam* in many couplets in the "Second Book" (entitled Porutpāl) of his work (see 39.4; 45.1; 64.5; 65.4; and 76.4). It must be admitted, however, that the terms *aṟam* and *aṟan* are used interchangeably in the Aṟrattuppāl, the "First Book," as, for instance, in couplet 9 of chapter 5 and couplets 2, 7, and 10 of chapter 15. This would add strength to the argument that the institutionalization possibility is ingrained in the very structure of *aṟam*.

18. This idea can be substantiated by a reference to many couplets in the *Kuṟaḷ*, but a reference to just two of them should suffice to make the point. It is significant that even in the fourth couplet of chapter 39, though the term *aṟan* is used, Turivaḷḷuvar carefully uses the term *aracu* (which refers to the institution of kingship) rather than *aracan*, while defining "king" as one who does not swerve from virtue and refrains from vice. The obvious intention of Tiruvaḷḷuvar in using the abstract term *aracu* in this couplet (even though he uses the term *aṟan* instead of *aṟam* to indicate morality or the institutionalization of it) is to impress upon his readers that even when he is referring to the application of the grand ideal of *aṟam* to the day-to-day life of a society, he does not want to be mistaken as dealing only with the actuality of an ethics of the king rather than with the ideal of goodness. (See Parimelaḻakar's commentary on 39.4.)

19. See, e.g., 45.1. When the "prince" is asked to acquire the friendship of the virtuous and the supremely wise, the reason, as Parimelaḻakar comments, seems to be that virtue or *aṟan* is to be known not merely through the sacred books but also through coming into contact with those who, through maturity and good conduct, possess a knowledge of it (see Parimelaḻakar's commentary on the couplet). It seems that the clear meaning of this couplet is that society is a definite source of morality. The insistence on the maturity and good conduct of those who are the sources of morality again signifies that it is not just following the social codes blindly that is meant here.

Bibliography

Sources

Aiyar, V. V. S. *The Kural or the Maxims of Tiruvalluvar*. Tiruchirapalli: V. V. S. Krishnamoorthy & Co., 1952.

Bharati, S. S. *Tiruvalluvar*. Madura: Tamil Sangam Power Press, 1929.

Ellis, E. W., trans. *Tirukkural on Virtue with Commentary*. 1812. Madras: University of Madras, 1955.

Iraiyanar. *Valluvar Kolkaiym Vatavar Kolkaiym*. Trichy: Tamilakam, 1959.

Kavijnar, Namakkal. *Valluvarin Ullam*. Madras: Inpa Nilayam, 1963.

Maraimalai Atikal. *Tirukkural Araychi*. Madras: Pari Nilayam, 1957.

Parimelalakar, Manakkutavar, Parithiyar, Kalinkar. Commentary on Tirukkural (Arattuppal). *Tirukkural Uraikkotthu*. Thiruppanandal: Kasi Mutt, 1969.

Parimelalakar, Manakkutavar, Paripperumal, Parithiyar, Kalinkar. Commentary on Tirukkural (Porutpal). *Tirukkural Uraikkotthu*. Thiruppanandal: Kasi Mutt, 1960.

Parimelalakar, Manakkutavar, Paripperumal, Parithiyar Kalinkar. Commentary on Tirukkural (Kamattuppal). *Tirukkural Uraikkotthu*. Thiruppanandal: Kasi Mutt, 1970.

Pope, G. U., and others, trans. *Tirukkural*. Madras: The South India Sāiva Siddhandta Works Publishing Society, Tinnevelly Ltd., 1962.

Sethu Pillai, R. A. P. *Tiruvalluvar Nool Nayam*. Madras: Tirunelveli Saiva Siddhanta Publishing House Ltd., 1961.

Studies

Appadurai, K. *The Mind and Thought of Tiruvalluvar*. Madras: Sekar Pathippakam, 1966.

Gopalan, S. *Hindu Social Philosophy*. New Delhi: Wiley Eastern Ltd., 1979.

——. *The Social Philosophy of Tirukkural*. New Delhi and Madras: Affiliated East-West Press Pvt. Ltd., 1979.

Meenakshisundaram, T. P. *A History of Tamil Language*. Poona: Deccan College of Post-Graduate and Research Institute, 1965.

Purnalingam Pillai, M. S. *Critical Studies in Kural*. Tinnevelly: The Bibliotheca, 1929.

Vaiyapuri Pillai, S. *History of Tamil Language and Literature*. Madras: The New Century Book House, 1957.

Venugopaula Pillai, M., ed. *Thirumathi Sornammal Endowment Lectures on Tirukkural*. Madras: University of Madras, 1971.

7

The Spiritual Quest of Āṇḍāl

P. T. Saroja Sundararajan

THE RECENT INTEREST in the religious and spiritual lives of women is multidisciplinary in its implications and premises. These new explorations of feminine spirituality may widen the range of the sociology and history of religions and similarly add a new dimension to the psychology of religion. Moreover, the consequences for philosophy of religion and philosophical theology are likely to be momentous. Here it is not merely a question of adding a new chapter or introducing new research areas; it is rather a question of a reformulation and a new understanding of the significance of the spiritual quest. A philosophically sensitive study of feminine religiosity may lead to a paradigm change in our understanding of the nature and forms of spiritual life.[1] Such a reformulation affects two important dimensions of the spiritual life: the soul's relation to the Lord and the idea of God. The first of these has been treated in studies of feminine religiosity. The particular warmth, intimacy, and loving devotion of the great women saints of the Hindu faith have been universally noted and remarked upon. Women such as Āṇḍāl and Mīrā have been taken as exemplars of loving devotion to the Lord. These illustrious women have been considered to be, as it were, actualizations of possibilities that are open to all. Perhaps in such an interpretation the distinctiveness and specificity of women's spiritual quest are somewhat marginalized. The specific forms of women's spiritual life are important also from the point of view of philosophy of religion and philosophical theology.[2] Furthermore, a sensitive and discerning phenomenology of feminine religiosity may provide clues to a somewhat changed understanding of our idea of God.

It is one of the important methodological principles of phenomenological analysis that there is a correlation between the kind of acts (cognitive and affective) and the nature of the object presented in and through those acts. Edmund Husserl calls this principle the noetic-noematic correlation a priori.[3] According to this principle, an object or entity of a certain kind of intentional act can be presented only by those kinds of acts; thus a material and physical object can be presented primarily only by way of perceptual acts and so on. Using this principle as our methodological clue, we can formulate a conception of the divine on the basis of a phenomenology of religious consciousness in general. A sensitive description of the modalities of the spiritual experience of women saints such as Āṇḍāl may hence be of a more than biographical significance, for such an account may provide insights into new forms in which we can think of the divine being and her nature. Proceeding in this way, we may be invited to think of a form of theism that is close to what in our days Charles Hartshorne has been arguing for as neoclassical theism.[4] Briefly put, the basic philosophical difference between classical or orthodox theism and Hartshorne's neoclassical theism is that classical theism is monopolar while new-classical theism is bipolar. Given the polarities of one and many, Being and Becoming, Active and Passive, Eternal and Temporal, Necessary and Contingent, the classical idea of God applies to only one of each of these pairs of predicates. Thus, God is paradigmatically said to be one without many, pure being or being as such, active and not passive, eternal, necessary, and changeless, whereas, according to Hartshorne, there is an eminent sense in which the other predicates also may be applicable to God. Thus, Hartshorne argues that it is logically possible and also religiously necessary that we must admit in some sense contingency, becoming, and variability in the divine nature, without diminishing the metaphysical perfections such as unity, constancy, and necessity. Thus, he suggests that while God's essence is necessary, the actuality or the concrete states of the divine essence may admit of variability.[5] The effect of substituting the logic of bipolarity for the logic of classical theism, in the ultimate analysis, would be a profound transformation of the idea of God, from that of the Absolute or Unsurpassable to that of a self-surpassing surpasser of all. Insofar as, in this conception, God would still be regarded as surpassing every being except God, His supereminence would be safeguarded; but there would now be a place for creativity in our understanding of His nature. Even with regard to the creatures, creativity involves self-surpassing; only now such creative self-transcendence would be given infinite dimensions. But Hartshorne's argument is not merely logical in the sense of outlining a different conceptual possibility in our attempts to interpret the idea of God. Much more importantly, he has argued that it is this idea of God that seems more suited to the needs and aspirations of the human spiritual quest. This suggestion will be the guiding idea in the present interpretation and understanding of the spiritual quest of Āṇḍāl.[6]

The Spiritual Quest of Āṇḍāl

Since Āṇḍāl's *Tiruppāvai* has not been given careful scholarly attention and analysis, precise biographical information about Āṇḍāl and her work is very scanty.[7] We have only a few clues in the popular tradition and stories that have grown up around her life.[8] Out of this traditional lore only a few firm facts stand out. Āṇḍāl lived in a village called Srivalliputtur in the interior part of South India. This village is a Vaiṣṇavite one with the presiding deity of Narayana in the form of Bathrasayee. For the Śrī Vaiṣṇavas, Āṇḍāl's father, Viṣṇucitta, also known as Periāḻvār, is one among a group of a twelve mystics known as the Āḻvārs. The generic name *āḻvār* connotes one who has been deeply immersed in the love of God. In the Śrī Vaiṣṇava tradition, *āḻvārs* enjoyed a unique and exalted place. They were considered to be "model devotees" who had surrendered themselves completely to the Lord. But the tradition goes on to say that even among the *āḻvārs*, Periāḻvār was considered most important (in fact his very title in Tamil, *periya*, signifies this importance). It is said that he was so much immersed in his devotion to God that he had lost the sense of himself as an individual needing salvation from *samsāric* existence. The tradition goes on to say that Āṇḍāl, his daughter, was even more exemplary in her devotion, because while all other saints and mystics sought to awaken souls from their ignorance, the *Tiruppāvai* of Āṇḍāl awakens God Himself to the need for bestowing grace on human souls (*Tiruppāvai*, introduction). The symbolism of *Tiruppāvai* is that of Āṇḍāl, along with other devotees, going up to the mansion of the Lord and awakening Him to their presence.

The tradition describes the supremacy of Āṇḍāl in another way also. In the Vaiṣṇavite tradition, the most intense form of *bhakti* is modeled on love. Rāmānuja's model of relation between the lover and the beloved (*nāyaki-nāyaka bhāva*) is taken as the supreme form of devotion (*bhakti*) and the *āḻvārs* expressed such devotion. But because they were born as men, the model of beloved does not have a spontaneous and natural application to them. They have to imagine themselves to be feminine before they can enter into the framework of *bhakti*. But Āṇḍāl, being born a woman, is more fit for the mode of devotion. It is also said that she represents the whole world of creation itself in its longing and aspiration for the Creator, since the created world is symbolized by a female deity, Bhūdevi (*Tiruppāvai*, introduction). According to the tradition, *bhakti*, or devotion to God, was innate for Āṇḍāl.

Of all the devotional works in Tamil, *Tiruppāvai* holds a special place (*Tiruppāvai*, introduction). The Vedas and the Upaniṣads also speak of the life of liberation, but being in Sanskrit they are inaccessible to the majority of people. But the works of *āḻvārs* were composed in their own mother tongue (Tamil) and were available even to children. Even among the works of *āḻvārs*, *Tiruppāvai* was held to be preeminent, since, consisting of thirty verses, it was neither too long nor too brief. In these thirty verses, *Tiruppāvai* includes all the values of human life, and, like many other devotional works, it is not extremely ascetic or world denying; it finds a room for pleasure and delight (*kāma*) and also for prosperity and affluence (*artha*). But it recognized the value of *kāma, artha*, and *dharma* only in relation to *mokṣa,* the ideal of liberation (ibid.).

According to *Tiruppāvai*, human life becomes significant only in relation to the value of liberation. *Mokṣa* here does not deny or negate the other goals of life such as *kāma*, *artha*, and *dharma*; on the contrary, it is their fulfillment. This relationship to *mokṣa* is seen in the *Tiruppāvai* as demanding commitment and discipline on the part of the individual. *Tiruppāvai* symbolizes this in the form of a ritual that the *gopīs* used to perform in honor of Kṛṣṇa. This ritual is to be performed in the month of December–January, and it involves forms of purification of mind and body. It is said that each one of the *gopīs* had her own personal end or aim for performing this ritual. Each one craved for something special and unique from the Lord. But Āṇḍāl did not live in the age of the *gopīs*. She was not one of them. But inwardly she performs the ritual in her own mind. She internalizes the past and in so doing, she identifies herself with every one of them. She relives in herself what all the *gopīs* wanted, and hence it is said that in her single person she sums up all the desires and aspirations of the *gopīs* (*Tiruppāvai,* introduction). According to the tradition, so great was the power of empathy of Āṇḍāl that although born in a cultured brahmin family, when she imagined herself to be a *gopī*, all her mannerisms of thought, feeling, and action were changed, and she lived and acted like a non-brahmin member of a cowherd community (ibid.).

In the first verse, the major objectives of the spiritual discipline into which Āṇḍāl is entering are set out; there is also an indication of those who are qualified to undertake such a discipline as well as the means or instruments necessary for it. The opening verse indicates also the results or benefits of such a discipline and the giver or source of such benefits. In this way, the first verse conforms to the classical model of the introduction to a treatise. According to classical Indian theory of literature, nonfictional texts were expected to indicate in the very beginning (a) the objectives of the treatise, (b) the people competent for it, (c) the means or instruments necessary, and (d) the objectives sought to be achieved. As far as *Tiruppāvai* is concerned, the discipline that Āṇḍāl is embarking on is the path of devotion (*bhakti yoga*). She indicates the people competent for *bhakti*, the means necessary for it, and the source of benefits from it. It is for this reason that the tradition sometimes speaks of *Tiruppāvai* as a *śāstra* (treatise)—*bhakti śāstra* (ibid.).

The *Tiruppāvai* moves simultaneously at two levels—the symbolic and philosophical. At the symbolic level, the discipline takes the form of a purificatory bath in the river Yamuna, cleansing and ornamentation of the body, singing and dancing. The objective or end is to receive a drum from Kṛṣṇa. The connection between the symbolic and philosophical levels is that the *gopīs* of old age performed this dance whereas Āṇḍāl internalizes the whole episode in her imagination. She recreates the sacred past and in so doing gives an inner spiritual meaning to external details.

The verse opens with the description of a full moonlit night in the month of *mārgaḻi* (December–January). This has some significance, for it seems to be a subtle reference to the *Gītā*, where Kṛṣṇa describes Himself as *mārgaḻi* among the seasons. Furthermore, it is in this month that the plants ripen in the field and become ready for the harvest. The idea is that our human destiny is now ripe and that we are fit to receive the grace of the Lord. It may also be noted that the opening verse celebrates the time and the place in which divine grace becomes possible. But there is no direct praise or celebration of God Himself in the verse. The Tamil commentators explain this as an implicit reference to Vālmīki's *Rāmāyaṇa*, where the month in which Rāmā was crowned (*citra*) is described in detail rather than coronation of Rāmā himself. The idea is that the event sanctifies the time. So also here the possibility of grace makes the time and the place themselves holy.

The first verse suggests also that all who desire to see the Lord are welcome, implying that there are no other qualifications such as birth or intelligence that are preconditions of devotion. In philosophical terms, *bhakti* (devotion) does not depend on *jñāna* (knowledge) or *karma* (action), but is autonomous. The Tamil commentators of *Tiruppāvai* come up with an interesting and profound explanation: according to them all other goals such as wealth and knowledge are in a sense external to the soul. Hence, the soul must discipline itself for the achievement of these goals. But the desire for God and liberation is natural and intrinsic to the human soul. All human souls, merely because they are human, are innately equipped for this end, and no other precondition or qualification is necessary. The commentators also explain this natural affinity of the human soul with the example of inheritance. For a son to inherit his father's wealth, nothing more is needed except that his be his son and acknowledge it. So also, to inherit divine grace, all that is required is that God be acknowledged.

The second verse indicates the kind of discipline of body, mind, and spirit that is the precondition for *bhakti*. The central idea here is that the discipline is at once bodily, mental, and moral. Bodily discipline such as keeping one's body clean and healthy is necessary for the exercise of superior virtues such as charity, generosity, and trust. Another significant point about this verse is that here Āṇḍāl talks of negative prohibitions and positive commandments in an interrelated manner. Unlike those who tend to emphasize moral prohibitions over moral prescriptions or vice versa, Āṇḍāl seems to suggest their interrelatedness. For her, the significance of the prohibition lies in its contribution to the possibility of the positive command. This point may be illustrated by an example mentioned in the second verse itself. The verse speaks of abstaining from certain kinds of food (ibid.), but the purpose of the abstinence is to make oneself capable of generosity toward others. The second example illustrates the same point. Here Āṇḍāl speaks of giving up bodily ornamentation and beautification such as wearing flowers. The point of this restriction is not to deny or undervalue the importance of beauty but precisely to make us capable of beholding the greatest beauty of all, namely, Kṛṣṇa Himself.

The third and fourth verses can be taken together, since they have a common theme, namely, *artha* (prosperity)—one of the desirable goals of life. In these verses, Āṇḍāl speaks of material prosperity and affluence as part of the grace of God. The basic idea is to give prosperity a moral and spiritual foundation. As is to be expected, *Tiruppāvai* thinks of wealth and prosperity in rural terms as a plentiful harvest and generous yield of milk. They are also perceived as gifts—immediately gifts of nature and ultimately gifts of God, who is Himself the Creator of all nature. The fourth verse elaborates this idea of human prosperity as a gift of nature. Āṇḍāl celebrates the elemental forces of wind and rain and gives them thanks for what they do for human welfare. Implicitly, there is an idea that we as human beings have to live in harmony with nature and receive all natural gifts as resulting from the grace of God. There is implicitly a recognition of what today we call an environmental ethics.

The fundamental theme of the fifth verse is *dharma*, but there is a certain continuity between this and the two earlier verses. In those verses, *Tiruppāvai* suggested that *artha* becomes a value only if it is seen as a gift that comes ultimately from God, for which we should be grateful. Similarly, here also *Tiruppāvai* links *dharma*, or human morality, with the spiritual or religious goal. Thus, constant meditation on God, which is one of the forms of *bhakti*, alone can remove all evil inclinations or dispositions that have entered our character as a result of our previous actions. In order to overcome the strength of these dispositions, we need a power greater than our own. *Tiruppāvai*, however, does not go to the Calvinistic extreme of regarding the human will as totally perverted or powerless. It has a certain autonomy of its own, but it can realize its freedom only by first turning toward the Lord. In Indian terms, it is *bhakti* that strengthens the will and makes it free. The verse states this point rather indirectly by saying that the very thought of Kṛṣṇa drives away all impurities in our character, like the first light of dawn driving away the forces of darkness before it.

In the next ten verses, the basic idea is the awakening of the soul and its turning toward God. These verses employ two root metaphors: (1) a young maiden asleep; and (2) light outside her bedchamber as the sun rises. In the chamber there is darkness, but outside that chamber there is light. Though the opportune moment has arrived, the human soul is still in the slumber of ignorance. In v. 6, Āṇḍāl speaks of the slumbering soul as a young innocent maiden, and the entire verse is a gentle remonstrance. There is no note of sin and guilt, for the underlying theme is that if only the human soul would awake, it would, because of its own innate tendency, begin to love God.

In the tenth verse, the preciousness of each individual again is addressed when Āṇḍāl refers to the lazy and sleeping maiden as a precious jewel that belongs to others. Furthermore, there is also an implicit idea that it is precisely this individual who may, perhaps, be the most precious to God. This idea is expressed by reference to a character in the epic *Rāmāyaṇa*. Āṇḍāl describes the sleeping girl as more indolent than Kumbakarṇa himself. At the popular level, Kumbakarṇa is a symbol of laziness, but this imagery moves at the spiritual level also. In the *Rāmāyaṇa*, when Kumbakarṇa wakes up, he has a vision of Rāma and ultimately receives Rāma's grace.

This idea becomes explicit in the eleventh verse, where Āṇḍāl directly calls the sleeping maiden the most beloved of Kṛṣṇa; the Lord Himself is waiting for her.

In the twelfth verse, Āṇḍāl talks about human foolishness in craving for ordinary pleasures of life when the supreme bliss of experiencing God awaits everyone. Here the soul delights in trivial pleasures, which are like dreams in sleep, and refuses to wake up to realize the most supreme happiness of receiving the grace of the Lord.

In the thirteenth verse, Āṇḍāl pleads with the slumbering maiden not to isolate herself from all her companions. To refuse God is also to refuse fellowship with all others.

In the fourteenth verse, Āṇḍāl reminds the maiden of her innate goodness. It is not as if her refusal to wake up is natural or intrinsic to her; for on the previous day, it is precisely this maiden who had promised to get up first and awaken her and awaken all the others.

The fifteenth verse celebrates the awakening of the sleeping one, but there is a little drama of hesitation on her part. She wakes up but does not yet have the will to join the rest. She asks others to wait and be sure that everyone has come. Āṇḍāl chides her gently and reminds her that it is the others who are waiting for her. In this little play is expressed the idea that sometimes one's will may not immediately be forthcoming, although one knows what one should do. This weakness of the will may even take the form of a rationalization, as in this verse, where the maiden expresses a seeming concern for others.

In the sixteenth verse, the *gopīs* proceed to the mansion of the Lord, but they must first meet with the gatekeeper and request his help. Before one is fit to receive God's grace, one must first pay one's respect to the sages and saints who are, as it were, the custodians of spirituality. The Hindu view of spiritual discipline is that there are stages in one's quest for God, and the first stage in this process is obtaining the grace of wise men and sages.

In the seventeenth verse, this idea of intermediary stages is still further developed when Āṇḍāl, in the form of *gopī*, waits upon Yaśoda (Kṛṣṇa's mother) and Balarāma (the elder brother of Kṛṣṇa).

In the eighteenth verse, the *gopīs* plead with Śrī (the consort of Nārāyaṇa) to intercede with the Lord on their behalf. It is the principle of Vaiṣṇavism that, without the grace of Śrī, the Lord cannot be approached. The tradition illustrates the necessity of obtaining her grace by means of the story of Sūrpanaka in the *Rāmāyaṇa*. Sūrpanaka sought to obtain Rāma's grace directly, scorning Sītā, and hence she had to be destroyed. If the Lord cannot be approached without Śrī, it is equally true that Śrī cannot be approached independently of the Lord. The present verse, therefore, is a prayer to Śrī.

In the nineteenth verse, there is a bit of symbolic play. Here we are told that Śrī, who is full of infinite mercy and love for the human soul, is prevented by the Lord from opening the door. The idea is that the Lord Himself desires to liberate the human soul and hence would not allow even Śrī to come between Him and His devotees.

The twentieth verse continues this idea by representing a kind of competition between Śrī and the Lord as to who would be the first to receive the *gopīs*.

In the twenty-first verse, the transcendence of God is expressed. Śrī receives the *gopīs* but declares that she is one of them and in relation to God they are equal. Traditional commentators have interpreted this verse in two ways. On the one hand, they point out that what the *Tiruppāvai* teaches here is the utter transcendence of God in His essence. In relation to His essential nature (*svarūpa*), even Śrī is only a finite part. On the other hand, some commentators say that the verse could also be understood as suggesting that so great is God's love for the human soul that He regards all human souls as equally deserving of His love with Śrī herself.

The twenty-second verse expresses the condition of the soul as it approaches God. It surrenders all its personal possessions and, thinking only of the Lord, seeks refuge in Him without any thought of its own personal will. The twenty-second verse is an expression of the state of total surrender of the soul to God. In this verse that there is an implicit reference to Vibhīṣaṇa's surrender to Rāma as described in *Rāmāyaṇa.*

In the twenty-third verse, Āṇḍāl describes the divine response to the surrender of the soul. The Lord meets the *gopīs* more than halfway and says that it is He who must seek them out and that they have indeed reminded Him of His lapse in this respect. This verse also contains an allusion to *Rāmāyaṇa*, where Rāma responds to the surrender of Vibhīṣaṇa in precisely these terms.

In the twenty-fourth verse, the *gopīs* celebrate the glory of God and entreat Him for the gift of a perfect life under His Lordship.

But in the very next verse, the *gopīs* correct themselves and tell the Lord that they have been hasty in making their request. They regret that even when they were in the presence of God, they for a moment were weak enough to think of themselves.

In the twenty-sixth verse, the *gopīs* declare that they want nothing except the favor of celebrating God's glory forever and contemplating His holiness. They do not want anything that does not contribute to this end, and conversely they want everything that is needed to achieve this end.

In the twenty-seventh verse, the *gopīs* state that the gift that they desire most from God is that He should receive them as His garland, so that they would always be in His presence.

The twenty-eighth verse described how the relationship between the soul and God is a bond that exists eternally. It is this relationship that draws the soul to the Lord in spite of itself; and it is this relationship that makes the Lord forgive and overlook the lapses of the soul.

The twenty-ninth verse again repeats the craving of the soul to be in continual relationship with God, in every birth that the soul takes. Āṇḍāl expresses this idea also in mythical terms when she says that what she wants is the blessedness to witness the infinite incarnations of the Lord in future time. In accordance with the spirit of Vaiṣṇavism, she aspires not after union but only after a relationship with the Lord.

The thirtieth verse is benedictory; here Āṇḍāl expresses the hope that whoever reads the *Tiruppāvai* may also receive divine grace and lead a life even more perfect and blessed than her own.

The *Tiruppāvai* as a Clue to the Idea of God

According to the Tamil commentators on the *Tiruppāvai*, the symbol of the drum, which occurs in the verses as the boon that Āṇḍāl and the *gopīs* seek from the Lord, is the fulfillment of the yearning of their spirits; it is the fullness of life that is the boon sought for. Traditionally this the fullness or perfection of life is seen in the ordered fulfillment of the four goals of life—*dharma*, *artha*, *kāma* and *mokṣa*.[9] While this general philosophical interpretative motif may be accepted, yet we must also keep in view the specificity of the literary form and texture of the poem. The *Tiruppāvai* is the celebration of the search of the *gopīs*—the infinitely varied young maidens of Brindāvan—for Kṛṣṇa, here the Supreme Lord. Each one of them is seeking to fulfill her yearning in her own way. Translating this into philosophical language, we can say that different individuals pursue the goals of life differently and that there is a plurality proportional to the richness and complexity of human nature. Therefore, the spiritual quest of humans has to be seen also as a unity in diversity. From one point of view it is proper to say that all beings aspire after the four goals of life, but from another angle this unity must be seen in its diversity and polyvalent manifestations.[10] It is against this infinite variability and plurality of human need and talent that we must see the divine response.

Multiplicity is not only among different human beings but within the same soul. There are different faculties, each with its own specific demands and exigencies.[11] There is the intellect, with its demand for certainty and necessity; and there is the moral sense, with its ideal of perfection. There are also the feelings, with their yearning for intimacy and participation. If, following Āṇḍāl's testimony, we think of the Lord as the one who alone can completely satisfy all the demands of the human soul, then we must think of Him as both the ideal of thought and the perfect response to the heart. We must think of Him in many dimensions but always as eminent or supreme. Thus, He is the ideal fulfillment of thought; this means that He is that of whom one can be certain, a being than whom a greater cannot even be conceived. *Tiruppāvai* puts this in temporal terms, as the one whom the soul has known in innumerable births—the necessity and eternity of the bond between the soul and God is represented as an ancient and ever-continuing friendship.

As the one who can fulfill the demands of the intellect, the Lord must be thought of as supreme or supereminent in every way. His supremacy or eminence is, as it were, a double one. On the one hand, unlike any created thing, the Lord has infinity of perfections; in the Vaiṣṇava tradition of Āṇḍāl, He is said to possess an infinity of auspicious attributes. On the other hand, in each one of these perfections themselves, He has, as it were, an infinity; thus He is infinite knowledge, infinite power, and infinite goodness. Further, all these infinite perfections do not exist in Him as a multiplicity, but they exist in their unity, as the ineffable divine essence. The infinity of perfections is composed in the unity of His nature, and this divine essence itself is one with his being or existence.[12]

As to how this integration takes place, as to the nature of this divine simplicity, we cannot know; that is the superessential form of the Lord beyond all manifestations and incarnations. The intellect cannot grasp this, although it craves to "see" it; the spirit yearns to behold Nārāyaṇa in His utter transcendent state itself. The intellect demands transcendence, for only a transcendent being can be beyond the vagaries of space, time, and becoming. Insofar as the intellect, in its commitment to the idea of perfection, radicalizes the differences between the finite and the infinite and seeks in God the utterly Transcendent, there arises as a counterpoint, the need for intimacy and fellowship. The spirit yearns not only to understand but also to feel a closeness and to participate in the fellowship with the Lord. The purity and perfection of the logical ideal are transformed into the notion of a perfect and unfailing love. Hence arises the complementary demand of responsiveness and recognition on the part of the Supreme. To this dialectic of the demands of the intellect and of the feelings are added the exigencies of the moral will and the moral sense. One's sensibility to the moral good is also touched and heightened in the spiritual quest such that one thinks of God as the fulfillment of the moral life, as one in whom alone one can find all the virtues in their perfect harmony and interrelationship. What are separate virtues in the case of humans, and hence potentiality capable of giving rise to tensions and contradictions in the soul, such as justice and mercy, steadfastness, and responsiveness, are in Him united and integral. Hence, if one can understand the depth and complexity of the soul's quest, if one grasps the many dimensions of the soul's yearning, then one can have an idea of what could fulfill the human heart.

It is in this sense that texts such as that of Āṇḍāl's *Tiruppāvai* become precious in helping us to give depth to the idea of God. The basic or underlying theme of *Tiruppāvai* is that the Lord must be thought of as the most adequate fulfillment of every power and faculty in us. But his simple formula is fecund in its implications, if only we first understand clearly the depth and width of the human yearning for God. It is precisely such an understanding of the manifoldness of the human capacity for love that is the gift of the *Tiruppāvai* to us. Guided by an understanding of the variety and richness of the aspirations the human spirit is capable of, we can attempt to deepen our philosophical and theological conceptions. Thus, if we think of God as one, we should also think of this single or simple essence making itself available to each one in her/his own unique way. The Lord presents Himself in an infinity of ways, and yet His manifold incarnations and presences do not negate His constancy—the tranquillity and repose of Nārāyaṇa. Again, if we think of Him as the knower of all, as the omniscient, as the Infinite subject, we should also think of Him as the infinitely *known*. Every living thing, in its vitality and movement, is really seeking Him, for all life is stirred by Him. In all that they do, and in all that they know, creatures are really knowing Him. But yet they do not know that they are seeking Him, and from this point of view He is infinitely accessible and infinitely open. Other beings close themselves beyond a point and become impervious and inaccessible, but the Lord is perfect lucidity, and hence He is knowable by all. Every being in its own proper way and according to its own proper measure has participation in His life and is present to Him. If He is the Infinite knower, He is also the Infinitely knowable—knowable by every form of awareness and sentience. He is the Perfect Subject and also the Perfect Object. Similarly, He is also the Most Active and also the Most Receptive. If He is the doer of all, every action, every event makes a difference to Him. For Him everything matters, and He has a special concern for each and every little being that stirs on earth. Finally, such is the creative upsurge of the Divine Life that there is a constant creative self-transcendence in Him. But in the divine economy this process in Him does not in the least diminish the distance between Him and every other being. He continues to surpass everything—only He is to be thought of as the self-surpassing surpasser of all.[13]

Notes

1. In the usual studies of the forms of spirituality in different faiths, the goal of such a spiritual quest, namely, the understanding of the nature and essence of God, is taken as given. Usually this conception of the divine is a male-centered one. I would like to deal with the possibility of a more "feminist" understanding of the divine nature. The description of the spiritual quest of Āṇḍāl is a first step in this direction.

2. See, e.g., the discussion of Āṇḍāl's religious quest in S. N. Dasgupta, *A History of Indian Philosophy* (Varanasi: Motilal Banarasidass, 1975), vol. 3, chap. 17.

3. Edmund Husserl, *Ideas Towards a Pure Phenomenology and Phenomenological Philosophy* (The Hague: Martinus Nijhoff, 1983).

4. Charles Hartshorne and William Reese, *Philosophers Speak of God* (Chicago: University of Chicago Press, 1953).

5. Ibid.

6. The present interpretation of Āṇḍāl's work is a revised version of my "An Essay on the Tiruppāvai," *Journal of Religious Studies* 21 (1992).

7. Even such a scholarly work as that of S. N. Dasgupta does not give the dates of Āṇḍāl and Periāḻvār (*History of Indian Philosophy*, vol. 3).

8. For details, see Shri Rangaswamy Ramanuja Dasa, *Tiruppāvai*, Tamil Commentary (Madras: Alwar Amuda Nilayam, 1984). Subsequent references in the text are to this version.

9. The Tamil commentators of the *Tiruppāvai* interpret the metaphor of the drum as standing for the fourfold *puruṣārthas*. See Ramaswamy Ramanuja Dasa, *Tiruppāvai*, introduction.

10. For the idea of multiple forms of pursuit of the *puruṣārthas*, see R. Sundara Rajan, "Towards a Phenomenology of Forms of Life," in *The Quality of Life*, ed. Amlan Dutta and M. M. Agrawal (Shimla: Indian Institute of Advanced Study, 1992).

11. *Tiruppāvai*, at the symbolic level, is the representation of the ritual performed by the *gopīs* of Brindavan in the times of the incarnation of Kṛṣṇa. Legend has it that each one of the *gopīs* had her own distinctive and unique spiritual talent and need and that Kṛṣṇa appeared to each one of them in the form best suited to her. But Āṇḍāl now internalized all the *gopīs* in her song. With this poetic-philosophic internalization, the multiplicity of needs of the *gopīs* becomes the inner multiplicity within Āṇḍāl herself; each aspect of her total person demands fulfillment and perfection in the experience of the divine, and Kṛṣṇa appears as the one who alone can satisfy the whole of our personalities—in word, thought, deed, and emotion. He is the one in whom alone we can find the fullest response.

12. The Viśiṣṭādvaita tradition is perhaps, in its own way, a perfect expression at the abstract level of philosophy of the logic of complementarity. Thus, on the one hand, there is the demand of unity and identity represented by Advaita Vedānta, and on the other hand, the demand of difference represented by Dvaita Vedānta. By means of its doctrine of fellowship with the Lord, the difference is maintained but at the same time, because the Lord is seen as *antaryāmin* (inner presence), the "consubstantiality" of the soul with the Lord is also maintained.

13. The notion of the self-surpassing surpasser of all implies first of all that the Lord must be conceived of as "Person," for only persons with spiritual identities of their own can be said to transcend themselves. Second, insofar as humans too may be said to have a measure of such self-surpassing, there is a certain commensurability between the finite and the infinite. Third, this commensurability is to be seen in terms of the best or the noblest in us, namely, our creativity. Finally, within the divine economy itself we must now make a distinction between the divine essence, which is perfect and unchanging, and the variable states of actualization of that essence; in short, we must distinguish with regard to God, as with any being whatsoever, between essence, existence, and actuality. Essence is the nature of God; actuality is the concrete total manifestation of the essence; and existence is the concrete appearance of the Lord in some form or other.

In theological terms, we must distinguish between the *para* (Highest) and the *avatāra* (incarnational) forms of Nārāyaṇa.

Bibliography

Sources

Simha, S. L. N. *Tiruppavai of Goda*. Bombay: Anathachara Indological Research Institute, 1982.

Venkatachariar, Karapangadu. *Tiruppavai* (in Tamil). Madras: Alwar Amuda Nilayam, 1975.

Studies

All India Seminar on Āṇḍāl 1983. Madras: Sri Ramanuja Vedanta Centre, 1985.

Deheja, Vidya. *Antal and her path of love: Poems of woman saint from South India*. Albany: State University of New York Press, 1990.

Jagannathachariyar, C. *The Tiruppavai of Sri Āṇḍāl: Texual, Literary & Critical Study*. Madras: Arulmigu Parthasarathy Devasthanam, 1982.

Varadachari, K. C. *Alvars of South India*. Bombay: Bharatiya Vidya Bhavan, 1966.

8

Mīrābāī: The Rebel Saint

Braj Sinha

Mīrā Bāī has been acclaimed as the greatest woman saint-poet of the medieval times in northern India. She was a princess of Mewār, modern Udaipur in the northern state of Rajasthan.[1] Deeply steeped in her devotion for Lord Kṛṣṇa, Mīrā rebelled against the prevalent social and cultural norms by refusing to consummate her marriage to Prince Bhojarāj of Mewār, claiming that Lord Kṛṣṇa was her true love to whom she was eternally wedded in mind, body, and spirit.[2] She challenged the might of the ruling clan of Śisodiyās of Mewār by publicly proclaiming her love for Lord Kṛṣṇa. In reality her entire life was lived in a constant struggle against the patriarchal value structure of the feudal system of Rājpūts (the warrior caste) of Rajasthan.[3] The Śisodiyā clan was the most prominent political power that ruled the state of Mewār in Rajasthan during the fifteenth and sixteenth centuries. Infused with deep spiritual yearnings, even during her early childhood, Mīrā had come to dedicate herself to Lord Kṛṣṇa, whom she looked upon as her true Lord and on whom she poured all her loving devotion.[4]

Mīrā's devotion to Lord Kṛṣṇa is an epitome of intense emotional relationship that embodies the highest level of conjugal love. In her poems Kṛṣṇa appears not only as the Supreme Lord of the *Bhagavad Gītā* but also as the beloved One for whom she feels pangs of love so strong that they verge on ecstatic madness of human spirit seeking to be united with the Divine. Mīrā's Kṛṣṇa is her beloved Lord, separation from whom makes her heart yearn with the greatest urgency for union with Him. Her lyrical outbursts are only the cry of an agonized soul who, in each moment of separation, also experiences the intense ecstasy that this experience of pain and anticipation of joy that the union with Lord will bring.[5] Thus, her poems are imbued with direct, immediate, and intense emotional fervor that sets her apart from many other great saint-poets of medieval northern India, including Kabīr, Sūrdāsa, and Tulsīdāsa. Mīrā is without doubt one of the most significant expressions of medieval Hindu spirituality in North India, and hers is the most prominent female voice giving vent to the unflinching devotional aspirations focused on the person of Lord Kṛṣṇa, which, since Mīrā's times, have reverberated throughout northern India from Rajasthan to Bengal, including Maharashtra, Gujarat, Punjab, Uttar Pradesh, and Bihar.

Mīrā lived in an age marked by political uncertainty created by the expansionist mood of the Mughal empire ruling from Delhi and engaged in constant battle with the courageous and proud Rājpūt principalities of Rajasthan, as well as the internecine warfare and interstate vendetta that prevailed among various ruling Rājpūt princes of Rajasthan.[6] The clashes of Muslim and Hindu forces in the political arena were also reflected in the attendant clashes of ideas and values in both the social and the religious realm. In the religious arena Hinduism displayed a peculiar paradox. On the one hand, the developments of *saguṇa bhakti* that marked this period can only be identified as an attempt at the spiritual regeneration of Hinduism from within in a manner that tended to reinforce and solidify Hindu identity. There were also forces of reconciliation symbolized by the proponents of *nirguṇa bhakti*, which looked beyond the exclusive pale of Hindu orthodoxy and sought to bring together Hindu-Muslim religious ideas and spiritual aspirations in a creative synthesis. On the Muslim side, some Sūfi mystics of India were making significant contributions to Indian spirituality by incorporating ideas and ideals in their poetic and musical compositions informed by Hindu themes. On the other hand, many Hindu saints inspired by *nirguṇa bhakti* were offering a critique of institutional religiosity and orthodoxies of both Hindu and Muslim faith, extolling the masses to realize the principle of divine unity as the hallmark of deeper spiritual yearnings.[7]

In a significant way the two forms of Hindu responses, *saguṇa bhakti* and *nirguṇa bhakti*, were both externally inspired by the challenges of Islam and internally required by the spiritual degeneration that Hinduism had suffered during the early part of this millennium. The Hindu social system had become extremely rigid, strictly enforcing the *varṇa* system, which continued to perpetuate social and religious inequality. The idea of ritual and social pollution that proscribed intercaste commensality, especially between members of the higher *varṇa* and lower *varṇa* and also significantly enough even within the realm of the higher *varṇa* between different subgroups, had caused the Hindu social system to suffer a stagnation that needed a jolt from within to provide an impetus for spiritual regeneration. An initial attempt at regeneration of Hindu spirituality came from the famed Rāmānanda. Rāmānanda's reformist effort was directed toward the spiritual regeneration of Hinduism by challenging its ritual excessiveness and institutional inequities. This was continued by his disciples, including Kabīr, Dhannā, and Rāīdāsa, all of whom belonged to lowly untouchable castes and made very significant contributions to making Hinduism relevant to an expressive spirituality of the masses. Mīrā belonged to this galaxy of religious rebels who sought to transcend the boundaries of social rigidities and institutional religiosity by challenging the Hindu social structure.[8]

Mīrā: Affront to Patriarchal Values

To this tradition of spiritual regenerators Mīrā lent the lone female voice rebelling against ritualistic institutional religiosity and also the social and political structure that tried to stifle her quest for expressive spirituality outside the boundaries of the feudal patriarchal value system. The existing social and political structure denied this remarkable woman saint freedom of body and spirit by trying to confine her within the narrow precincts of the palace of the Rāṇā (king) of Chittor and by enforcing a rigid patriarchal value system. The Rāṇā of Chittor and his family sought to control Mīrā's body and spirit by proscribing her from getting out of the precincts of Rāṇā's palace to mingle with the common folks and itinerant saints engaged in expressive spirituality. Mīrā was censored and subjected to various abuses for even inviting these itinerant saints and seeking their company within the confines of the palace to engage in *satsang* with fellow seekers in the path of spirituality.[9]

The restrictions and reproaches that Mīrā was subjected to in the later years of her stay at Chittor were probably triggered by her initial refusal to renounce her *Vaiṣṇava bhakti* focused on the person of Kṛṣṇa in order to accept the royal cult of Śaiva and Śākta worship espoused by the members of the ruling Śisodiyā clan of Chittor.[10] Equally important is the fact that, at least in her own mind, Mīrā never seems to have accepted Prince Bhojarāj of Chittor, to whom she was married by her parental family reigning at Medatā, as her husband. In her mind she was eternally wedded to her own beloved of many births, Lord Kṛṣṇa; and she reportedly refused to consummate the earthly marriage to Prince Bhojarāj which was in accordance with the norms and customs of her own class and caste.[11] Had she accepted her husband Prince Bhojarāj as her Lord by matrimony and continued to worship Lord Kṛṣṇa in a conventional manner prescribed for upper-class Rājpūt women, she probably could have been spared the ordeal that she suffered for most of her adult life, during the period of her matrimony as well as widowhood after the death of her husband. But it was precisely her denial to accept any earthly husband and her refusal to renounce her love for Kṛṣṇa as her only Lord that caused anguish in her husband's family. Hence, Mīrā was relentlessly persecuted by her in-laws for her devotion, love, and commitment to her chosen beloved, Lord Kṛṣṇa, before whom she was not willing to accept any other Lord.

Thus, the ruling family of Chittor denied Mīrā not only the freedom of body but also her spiritual freedom by asking her to accept the royal cult of Chittor and to pursue a conventional form of religious worship. But Mīrā's rebellious spirit and unfaltering devotion to Lord Kṛṣṇa gave her spiritual strength and courage to endure all the pain and suffering that she sustained at the hands of those who despised her for her spiritual convictions and commitment. Mīrā was, for her love for Kṛṣṇa, willing to sacrifice anything, to bear the wrath of her husband, Prince Bhojarāj, and her brother-in-law, King Vikramājīt, to suffer the censure of her mother-in-law and sister-in-law, and to endure degrading experiences of encounter with many religious leaders of her time. Praise and blame did not matter to her (vv. 13, 18, 25, 33, 42). Nor did patriarchal social customs and norms. Mīra's deep-rooted distrust of the institutionally sanctioned religious notions and practices caused her to revolt against them and shocked the political and religious authority of her time. Her sustained and purposeful flouting of the dictates and wishes of successive Rāṇās of Chittor and other members of the ruling family brought down on Mīrā their vicious vendetta that even sought to physically eliminate her by attempting to poison her. There were attempts on her life by the Rāṇā Vikramājīt Singh and his stooges who reportedly tried to force her to drink from a cup of poison, sent to her a basket containing a venomous snake, and asked her to lie down on a bed of spikes (vv. 36–41). These attempts on her life did not succeed in silencing her songs, calling on her beloved Lord Kṛṣṇa. Like the proverbial incessant call of the rain bird (*papihā*) for the beloved (*piu*), they reverberated throughout the land of Rajasthan and beyond.

Mīrā: Challenge to the Misogynistic Stances of Medieval Bhaktas

Mīrā's exclusive devotion to Lord Kṛṣṇa and her pride in her womanhood, which found its ultimate expression in her exclusive love for Him alone, pitted her against not only the ruling Śisodiyā family of Chittor but also some leading religious personages and spiritual leaders of her time. Mīrā had particularly unpleasant experiences with the followers of the *Puṣṭi-mārga* propounded by Vallabhācārya, who seems to have been her contemporary.

The *Chaurasī Vaiṣṇavana Kī Vārtā* cites several of such encounters in which Vallabhācārya's disciples had snubbed this woman devotee of Lord Kṛṣṇa, precisely because she had declined to acknowledge the supremacy of Vallabhācārya as a great Vaiṣṇava teacher.[12] This text relates that Govind Dubey, who was a follower of *Puṣṭimārga*, was once staying at Mīrā's place engaging in religious discourses with Mīrā. Vallabhācārya did not approve of this and sent a messenger with a *śloka* (verse) reproaching Govind Dubey for this indiscretion. Govind Dubey immediately left Mīrā's company, despite her heartfelt pleadings. Rāmadāsa, another follower of *Puṣṭimārga*, was a priest at the temple of Lord Kṛṣṇa where Mīrā used to perform her worship. One day during a session of devotional singing, Rāmadāsa sang a *bhajan* (devotional song) composed by Vallabhācārya, who was called by his disciples *mahāpraphu* (the great lord). Mīrā's discerning mind did not accept Vallabhācārya as her mentor, and it seems that she was not overwhelmed by the devotional composition of the great *ācārya*. Mīrā is reported to have requested Rāmadāsa to sing another *bhajan* to the Lord. Rāmadās became extremely agitated and reprimanded her by saying: "Look O widowed woman! Who do you think this hymn was addressed to . . . ?" Angered at her disinclination to accept Vallabhācārya as her mentor and spiritual lord, Rāmadāsa left the palace saying: "I will not see your face again." From the same Vaiṣṇava source we also learn about another incident in which Mīrā was snubbed by one Krishnadās Adhikārī, another member of Vallabhācārya's *Puṣṭimārga* sect. On his way to Vṛndāvana from Dwārakā, Krishnadās Adhikārī arrived at Mīrā's place, where many other Vaiṣnava devotees had gathered. Mīrā offered her hospitality to Krishnadās and requested him to accept a gift of a few gold coins (*mohar*) to be taken to Vṛndāvana. Krishnadās declined the hospitality and gift of Mīrā by saying: "since you are not a servant of great lord (Vallabhācārya), I will not even touch your gift with my hands."

Another significant incident shows Mīrā's unwillingness to submit to the misogynistic oppression of her contemporaries. Jīva Goswāmī was a prominent member of Caitanya *sampradāya* (sect) residing at Vṛndāvana. After leaving Medatā, Mīrā's parental home state, Mīrā had visited Vṛndāvana on her way to Dwārakā. There she probably first went to meet Jīva Goswāmī, who was well known for his devotion to Lord Kṛṣṇa. It is reported that the famed Goswāmī declined to meet her, stating that he had taken a vow not to meet with women. Hearing this, Mīrā asked the messenger to tell the Goswāmī that she thought that in Vṛndāvana Lord Kṛṣṇa was the only male, that all others were *gopīs*, rejoicing in their love for Lord Kṛṣṇa, and that she was surprised to learn that there was another male in Vṛndāvana. This reproach indeed was quite educational for this famous teacher of Caitanya *sampradāya* (sect). Since Śrī Caitanya's days, the

Caitanya *sampradāya* had propagated a form of devotion called *parakiyā bhakti* in which devotees were asked to look at themselves as *gopīs*, womenfolk of Vṛndāvana during Kṛṣṇa's time, who were madly in love with Lord Kṛṣṇa, even though Lord Kṛṣṇa was not their wedded husband. Within the Caitanya tradition this form of devotion has been interpreted to mean that all human souls are female before Lord Kṛṣṇa, who is the only male principle in the world deserving devotees' total devotion. Mīrā's reproach to Jīva Goswāmī was a sharp reminder to him of this truth and probably also a jolt to his male ego. Unlike the arrogant followers of Vallabhācārya, Jīva Goswāmī was suitably impressed by Mīrā's reproach, came running to greet her, and offered her hospitality at Vṛndāvana for some time.[13]

While there is ample evidence of Mīrā having spurned any sectarian allegiance, many of the sectarian movements of the medieval Hinduism tried to incorporate her into their fold, Caitanya *sampradāya* being no exception.[14] Among the followers of Caitanya it is believed that Mīrā was initiated into Caitanya *sampradāya* by Jīva Goswāmī, who was her guru.

These incidents raise the question of why Mīrā was mistreated by her contemporaries and compatriots of the Vaiṣṇava faith. Probably part of the answer lies in her refusal to accept any of the established teachers (*ācārya*) such as Vallabhācārya as her mentor and guru. This may have been a pardonable sin for there were other contemporary leaders of medieval *bhakti* movements who maintained somewhat independent religious stances. But what seems to be particularly problematic for many of the leading religious personages and leaders was the fact that such a stand was being taken by a woman—and a widow at that! Had Mīrā accepted the subservient role deemed appropriate for a woman devotee by accepting the superiority and spiritual lordship of any of the Vaiṣṇava *ācāryas* of her time, she probably would have been forgiven for her various transgressions of established social and religious norms. Her distinctively independent stance and her ability to carve out an unique niche within the religious psyche of the populace were seen as an affront to the male hegemony in the realm of the Vaiṣṇava *bhakti* movement of her times. Many spiritual seekers (*sādhūs*) naturally gravitated to Mīrā as a prominent and vocal spokesperson for an intimate and unmediated devotional relationship with God.

The fact that many followers of Vaiṣṇava and non-Vaiṣṇava sects subsequently tried to claim Mīrā for their sectarian traditions is a testimony to her spiritual accomplishments and the reverence that she commanded in various quarters of medieval *bhakti* movement. As the subsequent history of *bhakti* movement in northern India was to show, many spiritual leaders acknowledged and praised the depth of her devotion and the unsurpassed heights of her spiritual accomplishments.[15]

The Appropriation of Mīrā: A Patriarchal Strategy

Despite Mīrā's refusal to confine herself to any specific spiritual lineage or to concede allegiance to any guru, attempts to put the stamp of an established religious *sampradāya* (sect) or guru on her continued in the period immediately following her life. The most prevalent mode of such appropriation was the composition of devotional hymns in Mīrā's name that tried to link her with one or another spiritual teacher in a subservient way. Even the followers of Tulsīdāsa, the celebrated devotee of Lord Rāma and probably the most powerful influence on the popular religiosity in the northern India, have not lagged behind in this enterprise. Hagiographic accounts of Tulsīdāsa's life and teachings claim that Mīrā had corresponded with Tulsīdāsa at a crucial stage in her life.[16] It is stated that Mīrā, frustrated with various impediments to her devotion to Lord Kṛṣṇa put forth by her husband's family at Mewār, sought advice from Tulsīdāsa as to the right course of action. Tulsīdāsa supposedly responded to her by composing a *pada* (verse) in which he advised her to renounce her family, which was a stumbling block in her pursuit of devotion to God. Scholars, however, hold that the verses attributed to Mīrā that she is supposed to have sent to Tulsīdāsa seeking his advice are spurious. Further, close examination of chronology renders such hagiographic accounts highly improbable.[17] The sectarian traditions associated with Tulsīdāsa, however, have continued to affirm the authenticity of this legend.

The history of the *bhakti* movement during the medieval period in North India is replete with such obstinate and dogged effort to deny independence and freedom of spirit to the most prominent female spiritual leader of this period. The account described above denies Mīrā the dignity of independently making a decision to renounce her in-laws and the prestige of the imperial palace, which stood in the way of her devotion to Lord Kṛṣṇa. It is intriguing to note that the above incidence refers to a mature Mīrā, a woman of iron will and perseverance who had incessantly struggled against the oppressive treatment meted out to her by her in-laws, had successfully endured persecution at the hands of successive Rāṇās of Mewār for decades, and had acquired wide acclaim and reputation for her one-pointed devotion to Lord Kṛṣṇa. By this time her spiritual accomplishments and love for Lord Kṛṣṇa had gained for her fame in her own right, and many devotees and prominent spiritual seekers from far and wide were converging to Mewār to seek her inspirational company. It is this Mīrā who commanded deepest respect from the populace and who was the source of inspiration to a large number of spiritual seekers.

The self-serving sectarian attempts to incorporate Mīrā into different groups and to deny her legitimate status as an independent religious figure was not confined to the proponents of *saguṇa bhakti.* Even the proponents of *nirguṇa bhakti* attempted to subject Mīrā to a secondary status by declaring her to be a disciple of Sant Rāīdāsa or Rohidāsa, a direct disciple of Kabīr, and belonging to the untouchable caste of leatherworkers (*chamār*).[18] Given Mīrā's iconoclastic tendencies, it is quite probable that she would have associated in *satsang* (religious congregation) even with members of the untouchable castes, and definitely with someone of the status of Rāīdāsa. Rāīdāsa, like Kabīr, Senā, and Dhannā, was a member of the low caste and a follower of Rāmānanda, who had struck at the very core of Brāhmanic orthodoxy by declaring that caste distinctions were irrelevant, and that in the eyes of God all devotees were equal. These leading figures, including Rāīdāsa, not only challenged the religious hegemony of Brahmins and the caste hierarchies that had caused severe fissures in the Hindu social fabric but also had protested against prevalent modes of institutional religiosity and had tried to bring about a spiritual regeneration of Hinduism by giving Upaniṣadic/Vedāntic spiritual wisdom a popular expression accessible to common people. The movement specifically known as *sant mat* had a growing following during Mīrā's lifetime, and, like many other contemporary streams of *bhakti* movement, found its place in Mīrā's expansive spiritual horizon, which was unrestricted by any sectarian allegiance.

Mīrā spurned the institutional inequity of caste hierarchy by stating that a person is to be known not by his or her caste but by personal worth, devotion to God being the most appropriate index of a person's worth. On this point one might concede that Mīrā was influenced by the teachings of Rāīdāsa, but she also incorporated many themes and ideas from varied sources of Hindu spirituality, ancient and contemporary. Any attempt, however, to link her with Rāīdāsa in a *guru–śisya* (teacher–disciple) relationship or to place her within the *sant sampradāya* does an injustice to Mīrā's independence.

Another difficulty for Mīrā was prejudice against a woman, especially a widowed one who had renounced and rejected caste, class, and family traditions to pursue her spiritual goals in response to the call of Lord Kṛṣṇa. Male religious leaders could not deny the authenticity of her devotion and the courage of her convictions. What they needed was somehow to sanctify Mīrā, to exorcise her of her independence and freedom, to purify her of her womanhood, and thus to make her palpable. To find a place for Mīrā within the mainstream of officially sanctioned religion, male leaders continually tried to subjugate her to one or another religious teacher or the *sampradāya.* Yet Mīrā defied all categories, transcended all boundaries; with a free spirit, a discerning mind, and an open heart, she sought spiritual inspiration, wisdom, and comfort from all sources available to her. But she never totally committed herself to any earthly being, whether her husband, a Rāṇā of Mewār, or a spiritual mentor. Fully saturated with her love for Lord Kṛṣṇa, completely immersed in her devotion for her only Lord, to whom she was committed in body, mind, and spirit, she was both an enigma and a challenge to the religious teachers and lineages of her time.

Mīrā's Devotion and the Love of the "Absence"

Mīrā's unorthodoxy and courage of spirit are reflected also in the *bhakti* paradigm that emerges out of her devotional songs to Lord Kṛṣṇa. From her songs it is evident that she is totally enamored with Lord Kṛṣṇa, whom she considered to be her only and truly beloved Lord. Her truly beloved Lord was also her truly wedded husband, with whom she had had a relationship since ancient times that went back to many previous lives. Her devotion to Kṛṣṇa was that of a loving wife who was willing to sacrifice anything and everything for her beloved husband. So immersed was she in this love that she forgot all the socially sanctioned norms governing a woman's devotion to God. She was not content with offering her prayers in a temple within the palace of the Rāṇā of Mewār, nor did she find fulfillment in the endless cycle of institutionally approved, ritualistic worship in which a Hindu woman was supposed to be engaged in the confines of the courtyard of the family dwelling. Intoxicated with her love for Lord Kṛṣṇa, she broke loose from the traditional expressions of feminine spirituality and boldly charted her own course of loving devotion to Kṛṣṇa. She willingly and purposely crossed the threshold of the palace and the confines of the courtyard to proclaim to the world the news that Kṛṣṇa was her only love. Crazed with her longing for Kṛṣṇa, she announced her love to the world in agonizing songs and ecstatic dances for the world to witness. She did not want to keep her love for Kṛṣṇa concealed from the world; her public renderings of love songs to Kṛṣṇa and the tinkling of dancing bells on her anklets are pictures of total defiance of the worldly norms and conventional religiosity that had governed Hindu women's devotion in Mīrā's time (vv. 7, 9, 13–14, 17–22, 24, 26, etc.).

It was not, however, public singing and dancing expressing one's love for Lord Kṛṣṇa that were problematic; nor giving vent to one's passionate love and unsatiable longing for Kṛṣṇa that would have created a social flutter and evoked censure. Indeed, Mīrā was not the only one, and definitely not the first one, to indulge in such luxuriating devotional practices. She was in the good company of several illustrious devotees of medieval times, including Narsimha Mehtā, Candīdāsa, Vidyāpati, and Caitanya. They were the forerunners, the trendsetters of unorthodox expressions of a parallel spirituality that did not find itself constrained by conventional religiosity and institutional affiliations. They celebrated passionate love for God and rejoiced in the expression of conjugal love of the human soul for God. In many cases they flouted the institutional gender taboos and caste hierarchies. Narsimha Mehtā, a Brahmin from Gujarat, reportedly sang and danced expressing his love for Lord Kṛṣṇa, his devotional singing and dancing knowing no barriers of caste and gender among his audience. Such was also the case with Caitanya in Bengal, whose disciples formed devotional singing groups that marched through the streets of his hometown in procession singing and dancing in frenzy, attracting a mass of people by their devotional outpourings of love for Lord Kṛṣṇa. Candīdāsa in Bengal and Vidyāpati in the Mithila region of Bihar luxuriated in an expansive, emotive mood that employed erotic imagery to capture the depth and intensity of love of *gopīs* of Vṛṇdāvana for Kṛṣṇa. *Gopīs* symbolized the human soul seeking fulfillment in sensual passion and love directed toward Kṛṣṇa.

Mīrā differed from all these eminent devotees of Kṛṣṇa in one important respect. Mīrā was a woman, and she belonged to the powerful ruling family of the Mewār. In this lies the true source of both the challenge and the power of Mīrā's Kṛṣṇa *bhakti.* It captures the imagination of those who understand and appreciate the originality and depth of emotional richness that her songs express. Other medieval Kṛṣṇa poets and devotees composed or sang beautiful hymns that gave expression to human soul's longing for Kṛṣṇa's love. But their songs, though rich in imagery and full of emotional depths, were products of powerful imaginative flights in which they appropriated a female *persona* by identifying themselves with the *gopīs* of Vṛṇdāvana or by assuming the personality of Rādhā. For them, *gopīs* of Vṛṇdāvana or Rādhā symbolized the human soul seen as a feminine principle seeking its fulfillment in conjugal love for Lord Kṛṣṇa, the only and true male principle. Mīrā, on the other hand, speaks from the depth of her own soul, moved by her own yearnings. She does not need to identify with the *gopīs* of the Vṛṇdāvana or Rādhā; she does not need the power of imagination to capture love and pangs of the heart; her poems embody her own feelings of love for Kṛṣṇa in a very direct way and her own experience of the heart. She feels this love and yearning in the very depths of her soul, in her bones and marrow, with her entire being. In a way she is a *gopī;* she is the Rādhā.

Her intense love for Lord Kṛṣṇa and her willingness to proclaim it pitted her against the religious and political authorities of her age. It was acceptable for a male devotee such as Narsimha Mehtā or Caitanya to sing and dance in ecstasy proclaiming passionate conjugal love for Kṛṣṇa. Their assumed female identity, and therefore their conjugal love for Kṛṣṇa, did not threaten the social and familial structure that demanded from women exclusive love and subjugation to their earthy lords, their husbands. Male devotees such as Caitanya and his followers may even have evoked appreciation and admiration for their willingness to forsake their families and renounce their wives for the love of Kṛṣṇa. But this could not be tolerated in a woman, however authentic and genuine her love for Kṛṣṇa might be, for a woman could not and must not love anyone apart from her wedded husband. A woman could have devotion to Kṛṣṇa, but not love for Kṛṣṇa. In Mīrā's mind there was no conflict, for she was indeed wedded to Kṛṣṇa, before whom she was not willing to accept any other Lord.

The patriarchal value structure built on the principle of the inequality of genders does not simply ask for the physical submission of a woman's body but demands subjugation of her heart and spirit as well. It may be possible for a married woman to feel an emotional affinity for a man other than her husband, but she must bury that deep within the recesses of her heart so that no shame is brought to the *kula* (family). Mīrā, however, was not only in love with Kṛṣṇa; she loved Him so dearly and intensely that she could not keep this secret from the world. Thus she brought shame to the *kula* (family) and so was declared to be *kulanāsī* (destroyer of the family) (vv. 35–38, 40, 42). Mīrā's sin was to challenge the very foundation of a patriarchal value system by declaring and rejoicing in her love for Kṛṣṇa rather than her husband. Thus, intensity of emotion and loving devotion patterned on conjugal love of *gopīs* for Kṛṣṇa, which was seen as testimony of great devotion of Narasimha Mehtā and Caitanya, became the cause of sustained ridicule, abuse, and persecution of Mīrā. Mīrā, however, was not deterred by this abuse and persecution and remained steadfast in her loving devotion to Lord Kṛṣṇa, flouting all socially sanctioned norms and bravely challenging the authority of the Śisodiyā clan and the might of the Rāṇā of Mewār.[19]

The conjugal love for Kṛṣṇa that Mīrā professed and practiced was also distinctively different in its approach and orientation from that of Jayadeva, Vidyāpati and Candidāsa, the other celebrated poets who had earlier composed love songs dedicated to Kṛṣṇa.[20] These love songs, in which the amorous sport of Rādhā and Kṛṣṇa are portrayed with eroticism, are markedly different from Mīrā's love songs for Kṛṣṇa. Mīrā's poems are distinctively devotional without any element of eroticism. For Mīrā, Kṛṣṇa remained the Supreme Lord, Creator, Sustainer, and Deliverer from the world process (*samsāra*) (vv. 1–5, 31, 48, 50, 61–63, 96, 101, 106, 109, 113, 117, 128, 131, 133–41, etc.). She called Kṛṣṇa her only Lord and truly wedded husband, but this did not compromise the majesty, grandeur, and "wholly other" character of Kṛṣṇa as the Lord of the world union. Mīrā's conjugal love for Kṛṣṇa is expressed in a language that is well within the bounds of a devotional paradigm that preserves the personhood and autonomy of both the Divine and the devotee and thus provides a basis for intimate and immediate emotional affinity.[21]

Mīrā speaks about being united with Lord Kṛṣṇa in wedlock. The wedding she refers to takes place in a dream (v. 27), and the wedding is the fulfillment of a dream that she had entertained since her childhood.[22] The fact that this union takes place in a dream—in other words never translates into a reality in her life—gives a totally different dimension to Mīrā's love for Kṛṣṇa. It is the love of a woman for her beloved, who, while never absent from her heart, is at the same time never present. It is the presence of this "absence" (*viraha*) that accounts for Mīrā's lifelong quest for Kṛṣṇa; wanting to overcome her separation from Kṛṣṇa, she earnestly seeks eternal union with Him. It is the love of this "absence" that gives meaning and significance to her pain, which she finds both sweet and unbearable. Her love for Kṛṣṇa is tinged with a pain, a throbbing of the heart, the pang that the soul feels deeply and intimately. But it is a pain that Mīrā does not shun, for her pain is surely the sign of her unfathomable and profound love for Kṛṣṇa, which never lets her forget her beloved.

In Mīrā's formulation, conjugal love and the attendant feeling of pain at separation from the Lord are analogous to the relationship between sun and the sun-rays (v. 114). Indeed, it is a relationship of ultimate affinity and fundamental unity of the human soul and the Divine. But the human soul retains its distinctive identity in separation from its ultimate source, to which it wants to return to be reunited. Conscious of this separation, the human soul is willing to sacrifice all worldly relationships as an offering to the Lord, with whom it seeks its reunion. Mīrā, thus, like the *gopīs* of the purāṇic literature, makes an offering of all that she has—body, mind, and soul—totally dedicating herself to her beloved Kṛṣṇa with whom she has had an ancient love relationship going beyond the present birth. It is for this old love, love for the Lord that she has entertained in many previous lives, that she is willing to forsake all that she has. Every moment of her life is lived precisely in memory of this old love, which is her precious possession and for which she is willing to pay any price (vv. 17, 20, 22, 42, 59–60, 80, 101, 104, 106, 123, 129, 150–51).

The price that Mīrā pays most fervently is the price of total consummation in the experience of constant feeling of separation and the pain that ensues from this separation. In a sense it is this all-consuming pain rather than a sense of erotic love and passion that has besieged her body and soul. To love is to suffer this pain. It is the pain that only one who has suffered in love can know. There are no physical symptoms of this pain; there is no injury to the body; and there is no external indication. But, it is a pain that permeates one's entire being, that seeps through every pore of one's body and bleeds one's heart. The irony is that no one can see it, no one can know it, and no one can understand it except the one who has endured it. The physicians of the world may try in vain to diagnose Mīrā's ailment by gauging the pulse, but they are never able to ascertain the cause of the pain. Lord Kṛṣṇa alone knows the cause of her pain; for it is the pain of separation from Him that has seized her heart. Life without Kṛṣṇa cannot be endured; the pain of separation from Him is unbearable; there is no joy without the Lord (vv. 66–76, 83–92, 94–104, 107–8, 125, etc.).

A significant portion of Mīrā's poetry is colored by this intense feeling of pain caused by the presence of an "absence" that has gripped her entire being. Her depiction of this deeply felt pain at the separation from the beloved Lord is rich in its imagery and at the same time expresses in a very intimate way the physicality of this pain. But the agonizing physicality and subjectivity of this personally felt pain emanating from her devotion to Kṛṣṇa must be seen in the context of Mīrā's overall orientation as a devotee *par excellence* who is seeking union with the Lord. Mīrā's love, though expressed in a physical and embodied fashion, is fundamentally spiritual in its character, because its subject matter is God. This holds true also for the pain, which, though she feels in a very acute manner its physicality, is ultimately spiritual in its orientation. It is precisely the emergent awareness of the original separation of the soul from God that infuses the soul with an acute sense of anxiety and desire to become united with God. Mīrā's overwhelming experience of this pain and her lifelong quest for union with her Lord also suggest the human soul's total dependence on God's grace for realizing the ultimate union with the Divine. For Mīrā, constant seeking, the ongoing quest, incessant searching are what the human soul can do. Transforming this seeking into a unitive experience in which one ultimately loses oneself in the joy and bliss of an eternal communion with the Divine is God's making; it is a gift, a favor that is both spiritually fulfilling and personally liberative (vv. 114, 116–17, 119, 142–44, 146, 148–51, etc.).

Notes

1. It is difficult to construe a systematic and reliable account of Mīrābāī's life. Historians and scholars have widely diverged in their assessment of exact dates and events pertaining to her life. Hindi critical scholarship generally accepts 1498 C.E. as the year of her birth and places her death sometime during 1546 C.E. All references to Mīrā's poems by verse numbers are from *Mīrānbāī Kī Padāwalī*, ed. Acharya Parshuram Chaturvedi.

2. Scholars disagree on whether Mīrā's marriage to prince Bhojarāj was a happy one.

Prince Bhojarāj died sometime in the year 1527, and the marriage was childless. Mīrā has referred to herself as a virgin in at least two verses (51 and 77).

3. This aspect of Mīrābāī's life is well reflected in many of her poems, notably vv. 9, 13, 18, 24, 29–30, 32–42, and so on. For further confirmation of this being an important element in people's perception of the life and purpose of Mīrā, at least as it is preserved in the legends and memory of common folks, see Parita Mukta, *Upholding the Common Life*. This fine piece of ethnological research, based on extensive fieldwork in Rājasthān, came to my attention after I had completed the manuscript of the present work.

4. Acharya Parshuran Chaturvedi, *Mīrānbāī Kī Padāwalī*, 19; Desharaj Singh Bhati, *Mīrābāī Aur Unakī Padāwali*, 30; Bhagavandas Tiwari, *Mīrān Kā Kāvya*, 34.

5. This genre of devotionalism in Hindu literature, in which the devotee relates to the Lord as the beloved separation from whom causes feelings of intense pain and desire to be reunited with Him, has been called *viraha bhakti*. *Nārada Bhakti Sūtra* has included this as one of the eleven forms of attachment to the Lord. It constitutes transcendental love (*parama prema*) felt by the devotee toward the Lord (see *Nārada Bhakti Sūtra* 82). It is equally important to recognize that Hindu devotional literature has acknowledged that even the feeling of pain in the devotee is ultimately to be seen as a form of joy that permeates the devotee's entire being as the experience of pangs of love for the Lord (*Bhakti Rasāyana* 3–5).

6. Tiwari, *Mīrān Kā Kāvya*, 16–17.

7. Ibid.

8. Ibid., 18.

9. *For Love of The Dark One: Songs of Mirabai*, trans. Andrew Schelling (Boston: Shambala, 1993) 18–19; Tiwari, *Mīrān Kā Kāvya*, 24.

10. In his commentary on *Bhaktamāl*, probably written by Nābhādāsa sometime in the latter part of the sixteenth century, Priyadāsa mentions the incidence in which Mīrā's mother-in-law asked Mīrā to worship the Goddess (Devi), but Mīrā declined. See Bhati, *Mīrābāī Aur Unakī Padāwali*, 31; also pada 30.

11. See n. 13 below.

12. *Chaurāsī Vaiṣṇavan Kī Vārtā*, a sectarian text belonging to the *Puṣṭimārga* of the Vallabha *sampradāya*, was written by Goswāmī Gokulanātha during the later part of the seventeenth century. Goswāmī Gokulanātha's disciple Harīrāī wrote a commentary on the original *vārtā*. Three specific incidents involving Mīrā and the followers of *Puṣṭimārga* of Vallabhācārya are recorded in the *vārtā*. For further detail, see *Chaurāsī Vaiṣṇavan Kī Vārtā*, ed. Dwarkadas Parikh (Mathura: Śri Bajarang Pustakalay, 1970).

13. The incident is narrated by Priyādāsa in his commentary on *Bhaktamāl* of Nābhādāsa. Nāgaridāsa also has mentioned this incident (see *Bhaktamāl Satīk* [Lucknow: Nawalkishore Press, 1940] 247).

14. See Chaturvedi, *Mīrānbāī Kī Padāwalī*, 221.

15. Tiwari, *Mīrān Kā Kāvya*, 221.

16. Chaturvedi, *Mīrānbāī Kī Padāwalī*, 212ff.; also Tiwari, *Mīrān Kā Kāvya*, 38.

17. Tiwari, *Mīrān Kā Kāvya*, 38.

18. A few verses, e.g., 23, 153, 193, as well as many other verses attributed to Mīrā in the popular legend make reference to Raīdāsa as Mīrā's teacher. Their popularity, especially among the followers of Raīdāsa belonging to the untouchable caste of *chamārs* (leatherworkers), has been the basis for the suggestion that at least in the mind of the

populace Mīrā was a direct disciple of Sant Rāīdāsa. See Parita Mukta, *Upholding the Common Life,* 79ff. But scholars have challenged the validity of such claims, because historical evidence places Rāīdāsa's time period at least fifty years before Mīrā's birth. See Chaturvedi, *Mīrānbāī Kī Padāwalī*, 223.

19. See Mukta, *Upholding the Common Life,* 115ff.

20. Jayadeva, Vidyāpati, and Caṇḍīdāsa excelled in composing love songs dedicated to Lord Kṛṣṇa in which they all seem to profess *kāntāsakti,* a form of *bhakti* in which the devotee looks at himself as a woman and the Lord as the man. This form of devotion has been recognized in the classical formulation of Hindu devotionalsim in the *Nārada Bhakti Sūtra.* What distinguishes the love songs of these poets from that of Mīrā is precisely the preponderance of erotic imagery in their poems, which is generally absent from Mīrā's devotional songs.

21. A. J. Alston, *The Devotional Poems of Mīrābāī,* 20.

22. Verse 100 mentions Mīrā's childhood love for Kṛṣṇa. There are popular legends stating that even as a child Mīrā always thought of herself as a bride of Kṛṣṇa. See Desharaj Singh Bhati, *Mīrābāī Aur Unakī Padāwali,* 30; Chaturvedi, *Mīrānbāī Kī Padāwalī*, 19; Mukta, *Upholding the Common Life,* 117ff.; Tiwari, *Mīrān Kā Kāvya,* 34.

Bibliography

Sources

Alston, A. J. *The Devotional Poems of Mīrābāī.* Delhi: Motilal Banarsidass, 1980.
Bhati, Desharaj Singh. *Mīrābāī Aur Unakī Padāwali.* Delhi: Ashok Prakashan, 1995.
Chaturvedi, Acharya Parshuram, ed. *Mīrānbāī Kī Padāwalī*. Prayag: Hindi Sahitya Sammelan, 1993.
Schelling, Andrew, trans. *For Love of The Dark One: Songs of Mirabai.* Boston: Shambala, 1993.

Studies

Mukta, Parita. *Upholding the Common Life: The Community of Mīrābāī.* Delhi: Oxford University Press, 1994.
Pande, Susmita. *Medieval Bhakti Movement.* Meerut: Kusumajali Prakashan, 1989.
Shabanam, Padmāvate. *Mīrān: Ek Adhyayan.* Benaras: Lok Sevak Prakashan, 1951.
Tiwari, Bhagavandas. *Mīrān Kā Kāvya.* Allahabad: Sahitya Bhawan Private, 1990.

Part Two

THE SPIRITUALITIES OF THE PURĀṆAS, ĀGAMAS, AND TANTRA

9

Purāṇic Spirituality

GIORGIO BONAZZOLI

THE PURĀṆAS ARE ON A SMALL SCALE what Hinduism is at large: they contain a wide range of doctrines and paths of realization, some of them barely in harmony with one another and in a few instances even apparently contradictory. The range of time and space in which they developed is so vast that trying to make a brief summary of all their teachings would be unfair to the real nature of the Purāṇic message. We shall be satisfied, then, with presenting only a few general trends of this anonymous literature, traditionally ascribed to Vyāsa Kṛṣṇa Dvaipāyana and his disciples.

It has to be strongly emphasized from the outset that the Purāṇic message is not something belonging to the past or referred to in ancient sacred texts only. It is, rather, the living guide for the average Hindu of the modern age, at least in the sense that whatever the average Hindu does nowadays in any field of life is based on the Purāṇic prescriptions and is performed in the light of the Purāṇic ideas. This statement is valid even if one is totally unaware of the Purāṇic roots of one's behavior and beliefs. The spirit of the Purāṇas, indeed, pervades even modern India more than it is usually realized. Their perusal, then, puts us in contact with a living tradition, even as they offer valid material for understanding the historical development of Indian culture from ancient times. The Purāṇas, indeed, constitute one of the links between the past and the present, so that their study is somewhat halfway between a peep into the traditional roots of Indian culture as one would expect from reading ancient texts and a fieldwork, as if the Purāṇas were reports on the spiritual content of modern life. It is important to keep in mind this fact if we do not want to be puzzled by the continuing fluctuations and instability of the texts we are going to study.

The word *purāṇa*, which means "old" or "ancient," generally denotes a class of eighteen works, sometimes referred to as *Mahāpurāṇas,* or major

Purāṇas, to distinguish them from a series of eighteen other similar works called *Upapurāṇas,* or minor Purāṇas. The names of the eighteen *Mahāpurāṇas* (from now on designated simply as Purāṇas) are *Brahma*, *Padma*, *Viṣṇu*, *Śiva* (sometimes substituted with *Vāyu*), *Bhāgavata*, *Nāradīya*, *Mārkaṇḍeya*, *Garuḍa*, *Agni*, *Bhaviṣya*, *Brahmavaivarta*, *Liṅga*, *Varāha*, *Skanda*, *Vāmana*, *Kūrma*, *Matsya*, and *Brahmāṇḍa* (see *Vi* III.6). According to a common definition available in the Purāṇas themselves, they should deal with five topics (*pañcalaṣaṇa*),[1] but they in fact deal with many more subjects than these five.

The Purāṇas do not form a unified class of works; they belong neither to one period of time nor to one cultural and geographical area. In fact, only in a few cases is it possible to fix a date and a place for a Purāṇa, although it is a rather common belief among Purāṇic scholars that the bulk of the present corpus of Purāṇas was compiled in the Gupta and post-Gupta periods, namely, between the second and tenth centuries C.E. The text of eighteen Purāṇas, as it is available today, is only a remnant of a huge literature of similar texts collated down the centuries in different places, continuously taking new shape under the influence and needs of different people and times. The Purāṇic authors more than once tried to fix a Purāṇic canon along the centuries to stop the continuous floating of the text but without lasting or even appreciable results. On the other hand, the claim that the Purāṇic stories or subjects are linked with the hoary past through a long tradition (*paramparā*) of famous persons of ancient times is also common. Even more, the Purāṇic authors clearly affirm in many places that what is reported in the Purāṇas is linked to God Himself as a revelation. The Purāṇas, consequently, propose themselves as religious and authoritative texts and as an expansion of the Vedas or even the Vedas of the present time, meant for the common person as well as for the *śūdras*, that is, the fourth caste, for women and bad brahmins, who are not allowed to read or listen to the original ones. The Purāṇas, therefore, can authoritatively instruct people and claim respect and obedience, even if it is commonly accepted that their authority is not independent of the Vedas.

The style of writing in the Purāṇas is popular but far from simple. It is rather a very refined way of presenting doctrines through narrations, that is, *kathās*.[2] A narrative in the Purāṇas can reproduce or adapt a previous myth or can even give origin to it. The narration can be an illustrative story, a kind of life of saints, or simply a recreative account. More frequently, however, a narration is a model proposed to the listeners to elucidate a cultic or doctrinal message or to inculcate the practice of moral and religious precepts. The Purāṇic authors and their followers were, then, people who use narrations as a common means of conveying their philosophy, their religion, their moral teachings, their beliefs, and even scientific or secular subjects such as geography, medicine, and so on.

The Purāṇas, then, are molded by the narrations, which have an authoritative impact on their listeners even nowadays. A narration, indeed, whether it takes the hearers back to the origins or attracts them toward the future, is a revelation of the Lord Himself transmitted and duly adapted down the centuries to fit into the needs of a specific people, time, and place. The Purāṇas, therefore, contain a spirituality modeled on, or adapted by means of, narrations.

For the purpose of this essay the wide-ranging topics of the Purāṇas are subsumed under three main headings: (1) the presuppositions of the spiritual message of the Purāṇas; (2) the basic doctrines of this message; and (3) the means of attaining spiritual life in accordance with one's needs and abilities.

Presuppositions

An Ideal of Fullness: Bhukti and Mukti

It has been pointed out that the combination of the ideal of a "householder's way of life leading to the enjoyment of worldly pleasure" (*bhukti*) with the ideal "of renunciation proper to the life of a recluse" was "perfected by the Bhāgavatas in the form of *bhuktimuktipradam*,"[3] namely, that which confers *bhukti* (enjoyment) and *mukti* (release). Such an ideal of *bhukti* and *mukti*, however, implies much more than that. *Bhukti* in the Purāṇas is surely more inclusive than a "householder's way of life" and is usually less philosophical than a mere "enjoyment of the fruits of *karman*" (i.e., one's actions). The Purāṇas, indeed, besides promising to their reciters or listeners sons, absence of diseases, science, luck, glory, removal of fear and sins, similarity to divine beings, claim also to confer the fulfillment of all desires, however difficult to reach they might be.[4] *Bhukti*, therefore, is any kind of enjoyment on this earth (*iha*) and in heaven (*amutra*) and is overcome or completed by *mukti*, the final release from rebirth or, in a more basic understanding, the perpetual union with the Lord. So the Purāṇic ideal is a program of fullness (*sarva*, *A* 23.1). An ordinary person passes his or her life intent on carrying out the *trivarga*, or the three human pursuits, that is, accomplishing his physical and emotional needs (*kāma*), his social, economic, and political obligations (*artha*) and his duties (*dharma*), as an individual, a family man, and a caste man. Moreover, he will always have to aim at attaining his final realization—namely, *mokṣa*—which, according to the Purāṇas, can be realized even without going to the forest, by simply remaining at home and being engaged in one's duties pertaining to one's daily life.[5]

The Purāṇas cater to the needs of every person throughout the course of his or her life. If one desires *bhukti*, one will find in the Purāṇas the means for realizing it; and if one wants *mukti*, one will also find help in them and means to reach it.[6] The ideal of *bhukti-mukti*, therefore, is neither a disembodied spiritualism nor a refined hedonism; but rather a "holistic" realism. Humanity is in a concrete situation of development, but is on the way toward its final realization. The Purāṇas are there to help humans in the measure he needs and as he desires, but they encourage him to proceed ahead in full earnestness.

The ideal of *bhukti-mukti* touches the very roots of the Purāṇic message, which is concerned with the whole person, because it teaches harmony in all aspects of behavior, in a balanced bipolarity of the human and the divine, the temporal and the a-temporal, of here and there, of material and spiritual, of worldiness and renunciation, and so on. This message of "totality" oscillates continuously between the two mentioned poles and harmonizes them, putting them always either in reciprocal relation, or parallel, or in subordination to one another or mutually explanatory. The Purāṇas, indeed, never try to make of the two one; they stress one over the other at times, for the sake of making it stand out clearly. It is a characteristic process of Indian thought that the topic to be praised is in turn considered superior to all the others. It is not meant to be exclusivistic because different possible combinations of the two poles are left to the choice of the single individuals.

A person imbued with Purāṇic mentality, then, tends always toward the highest, the *mokṣa*, or the immersion in the Supreme and yet is always fully merged in worldly life wholly integrated in one and harmonized with everything.

Pluralism

The word "pluralism" is here used to describe a peculiar attitude of the Purāṇas that makes them incorporate different ways of conceiving life, different approaches to reality, different degrees of evolution, doctrines, morals, and the like. As stated above, these are all blended into a harmonious whole, allowing each element to preserve its peculiar significance. This assimilation or integration takes place continuously but smoothly, leading each element to combine with all the others. The average Indian's understanding of spirituality, one may say, is the result of such a Purāṇic attitude.

Gaṇeśa

Arjuna's Penance

It is a common opinion among scholars that the Purāṇas are sectarian. Such a statement does not do justice to the real nature of the Purāṇas as a whole and is not in tune with the general Purāṇic attitude we have just pointed out, namely, that while describing something, the Purāṇas, like the average Indian, tend to exalt it above all to the point that everything else becomes subordinate to it. This attitude is so constant in all the Purāṇas that what has been considered subordinate in a previous description can become predominant in the immediately following one. The resulting "contradictions" do not bother the authors; rather, they are not considered as such. This attitude is the key to understanding the whole Purāṇic message and is, in its turn, based on the soundest Indian tradition. So when a Purāṇa insists on the greatness of Śiva, for instance, even in a quite strong sectarian way or polemically, it does not hurt, really, the devotee of Viṣṇu, who will extend his indulgence toward the Śaivaite, and vice versa.

It is a rather peculiar pattern of the Purāṇas that after having exalted the importance of a thing, the opposite is also immediately praised:

> Those people who have destroyed the result of their actions (leading to rebirth) by means of wisdom, enter into you, O Śambhu, (Śiva) *by meditating* on you.
>
> It is not one's caste's duty, nor the Vedic science *nor meditation* nor the *samādhi* (which lead to you). I will bow to you (. . .) with devotion. (*B* 122.76–77)

It is a normal process that a deity assumes within itself all the opposite attributions and the qualities of all the other deities.[7] So in the list of the one thousand names of Viṣṇu, the attributes and the names of Śiva are also given, and in the lists of the one thousand names of Śiva the attributes and the names of Viṣṇu are also introduced.

> I am not Brahmā, nor Rudra (Śiva), know me as the Supreme Purusa (Man)

says the Lord in the *Brahma Purāṇa* (51.2), but he adds immediately:

> I am indeed Brahmā himself, I am Viṣṇu and also Śiva. . . . (*B* 51.4)

God is one and many (*Pd* V.25.79–83), affirm the Purāṇas, and He is identifiable with everything, even if He changes forms or is given different names by different persons; all the gods are in fact one God, who divided Himself for the sake of creation or for the sake of pleasing His devotees.[8]

> "There is no difference between Śiva and Viṣṇu.
> The Supreme Spirit has only one form . . .
> We praise Śiva in the form of Viṣṇu and
> praise Viṣṇu who has the form of Śiva.

> Viṣṇu is in Śiva's heart and Śiva in
> Viṣṇu's heart."
>
> "O great King, you are a devotee of Śiva and
> at the same time a devotee of Viṣṇu; for
> this reason the gods Brahmā, Viṣṇu, Maheśvara
> (Śiva) are happy with you."
>
> "To adore one is to adore the others too."
> (*Pd.* II.71.18–19, 21).

The *Brahma Purāṇa* (56.65ff.) in a Vaiṣṇava context says that Viṣṇu ordered Mārkaṇḍeya to build a temple to Śiva to prove that there is no difference between the two and that by establishing one, the other also is established.

Cases of synthesis are also rather frequent in the Purāṇas. The best known are the depiction of many gods into one symbolic representation. The first one is the unification or systematization of five deities in one group for the sake of worship; they usually are Gaṇeśa (the Elephant God), Sūrya (the Sun), Viṣṇu, Śiva, and the Goddess.[9] In this unification called *pañcāyatana*, each one of the gods can be put at the center, while the others occupy the four corners of an ideal square gathering all of them into one unity. The god in the middle changes according to the particular devotee's affiliation to a specific way of worship.

Another synthesis is the well-known *Trimūrti*,[10] in which the three forms or images of one God, as the word literally means, are represented by Brahmā, the Creator; Viṣṇu, the Sustainer; and Śiva, the Absorber. But the synthesis *Trimūrti* is only one aspect of a large Purāṇic vision which considers all the gods equal, that is, as we have already seen, all forms of the one God. Such a vision of equality is not a vague theism or a cheap syncretism; it is rather the concrete way the Purāṇas follow to instill a more general conviction that from whatever point of view one starts it is possible to build up a synthesis of the whole religious, moral, and spiritual world, doctrine, and practice. In other words, the starting points can be innumerable as they are peculiar to each person or groups of persons, but each one of them, once it has been chosen, helps in reconstructing the whole reality from a particular point of view and has, therefore, to be followed consequently up to the end.

> The Vedas ultimately treat of Vāsudeva (Kṛṣṇa); the sacrifices aim at the attainment of Vāsudeva; the various kinds of *yogas* eventually lead to Vāsudeva; and all sorts of rituals too have their end in Vāsudeva.
> All wisdom has its culmination in Vāsudeva;
> all austere penance has Vāsudeva as its goal;
> all religion (*dharma*) aims at the realization of Vāsudeva.[11]

Something similar is said of Śiva, Sūrya, Gaṇeśa, and the Goddess also. Thus, the particular form of God chosen by a person (*iṣṭadevatā*) is a perspective, a help toward a concrete synthesis, a way of recovering the oneness lost in the multiplicity of creation.

It may be said that the concept of *iṣṭadevatā* is central to the whole Purāṇic teaching. Through it stress is laid on individual choice and a door is opened for introducing new ways of conceiving the deity. Thus, although one remains in the broad riverbed of tradition, the form of the deity and the way of venerating it are left to the particular spiritual aspirations of the individual who takes refuge with that particular image of God which is dear to his or her heart and uses those rituals that go with its worship. There are, therefore, so to say, as many ways of worshiping as there are individual choices, but each one of these paths is already foreseen and prescribed in the tradition.

This is true not only of the concept of God but also of the means to reach Him. One can start from any one of them, such as *dharma*, ritual, knowledge or wisdom, devotion, meditation, yoga, *bhukti*, *mukti*, etc. Through each one of them all the others are gained so that each is at its right place and serves the right purpose, because they are aspects of one reality, even if they operate at different levels.

The same can be said, to give one more example, about the channels of divine revelation. Such channels or means are at different levels, so there are the Vedas (or *śruti*), the Tradition (or *smṛti*), and the *probi viri*'s behavior (*śiṣṭācāra*). Each preceding one is superior in importance and authoritativeness to the subsequent one; yet each one can be taken as a point of perspective to unify all the others in a synthesis.

The Purāṇic "pluralism" is not limited to the concept of God and related topics, such as rituals, vows, *dharma*, and festivals, but it extends even to the ways of conceiving the world, creation, time, final dissolution, and means to escape from it.[12] Even more, not only is the sacred and secular society of this world pluralistic, but also the inhabited worlds themselves and the universes are many, each having different shapes and its gods, its type of life, and so on.[13] The Purāṇic vision goes far beyond the limits of our universe.

The Purāṇas, in this way, are contemporaneously manuals containing different opinions and rituals and also books of spirituality, which form people to open themselves more and more to different situations and tendencies and to overcome even the differences between paths of realization or stages of development. They encourage everyone to do what one can do in that particular moment of one's evolution and life and suggest concrete means such as a festival, a fast, veneration of a place, a prayer, a meditation, an almsgiving (*dāna*), attending to a narration, taking a dip, eating, loving, going on a pilgrimage, and so on for reaching each one's peculiar scope. We can speak, then, of an *individualized* message of the Purāṇas.

Thus, pluralism applies not only to religious points of view but also to persons, time, situations, places, actions, and so on, and is far from creating a vague, indistinct attitude of indifference toward everything; it is, rather, conducive to a quite definite individualization. Pluralism in this way appears to be the background of any Purāṇic text and one of the most deep-rooted Purāṇic attitudes.

Spiritualization as Interiorization

The union between God and the spirit does not come from external elements, affirm the Purāṇas, but is reached by means of internal dispositions (*G* I.235.53). So every action has to be done with the highest effort, all the while meditating that the Supreme is in one's own heart.[14] One has not only to fix one's mind—that is, concentrate on *Brahman*, the Supreme—but one has also to give one's attention to the ritual one is performing, to one's duties, to oneself, and so on.[15] Every action must be done with full awareness and due consideration.

The *Agni Purāṇa* (59.1ff.) describes a long process through which the mind is slowly retracted both from external and from internal things and becomes fully itself. The process, well known in the yogic circles, is described several times in the Purāṇas. What is peculiar to our texts is that they extend this process of interiorization and spiritualization to every circumstance and field of life. A few examples are given below:

The water that really purifies is the knowledge of the Real (*G* I.83.13), and so those who have controlled their senses use the waters of real knowledge to purify their spirit. If one realizes that this world is *Brahman*, everything becomes for one a means to reach the Beyond (*G* I.81.26). Even a stone is divine because, although as such it is not divine, it becomes divine when it is sanctified, and so it is, in fact, the Unmanifested itself in the form of a stone. A river is the liquid form of God, and a place is God's body.[16] Moreover, all the rituals for the worship of the deity are very often deeply interiorized (*G* I.11.1ff.). In this connection the Purāṇas affirm that the real *tīrtha* (holy site), that is, the spot that makes a person ford to the other shore of reality, is the pure mind, and the famous spots of pilgrimage (*tīrthas*) such as Kurukṣetra, Prayāga, Puṣkara, and so on are all present, indeed, in a person who controls the senses (*B* 25.3, 6).

The Purāṇic attitude, however, is always very realistic. The quoted *Brahma Purāṇa*, after having stressed with impressive words that *tīrthas* are internal to a person's body, continues unexpectedly with descriptions of the concrete, external, material *tīrthas* as well. In the same way, after having exalted the importance of knowledge and having stressed the supremacy of the nondualistic doctrines, the Purāṇas are careful not to limit themselves to these extreme statements but to expound also on ritualistic subjects. An example from the *Garuḍa Purāṇa* will illustrate this point, which is of great importance for a correct understanding of the Purāṇic attitude. *Garuḍa Purāṇa* I.91 of the said Purāṇa exalts the Supreme in its unmanifested form and concludes that by meditating on it one becomes *Brahman* (91.17). The subsequent chapter describes the Supreme in its visible and manifest aspects and concludes that if one meditates on it one will reach the Supreme realization (92.17), to attain which, anyway, continues the Purāṇa, it is enough to read only the description of it. At this point the Purāṇa speaks of the rules of conduct, giving many details for each caste and the periods of a person's life, as if what it has just affirmed about the final realization through meditation in the previous chapters had not been said. For the Purāṇas, the identification with the Supreme is the utmost aim, no doubt, but only in a somewhat ideal way. In fact, many persons are still on the way to such a realization and are in need of the spiritual guidance that the Purāṇas provide.

The process of interiorization is very pervasive. *Dharma* is Viṣṇu himself, and even the threads of the brahmanical cord have names of gods (*G* I.42.1ff; 223.3). Each part of the body, affirm the Purāṇas, following the pattern laid down by the Tantras, can be made a dwelling place of one of God's forms through a ritual formula (*nyāsa*) (*G* I.48.48ff.). The Lord lives in heaven as well as in the lower regions, in divine beings, in the elements, in the human heart. He is the pilgrimage place itself; He is time; He is space; and so forth.[17] Even the so-called profane subjects can be used to reach the Absolute, and if they are described in the Purāṇas it is because by reading such subjects one gets spiritual benefits (*A* 283.51). In this light, geography is described, as well as history, astrological matters, medicine, different sciences, eclipses, and even grammar, art of buildings, and so on.[18] The Purāṇas want surely that one should possess every kind of knowledge in addition to the spiritual science (*vidyā*) (*A* 347.40); but they mean more than that. They want each element of the universe to come under the control of the spirit. This can be the reason behind such curious statements as the one of the *Kūrma Purāṇa* (II.12.6), affirming that wool was discovered just to prepare the brahmanical cord or that castes were created for sacrifice (*Vi* I.6.7f.). For the Purāṇas, in fact, one lives in a religious time and in a cosmos where one is identifiable with the Supreme. Between the human being and the Supreme, as well as between the cosmos and spirit, time and non-time, manifested and unmanifested, activity and stillness, the profane and the sacred, there is no discontinuity; one is permanently in the way of dissolving into the other. More than in any other field, the Purāṇas show here that they put themselves between the not yet fully spiritualized and the already spiritual, the no longer profane and the not yet fully religious. They are like channels through which one element flows, or is absorbed, into the other.

At this point a word of warning has to be sounded. It may appear from what has been said in this last section that the Purāṇas do not distinguish between the sacred and the profane and that their attitude is close to the one better known among the people at the ethnographical level, where such a distinction is still lacking. Such an understanding would be, however, irrelevant, because the Purāṇas follow rather the opposite tendency. Profane topics clearly distinct from the religious ones and available in separate treatises are incorporated by them into the religious field. The Purāṇas write about profane topics purposely, indicating a pattern of how to approach reality and shaping all those that enter into their atmosphere, into a deep spiritual understanding of the universe.

Basic Doctrines

The Purāṇas have hardly a doctrine that is not dealt with also in other texts, usually in a better way or in a larger context; for instance, the Purāṇas contain Vedic doctrines, moral teachings (*dharmaśāstra*), Tantrism, Vaiṣṇavism, Śivaism, philosophical doctrines such as Sāṁkhya, Yoga, Advaita, rebirth, histories of God's descents (*avatāras*), the ways of devotion, and so on. The Purāṇas take all these doctrines from different sources, written or oral, and develop and organize them according to their own perspective. These topics may be grouped under three main headings for clarity.

At the Beginning of Things: Creation

Sarga, that is, creation—or, better, "emanation"—and *pratisarga* in its meaning of both re-creation and destruction are two of the five topics or *pañcalakṣaṇas* of the Purāṇas. The Supreme is one and undivided at the beginning, but it becomes twofold—namely, *saguṇa* (adorned with attributes or qualified) and *nirguṇa* (devoid of all properties), or masculine and feminine—and manifold for the benefit of His devotees.[19] God has a cosmic form and a cosmic body; all the gods are His equal and at the same time His forms; everything is God; divisions or distinctions are only fruits of our human activity.[20] God's energies (*śaktis*) are often thought of as God's wives (*Vi* I.7.10ff.), and the Supreme itself contains manhood and womanhood as its constitutive parts: He is half man and half woman, or *ardhanarīśvara*, as the Śivaites would define Him (*L* I.5.28ff). The Supreme itself is conceived of at times as neuter (*Brahman*), at times as masculine (Śiva, Viṣṇu, etc.), and yet at other times as feminine (the Goddess) according to different perspectives; but these ways of conceiving the Supreme are eventually all equal:

> What is Śiva that is Goddess
> What is the Goddess That is Śiva. (*L* I.75.34f.)

This implies that for the Purāṇas the particular concept of the Supreme as this or that God or Goddess is less important than the general understanding of the Supreme as the only Reality:

> From me everything
> In me everything
> I am everything. (*Vi* I.19.85)
> As drops of water, raised by wind from the
> earth, sink into the earth again when the
> wind subsides, so the varieties of gods, men,
> and animals which have been detached by the
> agitation of the qualities, are reunited,
> when that disturbance ceases,
> with the eternal. (*Vi* III.7.16ff.)

This perfect identity of God and things is used as a support for venerating every element of the world. The Purāṇas, indeed, use the nondualistic doctrines for their purpose of helping everyone toward full realization through devotion, because such teachings very often conclude with hymns of praise (*stotras*), which means that they are introduced as means of prayer and praise. The tendency of transforming every teaching into a praise of the Lord is constant in the Purāṇas, and it is found not only when they describe the Supreme but also when they introduce other topics.

It is with this idea that *sarga*, or creation, is described in the Purāṇas. They affirm that the Supreme, before emitting the Universe, takes a body just for the sake of creation.[21] Such a creation, moreover, is considered a play (*līlā*), a pleasure for the Lord Himself, or a dance (*K* II.4.54; *Pd* IV.83). Moreover, good and bad things alike are produced by the Supreme; so also negative qualities such as violence, injustice, fear, illusion, and death are said to have come forth from the creator, that is, Brahmā.[22]

Brahmā is not the only Creator, although he is the usual one. Several other gods, men, Manus (i.e., the world's ancient ancestors and rulers), as well as Viṣṇu, Śiva, the Goddess, and so on can also be creators, and the gods create one another reciprocally (*K* I.9–10). Everything, even the smallest or the most insignificant element is considered to be directly derived from the Creator, as is the whole universe. The world, therefore, as well as every action, has concretely emanated from God Himself—or, better, is one of His parts (*aṃśa*); the trees are His hairs; rivers, His veins; and so on.[23] But this, let us say it once again, is not a sterile pantheistic vision of the world, but is a concrete support to the devotee, and possibly an invitation to mystical experience.

The Purāṇic vision of time, or *kāla*, deserves special attention. *Kāla* is first of all a sequence of instants that can be measured and that serve to define the existence of each being, even of the creator Himself, and to delimit the particular temporal "place" in which religious actions are performed. *Kāla*, therefore, has a cosmic and socioreligious dimension.[24] Emphasis, however, must be placed on *kāla*'s active import. It intervenes at creation, as it is one of *Brahman*'s forms and stirs its dormant qualities, or its *prakṛti*, that is, its potentiality.[25] During the course of the world's existence, *kāla* provides one occasions to perform one's *karman*, activity, but also causes one to sin (*Vi* I.6.14, 29) and provokes the continuous slow degradation of ages, *yugas*. *Kāla*, finally, is the active agent of destruction, or *pralaya* (*B* 212.57ff.). Thus, time is one of the causes of multiplicity; its end brings back the lost oneness. *Kāla* is not the first element to be created, so those who precede it, like Śiva, are reabsorbed into the Absolute only after the destruction of *kāla*; they are not born nor do they die.

Time (*kāla*) has a role also in the Purāṇic view of *bhukti* and *mukti*. Time, indeed, is to be used for completion of rituals and as a means in the process of purification through rebirth. Time has to be overcome so as to reach absorption into the Supreme. One can escape *kāla* only after having enjoyed it through all its levels or forms; so one has to enjoy it, passing through human time and then the forefathers' time and finally the divine time. These three times are not only unequal in length but apparently also in quality.

The Purāṇas are definite about the influence time has on human beings. They affirm that to each period of time corresponds its own *dharma*.[26] Our age, called *kali yuga*, is usually depicted in very dark colors (*B* 229.8ff.). Eulogistic descriptions of it, however, are not lacking.

> The fruit of penance, of continence, of silent prayer and the like, practised in the *kṛta* age for ten years, in the *tretā* for one year, in the *dvāpara* for a month, is obtained in the *kali* age in a day and night; therefore, I exclaim: "Excellent, excellent is the *kali* age."

> The reward, which a man obtains in the *kṛta* by abstract meditation, in the *tretā* by sacrifice, in the *dvāpara* by adoration, he receives in the *kali* by merely reciting the name of Keśava (Kṛṣṇa). (*Vi* VI.2.15–18)

Even the worst of times can have positive aspects because what matters is to go forward toward one's realization by any means, choosing the fittest ones according to circumstances of time, place, situation, and people. But time can also be transformed. There seem to be three ways of taking time back to its original purity: the ordinary way is that of accepting its course and its effects fully. This imparts meaning to what are called auspicious moments or days (*muhūrtas* or *tithis*) in which festivals are to be celebrated, rituals performed, and actions undertaken. It may happen that one may have to suffer, but through one's sufferings in time one gets detachment; from detachment one gets understanding; and from understanding, *dharma* arises in its complete form (*B* 230.45ff.). And so the original time of innocence, or *kṛta yuga,* starts afresh.

Another way of transforming time, or *kāla,* is by conquering it. King Parīkṣit subdues *kali,* as every good ruler should do (*Bhg* I.17f.), so that although the conditions of time and the situation around are bad, the time in which people live under such a ruler is indeed different (*Vm* 49.4ff.), resembling the original good age.

Yet another way to overcome the negative influence of the degrading time is God's own intervention in the world. God Himself, in fact, intervenes both to keep time going and to help humans overcome its bad effects. This He does through His descents (*avatāras*). When goodness is in danger and ill is augmenting, God prepares for Himself a body and comes to the rescue of *dharma* or what represents it. The topic of the *avatāras* is a central one in the Purāṇas and deserves close attention.

Participation of God in Time: The Avatāras

The word *avatāra* means descent, and it is used in the Purāṇas to describe the intervention of the Supreme mainly in this world. God appears not only as *avatāras* but in many other ways and shapes (*B* 213.20ff.; *Bhg* I.3.26–27). The world is the Lord Himself, and there is no place where He is not present nor any object that is not He. The Lord, however, does descend for the protection of the good and the destruction of evil or for giving solace to the earth (*bhārāvataraṇa*).[27] The Purāṇas add that He comes dividing Himself or through one of his aspects (*aṃśas*, *kalās*) and He comes out of compassion or to enhance the glory of His race, at the request of his earthly parents, or in response to Brahmā's prayer, to let His glory be spread among humans.[28] The idea that is more congenial to the Purāṇic spirit is that the Lord descends for His own and His faithful's sport (*līlā*) or to please His devotees and be praised by them.[29] The account of *avatāras*, indeed, ends very often with a hymn of glorification to the descended Lord; and the joy of the devotee at seeing the Lord's face or at being personally and individually with him is often described.[30]

The Lord has already descended several times, notably as Rāma and Kṛṣṇa, and will descend again. The number of *avatāras* is given differently in different passages; it can be seven or, more frequently, ten, but also twelve, twenty-two, or twenty-four.[31] Although the usually known *avatāras* are those of Viṣṇu, the Purāṇas speak of the *avatāras* also of other divine beings, such as Vyāsa, the Goddess, Bhṛgu, different gods, the Sun, and even Śiva.[32] The *avatāras* are, indeed, numberless[33] and so their number is not yet complete. Gods, humans, sages, and "all those who possess great power" are often thought of as rays (*aṃśas*) of God. For the *Brahmavaivarta Purāṇa* (IV.15.105.67.67) every man is a ray of Kṛṣṇa, namely, of the Supreme, and every woman is a ray of Rādhā, namely, of the complementary aspect of the Supreme and herself the Supreme. Thus, the concept of *avatāra* is almost all-pervasive, and one sees the Lord present everywhere and experiences His *avatāras* in everything.

The *avatāras* can also be for deluding the enemies of the god; that is, they may have mainly a negative purpose. This is the usual interpretation given to Viṣṇu's *avatāra* as the Buddha.[34]

The *avatāra* is not necessarily in human form; it can also be in animal or divine form. The ten *avatāras* of Viṣṇu—fish, tortoise, boar, dwarf, man-lion, Paraśurāma, Rāma, Kṛṣṇa, the Buddha, Kalki (at the end of *kali yuga*)—have been interpreted by some scholars as symbols and propellent agents of evolution.[35] But human *avatāras* are emphasized, and the most popular of them are those of Rāma and Kṛṣṇa.

The *avatāras*, then, are the visible links between the divine, the human, and the subhuman world, and as they are the object of devotion they help, more than all the other means, to rebuild the original unity of the Supreme, which was dispersed in multiplicity at the moment of creation.

The End of Things: Dissolution

Everything is a product of time: everything is created by it and is brought to the end by it. "If a man realizes that everything is temporal, namely, transient, he obtains peace" (*Vi* V.38.37). Time reaches its scope (*gati*, *Bhg* XII.4.38) when it has led everything to its consummation, or *pralaya*. A person passes through a long chain of pains (*tāpas*) of different origins,[36] which are produced by our actions. Such actions can lead us to a temporary heavenly happiness or to a temporary hell and then in both cases to a coming back again sooner or later to this earth.[37] "He who dies is born again and he who is born dies again" (*Bhv* IV.4.22). One must realize the emptiness of earthly and otherworldly enjoyments (*Bhg* XI.10.1ff.). By the means of *jñāna,* or wisdom, and by destroying one's attachment and passions, one gains *mokṣa* (BD III.3, 58). One can get immediate *mokṣa,* no doubt, but it is more probable that one will reach it gradually. The Purāṇas are meant for the persons who will pass through the latter type of realization. The Purāṇas have long descriptions of heavens (*svargas*) and hells (*narakas*), to encourage people to practice *dharma* and reach wisdom through the daily exercise of religious duties, charity, and ascetic effort or yoga.[38] Yoga will destroy the worldly pains, and wisdom will make the light of the Supreme shine (*A* 372–80). If one marches on this path, one will have the ideal death, like that of Kṛṣṇa or other illustrious persons,[39] who unified themselves with the Supreme by reproducing in themselves the process of creation in the reverse, namely, gathering in themselves one by one all the elements that had emanated from the original creator and thus pass from multiplicity to oneness. In other words, such a person will be in his or her death an image of what happens at the time of dissolution of the world (*pralaya*).

For the Purāṇas, death is a form of life which manifests itself in a different aspect. Death prolongs and even consolidates those ties that were already present in life. The dead person continues his or her purification also after death but no longer alone, that is, trusting only in his or her own capacity and merits. That one depends on those who remain on earth for constant help—first for the formation of one's subtle body and then for the food and strength needed for the journey toward the kingdom of Yama (the king of the dead). This full dependence of the dead on the "living" relatives through the performance of *śrāddha,* ritual offerings for the dead, constitutes a basic element in the total formation of the Purāṇic person. That one is called not only to embrace the whole universe, as we have seen, but also to go beyond the borders of life on earth. Such persons have the duty to generate offspring for their own benefit, that is, for having a helper after their death. At the same time, they must be deeply linked with their ancestors, who depend on them. A close bond of vertical relationship is thus formed, making a person fully established in the flow of life, which one has received from one's ancestors and has transmitted to one's successors. In this way, the *śrāddha* one must perform for the dead, as well as the descriptions the Purāṇas give of the long journey involved for the dead person in reaching the realm of Yama, builds up in every follower of the Purāṇic vision of life a strong sense of unity with others and highlights the responsibilities of the living in doing everything possible for the successful completion of the journey undertaken by the dead in the "afterlife." Thus one's link with the dead becomes a concrete step toward a deeper ascetic life as well as a means for opening oneself to the social dimension of one's spiritual realization. The perfection proposed to a follower of Purāṇic doctrine, in the light of one's duties toward one's ancestors, is marked by deep love of others and a new understanding of "life" and "death." Death, indeed, is not a breaking point between here and there, but only the night of rest between two days in one's journey toward final realization; death enters as an essential element of the necessary purification to reach realization. Death is not the end of this life but only a suspension or another face of it, from which one continues to return until one is ready to merge into the Absolute (see esp. *G* II).

Pralaya, or dissolution, is an important theme for several Purāṇas and has a meaningful bearing on Purāṇic attitude toward life. Four types of *pralayas* are usually described. Two refer to the universe: (1) intermediate or occasional (*naimittika*) dissolutions at the end of a cosmic period; and (2) dissolution at the end of the creator's life (*prakṛta*). The other two, parallel to the first ones, refer to individuals: (1) called *nitya*, or continuous, describes the individual death repeated after each rebirth; and (2) called *atyantika*, or definitive, which is a synonym of *mokṣa*, or final deliverance.[40] The one who has reached detachment through wisdom will meet this last end, or *laya*.

The Means toward Realization

The Purāṇas propose several means toward final realization, which are taken from many different sources. The general means to one's realization is the *sampradāyas* (sects), which stress a particular way of belonging. A person is not an abstract entity for the Purāṇas. A person has a family (*kula*) and a caste (*varṇa*, *jāti*), is in a particular stage of life (*āśrama*), in a concrete time and territory (*kāladeśa*), is linked to a specific chain of people (*paramparā*), transmitting to that person what has been seen and heard (*śruti* or Veda) and remembered (*smṛti*) down the centuries. A person is attached to a system of customs and rules (*dharma*), which one can know through the conduct of most respectable persons of one's territory (*śiṣṭācāra*). All this complex of elements gives one what one needs for one's spiritual, moral, social, and individual life. The human person belongs to this complex. This complex is not neuter; it has rather definite delimitations, is very well organized, and adapts itself continuously to different situations of people, time, places, doctrines, behaviors, and so on, though remaining constantly faithful to an eternal truth (*sanātana dharma*), which develops, grows, produces fruits according to necessity. Such a complex, which takes different shapes in different places and times, is called *sampradāya*. There are, of course, as many *sampradāyas* as there were different faucets for drinking the same water of truth. These *sampradāyas*, or currents, can remain different from one another or mix their waters all together; they are mobile, although at times they have become, in some places at least, rather stiff. It is possible that people may not be fully aware as to what *sampradāya* they really belong, and to which peculiar proposals their *sampradāya* adheres. Yet these currents have been extremely important in the formation and development of the Purāṇas. The feeling of belonging to one or another *sampradāya* is always very strong, although this feeling might take the shape, as it does very often, of belonging to all the *sampradāyas*, as in fact all the gods are equal.

Bhakti

Bhakti, or what may be approximately translated as devotion, is a central theme of the Purāṇas. *Bhakti* does not exclude the ascetic effort, which is very often linked to it. One who has a pure mind, sense subdued and stable in decisions, is required to follow the path of *bhakti*. Moreover, if *bhakti* proposes to one the ideal of serving, loving, and being immersed in the Lord, it does not absolve one from the duty of a constant attention to the more negative aspects of sin and time that keep one in bondage to the world (*samsāra*) and rebirth (*punarjanma*).

Bhakti is certainly one of the central means the Purāṇas propose for reaching final realization, yet it is far from being the only one.

The Purāṇas are indefatigable in citing examples of persons who had an unshakable devotion, through which they obtained the most extraordinary results. These accounts, like the stories of saints (hagiography), propose continuously to the devotee concrete examples from which the devotee can learn and which the devotee can be encouraged to imitate. The *Padma Purāṇa* (I.50.35) calls *Haribhakti* (devotion to Kṛṣṇa) a *karmayoga*, a path of action, emphasizing the active part of the person rather than total surrender.

Dharmaśāstras, or Treatises on Dharma

The Purāṇas have incorporated many topics referring to the field of *dharmaśāstra* since the remotest times and have themselves been considered authorities on *dharma* at least by the epitomists (*Nibandhakāras*). Purāṇic spirituality is largely based on *dharma*, which is considered the Lord Himself (*G* I.223.3). The human person is born alone and dies alone; only *dharma*, say the Purāṇas, helps one and follows one after death.[41] *Dharma* is the source of everything, even of wisdom (*jñāna*) and of *mokṣa*, and it must be considered modifiable, as there may be traditional views on it as well as new approaches.[42] The basis of every *dharmic* behavior is the *śruti* (the Vedas), enlarged by the *smṛti* (tradition), which includes the *dharmaśāstras*, the Purāṇas, and the epics, or *itihāsa*, and by the *śistācāra*, or the behavior of the *probi viri*, in case of controversy or doubt. The Purāṇas insist constantly on the necessity of following *dharma* and give norms for each category of persons and situations.[43]

The subjects that enter in the field of *dharmaśāstra* are many and important; we shall gather them, for clarity's sake, into three main items: rituals, or *karmakāṇḍa;* hymns of praise, or *stotras* and *mantras;* and rules of *dharma*. We shall deal with the magnifications or *māhātmyas* and the places of pilgrimage (*tīrthas*) in a different section, though they also belong to the field of *dharmaśāstra*.

Rituals, or Karmakāṇḍa

The entire system of rituals is based on a spirituality of action, of doing. The Purāṇas propose an ideal of completeness (*bhukti-mukti*), and they keep a balanced attitude between renunciation (*nivṛtti*) and full involvement in the worldly life (*pravṛtti*). Action (*karman*) is not considered by them to be negative or condemnable, as it is in many nondualistic traditions. Gifts, almsgiving, and help to others are prescribed;[44] but the actions that are especially emphasized are the performance of one's duty (*dharma*) and the conduct of the religious activity including rituals, pilgrimages, and praises of the Lord.

Ritual in the Purāṇas oscillates between two poles: exaltation of any worldly object, however unimportant it might appear; and a strong spiritualization or interiorization of the whole ritual. Thus, the spot where one sits for performing one's ritual is to be purified and the earth venerated. The light, the incense, the bells, the utensils, the books, the water, the clothes, and so on are to be purified before being used; they are thought of as representing, and being a form of, the Supreme itself.[45] The body of the one performing the ritual is thought of as being made up of different forms of the Supreme: the hands symbolize divine attributes; his vestments are made of the Divine (*G* I.22, 26, 30, 42ff.). According to Sāṁkhya philosophy, followed by the Purāṇas, all the parts of the body are presided over by different deities at the moment of the constitution of the body; so at the beginning of the ritual action, the performer is required to reenact this constitution of the body (*G* I.48.48ff.) through particular invocations (*nyāsa*).

The performer is to become aware of being God, because only God can worship God (*Ś* VII.2.22.42–43). Yet this process of exaltation of the ritual is meant for those who still need a ritual for entering into contact with the Supreme. For them, however, and for those who no longer need rituals, another path is proposed, which leads to finding the Supreme not externally but in one's own self and teaches that the external ritual is only an intermediate stage which has a value until one has realized in one's own heart the Lord present in all beings.

Innumerable are the rituals one is supposed to perform. For high-caste people, the Purāṇas lay down the scheme of the daily performance of five sacrifices (*pañcayajña*), as laid down in the *dharmaśāstras*—namely, sacrifice to the gods, to the spirits, to the ancestors, to humans, and to the Supreme (*Brahman*) (*N* I.27.76). In addition, there are vows to be taken, gifts to be made on special occasions, and festivals to be observed during the year. There are no fewer than than sixteen sacraments that every good brahmin receives from the moment of conception in one's mother's womb to one's death. Thus, any follower of the Purāṇas has clearly in mind what one has to do. One has learned it by tradition, in one's own family, and in the society to which one belongs.

Hymns and Sacred Formulas, or Stotras and Mantras

Stotras and *mantras* are used mainly during a ritual, but both have developed also independently of it. *Stotra* is basically a hymn of praise that very often has the scope of moving the praised one and making him or her well disposed toward the devotee. The satisfaction of praising and exalting someone, however, surpasses at times the desire to move the praised one. Frequently, indeed, there is a great disproportion between the sublime praise and the requested grace. A *stotra* is, for the Purāṇic mentality, an occasion for letting oneself be absorbed in the pleasure of describing and contemplating the Absolute. It is, indeed, because the Absolute reaches us in every way that any person and object can be identified with it. In this perspective different gods are often invested with the same attributes. In fact, everyone is everything; the difference is only in the names, not in reality.[46] Yet a distinction is always to be kept among the different aspects, and the devotee is asked to imagine in his or her heart a spiritual image of the deity to be honored with all the details prescribed in the scriptures. In that way the praise becomes liturgical—that is, public. The hymn, indeed, is very often said to have been revealed by some deity or seer of the past and is preceded by the name of the presiding deity of that hymn, its revealer, the meter in which it is recited, and the like.

Benaras (Vārāṇasī)

Mantras, or sacred formulas, are used in two different contexts: *indrajāla,*[47] or magic; and religion. Religious *mantras* are used in rituals and are linked also with the practice of repeating the names of God (*japa*). A faithful follower of the Purāṇic teachings is also a master of the rhythmic and uninterrupted recitation of the name of God and can select in the Purāṇas the *mantras* according to one's *sampradāya.*[48] Thus, *mantras* are on the borderline between magic and religion because they are empowered invocations. Although the Purāṇas do not deny the former, yet the proper use for them lies in a religious context. They are considered to be gods themselves or the ingredients of which the gods are made. Thus, the power of the *mantra* opens up the possibility of *mokṣa* itself.

Dharma

Dharma occupies a large part of the Purāṇic texts and teachings. One's own *dharma* is the only way of praising and serving the Supreme (*Vi* III.8.12). If one does not follow it, one cannot reach the other aims of life and will have to suffer hell.[49] By following it, instead, one will have a long life and glory, will reach the highest realization, and will attain all the aims of life, which are subordinate to *dharma*, and finally *mokṣa.*[50] The Purāṇas determine accurately the personal *dharmas* and the *dharmas* linked to one's caste, stage of life (*varṇāśrama*), and family (*kulācāra*).[51] There are *dharmas* for married people and for ascetics, for students and for women, and even for gods.[52] Each act of life is under the control of *dharma*; what one can eat or not, what one has to do for one's ancestors, when to make love to one's spouse, how to take a bath or present a gift, how to reign over a kingdom or live one's daily life. The land where we live is holy (*puṇyabhūmi*), and it is what sustains us in our struggle toward *mokṣa* or at least heaven (*phalabhūmi*) (*Pd* II.95). Humans commit sins, for which reparation is sometimes not possible (*Bhv* IV.5). For a few of them the whole punishment must be gone through in several rebirths; but the end for everyone is the final *mokṣa.*

Among one's duties there is also the concern for others (*Vi* III.8.13ff), at least for those who deserve it. Merits can be transmitted, especially to one's ancestors or descendants (*G* II). A certain transmission of demerits is also described (*K* II.16.30). Long lists are given presenting the good results one gets by performing certain acts, practicing certain penances, accomplishing certain vows (*A* 38), and so on.

Two attitudes characterize the Purāṇic teaching in the field of *dharma.* The first is the constant effort to spiritualize every act.[53] This effort has produced, historically, two important effects that are clearly visible today in

India. One is the importance given to *ahimsā*, or nonviolence; the other is the relevance of *satya*, or truth, as the supreme *dharma* (*Pd* V.45.95). The second attitude is the readiness to change because every age has its own *dharma*,[54] which is in the process of modification. A follower of the Purāṇas, therefore, is firmly attached to the past and tradition, on the one hand, but on the other, he or she is always moving toward the future, but within the logic of the tradition. Although the Purāṇas and their proposals have been changing through the centuries, they have remained constantly faithful to themselves. As the Purāṇic tradition is still alive, any change in present Hinduism—for example, in the understanding of caste relations, the position of women or outcasts, government, relations with foreigners—must be labeled Purāṇic as long as it remains in the spirit of the Purāṇas, although it might be rather different from what is actually available in the written tradition of the present Purāṇas. There is no doubt, indeed, that the actual Hindu or *sanātana dharma* is still basically a "Purāṇic *dharma*."

Pilgrimage Places, or Tīrthas, and Glorifications, or Māhātmyas

At the present time, *tīrthas*, or pilgrimage spots, are attracting the attention of scholars of different fields. Indeed, not only are they still alive in our times, but they are on the increase. The written Purāṇas have already given the main points for a development of a full-fledged doctrine based on *tīrthas*. In addition, the *māhātmyas*, or "magnifications," of pilgrimage spots as well as of festivals, auspicious days, vows, and so on have also increased in the Purāṇas to such an extent that it is possible to build up a whole specific understanding of life based only on such passages.

As God lives everywhere (*Vm* 62.56; 63), the *tīrthas* are in reality everywhere as they are God Himself (*Pd* I. 1.15). Moreover, everything can be considered a *tīrtha*, namely, a fording place to the Beyond, as the root of the word points out: the forefathers, one's guru, one's mother and father, one's spouse.[55] In fact, all the *tīrthas* are in one's pure mind and in the control of one's speech and senses (*B* 25.3). This strong spiritualization of the *tīrthas*, however, does not bar the Purāṇas from dealing with specific places of pilgrimage, the most famous of which are Vārāṇasī, Prayāga (Allahabad), Gayā, Kurukṣetra, Naimiṣa, Puṣkara, Vrindāvana, Mathurā, Ayodhyā, Gaṅgā, and Narmadā. These and related topics are dealt with at great length in the Purāṇas. A whole religious topography is easily reconstructable by reading the *tīrtha-māhātmyas*. A person in a *tīrthas* as described in the

Purāṇas, is immersed in a sacred universe where every stone, any piece of water as well as any tree is God Himself.[56]

The Purāṇas themselves are the real pilgrimage toward total and final realization—a pilgrimage that has surely different paths and different intermediary steps but leads everyone to the same point, which is already present figuratively in every spot of the pilgrimage. The Purāṇas take care of the pilgrims by showing them the different ways and the unique goal, which is contemporaneously distinct for each person, yet the same, in front and inside, in the future and already present.

The Purāṇas have a message for humanity that goes beyond the time in which they were composed, a message which by intent, as one may see through air of anonymity, crosses the borders of the land from which the Purāṇas sprang and the culture in which they were formed. Their psychological intuitions put them in tune with modern sensibility, which is so attentive to the need of the individual. The twentieth century, which is so sensitive to human values, can easily appreciate the ideal of totality presented by the Purāṇas. Moreover, a faithful adherence to the basic message of spiritualization in the Purāṇas is a constant source of encouragement for one to do one's best and to use any means in order to advance toward the final goal. The Purāṇas have an impelling influence of enthusiasm and optimism that affects everyone coming in touch with them.

> This wonderful world had origin from the *Purāṇapuruṣa* and the literature had origin from the Purāṇas . . . . What is not seen in the Vedas nor does it appear in Tradition (that) is available in the Purāṇas. (*N* II.24.15ff.)

Notes

1. The five topics are primary creation (*sarga*), destruction or secondary creation (*pratisarga*), families of the patriarchs, periods of the Manvantaras, and genealogical histories of kings (see *Vi* VI.8.2).

2. See *Vi* III.6.15: "Vyasa compiled a Purāṇic collection (*samhitā*) consisting of stories (*ākhyānas*), tales (*upākhyānas*), songs (*gāthās*), and accounts of periods called kalpas." These four elements, especially the first two, are called *kathas* (accounts) in general.

3. V. S. Agarwala, *Matsaya Purāṇa.*

4. *A* 25.50; 32.12; *B* 245.31; 226.7; 245.19, 30.

5. *A* 271.19ff.; *B* 88.15; *Pd* V.19/316ff.

6. *A* 24.59; *B* 136.26; *Vm* 18.24.

7. This attitude of predicating any perfection of a thing when it is praised is found also in the Vedas and other works and can be considered one of the basic attitudes of Indian mind.

8. *K* I.15.152; II.11.111; 44.29ff.; *Pd* IV.73.14–34; *S* IV.1.15–17 *Bhg* V. 25.10; *Vm* 41.42ff.

9. *A* 327.13; *N* II.41.29, 59. *Bv* II.4.35–36.

10. The word *Trimūrti* (*B* 138, 341; *K* I.10.80 etc.) is not very common in the Purāṇa, though the concept is all-pervasive: see *B* 123.25; 131.40; *K* I.4.49ff.; 10.75; *Bd* I.27.52; *Vi* I.2.66.

11. *Bhg* I.2.28–29; II.5.15–16 (repeat the same words changing Vāsudeva with Nārāyaṇa).

12. *Vi* I.4.38ff.; *Vi* II.2ff.

13. *A* 17; *K* I.11.312; II.8.17; *Vi* I.4.38ff.

14. *G* I.22.6–9; 31.30; 32.14.40; *Vi* V.8.90.

15. *G* I.44.1; 49.40; 92.16; *K* I.11.262.

16. *B* 123.124ff.; *Bv* II.11.80ff., 121; *Pd* IV.69.6ff.

17. *Bhg* II.1.24ff.; III.6; 29.38ff.; *Vi* I.20. 10ff.; *Vm* 62.56ff.; *L* I.31.3ff.; *Pd* I.1.15.

18. *A* 18–19; *B* 2–17; *G* I.46; 205ff.;*Bhv* III.1.4; *K* I.12–14; *Vm* 14.50 etc.

19. *Bd* II.42.47; *Bhg* I.2.32ff.; *Bv* II.2.29; *K* I.4.55; *L* I.31.9; *Pd* IV.81.55ff.; *Vi* I.2.66.

20. *B* 56.70; *Bd* II.42.48; *Bhg* II.1.24ff.; *G* I.2.13ff.; *L* I.75.7; *Vi* I.4.19–24; 5.48ff.

21. *Bd* I.31.1; 27.72; *Bhg* III.12.27; *G* I.4.8.

22. *A* 20.17ff.; *K* I.4; *L* II.6.31ff.

23. *Bhg* II.1.24ff.; *G* I.2.13ff.; *L* I.75.7; *Vi* I.5.48ff.

24. Madeleine Biardeau, *Hinduism: The Anthropology of Civilization* (Delhi: Oxford University Press, 1981; English ed., 1989) 2.

25. *Bhg* III.6; *K* II.2; *Vi* I.2.15ff.

26. *Bhg* I.16–17; XII.3; *Bv* II.7.68–69; *G* I.223; *K* I.26–28; *Pd* I.7; IV.110.390ff.; *Vi* VI.1ff.

27. *B* 181.1.14; *Bhg* I. 158.13–14, 145; *Vi* V.7.39 etc.

28. *B* 181.39; 182.4; 188.40; *Bhg* I.1.13, 17; 3.5; etc.

29. *B* 206.42; *Bhg* I.1.17–18; *Bv* II.7.88; *Vi* I.19.80.

30. *B* 189.13ff; *Bhg* I.8.30–31, etc.; *Bv* IV passim.

31. *Bhg* II.7.1–38; VI.8.13–18; XI.4; *Mt* 47.39, 105; *Vi* III.1.35ff.; *Vy* 97.137–42; 98.70–105; etc.

32. *B* 181.28; *Bhv* I.157, 159; *K* I.50; 51.1; *L* I.24. 141; *Pd* I.20.82; *Vi* I.10.142ff.; 13.45. Śiva's *avatāras*, although they are disclaimed by the Śaivaites, are clearly stated by the Purāṇas; see *K* I.51.1ff.; *L* I.24.130ff.; *S* III.1, 17, 20; VII.2.9.

33. *A* 16.12; *B* 213.20; *Bhg* I.23.5,23ff.

34. *A* 16.2–3; *Bhg* I.3.24; *G* I.1.32; *Pd* V.73.93; *Sk* V.151.22.

35. Upadhyaya (1965) 177–78.

36. *A* 371.38ff.; *Vi* VI.5.

37. *Bhv* IV.4; *G* I.225; *L* I.7.3.

38. *A* 371.38f.; *B* 22; 215; *Pd* III.12.2, 63; 24.37, 41, 50.

39. *B* 211.10ff.; *Bhg* I.15.39ff.

40. *A* 368; *B* 231–33; *Bhg* XII.4; *G* I.224; *Vi* VI.3ff.

41. *B* 217.4–7. The same statement is repeated, more often, for *karman*, or action.

42. *B* 245.38; *G* I.213.9; *Pd* I.54; II.61.47.

43. P. V. Kane and R. C. Hazra have dealt at length with this problem. More

recently M. Biardeau has also devoted particular attention to it, especially in its relation to *bhakti* in the *Mahābhārata*, the epic that is many points similar to the Purāṇas.

44. *B* 158; 172; 174; 218.9ff.; *Pd* III.12.2ff.

45. All the description of rituals contain such details or a few of them.

46. *B* 243; *Vi* I.4.19–24;22.10ff.; II.12.37ff.

47. *A* 123ff.; 142–48; *Bd* II.36.58; *G* I.27; *L* II.52–53.

48. Even the nowadays famous "*Hare Rama, Hare Krishna, Krishna Krishna*" etc., is found in the Purāṇas (*Pd* IV.80.2).

49. *K* II.15.14, 39; *Pd* I.54.38.

50. *B* 245.38; *Bd* I.16.14; *K* II.23.93; 25.20.

51. *A* 152ff.; *B* 223.55ff.; *Bd* I.7ff.; *Bhg* XI.10.1; 17; *G* I.49ff.; 213ff.; *K* II.12ff.; *Pd* I.54.38; V.15.163; *Vi* III.8.21ff.; *Vm* 14.

52. *L* I.20; *Pd* V.19.74ff.; *Vm* 11.14ff.

53. *A* 27; *B* 224.30ff.; 225.49ff; *G* I.223.3 etc.

54. *Bd* I.30.5, 62; *Bhg* XII.3.52 etc.

55. *Pd* II.59–63; 85.13; 123.52.

56. *A* 109.3ff.; 111.1ff.; *Pd* I.11.20–36.

Bibliography

Sources

The following abbreviations of sources are used: *A* = *Agni Purāṇa; B* = *Brahma Purāṇa; Bd* = *Brahmāṇḍa Purāṇa; Bhg* = *Bhāgavata Purāṇa; Bhv* = *Bhaviṣya Purāṇa; Bv* = *Brahmavaivarta Purāṇa; G* = *Garuḍa Purāṇa; K* = *Kūrma Purāṇa; L* = *Liṅga Purāṇa; Mk* = *Mārkandeya Purāṇa; Mt* = *Matsya Purāṇa; N* = *Nārada Purāṇa; P* = *Padma Purāṇa; S* = *Śiva Purāṇa; Sk* = *Skanda Purāṇa; Vi* = *Viṣṇu Purāṇa; Vm* = *Vāmana Purāṇa; Vr* = *Varāha Purāṇa; Vy* = *Purāṇa.*

The most common editions of the Puranic texts are from the following publishers: Venkateshwar Steam Press, Bombay; Ananda Sanskrit Series, Poona; Gurumandala Series, M.S. Mor, Calcutta; Jivananda Vidyasagara Bhattacharya, Calcutta. Only the Venkateshwar Steam Press, Bombay, has published all the eighteen Mahāpurāṇas. Reprinting of the Purāṇas that have gone out of print has been started both in India and abroad. For example, critical editions of the Vāmana, Kūrma, and Varāha Purāṇas have been published by the All-India Kashiraj Trust, Ramnagar, Varanasi (India).

Not all the Purāṇas have been translated. Translations into English are still in process, especially by Motilal Banarsidass, Delhi; and Chowkhamba, Varanasi. Old translations are also reprinted both in India and abroad.

Bhāgavata Purāṇa. Text and translation. 2 vols. Gorakhpur: Gita-Press, 1952, 1960.

Dimmit, C., and J. A. B. van Buitenen, eds. and trans. *Classical Hindu Mythology: A Reader in Sanskrit Purāṇas.* Philadelphia: Temple University, 1978.

Viṣṇu Purāṇa. Translated by H. H. Wilson. Reprint. Calcutta: Punthi Pustak, 1961.

Studies

Agarwala, V. S. *Matsaya Purāṇa: A Study*. Benaras: All-India Kashiraj Trust, 1963.
Bhattacharji, S. *The Indian Theogony: A Comparative Study of Indian Mythology from the Vedas to the Purāṇas*. Cambridge: Cambridge University Press, 1970.
Brown, C. M. *God as Mother: A Feminine Theology in India: An Historical and Theological Study of the Brahmavaivarta Purāṇa*. Hartford, Vt.: Claude Stark, 1974.
Dikshitar, V. R. Ramchandra. *The Purāṇic Index*. Madras: University of Madras, 1958.
Hazra, R. C. *Studies in Purāṇic Records of Hindu Rites and Customs*. 2nd ed. Delhi: Motilal Banarsidass, 1975.
——. *Studies in the Upapurāṇas*. Calcutta: Sanskrit College, 1958.
Kirfel, Willibald. *Purāṇa Pañcalaṣana*. Benaras: Motilal Banarsidass, 1963.
Mani, Vettam. *Purāṇic Encyclopaedia: A Comprehensive Dictionary with Special Reference to the Epic and Purāṇic Literature*. Delhi: Motilal Banarsidass, 1975.
Pusalker, A. D. *Studies in the Epics and Purāṇas*. Bombay: Bharatiya Vidya Bhavan, 1963.
Rocher, Ludo. *The Purāṇas*. Wiesbaden: O. Harrassowitz, 1986.

10

Mysticism in the *Śaivāgamas*

Hélène Brunner

The Śaivāgamas and the School of Śaiva Siddhānta*

IT IS WELL KNOWN to any student of indology that Southern Śaivism is based on a corpus of Sanskrit texts that were probably written before the eighth century and go by the name of Āgamas, more correctly, Śaivāgamas. Their relatively recent discovery by the world of scholars is due mainly to the efforts of the great French indologist Jean Filliozat, and to the work of the French Institute of Indology, which he founded in Pondicherry in 1956.[1] We have talked about this elsewhere and there is no need to expatiate on the subject. It is better to insist on the permanence of the tradition that has its roots in the Āgamas, for these are not dead texts. Even though the priests of the Śaiva temples (the *gurukkals* of the Tamil land), or the initiates who perform private worship, do not draw the instructions they require directly from these works but take them instead from (Sanskrit or Tamil) manuals, which are easier to use, yet it is a fact that these manuals transmit the formulas, the acts, the meditations, and the theoretical explications that were first given in the Āgamas. Moreover, whoever belongs to the sect can, if he or she wishes to, consult the Āgamas themselves, since a good number of them have come down to us, having

*This article first appeared in French in the issue of *Studia Missionalia* devoted to mysticism (26 [1977] 287–314). For the English translation given here, I have, besides making some minor corrections, omitted some passages and simplified others, in order to comply with the editorial instructions regarding the length of the paper. For similar reasons, I have canceled most of the notes of the French version, to which the reader is therefore directed, both for Āgamic references and for discussions. Finally, I also had to omit the Addendum I had prepared, which contained some new reflections, partially inspired by the general theme of the volume at hand: a new evaluation of the *bubhukṣu's* discipline, and some observations on the place of the temple in the spiritual life of the Śaivas.

been faithfully recopied by successive generations of masters. Almost every Śaiva priest owns, hidden somewhere in his house, carefully tied bundles of palm-leaf manuscripts in which his ancestors have recorded in writing some texts of their tradition. Those *gurukkals* who still know sufficient Sanskrit read these works and exchange them among themselves; some of them even continue to recopy them—nowadays on paper. Some have understood the advantage of printing: even before the Western world took over, four fundamental Āgamas (*mūlāgamas*) and several secondary Āgamas (*upāgamas*) had been published in India.

Thus, the tradition remains alive. As far as the ritual is concerned, it is in the hands of the Śaiva initiates, particularly the masters or *ācāryas*, mostly temple priests, whose uninterrupted lineage goes back to the epoch of the Āgamas—in other words, back to Śiva, since the Āgamas are supposed to have been enunciated by Him. As far as the doctrine is concerned, the tradition has split into a Sanskrit branch, which rests solely on the Āgamas, and the Tamil branch—by far the better known[2]—which has included in its canon texts of a different origin which the other deliberately ignores. The two schools have the same name, Śaiva Siddhānta, which is the technical name by which the Āgamas themselves denote the kind of Śaivism they teach. We shall consider here only the Sanskrit Śaiva Siddhānta, the sole direct heir of the Āgamas. Our sources will, therefore, be the Āgamas themselves with their commentaries, and the Sanskrit manuals based on them. To this list one should also add a few independent doctrinal works, the most important of which were written between the ninth and the eleventh centuries.

The fact that we rely on the written word alone does not mean that we totally ignore present-day Śaivism. It is our firm conviction, however, that a study of the texts written when this religion was in full vigor is bound to yield far more interesting results than an ethnological approach of the weakened Śaivism we meet with in South India in our days.

At first sight, nothing seems less mystical than the Āgamas, these voluminous encyclopedias of rituals, in which are recorded the details of all the rites that the initiates may have to perform in their life. The obligatory and daily (*nitya*) rites take comparatively little space, weighed down as they are by the enormous mass of the others: firstly, the occasional (*naimittika*) rites, which include rites of atonement, season rites, the rites that are called for by some exterior event, and especially the establishments of temples and divine images of all types; second, the optional (*kāmya*) rites, which are destined to ensure success, mostly in mundane enterprises, or immediate benefits of a general nature, such as peace and prosperity to a community. This "section on rites" (*kriyāpāda*) forms not the totality but the quasi totality of an

Āgama. There is also a "section on behavior" (*caryāpāda*), which deals with the specific duties of the members of the sect, but is often inextricably mixed with the previous one, instead of forming a separate quarter (*pāda*). An Āgama should also in principle include two other sections of theoretical content: a "section on knowledge" (*vidyā-* or *jñānapāda*), in order to set forth the beliefs particular to the school, namely, the nature of Śiva, the nature of souls, the description of the shackles by which they are bound, and of the path to salvation; and a "section on yoga" (*yogapāda*), which aims at describing the structure of the subtle human body and the practices that are supposed to result in its control. In most cases, the two latter sections are missing, either because they never existed or because they have been lost.[3] The section on rites generally makes up for this deficiency quite well. The doctrine associated with the ritual is sometimes explained as part of the description of the ritual itself. Often it quite clearly shows through the rite, and, if necessary, the commentators recall the essential points of the beliefs on which the rite is built.

This situation—the general absence of the theoretical section and the ease with which one can do without—clearly reveals the character of the religious life that is taught by the Āgamas, which is pure ritualism. Not, however, a ritualism of the Vedic type, where the rituals had either a cosmological function or a selfish aim, but a ritualism one aspect of which, as we are going to show, constitutes a path to liberation for the individual. This liberation is the effect of the rite itself; the intellectual knowledge of the dogmas and of the psychosomatic structure of the individual is but preliminary to the effective practice of yoga and, above all, to the performance of the rites in which this yoga is integrated. As for the discipline, it conditions the success of the ritual itself. Certainly no one can act efficiently without the theoretical knowledge on which one's acts are based; but it is more important to emphasize the point that intellectual knowledge alone is in vain if it does not express itself by acts, and that the mediation of acts is necessary for the discipline to attain the proposed objective. Everything leads to the rite.[4] Therefore, it is following a serious deviation that the Tamil Śaiva Siddhānta presents the development of the spiritual path of the disciple as a progressive passage from *caryāpāda* to *kriyāpāda*, from *kriyāpāda* to *yogāpāda*, and from this to *jñānapāda*, each stage corresponding to a particular initiation.[5] All the Āgamas that we know deny such an interpretation of their teaching. Hence, we come to the following conclusions: (1) we shall look for mysticism in the texts and not in the beliefs or behavior of present-day Śaivas; (2) we shall seek it in the ritual parts of the Āgamas and of the manuals, not in their doctrinal sections; and (3) taking into account the fact that the occasional rites are derived from daily rituals and do not shed any fresh light on the inner attitude of the officiant, and that the rituals that are aimed at some profit generally imply an attitude that is contrary to that of the mystic, one can restrict oneself to the analysis of the daily ritual, which will be completed by a study of the act that renders it possible and makes it a path to Śiva: the intiation or *dīksā*.

The Promises of the Āgamas

With the preceding statements, we have given in advance the conclusion of our inquiry: a path that leads to Śiva is a mystical one, and the person who follows it is a mystic. But the Āgamas do not present union with Śiva as the sole aim of the religious techniques they describe. Their authors were too sensible to do that. They knew that while everyone seeks happiness, this happiness is far from having the same form for each person. For the majority, it amounts to the possession of worldly goods or of the less ephemeral boons that lie ahead in various paradises. The Āgamas admit to satisfying these "lovers of enjoyments," these *bubhukṣus*, and to offer them different paths to realize their aspirations. But they note that this type of fruit was also promised by the Vedas. Certainly, it could never be a fruit as delicious as some of those which the Āgamas propose, since the Vedic school[6] did not know the purest worlds to which the Śaiva initiation can lead;[7] but, nonetheless, paradisiac sojourns were offered to those who abided by the ancient law. The path proclaimed by Śiva in the Āgamas is new in that it gives access to enjoyments (*bhukti*) as well as to liberation (*mukti*). This contrast between the so-called Vedic path, which can lead only to *bhukti*, and the Śaiva path, which offers both *bhukti* and *mukti*, is considered to be essential and is recalled constantly.

Bhukti

Within Śaivism itself, the distinction between enjoyments (*bhukti*) and liberation (*mukti*) and, accordingly, between the aspirants of enjoyments (*bubhukṣus*) and the aspirants of liberation (*mumukṣus*) is not so clear-cut; with the result that it is not possible for us to reject completely all the *bubhukṣus* from our field of investigation, under the pretext that one cannot imagine any mystics whose ideal is limited to obtaining pleasures.

Indeed, there is a whole range of "enjoyments" that the Āgamas can satisfy and, thus, a whole hierarchy of *bubhukṣus*. Some dream only of acquiring powers in this world, which allow them to cure or to kill, to cast spells or to exorcise, to ensure the victory of the king or to crush his enemies. These are the *bubhukṣus* of the inferior type. Others aim at access to worlds which, though better than ours, are nevertheless "impure" because they belong to the inferior part of the cosmos, which is a production of the opaque *māyā*.[8] There the effects of previous deeds (i.e., *karman*) follow the individual and, consequently, shadow mingles with light, suffering with happiness. Some disciples wish to take up their abode in these worlds, in order to exert there a sovereignty conceived on the model of earthly kingship. The desires of the *bubhukṣus* of this intermediate category do not differ essentially from those of the former. Nor does their future. At the next dissolution of the universe, both groups will suffer the fate of the worlds they inhabit; that is to say, they will disappear in the eternal *māyā*, only to emerge from it at the next creation, which will tie them anew to the wheel of becoming—unless they have been able to find the path leading to Śiva through the intervention of an initiating guru.

It is another matter as regards the last category, which we shall call the superior *bubhukṣus*. These are disciples who wish, first, to experience superior enjoyments; and later only, to attain that supreme aim which is liberation.[9] In other words, although they are named *bubhukṣus*, they are such only for the time being: in reality they are aspirants to deferred liberation. The refined enjoyments to which these *bubhukṣus* aspire are described as access to the "pure" worlds, situated beyond *māyā*. In these worlds of light, the stuff of which is an extremely subtle reality called *bindu* (or *māhāmāyā*, the Great *māyā*), *karman* does not follow the soul, nor is any *karman* sown by the gentle activity of the "pure" bodies, also made of *bindu*, which the soul takes on; and all experiences are blissful. These worlds are really paradises, of which the highest ones are abodes of great beatitude pervaded by Divine Light. Some souls enter there spontaneously: those who, in some way or another—but before their congenital stain (the *mala* about which we shall speak later) has become "ripe"—have been able to get rid of their burden of past *karman*. When the time has come, Śiva will grant them His liberating grace in the form of a direct initiation, which dispenses with the intermediary of a guru. The *bubhukṣus* we are concerned with are led to these worlds by their earthly guru, who confers on them an initiation adapted to the desires they manifest. This *dīkṣā* resembles the one given to the pure *mumukṣus*; but it is supposed to guarantee to those who receive it, provided they submit themselves to strict discipline, first *bhukti* and then *mukti*, without Śiva having to intervene any more, and without the risk of these purified souls falling back into the sub-*māyā* worlds. The liberation of one of these souls can take place at any given moment, if the desire for pleasures or powers becomes totally extinct. At the latest, it takes place at the time of the great cosmic dissolution, when the pure worlds themselves disappear, absorbed in their Cause (namely, *bindu*). Since this final liberation is certain, the abiding in the "pure" levels of the cosmos is sometimes called "inferior liberation" (*aparamukti*); but it would be better called "deferred liberation."

One sees why it was impossible to affirm, at the outset, that only *mumukṣus* could belong to the group of mystics. The superior *bubhukṣus* can display the same dispositions; however, the divinity toward which their love goes and with which they aspire to be united at that stage is not the supreme Śiva in whom all desire and all manifestation of power are absent, but rather one of the more easily accessible forms of Śiva, which are supposed to possess the very qualities or powers that the *bubhukṣus* seek, and which precisely govern the "pure" worlds, or else one or the other of the numerous divinities that populate these heavens. Except for this difference, which is not negligible, what will be said about the lovers of liberation is, *mutatis mutandis*, applicable to the superior *bubhukṣus* also.

Mukti

What then is this liberation that will occupy us from now on? One can define it negatively by saying that it consists in the falling away of the shackles that cause an ordinary being to be limited in its capacities of knowing and acting, and to be denied beatitude. These shackles are sometimes compared to bonds (*pāśa*) and sometimes to stains (*mala*). There are three of them.[10] The first and most fundamental one is a material impurity, which has always obscured the soul (*ātman*, *aṇu*), masking its natural faculties of knowledge and action, which are really infinite, like those of Śiva. One calls it *mala* (the impurity *par excellence*) or, to put it more precisely, *āṇavamala* (the impurity characteristic of the *aṇu*). This *mala*, though being eternal and one, nevertheless attaches itself separately to multiple *aṇus*, each of which must liberate itself from its hold. They cannot do it through their own forces, paralyzed as they are by this very *mala*. Śiva alone can detach this impurity from them, when time has sufficiently "ripened" it. Just as a surgeon removes the ripe cataract from a sick eye with a sharp instrument, Śiva removes the *mala* from the *ātman* with the help of His saving power, *anugrahaśakti*. The second of the bonds is *karman*, that is to say, the sum of the effects of past deeds, the mass of which, always being reconstituted, would never become exhausted if one were not to take the necessary measures. *Karman* is an inevitable evil and without beginning, adhering less intimately to the soul than *mala*, but more tenaciously than matter. The Śaivas have no original doctrine regarding it, but they propose, as we shall see, an original method for its destruction. The third bond is constituted by matter—that is, *māyā*, or, more exactly, what it produces, the worlds and the bodies. At every new creation, Śiva Himself adds it to the other two bonds by precipitating the souls into the worlds which He at that time makes *māyā* beget. He does it for the benefit of the *ātman*, because this is the only way for it to "consume" its *karman* and to cause its *mala* to ripen.

The individual is free, or rather freed, when the three preceding bonds have fallen. He or she was like cattle (*paśu*) fastened by ropes (*pāśa*). He or she becomes the Master (*pati*), the equal of Śiva. The usual Sanskrit terms for liberation—*mukti* and *mokṣa*—connote exactly this phenomenon of the disappearing of the shackles.

The liberation also has a positive aspect: that is the transformation, to which we have already alluded, of *paśu* into *pati*, of non-Śiva into Śiva. One must insist on that bold doctrine of the Āgamas, for it is little known, not having been accepted by the Tamil Śaiva Siddhānta, except by some rare masters who are considered heterodox. In fact, the Tamil school is anxious to safeguard its ideal of *bhakti* by maintaining a sufficient distance between the worshiper—even at the end of his ascent—and the Worshiped; and it is also certainly anxious to stress its refusal of Śaṅkara's nondualism. Nevertheless, the Āgamas are definite: the only difference between a liberated soul and Śiva is that Śiva has always been free, whereas the soul has become free at a certain point in time, and by the intervention of Śiva, who lets His Grace (*anugrahaśakti*) fall on the soul.[11]

The act by which Śiva, operating through the medium of a consecrated master who lends Him his body, breaks the chain of existences of an individual by making him leap into the eternal, is called *dīkṣa*—an untranslatable term, usually rendered by "initiation." More exactly, it is the *nirvāṇa-dīkṣā*, or "liberating initiation," the highest of all the *dīksās* that the school recognizes.[12] The term *nirvāṇa*, taken from Buddhism, is here charged with an essentially positive content, since it designates the soul's obtaining the state of Śiva Himself, *śivatva* (being-Śiva or śivahood), which has always been its own, but had been clouded by the presence of *mala* since the inconceivable beginning of the series of existences.

That is the aim assigned to the most fervent followers of Śiva: realizing their identity with God. This identity permits the intimate union of the soul with Śiva; it is not the fusion of the soul into Śiva. Surprising as it may seem, the Śaiva thesis on this point is clear: a liberated *ātman is* Śiva; it can unite with Śiva but does not disappear into Him. This is not the place to explain how the scholars of the sect try to remove the difficulties that such a conception of liberation entails. Let us just accept the idea that, according to them, a liberated soul can "feel" itself to be the equal of Śiva without blending into Him, and without being anymore limited by Him, since it possesses the same infinite power of knowledge and action. Let us concede, too, that one day it can discover that it had always been Śiva without feeling that its previous experiences as well as the world in which it was then plunged, as the other beings still are, were illusory.

The Liberating Initiation

The double affirmation of the essential identity between an *ātman* and Śiva and of the possibility of its actualization is the basis of the whole Āgamic ritual. That, at least, is the profound significance it has for true initiates. So now we turn to the initiating rites that introduce the devotee into a regular religious life and at the same time give it its meaning.

By a first initiation, the *samaya-dīkṣā,* or "regular" initiation,[13] the guru, inhabited by Śiva, introduces the disciple into the Śaiva family by a very simple act: by laying his hand—the hand of Śiva—on the head of the disciple. The details that surround this central act need not be discussed here. Suffice it to call attention to two points. First, it is after this *dīkṣā* that the disciple, called a *samayin*, must daily offer a regular worship to Śiva, to the Fire, and to one's guru, and must scrupulously follow the discipline imposed on all intitiates. Second, it is clear that this first *dīkṣā* is not a "transforming" rite, despite certain formulas used in the ritual, which could give rise to confusion. The disciple who has received it remains a *paśu*, for whom neither the path of *bhukti* nor that of *mukti* is open. One simply hopes that his (or her) *mala* will ripen, thanks to the ritual activity of an absolutely unselfish nature (for it does not sow *karman*), which he (or she) is going to perform under the protection of Śiva. This will result in a progressive modification of his* inner dispositions, in an increase of virtues and in a parallel decline of deficiencies and, above all, in an outbreak of a strong love for the Lord, accompanied by a more and more intense desire to rejoin Him.

When, at the end of a certain probationary period, the disciples show indubitable signs that their *mala* is ready to fall and that they are therefore ready to receive divine grace, the master proposes a higher *dīkṣā*, which can take the two forms already mentioned.

To the disciples eager for enjoyments or powers, the *bubhukṣus*, the guru gives a *dīkṣā* that is capable of leading them, after a long period of ascesis, to unite with a divinity of their choice in one of the pure worlds, from which one does not descend anymore. An adequate consecration makes these initi-

*From now on, masculine pronouns only will be used, for the sake of simplicity; but one may not forget that there were also some female initiates.

ates into *sādhakas*, a term that, in this context, is reserved for those *bubhukṣus* of the superior type, whose liberation is only deferred.[14]

To the others, the *mumukṣus*, whose sole desire is to unite with *niṣkala-Siva*,[15]—Śiva who transcends all forms—and who reveal to the perspicacious eyes of the master the purity of their intentions by certain characteristic traits of their conduct (a disgust with the world is most often required, together with an immense love for Śiva), the guru grants that liberating *dīkṣā* which we have alluded to above.

This is an immense purification, the essential part of which is the forced consumption—forced by the *mantras* carrying the power of Śiva—of all the *karman* accumulated by the disciple during previous lives. The guru, acting in the name of Śiva or, more exactly, as Śiva, makes all the fruits of this *karman* ripen at once, in whichever worlds they may be;[16] he then makes the disciple consume them by letting him be born in each of these worlds, live the life that awaited him there and undergo the corresponding lot of pains and pleasures. During this time—a time that is condensed into the few moments of the *dīkṣā* but is equivalent to hundreds or thousands of lives—the disciple obviously sows *karman*; therefore, he is not allowed to leave any world without the guru having carefully destroyed the germs of this *karman* "yet to come." All these births and all these experiences take place simultaneously in all the worlds that belong to the same cosmic level. But the process must be repeated at every level, with the whole staging (which we have not described), which makes the infinite matrix of the Śakti of Śiva intervene, as a symbol and substitute for all the matrices necessary for all these births. The cosmos can be divided in six different ways, and so there are six types of *dīkṣās* possible or six paths by which an initiate can be led from the earth to Śiva.[17] The most common *dīkṣā* utilizes a division of the cosmos into five strata, each reigned over by a power called *Kalā*: one then talks of a *kalā-dīkṣā* (initiation by the "Path of *Kalās*").

At the end of the ascent, when the soul emerges from the last envisaged domain, it is relieved of all the past *karman*, free of all future *karman;* and, at the same time, it has freed itself from its subjection to matter, which was solely due to the presence of *karman*. Moreover, since the *dīkṣā* was undertaken only when the *mala* of the disciple was sufficiently ripe, one imagines that it falls off by itself during the ritual, having attained perfect maturity under the effect of the Śakti of Śiva. Some special rites emphasize this result.

A soul free of all bonds, however, *is* Śiva, and this identity permits the union of these two infinites. The guru effects it by a complex process in which a butter libation accompanies a very peculiar yoga exercise, during which the syllable representing Śiva (HAUṂ in most cases, sometimes KṢAUṂ) is first joined with the soul (*ātman*) of the disciple within the guru's heart, then made to ascend along the guru's central *nādī* (*suṣumnā*) up to the domain of the transcendent Śiva—a place called *dvādaśānta*, for it is imagined twelve inches above the cranium. Afterward, the guru retrieves the soul from Śiva, in order to put it back in its previous place, the heart of the disciple.

As a matter of fact, one shackle escaped the purification that was accomplished by the *nirvāṇa-dīkṣā*: the *karman* that is neither past nor yet to come, namely, the one that the disciple is consuming in the present life, which is called *prārabdha-karman* or *prārabdhakārya-karman* (the *karman* of which the effects have begun to manifest themselves). This *karman* cannot be destroyed by any of the usual *dīkṣās,* but must be consumed until it is used up. Among the numerous passages of the Āgamas that state this truth, the most famous one is a verse of the *Kiraṇa*, quoted untiringly by all the masters: "Innumerable past *karmans* are burnt like seeds by the *aṇus* (here, the *mantras* utilized during the *dīkṣā*); the *karman* yet to come is prevented; with regard to the one by which "this" (our actual body) exists, only by consuming it one wipes it out."[18] Now, in order to consume this *karman*, the disciple must live out his present life; and this is why the guru restores his *ātman* to his body, instead of leaving it united with Śiva. This reincarnation, however, does not in the least affect the acquired glory, the śivahood that is finally realized. The guru affirms this truth by loudly proclaiming the perfections with which the free soul is now endowed: these are the very perfections of Śiva.

The Private Ritual Life

An incorporated Śiva who will be entirely Śiva only after death: such is now, after the liberating *dīkṣā*, the status of the initiate—henceforth called *putraka*, the Son.[19] The years during which his present body will continue to exist are not years of idleness for the *putraka*; because his *dīkṣā* will bear its fruit—that is, the total and definitive liberation—only if he manages not to spoil the accomplished work. Now, one sole but serious danger awaits this initiate: the one entailed by the actions that he, of necessity, will have to perform. If these acts sow *karman* and one does not prevent its fructification, new lives await the disciple, whose *dīkṣā* will have been a vain act. That means that the initiation is liberating only if certain conditions are fulfilled. This is why it is called "conditional" (*sāpekṣā*), a qualification that contrasts it to the initiations (termed *nirapekṣā*) given to physiologically and psychologically deficient individuals, which are not furnished with rules.

The requirements imposed on the initiate are of two types. On the one hand, he will submit during his whole life, without weakening, to a discipline that is very strict, though not ascetic. On the other hand, he has the absolute obligation to fulfill certain religious duties, the most important ones being, as we have said, the daily worship of Śiva, of the Fire, and of the guru.

We shall not speak of the discipline, except that no initiate, however spiritually advanced, can escape its imperatives. There is no place in the Āgamas for a condition "beyond the rules"—which sufficiently proves that the *caryāpādas*, in which the rules are laid down, are not destined for beginners only.

On the contrary, we shall insist on the ritual life, not without mentioning in passing that it is but an aspect of the discipline in the wide sense of the term—and this is probably the reason why some Āgamas describe the daily private rites in their *caryāpāda* instead of including them in the *kriyāpāda*, as is the general rule. The ritual life is not the prerogative of the *putrakas*. It concerns all the initiates, including the *samayins*; but since it gets its full meaning only after the *nirvāṇa-dīkṣā*, we shall limit our inquiry to the rituals of these full-fledged initiates. It is not necessary to examine them all. The cults of the Fire and of the guru are, in fact, a worship of Śiva under the form of the Fire or of the guru: it will suffice, therefore, to consider the worship of Śiva on any image (and generally it is a *liṅga*), insisting on those aspects of it which make it a mystical event, or which give room for the expression of a mystique.

The two actors of the drama have been presented: the *putraka* (or the *ācārya* he might have become) and Śiva. But Śaivism recognizes as an agent only the spiritual part of the being. In the case of the *putraka*, this spiritual part, the *ātman*, has become Śiva. The *putraka*'s worship is thus an adoration of Śiva by Śiva. It could not be anything else. We read in our texts: "In order to worship Śiva, one has to become Śiva" (*śivībhūya śivaṃ yajet*). And also: "The one who is not Śiva should not worship Śiva (*nāśivaś śivam arcayet*) (see SP1, 130). The requirement thus expressed is so fundamental that even the *samayins*, that is, the initiates who are still *paśus*, must "become Śiva" for the duration of the worship, through appropriate rites. Thus, the worship must not be seen as a homage that an inferior (a human) does to a superior (Śiva), but as the expression, and even the consequence, of the identity of the soul and of Śiva.

A preparatory phase actualizes this identification for the *samayin*, where it is still masked by the stains; for the *putraka*, it reactualizes it, if one may say so, by suppressing the opacity of the body, which is liable to make one forget it. The worship proper expresses it.

Śiva

Worship of Śiva as Liṅga

The performance of the ritual as it has been fixed by the tradition could, not doubt, lead a profane observer astray. It can even deceive the officiant, who, not yet distinctively perceiving his "śivahood," has a natural tendency to place himself in the position of an infirm being—of a sinner, as the Christian would say—and to express a humility that has no place in the worship but conveys what his whole physiological and mental being cannot help feeling. Therefore, the Āgamas and the manuals persistently remind him: "You are Śiva!"

Should we be surprised or even indignant at this conception of worship? We see here, rather, the logical corollary of a metaphysical theorem that is acceptable to all, namely, the incommunicability of two realities that are situated on different ontological levels. The communication demands the displacement of one of them: God must descend toward man, or man must ascend to God. For the Śaivas, the immutable Śiva cannot "descend" to the level of a tainted soul. So it is necessary that the soul, freed from its stains, rise to the level of Śiva. It does not do it by its own powers. It is the power of Śiva which draws it toward Him at the time of the *dīkṣā* and of every worship. Nonetheless, the soul is led to the supreme level, where it beholds Śiva face to face.

Preparation for the Worship

The officiant must thus become Śiva again before beginning worship. This episode is called "transformation into Śiva" (*śivīkaraṇa*), a process that comprises two stages.

(1) The first is destructive. It is the *bhūtaśuddhi*, the "purification of elements" or, better, the "destruction of elements." The method varies with the authors; sometimes the *bhūtaśuddhi* is viewed as a vast conflagration that evokes the destruction of the world at the time of *pralaya.* Sometimes the process is more intellectual, but the effect is always the same: it is the total abolition, through the power of the recited *mantras*, and only with respect to the person concerned, of everything belonging to earth, water, fire, air, and ether in succession. Not only is the gross body supposed to disappear during this great purification, but also the five levels of the cosmos over which these very elements reign—which are none other than the five domains governed by the *Kalās* which the *dīkṣā* brings into play. The officiant must take care beforehand to shelter his *ātman* in a place that escapes the annihilation: generally, in the very sojourn of the transcendent Śiva, the aforesaid *dvādaśānta*.

In the case of the full-fledged initiate, whom we are now discussing, the *bhūtaśuddhi* should be regarded not only as the necessary disappearance of the body but as a kind of daily repetition of the liberating intiation, justified by the fear that some seeds of *karman* were unfortunately sown in certain worlds by an inconsiderate act of the disciple.

(2) After such a total destruction, a reconstruction, now concerning only the body, is needed. The purpose is to create in the place of the body that has disappeared a pure body, where Śiva will be able to establish His abode. In other words, the body "made of *māyā*" will be replaced by the very body of Śiva. It is clear that Śiva, who is purely spiritual, cannot have a body, subtle as its stuff might be. However, when God must assume a form, in order to perform a certain activity or to become an object of contemplation, what serves as His body is a collection of powers, called Mantras, which are aspects of His one and undivided own power. It is then said that Śiva has a "body of power" (*śāktadeha*), or a "body of Mantras" (*mantradeha*), or else a "body of Vidyās" (*vidyādeha*—the term *vidyā* in this case being the feminine equivalent of the masculine *mantra*). That is the body which the worshiper must construct in the place of his own. He does it by reciting on every part of his own body (which is supposed to have disappeared, but this is of little importance), the *mantra* (formula) that calls into being the Mantra (Energy) that is to replace the organ in question. The process varies according to whether one operates "broadly" or "in detail." In the first case, the worshiper recites merely the fundamental *mantra* of Śiva and those of His "Members" (sometimes adding the *mantras* that evoke the five faces of the Divine Form, Sadāśiva); in the second case, the worshiper recites thirty-eight formulas which create in succession all the parts of God, seen under the aspect of a human being. Since these parts are called *kalās*, the act is called *sakalī-karaṇa*, that is, "creation of parts" (parts of the body of Śiva). The subject of this rite can be anything. Here it is the body of the officiant, which thus becomes a "body of Mantras."

The officiant is now ready to worship his God.

Mental Worship

The first phase of the cult is completely interior. The devotee worships the Śiva-who-is-in-him by mentally accomplishing all the acts of the external worship that serves as the model, without omitting any detail. He likewise worships Śiva in the inner Fire, on the model of the worship of Śiva in the outer Fire.

The interior phase of worship is obligatory. It is the logical result of *śivīkaraṇa*, the necessary homage to the Śiva who dwells in the initiate: for every form of Śiva must be recognized as such and be treated with the same respect. Certain texts even make this inner worship (*antaḥpūjā*) an integral part of the "becoming-Śiva," which it crowns; for only after this worship of the Śiva-who-is-in-him is the officiant in a position to worship, as an equal, the Śiva-who-is-elsewhere, that is to say, in a concrete image.

Exterior Worship

The worshiper must beforehand purify in turn (in the same way as he has purified himself) the place, the material, the *mantras*, and the image that will serve as a support for the *pūjā*, so as to make them worthy of coming into contact with the Divinity. The initiate is invited to forget the apparent form of things (the room where he sits, the flowers and other offerings that he will handle, the words that he is going to utter, the cylinder of stone or metal that he will worship), and consider their "pure" form only. He should particularly imagine the place he occupies as being situated beyond *māyā*—in this region of the cosmos where matter is so subtle that it does not represent an obstacle to the radiance of God.

The initial act of the worship, however, makes the officiant come down from these heights for a time. For he must construct a throne for Śiva, mentally and through the power of the Mantra. Now, this throne, which is to be projected on the pedestal of the divine image, occupies the whole range of the cosmos; it is the cosmos itself, over which Śiva reigns, and therefore it entails an "impure" part as its foundation. But its top projects into the luminous part, where the worshiper stands and where the worship proper will take place.

The officiant first invites Śiva to come and dwell in the image that is in front of him or, in other words, to come and be seated on the throne. But Śiva, being pure Spirit, can appear only in a body: this will be the body-of-Mantras, which was mentioned above, the form (*mūrti*) known by the name of Sadāśiva. The worhsiper evokes this form, by reciting a particular *mantra* while intensively visualizing all the details: the five faces, the ten arms with the various attributes they hold, and so on.[20] He then "sees" Śiva in front of him, Śiva seated on the immense throne.

But this form is still only an empty form. Giving Him a soul means making Śiva descend therein in His absolute aspect, "without parts" (*niṣkala*). To this end the officiant performs a yogic exercise which reinforces or reaffirms his identity with Śiva. By slowly reciting the root syllable which represents Śiva (HAUṂ in most cases, as we have seen), split up in parts of increasing subtlety, the officiant makes it "rise" by the force of the breath from his heart to the invisible place twice mentioned, the *dvādaśānta*. There the *mantra* HAUṂ unites with the supreme Śiva. The officiant now has just to "deposit" this Pure Spirit in the form that it animates.

Such is, in brief, the rite called *āvāhana*, or Invocation. It must be completed by a series of rites, the aim of which is, in succession, to assure that Śiva is well-disposed toward the worshiper; that He will not, before the end of the worship, leave the image He was made to enter; finally, that He is well "protected," that is, that none other than a real devotee can see His true form. The officiant then solemnly gives Him Members (in the form of Mantras) which are the expression of His Glory.[21] Now the God is ready to receive the homage due to Him.

This is the part of the ritual that is best known. All the rites so far described can indeed pass unobserved to an outside witness, especially if they are performed somewhat quickly, as is the general rule nowadays. The subsequent "services," which range from washing the feet to giving a feast and include elaborate ablutions are, on the other hand, clearly visible and sometimes quite impressive when they are done in public in the temples. It would be quite wrong, however, to think that they form the core of the ritual. If the worshiper has invoked his God in the way described above, it is certainly not in order to render Him these "services," which He does not require. Rather, it is because he invokes Him daily, that is to say, "recalls" (in the literal sense) His Presence into the interior of himself (mental worship) and in the world around (exterior worship), that the worshiper does God homage by bestowing a series of attentions on Him, of the kind a host lavishes on any person of distinction who has entered his home.

The idea is not to declare that this part of the worship is superfluous. It certainly aids the worshiper to convince himself of the real existence of Śiva as he washes Him, dresses Him, anoints Him with perfumes, feeds Him, and so on. The Āgamas even insist that these acts of homage be effectively accomplished, even if one would have to replace costly objects—if one lacks the necessary resources—by some grains of rice or by a blade of grass. But to emphasize these "services" would be inconsistent with the affirmation that the worshiper is Śiva. In this context it will be noted that when an uninitiated person is authorized to show devotion to the Lord, directly or through the intermediary of a specialist, that person is permitted to perform or have performed for him, only these very acts, especially the offering of flowers, fruits, incense, or other things. For this simple devotee, the significance of this homage is very great. It is evidently less so, the nearer the worshiper is to Śiva.

One can say the same about the hymns of praise that are chanted at this stage (sometimes later) in the longer rituals. The most intense devotion can express itself through them and even culminate in a kind of ecstasy of the singer. But the Āgamas do not encourage these manifestations. They pertain to the domain of the pure *bhakti*, which is not regulated by our texts, and which consequently, we do not have to deal with.

The worship concludes with a *japa*, which consists in reciting the *mantra* of Śiva and those of His members, as many times as possible (for a *sādhaka*, it would be the *mantra* of the godhead which he serves especially). The initiates repeat their *mantra*—particularly the fundamental syllable called "seed," which makes it effective and can even replace it—as the guru has taught them on the occasion of the *dīkṣā*. Every repetition, and there can be hundreds of them, therefore involves a real yogic exercise, which results in a reinforcement of the identification between the *ātman* and Śiva, already brought about by the *śivīkaraṇa*. For a devotee who has chosen the path of powers (a *bubhukṣu*), the *japa* is an act sowing good *karman*, the effects of which must be carefully preserved, since it is their accumulation which will constitute the "capital" that he needs, to "buy" the results he seeks. He, therefore, daily recites the formula many times and entreats Śiva to take this act into account and to protect its fruits. The initiate who aims solely at liberation does not need such a capital: that one totally abandons the fruits of his *japa* to Śiva. For him, the *japa* is only one of the numerous occasions offered by the worship to identify with Śiva. Perhaps it is the best one. In any case, it is considered an essential phase of the daily ritual. An eloquent though somewhat mysterious verse concludes the gift of this ritual to Śiva, bestowed by the pure among pure ones: "Śiva is the giver, Śiva is the enjoyer, Śiva is the whole world; everywhere, Śiva is the one who worships—and this Śiva, verily, I am."

Such are the main phases of the worship of Śiva, whatever image it may use as concrete support.

Is This Ritual Path a Mystical One?

At this point of our discussion, the reader might feel somewhat disappointed: Is that all the mysticism to be found in the Āgamas and the texts derived from them, and is it a mysticism at all?

Evidently everything depends on what is understood by this term. If one insists on regarding as mystical only outpourings of adoration directed from "the bottom to the top"—from worshipers toward a God whom they feel to be immensely superior to them—or again those fulgurating encounters of the soul with the divine that are not conditioned by any rite and where the main component is love, then the attitude of the initiate, as described by the Āgamas, will not be called mystical. In the same Śaiva religion, mysticism would rather be found in the pure *bhaktas* (devotees), in those enthusiastic votaries of a personal God whose profound devotion, often accompanied by visions and dreams, rejects the ethical obligations and the ritual acts as useless burdens. South India has known many of them, and very great ones too, who are certainly more understandable to Christians than the disciplined initiates whose techniques of worship we have described.[22] Some have viewed Śiva as their Master, others as their Friend, and still others as their Lover. They have chanted His praise in verses bearing the stamp of an undeniable religious experience. They have refused the idols in the name of the omnipresence of God, the offerings in the name of His plenitude. They have often preferred the simple Name of Śiva to the traditional *mantras*. They have also generally ignored the dogma taught by the scriptures. Such devotees, no doubt, have their place in Śiva's paradise. But it is not about them that the Āgamas speak.

The Āgamas describe initiates whose whole life is regulated by rigid obligations, whose spiritual discoveries are, as it were, programmed in advance and whose emotions express themselves through the channel of well-structured rites. Still they proclaim that the path they teach is a path leading to Śiva. Let us listen again to the teachings that concern the purest disciples, those who receive the "liberating" *dīkṣā*. Before even being given this initiation, the devotee burns with the desire to unite with his God. During the ritual, the guru, inhabited by the power of Śiva, raises him to the level where the soul, laid bare, recognizes its complete identity with Śiva and unites with Him. Thereafter, daily throughout life and without flinching, the *putraka* expresses his conviction in the course of his private worship by acts that were taught to him, the indefinite repetition of which, far from being considered a hardening factor, is compared to the slow polishing of a precious stone; and also by formulas that were taught to him, the indefinite repetition of which, acting like an incantation, causes adventitious thoughts to be dispelled and the mind to be focused on the sole Reality. With faith and perseverance, he daily strives to regain the contact with Śiva, to experience it in all its intensity. Why doubt that some succeed? Now, if one is willing to admit that all direct contact with the supreme Reality is a mystical experience, one must say that these initiates are mystics. They are mystics as rightfully as those who have at the outset rejected the burden of the discipline and the apparatus of the rites as being useless. One would like to think that it was so with the authors of the Āgamas; and it seems that many subsequent masters, authors of commentaries or of manuals, speak from experience when they describe the beatitude in which the soul is plunged at the time of its union with Śiva.

That this is not valid for all initiates is probable and even certain. The affirmation "I am Śiva" must be more often the expression of a hope rather than of a certainty; and many yoga exercises that are directed at the union must remain inchoate. The Āgamas, however, seem to admit that if the sincerity is unquestioned, and if the required discipline is strictly observed, the efforts of these *mumukṣus* would not be in vain. Any *dīkṣā* rightly performed must yield its fruits. Therefore, even in the case of the less-advanced disciples one can still speak of mysticism, but a mysticism of sustained mental exertion, in which the mystical experience is postponed to the end of a long series of unfruitful efforts.

Such a confidence in the efficacy of the rite may look surprising, but one must keep in mind that the conditions the Āgamas imposed on the candidates of the *nirvāṇa-dīkṣā* were quite difficult to satisfy, so that these initiations must have been very rare. Their promises were taken seriously—a fact that is attested by the texts' abundant caution, and even threats heaped on the *ācāryas.* All those who out of greed, weakness, or lack of discrimination bestow a liberating *dīkṣā* on an unworthy disciple, will go to hell for thousands of years. Although these hells are not eternal, such a prospect should suffice to make the masters hesitate to give the initiation lightly. Hence probably the lofty optimism with which they assure that the fruit of the *dīkṣā* is certain.

The situation that we see nowadays is entirely different. The "liberating" *dīkṣās* are easily granted because one no longer considers them paths leading to Śiva, but paths leading to the function of an *ācārya*, considered to be a good "job."[23] One cannot then be surprised that the initiates, and even the masters with whom one comes in contact, so rarely give the impression of being mystics. But nothing could be more unfair than to judge the value of the Āgamic religion through them.

Conclusion

We shall conclude by pointing out the originality of the mystical path taught by the Āgamas. To be sure, it is less exalting than the direct way that is reserved for exceptional beings who can, without the risk of falling, attain the peak without detours, remain there as long as they like, and return there easily, either by relying on their innate talents as alpinists on the path of pure knowledge, or by placing their trust on the wings of a faultless *bhakti*. Yet the method of the Āgamas is perhaps safer. It is the difficult way, but clearly charted and blazed, destined for the courageous and persevering mountaineer whom his guide has one day taken to the top, where complete liberation awaits him, because he proved worthy of it and made himself light—so that he might *see,* and who was by the same guide taken back again to the plains, where he has a mission to fulfill. Daily he should, at least partially, perform the same ascent, and daily find himself again as a human being at the foot of that mountain on the summit of which he is God—and this until his soul, freed from the body, takes up its eternal abode there. The daily worship constitutes the ascent, and the discipline is the railing preventing the fall. The love for Śiva, stirred up by the first experience, and the profound faith in His teaching give the necessary strength for the journey and, above all, maintain the permanent tension of the still incarnate soul toward the Aim that it knows it will reach, and where its definitive liberation will take place. This liberation, as we have seen, is neither the contact between two different realities nor the fusion of the one into the other, but the union of two identical Spirits which, mysteriously, remain distinct.

Success implies the theoretical knowledge of both the aim and the means, which belongs to the *jñānapāda* and the *yogapāda*, and the practical knowledge of the path, which belongs to the *kriyāpāda* and the *caryāpāda*. That is why one cannot isolate the four sections of the Āgamas from one another; and that is why it would be futile to look for the mysticism of the Āgamas exclusively in the first two sections mentioned, as one could be tempted to do at the outset.

Let us point out finally that with a different philosophy (namely, that the stuff of the worlds results from a transformation of Śiva, and that the liberating Union is a fusion into Śiva), the Northern Śaivism recognizes a path very similar to the Āgamic one and teaches it in Tantras, the ritual part of which often exactly corresponds to that of the Āgamas. The same is valid for the Vaiṣṇavite Pāñcarātra. Our conclusion, according to which the path of Śaiva ritualism does not at all exclude mysticism but, on the contrary, presupposes and encourages it in the most gifted disciples, is therefore certainly valid for all the ritualistic paths of Hinduism. Perhaps this observation will contribute to a reevaluation of a still little known aspect of the Indian religion.

Notes

1. References in the following notes will be mostly to my edition with translation of the eleventh-century manual by Somaśambhu: *Somaśambhupaddhati* (3 vols., 1963, 1968, 1977, and vol. 4 in the press) (referred to respectively as SP1, SP2, and SP3). For a general presentation of the Śaivāgamas, see Jean Filliozat, "Les Āgama çivaïtes," introduction to *Rauravāgama*, Publ. IFI No. 18 (Pondicherry, 1961); Hélène Brunner, "Importance de la littérature āgamique pour l'étude des religions vivantes de l'Inde," *Indological Taurinensia* 3–4 (1975–76) 107–24.

2. During the past centuries, the Tamil school had actually an abundant literary pro-

duction, whereas the Sanskrit school almost stopped bringing out works or commentaries after the sixteenth century. Moreover, the European missionaries became acquainted with the Tamil texts, whereas the Sanskrit literature of the school was out of their reach, being jealously reserved for the members of the sect. So for a long time the name "Śaiva-Siddhānta" has been used for the Tamil school alone.

3. See my "The four *pādas* of Śaivāgamas," in *Journal of Oriental Research: Dr. S. S. Janaki Felicitation Volume* (Madras, 1992) 260–78.

4. See my "Jñāna and Kriyā: Relation between Theory and Practice in the Śaivāgamas," in *Ritual and Speculation in Early Tantrism: Studies in Honor of André Padoux*, ed. T. Goudriaan (Albany: State University of New York Press, 1992) 1–59.

5. See, e.g., Shivapadasundaram, *The Śaiva School of Hinduism* (London: George Allen & Unwin, 1934) 175–80; V. A. Devasenapathi, *Śaiva Siddhānta* (Madras: University of Madras, 1966) 250; K. Sivaraman, *Śaivism in Philosophical Perspective* (Delhi/Patna/Varanasi, 1973) 385, 393. As shown by these works, the path taught by the masters of Tamil Śaiva Siddhānta is notably different, in this and other respects, from the path shown by the Āgamas.

6. The Śaivites call "Vedic" any school that recognizes the Vedas and the texts derived from them as its scriptures. They themselves, on the contrary, give the Āgamas an absolute authority and accept the authority of the Vedas only secondarily and for questions that are not essential.

7. Śaivism (and Tantrism in general, to which almost everything I am going to say applies) affirms the existence of a very high number of worlds (the number 224 is given most often) which are piled up from the infernal worlds to Śiva, distributed on the ladder of the secondary realities (the *tattvas*). All the worlds that exist in the eleven *tattvas* which Tantrism adds (at the top) to the classical list of the Sāṃkhya are declared to be unknown to the Vedas. See SP3, Tables VIIA to VIIE.

8. One should remember that, according to Southern Śaivism, *māyā* is not only a power of illusion; it is an eternal, very subtle matter, out of which Śiva causes the emergences of the "impure" worlds. See SP1, introduction, xvi ff.

9. I deem it highly probable that this conception of a *bubhukṣu* who at the same time is also a *mumukṣu* is not old. It is found, however, in numerous Upāgamas (see *Mṛgendra*, *kriyāpāda*, 8, 6–7) and in some Āgamas, and it has been generally accepted by the school. The Āgamic conception of the *bubhukṣu* is actually difficult to grasp. We meet with contradictions within the same text, and with considerable variations from one text to another. For a first attempt to clarify this problem, see H. Brunner, "Le *sādhaka*, personnage oublié du śivaisme du Sud," *Journal Asiatique* (1975) 411–43; see also SP3, introduction and section VII.

10. These are the three main ones. To them are generally added: (1) *bindu*, which, though it is very pure, is an impediment for the souls aiming at absolute liberation; (2) Śiva's power of obstruction (*rodhaśakti*), which gives the bonds the power of binding. See SP3, introduction, iii–vi.

11. This descent of divine grace on the disciple is called the "fall of power" (*śaktipāta*, *śaktinipāta*). For most of the Āgamas, it takes place during the *dīkṣā* itself. For the later authors, it should happen before, and *nirvāṇa-dīkṣā* cannot be granted to one who has not received it. In other words, the guru performs the liberating rite only with regard to

the disciples on whom God has bestowed His grace. See SP3, introduction, viii. See also *Kiraṇa, vidyāpāda, patala* 5.

12. This point must be emphasized, for one too often forgets that the consecrations (*ācāryābhiṣeka* and *sādhakābhiṣeka*) which may eventually follow the initiations are not *dīkṣās*: they do not alter the status of the disciple's soul.

13. This *samaya-dīkṣā* is divided into two in most of the hand-books: a *sāmānya-samaya-dīkṣā* and a *viśeṣa-samaya-dīkṣā*—names often shortened into *samaya-dīkṣā* and *viśeṣa-dīkṣā*. See SP3, introduction, xxx–xxxvi. For a general treatment of *dīkṣā*, see SP3, chaps. 3–5.

14. On the *sādhaka*, see my "Le *sādhaka*." Let us emphasize the fact that the discipline demanded from *sādhakas* is much harder than the one the *putrakas* and *ācāryas* are submitted to—as if it were more difficult to obtain powers and enjoyments (both being linked) than "mere" liberation.

15. *Niṣkala* (literally, "without parts") is opposed to *sakala* ("with parts," and therefore divisible and in particular endowed with form). The God who is the object of worship with the Śaivas is Sadāśiva, defined as *sakala-niṣkala*, "with and without parts."

16. Let us recall that an act performed in a certain world (say, our world) produces a "fruit" that appears generally in another world, where one must therefore be reborn in order to consume it.

17. Paths of *kalā, tattva, bhuvana, varṇa, pada,* and *mantra*. This conception of *ṣaḍadhvan* is common to Southern and Northern Śaivism. For the latter, see A. Padoux, *Recherches sur la symbolique et l'énergie de la Parole* (Paris: Publ. de l'Institut de Civilisation Indienne, 1963) chap. 6; R. Gnoli, *Luce delle Sacre Scritture* (*Tantrāloka*) (Turin, 1972) chaps. 8–11. For Southern Śaivism, where the perspective is quite different, see SP3, introduction, xiii–xxii.

18. *Kiraṇa, vidyāpāda*, 6, 13b–14a (quoted in SP3, introduction, xxiii n. 40).

19. For the term *putraka*, see my "Le *sādhaka*," 412–16; and SP3, 416–25, n. 457. One will note the very peculiar status of this disciple. He reminds one of the *jīvanmukta* of Advaita Vedānta, except that the terrestrial life he leads is not deemed illusory and the danger of falling back indeed exists for him—a fact that, by the way, is difficult to reconcile with the assurance that his *mala* has detached itself during the *dīkṣā*.

20. The Āgamas do not give any detail about the technique to be used for obtaining this vision. In all probability, it would not be just a mere evocation of a mental image, but something similar to those exercises of "materialization" of divinities which form part of the training of adepts of Tibetan Buddhism, for instance. The instructions regarding this point were probably given orally to the Śaiva initiates.

21. Our texts do not agree with each other as to the symbolism and signification of these "members" (Aṅga). See SP1, 194–96; SP3, 393; and, above all, my "Les Membres de Śiva," *Etudes Asiatiques* 40 (1986) 89–132.

22. See Oliver Lacombe, "Le brahmanisme," in *La Mystique et les mystiques* (Paris: Desclée de Brouwer, 1965) 731–827, esp. 792–97; Carl Keller, "Aspiration collective et expérience individuelle," *Numen* 31: 1–21; idem, "Témoin de Shiva: Le rôle social et culturel d'un mystique tamoul," in *Mystique, culture et société*, ed. Michel Meslin (Paris, 1983).

23. See my "L'*ācārya* śivaite: Du *guru* au *gurukkal*," in *Bulletin d'Etudes Indiennes* [Paris] 6 (1988) 145–76.

Bibliography

Sources

The following Āgamas are available in critical editions (in *nāgarī*) issued by Pandit N. R. Bhatt in the Publications de l'Institut Français d'Indologie, Pondicherry (India):

Ajitāgama. 3 vols. 1963, 1967, 1991.
Mataṅgapārameśvarāgama. With commentary of Rāmakaṇṭha. 2 vols. 1977, 1982.
Mṛgendrāgama, *kriyāpāda* and *caryāpāda*. With commentary of Narāyāṇakaṇṭha. 1962.
Rauravāgama. 3 vols. 1961, 1972, 1988.
Rauravottarāgama. 1983.
Sārdhatriśatikālottarāgama. With commentary of Rāmakaṇṭha. 1979.

The following Āgamas have been translated:

Kiranāgama, vidyāpāda. Translated into Italian with edition by M. P. Vivanti. Naples: Istituto Orientali di Napoli, 1975.
Mṛgendrāgama, vidyāpāda and *yogapāda*. Translated into French by M. Hulin. Pondicherry: Publ. IFI No. 63, 1980.
Mṛgendrāgama, kriyāpāda and *caryāpāda*. Translated into French by H. Brunner. Pondicherry: Publ. IFI No. 69, 1985.
Svāyaṃbhuvasūtzasaṅgraha, vidyāpāda. With Sadyojyoti's commentary. Translated into French with edition by P. S. Filliozat. EPHE-IV section. Geneva: Droz, 1991.

11

Tantric Spirituality

H. N. CHAKRAVARTY

THE STUDY OF TANTRISM is essential to the understanding of the historical development of Hindu spirituality, for Tantra and *āgama*, next to the Vedas, have influenced every aspect of the spiritual life and ritualistic behavior of Indian people.

If we study carefully the gradual development of Hindu culture, which is of composite nature, a few distinctive layers are clear. The most salient of them is the presence of Vedic thought, but along with it there are many non-Vedic and even non-Aryan thoughts that have shared and shaped the lofty edifice of Hindu spiritual thought.

The delineation of the history of the Tantric tradition is made difficult by the paucity of reliable data. It is the general opinion of scholars that the cult of Śakti, the most important feature of Tantra, was a very ancient tradition. Some scholars believe that the female icons recovered in the Indus Valley prove the prevalence of this cult in India even before the rise of Vedic civilization. Others see the origin in the Vedas,[1] especially in the *Atharvaveda*, where we find ideas such as the earth as the mother and also the rudiments of rituals that are to be found in the Tantric texts. These notions and practices have been termed popular, practical, and more or less magical, relying heavily on sacred formulas, specific arrangement of limbs as a mark of divine attributes, sacred diagrams, and the fixation of sacred syllables on different limbs of the body of the worshiper for the purpose of realizing the worshiper's identity with the Divine.

The rudimentary notion of Śakti can be traced even to the *Ṛgveda*. For example, *vāk*[2] (speech), which has been given a highly spiritual interpretation in the *āgama* and Tantra, is considered to be the "Mother of the Vedas." She is most frequently identified with Bhāratī or Sarasvatī, the goddess of speech.

In Śaiva and Śākta systems, Supreme *Brahman* is pure consciousness in essence. Everything evolves out of It and has its final rest in It. Those who consider the supremacy of Śakti consider it to be the very source of everything, the Supreme illuminative consciousness (*parāsaṃvit*).[3] She not only transends the universe but is immanent in every entity. The pure illuminative consciousness (*saṃvit*) extends itself as the universe, then withdraws it within, and finally takes rest in itself. Identification with the Supreme Deity is the chief aim of the seeker. Therefore, the main trend of Tantra, especially of Śākta-tantras, has always been directed toward realization of the dynamic energy of the divine Śakti.[4]

This view of Śakti is maintained and discussed in different Tantras. Lending support to the view of the supremacy of Śakti, Śaṅkara writes: "Only if conjoined with Śakti would Śiva earn the privilege to become overlord, otherwise the Lord is not able even to stir" (*Saundarya-Laharī* 1). The *Vāmakeśvaratantra*, even when emphasizing the supremacy of Śiva, states that Śiva dissociated from Śakti is unable to perform anything, whereas associated with her he is capable of action (*Nityā-Ṣoḍaśikārṇava* IV.6).

The Supreme Śakti in Her autonomy expands Herself as the universe (*svecchayā viśvarūpiṇī*), says *Yoginī Hṛdaya*.[5] She is further said to have the capacity of manifesting myriad phenomena in order to display Herself externally. She manifests Herself in Her creative upsurge as will (*icchā*), consciousness (*jñāna*), and activity (*kriyā*) on the transcendent level; as *vāmā*, *jeṣṭḥa*, and *raudrī* at the subtle level; and as Brahmā, Viṣṇu, and Rudra at the gross level. It is emphasized by Prabhākara, Bhāsarvajña, Vācaspati, and other thinkers that "it is by virtue of *saṃvit*, the Goddess, the real nature of the thing, is ascertained by us" (*Pañcadaśī* I.7).[6] If *saṃvit* is taken to mean knowledge, even then we may say along with the author of *Pañcadaśī*: "This *saṃvit* never rises, nor does it set, this self-luminous singular Light ever remains ablaze." She is none other than *Saccidānanda Parabrahman*, the Absolute, Being, Consciousness, and Bliss. Her general name is Mother, the primordial Creatrix, and it is She who deludes and causes obstacles on the way of highest realization. Even so, She is the basis of knowledge as it is stated in *Śivasūtra* (I.3): *jñānādhiṣṭḥānam mātṛkā*.

During the historical period, we find the names of *mātṛs* (Mother Goddesses), and mention has been made of Tantra as a specific kind of sacred text. The Gaṅgādhara stone inscription of Viśvavarman (424 C.E.) refers to *mātṛs*. The *Bṛhat Saṃhitā* mentions a number of *mātṛs* who are worshiped in various places. *Viṣṇu Purāṇa* speaks of Viṣṇu as the highest *Brahman* who is endowed with Śakti and enumerates some of the names of Durgā as Āryā, Vedagarbhā, Ambikā, Bhadrā, Bhadrakālī, Kṣemadā, and Bhāgyadā (I.86).

Tantric Literature

In Tantra, the Supreme Being is visualized as the Supreme Goddess, or Śakti, and therefore it may be called Śāktism. In fact, *śaktivāda*, the theory of Śakti, is implicit in Tantra. Tantric literature is vast, and reference will be made here to only a few of the published Hindu Tantras: *Rudra Yāmala, Kulārṇava*, *Kulacuḍāmaṇi*, *Svacchanda Tantra*, *Netra Tantra*, *Vāmakeśvara Tantra*, *Yoginī Hṛdaya*, *Mālinīvijaya Tantra*, and *Mṛgendra Tantra*. In the above list some are *āgamas*, though mentioned as Tantra, for *āgama* and Tantra are interchangeable.

The word *tantra* is derived from *tan*, "to spread," and *trai*, "to save." It "spreads" many matters, including the categories (*tattvas*) and sacred formula (*mantra*). Technically, Tantra is a system that combines spiritual and ritualistic practices in order to attain worldly and otherworldly pleasures (*bhoga*) and, ultimately, liberation (*mokṣa*)—unity with the Divine. The Divinity, for a Śākta aspirant, is represented by a sacred seed *mantra* (*bīja*), which one receives from the spiritual teacher during *dīkṣā*, initiation.

It is held by some scholars that while Śakti is the focus in Tantra, Śiva is the predominant figure in the *āgamas*, but *āgamas* and Tantras are interchangeable terms. Tantra elucidates in detail methods for achieving the highest goal of human life, by recourse to Śakti, the ever-pulsating divine power, and by focusing on Śakti as the Supreme Consciousness for which an "awakened" aspirant finally strives. This Supreme Consciousness is known as *parāsaṃvit* in the Śākta tradition; in the *āgamas* it is known as *parama* Śiva.

Even where the Absolute or the transcendent is stated to be Śiva, Śakti is considered to be Śiva's self-reflective nature (*sphurattā*). Without self-reflection nothing becomes manifest, for the unlimited light is of no help to the spiritual aspirant. Hence, one should make an effort to identify oneself with Śakti. According to *Vijñāna Bhairava* (20):

> When one who enters the state of Śakti (i.e. who is identified with Śakti), there ensues the feeling of non-distinction between Śakti and Śiva; then, one acquires the state of Śiva, (for) here, she (Śakti) is declared as the door of entrance (into Śiva).

While initiating a disciple, the spiritual teacher connects the (limited) consciousness of the disciple with Śakti, since She is the bestower of all fruits. It should not be connected with *puruṣa*, that is, the limited subject, or with the Supreme Absolute. The connection is done through *mantra* given to the disciple at the time of initiation.

Śakti, pure consciousness and bliss in essence, is inseparably united with Śiva. Śakti is the single illuminative consciousness. She is of the nature of knowing agent (*upalabdhṛ rūpā*). She vibrates as I-consciousness—that is Her Supreme nature.[7] The Śiva aspect is static, while the Śakti aspect is dynamic. The former is *aspanda* (nonvibrative) and the latter is *spanda* (vibrative). The one is *bindu*, and the other *visarga*, contraction and expansion. But when this swing from *bindu* to *visarga* is absent, *mahābindu*, the Supreme equilibrium, flashes forth. It combines together both *bindu* and *visarga* as an integral unity. This equilibrium is called *bindu* in the sense that here two opposing forces have stopped polarization and remain in an unbroken unity (*sāmarasya*).

According to the Śākta viewpoint, the integral unity known as the perfect equilibrium of Śiva-Śakti (*parama sāmarasya*) lies in the background of the entire creation. But when a break occurs, the static principle, Śiva, remains changeless, while Śakti becomes the material and the very being of the universe. Śakti is not only the prime mover but also the thing moved and the movement itself—these three are Her manifested form!

The universe is seen in three distinct stages—gross, subtle, and causal. They are nothing but the solid and rarefied forms of Śakti. When this very Śakti becomes "introvert," when the play of contraction becomes predominant, Śakti is then called *bindu*. The Tantric yogi, in his internal journey, must attain equilibrium in these different stages, namely, in gross, subtle, and causal levels. His final aim remains unattained so long as he is not able to experience equilibrium in these three levels. When he is able to pass beyond them, the fourth, the Supreme equilibrium, flashes forth and he is able to realize his identity with It. This is indeed the highest aim of one's life. It is the experience of total unity. According to Gopinath Kaviraj, "Without proper propitiation of Śakti it is quite impossible to attain balance (*sāmya*) in the gross level, what to say of equilibrium at the subtle and causal levels."[8] It is also held by the Śākta thinkers that Śakti is the doorway to Śiva, and the worship of Śiva is really the worship of *Śakti*.

As has been stated, *mahābindu*, on account of creative urge, experiences an apparent break in the equilibrium, with the result that one single *bindu* begins to function as three *bindus*. Two opposing *bindus* operate even while the middle-most *bindu* itself remains in equilibrium. From these three *bindus* three lines come into being. Out of these three lines and their interrelationship a triangle is formed, which is the womb (*yoni*), the *mātṛmaṇḍala*, the circle of Mother.

When we try to penetrate the mystery of creation we find that the entity from which everything originates is without parts or undifferentiated and is free from vibration (*spanda*), but on close observation, the aspect of differentiation (*sāṃśa*, with parts) also comes into view. The differentiated is made up of two further aspects, one in which the "Śiva nature" predominates, and the other in which the "Śakti nature" is predominant, although actually both are of the nature of Śakti, since both are parts of the differentiated (*sāṃśa*). They are named *ambikā* and *śāntā* respectively. Out of the union of both, a flow is emitted from which the universe is born. The union of the two is known as *kāmabindu* or *mahābindu*. It is otherwise called the supreme speech (*parāvāk*) in which all the principles lie latent like the tree in a seed. When the latent universe is born or thrown outside, the two *śaktis* that function in the process are called *vāmā* and *icchāśakti*. Out of their coalesced union, *paśyantī-vāk* (the "seeing" or intuitive speech) is born. Similarly, out of the balanced union of *jyeṣṭhāśakti* and *jñānaśakti* (energy of knowledge), *madhyamā vāk* (the mental speech or interior word) is born. In the same way, out of the union of *raudrīśakti* and *kriyāśakti* (energy of activity), *vaikharī vāk* (the external speech) is born. Symbolically, this is presented by a triangle thus.

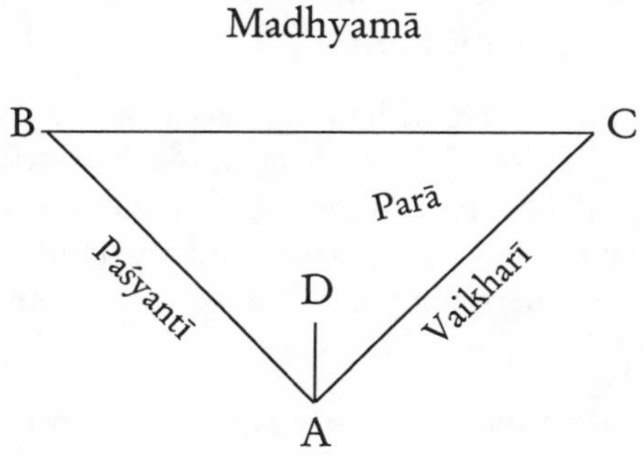

Here, DA represents the creative flow known as *citkalā;* AB, creation; BC, maintenance; CA and AD, dissolution. This triangle is the source of words and objects, and all the vowels of the Sanskrit alphabet, from *a* to *am*, constitute the three sides of the triangle. The last—that is, the sixteenth vowel—is the seat of the Lord and His consort, who remain ever in union. Śiva is the fire that consumes the entire creation. This fire is really the transcendent light, which is technically known as *a*. The last *kalā* is known as *hārdhakalā*, that is, *ha*. The inseparable unity of both is known as *aham*—"I." The supreme goal of all things is to attain perfect equilibrium, the unity of Śiva-Śakti, which encompasses in its cosmic sweep all diversities of time, space, and objecthood.

The principal sources of Tantric doctrine are both the *Śaivāgamas* and the *Śāktāgamas,* including the treatises known as Tantra. Two trends are discerned in this body of literature. One trend develops fully in accord with the Vedic tradition, but parallel to this is another trend, which preaches and presents such thoughts and practices as are disparaged in the Vedas. The former accepts five *āgamas* as sacred, which are called the "five auspicious *āgamas*" (*śubhāgamapañcaka*). The latter bases its doctrine on sixty-four Tantric texts, the names and numbers of which vary in accordance with the divisions and subdivisions of regions called *krāntās*. The followers of the former are called *Samayācārins*. There is also a middle position, which is an amalgam of both trends and is known as the way of *Kaulikas*.

From the Śākta or Tantric standpoint, Tantra and *āgama* texts are as sacred and authoritative as the Vedas. Hence, scholars such as Nārāyaṇakaṇṭha, in the introductory portion of the *Mṛgendrāgama;* Jayanta Bhatta, in his *Nyāyamañjarī;* and Kulluka Bhaṭṭa, the famous commentator of the *Manusaṃhitā,* speak highly of the *āgama* as the most dependable testimony for the removal of the basic impurities of the soul. Abhinavagupta places the *āgama* in the dimension of *vimarśa* and argues forcefully in favor of the *āgama* being of the nature of unlimited light of God in whose Being it abides inseparable as self-reflection.

> In this universe composed of the light of consciousness which essentially is of the nature of self-reflection and which again is characterized by the nature of sound (speech), the deliberation regarding all the entities abiding in the Universe having diverse relations of deeds and their effects lying therein, is known as scriptures—therefore the entirety of scriptures is inseparable with the essence of the Lord. (*Tantrasāra* XIX)

We see that the late advent of the written accounts of the Tantric teachings do not affect the high regard accorded to this tradition by scholars, ancient and modern. The worship of the Goddess as Supreme Reality blends in homogeneously with the Vedic as well as the *Smārta* and Purāṇic traditions of India.

The Tantric tradition aligns itself with the Vedic tradition by giving recognition to the *Devī-Sūkta* of the *Ṛgveda* as one of the authenticating sources of its theology. The Supreme Śakti manifests Herself whenever Her presence is especially required by gods. The appearance of Umā Haimavatī to indicate to gods the presence of a power beyond them (*Kena Upaniṣad* III) and the manifestation of Durgā on snow-capped Himalayas to grant reassurance to troubled gods against the forces of evil are instances of the compassionate concern of the Mother for her creation.

In the *Devī Māhātmya*, the Divine Cosmic Energy has been eulogized in the following manner:

> O Devi, Thou art (personified) in all knowledge; all women are Thy parts. Thou art immanent in this entire universe. How can one over praise Thee! (II.6)

Ardhanārīśvara

The Emergence of Tantras and *Āgamas*

According to *āgamic* tradition, all the sacred texts descended to earth from Śiva, the self-refulgent light. The seers who perceive the Truth state that *vāk* (speech) is inseparably united with the Absolute as Its self-reflection (*vimarśa*).

> This Śakti, named *unmanā* keeping the indicative vibration (*vācya spanda*) within, upsurges in the beginning as the indicative sound of *nāda*. That *nāda* is called the highest Lord Sadāśiva. (*Netra Tantra* 2:287)

When creation starts, the transcendent Word comes down in three successive stages—*paśyantī*, *madhyamā*, and *vaikharī*. In the *paśyantī* level the relation between the thing signified (*vācya*) and the signifier (*vācaka*) is still identical, whereas in the *madhyamā* level a clear distinction between the speech, as the signifier, and the thing signified takes place. The relation in this stage is that of difference-in-identity (*bhedābheda*).

It is from here that all the sacred texts start to descend. According to tradition, the Great Lord divides Himself into two—one as the teacher, and the other as the disciple. Here the teacher is Sadāśiva, the Lord of *nāda*, the undivided current of Sound. Truly speaking, according to the nondual tradition of the Tantra and the *āgama*, both the teacher and the disciple are identical. The characteristic of both is pure consciousness, but in the creative process this pure consciousness imposes on itself the veil of limitation and takes up the role of Śiva as the teacher and Śakti as the disciple. Abhinavagupta writes in his *Tantrāloka* that in truth the distinction of the teacher and the disciple, their dual objectivity is only apparent and not real. "The inquirer and the reply given by the other are the same consciousness abiding in her refulgent nature" (I.256). Vedāntadeśikā in his *Tattvamuktākalāpa*, while supporting the same view, states that in order to show grace to the world the Great Lord assumes the role of the teacher and the disciple. Amṛtānanda in the beginning of the commentary on *Yoginī Hṛdaya* speaks on the spiritual descent of Tantra thus:

> The divine teacher of the universe has Śakti with the nature of reflective consciousness who remaining ever united with Him as one shines in multifarious names and their imports.

He writes further:

> I, indeed, the Supreme Lord with the characteristic of light, in order to bestow grace to the universe engage myself with the order of *parā*, the beyond, *paśyantī*, *madhyamā* and *vaikharī*, assume the nature of the inquirer with the portion of *vimarśa*, self-reflection, and with the portion of light *prakāśa* become the giver of the reply. Thus I bring down Tantras.

At the start, the flow begins with five currents representing five faces of Śiva. These five faces are none but Śiva's five *śaktis: cit*, *ānanda*, *icchā*, *jñāna*, and *kriyā* (consciousness, bliss, will, knowledge, and activity, respectively). The five currents, according to *Kiraṇāgama*, connected with five faces each, give birth to ten *Śivāgamas* and eighteen *Rudrāgamas*. In *Tantrāloka* of Abhinavagupta it is stated that the sacred texts of the Lord are divided into ten, eighteen, and eight into eight, that is, sixty-four (I.18).

In the opinion of the nondual *āgamas,* all the sacred texts that have appeared in the world and those that have not appeared yet are existing as the highest *vāk* (speech) in inseparable oneness with I-consciousness. In the Tantric tradition the meaning of *āgama* and *nigama* is given in the following way: In the *āgama*, the inquirer is the consort of Śiva, and the reply given to Her is by Śiva himself. In *nigama*, the inquirer is Śiva, and the giver of the reply is Śakti, the consort.

The revelation of the holy texts takes place on Mount Kailasa, cloistered in the snow-capped Himalayan region. The symbolic Kailasa is not located on the earth, but is something beyond all principles, where Śiva dwells in his refulgent light as if seated above the aperture of the crown of the yogi's head. Hence John Woodroffe has aptly commented in his *Introduction to Tantra Śāstra*: "His mystic mount is to be sought in the thousand-petaled lotus in the body of every human *jīva.*"[9]

The Nature of Ritualistic Worship

In this world everyone longs to fulfill his or her desires. Broadly speaking, human desires may be divided into two groups: (1) enjoyment of pleasures (*bhukti*), and (2) attainment of liberation (*mukti*). Śiva, the Lord, fulfills them by means of Śakti, who is nondifferent from Him. Bhoja says, "The Great Lord Śiva, who is able to give the object of enjoyment and liberation to the souls in bondage, hence I bow to that Śakti, the beginningless one who is of the form of pure consciousness" (*Tattvaprakāśa* I.3).

It is proper that in order to gain the fruit of worship of Śiva, the worship of Śakti is essential. It is to be known that Śakti, though inseparable and nondifferent from Śiva, is an aspect of Śiva Himself, like the power of burning and cooking are nondifferent from fire itself (cf. *Netra Tantra* I.26). The five functions that are related to Śiva—creation, maintenance, dissolution, veiling, and grace—are nothing but the outer mainfestation of Śiva as Śakti.

The worship of Supreme Śakti is of two kinds: external and internal. The external worship is of two types: one type follows the Vedic tradition supported by *Smṛti* and Purāṇas; the other type, which is Tantric in kind, is supported by *āgamas*. These two traditions follow two different views.

While those who follow the Veda and Purāṇas gain competence to worship with the performance of purificatory rites prescribed in the Vedic tradition, those who follow the Tantric path gain competence to worship only after receiving initiation from their teachers.

The Tantrics use *mātṛkās* for making offerings to their deity, for they hold that it is the *mātṛkā* that leads a *mantra* to its intended goal. *Mātṛkā* is of three kinds: gross, subtle, and subtlest. The highest kind of *mātṛkā* is *spanda* (vibration), which manifests itself in *mūlādhāra*. This is the subtlest form of sound, known as *parāvāk*, the highest speech. When it goes upward, it is called *paśyantī*. In one of these two forms of speech, the *mantra* is totally identified with the deity that the person worships, while in the other the *mantra* is partly separate and nonseparate from the deity worshiped. In the *madhyamā* stage that follows *paśyantī*, the *mantra* loses its identification with the deity. In the *vaikharī* stage, which follows *madhyamā*, the *mantra* loses its identification with the deity and also with the worshiper. At this stage one worships the deity only with gross letters.

Śakti, though considered the all-pervading dynamic energy, shines in three distinct aspects for the worshiper. In the first aspect She is distinctly separate from the aspirant. In the second aspect the aspirant is able to realize nondifference-in-difference; in the third aspect, all differences merge in the light of nonduality. In spite of this truth, the Tantric worshiper worships Śakti alone and tries to unite the *mantra* with Śakti. It is instructed that the aspirant should unite the *mantra* neither with *puruṣa* nor with the Supreme Reality, but should unite it with Śakti; for the *mantra* becomes inert when it is united with *puruṣa* and becomes fruitless when it is united with the Supreme Reality; however, when united with Śakti, the *mantra* yields fruits of all sorts. It is further stated in *Vijñāna Bhairava* (v, 20):

> When in one who enters the state of Śakti (i.e., who is identified with Śakti) there ensues the feeling of nondistinction between Śakti and Śiva, then he acquires the state of Śiva. For in the *āgamas*, she (Śakti) is declared as the door of entrance (into Śiva).

The deity one worships is contemplated as having a body, but, unlike a human body, it is made of alphabets arranged in such a way that they represent different limbs of the deity's body with specific postures, having in her hands a jar of nectar, a book, etc. She has assumed this form from the light that has emerged from *mūlādhāra* going upward. When the worshiper has in mind a particular form to be meditated upon, that form is the supporting ground. It is called *sādhāra* (with a form), while another kind of worship is performed without any supporting ground (*nirādhāra*). One worships formless pure consciousness (*saṃvit*), which is nondifferent from the worshiper himself. One worships the deity by means of the sacred formula, which may be *om* or *hrīm* with its seven or twelve components. These stages, when properly contemplated, lead the worshiper from determinate thoughts (*vikalpa*) to indeterminate, pure consciousness. In the beginning the worshiper fixes attention on the constituents of *mantra* syllables in order to get rid of mental fluctuations. Then the worshiper plunges into pure consciousness. When full absorption occurs, the meditation, the mediator, and the object of meditation are all dissolved in one great expanse of pure consciousness. This is considered to be one of the highest forms of worship.

The esoteric meaning of *mantra*, consisting of a set of syllables, is in essence the Supreme I-consciousness. It is permeated by the highest light. All the syllables beginning with *a* and ending with *ha*, the first and the last of Sanskrit syllables—nay all words, names, and thought constructions—are made of them, and even from Brahmā to the gross physical world are born of them. For this reason syllables are considered to be the *mātṛkā*, the Great Mother of the universe, the gross, the subtle, and the transcendent. All *mantras* have their source in "I" (*aham*), for it is stated in *Tantrasadbhāva* that all *mantras* have the characteristic of letters that again are forms of Śakti.[10] This Śakti is known to be *mātṛkā*, the mother.

The number of *mātṛkās* (letters) is fifty, beginning with *a* and ending with *ha*. They are not only the basic element of all the principles, but the human body is made of them. They lie within the body forming *cakras* in order to create thought-constructs (*vikalpas*) and thus push the *jīvas* to remain in bondage. But as soon as their real nature is realized, they become Śakti and thereby providers of release or freedom (*mokṣa*) (*Śivasūtra*, commentary on II.3).

The yogi tries to attain full concentration of the mind, but so long as the *mātṛkās* remain in the respective centers functioning through the channels of *iḍā* and *piṅgalā*, they create only a curving movement. When, by the effort of the yogi or by any means, the *cakra* (plexus) in the lower level (i.e., in the *mūlādhāra*, which is made of four letters) merges in the *bindu*, the *bindu* moves upward. The movement of the lowest *bindu* has its terminating point in the next upper *bindu*, but here again the yogi finds a plexus where another set of *mātṛkās* is functioning. The yogi's effort continues in order to melt them into *bindu* by the help of the causal sound called *nāda*. This *nāda* takes him to the final terminating point in the center of the two eyebrows, from where he finds the path to reach *mahābindu*, the origin of all the *bindus*.

The Worship of Tripurasundari

The three forms of Śakti—Kāli, Tārā, and Ṣoḍaśī—occupy a unique place in the Tantric form of worship. Ṣoḍaśī is also known by the name Tripurasundarī or Lalita. She is regarded as the Supreme Śakti. She is beyond the thirty-six principles, but at the same time it is She who assumes the form of all the principles, individually and collectively. The Supreme Goddess is worshiped both externally and internally. The former is done by the repetition of the *mantra*. The latter is regarded as the highest kind of worship, where meditation is its principal form. Bhāskara Rāya in his commentary on *Yoginī Hṛdaya* speaks of three forms of worship. The highest form of worship is one where manifestation of duality never arises. The second form, (*parā-parā*), the nondual-dual, dissolves into nonduality by rigorous practice.[11] In the third form one does not get even a glimpse of nonduality.[12] However, even those who have advanced a great deal in the path should perform external mode of worship, since the final truth is nonduality. "Wherever the mind goes whether toward the exterior or toward the interior, O dear, everywhere there is the highest stage, for it is all-pervading, where can the mind go" (*Vijñāna Bhairava*, v. 116).

The meditation of the Great Goddess (Tripurasundarī) is performed in six different ways. It starts with the meditation on how the Great Goddess has manifested Herself in the form of the universe—gross, subtle, and causal. The *cakra*, the magical diagram, known as *Śrīyantra*, represents the universe, on the one hand, and, on the other, it is Her own manifestation. This *cakra* consists of nine triangles, five with vertices downwards and four with vertices upwards. The former represents the creative aspect called *śakti*, and the latter called "Fire" stands for its destructive phase or Śiva.

The *cakra* originates because of the will for self-revelation on the part of the Supreme Śakti. In the introduction to *Yoginī Hṛdaya*, Gopinath Kaviraja writes:

> Śiva and Śakti are known as Fire and Moon, and their equilibrium, where the difference is obliterated, is called Sun, otherwise known as *Kāma* or Supreme *bindu*. It is said that as in contact with fire, *ghee* (clarified butter) melts and flows out, similarly the contact of Fire or Śiva causes the Moon or Śakti to melt and flow out. This outflow from between the two *bindus* is called *hārdhakalā*. *Kāma* as associated with the *hārdhakalā* gives rise to the first *cakra*, called *Baindava*, which is the source of all kinds of subsequent waves. (p. xi)

The worship of Tripurasundarī is performed either externally in the mystical diagram of *Śrīyantra*, or internally within the body. According to the *samaya* method, internal worship is considered to be the real one. Here the six centers beginning with *mūlādhāra* and so on inside the human body constitute the inmost triangle in *Śrīyantra*. The quadrangle in *sahasrāra*, the thousand-petaled lotus, is the location of the disk of the moon, inside which is *bindu* in the center. This *bindu* is described as the ocean of nectar. In the Vedas it is known as *saragha*. The followers of the *samaya* method meditate on the unification of *samaya* and *samayā*. Here *samaya* means Śiva and *samayā*, Śakti. The literal meaning is given in the following way: *Samam* = *sāmyam* = identification, *yāti* = attains. Hence, the significance of the term is total identification of both. For this reason, Śakti being united with Śiva is called *samaya*, and Śiva being united with Śakti is known as *samayā*. The worshipers of *samaya* and *samayā* are thus known as *Samayācārins*.

The unification of Śiva-Śakti is of five kinds: equality of place, equality of state, equality of origination, equality of forms, equality of names.

According to *Samayācārins*, the principal worship of the Goddess is to be performed in the thousand-petaled lotus by meditation. But those who are not so competent should worship Śiva and Śakti in six centers of the body in descending order. This should be done from *ajñā* to *mūlādhāra*. According to them, *mūlādhāra* and *svādhiṣṭhāna* are the regions of darkness where *Kaulas* perform worship; hence *Samayācārins* possessing the highest competency should avoid worshiping in these regions, but those who are not so competent can do the worship of Ānandabhairva and Ānandabhairavī even there.

According to Lakṣmīdhara, the worship is of two kinds, the one that follows the Vedas, and the other that does not follow the Vedas strictly. The *Samayācārins* follow the Veda in their worship and do not use those articles that are forbidden in the Veda, whereas *Kaulas* use meat and wine in their worship.

The *Kaulas* are of two kinds: *pūrva* and *uttara*. Both of them worship in the triangle, the location of *bindu* which is Śakti. This triangle is of two kinds, the one with the *bindu* inside the central triangle of *Śrīyantra*, and the other, the private organ of a woman. The *Kaulas* belonging to the *pūrva* (novice) class paint the *Śrīcakra* either on the birch leaf or on a gold plate and worship *bindu* there, while *Kaulas* of the *uttara* (advanced) order worship *bindu* in the female organ following the left-hand method (*vāmācāra*). Both of them perform internal worship of *kuṇḍalinī*, the coiled Śakti in *mūlādhāra*.

The Repetition of the Sacred Formula (*Japa*)

In Tantric worship, *mantra*, the sacred formula, occupies a very significant place, for it is believed that when a *mantra* is properly meditated upon, it rescues a person from distress. Generally, a *mantra* is muttered either audibly or in a low voice so that nobody can hear it. The number of *mantras* being repeated is counted either by fingers or in rosary beads. A sacred formula may consist of more than one syllable, ending in *m* or *h* and of a composite form like *k l i m*, *h r i m*, etc. They are known as seed *mantras*, which are intended to be mediated upon and not simply be "mechanically" repeated. By meditating on the *mantra* syllables and unifying them, one is able to arouse the deity itself and raise one's own level of consciousness from the lower part of *mūlādhāra* to the center of the thousand-petaled lotus located in the head. Then one is able to visualize the desired deity in the *maṇipūra* region.

The body of the worshiper is said to fall under three sections: the circle of the fire, of the sun, and of the moon. The circle of the fire has its root in *mūlādhāra* from where a *mantra* arises. The syllables of a *mantra* in their ascending order end in the peak of *kāmakalā*, that is, *ī*, which again constitutes *hārdhakalā*(*m*). The yogi meditates on this *kalā* with *nāda*, and *nāda* with the coiled state of fire. Besides the constituents, namely, the subtle syllabic sounds that begin with *m*, are thought to have merged and unified with the next group of *mantra* syllables and so on. Thus, the yogi goes on meditating and his inner journey continues. Finally, he meditates that the syllables are lying in the circle of the moon from the root of *viśuddhi* to *ajñā*. Then the syllables rise from the coiled state of the moon to ascend beyond *brahmarandhra* (the cavity of the cerebral orifice). The yogi contemplates that the moon and the *kāmakalā* have become one and all the nine subtle syllabic sounds have been dissolved in *unmanī*, the state that transcends the mind.

Daily Practice of the Worshiper

Generally Śākta worshipers are given initiation in the *mantras* of Kāli, Tārā, or Ṣoḍaśī. They are known as three *śaktis*. Though the mode of worship varies, there are some broad and general areas of similarity.

In the early morning when the worshiper rises from bed he meditates on his teacher on the pericarp of the thousand-petaled lotus located on the head. The lotus faces downward. In the center there is a twelve-petaled lotus and a triangle called *vāgbhava* (the source of speech) where the seat of the guru (teacher) is imagined to be located. The teacher is supposed to have his seat on the disk of the moon. He is white in complexion and clothed in white silk. His "Śakti" is seated at his left embracing him with her right hand, while holding a red lotus in her left hand. The guru has a smiling face looking gracefully toward the disciple with the posture of assurance and blessing by his two hands, and his eyes expressive of his inner blissful nature.

Thus meditating, the worshiper makes certain offerings to his guru mentally and repeats the *mantra*. Then taking leave of his teacher, he meditates on *kulaśakti*, his desired deity with a luminous form but very subtle like the thread of a lotus stalk, coiling round the *svayaṃbhu liṅga* thrice and a half. She is lying asleep in *mūlādhāra*. The worshiper rouses her by uttering the *mantra huṃ haṃsaḥ* and leads her moving upward along the *suṣumnā* path. Her journey terminates in union with Śiva. After that he meditates on the gurus of his tradition on the moon's disk.

Then he goes to the riverside, performs "ritual bathing" by reciting a *mantra*. It is followed by actual bathing in water, while imagining that all holy rivers have come down from the sun's disk and joined in the water. He sips water thrice uttering the seed *mantra* of his goddess adding *ātmatattva*, *vidyātattva*, *śivatattva* separately. Then closing the seven openings of his face, he plunges into the water.

He performs both the Vedic and Tantric *sandhyā* rites. Then he takes some water in the left palm and covers it with the right palm, charges the water with the seed syllables of Śiva, air, water, earth, and fire thrice, then sprinkles seven times with the water that drops through the crevice of his fingers. This he does with *tattvamurdrā* over his head. Then he collects the rest of the water in his right palm. He thinks that the water is fiery. He brings the water near the left nostril and inhales it. The water goes inside a little and thus purifies the inner self. Then the water that has gone inside is exhaled through the right nostril, and, collecting it in the right hand, he flings it on the ground with a *mantra*, while thinking that the sin personified has thus been crushed to death.

Offering to the Sun

As in Vedic rituals, offering to the Sun is considered to be essential; in Tantric form, the Sun is worshiped as Bhairava. But before offering *arghya* consisting of *dūrvā* grass, red flowers, and a little quantity of washed rice grains, one offers water to one's teacher, located in the northeast; to the grand-teacher, in the southeast; to the great-grand-teacher in the southwest; to the great-great-grand-teacher in the northwest; and, in the center, to his own deity. This is followed by an offering of water to his departed ancestors, who are thought to be of the form of Bhairava. The Sun also is thought to be of the form of Bhairava accompanied by his Śakti. The worshiper thinks that his own deity is present in the disk of the sun with *mahākāla*. He offers water to Her and recites the *Gāyatrī mantra*.

For a Tantric worshiper, everything that he sees, the sound he hears, the articles he offers to the deity, the deity itself, and his own being, is none but Bhairava. While this is one of the ways of looking at things, there is another way in which he is required to think: that he is one with *kula* or Śakti. For this reason, the *dūrvā* or *kuśa* grass is for him *kuladarbha*, the mystical diagram he draws is *kulacakra*, the holy spots are *kulatīrtha*, and the seat is *kulāsana*, and so on.

His external worship does not end here. He places alphabets on his limbs elaborately for the purpose of creating a body made of letters of alphabets. He knows that the letters he fixes in different parts of his limbs have all emanated from the original source, the source being the union of *prakāśa* (light) and *vimarśa* (reflection), which represents a luminous lamp from which another lamp has been lighted. By means of his *nyāsa* rite, by the fixation of syllables on the body, his own self becomes one with the deity, on the one hand; and his physical body, on the other, becomes the surrounding deity.

Mental Worship (*Antaryajana*)

Before performing an external form of worship, it is essential for the worshiper to perform an internal worship, for without it all external rituals will remain ineffective. At the beginning of this internal (mental) worship one meditates on the guru as described earlier. After this he (mentally) bathes in the water flowing down from *bindu*, conceiving it to be nectar coming down from the joint of the two eyebrows. Thus, the internal bath being complete, he performs *sandhyā* (twilight rituals). According to the Tantric tradition, when the union of Śiva and *Śakti* occurs, it is considered to be an auspicious moment for performing *sandhyā* rite, and it is judged as *sandhyā* proper. Then the worshiper meditates that *kuṇḍalinī* has ascended and reached up to the point of *bindu* and penetrated it. With the penetration of *bindu*, a flow of nectar begins to descend. When this downward flow continues, the worshiper thinks that by this process the deities located in different conscious centers of his body have become refreshed. This is called *tarpaṇa*.

Fixation on Six Limbs

After having the deities refreshed, the worshiper proceeds with the "fixation of six limbs" (*saḍaṅga nyāsa*). The syllables of letters are thought of as being located in six centers—*mūlādhāra*, *svādhiṣṭhāna*, *maṇipūra*, *anāhata*, *viśuddhi*, and *ajñā*—in the following order: *va*, *śa*, *ṣa*, *sa* are fixed in *mūlā-*

dhāra; ba to *la* in *svādhiṣṭhāna; ḍa* to *pha* in *maṇipūra; ka* to *ṭha* in *anāhata; a* to *ah* in *viśuddhi;* and *ha* and *kṣa* in *ājñā*. All these are meditated upon carefully by the worshiper.

Then one proceeds to meditate on the light that abides in a halo, in fire, in the moon, in the sun, and in the void. It is free from all attributes and other qualitative distinctions. When one conceives that this light has its abode in the core of one's heart, by constant practice one is able to see the light. After this one places different articles of offering to one's deity. The seat one offers is one's heart for cleansing the deity's feet and for bathing the deity one makes an offering of nectar that flows from the thousand-petaled lotus. Here, the principle of ether stands for the deity's clothing, and the subtle element of smell represents the sandal paste that is applied to the deity's body. The *citta* (mind) comes to represent flowers; the vital air, incense; and for the lamp, the fire element is offered. Again, the food-offering is the sea of nectar; the causal sound (*anāhata*), the bell; the air element, the chowri (*cāmara*); and the activity of his senses and the mind, acts of dancing. For the purpose of retaining steadiness of mind in one's disposition, the worshiper should offer "flowers" of nonviolence, restraining of senses, mercy, forgiveness, and knowledge.

Oblation into the Fire (*Homa*)

For the Tantric worshiper the ritual is not considered effective without making an oblation into the fire. Externally it is performed on an altar specially made for making an oblation. It may be square, round, or of any other shape, according to the purpose of the worshiper. The worshiper imagines that the square-shaped *mūlādhāra* represents the altar. The girdle (*mekhalā*) of it is bliss; the triangle located in the center is the *yoni* (the female organ). Thus meditating, the worshiper further conceives that *iḍā* is lying in the left, *piṅgalā* to the right, and *suṣumnā* in the middle. There one conceives that merits and demerits are the clarified butter with which one mixes the functions of one's senses as the food to be offered into it. Then the worshiper utters: "The fire of consciousness has blazed up in the navel into which I offered the functions of senses along the path of *susumnā*, gathering them together in the ladle of my mind" (*Yoginī Hṛdaya* III; *Gandharva Tantra*, chap. xxxvi.62). In this way the worshiper makes offerings five times conceiving fire as consciousness, as his self, as knowledge, as *saṃvit*, and as Supreme Consciousness.

At the first and second stage he offers only objects of his sense experience, but later on, as he advances, he leaves the mind behind. The ladle is no longer his mind, for he has already transcended it. The ladle is now *unmanī*, by means of which he offers the subtle residual traces of senses into the fire of knowledge. In the fourth stage he realizes that pure consciousness is ever ablaze in the heart. It is unique and very unlike other fires; it is the light of all lights and it has the character of opposing all kinds of delusions. He offers in this fire the entire universe beginning from the earth to Śiva at the end. At the fifth stage he realizes his identity with full I-consciousness before which there remains "Thisness" as a whole. He now fills his ladle with the essence of "this" as nectar and puts it into the fire of Supreme I-consciousness.

This, in short, is the internal form of sacrifice. When it is performed well, only then the worshiper earns competence to perform external forms of sacrifice. It is stated that without performing the mental sacrifice that helps one to attain Śiva-nature, if one strives to perform oblation, it fails to lead the "animal" to get its release (*Svacchanda Tantra* III.32).

We shall present very briefly how a Tantric worshiper performs oblation in the sacrificial altar. First of all, the worshiper makes a pit (*kuṇḍa*) according to the measurement prescribed by the text. When the pit is prepared, he is said to look at it with divine glance. Leaving a square in the middle, four alleys, from north, south, east, and west, are drawn, along with an enclosure in the northeast. He covers the whole space with *kuśa* grass, thinking them blazing. Then the worshiper invokes Ambika (Śakti) and places Her in the seat and worships Her. Then he brings fire, which is thought to be the semen, and places it in the womb of Śakti. Then the fire is kindled. The worshiper makes a *mudrā* called *jvālāmudrā* and then performs some rites for bringing forth a male child, namely, the rite of parting of the hair, the rite of birth of the child (here fire), the rite of name-giving. He does this by means of giving an oblation for each. Then he purifies the two ladles, one representing Śiva and the other Śakti, takes leave of the mother of the fire, conceives the pit as a hole, as the mouth of fire, and proceeds to offer food into it.

The Nature of Tantric Ritual Worship

According to Tantric tradition, there are seven kinds of ritualistic practices: *vedācāra*, *vaiṣṇavācāra*, *śaivācāra*, *dakṣiṇācāra*, *vāmācāra*, *siddhāntācāra*, and *kulācāra*. The first three of these are followed by those in whom spiritual growth has not yet shaken off their innate animality and has not attained the proper stature to follow the heroic form of ritual practice. Those who follow *dakṣiṇācāra* are supposed to have gained the preliminary competence to follow the heroic line of worship. The *dakṣiṇācārin* worships Śakti as the Supreme Divinity, identifying oneself with Śiva. Hence the saying goes, *Śivo bhūtvā Śivām yajet* ("after identifying oneself with Śiva one should worship Śivā"). In *vāmācāra*, the worshiper thinks himself to be one with *vāmāśakti* and worships Śakti by identifying himself with Śakti.

The truth is that the Supreme is neither male nor female: it is the unity of knowledge (*jñāna*) and activity (*kriyā*). When one conceives of the Supreme Truth as the coalesced union (*yāmala*) of light and activity, lying in the left and the right sides of one's deity, one is inclined to add predominance either to the left or to the right. The right portion of the deity is *kriyā* (activity), for this reason rituals are elaborately performed by the followers of the "right-hand" path. The left half of the deity is *jñāna*, hence the followers of *jñāna* worship the deity following the "left-hand" procedure where knowledge is predominant.

Yet it is true, the *Kaulas* say, that *icchā* (will), which lies in the middle, is the origin of both *jñāna* and *kriyā*. Hence, the spiritual aspiration of the *Kaula* is to merge oneself into the "will," which is the middle. For the *Kaulas*, the ritualistic form of worship is neither to be discarded nor to be accepted. Here the practitioner tries to sublimate all the activities to *icchā* (will)—in this effort he thinks it will lead him to the Divine. When the middle path opens up, he sees no distinction between the sandal paste and mud, between an enemy and a friend, between the cremation ground and a palatial building, or between gold and grass. He remains always merged in blissful self-awareness and looks at the world as his own self since everything converges on the self.

From Time to Timelessness

We shall discuss here how a yogi tries to go beyond time to arrive at timelessness. We know that the life of worldly people passes through three levels of consciousness: the waking state, the dreaming state, and the state of deep sleep. Our life passes through these cycles of consciousness, and we are unable to proceed to a fourth level beyond these three states of consciousness. For this reason it is proper to say that ordinary consciousness is made of these three. Yogis say that one half of the human mind is occupied with worldly affairs and the other half remains unoccupied. By means of certain practices, yogis try to go beyond these three states. They do this by means of one-pointedness of the mind. When one is able to make the mind one-pointed, one is able to go beyond these three states and arrive at the level of *bindu*, located at the region above the joint of the two eyebrows. At this level one can grasp the entire world at a single glance. Here one realizes that one's mind has become "half." In the language of Tantra, the mind is, as it were, global in shape, like the full moon. When it is broken in half—that is, when a yogi with his effort is able to make his mind fully one-pointed in the center of the two eyebrows—he is able to hear the causal sound permeating in the source and origin of causal, subtle, and gross bodies.

The causal sound is the seed of the entire universe and is said to be the life force of all. It is called the Supreme Seed (*anacka ha*) and has three states. The first is known as the highest coiled *kuṇḍalinī* state, where even *nāda* as the Causal Sound remains unmanifest and, as a result, the entire universe remains in its womb. When it is manifested in the form of *nāda*, the Causal Sound, it is then called the coiled state of syllables (*varṇakuṇḍalinī*). Finally, when its characteristic state of Sound plunges into deep sleep, it is then known as the coiled state of the vital energy (*prāṇakuṇḍalinī*).

Even then, this vital energy (*prāṇa*) by its inherent nature begins to wander up and down with the sound of *ham* (exhaling) and *saḥ* (inhaling). This is described as a swan (*haṃsa*). The sound *a* helps *anacka h* to manifest. The two syllables (*ham* and *saḥ*) by the grace of guru are transformed into *so'ham* (I am that). Then, further, in a strange way both *sa* and *ha* portions are dropped, and *om* is left. Here *ham* denotes "I" and *saḥ*, "he." When their position is reversed, that is when *saḥ* comes first and *ham* follows it, then according to the rule of euphonic combination, the order becomes *sah* + *aham* = *so'ham*, which according to Tantric symbolism is known as a *mantra* of great efficacy. *Praṇava* (*om*) consists of three syllables, namely, *a*, *u*, and *m*. The letter *a* represents the head of the *haṃsa* (swan), and *u* its feet. When *u* comes in contact with *a*, the manifestation of *bindu*, *m*, begins, and by the grace of guru, *kuṇḍalinī* also wakes up and then the vital air and the mind give up their dual nature and start to flow upward along the *suṣumnā* path. Then the yogi begins to hear different kinds of sound. These are said to be of nine kinds, but he avoids all the nine sounds and tries to listen to the tenth, the one that is free of differences of measure and character. By continuous practice, the sound becomes subtle, and as a result, the vital air begins to leave its contact with all the other passages (*nādis*). Similarly, the gross, the subtle, and the causal measures (*mātrā*) of *a*, *u*, and *m* become one, leaving aside their differences, and assume the form of *bindu*, which is the total unit of the objective experience. It is the doorway to the domain of the Divine. From *bindu* on, the real journey of the yogi begins. As there are nine *nādas* below *bindu*, so also the yogi must pass through nine stages of experience. These nine are also known as nine *nādas*. The time that is needed to utter a short vowel sound is supposed to be of one measure, but for *bindu* it is half of it, while for the next, it is one-fourth. This, in other words, is a process by which the mind is made subtle and is freed from time duration, as the yogi's upward journey continues. The fartherst limit of the journey is the stage of *unmanī*, where the trace of the mind is totally gone.

At this stage, the yogi has transcended mind and time and has become one with the Divine.

Conclusion

In conclusion, some comments on the status of Tantra in the changing situation of modern India seem relevant. Tantra, as well as all spiritual traditions of India, appears to have lost some ground in our times. There are only a small number of people who have made serious efforts to delve into the mystery of Tantric *sādhana* and have followed the tradition earnestly and with fervor. In the light of the paucity of Tantric teachers well-aquainted with the theory and practice of *Tantra*, it is quite difficult for the seeker to get proper guidance.

The spiritual tradition of Tantra is indeed vast. In this paper the salient features of Tantric spirituality have been dealt with in a summary fashion. Topics such as *nyāsa* (fixation of syllables) in the body of the aspirant; *puraścaraṇa*, repetition of a *mantra* for a specific number of times; *bhūtaśuddhi*, purification of elements in the body of the aspirant; *yantra*, the sacred symbolic diagram; *mudrā*, symbolic gesture; and *maṇḍala*, the sacred diagram on which rituals are to be performed have not been dealt with for brevity's sake.

The practice of Tantra leads not only to *bhoga* (enjoyment while living) but also to *mokṣa*, freedom from *saṃsāra*. The Tantric path has influenced and shaped significantly the spirituality of the Hindu tradition, by highlighting the feminine models of divinity and formulating a philosophy of nonduality based on the union of Śiva and Śakti. Hence, the study of Tantric spirituality becomes very important when we attempt to trace the development of Hindu spirituality in its postclassical period.

Notes

1. E.g., "Like your own son upon his parents' bosom, protect us Heaven and Earth, from fearful danger" (*Ṛg* I.185.2); "This great earth is my kin and Mother" (*Ṛg* I.164.33); "O Earth, what is thy middle, what thy navel, the energy that has emerged and spread over, establish us steadily there, fill us with fragrance, purify us, I am the son of Earth" (*A V.* 12.1.12).

2. Though the divine energy is stated to be the speech, she is the source of everything. Therefore she utters boldly: *aham suve pitaram*, "I give birth to *dyaus*, the upper heaven." As the immanent energy, she exists everywhere pervading all. See A. Padoux, *Vāc*.

3. In the commentary of *Śivadṛṣṭi* of Somānanda, Utpala in the beginning of chapter 3 quotes a verse in which it is stated "that of the unconditional light to whom the name Śiva is given, to that transcendent one, O Mother, we pay our homage." This verse

alludes to the fact that there had been two schools of Tantra, the one in which Śiva is held to be the Supreme, the other in which Śakti is held to be the Supreme.

4. Bhaṭṭa Dāmodara states: "The energy that is the dynamic force designated as Vāmeśī and so on who preside over inner and external sense organs and also abiding in objects bestow pure light of consciousness and bestow liberation when they are perfectly known. While in the absence of right knowledge regarding them they create bondage" *(Pratyabhijñā Hṛdaya* commentary).

5. When that Supreme dynamic energy, in order to assume the nature of the universe in her will, feels her own vibrative stir, then the *cakra* emerges (*Yoginī Hṛdaya* I.9).

6. This ever-rising state of the light of consciousness is also mentioned in *Chāndogya Upaniṣad*: "Henceforth, after having risen in the zenith, it will no more rise nor set. It will stand alone in the middle" (3.11.1–2).

7. a. *Ekaiva saṃvit upalabdhṛrūpā ahamiti sphurantī pāramārthikī* (*Spandakārikā*); b. *na pumsi na pare tattve śaktau mantraṃ niyojayet puṃstattve jaḍatameti pare tattve tu niṣphalaḥ* (Jayaratha's commentary on *Tantrāloka* V.116).

8. Gopinath Kaviraj, *Tantrik Vāṅgmay me Śāktadṛṣṭi*, 73.

9. John Woodroffe, *Introduction to Tantra Śāstra.*

10. Quoted in *Spanda Pradīpikā*, p. 83 (the source is Kulayukti).

11. Here all kinds of ritualistic activities are performed in such a way that they may get rest in consciousness. The yogi thinks that all sorts of *vikalpas*, determinate thoughts, are thrown into a mass of light, like throwing clarified butter into the fire.

12. *Dvaitabhānasāmanyābhāve para* (Bhāskara Rāya's commentary, *Setubandha*, p. 196). *Yoginī Hṛdaya* (Varanasi: Sampurnananda Sanskrit University, 1979).

Bibliography

Sources

Abhinavagupta. *Isvara Pratyabhijñā vimarśinī.* Edited by K. A. S. Iyer and K. C. Pandey. Prince of Wales Saraswati Bhavan Texts 70, 83, and 84. 1938, 1950, 1954.

———. *Parātrīśikā Vivaraṇa.* Edited by M. Kaul Sastri. Srinager: Research Department, Jammu and Kashmir State.

———. *Parātrīśikā Vivaraṇa.* Edited by B. Baumer. Translated into English by Jaideva Singh. Delhi: Motilal Banarsidass, 1988.

Tantrāloka with Vivaraṇa of Jayaratha. Edited by M. Kaul Sastri. 12 vols. Srinagar: Government Press, 1921–1938. Reprint by R. C. Dwivedi and N. Rastogi. Delhi: Motilal Banarsidass.

Tantrasāra. Edited by M. R. Shastri. Srinagar: Government Press, 1918.

Aṣṭa Prakaraṇa. Edited by V. V. Dwivedi. Varanasi: Sampurananada Sanskrit University, 1988.

Bhāvanopaniṣat: Text and Commentary of Bhāskara Rāya. Translated by S. Mira. Madras: Ganesh & Co., 1976.

Devībhāgavatam. Kasi: Published by Pandit Pustakalay, 1956.

Devīmāhātmya Durgā Saptaśati with Seven Sanskrit Commentaries. Edited by Harikishan Sharma. Chowkhamba: Surabharati Prakashan, 1988.

Gandharvatantra. Edited by R. P. Tripathi. Varanasi: Sampurnananda Sanskrit University, 1992.

Kṣemarāja. *Spandanirṇaya.* Translated by Jaideva Singh. Delhi: Motilal Banarsidass, 1980.

———. *Pratyabhijñā Hṛdayam.* Translated by Jaideva Singh. Delhi: Motilal Banarsidass, 1973.

Kula Cudāmani Tantra. Edited by Arthur Avalon. Madras: Ganesh & Co., 1956.

Kularnava Tantra. Edited by Taranatha Vidyaratna with Introduction by Arthur Avalon and Readings of M. P. Pandit. Delhi: Motilal Banarsidass, 1965, 1984.

Mahārtha Mañjarī with Parimala of Maheśwarānanda. Edited by V. V. Dvivedi. Varanasi: Varanaseya Sanskrit Visvavidyalaya, 1972.

Mālinivijaya Tantra. Edited by M. K. Shastri. Sringar: Government Press, 1922.

Mṛgendrāgama (Kriyāpāda and Caryāpāda) with Commentary by Bhatta Nārāyaṇakaṇṭha. Edited by N. R. Bhatt. Pondicherry: Institut Français d'Indologie, 1962.

Mṛgendra Tantra (Vidyāpada and Yogapāda). Edited by M. Kaul Śastri. Srinagar: Research Department, Jammu and Kashmir State, 1930.

Netra Tantra with Udyota of Kṣemarāja. Edited by Kaul Sastri. 2 vols. Kashmir Sanskrit Series. 1926, 1939.

Nityāṣoḍaśikārṇava with Two Commentarties. Edited by V. V. Dviveda. Varanasi: Sampurnananda Sanskrit University, 1968.

Śaṅkarācārya. *Prapañcasāratantra.* Revised by A. Avalon. Delhi: Motilal Banarsidass, 1981.

Śivadṛṣṭi of Somānanda with vṛtti of Utpalācārya. Edited by M. Kaul Shastri. Srinagar, 1934.

Śivasūtra Vimarśinī. Edited and translated by Jaideva Singh. Delhi: Motilal Banarsidass, 1979.

Spanda Kārikā with vivṛti of Rāmakaṇṭha. Edited by J. C. Chatterji. Srinagar: Research Department, Jammu and Kashmir State, 1913.

Svacchanda Tantra with the Uddyota commentary of Kṣemarāja. 7 vols. Srinagar: Government Press, 1921–35.

Tantrasāra—Kṛṣṇānanda Āgamavāgīśa. Edited by P. K. Sharma. Calcutta, 1910.

Utpalācārya. *Spandapradīpikā.* Edited by G. Kaviraj. Varanasi: Varanaseya Sanskrit Visvavidyalaya, 1970.

Studies

Kaviraj, G. N. *Tantrik Sāhitya.* Lucknow: Hindi Bhavan, 1972.

Padoux, André. *Vac—The Concept of the Word in Selected Hindu Tantras.* Translated into English by Jacques Gontier. Albany: State University of New York Press, 1990.

12

The Way of the Siddhas

T. N. GANAPATHY

Who Are the Siddhas?

FROM A HISTORICAL POINT OF VIEW the Siddha tradition is timeless. It is not confined to a particular school of philosophy or religion, for the Siddhas do not believe in system-building techniques leading to narrowness of appeal, but are freethinkers having an appeal to all humankind and all races. Hence, the typical features of the Tamil Siddha doctrines cannot be explained in terms of one historical line; for the Siddhas never trod on the beaten path. The questions raised by them cannot be put into an either-or pattern, and their answers cannot be reduced to any one view. It is an open system and as such does not give room for any reductionist doctrine. Yet the Siddhas form an integral part of the pan-Indian tradition, a tradition in which transgression of time and eternal living constitute one of the major themes.

The term "Siddha" has various connotations. It is a Sanskrit term meaning "fulfilled." A Siddha is a completed one, fulfilled and accomplished, a God-realized being alive in the world for the sake of humankind and all living beings. The term is also used to refer to the master-teachers who live perfectly in God while they are active in the paradoxical and spontaneous functions of the Divine in the created world. The Tamils refer to four types of *mukti* (liberation): *sālokya* (the status of living in the world of God), *sāmīpya* (the status of being near God), *sārūpya* (the status of getting the form of God), and *sāyujya* (the status of being one with God). The Siddhas are those who have attained the last type of liberation. The first three types of liberation are called *padamukti* by Saint Tirumūlar, a Tamil Siddha *par excellence*, and the last one is called *siddhi*.[1] Those who have attained this state of *siddhi* are called the Siddhas. Using the expression of Mircea Eliade, we may say that the Siddhas are those "who understood liberation as the conquest of immortality."[2]

A Siddha is a yogi. Saint Tirumūlar says that those who live in yoga and see the divine power and light through yoga are the Siddhas (*Tirumantiram*, v. 1490). The Siddhas are yogis who attain perfection by rousing the *kuṇḍalinī*, the master energy. A Siddha is an experimental yogi who attains perfection by self-effort. It is, therefore, possible for him to explain the different types of *anubhava*, or experience, at every step of his spiritual journey. In Tantric literature, the practitioners of Tantra are divided into two classes—the *samayins*, who attempt to reach godhead by awakening the *kuṇḍalinī* by yoga, and the *kaulas*, who venerate and worship the *kuṇḍalinī* and employ concrete rituals. The Tamil Siddhas belong to the former variety; their aim is to arouse the *kuṇḍalinī śakti*, the supreme power inside us, to attain freedom.

According to one ancient tradition, ascetics who strive to gain liberation are classified into four classes. They are *kuṭīcakas*, *bahūdakas*, *haṃsas*, and *paramahaṃsas*. Of these, the last represents a most ancient ascetic order. They live under trees, in graveyards, or in deserted houses. They go naked or clad. They are indifferent to everything in the sense that they are disinterested. They look at a clod of mud or of gold with the same dispassion. They accept food from people of any caste. They practice a kind of yogic Tantrism. The Siddhas of Tamilnadu come very close to these *paramahaṃsas*.

A Siddha is a freethinker and a revolutionary who refuses to allow himself to be carried away by any religion or scriptures or rituals. A Tamil Siddha says: "A Siddha is one who has burnt the śāstras."[3] This is to be interpreted not in the literal sense but in the sense that, for a *jñānin* (one who is liberated), "Vedas are no Vedas." A Siddha is one who has attained a stage of realization where he is not bound by the injunctions of the *śāstras* and where he has gone beyond the Vedas. The Siddhas wanted to convey their spiritual experiences directly to the people without the medium of the *śāstras* and rituals. There is always a gulf between words and the experience they represent. The truth expressed in the Vedas and languages is like the truth in echo or reflection of the moon in water. Of course, the Vedas point to the goal, but they do not contain it. Veda is like a finger pointing at the moon; it would be a calamity if one took the finger for the moon. Siddhas want us to move beyond the "descriptive experience" of truth in the *śāstras*, to a stage where we personally "experience" the truth. This experience must be gained by one's own effort, though the path is "pointed to" by the Siddhas. Truth is a felt experience; truth once expressed in words loses its value as an experience. Though the Siddhas seem to be opposed to the scriptures, still their temper is surely devout! They are "pious rebels" and certainly not atheists. Kārai Siddhar draws a distinction between a Siddha and a non-

Siddha by saying that a Siddha points to the path of experience whereas a non-Siddha points to the path of scriptures (Kārai Siddhar, 205, p. 183).

A Siddha is one who has attained *siddhi* (special psychic and supernatural power), which is stated to be eightfold in Yoga.[4] *Siddhis* indicate whether the practitioners of yoga have attained a stage where they could reach the ultimate goal, namely, liberation. It is wrong to think that the Siddhas are simply magicians or uncouth ascetics credited with supernatural powers. They are really seers and highly evolved souls. They are not atheists or agnostics, as is commonly believed. They believe in God, but not a God of this or that religion. A genuine Siddha is beyond atheism and faith alike. Saint Tirumūlar says that one whose mind is serene and clear like an ocean without waves is a Siddha (*Tirumantiram*, v. 2955). In short, a Siddha is an individual who believes that by practicing detachment and disinterestedness one becomes free. He is a mystic because he believes that he can become one with the eternal Reality.

What Are Siddhis?

According to the *Tamil Lexicon*, *siddhi* means "realization," "success," "attainment," "final liberation."[5] *Siddhi* is an accomplishment on the psychic plane. In Tamil, *siddhi* may also mean mysticism. In Tamil literature a list of *siddhis* is to be found in Parañjoti's *Tiruvilayādar Purāṇam*,[6] Tayumānavar's *Tejōmayānandam* (v. 8)[7] and *Siddharganam* (v. 1), Pāmbātticittar's songs (vv. 25–34; 35–39; vol. 1, pp. 184–86), Saint Rāmalingam's *Tiruvarutpā*,[8] and Saint Tirumūlar's *Tirumantiram* (vv. 640–711). The *Yogatattvopaniṣad* also discusses a long list of *siddhis*.[9] Buddhism also provides a list of *iddhis* (the Pali word for *siddhis*). These *siddhis* are integral elements of the yogic practice. They are not merely negative by-products, as has been often asserted, but rightful phenomena in a successful practice of the yoga. The *siddhis*, however, have been considered hindrances to yoga and *samādhi* (concentration). The desire of attracting popular notice through a display of *siddhis* shows immaturity, but to the genuine Siddhas, these *siddhis* are of immense value. True Siddhas neither look for these nor are eager to display them. Though the possession of *siddhis* is not equivalent to liberation, they do indicate for the Siddha that he is no more under the clutches of the laws of nature which condemn him to suffer the "karmic determinism" for ever. The *Siddhis* constitute valuable indications of the aspirant's spiritual progress, yet at the same time they are dangerous in the sense that they may tempt him with a vain mastery of the world. Thus the possession of *siddhis* is not harmful in itself but one should be careful not to succumb to them, by avoiding exhibition of these powers.

The Classification of Siddhas

The *Haṭhayoga-pradīpikā*, a classical text on *Haṭha* Yoga contains a list of Great Siddhas (*mahāsiddhas*) beginning with Ādinātha.[10] Ādinātha is the mystical name for Śiva. The Siddhas belonging to the school of Ādinātha are called Nātha Siddhas. They are also known as *kaṇ-phatta*, because they have to pierce the cartilages of their ears. The Nātha Siddhas originated in North India. The Siddhas from the South are known as Maheśvara Siddhas, who advocate the pure method (*śuddha-mārga*) of Tantra. All Siddhas insist on the value of Tantric yoga as a means for the conquest of freedom and immortality. The term *tantra* is a polysemous word that contains layer upon layer of meanings. Tantrism in India has developed along two main lines—the *vāma* (left) and the *dakṣiṇa* (right). The *vamaśrota* (left current) sticks to the earlier traditions of Tantra, which are more involved in mystic rites, in the five *M*'s, which include blood sacrifices, drinking, and female consorts.[11] The *dakṣiṇaśrota* (right current) stresses *vidyā* (knowledge) through yogic practices. Hence, it is called the pure way (*śuddha-mārga*). The Tamil Siddhas belong to the *dakṣiṇaśrota*.

It is customary among the Siddhas from the Tamil area to trace their origin to Lord Śiva, who is also called a Siddha. The *Tevāram* refers to Śiva as Siddha (5.2.5; 5.4.3). The Lord in the Meenakshi Temple at Madurai is called the "all-powerful Siddha." The Tamil Siddhas view Lord Śiva as a guru (teacher), not a guru as *mūrti* (embodied physically and mentally) but as a *tattva* (a principle).

There is no agreed view as to the exact number of Siddhas. In Tamilnadu, however, tradition speaks of the eighteen Siddhas (*aśṭādaśa siddhas*). A few writers say that the number eighteen has no special significance, but others have given various interpretations as to the number. For them, it refers to the eighteen *siddhis*. The Tamil Siddhas, on this interpretation, are those who possess the eighteen *siddhis*. That there are eighteen *siddhis* is referred to in the *Bhāgavata*, where Lord Kṛṣṇa says that eighteen are the *siddhis* declared by those who are thoroughly successful in the yoga of concentration.[12] In comparing Swami Vivekānanda with other spiritual luminaries of his time, Śrī Rāmakrishna said of him that he had eighteen powers in the fullest measure.[13]

The Siddhas of Tamilnadu are freethinkers whose origins have never been dated or traced. In the *Rāmāyaṇa* of Vālmīki there is an oblique reference to the Tamil Siddhas, where Sugrīva advises Hanumān to offer his obeisance to those good people in South India who go to heaven (*svarga*) with their bodies ("Kiṣkindākāṇda," chap. 41). Most of the works of Siddhas refer to Sage Agastya as a preceptor of the Tamil Siddha doctrine.

Agastya is also called by different names as *kumbhamuni, kalaśamuni, kuḍamuni*, and so on. These names are symbolic, referring to the individual who has attained immortality by raising the *kuṇḍalinī* to the highest stage of perfection. In Tamil literature and philosophy there are references not to one but to several Agastyas. Similarly, we have more than one Paṭṭinattār mentioned in Tamil literature. The recurrence of the same name goes to show that most of the names of the Tamil Siddhas are acquired ones. It seems that once siddhahood is attained, the saint gives up his family name or the name given to him by the parents and acquires a new name to show that he has become one with God. By the attainment of siddhahood he is "born" into a "new experience" and hence must shed his old name and acquire a new name befitting the spiritual level. In the North Indian Nātha tradition, the term *nātha* has sometimes been used to refer to some transcendental state of consciousness attainable through the practice of yoga. Matsyendranāth, Goraknāth, etc., are not family names but names bestowed on every saint when that saint reaches a certain stage of spiritual perfection. "Matsya," for example, means "fish"; in Tantra it stands for the senses. "Matsyendranath" means "one who has mastery or control over the senses" (*indriyas*). In the same manner we may construe the name "Pattinattār" as "Patti + nāthar," a man who can save the souls. *Patti* in Tamil means "herding of cattle"; it may also mean "herding of souls," souls wallowing in darkness. Paṭṭinattār is one who helps and guides these souls by providing a method to get out of the "pond of the world and the senses" and get liberated.

Pāmbāṭṭiccittar is one such name. *Pāmbu* in Tamil means "snake." The snake here referred to is the coiled *kuṇḍalinī*. A Siddha who has perfected *Kuṇḍalinī* Yoga is a *pāmbāṭṭi*. There was another Tamil Siddha by name Kudambai. In Tamil this word means "earring" and stands exactly for what is meant by *kaṇ-phatta*, piercing the cartilages of the ear. This expression is a pan-Tantric, Indian term. Most of the names of the Tamil Siddhas can be shown as acquired names. When such is the case, it is difficult to decide the place and year of birth of these Siddhas. We may just say that the writings of the Tamil Siddhas span many centuries, and historians of Tamil literature prefer to put the period of Siddha poetry from fifth century C.E. on. We may remain satisfied in mentioning some of the names of the individual Siddhas without entering into a discussion of their period. Tirumūlar, Śivavākkiyar, Paṭṭinattār, Bhadragiriyār, Pāmbāṭṭiccittar, Iḍaikkāṭṭuccittar, Kundambaiccittar, Agappeyccittar, Alukanniccittar are some of the very important Tamil Siddhas.

The Siddha Attitude

In India in general and in Tamilnadu in particular there is a prevailing antipathy to the Siddhas. In Tamil literature, due place has not been given to their poems and songs. The deep-rooted prejudice against the Siddhas among the orthodox Hindus results in the misinterpretation of the Siddha doctrines. The secret and symbolic language used by the Siddhas has been one of the causes for a deep mistrust of their doctrines by the other classical systems of philosophy and religions in India. The Siddhācāryas were required not to unfold the secrets of their knowledge to anybody, and hence they had to couch their ideas in symbolic language; but at the same time they wanted to make their ideas readily available to anyone who genuinely sought them. So the secrets were written in the ordinary language of the masses in a symbolic form, sometimes using sexual imagery very freely. The aim of rendering such great truths in symbolic yet in simple language is (1) to prevent the uninitiated from being satisfied with the superficial meaning; (2) to preserve the real messages intact by making the people sing them in popular folk-song forms, and (3) to make the message reach anyone interested in it, without any discrimination of sex or caste. People who oppose the Siddha doctrines have highlighted only the seemingly obscene and obscure elements of language used by the Siddhas and have not gone deep into their inner meanings. The symbolism of sex and the imagery of women are used often in Siddha poetry because the Siddhas have felt that by giving a true picture of a woman, a man is liberated from the tyranny of the senses and the sensuous feelings. In India a woman is always viewed from two aspects—the *vigraha* and the *agraha*. In the *virgraha*, or formal, aspect she belongs to her husband (as a sex object) and to her children (as mother). In the *agraha*, or ideal, aspect she stands for cosmic energy, and in every individual human being she is represented as *kuṇḍalinī śakti*. A man who treats a woman in the first aspect and a woman who allows herself to be treated so insult womanhood; hence, they are condemned by the Siddhas. Further, the homology between the bliss enjoyed by the *sādhaka* at the supreme state and the enjoyment in sexual union is a common feature found in all mystical expressions; and the Siddha language is no exception to this.[14]

The seeming vulgarity of the Siddha poems, their esoteric teachings, their intentionally obscure language and symbolism all contributed to a lack of coordinated approach to the sources and their philosophy. Because Siddhas scoff at the Vedic sacrifices and rituals and all forms of worship of icons, they are considered to be iconoclasts. They are constantly at war with the upholders of caste system and violently oppose the practice of untouchability. A Tamil Siddha scoffs at untouchability by raising a pertinent question whether the bones, flesh, and skin of an upper-caste woman (brahman) and those of a lower-caste woman (*paraiya*) are distinguishable on the basis of caste. He asks: Are they numbered accordingly on the basis of their castes? (Śivavākkiyar, v. 38; vol. 1, p. 123). Because of all this the Siddhas are, in the eyes of the religious orthodoxy, *pāṣaṇḍas*, that is, heretics and infidels. Further, though devotees of Śiva, Siddhas deride the externals of the cult of Śiva such as wearing of a *liṅgam*, observance of fasts, and so on. The followers of traditional Śaiva Siddhānta in Tamilnadu opposed this attitude of the Siddhas, and they prevented successfully the popularity of the Siddha doctrines and blocked people from getting at their sources. Added to all these things, the Siddha way is terse, difficult, ascetically ordered, and admits of no charlatanism. Its Tantric way demands courage and is unemotional and appears to be less human. On the contrary, Āgamic Śaivism is human, emotional, and relaxed. Because of this the Siddha doctrines and poems do not get the official sanction from the elite and the educated, though their songs are popular in Tamilnadu even today. One special feature of the Siddha doctrines in Tamilnadu is that they are in the spoken language of the people, a claim no other doctrinal theories can make.

Some of the songs of the Siddhas are against the superiority of the higher castes. In many of their poems they have adduced arguments to show the illogical basis of the caste system. Casteism is perpetuated through the theory of rebirth, and the common person believes that those who do right actions in this birth are reborn in a higher caste in the next birth. In order to have a dig at casteism Śivavākkiyar goes to the extent of denying rebirth (v. 46; vol. 1, p. 124). The denial of rebirth emphasizes the fact that there is no connection between one's birth and caste. The Siddhas ridicule many of the Hindu rituals, social customs, and practices. Śivavākkiyar laughs at those who bathe for the sake of cleanliness and yet are impure in their hearts (ibid.). To the Siddhas, religious institutions, festivals, rituals, and conformity of any kind are unimportant. In short, they are haters of popular theology and practices. Yet they are not *nāstikas* (anti-Vedic). We may call the theology of the Siddhas a discourse on the Divine bereft of rituals and all popular modes of worship. Many Siddhas are also critical of the role played by women in the Hindu religious life. They consider women to be the determined opponents of religious reform of any kind. Women's innate conservatism and their blind acquiescence to traditional customs are contrary to the efforts of the Siddhas, who condemn ritualistic worship and casteism. Moreover, the Siddhas condemn the *vāmācāra* (Left-Handed) school of Tantricism, and women play an important role in the *vāmācāra* practices. The real aim of the Siddha criticism of higher caste is to show that the doors of yoga have always been open to all castes, to all men and women, irrespective of their birth, upbringing, tradition, culture, or education. At the hands of the Siddhas, yoga has become India's primary tool for self-reconciliation in the face of society's contrary pulls.

The Method of the Siddhas

In the history of Indian thought there has always been a tension among the adherents of the path of devotion (*bhakti*), those of the path of knowedge (*jñāna*), and those of yoga. The Siddhas are antagonistic toward *bhakti;* they accept yoga as the only method of final realization. The Tamil Siddhas have developed an openly negative, iconoclastic attitude toward the worship of divine images (*arca*), which is important to the path of devotion (*bhakti*). This naturally makes them critical of *bhakti* as a mode of final realization. In India, saints and seers generally speak of three mistakes of those who worship the icons.[15] (1) The worshiper reduces the Formless by giving It many forms. (2) The worshiper limits the limitless by singing its praise in words of prayer. (3) The worshiper confines the Infinite by thinking that it resides in certain sacred places such as temples, and so forth. The Tamil Siddhas totally agree with these comments. They do not consider the following to be essential requisites of inner religious life: worship of God in temples; singing His glory; and observance of certain rules and practices such as smearing the body with holy ash, wearing *rudrākṣa*, and so on. The wearing of *rudrākṣa* and the like is intended to make one firmly grounded in the path of devotion. By negating the importance of these emblems the Siddhas stand in striking contrast to the classical *bhakti* schools and literature. In Tamil Siddha literature there is almost total absence of any local cult of the deity.[16] The Tamil Siddhas have not been bound by religious dogma of any sort, nor have they used any regular place of worship. They have no sacred city, sacred river, monastic organizations, or any religious instrument. According to Agastya, if the mind is of the right disposition, it is unnecessary to chant hymns (*Jnanam-2,* v. 1; vol. 1, p. 295). The *Tirumantiram*, a work of Saint Tirumūlar, is almost free of the lover–beloved conception of God and humankind, which is characteristic of the *bhakti* schools. The Siddhas, in general, disapprove of the ultra-emotional type of *bhakti* toward a personal God. According to them, a rigid theism focusing on one Supreme "personal God" has been a divisive factor responsible for a good deal of controversy and hostility among the followers of the various theistic faiths (Śivavākkiyar, vv. 218, 128; vol. 1, pp. 145, 135; *Tirumanti-*

ram, v. 1087). Siddhas could not accept worship of divine images, since, according to them, a deity could be adored only by one becoming the deity itself. Yet the Siddhas are not atheists, as they are often represented. For most of them there is God, *Śiva*, without any limitation or attributes, grammatically and philosophically an impersonnal conception. Ideally, Śiva should be seen as "It" or *Atu*, "Thatness" or "Suchness."

Yoga is the method of actualizing what is always potential in human nature. It enables one to recover one's divine nature. Almost all yoga systems find seven components in the human being in the following order: (1) the physical body, (2) vitality, (3) the astral body, (4) the animal or sentient body, (5) the intelligence or human soul, (6) the spiritual soul, and (7) the divine soul. Body is an important component in the yoga system. According to Tantra, the human body is not merely a thing in the universe; it is an epitome of the universe—a microcosm in relation to the macrocosm. There is nothing in the universe that is not present in the body of the human being. This homology has been adopted by the Tamil Siddhas. Saint Tirumūlar says that the body is a temple and that one goes about searching for God everywhere not knowing that God resides within oneself (*Tirumantiram*, vv. 121, 307, 724–25, 1823, 2550). The Siddhas are yogis who continue to dwell in the physical body after "realization." For a Siddha, the total truth of the individual body lies in the infinitely diversified and organized cosmic body of Śiva; and the real glory of the human body lies in the possibility of realizing the presence of this whole universe in it. In short, yoga is the method of realizing the macrocosm in the microcosm. *Śiva-saṃhitā* says that an enlightened yogi can experience within his own body the presence of all *lokas* (all phenomenal existence, i.e., universe).[17] The Tantric practitioner locates the sun, the moon, the stars, mountains, islands, and rivers of the external world within one's body. Thus, the body is treated as the best medium of realizing the ultimate truth. Through yogic meditation, the material human body is transformed into microcosmos; appropriately, Mircea Eliade refers to yogic *sādhana* as "cosmophysiology."[18] The forces that govern the cosmos on the macro-level (*aṇḍa*) are the same that govern the individual in the micro-level (*piṇḍa*). Yoga recognizes the underlying unity—nay, *sameness* or *oneness*—between the cosmos and the individual and helps one to extend the ego-boundary and liberate one from a limited attitude, toward a cosmic vision. Once this feeling of oneness is developed, the internal and the external are no longer polarized and one sees the universe as though it were within oneself. Yoga is thus an effort toward the "cosmicization" of humanity and the "humanization" of the universe. This unity has been expressed in great Upaniṣadic texts such as, "the One alone exists without a second" (*ekameva-advitīyam*); "All existence is one" (*sarvam khalvidam-brahma*), "You are that One" (*tat tvam asi*), and, "This self is Brahman" (*ayam-ātmā brahma*).

The different schools of yoga study the various aspects of the human being. *Hatha* Yoga gives one a mastery of physical body and vitality; *Śakti* Yoga, power over energizing forces of nature; *Mantra* Yoga, power of thought processes; *Jñāna* Yoga, power of intellect; *Kuṇḍalinī* Yoga, power of psychic and nerve forces; and *Samādhi* Yoga, power of ecstasy. Yoga helps one tap the untapped silent areas of one's consciousness. Mircea Eliade makes an interesting comparison between the yogi and the alchemist.

> The yogi works on his own physiology. . . . Through ascesis practised on his own body he achieves a refinement of matter exactly comparable with the alchemist who "tortures" metals—that is the expression used—and purifies them in his laboratory. In both cases a state of complete spiritual autonomy is reached in the end, because the spirit is no longer conditioned by psycho-physiology or by the external material world.[19]

In Tamilnadu, the Siddhas are identified with the alchemists, and in Tantrism we find distinct reference to alchemy. One Tantric text mentions *rasa rasāyāna* as one of the *siddhis*.[20] Just as the alchemist works on base metals and turns them into gold, the Siddha transmutes his psychophysical life into a free autonomous spirit. In India gold symbolizes immortality.[21] Viewed in this way, every Siddha is a spiritual alchemist *par excellence* and his *sādhana* is *kāya sādhana*, that is, cultivation of the body or transformation of the body into immortal essence. The Siddha alchemy is no mere pre-chemistry, no mere science in embryo, but a spiritual technique to bring about spiritual deliverance and automomy. In describing the spiritual techniques, the Siddhas freely use metaphors taken from old writings on alchemy. They liken the changes brought about by the mixture of metallic powders by heat to the change that takes place in ourselves by our inner yogic *sādhana* for awakening and liberation. Because of their soteriological nature, there is a correspondence between the yogic and the alchemic techniques. The yogis call their technique *sādhana,* which is a sort of internal spiritual alchemy.

The yogic *kāya sādhana* ("body culture") is to be distinguished from physical culture, which aims at developing the athelete's prowess. *Kāya sādhana* aims at developing the spiritual power, a power that electrifies consciousness. *Kāya sādhana* is an attempt to bring about the transubstantiation of the body, the attainment of what is called *siddha deha*, a perfect body. This attaiment is not an end in itself but is a means to achieve a *divya deha*, an immutable spiritual body, or "Śiva-hood." The Siddhas considered the body to be a sacred passage to the ultimate Reality, similar to the sacred rivers, temples, mountains, and so on. They ask why we should go out to these places when the threshold is within us (Śivavākkiyar, vv. 17–18, 33; vol. 1, pp. 120–21, 123). Similarly, the guru is another threshold in the Siddha tradition. In a small Sanskrit text, *Yoga-vīja*, two kinds of body are distinguished—that which is "ripe" (*pakva*) or matured and that which is "unripe" (*apakva*) or not matured.[22] The former body has been hardened by yoga and hence is called *yoga-deha*. *Hatha* Yoga tells us the methods by which one can prepare the body for attaining *yoga-deha*. It advocates two techniques for promoting the health and strength of the body, namely, *āsana* (posture) and *mudrā* (gesture) or *bandha* (constriction). Thirty-two *āsanas* and twenty-five *bandhas* (*mudrās*) are usually mentioned as best suited for most aspirants. These *āsanas* and *mudrās* render the body supple and fit, so that there may not be physical problems when one comes to practice meditation. As Mircea Eliade put it:

> On the plane of the "body," *āsana* is an *ekāgratā*, a concentration on a single point; the body is "tensed," concentrated in a single position. Just as *ekāgratā* puts an end to the fluctuation and dispersion of the states of consciousness, so *āsana* puts an end to the mobility and disposability of the body, by reducing the infinity of possible positions to a single archetypal, iconographic posture.[23]

The heart of yoga practice is the disciplining of respiration, *prāṇāyāma*. The aim of *prāṇāyāma*, also called *vāyu-yoga* or *sara-yoga* in Tamil, is to grasp the nature of mind. Mind, which in the case of the ignorant leads to bondage, leads yogis toward enlightment. *Prāṇa* means vital force, life-breath, the energy that is everywhere—within us, in the environment, in every atom of the universe, in all substances and forms. It circulates in the body through channels called *nāḍis*.[24] Among the *nāḍis*, *iḍā*, *piṅgalā*, and *suṣumnā* are of special significance. *Prāṇāyāma* is the control of breath; it is the practice of ordered breathing. According to the Tantric text *Rasārṇava*, the body can be kept alive indefinitely if one learns how to control the breath.[25]

Prāṇāyāma is a technique that promotes meditation. While practicing *prāṇāyāma*, the yogis meditate on the *cakras*,[26] which are centers of spiritual energy that are located in the body. They are depicted as (lotus) flowers rather than as wheels, and have petals through which the *yoga-śakti* flows, producing various spiritual phenomena in life, body, and consciousness. There are six important *cakras*. These are also called *ādhāras*. They are: (1) *mūlādhāra* (the root center) located at the lower end of the spinal cord, i.e., anus, containing four petals; (2) *svādhiṣṭhāna* (the support of the life center) at the genital organs, having six petals; (3) *maṇipūra* (the jewel city center) at the navel with ten petals; (4) *anāhata* (the unstruck sound center) at the heart with twelve petals; (5) *viśuddha* (the great purity center) at the throat, with sixteen petals; and (6) *ājñā* (the command center), between the two eyebrows, with two petals.

The seventh *cakra* is known as *sahasrāra*, located in the brain, which contains a thousand petals. The doctrine of the six *ādhāras* or seven *cakras* is very important because all yoga techniques ultimately aim at the awakening of the *kuṇḍalinī*, the master energy, the supreme consciousness, and her passage through the *cakras*. All the *cakras* are upside down except when the *kuṇḍalinī* passes over them, when they are right side up. The six mystical circles (six *cakras*), or lotuses, are to be passed through by a *sādhaka* (aspirant) before he/she reaches the final goal and attains beatitude. The piercing or passing through these lotuses is called *kamala-vedha*. The *kuṇḍalinī* is called "serpent power" and is symbolized by a serpent motif because it is as dangerous as playing with the tempers of a hydra-headed serpent. The idea of Lord Kṛṣṇa dancing on the hood of such a monster is to show him as a *sādhaka par excellence*. *Kuṇḍalinī-yoga* takes one to immortality or *amṛta*. If by death we mean change, then "immortality" means a state that is not subject to death or change. So to be immortal means to persist in existence which is absolute and unchangeable. This is what is called *siddhi* in Tantric literature. *Siddhis* are not contrary to nature. They appear to be supernatural since the "normal" human being does not care to cultivate them. In the *karma-yoga* of the *Bhagavad Gītā*, *naiṣkarmyam* and *siddhi* connote the same—they mean success, perfection.

In Siddha literature, as we have already stated, the body is an important instrument, for in it resides the true spirit of humanity. It should be the threshold of human liberation. The *Kulārṇavatantra* says that as one falls on the ground one must lift oneself by the aid of the ground.[27] In the same way, the body should be the elevator leading to one's liberation. Eternity is within the body: it is not the body itself, but it is in the body. Almost all systems of Indian thought accept three bodies (*śarīras*) in human beings. They are the gross or physical body (*sthūla-śarīra*), the causal body (the *kāraṇa-śarīra*), and the subtle or ethereal body (the *sūkṣma* or *liṅga-śarīra*). According to the Tamil Siddhas, the *liṅga śarīra* consists of the *praṇava*, or *mantra-tanu*, and *jñāna*, or *divya-tanu*.[28] These bodies are free from gross matter and all impurities. The Siddha, by yogic *sādhana*, transmutes the gross physical body into the body called *praṇava* or *mantra-tanu*, one consisting of the sacred formula *Om*. This body is a refined, transphysical, incorruptible, transfigured body of glory and power. The person with the *praṇava-tanu* is a *jīvanmukta*, a Siddha or a yogi. In a *jīvanmukta*, the senses continue to function, maintaining contact with the external world, but the inner consciousness refuses to take note of it and persists in the exclusive enjoyment of the bliss of its own light. That person moves in the everyday world and yet "lives" in "Reality" exclusively. One no longer possesses a personal consciousness, but only a "witnessing consciousness." The *praṇava-tanu* is transfigured into an "eternal spiritual body," called the *jñāna* or *divya-tanu*. When the Siddha attains this spiritual body he becomes a *para-mukta*, a deathless, spiritual being who becomes one with the ultimate Reality. He becomes a permanent "Enlightenment-Consciousness." This stage is beyond all concepts and spatiotemporal relations. Since a Siddha goes out of the ravages of time through the method of yoga, he is often referred to as *kāla-atīta*, "one who has transcended time." As a *jīvanmukta*, he does act in this world; but he does not have the consciousness, "I act."

Mysticism of the Siddhas

This is best exhibited in their conception of the Absolute. According to Śivavākkiyar, true Reality is indescribable. He asks a pertinent question as to how he can explain in words that which is beyond words and speech. He also says that the Absolute is nondual. To him there is no point in describing the Absolute as this or as not this, which leads to confusion only (Śivavākkiyar, vv. 11, 287, 415, 218; vol. 1, pp. 120, 153, 168, 145). Agappeyccittar says that *Śivam* is only for those who have attained self-realization (v. 55; vol. 1, p. 221). As Arthur Eddington pointed out, "I know" of the mystic is like the idempotent symbol of modern mathematical physics the square of which is equal to itself ($J^2=J$).[29] Saint Tirumūlar had leanings toward viewing the Absolute as nondual. He speaks of the "Brahman-*Ātman* equation" when he says that for those who have attained clear spiritual stature, *jīva* and *Śiva* are the same (*Tirumantiram*, v. 1823). When subject to change, it is *jīva*; when subject to no change, It is Śiva. The mystical equation of Self and the Absolute does not refer to a numerical or logical identity. It is the assertion of a metalogical identity. When the mystic has realized this equation of the ultimate Reality within himself, he becomes a *paramahaṃsa*, a "Supreme swan." This title may have two explanations. First, it refers to the swan which is able to drink pure milk alone out of a mixture of milk and water. The second is an esoteric explanation based on the mantra *saḥ aham*, meaning "He is I." If *saḥ aham* is repeated several times, we read back as *haṃ sa*, that is, swan. The identity between *jīva* and Śiva belongs to experience or direct apprehension and not to the interpretation. The "oneness" is an experienced certainty. It is an experience of "seeing" all in each and each in all. It is an experience of the dissolution of the separate individuality, a fading of the "I" into the Boundless Being.

The oneness between the "I" and the "Absolute" is of an extraordinary character. It does not add anything, as nothing can be subtracted. For want of a better expression, this oneness is termed "superunion," and this is what is termed "yoga." Yoga, in essence, is oneness. As a method it makes us realize this oneness. The superunion is not a stage in the annihilation of the self, because the Self is immortal. The immortality of the Self is experienced when the self is free from the bondage of "I-ness." The oneness is, therefore, a case of spiritual impersonality. In one sense, the oneness is "selfless," because in the broadest sense it is not "selfish"; that is, it does not have the element of ego or "I-ness" in it. In another sense the oneness is the supreme Self, because it is no other than one's own self in a new dimension, the newly discovered self. This mystical oneness or unity between the "self" and the "Self" is an undivided oneness and may be called the original prebiographical unity or oneness.

Almost all the Tamil Siddhas refer to the mystical *mantra*, *namah śivāya*. The sacred five letters are *ci-va-ya-no-ma*. This is a *mahāvākya*. *Śiva* stands for *tat*. *Nama* stands for *tvam*, and *aya* stands for *asi*. Hence, *Śivāyanama* means *tat tvam asi*, "That Thou Art." In some Siddha poems the five letters are referred to as *ci-va-ya-va-ci*, which can be read in both ways as the same. Hence, some of them refer to this term as the "two-pronged fire," *irutalaittī*, which burns both birth and death. Śiva (Absolute) is visualized by many Siddhas as a mighty and moving blaze of light (*oli*) which dispels ignorance. Generally Indian spiritual thinkers often use the simile of light when talking about consciousness.

In Tamil Siddha literature, liberation is referred to as *vettaveḷi* or *uyarveḷi* or *peruveḷi* or *kaḍuveḷi*. The ultimate Reality is conceived by them as *vettaveḷi*, which in ordinary language means "plain, clear, or light space," while in yoga it stands for the liberated state. *Vettaveḷi* stands for expanse, an ideal transcendental region. It stands for an infinite, transcendental awareness; it is not *our* awareness but the awareness of Being itself. It is stored consciousness, something incorruptible by concepts, and is beyond the space-time matrix. It is "is-ness" everywhere. It stands for freedom from time. At that stage the terms "before" and "after" become entirely meaningless and there is only an "eternal now." In that vast realm of spaceless-timeless *vettaveḷi*, the small personal pronouns become meaningless. *Vettaveḷi* is bliss; it is spaciousness of freedom; it is a state of *kaivalaya* or isolation, a Great Aloneness. It is a state where the soul is one with the ultimate Reality. *Vettaveḷi* also means space in the sense of an all-embracing principle. In Tamil, *Iṛai* means "to pervade"; hence God is called *Iṛaivan*. *Vettaveḷi* is that which can contain and embrace anything and everything. There is nothing that exists outside it. It is in opposition to the principle of "substance" or "thingness," which stands for distinction and differentiation. *Vettaveḷi* also stands for *oḷi,* or blazing light, since it is *ākāśa* and the root word of *ākāśa* is *kāś*, which means "to radiate, to shine." *Vettaveḷi* also means "stainless sky" and symbolically it stands for a state where all the senses are asleep. The term *vettaveḷi* has been used by the Siddhas to suggest that even the idea of "having nothing" (*śūnya*) ought to be done away with.

The term *vettaveḷi* stands for indescribability. The Siddha view of *vettaveḷi,* or the Absolute, may be best described in the words of Vidyāpati, a Vaisnava saint: "Don't ask, I know; ask, I know not."[30] This is best described by a Tamil Siddha as those who know Him cannot explain Him and as those who explain Him do not know Him.[31] When something is indescribable, one must remain silent. The term *vettaveḷi* gradually came to convey the meaning of silence. The concept *cummā* in Tamil Siddha literature refers to this silence. It is not *śūnya* in the sense of nothingness. It is a state that is free of all supports, whether external existents such as jar, flower, and so on or internal subsistents such as pleasure, pain, and the like—a state free of all constituent elements of thought and action. Whenever we cannot speak or express fully, we must be silent. *Cummā* is the silent language of the heart; it is the negation of all determinations, but not a negation of "is-ness" as such. Silence is a mystical metaphor often used for distinctionlessness. It is a state in which the Absolute is not an ultimate but an intimate. There is a Tamil proverb, *monam enbadu jñānavarambu*, which means silence is the indication of *jñāna* (knowledge). Silence is the absolutely motionless state of mind; a stage of "sleepless sleep" (Bhadragiriyār, *Meijñānappulambal,* v. 1; vol. 1, p. 102). It is the "still point" to which T. S. Eliot refers.[32] It refers to a state of "actionless action," a state of restful alertness; it is the deepest depth. It is an egoless, nondualistic state where Reality is without any "otherness"; it is a state of "not-two-ness." It has no content except itself; it is a state that is beyond the manifest. *Cummā* stands for imageless liberation. Tamil Siddhas call this as a state "Beyond, beyond the beyond" (Śivavākkiyar, vv. 9, 12; vol. 1, p. 120). The term "beyond" means exceeding or wider than relation. The Absolute includes all relations but is not exhausted by any one of them or their sum total. Whereas "you" and "I" as persons have "sets" of relations, the Absolute does not have such a set. In this sense, it is an "alogical whole" not determined by any set of relations, even though all sets of relations are contained in it. Since it is beyond relations, one cannot even speak about it. Śivavākkiyar says that once God has entered his heart, he does not open his mouth afterwards (v. 31; vol. 1, p. 122). This is because the name that can be named cannot be the eternal name; for names set bounds and imply relations. So the silence adopted by Siddhas like Śivavākkiyar should be construed not as ignorance but as soul's highest and best form of knowledge. We may compare the silence to the "instructed or learned ignorance" (*docta ignorantia*) of Nicholas of Cusa, or the silent desert of the Godhead (*stille Wüste der Gottheit*) of Meister Eckhart, or Swāmi Vivekānanda's "joy that never spoke." This type of mystical experience is unconceptualizable because concepts depend on multiplicity and they are not adequate to describe a felt, unitary experience. To view the Absolute as nondual is also a Tantric tradition. Both Hindu and Buddhist types of Tantrism visualize the Absolute as supreme Nonduality, *advaita* and *advaya* respectively. Nothing numerical can pertain to the Absolute. In the state of absolute Bliss, it is not that something different is seen but that one *sees* differently. It is a state of "I am Thou," where the copula "am" is not a logical one but a mystical copula. To use Rudolf Otto's word, mysticism has its own "wonder" logic. The oneness expressed is the fullness of all manifestations.

Like other mystics throughout the world, the Siddhas also express their mystical experience in a paradoxical language. The Tamil Siddhas have expressed their experience in the form of folk songs, which are characterized by deceptive simplicity. These folk songs are written for both the uninitiated and the initiated. They are noted for using pedestrian symbolism, that is, symbols and words used by ordinary people. They really conceal the spiritual doctrines, especially the *kuṇḍalinī yoga* from the uninitiated. The language of the Siddhas, then, operates at two levels—popular and esoteric. In addition to using words in a dual sense, the use of numerals to denote facts, ideas, or allusions is a favorite device of the Tamil Siddhas. The ordinary terms, words, and numerals used in Siddha language have hidden meanings. The use of double-meaning language by the Tamil Siddhas has an unbroken history for centuries and fits very well into the Tantric pattern of *sandhyā-bhāṣā*, which has been translated variously as "enigmatic language," "mystery," "hidden sayings," and "twilight language." We may use the term "intentional language" for *sandhyā-bhāṣā*, a language that seeks to conceal the message from the uninitiated and at the same time helps to project the yogi or the *sādhaka* into a paradoxical situation indispensable to his training. Religious symbolism has a characteristic feature, namely, "multivalence"—to use the expression of Mircea Eliade, that is, the capacity to express at the same time a number of meanings.[33] "Lotus" is a symbol used in Siddha language. It stands for the unfolding of the expanding consciousness. The tasting of the *amṛta* (nectar) that is produced in *sahasrāra* is called "the flesh of the cow" that the yogi eats (*Hathayogapradīpika*, chap. 3, 47–49). This expression "eating of cow's flesh" is used just to show that a true Siddha, as a participator in "transcendence," goes beyond the Hindu prohibitions (eating cow's flesh), that he is no longer conditioned by its ethical codes, and that he is no longer "of this world." The term *paramahaṃsa* is also symbolic. Figuratively it is said that the swan (*haṃsa*) is playing in the waters of the Gangā and the Yamunā. The Gangā and Yamunā stand for the in-going and out-going of the vital air, namely, *idā* and *piṅgalā*. *Paramahaṃsa* is a person who has stopped playing in these rivers and has chosen the course of the middle stream, that is, *suṣummā*, thus leading one to *sahasrāra*, a place of infinite and immutable joy. The use of symbolic language is not merely a protection against the profanation of the sacred by the ignorant but also a suggestion that language, however enriched, is incapable of expressing the highest experiences of the spirit. In terms of Sufi terminology, any attempt to convey the inner meaning of one's spiritual experiences in a conventional language is like "sending a kiss by a messenger"!

According to the Siddhas, the esoteric teaching must be learned from master-teachers, gurus, and almost all Siddhas refer to their tradition of gurus (*guru-paraṃparā*). A guru is one who guides the disciple in the onward path of spiritual progress through yoga and *jñāna*. What characterizes yoga is not only its practical side but also its initiatory structure. *Dīkṣā*, or initiation (literally, "empowerment"), is a philosophical apprenticeship. Sometimes it is symbolically referred to as a gynecological term, and we speak of "rebirth," of "new person," after initiation. In this sense every guru is a midwife, for he aids in the birth of "a person who knows."

The Tamil Siddhas considered it a fallacy to regard mysticism as necessarily linked with the denial of the world and its welfare. They are noted for their altruism and are very much concerned with the welfare of the people around them. They did not fail to see in their neighbor's face their own unanswered agonies. Their *mantra*, *Śivāya nama*, is not merely a philosphical-mystical concept but a social one as well. *Nama* means *tyāga*, or "sacrifice"; "Śiva" means *ānanda* (bliss); and *aya* means "income" or "result." The term *Śivāya nama* therefore means "the result of sacrifice is bliss." The Tamil Siddhas felt the bliss in "sacrifice," and they construed "sacrifice" as an opportunity to serve. By this they discovered that the self in others is an enlargement of their own consciousness and being. The social concern of the Siddhas has provided them with one more path for the discovery of the self. The *āṟṟuppaḍai* concept that we find in Tamil literature has acquired a socio-philosophical meaning at the hands of the Tamil Siddhas. Their songs are "indicators" of the path of self-realization for a seeker after truth. They are meant as guides to common people, to direct them to the path of spirituality. The Siddhas wanted every one to "enjoy" what they have "enjoyed."

Saint Tirumūlar wants the universe to enjoy the bliss that he has enjoyed (*Turumantiram,* v. 85). Hence, the poems of the Siddhas are not mere expressions in language, but they contain in them the elevated *āṟṟupaḍai* concept of directing or showing the path to one and all. Thus, we find here the Siddhas' concern for the well-being of all (*lokasaṅgraha*). To a Siddha, a neighbor is not merely a human being who lives nearby, but *every* living being whom he encounters. His mystic way of salvation finds its necessary corollary in the concept of service to humanity. To him genuine freedom is not isolation. Cosmic gregariousness is one of the instincts of a genuine Siddha. A Siddha prefers the ideal of service to the ideal of gaining his own personal salvation (*mokṣa*). Hence, they put their ideas into the common language of the people, and their social concern is best exhibited in their systems of medicine.

In conclusion we may say that the Tamil Siddhas are in a sense "rebels" inside the theistic fold; they are pious rebels. They have influenced the later orthodox saints and seers also. To a Siddha, religion is not a creed or a code but an insight into, and a profound encounter with, Supreme Reality. The Siddha philosophy with its social attitude may well constitute the point of departure for a new humanism on a world scale with its fount deeply enbedded in a philosophy of the spirit that is not confined to any notion or nation, religion, or community—which, indeed, is the common spiritual treasure trove of the entire human race.

Notes

1. Tirumūlar, *Tirumantiram* (Sri Vaikuntam: Sri Kumaraguruparan Sangam, 1968) v. 2525. Hereafter, references to *Tirumantiram* are from this edition.

2. Mircea Eliade, *Yoga: Immortality and Freedom,* trans. Willard R. Trask (New York: Bollingen Foundation, Princeton University Press, 1969) 302.

3. Agastya, *Jnanam-2*, v. 5 in *Siddhar Padalgal*, ed. Aru. Ramanathan (2 vols.; 4th ed.; Madras: Prema Presuram, 1984) 1:296. Hereafter the references to Siddha songs are from this collection.

4. The eight *siddhis* are (1) *animā*, the ability to become as minute as an atom; (2) *mahimā*, the ability to expand infinitely; (3) *laghimā*, levitation or the ability to float through the air; (4) *garimā*, the ability to reach everywhere; (5) *prākāmya*, freedom of will or the ability to overcome natural obstacles; (6) *īśitva*, the ability to create or control; (7) *vaśitva*, dominion over the entire creation; and (8) *kāmāvaśāyitva*, the gift of wish-fulfillment or the ability of attaining everything desired or to attain the stage of desirelessness. *Aṣṭa siddhi* is of three orders: two *siddhis* of knowledge (*garimā* and *prākāmya*), three *siddhis* of power (*īśitva*, *vaśitva*, and *kāmāvāśayitva*) and three *siddhis* of the body (*mahimā*, *laghimā*, and *animā*).

5. *Tamil Lexicon*, vol. 3, part 1 (Madras: Madras University, 1928) 1412.

6. Parañjoti, *Tiruvilayādar Puraṇam, Kūdarkāṇḍam*, sections relating to *ellām valla cittarāna paḍalam, kallānaikku-karumbaruthiya paḍalam,* and *attamāsiddhi upadesitha paḍalam*.

7. *Tiruppādarrirattu* (Madras: Rathina Nayakar & Sons, n.d).

8. Rāmaliṅga Adigal, *Tiruvarutpā*, ed. Ooran Adigal (Vadalur: Samarasa Sanmarga Araychi Nilayam, 1972) 3.8.4, p. 450; *Tirumantiram*, vv. 640–711.

9. *The Yoga-Upaniṣads,* trans. T. R. Srinivasa Ayyangar (Madras: The Adyar Library, 1938) 311, 313.

10. *The Hatha Yoga Pradipika*, trans. Pancham Sinh (2nd ed.; New Delhi: Oriental Books Reprint Corporation, 1975) chap. 1, pp. 5–8.

11. The five *M*'s called *pañca makāras* in Tantric literature are: *madya, matsya, māṃsa, mudrā,* and *maithuna*. In *vāmaśrota* these terms refer to their literal meanings, that is, wine, fish, meat, parched cereal, and sexual union respectively. But in *dakṣinaśrota* they are hypostatized into mental configurations and are intended to denote a progressive course of *sādhana* leading to the realization of the absolute Self. *Madya* becomes the symbol for intoxicating knowledge; *matsya* is symbolic of *prāṇāyāma; māṃsa* stands for control of speech and withdrawal from world phenomena; *mudrā* refers to the yogic state of concentration; and *maithuna* is the merging of the *sādhaka* with the Reality.

12. *Uddhava-Gītā,* ed. Swami Madhavananda (3rd ed.; Calcutta: Advaita Ashrama, 1971) 141–42.

13. See E. R. Marrozi, "The Making of Swami Vivekananda," in *Swami Vivekananda in East and West* (London: Ramakrishna Vedanta Centre, 1968) 11.

14. In the *Bṛhadāraṇyaka Upaniṣad* the realization of Self has been compared to the transcendental realization of bliss arising through the deep embrace of a woman. "As, when deeply embraced by the dear woman, one knows neither anything external nor anything internal—so also a man deeply embraced by the *ātman* through perfect knowledge knows neither anything external nor anything internal" (4–3.21). Śrī Rāmakrishna Paramahaṃsa says: "*Nityaśuddha-bodharūpam*—the Eternal and Ever-pure consciousness—How can I make it clear to you? A young girl once asked her friend: 'Well, friend, your husband is here. What sort of pleasure do you enjoy with him?' The friend answered: 'My dear, you will know it for yourself when you get a husband. How can I explain it to you?'" (*The Gospel of Sri Ramakrishna*, trans. Swami Nikhilananda (abridged ed.; New York: Ramakrishna Vivekananda Centre, 1980) 440.

15. The three mistakes of the image worshiper are referred to by Vyāsa in *Bhāgavata Purāṇa*.

16. No genuine Siddha in Tamil literature, including Saint Tirumūlar, has sung in praise of any local God or Deity. I am of the firm conviction that one of the ways of separating a "genuine Siddha" from a "pseudo Siddha" is to ascertain whether one has songs in praise of any local God or Deity, in which case one falls under the category of "pseudo Siddha"! According to Śivavākkiyar, a Siddha does not worship any deity in the temple (*kanda koyil deyvam enru kaiyeduppad-illaiye;* Śivavākkiyar, v. 26, vol. 1, p. 111). The *vāmācāra* system was current among the worshipers of Ganesa, Viṣṇu, Rudra, Śiva, Bhairava, Kāpalika, Pasupata, Aghora, etc. It is probable that Tamil Siddhas did not worship any deity or go to temples just to distinguish themselves from the practioners of the *vāmācāra* tradition.

17. *The Esoteric Philosophy of the Tantras: Shiva Sanhita*, trans. Srischandra Basu (Calcutta: Heerabal Dhole, 1887) chap. 2, vv. 1–5.

18. Eliade, *Yoga*, 236.

19. Mircea Eliade, "The True Dreams of Mankind—A Conversation with Mircea Eliade," *Span* (April 1981) 38.

20. *Sādhanamālā*, ed. B. T. Bhattacharyya (2 vols.; Oriental Series 27, 41; Baroda: Gaekwad, 1925, 1928) 1:350.

21. *Amṛtam āyur hiraṇyam* (*Maitrāyani Saṃhitā*, II, 2,2; *Śatapatha Brāhmaṇa*, III, 8, 2, 27; *Aitareya Brāhmaṇa*, VII, 4,6).

22. Referred to by S. Dasgupta in his *Obscure Religious Cults* (Calcutta: Firma K. L. Mukhopadhyay, 1969) 253.

23. Eliade, *Yoga*, 54–55.

24. *Nāḍi* is a technical term in *yoga* and does not stand exclusively for the nerve. It stands for energy in motion or *prāṇic* force.

25. *Rasārnava*, cited in *Sarvadarśanasaṁgraha* of Mādhva, trans. E. B. Cowell and A. E. Gough (6th ed.; Varanasi: Chowkhamba Sanskrit Series, 1961) 137–44.

26. *Cakras* are inner power phenomena and indicate the levels of consciousness and of absorptive concentration. There cannot be any real identification of them with the nerve plexuses as advocated by Vasant Rele in his *Mysterious Kundalinī* (3rd ed.; Bombay: Taraporewala, 1931).

27. "Success is attained by those very things which lead to fall" (*Kulārṇava Tantra*, ed. John Woodroffe and M. P. Pandit, with introduction and readings (rpt., Delhi: Motilal Banarsidass, 1984) 8.

28. The Siddhas of Tamilnadu who belong to the *śuddhamārga* ("the pure way") distinguish two kinds of incorruptible bodies, *praṇava-tanu* and *divya-tanu*. The yogi with a *praṇava-tanu* is a *jīvanmukta* (a man who is liberated in life), and the one with a *divya tanu* is a *paramukta*, with a "body of pure light" (*cinmaya*) or "divine body."

29. Arthur Eddington, *The Philosophy of Physical Sciences* (Cambridge: Cambridge University Press, 1939) 162, 202.

30. Quoted by S. Bhattacharya, *Saivism and the Phallic World* (2 vols.; New Delhi: Oxford & IBH Publishing Co., 1975) 1:377.

31. *Agattiya Mahā Munivar Paripoornam 400*, ed. Vadivelu Mudaliar (Madras: Vidyaratnakara Press, 1903) 16; Ganapathy Dasar, *Nenjaneri Vilakkam*, v. 39; *Siddhar Padalgal*, vol. 1.

32. T. S. Eliot, "Four Quartets," *The Complete Poems and Plays of T.S. Eliot* (rpt., London: Faber & Faber, 1970) 173.

33. Mircea Eliade, "Methodological Remarks on the Study of Religious Symbolism," in *The History of Religions: Essays in Methodology*, ed. Mircea Eliade and Joseph M. Kitagawa (Chicago: University of Chicago Press, 1959) 99.

Bibliography

Studies

Aijar, A. V. Subramaniya. *The Poetry and Philosophy of the Tamil Siddhars.* Tirunelveli: S. Mahadevan, 1957.

Arunachalam, M. "The Poetry and Philosophy of Siddhar Sivavakiyar." *Saiva Siddhanta* 8/2 (1973) 68–77.

———. "The Siddha Cult in Tamilnad." *Bulletin of the Institute of Traditional Cultures* (January–June 1977) 8–21, 85–94.

Buck, David C. "Siddhanta: Siddha and Saiva." In *Experiencing Siva: Encounters with a Hindu Deity*, edited by Fred Clothy and Bruce Long. Delhi: Manohar, 1983.

Ganapathy, T. N. *The Philosophy of the Tamil Siddhas.* New Delhi: Indian Council of Philosophical Research, 1993.

———. "The Twilight Language of the Siddhas." In *Indian Philosophical Annual*, vol. 17. Madras: University of Madras Radhakrishnan Institute of Advanced Study in Philosophy, 1984–85.

Gover, Charles E. *The Folk Songs of South India.* 1872. Reprint. Madras: South India Saiva Siddhanta Kalagam, 1959.

Jaya, P. "Works of Cittars and Their Place in Hindu Religious Thought in Tamil Literature." Ph.D. Thesis. Tamil Department, Kerala University, Trivandrum.

Jones, Franklin. *The Method of the Siddhas.* Los Angeles: The Dawn Horse Press, 1973.

Narayanan. K. *Siddhar Tattvam* (in Tamil). Madras: Tamil Puthakalayam, 1988.

Pampatti-Cittar. *Dance, Snake! Dance!* Translated by David C. Buck. Calcutta: Writers Workshop, 1976.

Sastry, V. V. Ramana. "The Doctrinal Culture and Tradition of the Siddhas." In *The Cultural Heritage of India*, vol. 4, edited by H. Bhjattacharya. Calcutta: Ramakrishna Mission Institute of Culture, 1962.

Part Three

THE SPIRITUALITY OF MODERN HINDUISM

13

The Spiritual Vision of Rāmaliṅgar

V. A. DEVASENAPATHI

RĀMALIṄGAR, popularly known as *Arutprakāsa Vaḷḷalār*, was a spiritual luminary of the nineteenth century. He was a contemporary of Rāmakrishna Paramahamsa. Born in 1823 in Marudur, near Cidambaram, he moved on to Madras in 1825 after the death of his father. After a stay of thirty-three years in Madras, he went to Karunguli in 1858. Leaving this place in 1867, he went to Vadalur, where he stayed till 1870. Thereafter he stayed in Mettukuppam, very near Vadalur, until 1874, the year when he withdrew his physical presence from this world.

In the divine dispensation, India was blessed to have two saints, one in the North in Rāmakrishna Paramahamsa and the other in the South in Rāmaliṅgar, to give a clear lead in promoting concord and religious harmony among the various religions that met on this soil. The message of these saints was essentially that of the Vedas, which proclaimed the truth: "Reality is one. Sages call it by various names." By the nineteenth century, India had to accommodate religions such as Christianity and Islam, and it became imperative to develop and promote religious harmony. Rāmakrishna showed the validity and value of all approaches by his personal experience of each of them. Rāmaliṅgar spoke and sang about concord and established an institution to promote this ideal. Both of these saints were firmly rooted in their tradition, which, without being hidebound, has an innate elasticity and capacity for growth. It is no untenable claim that the currently popular concept of dialogue has been a basic belief of the Hindu tradition from Vedic times. These two saints gave a clear call for concord in the last century. It is a pity that it has evoked a response only during the last two decades in world circles. In regard to dialogue, we are slowly realizing the wisdom behind the witty remark that two monologues do not become a dialogue. Dialogue or multilogue—call it what you will—must be conducted for mutual understanding and enrichment.

Rāmaliṅgar was the fifth child of his parents, Ramiah Pillai and Cinnammai. It is said that when Rāmaliṅgar was taken as a baby to the Cidambaram temple, he laughed in joy when the screen in the temple was lifted to show the divine mystery (*Cidambara rahasyam*). When he lost his father, he was taken to Madras by his eldest brother Sabhapati Pillai. The attempts of Rāmaliṅgar's brother to give him a formal education did not meet with great success. To teach Rāmaliṅgar a lesson and to get him interested in schooling, his brother sent him out of the home. Rāmaliṅgar's sister-in-law used to give Rāmaliṅgar a meal in the back yard of the house without the knowledge of his brother. On the day of the annual death ceremony of his parent, when Rāmaliṅgar called as usual, his sister-in-law was moved to tears by the thought that while strangers were invited to dine with them, a member of the household had to be treated as an outcast. Moved by her tears, Rāmaliṅgar said that if he was given a separate room in the house, he would apply himself to his studies. This was done. Rāmaliṅgar placed a mirror in the room and, sitting in front of it, practiced contemplation. The figure of Lord Subrahmaṇya, the presiding Deity of Tiruttani (a famous pilgrim center, about fifty miles from Madras) appeared on the mirror.

How is this to be explained? We may hazard a guess. In contemplation, when the mind is initially stilled by the withdrawal of the senses from external objects, it becomes like a mirror without any object before it—a blank surface. Then it becomes possible for the object of contemplation to present itself. We may say that there is a reversal here. Instead of the senses presenting objects to the mind, now the mind presents objects to the senses. The purified mind dictates to the physical world, without allowing itself to be dictated to by the latter. Would this not be a streak of abnormality? Such experiences may be judged by the fruits of the spirit they produce to feed the world at all levels—organic, mental, and spiritual. One incident after this experience of Rāmaliṅgar may be said to vouch for its authenticity. Sabhapati Pillai use to give religious discourses. One day, unable to go, he sent Rāmaliṅgar just to read from a sacred text so that the gathering might not go away entirely disappointed. Rāmaliṅgar went on to comment on the passage to the amazement of the gathering. Sabhapati Pillai was informed of this matter. He sent Rāmaliṅgar again, but he himself went secretly to the place of the meeting and hid himself to listen to Rāmaliṅgar. As he listened, he realized that his brother was one far above all book-learning, that he had come to know *That* by knowing which everything else is known. Rāmaliṅgar spoke with the authority of his personal experiences to give authenticity to his utterances. Succeeding generations have had the benefit of listening to the voice of Rāmaliṅgar as recorded in his songs, outpourings, correspondence, commentaries, and prose pieces. They have a marvelous power to move the hearts of the lettered and the unlettered, the virtuous and the wicked.

Rāmaliṅgar expresses his gratitude to God for the gift of Tamil—a language easier than Sanskrit in regard to learning, pronunciation, and understanding. This should not blind us to the fact that Rāmaliṅgar wields Sanskrit with graceful ease. In one of his songs, the first part is a string of pure Sanskrit words (though given in Tamil characters); the second part is a happy blend of Sanskrit and Tamil words; and the concluding part is mostly Tamil words. His prose writings have been a model for subsequent generations. There are songs in lifting style to the tune of which small girls could dance, while the contents of the songs gently cast their spell on the minds of the singers and the listeners. There are also regular musical compositions. While on the whole his songs are easy to understand, a few of them have a profound musical tenor. Rāmaliṅgar gives us guidance for building a healthy mind in a healthy body as a prerequisite for a fruitful spiritual journey. Even details for one's day-to-day routine are given—from waking to sleeping. Rāmaliṅgar may be deemed to have broken the tradition of keeping the medicinal effects of greens and roots a closely guarded secret. He reveals their value in promoting health and curing ailments. The body, with its sensory and psychic equipment, is a precious gift of God to enable us to attain salvation. Hence, it must be used in a gentle fashion in whatever function it is employed. Eating, work, and sleep should be in moderation. Even while engaged in good action, violent exertion should be avoided. Diseases should be attended to promptly so that they may not lead to untimely death or senility.

In his correspondence with devotees, Rāmaliṅgar gives guidance in regard to the way one should behave with others. It should be in such a way as not to hurt their feelings. Expenses should be incurred only in proportion to income. But if debts are incurred, steps should be taken to clear them. Corporal punishment must be avoided in the process of teaching children. There should be a measure of detachment even in the midst of active worldly life.

Thus, in several ways Rāmaliṅgar endeavored to help one and all to live a full life and achieve its purpose. Did he preach and proclaim immortality for the physical body? Was this the reason he advocated burial of bodies instead of cremation? Was his own physical disappearance to be understood as his presence elsewhere? There is no unanimity in answering these questions. The late Justice M. Ananthanarayanan observed:

> In bringing out a critical and definitive edition of the Poet Saint's version, correspondence, prose and commentaries Sri A. Balakrishna Pillai is rendering a very great service not merely towards the people of Madras State and all

lovers of Tamil, but to the peoples of the world, if this work could fortunately reach them through the media of translations into European and other languages. For, though Sri Rāmaliṅgar Swamigal lived as recently as the closing decades of the nineteenth century, we do not know a great deal about him authentically and certainly we have not understood him.

He disappeared from the view of his devotees and of the world on 31-1-1874 (January 31, 1874) under circumstances which do suggest some experiment in "Creative Evolution," with strange affinities to the "Supramental" yoga to which Sri Aurobindo dedicated his life. More, it is not possible to hazard, from our faltering and inadequate knowledge. I am referring here, of course, to our ignorance of the true nature of the experiment and not to the Realization (*Anuboothi)* of the saint of which there is no doubt whatever. We know only somewhat of the outer host of the events: an objective, if necessarily superficial account of this will also be found in W. Francis's "South Arcot Gazetteer."[1]

Rāmaliṅgar founded institutions to promote his ideals: (1) *Dharma sāla* was begun to feed persons who are hungry; this institution has been functioning for over a century now. The highlight is on the Full Moon day in January-February each year. (2) *Vedapāḍasāla* was founded to teach the scriptures to the young. (3) *Satya-jñāna sabhai* was established as a place to practice meditation. A lamp whose bright flame could be seen when seven curtains are lifted was installed as a symbol of the effulgence that is divine grace.

Being a great seer, Rāmaliṅgar would have foreseen the day when it would be necessary and possible for all spiritually inclined to constitute—perhaps not officially or institutionally but nonetheless effectively—"the Association of the Good Path" (*Sanmārga Saṅgam*). The pervading spirit in the practice of the presence of the Real would be concord and harmony, avoiding polemics and acrimony. Tāyumānavar, a saint who preceded Rāmaliṅgar by two centuries, sang of the happy state of the concord of Vedānta and Siddhānta (*vedānta siddhānta samarasa nannilai*), so that there could be a judicious blend of metaphysical absolutism and theism. Rāmaliṅgar paved the way for a larger or universal concord. It would be a Parliament of Religions, so to say, whose edict would hold sway in the hearts of all those dedicated to the promotion of spiritual values. The Reality recognized by them is aptly described by Rāmaliṅgar as "the Great Effulgence of Grace" (*aruṭperum Jyoti*) which is compassion unique in its greatness (*tannipperum karuṇai*). We saw earlier that Rāmaliṅgar started his spiritual journey by meditating on Subrahmaṇya as his chosen Deity. Has he discarded this mode of worship as inferior or worthless? We are not justified in reaching such a conclusion. In one of his songs in the mode of "bridal mysticism," he sings, in reply, as the beloved to her maid-friend, "you want to know the name of my Lord and Lover? He is Brahmā, Nārāyaṇa, Hara, Parāśakti, Para Brahman, Arhat, Buddha. In fact, all names yours and mine, names of all things that are really His names. You ask, 'How can you give the names of alien gods?' Well, what name is inappropriate to the One who is known as a mad one?" We may note two points here. One is that all the names, whatever be the faith, are truly the names of the One Supreme Reality. We need not quarrel about the names. A rose is a rose by whatever name it is called. Second, the madness in question here is the madness of love, even exceeding in its sweep and strength the love of a mother, ever ready to forget and forgive all lapses. Thus, Rāmaliṅgar seeks to bring all devotees of God, irrespective of denominational differences, into one universal family. This family includes all souls irrespective of differences as human or subhuman. Human beings should feel kinship with every living thing. Rāmaliṅgar speaks of the privilege of unity through spiritual love (*ānmaneya orumaipāttu unmai*).

Rāmaliṅgar began his spiritual practice (*sādhana*) with devotion to Subrahmanya. He took as his preceptor (guru) the great Śaiva Saint Tirujñānasambandhar, who is considered to be the exemplar of "the path of the good son" (*satputramārga*). Various relationships enable us to feel proximity to God. Master–servant, parent–child, friend–friend, teacher–pupil, or lover–beloved, these are the broad categories. Tirujñānasambandar exemplified in his life and songs how a son could live to be considered worthy of divine parentage. We are all children of immortality (*amṛtasya putrāḥ*). Tirujñānasambandhar shows how we could live up to this title. It is natural that Rāmaliṅgar should propagate this lesson to the whole world by proclaiming God as the Father of the world family. Rāmaliṅgar feels that to be worthy children of God, we must have compassion for everything alive. He prays to the Lord,

> As I see the ways of the world in terms of compassion for all living things, I am seized by fear (at sight of callousness and cruelty). I have submitted to You and submit again that my life and compassion are indeed one, *not* two. If compassion departs, my life also will depart. I (make bold to) swear this at Your Feet.

Because God is compassion, as a corollary he sings, "If I forget You, my Father, will my life continue to exist in my body?" Thus, for Rāmaliṅgar his life is identical with compassion, which is identical with God.

Albert Schweitzer was searching for a long time for the key concept for future civilization, a concept that would guide the world to escape the ruin that will otherwise surely overtake it. He found it in the phrase "reverence for life." "That man is truly ethical who shatters no ice-crystal as it sparkles in the sun, tears no leaf from a tree, cuts no flower." Schweitzer's sensitivity in this matter reminds us of Rāmaliṅgar's active love and reverence for life, made memorable by his favorite phrase, *jīvakāruṇyam*. One of the ways by which this concern can be shown is "nonkilling." A practical expression of this concern is in regard to food habits—specifically, vegetarianism.

Nonkilling and truthfulness are both high ideals for our guidance. But if we are asked to choose between them, which shall we choose? Tiruvaḷḷuvar, author of the *Tirukkuṛaḷ*, says, "If it is to be only one (of these), it is nonkilling." He hastened to add so that "truthfulness" may not be eschewed thereby, "closely following it (nonkilling) is truthfulness." The reason for the choice of nonkilling is that while it may be in our power to take life, it is not in our power to give or to restore life.

Rāmaliṅgar was the embodiment of compassion for all life. He could not bear to see hunger, whether it was human beings or even vegetation thirsting for water. He sings that his spirits droop when he sees crops in the field wilting for want of water. The ache he felt made him start an institution called *dharma sāla*, for feeding hungry persons, and to initiate and encourage efforts to dig tanks to provide drinking water for animals.

Body and soul must be kept together for living a fruitful life. Hence, it is most essential to provide food. Rāmaliṅgar knows that there are other needs which cause as much suffering as the lack of food. How are we to relieve these wants? Rāmaliṅgar prays:

> Give me the nature not to stand before any one to beg. Grant me the capacity when some one asks, "Give me this," to give it, without pleading inability. Give me the state in which you will be ever present with me. Give me the path (of spiritual pursuit) which will ensure keeping You in my thoughts without a break. Give me the mind which will never covet the belongings of others . . . .

We may note here that Rāmaliṅgar advocates self-effort sustained by the grace of God. When a person enjoys the grace of God, he is given resources to meet legitimate wants. Whether it is food that is asked for, economic aid, intellectual help, moral support, or spiritual strength, a God-centered soul draws on God's unfailing source to supply that specific want. In the following, Rāmaliṅgar paints two pictures in contrast:

> My Father! The mouth of the demoniac person which does not glorify You is parched for lack of even gruel. The head of the fool, which does not bow before You in worship is fit only to carry faggot. The eye of the base person which has not beheld Your fragrant figure is one which sheds pails of tears. The ear of the vain person that does not hear your praise is one that perforce has to listen to dreadful news. The minds of the sinner which does not think of You in order to overcome all bondage is one that quakes in terror. The

> hand of the treacherous person that is not raised in worship in your presence is a long, wicked hand held forth to beg.

In sharp and shining contrast, Rāmaliṅgar gives us the following picture:

> Lord! The mouth of the blessed person that proclaims your excellence is the mouth that is delighted by tasting good crystal-clear nectar. Father! The head of the person that bows in worship of Your Feet, is a crowned head, held erect in (joyful) living. Oh Truth! The eye of the (spiritually) meritorious person that has beheld Your Sacred Form is an exceedingly bright eye! Oh, You with a javelin! The ear of the wise person that has heard Your glory is an ear that listens to auspicious news. Oh Pure One! The mind of the exalted person which contemplates Your Feet is a mind which is of the form of real joy. Oh Reality! The hand that is clasped in worship is the hand that distributes gold (in charity).

Rāmaliṅgar makes it clear that, given God's grace, we shall become channels of His grace to the benefit of all living things. Though human effort is necessary, it is thoroughly inadequate by itself. He sings:

> Even if the eyes are kept wide open, in the absence of radiant sunrise, there will be no result except weariness for the eyes. Even if I stir myself to strenuous effort repeatedly by skillful verbal urging, in the absence of Your great Grace to guide it, there will be no worthwhile result. But if You are pleased to bestow Your Grace, even a small straw can perform the (Lord's) five functions.

Again, he sings, "Of what avail my effort if You don't bestow Your Grace? Who am I? What intelligence have I? Whoever will give me any respect? In the absence of Grace even noble effort will be unavailing."

Rāmaliṅgar's songs praying for God's grace are like the *Tiruvācakam* of Māṇikkavācakar in their gentle power to move the hearts of listeners and readers. This is but natural, for Rāmaliṅgar could be said to have taken the *Tiruvācakam* as the *one* devotional work for his inspiration. He has sung in high praise also of the other three Śaiva *Samayācāryas,* and one of them—Tirujñānasambandhar—was especially dear to him as his guru. When he sings in praise of the *Tiruvācakam*, he becomes one with it. Indirectly he exhorts us also to enter into the spirit of *Tiruvācakam* when we read or listen to it. He says that even wild animals and birds develop a spiritual craving when *Tiruvācakam* is chanted. In several songs, he pleads for God's grace. The state of desolation in the absence of grace is vividly described. He sings:

> My mind is not under my control. My past *karma* has not also ceased to operate. I have no love for Your Feet. I have none, able to help me, except You. There is none to plead with You to be merciful to me as one in need of Your

> Grace. There is none also to stand before You to object saying "He is (spiritually) poor. Why be merciful to him?" There is no dearth of your Grace which bestows prosperity. There is nothing against grant of Grace. You never say "No" to those who come begging to You. You are not hard-hearted either.

In other words, even if no one intercedes on behalf of one longing for grace, there is none to oppose granting of grace. Why then is not the Lord moved to grant grace?

As in all devotional literature, here also we find the alternation of sorrow and joy. In moods of despair and desolation, the devotee feels that because of his depravity, God withholds the consolation of grace. In several songs, Rāmaliṅgar describes himself as one guilty of sins of the flesh and sins of the spirit. Could these references be taken as autobiographical? From the accounts that we have of Rāmaliṅgar's personal life, we gather that he was a spotlessly pure person. Though he married, owing to domestic pressure, sex played no part in his life. In regard to eating, dressing, and so on, austerity was natural to him. Why then did he describe himself as a vile sinner? It may be that any trivial lapse or even tendency to lapse stands out in glaring contrast to the white radiance of the Supreme. A hypersensitive soul like Rāmaliṅgar is bound to feel miserable by this contrast. More important is the factor that devotees like Rāmaliṅgar identify themselves spontaneously with every living thing, whatever its level—human or subhuman. Any lapse around them at the human level is felt sharply by them as their own lapse. So they pray to the Lord in repentance on behalf of these erring souls. This is no make-believe but a genuine identification. The tears they shed gush forth from their aching hearts. The tears shed by saints wash away the lapses of sinners and transform their character.

In some of his songs Rāmaliṅgar describes how the grace of God affords not only relief from misery but also positive joy. In one of the most popular of his songs, the imagery comes alive to those who know the severity of summer heat in a tropical country. He sings:

> You are the cool tree to rest under in the heat of summer, its shade, the fruit ripening in the shade. You are the sweet water welling forth in the rivulet. You are the fragrant flower that has blossomed on it. You are the gentle breeze caressing the resting ground. You are the joy produced by the breeze and the relish of that joy. You are the Bridegroom Who has wedded me.

A traveler walking along in the fierce heat of summer would be happy to find a tree to rest under. He would like the shade provided by the tree, sheltering him from the heat. He would welcome the branches wafting a gentle breeze. Sheltered thus, he would like to eat delicious fruit and to drink cool fresh water. As he reclines on a rustling ground, he would enjoy the smell of fragrant flowers. The imagery now calls for a shift in the sex of the traveler in terms of bridal mysticism. The happy consummation would be a young girl finding a handsome bridegroom ready to garland and wed her in the ideal setting described above. We may notice here the delight to the senses—cool shade in the glare of the sun (to the eye), the musical rustling of the leaves (to the ear), cool breeze (to the tactile sense of the body), the taste of sweet fruit and cool water (to the tongue), the small of fragrant flowers (to the nose). The overall joy of the presence of the bridegroom envelopes body, mind, and soul.

Rāmaliṅgar speaks of the devotees of God as constituting a sacred community:

> The tradition of the sacred community has been handed on from generation to generation. Am I not the only person in this line to be ignorant of its nature? Is the agony of this (spiritually) poor one acceptable to Your Divine Will? Is this proper? Is this just? Is this even righteous? Oh Lord dancing in the Sacred Expanse! Oh Munificent Giver! Am I not Your son? Are You not my Father by Divine Destiny? I can no longer bear to see the suffering in the world. Grant me the Light of Grace instantly.

Rāmaliṅgar feels that devotees of God actively engaged in service to His creatures constitute an unbroken chain. In the manner of plantain trees, where from the root of the parent tree a young one sprouts to grow up yielding fruits, devotees continue service from generation to generation. The suffering Rāmaliṅgar sees in the world wrings his heart. Rāmaliṅgar feels that the agony he suffers and witnesses is inconsistent with Divine Will. He asks piteously whether he is not God's child (like all souls) and, what is even more to the point, whether God is not his Father. In other words, it becomes the loving duty of the Father to help children to grow up in His likeness. If God is the embodiment of compassion, so should His children be. Rāmaliṅgar's prayer is that, as he is unable to stand as a helpless witness of the suffering in the world, he may be given the Light of Grace to enable him to see how best he could relieve suffering. It is not as if he cannot endure personal suffering. He is no coward in that respect. What has happened is that the identification now with everything around him makes him feel their sufferings as his own. Hence, when he sees the plants withering for want of water, the hungry being turned away empty-handed from house to house, persons whose illness is protracted, persons who grow weak in poverty as their matchless self-respect prevents them from begging—he suffers acute misery. He suffers agonies when the wicked commit murder. He is so sensitive that he cannot bear to see people setting out to catch fish. With so much suffering around him, he cannot bear to indulge in personal luxuries, such as lying on a soft bed. Hence, he prays that he may be blessed with the Light of Grace, which will fill his heart with love and illumine his understanding to give practical expression to that love. He prays, "My desire is that You should grant me as a boon the power of Your Grace to relieve suffering whenever and wherever there is opportunity." He prays for the power of grace to become the very embodiment of compassion, not only to relieve the intense suffering of others but also to enable souls to be rid of fears and enjoy happiness. We may remind ourselves that the long line of devotees from Vedic times has prayed and worked for removal of distress and attainment of joy at all levels of existence. When we hear now from scientists about ecology and the eco-system and how it is imperative to preserve wildlife and plant life, we realize with what prophetic foresight our ancestors have prayed and worked for peace and prosperty at all levels of life. We may recall the following from the *Vājasaneya Saṃhitā*, "May weal tend our bipeds and our quadrupeds" (36.8); "May alleviation be for plants, for trees, for all gods, for Brahmā." (36.17).

We have been using up at a prodigal rate the resources that nature took long millennia to store up in the world. Plants, trees, animals, and birds have been ruthlessly destroyed. Now that scientists are describing in detail how we are upsetting the balance, rhythm, and harmony in nature and polluting and poisoning the atmosphere and the rivers, we are waking up to the wisdom of seers and saints, of whom Rāmaliṅgar was a fairly recent one.

We have referred to the continuity of succession of saints from Vedic times. Those who go through the songs of Rāmaliṅgar may feel perplexed to find in some of them strong denunciation of the Vedas, *āgamas*, creeds, and so on. This leads a few to say that Rāmaliṅgar was a revolutionary, calling people away from the traditions of the past to a wholly new approach, that he started a new movement or institution. It happens that in the course of time accretions so gather around traditions that their living core is stifled. It is as a warning against such danger that great prophets call attention to the *spirit* of the "law," so that followers may not stop with conformity to its mere *letter*. Even more than at the time of Tāyumānavar, the nineteenth century needed a clarion call to religious harmony and fruitful coexistence of faiths. Rāmaliṅgar must have felt deeply hurt that Hinduism, forgetting its tradition of religious harmony and benevolent attitude of "live and let live" was stultifying itself by harmful polemics. Works devoted to "refutation," "refutation of refutation," and so on promoted only ill will among the followers of various faiths without enhancing the value of their respective faiths. When practice does not match precept, when conduct does not substantiate claim, a prophet is roused to righteous indignation. In the case of Rāmaliṅgar, we must keep in mind both his own early spiritual practice (*sādhana*) and his songs expressing rapturous appreciation of the songs of the four Śaiva *Samayācāryas*. If we find a remark or two referring to his early enthusiasm for Śaivism as yielding place to a non-sectarian universalism, we must not take it that he was disillusioned about Śaivism (or Hinduism). In the white heat of prophetic indignation at followers of faiths becoming so self-righteous and self-sufficient as to engage in a war of mutual destruction, even Rāmaliṅgar, who was compassion incarnate, had to take cudgels against intolerance. He was understandably impatient in regard to obstacles that stood in the way of religious concord and harmony. Similarly, Rāmaliṅgar's strong denunciation of the caste system should not be misunderstood. If the caste system promoted an unwarranted attitude of superiority for one's own caste and contempt or hatred for other castes, it required condemnation. Rāmaliṅgar's teaching emphasizes the need for treating a human (or living) being as a human (or living) being, entitled to reverence irrespective of social distinctions. Gradations may be necessary, but they should not become de-gradations.

We have noted earlier that Rāmaliṅgar was a staunch advocate of vegetarianism. Hence he sings that those given to killing and to nonvegetarianism are not be treated as kith and kin but only as outsiders. But even in their case help must be given to relieve their hunger. Should they suffer in some perilous situation, one must not rejoice but should help them to get over their sorrow and fear. It is pertinent to recall the contrast Rāmaliṅgar draws between the followers of the good path (*sanmārga saṅgattavar*) and the followers of the wicked path (*dunmārga saṅgattavar*). The former treat all living beings as their own children and talk like a mother. The followers of the wicked path become intensely bitter when they see others and, with strong inner resentment and ill will, bark like dogs at them. In light of such statements, we are not justified in reading into Rāmaliṅgar's songs rancor and deep-seated anger contrary to his nature. Rāmaliṅgar's mission was to make everyone ultimately a follower of the good path.

Rāmaliṅgar hails God as *the Joy* that is joy alike to the ignorant and the learned; as *the Eye* that gives vision to those who have not seen and to those who have seen; as *the Boon* granting boons to the powerful and to the weak; as *the Intellect* that gives intelligence to those who disregard (Reality) and those who do give regard (to Reality): as *the Just*, standing between the good and the wicked: as *the Good*, bestowing welfare on the celestial and the humans. God is the Auspicious One (Śiva) dancing on the ground common to all. Rāmaliṅgar stresses the universal, all-pervasive character of God. God, the Supreme Reality, the ground and goal of all existence, may not be restricted to any name and local habitation. Yet Rāmaliṅgar locates Him! The Lord is in the hearts of all those who, without the least feeling of difference, treat all living beings as themselves, who rejoice in according privileges alike to all. Rāmaliṅgar says that he has seen clearly the Lord in the form of Pure Intelligence dancing in their hearts. How do such persons act? How do they speak? They treat all living beings alike. In compassion they render help to all beings. Their acts are the acts of grace. Rāmaliṅgar longs to do joyfully the bidding of all those people of the Sacred Path. They are the virtuous ones of noble qualities and spiritual calm. The utterances of their sacred mouths are declared to be the beginning and the end of the compassion-filled Vedas and *āgamas*.

Rāmaliṅgar does not restrict his spiritual mission to this world:

> Oh my Father, listen to my prayer and grant Your Grace. I should express in action my love for all beings. I should go to the worlds everywhere, to worlds of all kinds and proclaim the Glory of Your Grace. I should direct the Light of Grace so that the pure Good Path may prevail in (as yet) undeclared exalted places. Even if I commit mistakes, You must graciously forgive me. I want also the state of never being separated from You.

Rāmaliṅgar left a bequest of nearly six thousand songs, not to speak of his prose writings, musical pieces, and correspondence. Even as he sings of God as *the Joy,* alike to the ignorant and the scholar, his own songs are sung by the unlettered and the lettered, the beginner and the spiritually advanced. We may conclude by giving the gist of one of his most popular songs. It is in the form of a prayer, universal in its scope.

> Grant me the company of those exalted one who with one-pointed mind, contemplate Your flower-like Feet. Let me avoid the company of those whose utterances do not match their thoughts and inner feelings. Let me speak of Your exalted Glory. Let me not utter falsehood. Let me take to walking on the Great Path. Let me not be seized by the demon of pride. Let me forget the desire for the company of women. Let me never forget You. Let me have wisdom. Let me have the treasure of Your Grace. Let me live a life, free from diseases.

Rāmaliṅgar's songs, even through the inadequate medium of translation, will serve as a rallying point for all those who pray for one family of all living beings, equal as children of God. May the lamp of grace that Rāmaliṅgar lit in the last century continue to shine everywhere and for ever!

Note

[1] M. Ananthanarayanan, "Appreciation," *Tiruaruṭpā* (1906) 316.

Bibliography

Sources

Thiruvarutpa. Translated by A. Balakrishna Pillai. Madras: Ramalinga Mission, 1966.
Twelve volumes of the works of Saint Rāmaliṅgam (in Tamil). Madras: Pari Nilayam, 1956–61.

Studies

Annalamalai, S. *The Life and Teachings of Saint Ramalingar*. Bombay: Bharatiya Vidya Bhavan, 1973.
Dayanandan, Francis. *Mission and Message of Ramalinga Swamy*. Delhi: Motilal Banarsidas, 1990.
——. *Ramalinga Swamy*. Madras: Christian Institute for the Study of Religion and Society, 1972.
Kuppuswamy, M. *Philosophical Works of Saint Vallalar: Compilation and Commentary*. New Delhi: M. Kuppuswamy, 1989.
Vaittiyanathan, K. N. *Arutpā Amudham* (in Tamil). Madras: Vairam Pattipakam, 1975.
——. *Vallalār kaṇta Vācakar* (in Tamil). Madras: Maninmani Puttaka Nilayam, 1970.
Vanmikanathan, G. *Pathway to God Trod by Raamalinga Swaamigal*. Bombay: Bharatiya Vidya Bhavan, 1976.
——. *Triology on Ramalingar*. Coimbatore: Ramalinga Mission, 1977.
The Works of Saint Ramalingam (Tamil), 12 vols. Madras: Pari Nilayam, 1956–1961.

14

The Spirituality of Rabindranath Tagore: "The Religion of an Artist"

SITANSU SEKHAR CHAKRAVARTI

RABINDRANATH TAGORE (1861–1941) was a poet, novelist, short story writer, composer of songs, painter, educator, social reformer, and, above all, a spiritual leader with his own views on spirituality. The keynote of all the multifarious aspects of his genius is his spirituality. He does not belong to any established school relating to the subject, nor does he have any dogmas regarding it. Spirituality to him is the dynamic principle touching every aspect of life, or any form of existence, for that matter, that touches human life. It is the supreme guiding principle of life that leads human existence from partiality to fullness, and from "darkness to light," to use the expression of the Vedas. There is a spiritual message even in those of Tagore's writings where he does not speak about God. We will discuss two of his plays, neither of which conveys a notion of spirituality in the traditional sense of its association with God, with or without form, but in the sense of attaining our real nature wherein we find the meaning of freedom and joy apart from the mundane existence of routines. Attaining our real nature does not mean renouncing the everyday world for a secluded place in order to look for perfection there. It means discovering the spirit of life in everyday activities by establishing our activities anew in conformity with our true nature. The message of the Hindu spiritual ideal of discovering joy as one's essential nature arising out of one's freedom from the dictates of the senses is very much present here, though independent of institutionalized practices. In a way, we may say that the endeavor of Tagore was to dissociate spirituality from its conventional moorings and equate it with life itself on its journey toward fulfillment through the creative interaction of an artist or a poet. God to him is a nonconventional concept, too, as we will see, at the level of the human value system, and not at the scientific or the metaphysical level. Although he has advocated what he calls "the religion of man," it is not a religion in the traditional sense. It does imply conversion, but no ritual of conversion is involved. No priests are there, nor are any scriptural dictates to be followed. Man is his own priest; his understanding is his scripture; and the existential involvement in the process is the only requirement.

The Religion of an Artist

Rabindranath Tagore was born into a Hindu Brahmin (priestly) family which was considered outcast because of certain restrictions in the hierarchy of the Hindu social system. His father, Debendranath, "the great sage" as he was called, had come into close contact with the regeneration movement among the Hindus of the eastern part of India, known as the Brāhma Samāj movement. He was converted to the new faith before the poet was born. This faith was very much inspired by the parts of the Vedas known as the Upaniṣads, abandoning the rest of the scriptures for their supposed involvement with rites and rituals. The Upaniṣads constitute the Vedānta, the end part of the Vedas, and are so called because they occur at the end of the Vedas. The Vedānta has several interpretations. The one in line with the Śaṅkara tradition, called the Advaita (nondualistic) Vedānta, says that *Brahman*—the Absolute—whose essence is bliss and who is without any qualifications, appears in a distorted way in all the manifestations. Raja Rammohan Roy, the founder of the Brāhma Samāj, was influenced by this interpretation of the Vedānta and opposed the worship of images. Through image worship, he thought, we circumscribe truth, which is without any limits. Debendranath was against image worship, too, but would not commit himself entirely to the Advaita interpretation. Since Tagore was brought up in the Brāhma Samāj atmosphere, he was quite saturated in the philosophy of this religion and must have acquired from his earlier years that reverence for the world which his father felt. He says:

> Salvation through the practice of renunciation
> Is not for me.
> I will taste of the freedom of joy in the midst of
> Innumerable ties.
> You will fill the earthen pot of this world several times
> With your nectar of color and fragrance. . . .
> Practice of yoga closing all the doors of the senses
> Is not for me.
> Whatever joy is in sight, smell or songs,
> Your bliss will be in its midst. (*Naivedya*, p. 37)

The Vedāntic endeavor of realizing the "original state," he says, by merging the personal self "in an impersonal entity," however laudable it may be "as a psychological experience," "is not a religion, even as the knowledge of the state of the atom is of no use to an artist who deals in images in which atoms have taken forms. . . . The concrete form is a more perfect manifestation than the atom, and man is more perfect as a man" (*Religion of Man*, p. 115). Spiritual pursuit implies a change in one's attitude to the world, which frees one from the dimension of pleasure and suffering, which are rooted in one's egotistic learnings, to that of *ānanda* or unconditional joy. The change for Tagore was not in ignoring nature as a nullity to the extent that the world is looked upon as false, as in the tradition of the Advaita Vedānta, but in finding oneness with nature, through the creativity of the artist, poet, or singer, wherein the meaning of life lies. "Man by nature is an artist," he says. "In order to be happy," he continues, "he must establish harmonious relationship with all things with which he has dealings. Our creation is the modification of relationship" (ibid., p. 131). Again, "Reality is human; it is what we are conscious of, by which we are affected, that which we express. When we are intensely aware of it, we are aware of ourselves and it gives us delight. We live in it, we always widen its limits. Our arts and literature represent this creative activity which is fundamental in man" (ibid., p. 132).

The human being needs to discover the beauty, the spontaneity, and the rhythm in nature in all its vitality, and in the mood of an artist become a part of the total creation and partake of the joy that is all around. Personal gains are the negation of this. The traditional Vedāntic practice follows the path of negation (*neti, neti*), whereas Tagore's spirituality lies in the affirmation of the common bond that harmonizes a human being with himself or herself, and with nature. He says:

> I am the poet of the world,—my flute responds to
> All the notes that rise at any corner there. . . .
> The grand orchestra of the universe has filled my heart
> In many a quiet moment in my imagination.
> The inaccessible snow-clad mountain peaks in their
> Infinite solitude of blue
> Have sent to my heart many an invitation
> For the unheard songs that they compose,—
> The unknown star above the antarctic pole,
> That is spending its long night in deep silence,
> Has touched my open eyes during the sleepless nights
> With the splendor of its glow. (*Janmadine*, pp. 14–15)

Spiritual pursuit, to Tagore, is quite different from the pursuit of science, and the point deserves special attention today when everything needs scientific sanction in order to have any credibility at all. The difference is that, to the scientist, the world carries information, whereas to the artist or the poet the world does not "merely carry information but a harmony" with one's being (*Religion of Man*, p. 34). This harmony is not a matter of factual knowledge conveyed through the language of formulae, but is a matter of realization brought about by changes in one's attitudes, which is never the object of scientific pursuit. The total harmony feels like the presence of "some being who comprehended me and my world" and "was seeking his best expression in all my experiences, uniting them into an ever-widening individuality which is a spiritual work of art." "To this being," he continues, "I am responsible; for the creation in me is his, as well as mine" (ibid., p. 94). It is this artistic mood that transcends the boundary of individuality for Tagore and unites the individual with the universal. Here is the concept of the Vedic *ṛta* in the context of human fulfillment in its creative mode. The process of the pursuit of the totality is what Tagore calls the "religion of man," during which the infinite becomes defined in humanity and comes close to the individual so as to need his love and cooperation.

Thus, truth is not exhausted by the scientific pursuit of knowledge. Physical science tries to explain facts—not the relation that they bear to us in the domain of our values. The message that a flower carries is not indicated in scientific analyses; it is one that enters our heart, a message of love and a message of unity and harmony in a more inclusive sense than is found in science. The domain of love is one of freedom and joy, an aesthetic domain of creativity in appreciation. Nature, according to Tagore, has two aspects: one is her workmanship, an engagement in continuous activity, the aspect which is the object of scientific investigation; the other is that of silence, peace, joy, and freedom, the object of spiritual pursuit.

In the Upaniṣads it is said, as Tagore quotes several times, "From joy are born all creatures, by joy they are sustained, towards joy they progress, and into joy they enter." Also, "The immortal being manifests itself in joy-form" (*Sadhana*, pp. 103–4). There are forms on which joy or freedom base themselves. "The joy of the singer is expressed in the form of a song, that of the poet in the form of a poem" (ibid., 104), and the forms are constituted by rules. But a song or a poem transcends the forms and rules that constitute it. If morality and spirituality reduce themselves to conformity to rules, then what remains is an imitation of science. Religions, Tagore warns, often degrade themselves into "irrational habits and mechanical practices," thereby deadening themselves into sectarianism "in a perverse form of worldliness" (*Boundless Sky*, pp. 269–70). As a result of such mechanization, morality and spirituality lose their freedom and joy.

True spirituality finds its expression, as we saw, in harmony, which is the keynote of aesthetic creation, including appreciation—a form of creation itself. A "spiritual vision . . . is the vision of the whole truth" (*Sadhana*,

p. 111). Freedom, the goal of spirituality, is signaled by joy "whose other name is love" and "must by its very nature have duality for its realization. . . . The amritam, the immortal bliss, has made itself into two. Our soul is the loved one. . . . The infinite joy is manifesting itself in manifold forms, taking upon itself the bondage of law, and we fulfill our destiny when we go back from forms to joy, from law to love, when we untie the knot of the finite and hark back to the infinite" (ibid., pp. 104–6). Truth and goodness for Tagore coalesce into one in the aesthetic domain, for in the beauty of harmony, which is the truth of human nature, lies its goodness. This is why one who has realized the highest state of spiritual harmony would be called "a poet" (*kavi* in Sanskrit) during the Vedic times. In the *Gītā* it is said: "Equilibrium and equanimity are what is meant by *yoga*" (*Bhagavad Gītā*, 2.48). This state of equilibrium is also a state of universal compassion and love. The concept of love transcends that of usefulness, for it is "an end in itself; it is for our whole being and therefore can never tire us" (*Sadhana*, p. 107).

The crisis of modern civilization lies in the fact that "we are frantically busy making use of the forces of the universe to gain more and more power . . . and thus to the end of our days we only try to feed upon it and miss its truth, just like the greedy child who tears leaves from a precious book and tries to swallow them" (*Sadhana*, p. 108). Enslaved by the value of usefulness, we turn human beings into machines and "cheapen" "man to his lowest value" (ibid., p. 109). Imperialism is a process of the cheapening of human values, and Tagore equates it with cannibalism. In his address "The Crisis in Civilization," at a time when the specter of the Second World War was looming, the poet could not but express his gradual loss of faith in the claim of some nations to civilization and his hope that the dawn of civilization would appear on the horizon of the East "where the sun rises."

Since spirituality pertains to the aesthetic realm, the God of Tagore is not claimed as a scientific or a metaphysical entity. He is not a scientific entity, because He is not a matter of information. He is not the object of intellectual pursuit but belongs to the highest level of human truth—that of values. God is not a metaphysical entity either, for He is not an objective entity to be discovered by intellectual reasoning of the metaphysical kind. He is a phenomenological entity truer than the scientific truths, because value is, in the ultimate analysis, more important to human beings than facts. Tagore calls his God "The Lord of Life" who is both personal and impersonal. God is impersonal in the sense of *ṛta*, or the objective principle that leads toward a fulfillment of the human soul in harmony with the infinite. God is personal in the sense of being the subject of prayer with whom we can have an existential involvement. This is a synthesis of the God of forms with the formless God. However, the personal God who is with forms is not a real person insofar as He is not an object in the inventory of the world; His criteria of identity are not the same as those of a real person, the subject as He is of prayer and reverence at the level of our realization of the highest values of human existence. The prayer to God is not for riches, but for the realization of equanimity and harmony. God, to Tagore, is neither omnipotent nor omniscient in the usual connotations of the terms, but is both a lover and an object of love.

The Lord of Life

Whatever reservations Tagore might have regarding the Vedāntic theory of *māyā*, the Vedāntic message that everything is *Brahman* and *Brahman* is consciousness and bliss is an underlying theme of Tagore's writings:

> Joy flows through the universe, . . .
> The sun and the moon drink of it
> A full measure.
> The light of the joy of goodness
> Stays ever effulgent. . . .
> Why are you all by yourself, confined to
> Your own ego? (*Rabindra Rachnāvali,* vol. 4, #326)

Again,

> Wake up to a new joy today
> With the new rays of the sun
> To a clean life which is good, beautiful and
> Sparkling with love. . . .
> The wind of peace today
> Carries the fragrance of the flowers of eternity. (ibid., #327)

Tagore was exposed not only to the Advaita tradition of Hinduism but to other traditions of the religion as well, of which the two that made the most permanent impressions on his mind and helped crystallize his thoughts throughout his life were Vaiṣṇavism and the Bāul sect of eastern India. The Vaiṣṇava tradition of love between Kṛṣṇa and Rādhā had made such a vivid impression on his mind that when he was only sixteen, Tagore composed a book of poems called *Bhānusimher Padāvali* in the pseudonym of *Bhānusimha*, in the Brajabuli dialect according to the tradition of medieval Vaiṣṇava poets.

Tagore was influenced also by the Bāul tradition, a nonorthodox faith that flourished in Bengal, with a philosophy very similar to that of Sufism. The simple but meaningful life-style of Bāul singers who wander around singing and dancing, always absorbed in the joy of life, deeply touched his emotions. The Bāuls have a directly mystic approach to God who, they believe, is the indwelling principle in human beings—"the man of the heart" as He is called—who keeps on sending His beckoning notes, to which we do not always pay due attention. Since the response to the inner call involves an understanding of one's innate nature, the path pursued in the tradition is also meant to be "the innate path," where there is no room for any artificial distinction of caste or sex. There are many songs that Tagore composed in the Bāul tune, such as:

> O my mind,
> You didn't wake up when the man of your heart
> Came to your door.
> You woke up in the dark
> At the sound of His departing foot-steps
> My lonely night passes on a mat on the floor.
> His flute sounds in darkness,
> Alas, I cannot see Him. (ibid., #550)

The idea in this song is very much in keeping with the Bāul spirit. The relation between the singer and God—"the man of the heart"—is very intimate.

In the songs generally, there are moods of intimacy, as in the Vaiṣṇava tradition. Sometimes God is "the eternal friend," and the poet begs Him not to leave him for a moment. At other times He is the "lover" whom he implores:

> . . . destroy all the hurdles on the path of love.
> Please do not, do not keep anything between us;
> Please do not, do not stay away. (ibid., #418)

At yet other times He is the "Lord" of whom he begs:

> If ever the door of my heart remains closed,
> Oh my Lord,
> Break it open and come near to me.
> If ever your dear name does not sound on the strings
> Of my musical instrument,
> Please remain my Lord, and never go away.
> If on any occasion
> My sleep does not break at your call,
> Wake me up my Lord, with the pain of the thunder,—
> Please do not ever go away. (ibid., #102)

Love, or surrender, as in the Vaiṣṇava tradition, is total, but not one-sided:

That is why you shower your joy on me,
That is why you have brought yourself down,
O the Lord of the universe,
For your love would have been false without me. . . .
That is why O the King of Kings,
You assume so many enchanting forms
To win my heart. . . .
That is why O my Lord,
Your form assumes the fullest manifestation
In the union where it is your love
That descends on to the love of the devotee. (ibid., #294)

This is Tagore's *Jīvan Devatā*, *The Lord of Life*, who appears to the poet sometimes as male, other times as female. In the poem entitled "Lord of My Life" he addressed the Lord thus:

Thou who art the innermost Spirit of my being
art thou pleased,
Lord of my life? . . .
I know not why thou chosest me for thy partner,
Lord of my life!
Didst thou store my days and nights,
my deeds and dreams for the alchemy of thy art,
and string in the chain of thy music
my songs of autumn and spring . . . ? (*Religion of Man*, p. 95)

The Lord of life is the guiding principle in Tagore's life, the dynamic value that keeps unfolding itself in the course of life's onward journey. The relation with Him is very intimate and is not circumscribed by any rites or rituals.

I keep on forgetting you in the show of your worship. . . .
I do not find the opportunity of touching your feet
From behind the garlands of flowers,
The light from the lamps,
And all the incense smoke. . . .
What is the use in frequenting the temple?
I will prepare my seat in the corner of my heart,
And beseech you in silence. . . . (*Rabindra Rachnāvali*, vol. 4, #132)

Tagore's spirituality is a synthesis of Advaita, Vaiṣṇavism, and the Bāul tradition. The genius of Tagore recognized the essences of the traditions and did not find any conflict among them. He was raised in the atmosphere of revolt against traditional Hinduism and image worship, yet we see him eventually composing songs on Lord Śiva. "O intense pain, wrath personified, O terrible one, Shankara, the destroyer," he says, "let everything static or dynamic be numbed by bites from the fangs of flame shooting out of your matted hair" (ibid., #233; cf. ##234, 236). Thus, the one with forms and the one who is formless, the one with images and the one who is imageless merge into each other and take the form of a nonexclusive totality. With the passage of time Tagore came to the opinion that he was a Hindu and that the followers of Brāhma Samāj were Hindus. He tried to interpret and incorporate in his philosophy the dynamism and inclusive character of the broader Hinduism that has evolved through millennia. In the poem "Pilgrimage That is India" he says that the land has accommodated all peoples of all cultures who have come to India through ages. "O my mind," Tagore reflects, "wake up in this place of pilgrimage on the shore of the great humanity that is India" (*Gitānjali*, p. 132).

Tagore's conception of the world's being a song does not mean that he did not perceive evils here. "Whoever does wrong, O Lord," he says, "or whoever tolerates it, let your hatred burn them like straw" (*Sanchayitā*, p. 442). He raised his voice many a time against the ruthlessness of the British rule of India and resigned his knighthood as a protest.

Tagore did not establish a church of his own, although at Santiniketan (literally, "the abode of peace") he founded his "Visva Bharati," the place for universal learning, as *brahmacharyāshram*, "the hermitage of self-restraint." He wanted the world to meet there in the twentieth century. In the attached temple, he used to give sermons, in which he would speak respectfully of other religions, including Christianity. He wanted Visva Bhārati to be "a wide meeting place where all sects may gather together and forget their differences" in search of their religion of man. "The individual man," he says, "must exist for Man the great, and must express him in disinterested works, in science and philosophy, in literature and arts, in service and worship. This is his religion, which is working in the heart of all his religions in various names and forms" (*Religion of Man*, pp. 14–15). At the end of one of his novels, Gora, the hero, who lost his parents at birth and was brought up by a Hindu Brahmin family, comes to know of his Christian ancestry and wakes up to a new awareness of his identity as a human being, neither Hindu nor Christian. This signifies Tagore's transcendence of specific religions in favor of the "religion of man."

Spiritual Message in Tagore's Secular Works

In Tagore's drama *The Post Office*, Amal, the little boy, confined in his room, is thought to be sick with his desire for the outer world, where freedom lies in all its expansiveness. The sickness is diagnosed as fatal, in accordance with the maxims of the science of medicine which protect the interest and point of view of a world that reduces life to the consideration of utility. He is forbidden from going out of the building, for "the autumn sun and breeze would act like poison to him." The medicine that has been prescribed for Amal is bitter, and consequently, is expected to "have a quick effect, like good advice does" on our moral life. The window that he sits behind permits him a glimpse of the outer world, though, and he is allowed a partial contact with the world from a distance. He is amazed at the joy that he thinks the activities of the world involve, but is bewildered when people passing by the window complain of his interrupting them in their business and wasting their time. However, once conversation starts, they seem to enjoy it and find a meaning in apparently purposeless gossiping, and promise to visit him on their way back from work. In one instance, the boy possesses intuitions regarding the home of a yogurt hawker in a beautiful, natural setting, which indicates, in the Upaniṣadic way of thinking, the a priori knowledge of *Ānanda* (Bliss) or *Brahman* that is innate (*sahaja*) to each and every person. But the normal and natural tendency toward unconditional *ānanda* is thwarted by the social system around us that is wrongly oriented and does not nurture us in the fulfillment of our real nature.

Amal sees a newly built royal post office across the street. He hopes to beg favors of the king when he gets well, whereupon an old man visiting him reassures him: "You don't need to ask of him, my dear; whatever he gives, he does on his own." So Amal feels much better while expecting a letter from the post office written by the king himself, a feeling the physician diagnoses as a worsening of the situation, for "he seems to have been exposed to the outside world." The physician recommends that he be sealed completely indoors. However much social customs, in conformity with mundane considerations, try to segregate us from our real nature, the attempts are doomed to failure. All of a sudden the messenger of the king appears, accompanied by the royal physician, who advises that all the doors and windows be flung open. Amal starts feeling better with the sight of the evening stars in the sky "appearing from the other side of darkness." He peacefully falls asleep awaiting the king's call, which appears to be a very bad omen to "the nonbeliever." The king, of course, is Tagore's "Lord of Life," whose irresistible call comes from the very depth of our heart.

Another of Tagore's most important plays with an underlying spiritual message is the *Red Oleanders.* Its setting is large-scale industry and technology—a theme still more disturbing today when survival of our own technological innovation is problematic.

The king is the human spirit of the modern industrialized civilization. The stage directions indicate that he is behind an opaque wall that is a product of industrialized society. It may be interpreted as *māyā,* representing the abstraction and isolation of the human soul today. In the kingdom of Yakshapuri everybody is trained according to the frame of reference of the kingdom, namely, profit and production. The presence of Nandini, who is apparently unrelated to the frame of reference, is incongruous in the life of the place. She represents the fulfillment of the human soul, the meaning of life, the inner urge that sustains our very existence. However, in the spiritually truncated life of Yakshapuri the inner joy that she stands for is utterly neglected. Her fulfillment, which lies in her union with Ranjan, her lover, is very much out of place in the kingdom. Yet even in the midst of his fragmented existence, the king yearns for *ānanda* and pines for Nandini from behind the screen. Since he has no means of self-satisfaction in the system he commands, except by forcefully extracting enjoyment, he does not understand Nandini's love for Ranjan, although he has an inkling that there is a difference between Ranjan and himself. He feels that he is attractive to Nandini for his strength, whereas Ranjan's appeal lies in the spontaneous charm of love. The king realizes that *ānanda* cannot be commanded at will and confesses that all his enjoyment had turned him into a thirsty desert, which is always expanding its insatiable thirst to new horizons. Nandini keeps pounding on his door, for the inner call of spiritual fulfillment is always present and persistent, however far one might have strayed from the truth of life. The king is attached to Nandini, no doubt, but he is afraid to face her. Every time she attempts to visit the king's apartment, he shouts out that the time is not yet ripe, for he is busy with his own affairs. The king, however, becomes restless in his urge to meet Nandini. This dissatisfaction on the part of the king with his own state of affairs worried his associates—the watch-dogs of the system—including the physician, who diagnoses the problem and prescribes cures for the "ailment." A vanguard of the system—the priest—counsels Nandini to conform to it, for, he says, it is only through conformity that peace can be achieved. One of the followers is punished for his rebellion against the conformist rule for seeking freedom from the material comforts that he considered an indignity. He understands that the suffering of human existence, when it arises out of a desire for *ānanda* lying beyond these comforts, has human value, whereas the suffering resulting from the craving for comfort is a debasement of the human spirit.

The situation becomes tense. A point is reached when the system conspires against its own head and leads the king to kill Ranjan unknowingly, thereby attempting to paralyze Nandini, who is distracting the king, by taking Ranjan—her life-force—from her. The king becomes very angry at the conspiracy of his subjects, and launches a crusade against the system hand in hand with Nandini awaiting the resurrection of Ranjan. He is ready to face death himself, if need be, having realized the meaning of life through death. All the workers join the king in the crusade.

The message is clearly Vedāntic in its essence, though the ideas are not mentioned explicitly. (It is interesting to note that Ranjan and Nandini remind one of the concepts of Kṛṣṇa and Rādhā in the Vaiṣṇava tradition.) So long as we pursue the selfish end of looking for comforts and prosperity on the plane of pleasures, we go against our very nature, which is of the essence of *ānanda*. The industrial system, which has perfected the exploitation of pleasures, has reduced the concept of love to pleasure itself and has dealt a deathblow to love, because this is the only way the system can confront love. The king, so long as he is within the system, has no way other than killing Ranjan, the personification of love. He must come out of the system in an attempt to resurrect Ranjan.

Spirituality and Humanism

Humanism is an inevitable direction as well as a strong foundation of Tagore's spirituality. He realized that the poor and the downtrodden needed his attention, for he was very conscious that he was "the poet of the world." He feels, however, that his life-style has separated him from the majority of the masses, and although he has often "ventured into their localities," he deplores his "lack of strength to go into their midst." "If life is not added onto life," he says, the "array of songs is replete with the futility of artificial merchandise" (*Janmadine*, p. 16). He waits for the poet who would take care of the sorrows and agonies of the hearts of all the people who are in total oblivion because of their inability to articulate personal feelings in words. Although Tagore's warnings were against "the hobby of the imitation of artisanship," he took an active interest in the lives of the masses and their economic and cultural advancement. He set up the model school of Sriniketan near Santiniketan, geared to the vocational education of the downtrodden. He also made sincere attempts at spreading general education among the masses through the medium of the language of the soil—as opposed to English, which was a colonial imposition for the medium of instruction at "standard" schools.

Tagore was against sectarianism of all kinds, including the religious dimension. He believed in religious diversity, for "religion, like poetry, is not a mere idea,—it is an expression." "The self-expression of God is in the varieties of creation; and our attitude towards the infinite must in its expression also have a variedness of individuality, ceaseless and unending" (*Boundless Sky*, p. 274). Religious sectarianism leads to tyranny of the imperialistic kind, he says, observing that the ruthless method of fascism rears its ugly head in religious matters in most parts of the world, "trampling flat the expansion of the spirit of man under its insensitive heels." The touchstone for the success of a religious creed is its ability to satisfy the most intense and universal human need. Thus, the test of a religion is in its humanitarian application.

In the *Sannyasi, Or The Ascetic*, we see the conversion of the *sannyāsi* from a strictly ascetic pursuit to a search that includes humanistic goals. The *sannyāsi* has renounced the world for the sake of the Truth and is not initially disturbed by the longing for friendship on the part of Vasanti, the little untouchable girl. He notices a strange similarity between them in that they are without friends or relatives. But when the girl expresses satisfaction over his paternal love, he thinks that, not being a renunciate, she is under an illusion regarding her expectations. Very soon the self-aggrandizement turns into the fear that he is falling into the trap of illusion himself, a renunciate though he is, and he becomes angry over the whole thing. The experience of anger makes clear to him the fact that his mind still is possessed by hidden things which do not spare even a renunciate supposedly free from bonds of any kind. This deliberation in its wake fills his heart with compassion for the child, a feeling arising out of a foreign world as it were, which he had banished totally from the surface of his consciousness. Soon he reverts back to his own self and makes up his mind to leave the girl very much against her imploring. Eventually it dawns on him that a *sannyāsi* must be free even from "the bodiless chain of Nay." The infinite that he is after, and for the sake of which he has abandoned the world, "is to be found in the finite itself through the magic touch of love." He realizes that he has to join once more the pilgrims in the stately ship of the world "which is crossing the sea of time." He starts looking for the little girl whom he forsook for fear of contamination, knowing he needs her now for his salvation. The spiritually esoteric yields to humanism.

"Reality is human," Tagore says in the *Religion of Man*, and adds that "man is more perfect as a man." The existentialistic attitude toward life is, we can say, the basis of his humanism.

Conclusion

At the time Tagore was born, attempts were already in progress for the regeneration of Hinduism and India. Raja Rammohan Roy had founded the

Brāhma Samāj. Pandit Ishwarchandra Vidyasagar was trying to carry out socioreligious reforms from within the fold of the religion. Sri Ramakrishna Paramahamsa was preaching the universality of religions, saying "As many are the views, so many are the ways." Rabindranath attempted in his own way to advance the regeneration of Hinduism. In the course of his onward journey, he addressed himself to the larger problem of the rebirth of humanity through the "religion of man," from which, he knew, a surer and truer Hinduism and India would emerge.

It is true that in spite of its breadth and charm, Tagore's religion never took any deep root in India, because it was too general and did not provide any technique or practical help. "The religion of man" provides no room for a guru who is supposed to come up with assistance at every step of the devotee's spiritual progress. The demands that his religion makes on the individual are high, for one has to be one's own guru. Nor did Tagore intend his religion for propagation and conversion. He was not after establishing a sect or a creed, for that would go against the very concept of the "religion of man," which is essentially existentialistic. "The religion of man" may be viewed as a guiding principle for all religions, rather than as a religion itself in the ordinary sense of the term. Work remains to be done to interpret specific religions in terms of these general ideas about religion as such. Tagore never claimed to be a philosopher in the technical sense. Although his writings are full of rich philosophical insights, studies are needed to relate his views, in a technical way, to philosophical trends—Eastern and Western—in order to uncover common grounds between the two dimensions of spirituality.

Bibliography

Sources

Tagore, Rabindranath. *The Boundless Sky*. Calcutta: Visva Bharati, 1964.

——. *Collected Poems and Plays of Rabindranath Tagore*. London: Macmillan, 1967.

——. *Crisis in Civilization*. Calcutta: Visva Bharati, 1941.

——. *The Cycle of Spring*. London: Macmillan, 1917.

——. *Gitānjali*. Calcutta: Visva Bharati, 1959.

——. *Gitanjali (Song Offerings)*. London: Macmillan, 1913.

——. *Janmadine*. Calcutta: Visva Bharati, 1952.

——. *Naivedya*. Calcutta: Visva Bharati, 1986.

——. *Rabindra Rachanāvali*. Calcutta: Government of West Bengal, Centenary Edition, 1961.

——. *Red Oleanders*. Calcutta: Macmillan, 1955.

——. *The Religion of Man*. London: Macmillan, 1931.

——. *Sadhana: The Realization of Life*. London: Macmillan, 1913.
——. *Sanchayitā*. Calcutta: Visva Bharati, 1975.
A Tagore Reader. Edited by Amiya Chakravarty. New York: Macmillan, 1961.

Studies

Ayyub, Abu Sayeed. *Pāntha Janer Sakhā*. Calcutta: Dey's Publishing, 1973.
——. *Tagore's Quest*. Calcutta: Papyras, 1980.
Dasgupta, Sashibhushan. *Upanishader Patabhūmikāy Rabindramānas*. Calcutta: A. Mukherjee & Co., 1975.
De, S. K. *The Early History of the Vaishnava Faith and Movement in Bengal*. Calcutta: K. L. Mukhopadhyay, 1975.
Dimock, Edward C., Jr. "Rabindranath Tagore—'The Greatest of the Bauls of Bengal.'" *Journal of Asian Studies* 19 (1959) 33–51.
Kripalani, Krishna. *Rabindranath Tagore: A Biography*. New York: Grove Press, 1962.

15

Śrī Rāmakrishna: At Play in His Mother's Mansion

WALTER G. NEEVEL, JR.

I

IN SEEKING TO UNDERSTAND and interpret the spiritual experience of Śrī Rāmakrishna, it is difficult to find an approach that deals adequately with both his particularity and his universality, with his determinative role as a distinctively Bengali mystic and ecstatic in the modern resurgence of Hindu religion and with his significance for the religious life of humankind. In another place, I have stressed that beginning with the latter—as is usually the case in writings on Śrī Rāmakrishna in English—leads to confusion and distortion.[1] The Indian psychoanalyst Sudhir Kakar suggests an avenue that relates Rāmakrishna's spiritual strivings concretely to his Hindu background but also allows us to see his ecstatic mystical experience as "a heritage of our condition as human beings." [2]

As Kakar points out, a crisis was precipitated in the young Rāmakrishna's personal and spiritual development by the death of his oldest brother and father-figure Rāmkumār, a loss that compounded that of his father while Rāmakrishna was still a boy.[3] If his father's death had drawn him closer to his human mother, the loss of his brother appears to have played a major role in driving him to an agonizing and frenzied quest for the presence of his Divine Mother Kālī. The theme of the "pain of separation" as leading to a "divine madness" and as an essential motivating factor in attaining the "bliss of the union" is a major one in the Bengali Vaiṣṇava tradition into which Rāmakrishna was born, as well as in the Goddess or Śākta tradition that he adopted.[4]

Confronting and attempting to overcome the crisis caused by the death of a loved one is, of course, also a universal aspect of our human condition in general and our religiousness in particular. Kakar relates this theme of separation to other universally human experiences of alienation and loss—for example, to the way in which our dependence on the artificial world created by language exiles us from non-linguistic reality and "being itself" and to the primordial rupture that occurs at birth with our separation from our mother's body.

Of particular significance for the interpretation of Rāmakrishna's religious experience is Kakar's account of the growing psychoanalytic awareness—overcoming the earlier "fixation" upon the Oedipus complex and the father—of the primary and foundational role of the relationship to the mother and of the dynamics of achieving a sense of separateness from and rapprochement with this primal figure. Moreover, in line with the "anti-reductionistic agenda" of such psychoanalytic theorists as Erik Erikson, Donald Winnicott, Wilfred Bion, and Jacques Lacan, Kakar invites us to view the continued struggling with the problematic dynamics of this mother–child relationship as not necessarily regressive or pathological but as an attempt to recover the "creative experiencing" that lies at the base of human existence and that is seen most clearly in the spontaneous and joyful play of a young child while her or his mother is close at hand.

Tragically, as we "grow up" most of us also grow away from and lose touch with this joyous creativity; but as Kakar suggests,

> Most of us harbor tantalizing "forgotten" traces of this kind of experiencing, an apperception where what is happening outside is felt to be the creative act of the original artist (or mystic) within each of us and recognized as such with (in Blake's word) *delight*. For in late infancy and early childhood we did not always see the world as something outside ourselves, to be recognized in detail, adapted, complied with, and fitted into our idiosyncratic inner world, but often as an infinite succession of creative acts. Mystical experience, then, is one and—in some cultures and at certain historical periods—the preeminent way of uncovering the vein of creativity that runs deep in all of us.[5]

In reading the autobiographical reflections of great creative artists (Rabindranath Tagore and Nikos Kazantzakis are the two that come to my mind), we often catch the sense that they have never lost touch with this "original artist," with their original sense of joy and wonder at the newness, the openness, the rhythm of life. The evidence is clear that Rāmakrishna was a child of precocious aesthetic sensitivity and power. If we are to appreciate the passion and power of his spiritual struggles, we must view them in the light of his refusal, in the face of separation and death, to lose that joyous and playful creativity that is the birthright of every human being.

II

Śrī Rāmakrishna was born in the mid-1830s as Gadādhar Chatterjee in the isolated village of Kamarpukur, and only once in his life did he venture outside of his native Bengal. His traditional Brahmin family had a predominantly Vaiṣṇava religious background, its tutelary deity being the Incarnation of Viṣṇu, Rāma. However, the family participated freely in the worship of the other deities of devotional Hindu religion, such as Śiva and the goddess Durgā.

The most striking characteristic of Rāmakrishna, one that was nurtured by the traditional ecstatic devotion of Bengali religion, was his aesthetic and emotional sensitivity and power. He attracted early attention as a singer of devotional hymns who could move both himself and others to tears. Equally striking was his dramatic ability; he loved to mimic others and came to take leading roles in religious dramas staged in the village. From at least his tenth or eleventh year he would regularly become so overwhelmed by beauty and emotion that he would lose consciousness. His followers record his description of the first such experience in the following words:

> One morning I took parched rice in a small basket and was eating it while walking. . . . In one part of the sky there appeared a beautiful black cloud charged with rain. I was looking at it while eating the rice. Very soon the cloud covered almost the whole sky, when a flock of milk-white cranes flew against that black cloud. It looked so beautiful that I became very soon absorbed in an extraordinary mood. Such a state came on me that my external consciousness was lost. I fell down and the rice got scattered. . . . People saw it and carried me home. This was the first time that I lost external consciousness in ecstasy.[6]

Rāmakrishna's father and mother, Khudirām and Chandra, were unusually elderly; and his father's death at the age of sixty-eight in 1843 (when the boy was perhaps seven, or at most nine, years old) was a major event for his early development. On the one hand, he was naturally drawn back into a strong relationship of dependence on his mother, a fact certainly of relevance to his mature view that the ideal religious devotee should be as a child restlessly yearning for his or her Divine Mother. As Kakar points out, his relationship with his human mother, although basically a positive one, may have had certain problematic aspects, given Chandra's increased burdens at this time, including the task of raising Rāmakrishna's younger sister.[7]

On the other hand, his father's death also led him to search for alternate father-figures, including the wandering *sādhus,* or holy men, who would pass through his village. With these ascetics he developed a habit, one that was to endure throughout his life, of entering into discussion with a wide variety of religious strivers and of experimenting with their diverse practices. This habit would provide the primary basis for his wide knowledge of the many schools of Hindu religion and philosophy and for the broad catholic appeal that his eventual integration or harmonization of these many, often conflicting, elements had among Hindus of all persuasions.

Śrī Rāmakrishna Paramahamsa

The formal role of a father figure, however, was assumed by his eldest brother Rāmkumār, who was some thirty years his senior. As Rāmakrishna admonishes a devotee later in his life, "The elder brother is like one's father. Respect him" (*Gospel,* p. 786). He also acknowledges his debt to Rāmkumār by listing among the favorable conditions necessary for attaining God that "his elder brother takes responsibility for the family," allowing the person to devote himself wholeheartedly to the spiritual quest (*Gospel,* p. 646; cf. p. 793).

In the years following his father's death, Rāmakrishna came to spend much of his time helping his mother around their house, and in this way he also developed close relationships with the other women of the village. He became their favorite, and they encouraged him to sing hymns for them and to recite and enact religious stories. He in turn came to identify with and imitate them, dressing as a woman and mimicking feminine movements so perfectly that he could pass undetected through the village, getting into a great deal of mischief in the process.

This tendency of Rāmakrishna to identify with the feminine was encouraged also by the popular Vaiṣṇava religion of the village, centering on Kṛṣṇa and his love-play with the *gopīs* or milkmaids. In this form of devotion, all human beings—men as well as women—are to see themselves as milkmaids longing for the lover Kṛṣṇa. It is also this form of Hindu religion that develops most fully the dynamic tension between the "pain of separation" and the "bliss of union" as central to the relationship between the Divine and the human self. It is said of the teenage Rāmakrishna that "often in his yearning for God he would transmute himself, so to speak, into a milkmaid . . . , forgetting his real self"[8] and that at the request of the women he would play the part of Rādhā, Kṛṣṇa's heavenly consort.[9]

Another major change in Rāmakrishna's family life occurred when Rāmkumār, after the death of his wife in childbirth, moved from the village to the city of Calcutta, opening a Sanskrit school in an effort to improve the family's declining financial situation. Several years later, in 1852, he brought Rāmakrishna, then in his late teens, to the city so he could play a greater role in supervising his younger brother's studies and development.

Three years later, an opportunity presented itself that was to have the impact of setting the stage for Rāmakrishna's religious development into a Hindu saint of an exceptionally broad appeal. A wealthy but low-caste widow named Rāṇī Rāsmaṇi, who was a Śākta (a devotee of Śakti, the divine power conceived of as the Great Goddess), was moved to build a major new temple dedicated to the Divine Mother in Her fierce form of Kālī and located on the banks of the Ganges at Dakshineswar in the outskirts of Calcutta. Because of her low caste, she had great difficulty finding

Brahmin backing for her project; and Rāmkumār, one of the few who had lent her advice and support and who previously had undergone the Tantric initiation qualifying him to perform ritual worship of Kālī, was appointed chief priest of the temple when it was consecrated in 1855. In addition to the main shrine to Kālī, the temple contained a series of small shrines to her consort Śiva as well as a large one to Kṛṣṇa in union with Rādhā; thus the new temple mingled elements from the three great strands of Hindu devotional and Tantric religion, the Śākta, the Śaiva and the Vaiṣṇava.

While Rāmakrishna as a Brahmin also initially resisted involvement with this temple, within a few months he was persuaded to become the priest for the Rādhā-Kṛṣṇa shrine. Unfortunately, Rāmkumār's health soon began a serious decline; and Rāmakrishna, whose intense devotion had already been noted, was prevailed upon to take training and initiation in Śākta ritual and to become the chief priest to Kālī, which he did shortly before his brother died in 1856.

Bereft of the one who had been like a father to him, Rāmakrishna was thrown into the crisis alluded to at the beginning of this essay and began the most intense and bizarre period of his long and arduous course of spiritual striving. In the face of Rāmkumār's death, he sought solace in compulsively fulfilling the task that his brother had bequeathed to him, performing the ritual worship of Kālī, the Goddess of Death.

The image of Kālī in the Dakshineswar Temple with its gaping mouth, sword, and garland of skulls reveals that on the surface She represents the dizzying dance of Time, who devours Her own children, forcing Her devotee to confront and accept the fact that our human existence is lived in the face of and surrounded by death. Yet the image, known by the name Bhavatāriṇī, the Saviouress of the World, also invites the devotee to penetrate beneath this surface and to realize through the symbolism of its two right hands, with their "gift-giving" and "fear not" gestures, that the Śakti or Power that takes life is the same as that which gives it and protects Her children in both life and death. As Rāmakrishna later says, warning us away from stopping with the superficial impression of the image, "Kāli, the Embodiment of Destruction! No, Nitya-Kāli, my eternal Divine Mother" (*Gospel*, p. 751).

Such insight in the face of his brother's death, however, was not easily or quickly won; and he descended into a period in which, as he would later attest, he "became positively insane"[10] and was driven to the brink of suicide. After completing his ritual duties, he would wander disconsolately in a wild area north of the temple that was deserted because it had been a Muslim graveyard. Often he would spend the entire night there, returning with his eyes swollen from weeping for his Divine Mother.

In this restless yearning for an immediate vision of Kālī, it is clear that Rāmakrishna was identifying with and following the example of Rāmprasād Sen, who is known as the poet of the cremation ground and who in the eighteenth century established devotion to Kālī as a major part of Bengali religion.[11] Rāmakrishna's biographers portray him as weeping, "O Mother! Where art Thou? Reveal Thyself to me. Rāmprasād saw Thee and obtained Thy divine grace. Am I a wretch that Thou dost not come to me?"[12]

He would sing before Kālī the songs of Rāmprasād, hymns such as the following, which remained his favorites throughout his life:

> My mind is overwhelmed with wonder,
> Pondering the Mother's mystery;
> Her very name removes
> The fear of Kāla, Death himself;
> Beneath Her feet lies Mahā-Kāla [Śiva]. (*Gospel*, pp. 302, 380)

But Rāmakrishna had much to endure before he could attain the vision that would remove the fear of Death. As he told his disciples, "Oh what days of suffering I passed through! You can't imagine my agony at separation from Mother. . . . I became mad for her."[13]

Rāmakrishna described the climax of this crisis to his disciples as follows:

> There was an intolerable anguish in my heart because I could not have Her vision. Just as a man wrings a towel forcibly to squeeze out all the water from it, so I felt as if somebody caught hold of my heart and mind and was doing so with them. Greatly afflicted with the thought that I might never have Mother's vision, I was dying of despair. . . . My eyes suddenly fell upon the sword that was there in the Mother's temple. I made up my mind to put an end to my life with it that very moment. Like one mad, I ran and caught hold of it, when suddenly I had the wonderful vision of the Mother and fell down unconscious. I did not know what happened then in the external world—how that day and the next slipped away. But, in my heart of hearts, there was flowing a current of intense bliss, never experienced before, and I had the immediate knowledge of the light that was Mother. . . . what I saw was a boundless infinite conscious sea of light! However far and in whatever direction I looked, I found a continuous succession of effulgent waves coming forward, raging and storming from all sides with great speed. Very soon they fell on me and made me sink to the unknown bottom. I panted, struggled and fell unconscious.[14]

It is important to stress that this vision of the Mother as a formless sea of consciousness, light, and bliss was not the culmination but only the beginning of Rāmakrishna's quest for a liberating vision of Kālī. He also would recount how during this early period he would lose "consciousness on account of unbearable anguish" and see "that form of the Mother with hands that give boons and freedom from fear—the form that smiled, spoke and consoled and taught me in endless ways!"[15]

These overwhelming early visions would come and go and did not satisfy Rāmakrishna's longing; rather they intensified his feeling of separation from his Mother during normal consciousness and his yearning for a *continual* awareness of Her presence. As his all-consuming and frenzied strivings continued for several years he was driven increasingly toward physical and mental breakdown. In 1859 he was persuaded by his mother, Chandra, and others to take an extended vacation with his family. In an attempt to establish him in a more normal way of life, Chandra and his family arranged a marriage for him. The bride, Śāradāmaṇī Devī was, however, only five years old and would continue to live with her family for many years after their marriage in May 1859, leaving Rāmakrishna free for his spiritual quest. The marriage was never consummated physically, although they developed a deep spiritual relationship in later years and Śāradāmaṇī Devī herself became a highly revered and influential figure after Rāmakrishna's death.

In 1860, Rāmakrishna returned to the Dakshineswar temple and his "divine madness and inebriation" returned also. He entered an extraordinary state of consciousness in which visions appeared repeatedly at the slightest provocation. He later told his disciples that during this period he was unable to sleep or even to close his eyes. His physical condition again deteriorated; when not possessed by a vision, he would feel shudders of physical pain. Fortunately help was soon to arrive that would channel his spiritual intensity in more positive and constructive directions.

In 1861, a remarkable woman called Yogeśvarī arrived at Dakshineswar. She was a wandering ascetic or renouncer also known as the Bhairavī Brāhmaṇī Brahmin devotee of the Śakti, or female aspect, of Śiva's terrible (*bhairava*) forms. An accomplished master of a Tantric form of discipline, she became Rāmakrishna's first *guru* and guided him through a transformation that brought under control the more self-destructive aspects of his devotion. Like a child to his mother, Rāmakrishna poured out to this middle-aged woman the anguish and pain caused by his constant striving for the Divine Mother, asking her "Mother, what are these things that happen to me? Have I actually become mad? Have I been seized with a fell disease for calling on Mother whole-heartedly?"[16] She reassured him that what he was experiencing was not ordinary madness but *mahā-bhāva*, the "great mood" of loving devotion that has characterized the lives of great saints such as Caitanya, who have come to be recognized as divine incarnations. The Bhairavī became his sponsor, attempting to convince other religious leaders that he too was an *avatāra* (divine incarnation). But more importantly, she for the first time subjected his religious struggles to a systematic, long-term discipline.

Tantric discipline is often considered disreputable because it employs as a means to liberation practices that from the viewpoint of Hindu social conventions appear to be immoral, shocking, and polluting, such as eating meat, drinking wine, or engaging in illicit but ritually controlled sexual activity (although the evidence is that Rāmakrishna participated in most of these activities only symbolically, as is often the case). The goal is to enable the aspirant to transcend the normal distinctions between pure and impure, good and evil, divine and demonic, and to realize that everything is a manifestation of Śakti, the divine creative power. Normally to Hindus death and the dead are polluting, so the first Tantric ritual through which the Bhairavī guided Rāmakrishna was one involving five skulls, including a human one, forcing him to overcome the fear of death and to see the Śakti at work in and through it. Eventually she is reported to have led him through all of the practices prescribed by the sixty-four major Tantras or ritual texts, including the discipline of *Kuṇḍalinī* yoga in which he learned to control the Śakti as present within his own being.

This Tantric course of training would appear to have had a major transformative impact upon Rāmakrishna. He told his disciples that "a root-and-branch change" came over him during this period.[17] In the following significant passages he describes what happened to him:

> I practiced the discipline of the Tantra under the bel-tree. At that time I could see no distinction between the sacred tulsi and any other plant. In that state I sometimes ate the leavings from a jackal's meal . . . . Sometimes I rode on a dog and fed him with luchi, also eating part of the bread myself. I realized that the whole world was filled with God alone. (*Gospel*, p. 544)

Before this realization he had experienced the immediate presence of the Divine only during overwhelming ecstatic visions that blotted out the normal world and that served to increase the agony of separation during his normal state of consciousness. The awareness "that the whole world was filled with God alone" provided him with a constant sense of the presence of his Divine Mother Kālī and transformed his self-destructive fervor into the joyful Play (*līlā*) of a child in his Mother's "mansion of mirth," as he came to see the world:

> . . . the Bhakti scriptures describe this very world as a "mansion of mirth." Rāmprasād sang in one of his songs, "This world is a framework of illusion." Another devotee gave the reply, "This very world is a mansion of mirth." As the saying goes, "The devotee of Kāli, free while living, is full of Eternal Bliss." (*Gospel*, p. 243)

This Tantric realization of the universal presence of the Divine also furnished the basic framework into which Rāmakrishna came to integrate all of his spiritual experiences, seeing all deities as forms of the Divine Mother and seeking through them to participate fully in all aspects of Her divine Play (*Gospel*, p. 667).

While the Bhairavī remained a major presence in Rāmakrishna's life for six years, until 1867, he did not give her his undivided allegiance. In 1864, he returned to explore more fully his Vaiṣṇava heritage, taking initiation from a holy man called Jatādhāri in the worship of the child Rāma, realizing fully the *vātsalya-bhāva*, the devotional mood of a loving parent toward God as his child. He also continued to pursue the *mādhurya-bhāva*, or erotic mood, dressing as a milkmaid and longing for the beloved Kṛṣṇa.

Another important stage in Rāmakrishna's spiritual journey began in 1864 or 1865 with the arrival at Dakshineswar of a naked renouncer called Totāpurī, a teacher of Śaṇkara's *Kevala-advaita*, "Strict or Absolute Nondualism." Śaṇkara's absolutistic idealism has never been very popular within the context of the devotional and theistic religion of Bengal because it teaches that all distinctions, such as that between a personal deity and the devotee, are illusory and ultimately unreal. Rāmakrishna, however, in his enthusiasm to explore all spiritual paths, accepted Totāpurī's offer of initiation, first having sought and received the permission of his Divine Mother, Kālī.

Totāpurī led him through the formal rite of renunciation and instructed him in the sole reality of the formless, impersonal Absolute (*nirguṇa Brahman*); the illusory nature of the manifest world and its distinctions, and the complete identity between his true self, *Ātman*, and the Absolute, *Brahman*. He then began to lead Rāmakrishna toward the experiential realization of these truths in meditation, culminating in the state of *nirvikalpa samādhi*, concentration in a state of consciousness devoid of all conceptual forms. Rāmakrishna could easily withdraw his mind from most forms, but met resistance as his mind repeatedly fixed upon the beloved form of Kālī. In frustration, Totāpurī ruthlessly forced Rāmakrishna to concentrate on the point of a broken piece of glass pressed painfully into his forehead. Thus was his mind torn from the Divine Mother's form and plunged into the trancelike state of *nirvikalpa samādhi*.

On this first occasion he remained in this state for three full days, an extraordinary length of time for a neophyte, being brought back to normal consciousness only by Totāpurī's repeated chanting of a *mantra*. Totāpurī stayed with Rāmakrishna for eleven months, attempting to establish him in a disciplined practice of *nirvikalpa samādhi*. However, after he left, Rāmakrishna was once again carried away by his enthusiasm and spent six months almost constantly in this abstracted state. The toll upon his physical health was again severe; and he survived only because another holy man attended him, periodically forcing him back to normal consciousness and shoving small amounts of food into his mouth. Finally, his body broke down under a severe attack of dysentery that lasted for another six months, threatening his life.

According to his biographers, Rāmakrishna returned from *nirvikalpa samādhi* because he received a command from the Divine Mother to remain on the threshold between absolute and relative consciousness for the welfare of the world. They also maintain that this experience of *nirvikalpa samādhi* represented "the highest pinnacle" of his spiritual quest,[18] and that this realization of the nondual Absolute provides the basis for his teaching of the unity of all religions as paths leading to this same goal.[19]

However, the record of Rāmakrishna's conversations during the last years of his life makes clear that his followers have overemphasized the significance of this episode. There he frequently stresses that a preoccupation with such a withdrawal from the world as "illusion" to realize the sole reality of *Brahman* produces a "knower" or *jñānī* who is dry, self-centered, monotonous, and negative. He regularly contrasted such an imperfect *jñānī* with his ideal of perfection, the *vi-jñānī*, a complete or full knower who has realized not only the reality of the impersonal *Brahman* but also the reality of the world as the Play of the Divine Mother:

> Brahman alone has become everything. Therefore to the vijnāni this world is a "mansion of mirth." But to the jnāni it is a "framework of illusion." . . . A mere jnāni trembles with fear. . . . But a vijnāni isn't afraid of anything. He has realized both aspects of God: Personal and Impersonal. He has talked with God. He has enjoyed the Bliss of God. (*Gospel*, pp. 478–79)

Rāmakrishna's mature judgment on his practice of Śaṇkara's nondualistic Vedānta under Totāpurī is given in the following comment made in 1885:

> Once I fell into the clutches of a jnāni, who make me listen to Vedānta for eleven months. But he couldn't altogether destroy the seed of bhakti in me. No matter where my mind wandered, it would come back to the Divine Mother. (*Gospel*, p. 779)

Thus, after his life-threatening excursion into *nirvikalpa samādhi*, Rāmakrishna at the command of his Divine Mother, returned to a level of threshold consciousness, once again able to explore and enjoy the many dimensions of his Mother's Play within the world. It was in this period (*ca.* 1866) that he began to expand his religious experience beyond the Hindu traditions. He became interested in Islam through a Hindu with Sufi leanings who frequented Dakshineswar. After a brief period of instruction and initiation, he adopted a Muslim's way of life, dressing like one and constantly repeating the name of Allah. After three days, he had a vision of the Divine similar to those he had had through the worship of Hindu deities. This experience, to be repeated some years later with Christianity, became the experiential basis for his claim that all religions can become paths leading to realization of the Divine.

It was in the mid-1870s that Rāmakrishna began to receive wide attention and to become involved in the issue through which he was eventually to have a worldwide impact, that is, the challenge of the Christian missionary movement, with its powerful European colonialist backing, to non-Christian traditions and cultures. Two major events should be noted. The first, which happened in *ca.* 1874, was his brief but intense experiment with Christianity, in which after four days he had a vision of Christ, who merged with him. This vision came to form the basis for his claim that Christianity can also be a true path, but not a unique one, since he had had the same visionary realization through the different Hindu paths and through Islam. The other event was his meeting in 1875 with Keshab Chandra Sen, one of the most well-known and controversial Hindu reformers of the day and the one person most responsible for making Rāmakrishna famous among the English-speaking and westernized intellectuals of Calcutta. Such intellectuals, who were rejecting much of Hindu culture and religion in favor of modern European and Christian ways, discovered in Rāmakrishna a spiritual intensity and authenticity, coupled with a simple but profound sensitivity and wisdom, that led them to reevaluate the worth of their own heritage.

It was from among such young English-speaking intellectuals that, in the late 1870s and 1880s, his main disciples were drawn, including Narendranāth Datta, who was to become the world famous Swāmi Vivekānanda. During the last years of his life, Rāmakrishna spent himself teaching and inspiring these disciples and a never-ending stream of visitors to Dakshineswar. His ecstatic life-style and incessant speaking continued to take a heavy toll on his health, and he died of "clergyman's throat," or throat cancer, on August 16, 1886. Fortunately, one of his disciples, Mahendranāth Gupta (generally known simple as "M"), a well-educated schoolmaster, recorded in his diary many of his master's teachings and conversations during the last four years of his life. Research is demonstrating that "M" was not simply a passive scribe and that he and Swami Nikhilananda, the translator of the English version published as *The Gospel of Sri Ramakrishna*, played an active role in presenting and structuring their master's message.[20] Nevertheless, it is to this published record of Rāmakrishna's *Gospel*, which has become the scriptural basis for the Rāmakrishna Movement and Mission, that we must turn for our best view of his mature teachings and religious worldview.

III

In opening *The Gospel* we enter the enchanted and joyful, if often bizarre and bewildering, world of a child at play in his Mother's "mansion of mirth." Rāmakrishna greets his visitors enthusiastically, engages them in lively and humorous conversation, answers their questions with vivid and dramatic stories and parables, breaks spontaneously into tears or hymns of praise to his Divine Mother, and may, at any time, suddenly lose consciousness, overwhelmed by the ecstasy of the moment. In all of this, we see illustrated the central point of his teaching, that everyone and everything is to be enjoyed as part of the Play of the Divine Mother.

But within this simple, childlike person, many sensed a depth, a sensitivity, and wisdom. He had struggled and suffered greatly and had a genuine empathy with the problems and sufferings of those who came to him. More importantly, he also had a supreme confidence that, if one's spiritual strivings were sincere and intense, all such problems could be overcome. Moreover, while he had little sympathy with dry academic learning or philosophy, he was a teacher with a fine mind and a broad and profound knowledge of all aspects of Hindu religion.

Basic to the enduring impact of Rāmakrishna's "Gospel" upon India and the modern world was his formulation of a broadly inclusive worldview that provided the basis not only for a coherent integration of the many different, and often conflicting, Hindu traditions but also, in the eyes of many in various parts of the globe, for a more positive understanding of the relationship between the different religions of the world. Among Hindus over the centuries a major divisive issue has been that of the relative reality, truth and value of the personal God (*saguṇa Brahman*, "*Brahman* with qualities"), seen as the creator of the manifest universe, on the one hand, and of the formless, impersonal Absolute (*nirguṇa Brahman*), on the other. Rāmakrishna's response to this issue was to assert the reality and truth of both. Drawing on an ancient Vedic theme, he says repeatedly that "Reality is one" (*Gospel*, p. 134) and that all that exists is to be affirmed as a manifestation or form of that one Reality. The eternal, unchanging, formless *Brahman* (to be experienced only in *nirvikalpa samādhi*) is real, but so is the dynamic Śakti at Play in the changing world of form:

> . . . Brahman and Śakti are identical. If you accept the one, you must accept the other. It is like fire and its power to burn. . . . Thus one cannot think of Brahman without Śakti, or of Śakti without Brahman. One cannot think of the Absolute without the Relative, or of the Relative without the Absolute. The Primordial Power is ever at play. She is creating, preserving, and destroying in play, as it were. This Power is called Kāli. Kāli is verily Brahman, and Brahman is verily Kāli. It is one and the same Reality. (*Gospel*, p. 134)

In this way Rāmakrishna affirmed the reality of the goal of the followers of Śaṇkara's Absolute Non-Dualism—*jñāna*, or Knowledge, of the formless *Brahman* in *nirvikalpa samādhi*; and he also acknowledged the value of this *jñāna* in realizing the unity of Reality. However, it must again be stressed that such a knowledge of the formless *Brahman* was *not* Rāmakrishna's own goal or ideal and that he felt that a preoccupation with such a limited knowledge led to distortions, as in the assertion of the unreality or illusory nature of the Śakti or Divine Mother and of the manifest universe:

> The jnāni, sticking to the path of knowledge, always reasons about the Reality, saying, "Not this, not this." Brahman is neither "this" nor "that"; It is neither the universe nor its living beings. Reasoning in this way, the mind becomes steady. Then it disappears and the aspirant goes into samadhi. This is the Knowledge of Brahman. It is the unwavering conviction of the jnāni that Brahman alone is real and the world illusory. All these names and forms are illusory, like a dream. What Brahman is cannot be described. One cannot even say that Brahman is a Person. This is the opinion of the jnānis, the followers of Vedānta philosophy.
>
> But the bhaktas [devotees] accept all the states of consciousness. They take the waking state to be real also. They don't think the world to be illusory, like a dream. They say that the universe is a manifestation of God's power and glory. God has created all these—sky, stars, moon, sun, mountains, oceans, men, animals. They constitute His glory. He is within us, in our hearts. Again, He is outside. The most advanced devotees say that He Himself has become all this. . . . (*Gospel*, p. 133)[21]

Rāmakrishna clearly identifies himself with these "most advanced devotees," such as Rāmprasād, who sings "Only through affirmation, never negation, can you know Him" (*Gospel*, p. 107).

As we have already seen, Rāmakrishna's own ideal was not *jñāna* but *vijñāna* or "Full Knowledge" that realizes the reality of both *Brahman* and Śakti, of both the Eternal (*nitya*) and the Play (*līlā*) aspects of the One that becomes All:

> What is vijnāna? It is knowing God in a special way. The awareness and conviction that fire exists in wood is jnāna, knowledge. But to cook rice on that fire, eat the rice, and get nourishment from it is vijnāna. To know by one's inner experience that God exists is jnāna. But to talk to Him, to enjoy Him as Child, as Friend, as Master, as Beloved, is vijnāna. The realization that God alone has become the universe and all living beings is vijnāna. (*Gospel*, p. 288)

Thus, Rāmakrishna's own religious emphasis was on *bhakti*, loving devotion to the personal manifestations of Reality (*saguṇa Brahman*) in the forms of Kālī and the other divinities of the Hindu pantheon. While in the above quotation he emphasizes relating to Kṛṣṇa or Rāma as Child, Beloved, and so on, he elsewhere makes clear that his "natural attitude has always been that of a child toward its mother" (*Gospel*, p. 116).

From his own experience he asserts that to succeed in the spiritual quest

> One must have for God the yearning of a child. The child sees nothing but confusion when his mother is away. You may try to cajole him by putting a sweetmeat in his hand; but he will not be fooled. He only says, "No, I want to go to my mother." One must feel such yearning for God. Ah, what yearning! How restless a child feels for his mother! Nothing can make him forget his mother. He to whom the enjoyment of worldly happiness appears tasteless . . . becomes sincerely grief-stricken for the vision of the Mother. And to him alone the Mother comes running, leaving all Her other duties. Ah, that restlessness is the whole thing. (*Gospel*, p. 673)

And when the Divine Mother has come running and revealed Herself as the Śakti at Play in the world, Her child can also participate joyously in Her activities.

Rāmakrishna has become known as a *paramahamsa*, one who has attained the supreme goal and is liberated while still alive (*jīvanmukta*). A *paramahamsa*, having realized the Divine, is a multifaceted being, appearing in many different forms just as does the Divine itself. He may appear to be a madman or a ghoul, but primarily:

> The paramahamsa is like a five-year-old child. He sees everything filled with Consciousness. . . . The paramahamsa is like a child. He cannot distinguish between a stranger and a relative. . . . The paramahamsa is like a child. He doesn't keep any track of his whereabouts. He sees everything as Brahman. (*Gospel*, pp. 490–91)
>
> "The devotee of Kāli, free while living, is full of Eternal Bliss."(*Gospel*, p. 243)

Notes

1. Walter G. Neevel, Jr., "The Transformation of Śrī Rāmakrishna," 53–57.
2. Sudhir Kakar, *Analyst and the Mystic*, ix.
3. Ibid., 11.
4. June McDaniel, *Madness of the Saints*, 9, 43–45, 90–91.
5. Kakar, *Analyst and the Mystic*, 29.
6. Swami Saradananda, *Sri Ramakrishna*, 101.
7. Kakar, *Analyst and the Mystic*, 26.
8. *Life of Sri Ramakrishna*, 35–36.
9. Saradananda, *Sri Ramakrishna*, 63.
10. *Life of Sri Ramakrishna*, 282.
11. McDaniel, *Madness of the Saints*, 137ff.; David R. Kinsley, *Sword and the Flute*, 115ff.
12. *Life of Sri Ramakrishna*, 68.

13. Ibid., 69–70.
14. Saradananda, *Sri Ramakrishna*, 140–41.
15. Ibid., 141.
16. Ibid., 186.
17. Ibid., 200.
18. *Life of Sri Ramakrishna*, 205.
19. Saradananda, *Sri Ramakrishna*, 258.
20. Jeffrey J. Kripal, "Revealing and Concealing the Secret," 248–51. See also Kripal's *Kālī's Child;* I regret that I received this major, groundbreaking study too late for use in preparing this article.
21. On the translator's preference for masculine pronouns for the Divine in contrast to Rāmakrishna's for the feminine, see Neevel, "Transformation of Śrī Rāmakrishna," 78 n. 66.

Bibliography

Sources

The Gospel of Sri Ramakrishna, Originally recorded in Bengali by M., a disciple of the Master. Translated into English with an Introduction by Swami Nikhilananda. New York: Ramakrishna-Vivekanada Center, 1952.

Studies

Kakar, Sudhir. *The Analyst and the Mystic.* Chicago: University of Chicago Press, 1991.

Kinsley, David R. *The Sword and the Flute: Kālī and Kṛṣṇa, Dark Visions of the Terrible and the Sublime in Hindu Mythology.* Berkeley: University of California Press, 1977.

Kripal, Jeffrey J. "Revealing and Concealing the Secret: A Textual History of Mahendranath Gupta's Srisriramakrsnakathamrta." In *Calcutta, Bangladesh, and Bengal Studies: 1990 Bengal Studies Conference Proceedings*, edited by Clinton B. Seely, 245–52. South Asia Series Occasional Paper No. 40. East Lansing: Asian Studies Center, Michigan State University, 1991.

———. *Kālī's Child, The Mystical and the Erotic in the Life and Teachings of Ramakrishna.* Chicago: University of Chicago Press, 1995.

Life of Sri Ramakrishna Compiled from Various Authentic Sources. 2nd rev. ed. Calcutta: Advaita Ashrama, 1964.

McDaniel, June. *The Madness of the Saints: Ecstatic Religion in Bengal.* Chicago: University of Chicago Press, 1989.

Neevel, Walter G., Jr. "The Transformation of Śrī Rāmakrishna." In *Hinduism: New Essays in the History of Religions*, edited by Bardwell L. Smith, 53–97. Leiden: E. J. Brill, 1976.

Saradananda, Swami. *Sri Ramakrishna the Great Master.* Translated by Swami Jagadananda. 3rd ed. Madras: Sri Ramakrishna Math, 1963.

Whitmarsh, Katharine. *A Concordance to Swami Nikhilanada's Translation of The Gospel of Sri Ramakrishna (New York Edition).* Santa Barbara: Vedanta Society of Southern California, 1985.

16

The Spirituality of Swami Vivekānanda

ANANTANAND RAMBACHAN

SWAMI VIVEKĀNANDA (1863–1902) is unquestionably one of the most influential interpreters of the Hindu Tradition in recent times.[1] Vivekānanda was the first to offer to the Western world a detailed and systematic exposition of some of the central claims of the Hindu tradition, and his vibrant participation in the 1893 World's Parliament of Religions marked a new phase in the history of Hinduism. While Vivekānanda was a champion of the Advaita (nondual) system of Vedānta, he made a broad impact on the Hindu tradition. He presented Advaita as the fulfillment of Hindu spirituality and employed its insights to generalize about the features of Hinduism. In any event, Vivekānanda was widely perceived, in his own time, as the representative and advocate of Hinduism and not of a particular branch of it. Vivekānanda's perceived success in the West enhanced his impact in India. In the colonial context of India, his activities in the West evoked genuine pride and self-respect and it is quite posssible that his influence in India would have been minimal without his sojourn in the United States. The theme of pride and spiritual conquest pervade the addresses presented to Vivekānanda after his return to India. The Raja of Ramnad spoke of observing with genuine pride and pleasure the "unprecedented success which crowned your laudable efforts in bringing home to the master-minds of the West the intrinsic merits and excellence of our time-honoured and noble religion." Vivekānanda was praised for having "crossed boundless seas and oceans to convey the message of truth and peace, and to plant the flag of India's spiritual triumph and glory in the rich soil of Europe and America."[2]

With few exceptions, the published studies on Vivekānanda are generally uncritical summaries of his lectures or adulatory accounts of his Western achievements. As Wilhelm Halbfass correctly notes, "critical assessments and attempts to 'demythologize' Vivekānanda are much more rare, and rarer still are examples of thorough historical analysis and hermeneutical clarifications of Vivekānanda's work."[3] Vivekānanda's widespread impact and continuing influence, however, make critical appraisal necessary, and it is with this aim in mind that certain salient features of his spirituality will be considered in the present discussion.

Spirituality as Realization

Perhaps the most prominent and reiterated characteristic of Vivekānanda's spirituality is his emphasis on religion as realization. This is an idea that he predictably underlines in almost everyone of his lectures. In his "Paper on Hinduism," presented at the World's Parliament of Religions on 19 September 1893, Vivekānanda spoke on this theme.

> The Hindu does not want to live upon words and theories. If there is a soul in him which is not matter, if there is an all merciful universal Soul, he will go to Him direct. He must see Him, and that alone can destroy all doubts. So the best proof a Hindu sage gives about the soul, about God, is: "I have seen the soul; I have seen God." And this is the only condition of perfection. The Hindu religion does not consist in struggles and attempts to believe a certain doctrine or dogma, but in realising—not in believing, but in being and becoming. (*Works* 1:13)

In his quest for common grounds in Hinduism, Vivekānanda repeatedly presented the notion of religion as realization or direct perception as belonging to all Hindu traditions.

> Mere believing in certain theories and doctrine will not help you much. The mighty word that came out from the sky of spirituality in India was *anubhūti* realization, and ours are only books which declare again and again: "The Lord is to be *seen*." Bold, brave words indeed, but true to their very core; every sound, every vibration is true. Religion is to be realised, not only heard; it is not in learning some doctrine like a parrot. Neither is it in mere intellectual assent—that is nothing; but it must come into us . . . therefore the greatest proof that we have of the existence of a God is not because our reason says so, but because God has been seen by the ancients as well as by the moderns. (*Works* 3:377–78)

Why does realization or the possibility of a direct perception of religious claims occupy such a prominent place in Vivekānanda's spirituality? It emerges from his lectures and writings that he was concerned to find a point of reference, by virtue of which the claims of religion could be moved from the level of faith and belief to fact. He felt the need to show that religious propositions can and must be endorsed by a process of verification not unlike that employed in the physical sciences. In seeking to do this, however, Vivekānanda advances a questionable hypothesis about the derivation of all knowledge from experience. The appeal of the physical sciences, according to Vivekānanda, lies in the fact that their claims can be referred to experiences that are accessible to all human beings.

> The scientist does not tell you to believe in anything, but he has certain results which come from his own experiences, and reasoning on them when he asks us to believe in his conclusions, he appeals to some universal experience of humanity. In every exact science there is a basis which is common to all humanity, so that we can at once see the truth or fallacy of the conclusions drawn therefrom. (*Works* 1:125)

The problem of religion, according to Vivekānanda, is that it is generally presented as founded on faith and lacking central and universal experiences by reference to which its claims could be verified. This is an assumption Vivekānanda questions. Religious beliefs, in his view, are also derived from certain generic experiences that ought to be repeatable.

> But if you go to the fountain-head of Christianity, you will find that it is based on experience. Christ said that he saw God; the disciples said that they felt God; and so forth. Similarly in Buddhism, it is the Buddha's experience. He experienced certain truths, saw them, came in contact with them, and preached them to the world. . . . Thus it is clear that all the religions of the world have been built upon that one universal and adamantine foundation of all our knowledge—direct experience. (*Works* 1:126)

Vivekānanda's understanding of the origin and authority of scriptural texts is consistent with his emphasis on the significance of realization or direct perception of religious truths. He characterizes the Vedas as a collection of spiritual laws discovered by different inspired sages (*ṛṣis*) at different times (see *Works* 1:7). The texts record the spiritual discoveries of others and the methods by which such discoveries have been made, but these findings must be personally rediscovered by each person before they are valid. The scripture, therefore, is only an indication of the way to the discovery of certain facts, and its teachings must be verified by a direct perception of its claims.

> The proof, therefore, of the Vedas is just the same as the proof of this table before me, *pratyakṣa*, direct perception. This I see with the senses, and the truths of spirituality we also see in a superconscious state of the human soul. (*Works* 3:253)

Scriptures are portrayed by him as second-hand religion. As a record of the experiences of others, it may stimulate our own desires, but even as one person's eating is of little or no value to another, so also is the record of another's experience until we attain to the same end.

Vivekānanda not only advocated the necessity for a direct perception of the claims of the Vedas but made such perception a necessity for properly understanding the Vedas. His justification seems to be that, as records of direct perception, they were not written for the intellect or for understanding through rational inquiry. The texts become useful only when one has lifted oneself to the same heights of perception. At that point, however, they are useful only to the extent that they confirm what one has known directly (see *Works* 4:165; 7:85, 89).[4]

The Diversity of Spiritual Paths

For the attainment of realization or direct perception, Vivekānanda proposes the four yogas of *karma*, *bhakti*, *jñāna* and *rāja*. He affirms that each method leads independently to the realization of nonduality. Vivekānanda does not see the different methods as being in conflict with one another. His rationale for a plurality of means is derived from the variety of human personalities. Each one is adapted to a different nature and temperament. Vivekānanda generalizes the variety of human beings into four types. First, there is the active, energetic temperament, the worker, for whom is meant *karmayoga*. Second, there is the emotional person, who discovers an appropriate method in *bhaktiyoga*. *Jñānayoga* is intended for the philosophical and rational mind, while *rājayoga* satisfies the mystically oriented person.[5] We can now turn our attention to his consideration of these different methods and the ways in which they lead to realization. My concern here is not to offer a comprehensive account of the characteristics of each method but to delineate its essential characteristics and validity as a means to nondual knowledge.

Karmayoga

There is no single discussion in the lectures and writings of Vivekānanda where one can turn to find a clear and comprehensive statement of his understanding of *karmayoga*. In searching for his central definition of *karmayoga*, the concept that emerges most often is the idea of unselfish action.

> It is the most difficult thing in the world to work and not to care for the result, to help a man and never to think that he ought to be grateful, to do some good work and at the same time never to look to see whether it brings you name or fame, or nothing at all. Even the most arrant coward becomes

> brave when the world praises him, but for a man to constantly do good without caring for the approbation of his fellow men is indeed the highest sacrifice man can perform. (*Works* 1:42–43)

Although Vivekānanda speaks of *karmayoga* as an attitude of indifference to the results of action, one must suppose that the unconcern is with personal selfish results only. A complete unconcern with results will make even action for the sake of others impossible, for it is difficult to see how any action could be initiated without some end in view.

In order to emphasize the distinction between *karmayoga* and *bhaktiyoga*, Vivekānanda insists that detachment in action is possible even for one who does not believe in *īśvara* (personal God). He insists that detachment may be accomplished by the force of the will and justifies this by a recourse to Sāṁkhya tradition, where *īśvara* is not posited. In this case, claims Vivekānanda, detachment is made possible by an attitude of the world as a temporary place of abode, meant only for the education of the soul. Instead of identifying with nature, it should be viewed as a book to be read and then disposed of (*Works* 1:56–57). For Vivekānanda, the essential factor about *karmayoga* as a method is its emphasis on work. It is meant for those whose minds cannot be applied on the plane of thought alone, and whose natures demand some sort of activity.

In order to strengthen his claim for *karmayoga* as an independent path of liberation, Vivekānanda distinguishes it, one supposes, from *jñānayoga* by describing it as being free from all doctrines and dogma. This is a conclusion he reiterates throughout his discussion of this method.

> The *karmayogi* need not believe in any doctrine whatever. He may not believe even in God, may not ask what his soul is, nor think of any metaphysical speculation. He has got his own special aim of realizing selflessness; and he has to work it out himself. Every moment of his life must be realization, because he has to solve by mere work, without the help of doctrines or theory, the very problem to which the *jñāni* applies his reason and inspiration and the *bhakta* his love. (*Works* 1:111)[6]

This is a troubling conclusion which critical examination of Vivekānanda's statements on *karmayoga* finds difficult to sustain. His views are clearly imbued with implicit and explicit doctrinal assumptions. It is obvious that one embarks on this path of detached activity only after certain conclusions about the nature of existence and the ultimacy of liberation (*mokṣa*). The lack of concern with personal rewards is not absolute, for *karmayoga* is presented as a method adopted with a definite aim in mind. Through unselfish action the aspirant hopes to be free. The *karmayoga* that Vivekānanda describes is intelligible only in the doctrinal context of Advaita and his dicussions are suffused with Advaita postulates and premises (see, e.g., *Works* 1:100–101). It appears that Advaita contentions have such an axiomatic character for him that they slip easily into his discussions as unquestionable propositions.

The most problematic aspect of Vivekānanda's discussion on *karmayoga* is the connection he tries to establish between *karmayoga* and *mokṣa*. Ignorance is presented as somehow falling away with the cultivation of selflessness. In making the connection between *karmayoga* and *mokṣa*, Vivekānanda's language becomes imprecise and hazy and there is a tendency to reformulate the nature of the problem and goal to be attained. Selfishness, for example, rather than *avidyā*, the customary way of defining the fundamental problem in Advaita, is described as the root of the bondage. The goal is presented as self-abnegation, and *karmayoga*, by its emphasis on the service of others, leads to this by encouraging self-forgetfulness and humility. This is identified by Vivekānanda with *nivṛtti* (renunciation).

> We become forgetful of the ego when we think of the body as dedicated to the service of others—the body with which most complacently we identify the ego. And in the long run comes the consciousness of disembodiedness. The more intently you think of well-being of others, the more oblivious of self you become. In this way, as gradually your heart gets purified by work, you will come to feel the truth that your own Self is pervading all beings and all things. Thus it is that doing good to others constitutes a way, a means of revealing one's Self or *ātman*. Know this also to be one of the spiritual practices, a discipline for God-realization. Its aim is also Self-realization. Exactly that aim is attained by *jñāna* (knowledge), *bhakti* (devotion) and so on, also by work for the sake of others. (*Works* 7:111–12)

In response to Vivekānanda, one may contend that from the Advaita perspective the fundamental human problem is not just one of exalting or humbling oneself. It is erroneous apprehension of the *ātman* in the form of *adhyāsa* (superimposition). Humility, which may be associated with the service of others, is certainly valued as necessary for the gain of nondual knowledge, but it is difficult to see how it can eliminate ignorance and lead to the kind of understanding which Advaita implies. The supposedly natural progression that Vivekānanda posits in the above passage from the service of others to a knowledge of the distinction of self and body, its nondual and all-pervasive nature, is difficult to understand. It is not at all clear how such far-reaching deductions can be made or how they are self-evident. A feeling of affinity with others is not the same as a knowledge of nonduality.[7]

Swami Vivekānanda

Bhaktiyoga

Vivekānanda provides several definitions of *bhaktiyoga*, showing that its singularity lies in love and worship, and that its aim is also nondual identity with the absolute.

> *Bhakti* is a series or succession of mental efforts at religious realization beginning with ordinary worship and ending in a supreme intensity of love for *Īśvara*. (*Works* 3:36)

> *Bhaktiyoga* is the path of systematized devotion for the attainment of union with the Absolute. (*Works* 6:90)

Whereas *karmayoga* is meant for the activity-oriented nature, *bhaktiyoga* is conducive to the largely emotional temperament who wants only to love and does not care for abstract definitions of God or philosophical speculation.

Vivekānanda continuously affirms that the advantage of *bhaktiyoga* is its naturalness and easiness as a means for liberation. In this path, the various human passions and feelings are not viewed as essentially wrong, but are given a new orientation in a relationship with God. The renunciation of the devotee, for example, is the spontaneous consequence of love for God.

> The renunciation necessary for the attainment of *bhakti* is not obtained by killing anything, but just comes naturally as in the presence of an increasingly stronger light, the less intense ones become dimmer and dimmer until they vanish away completely. So this love of pleasures of the senses and of the intellect is all made dim and thrown aside and cast into the shade by the love of God Himself. (*Works* 3:72)

In his discussion of *bhaktiyoga* Vivekānanda draws a great deal from the writings of Rāmānuja. He presents *bhaktiyoga* as progressing through two stages. The first is *gaunī*, or the preparatory stage, where there is still a necessity for myths, symbols, forms, rituals, and the repetition of names. From the preparatory stage, one moves to *parabhakti*, or supreme devotion, the most intense of all relationships possible with God. At this stage, the devotee does not even hope for salvation. It is the ideal of love for love's sake; God is loved because God is lovable and the devotee cannot help loving. The relationship is characterized by the absence of all fear.

There are obviously a few difficulties with Vivekānanda's account of the characteristics of *bhaktiyoga*. As noted, he draws from and acknowledges his dependence on Rāmānuja and other *bhakti* writers. Rāmānuja, however, challenged many of the premises and conclusions of Advaita, while Vivekānanda presents *bhaktiyoga* as leading directly to the conclusions and goal of Advaita.

Vivekānanda, however, is not very helpful in tracing the evolution from the duality of *bhakti* to nonduality. He appears to suggest a natural progression to nonduality and I can do no better than cite one such example.

> We all have to begin as dualists in the religion of love. God is to us a separate Being, and we all feel ourselves to be separate beings also. Love then comes in the middle, and man begins to approach God, and God comes nearer and nearer to man. Man takes up all the various relationships of life, as father, as mother, as son, as friend, as master, as lover, and projects them on his ideal of love, on his God. To him God exists as all these, and the last point of his progress is reached when he feels that he has become absolutely merged in the object of his worship. We all begin with love for ourselves, and the unfair claims of the little self make even love selfish. At last, however, comes the full blaze of light, in which the little self is seen to have become one with the Infinite. Man himself is transfigured in the presence of this Light of Love, and he realizes at last the beautiful truth that Love, the Lover, and the Beloved are One. (*Works* 3:100)

That the movement from the duality of *bhaktiyoga* to nonduality is a natural and inevitable progression is not at all clearly demonstrated in the above passage. It seems to fall into the general context of his claim that all religious quests will eventually end in nonduality. Unless this is accepted, the movement from duality to nonduality is not clear from his *bhaktiyoga* discussion. The discovery of nonduality occurs from the stage of *parabhakti,* but even at this level, from his own descriptions, there is a clear distinction between worshiper and worshiped.

Jñānayoga

In the lectures and writings of Vivekānanda, we are given only vague suggestions about what constitutes the distinctiveness and development of *jñānayoga* as a method of attaining liberation. He presents *jñānayoga* as a path suitable only for the highest and most exceptional minds—the brave, strong, and daring. In contrast with other paths, it is the most difficult, but also brings the quickest results.

> The object of *jñānayoga* is the same as *bhakti* and *rājayoga,* but the method is different. This is the Yoga for the strong, for those who are neither mystical nor devotional, but rational. (*Works* 8:3)

While selfless activity seems to be the chief distinctive feature of *karmayoga*, and loving worship of *bhaktiyoga*, Vivekānanda presents "pure" reason and reliance on will as the singular characteristic of *jñānayoga*. He describes it as the rational and philosophical side of yoga.

> As the *bhaktiyogi* works his way to complete oneness with the Supreme through love and devotion, so the *jñānayogi* forces his way to the realization of God by the power of pure reason. He must be prepared to throw away all old idols, all old beliefs and superstitions, all desire for this world or another, and be determined only to find freedom. Without *jñāna* (knowledge) liberation cannot be ours. (*Works* 8:3)

Occasionally, the way of *jñāna* is alluded to as the negative way, *neti, neti*, but the nature of this negative reasoning is not developed. On one occasion, Vivekānanda describes it as a method of mind control or destruction, after which the real discloses itself. Elsewhere his description suggests that it is a denial of the non-self and an assertion of the self (see *Works* 1:98; 5:300; 6:464).

His most consistent characterization of *jñānayoga* is his description of it as a method of reason and will. This definition, however, raises a number of problems within the context of his overall views. He does not, for example, indicate the source of the propositions upon which the aspirant exercises his reason, or whether these propositions are arrived at by reason itself. If we assume that the original propositions are derived from the Vedas, then the utility or possibility of reasoning on these statements seems to be undermined by some of Vivekānanda's own contentions. He has argued, for example, that the Vedas, as the product of an experience transcending reason, cannot be understood by reason.

The issue is further complicated by the fact that Vivekānanda argues also for the limited nature of reason. Its chief limitation, according to Vivekānanda, is its dependence on perception for its data. This constitutes its essential weakness and binds it to the realms of time and place. As an intellectual process, reason functions only after perception in the realms of both secular and spiritual knowledge.

> All argument and reasoning must be based upon certain perceptions. Without these, there cannot be any argument. Reasoning is the method of comparison between certain facts which we have already perceived. If these facts are not there already, there cannot be any reasoning. If this is true of external phenomena, why should it not be so of the internal? The chemist takes certain chemicals and certain results are produced. This is a fact; you see it, sense it, and make that the basis on which to build all your chemical arguments. So with physicists, so with all other sciences. All knowledge must stand on perception of certain facts, and upon that we have to build our reasoning. (*Works* 2:162)

The argument that reason becomes possible only subsequent to perception seems to undermine Vivekānanda's own claim about *jñānayoga* as a path of reason. If reason is the chief tool that the aspirant must employ from the inception, then it appears impossible to do so without a direct perception of spiritual truths. If, on the other hand, one directly perceives these truths, then, from the logic of Vivekānanda's own position, reason is redundant.

Generally speaking, because of the overriding importance that Vivekānanda places on perception or realization as a source of knowledge, he ascribes little importance to reason in his spirituality. He groups reason, along with theories, documents, doctrines, books, and ceremonies, as an aid to religion. In relation to realization, the role of reason is merely preparatory. It checks and prevents crude errors and superstition.

> The intellect is only the street-cleaner, cleansing the path for us, a secondary worker, the policeman; but the policeman is not a positive necessity for the workings of society. He is only to stop disturbances, to check wrong-doing, and that is all the work required of the intellect. (*Works* 2:306)

In the light of Vivekānanda's arguments that reason cannot operate before perception, it is not clear how it can accomplish even this negative role. There is no clear indication of the nature and source of the information on which the aspirant exercises reason, and no suggestion of the principles that should guide reason in this pre-perception stage.[8]

Rajayoga

Rājayoga, as described by Vivekānanda, is based primarily on the *Yoga-sūtras* of Patañjali. It is the method proposed by Vivekānanda for attaining direct perception of religious truths. In fact, he claims, this is the method advanced by all schools of Indian spirituality for gaining liberation. As with his claim for the method of *karmayoga*, he emphasizes that no faith or belief is necessary. It is not necessary to outline, in detail, Vivekānanda's interpretation of the eightfold system of Patañjali. The culmination of these spiritual disciplines is to be found in the experience of *samādhi*, and our discussion will concern itself primarily with the description and evaluation of his claims for this experience. The entire procedure of *rājayoga*, contends Vivekānanda, is designed to bring us scientifically to this all-important state.

> From the lowest animal to the highest angel, some time or other, each one will have to come to that state, and then alone will real religion begin for him. Until then we only struggle towards that stage. There is no difference now between us and those who have no religion, because we have no experience. What is concentration good for, save to bring us to this experience? Each one of the steps to gain *samādhi* has been reasoned out, properly adjusted, scientifically organized, and when faithfully practiced, will surely lead us to the

> desired end. Then will all sorrows cease, all miseries vanish; the seeds for actions will be burnt, and the soul will be free forever. (*Works* 1:188)

Samādhi, attests Vivekānanda, is the result of the awakening of the *kuṇḍalinī.* This is the single way, he claims, of attaining spiritual knowledge through direct perception. Although the *samādhi*-experience is derived by Vivekānanda from Patañjali, the latter does not refer to the *kuṇḍalinī.* The idea of the *kuṇḍalinī* appears to have been unknown to Patañjali and belongs to the schools of Tantra.[9]

Vivekānanda often describes *samādhi* by distinguishing three gradations of mental activity. The lowest of these is the level of instinctive behavior, most highly developed among animals. Here thought is largely unconscious and actions are unaccompanied by any feelings of self-awareness or egoism. Reason is a more highly developed instrument of knowledge than instinct. It is conscious mental activity accompanied by a sense of egoism and self-awareness. Even though its sphere of operation, says Vivekānanda, is much wider than the confines of instinct, it is nevertheless limited. Higher than instinct or reason is the superconscious state of mind, or *samādhi.* Here the mind transcends the limits of reason and instinct and apprehends facts inaccessible to these. He characterizes the superconscious as being infallible and far more unlimited in its scope than reason, while maintaining that it never contradicts reason.

As a means of gaining knowledge of the self, Vivekānanda presents *samādhi* as a method of concentration or meditation. He speaks in universal terms about the process of gaining knowledge, emphasizing concentration or observation as the primary act. In the physical sciences it is a question of concentrating the mind on external phenomena.

> There is only one method by which to attain this knowledge, that which is called concentration. The chemist in his laboratory concentrates all the energies of his mind into one focus and throws them upon the materials he is analysing, and so finds out their secrets. The astronomer concentrates all the energies of his mind and projects them through his telescope upon the skies; and the stars, the sun, and the moon, give up their secrets to him. (*Works* 1:130)

The unique characteristic of *rājayoga* as a method of gaining knowledge is that the observation is internal. The mind is the object as well as the instrument of knowledge.

In his description of *samādhi,* Vivekānanda alternates between identifying it as a state in which the mind is still operative at its highest level and one in which the mind ceases to function. Vivekānanda describes the goals of *rājayoga* as the total suppression of all thought forms in the mind. He speaks of the necessity to curb each thought as it enters into the mind, making the mind a vacuum. A disciple is advised by him to "kill the mind." Vivekānanda repeatedly contends that the knowledge of the self spontaneously follows the extinction of the mind (see *Works* 1:188, 212–13; 7:195–96; 8:40).

There are not many descriptions in Vivekānanda's writings of the actual state of *samādhi*. He describes it as "sensationless" and characterized by the cessation of all mental modifications. All duality disappears, and the knower and known become one (see *Works* 8:36; 7:140, 196; 5:336; 6:89). We are afforded, however, two personal accounts of this spiritual state by Vivekānanda, both strikingly similar. On the basis of Vivekānanda's own discussions, we can consider the first account, where even his ego-sense disappeared to be truer to the *samādhi* ideal. The confession of his inability to recollect anything in the absense of his ego-consciousness is significant.

> One day in the temple-garden at Dakshineswar Shri Ramakrishna touched me over the heart, and first of all I began to see that the houses—rooms, doors, windows, verandahs—the trees, the sun, the moon,—all were flying off, shattering to pieces as it were—reduced to atoms and molecules—and ultimately became merged in the *ākāsa*. Gradually again, the *ākāsa* also vanished, and after that, my consciousness of the ego with it; what happened next I do not recollect. (*Works* 5:392)[10]

The analogy almost invariably used by Vivekānanda to describe the gain of knowledge in *samādhi* is direct perception (*pratyakṣa*). He argues throughout for a direct perception of religious truths. This direct perception is particularly distinguished by him from intellectual assent or dissent and belief in doctrines. He is derisive toward religious commitment based on belief in doctrines. The goal is always affirmed to be direct perception, which alone constitutes real knowledge. What is required is superconscious or "superfine" perception.

> What is the proof of God? Direct perception *pratyakṣa*. The proof of this wall is that I perceive it. God has been perceived that way by thousands before, and will be perceived by all who want to perceive Him. But this perception is no sense-perception at all; it is supersensuous, super conscious, and all this training is needed to take us beyond the senses. (*Works* 1:415; see also 4:34, 167)

It is important to emphasize specifically the self-valid status Vivekānanda ascribes to knowledge gained through this process of direct perception. His disdain for dogma, doctrine, theory, books, and intellectual assent and dissent is directly related to his view of the self-valid nature of knowledge gained through realization. Throughout his writings, he upholds the supreme value of realization in contrast with all of these.

While *samādhi* is clearly of central importance in the spirituality of Vivekānanda, his characterization of this state and his claims for it leave many questions unanswered. His claims for *rājayoga* and *samādhi* appear to undermine his arguments for the yogas of *karma*, *bhakti*, and *jñāna* as direct and independent ways to liberation. We have seen his profession that direct perception is the only acceptable way of ascertaining religious truths and that this is attained solely through *samādhi* and *rājayoga.* Are we to understand all other ways as only preparations for *rājayoga?* Do they culminate in the experience of *samādhi?* Vivekānanda, however, has argued that the different steps of *rājayoga* are designed to lead the aspirant scientifically to the *samādhi* state. He has also cautioned us about the dangers of accidentally encountering this state without following proper methods. One is likely to be deranged; the source of knowledge will be misunderstood; and with knowledge will come superstition. Are these dangers not real for aspirants in other spiritual paths where Vivekānanda does not make the practice of *rājayoga* imperative?

Vivekānanda, as we have seen, equates the gain and verification of spiritual knowledge with the methods employed in science. The grounds on which he draws his parallels leave many unanswered questions.[11] While Vivekānanda's analogy with science is basically an analogy between religious experience and sense perception, there are obviously important differences between these two. Sense perception is not as simple as Vivekānanda makes it out to be, and it is certainly not always self-validating. The possibilities of sense illusion and deception are very well accepted. Even though these may not be readily apparent, there are definite criteria that are imbibed and employed in validating sense experience. It might be argued that there are definite criteria available for verifying religious experience. The problem here is reaching agreement with those criteria, since the criteria for evaluating religious experience in any particular community of shared beliefs may not be considered reliable in a different community. If one argues as Vivekānanda does, that the experience must be in accord with reason, other problems emerge. Whence are the agreed premises of reason to be derived? How can reason be employed in validating claims to which reason has no direct access? Does this mean that reason is being elevated to a status above that of experience? Vivekānanda's arguments about the self-valid nature of the experience and its infallibility appear under question.

In describing *rājayoga* as conforming to the methods of science, Vivekānanda is constrained to misrepresent the scientific process of gaining knowledge. When speaking of all knowledge as being derived from experience, Vivekānanda does not address the complexity of the "experience" through which knowledge is gained and corroborated in the physical sciences. The claims of science are not as easily verifiable in the experiences of ordinary people as Vivekānanda suggests. In the same manner, he speaks of all religious traditions as being derived from experience without taking into account the diversity among religions about their origins and authoritive sources. One of the significant points about his imprecise use of the term "experience" is the fact that, in respect of the *samādhi*, he is making claims for a singular and unique experience, totally unlike any other. He speaks of science and all other religions as being founded on experience and, ignoring all diversity, slips into making assertations about the distinctive experience of *samādhi*.

Vivekānanda speaks repeatedly about the necessity for a direct perception of the self if its existence is to be certified beyond any doubt. Perception, however, whether internal or external, involves the process of objectification. It implies a duality between the knower and the known. In the Advaita tradition, with which Vivekānanda identifies himself, the self is the only knower, incapable of being objectified by any faculty. There is no other knower for whom the self can become an object. To suggest, as Vivekānanda does, that the self must be known through direct perception is to posit the existence of some other knower. The objectification of the self by any other knowing entity would also signify its limitation, for only a delimited thing can be objectified.

We have already noted, at many points in this discussion, Vivekānanda's belittling of everything he considers to be doctrine and dogma. This attitude is directly related to the fact that he argues for a pure, self-interpretative experience. Contemporary studies on mysticism and religious experience have raised important questions about this assumption and have highlighted the complexity of the interplay between experience and doctrine.[12] While Vivekānanda contends that experience is followed later by the recording, in words, of its implications and significance, his writings reveal a more complex relationship. His writings on *rājayoga*, for example, are permeated with the doctrinal assumptions of the Sāṁkhya tradition. In fact, very important questions are raised by the fact that Vivekānanda turns to the *rājayoga* system of Patañjali to find the veridical experience on which he places so much emphasis. The system of Patañjali derives its doctrinal framework almost entirely from Sāṁkhya and exhibits fundamental differences with Advaita. Sāṁkhya is, of course, dualistic and posits a plurality of selves. The *samādhi* experience, therefore, has entirely different implications for the follower of Patañjali. If different conclusions can be inferred from the same experience, one may draw the conclusion that the meaning of the experience is not self-valid.

Spirituality and Religious Diversity

Vivekānanda's approach to the variety of religious belief and practice outside of Hinduism is basically the same as his approach to the pluralism within it. Diversity and difference are not accepted as absolute. The strands of his viewpoint on religious diversity are held together by the premise that the goal of all religious quest is the same. The world of religions is, as he puts it, "only a travelling, a coming up of different men and women, through various conditions and circumstances, to the same goal." For Vivekānanda, the goal of all religious quest is the discovery of the nondual reality underlying all existence. This knowledge, as we have already noted, is attainable through different religious paths, but the path, claims Vivekānanda, is not the goal. The unifying factor is the common goal, and diversity is expressed in the variety of means adopted for attainment.

> All religions are so many stages. Each one of them represents the stage through which the human soul passes to God. Therefore, not one of them should be neglected. None of these stages are dangerous or bad. They are good. Just as a child becomes a man, and a young man becomes an old man, so they are travelling from truth to truth; they become dangerous only when they become rigid and will not move further; when he ceases to grow. (*Works* 2:500)

This outlook, Vivekānanda feels, offers him the possibility of accepting all religious doctrines with the full conviction that "they are mainfestations of the same truth and that they all lead to the same conclusions as the Advaita has reached." Vivekānanda did not see spiritual diversity, either within or outside Hinduism, as negative. He valued differences as signs of the life of thought and feared a uniformity of views. His important argument, however, for a diversity of spiritual ways is that it widens the choice for the religious person. Because of the rich variation in human nature and temperament, diversity holds out the possibility of the individual discovering a form of religious life suitable to his or her mentality. While Vivekānanda welcomed diversity, he stood firm against exclusivism. He saw religious discord as the consequence of each religion adopting a narrow self-righteous position, refusing to take into account any other existing view.

Vivekānanda's own solution to the problem of religious conflict and dissension is his proposal of the idea of universal religion. By universal religion, however, he does not mean religious uniformity or the triumph of one religion over all others. Universal religion appears to be synonymous with the absense of exclusivism and includes a readiness to accept diversity.

> Just as we have recognized unity by our very nature, so we must also recognize variation. We must learn that truth may be expressed in a hundred thousand ways and that each of these ways is true as far as it goes. We must learn that the same thing can be viewed from a hundred different standpoints and yet be the same thing. (*Works* 2:382–83)

In spite of this diversity, according to Vivekānanda, religions are to be seen as expressions of a common struggle toward God.

> Through high philosophy or low, through the most exalted mythology, or the grossest, through the most refined ritualism or arrant fetishism, every sect, every soul, every nation, every religion, consciously or unconsciously, is struggling upward, toward God; every vision of truth that man has is a vision of Him and none else. (*Works* 2:383)

Vivekānanda saw the necessity of each tradition's striving to assimilate the spirit of the others while preserving its own uniqueness and individuality. He often pointed out how the contemplation of another tradition enhanced the understanding of one's own. In his view of universal religion, he represented each of the major religions as having a unique mission wherein its individuality is expressed. Each one utilizes its energy in typifying and embodying the dimension of truth which is its special concern. He portrayed the religions of the world as different forces in the economy of God working for the good of mankind.

In trying to assess the relevance of Vivekānanda's interpretations to contemporary interreligious dialogue, one must bear in mind that these were formulated during the last decades of the nineteenth century. In the light of recent discussions on issues of religious pluralism, however, many of Vivekānanda's arguments appear progressive. Among these are his readiness to admit a common source and origin for the world's religions and his claim that truth is not limited to any particular tradition. He rejoiced in religious diversity and saw the need to preserve the uniqueness and individuality of each tradition.

Vivekānanda rejects the patronizing attititudes to religious diversity found in the idea that one religion is the fulfillment of all others (see *Works* 4:184). He sees his position as being different from this in the sense that he is proposing a concept not merely of tolerance but of acceptance. He claims to be arguing that all religions are true and that religious growth is from lower to higher truth. It is important, however, to note that Vivekānanda takes his stand on a definite view of truth and one to which he is deeply committed. Advaita (nondualism) is the goal toward which all religions are evolving, representing different points along the way. In relation to other religions, therefore, Vivekānanda's spirituality is clearly inclusivistic and reflects the common problem of such theologies. This is the tendency to redefine the other in one's own image. R. W. Neufeldt is correct in his summary of the position of the Ramakrishna Mission on religious pluralism, a position largely shaped by Vivekānanda's interpretation.

> All traditions are to be understood as good or true because they point to Advaita and in pointing contain, at least implicitly, the truth of Advaita. But in order that we might see the Advaitin message in all traditions, they must be reconceived in terms of Advaita. This is made abundantly clear in the Mission's traditional interpretation of Gautama Buddha. I would see this as the most severe and problematical limitation in the Mission's response to pluralism. To understand the traditions correctly they are to be seen as Advaitin, either explicitly or implicitly. This serves to make adherents of various traditions into either conscious or anonymous Advaitins.[13]

Vivekānanda lived a short life during a time of great upheaval and tumult in the history of the Hindu tradition. Besides the specific challenge of Christian exclusivism, Hinduism was also responding to the multifaceted character of the impact of the West. In many different ways, his spirituality reflected his response to these challenges, and its different elements were not effectively integrated. One important element of his response to Christian exclusivism was his proposal that Hinduism included a variety of independent ways to liberation. I have attempted to show the problematic nature of this claim in relation to his Advaita premises. He responded to the findings of science and its methodology by trying to show that these were consistent with the main tenets of Hindu spirituality and its practices. His parallels are possible, however, only through a radical simplification of the scientific method. Vivekānanda achieved heroic status early in his short life and the deep pride which Hindus discovered through his work in the West did not encourage critical reflection on his spirituality. Standing on his feet, as it were, he responded to major challenges facing the Hindu tradition, with little time to assess and evaluate the overall consistency and persuasiveness of these responses.

Notes

1. The details of Swāmi Vivekānanda's biography are familiar. For a detailed discussion, see S. N. Dhar, *A Comprehensive Biography of Swami Vivekananda*. For a briefer study see Swami Nikhilananda, *Vivekananda: A Biography* (3rd Indian ed.; Calcutta: Advaita Ashrama, 1975).
2. *The Complete Works of Swami Vivekananda*, 3:144–45; hereafter cited as *Works*.

3. See Wilhelm Halbfass, *India and Europe*, 228.

4. Vivekānanda's understanding of the authority of the Vedas stands in radical contrast to Śaṅkara. For Śaṅkara, the necessity of the Vedas as a valid source of knowledge about *brahman* is explained by the inapplicability of all other means of knowledge. The Vedas would not fulfill the criteria of being a valid source of knowledge unless they were capable of producing a unique and self-valid knowledge. For a contrast between Vivekānanda and Śaṅkara on the authority of the Vedas, see Anantanand Rambachan, *Limits of Scripture*.

5. For elaborations of this argument, see *Works* 2:385–88; 6:16–17, 137–38.

6. Vivekānanda describes the Buddha as an ideal *karmayogi* because of his perceived doctrinal indifference.

7. For a critical assessment of Vivekānanda's treatment of *karmayoga*, see Anantanand Rambachan, "Is *Karmayoga* a Direct and Independent Means to *Mokṣa*?" *Religion* 15 (1985) 53–65.

8. For a detailed discussion of Vivekānanda's attitude to reason, as well as for analysis of specific examples of his reasoning, see Anantanand Rambachan, "The Place of Reason in the Quest for *Mokṣa:* Vivekananda's Conceptualization of *Jñānayoga*," *Religious Studies* (June 1987) 279–88.

9. The *kuṇḍalinī* is described by Vivekānanda as a coiled up, unmanifested energy lying at the base of the spinal canal. Its awakening through the practice of *rājayoga* leads to its upward movement through a subtle, nonphysical hollow in the spinal column (*suṣumnā*). As it progresses, it passes through seven centers of consciousness (*cakras*), each step marked by distinct spiritual experiences. When it reaches the seventh, the thousand-petaled (*sahasrāra cakra*), located in the brain, full spiritual illumination is gained. See *Works* 1:160–70. See also Agehananda Bharati, *The Tantric Tradition* (London: Rider & Company, 1965).

10. For the second account, see *Works* 7:139.

11. See Anantanand Rambachan, "Swami Vivekananda's Use of Science as an Analogy for the Attainment of *Mokṣa*," *Philosophy East and West* 40 (July 1990) 331–42.

12. See, e.g., *Mysticism and Philosophical Analysis*, ed. S. T. Katz (London: Sheldon Press, 1978).

13. R. W. Neufeldt, "The Response of the Ramakrishna Mission," in *Modern Indian Responses to Religious Pluralism*, ed. Harold G. Coward (Albany: State University of New York Press, 1987) 80.

Bibliography

Sources

The Complete Works of Swami Vivekananda. Mayavati Memorial Edition. 8 vols. Calcutta: Advaita Ashrama, 1964–71.

Studies

Arora, V. K. *The Social and Political Philosophy of Swami Vivekananda*. Calcutta: Punthi Pustak, 1968.

Baird, Robert, ed. *Religion in Modern India*. New Delhi: Manohar Publications, 1981.

Dhar, S. N. *A Comprehensive Biography of Swami Vivekananda.* 2 vols. Madras: Vivekananda Prakashan Kendra, 1975–76.

Ghanananda, Swami, and Geoffrey Parrinder, eds. *Swami Vivekananda in East and West.* London: Ramakrishna Vedanta Center, 1968.

Halbfass, Wilhelm. *India and Europe.* Albany: State University of New York Press, 1988.

Mahadevan, T. M. P. *Swami Vivekananda and the Indian Renaissance.* Coimbatore: Sri Ramakrishna Mission Vidyalaya Teachers College, 1965.

Majumdar, R. C., ed. *Vivekananda Centenary Memorial Volume.* Calcutta: Swami Vivekananda Centenary Committee, 1963.

Rambachan, Anantanand. *The Limits of Scripure: Vivekananda's Reinterpretation of the Authority of the Vedas.* Honolulu: University of Hawaii Press, 1994.

Satprakashananda, Swami. *Swami Vivekananda's Contribution to the Present Age.* St. Louis: Vedanta Society of St. Louis, 1978.

Williams. George. *The Quest for Meaning in Swami Vivekananda.* Chico, Calif.: New Horizons Press, 1978.

Part Four

CONTEMPORARY HINDU SPIRITUALITY

17

J. Krishnamurti: Traveler in a Pathless Land

Ravi Ravindra

> Truth is a pathless land, and you cannot approach it by any path whatsoever, by any religion, by any sect.
>
> Because I am free, unconditioned, whole, not the part, not the relative, but the whole Truth that is eternal, I desire those who seek to understand me to be free, not to make out of me a cage which will become a religion, a sect. Rather should they be free from all fears—from the fear of religion, from the fear of salvation, from the fear of spirituality, from the fear of love, from the fear of death, from the fear of life itself. . . .
>
> For two years I have been thinking about this, slowly, carefully, patiently, and I have now decided to disband the Order, as I happen to be its Head. You can form other organizations and expect someone else. With that I am not concerned, nor with creating new cages, new decorations for those cages. My only concern is to set men absolutely, unconditionally free.[1]

THUS ON 2 AUGUST 1929, at the age of thirty-four, Jiddu Krishnamurti announced his great renunciation. He dissolved the Order of the Star, an international organization that had been created by the leaders of the Theosophical Society, who had heralded him as the vehicle of the coming Messiah. Soon afterward, Krishnamurti dissociated himself from the activities of the society, although it is not clear whether he ever formally resigned from it. He wished to break away completely from the influence of those who had tried to mold him and to confine him within a traditional messianic role.

Jiddu Krishnamurti was born on 11 May 1895, the eighth child of a Telugu Brahmin petty official, in Madanapalle, a small town in Andhra Pradesh, India. Before he was born, his mother, an unusual and sensitive woman, had a premonition that he was to be remarkable in some way. A renowned astrologer who cast the boy's horoscope was convinced that

Krishna—as he was called as a child—would be a very great man indeed. The astrologer held to this conviction even when, to his father's great disappointment, Krishna turned out to be vague and dreamy and made little progress in his studies. From early childhood he was inclined to be religious, although he also had an aptitude for mechanical things. Generous by nature, he would often return from school having given away his pencil or notebook to some poor child who could not afford to buy one. After his mother died, when he was ten, it became evident that he was endowed with clairvoyance and other special powers, for he often saw her after her death.

When Krishna's father, a Theosophist, retired, he moved with four of his sons to the Theosophical Society's headquarters at Adyar. It was there one day in 1909 that C. W. Leadbeater, a leader of the Theosophical Society who was considered a great occultist, discovered Krishna playing on the beach. Leadbeater was struck by Krishna's aura, which he said was the most beautiful he had ever seen and was without a particle of selfishness. He was convinced that Krishnamurti was to be the vehicle of the Lord Maitreya, the coming World Teacher. Annie Besant, president of the Society, shared this conviction.[2] In order to prepare the body and the mind of Krishnamurti to serve as the proper vehicle for Lord Maitreya, Leadbeater and Besant took over the protection, care, and education of Krishna and also of his beloved younger brother, Nitya.

In 1910, their father transferred the legal guardianship of Krishna and Nitya to Annie Besant. Later he changed his mind and initiated litigation that dragged on for several years. He brought charges of sexual misconduct against Leadbeater, although the boys denied there was any truth in these allegations. The case went through several courts in England and was finally thrown out by the Privy Council, but by this time the father had become completely estranged from his sons. Later, when Krishna and Nitya returned to India after an absence of ten years, they made a special point of meeting their father in the hope of being reconciled with him. According to Krishna's biographer, Mary Lutyens, when Krishna and Nitya paid their visit, they prostrated themselves and touched their father's feet with their foreheads, as is the custom in India. Their father immediately went and washed his feet, declaring them defiled by the touch of pariahs.

Between 1909 and 1929, during the most formative years of his life, from age fourteen to thirty-four, Krishnamurti was almost constantly under the influence of the Theosophical Society. Soon after Leadbeater discovered him, the Theosophists formed a special group called the Order of the Star in the East (later the Order of the Star) to facilitate the mission they foresaw for him. The group, composed of the most senior members of the inner circle of Theosophy and many others, was designed to prepare people to receive the new Messiah, or World Teacher, who was to inhabit Krishna's body and speak through him. They launched a journal called *The Herald of the Star,* later *The Star Review,* with Krishnamurti as its nominal editor. It contained accounts of many past lives of the reincarnating ego of Krishnamurti under the "Star name" Alcyone. In these accounts, many of the leaders of the Theosophical Society, under their star names, played significant roles.

Krishnamurti and his younger brother spent most of this period in England, France, and the United States, with only a few visits to India to attend some Theosophical Society conventions. Wherever they went they were always in the company of other Theosophists, a situation that both of them sometimes found stifling, particularly owing to the pious and holy atmosphere associated with Theosophical circles. As they entered mature adulthood in this milieu, which allowed them no independence of time, money, or accommodation and did not allow for any youthful exuberance, the brothers began to find Theosophy and its demands quite tiresome. Nitya, with a nature more robust than Krishna's, began to develop a loathing for the whole thing and longed to escape from it, but they were completely beholden to the Theosophical Society and its president, Annie Besant, not only for the care, protection, and livelihood they needed but also for the acceptance and honor they were accorded in the Theosophical circles.

There were compensations, of course, for this captivity. Krishna and Nitya were the most valued and prized persons in the esoteric circles of Theosophy. At a time when a great many English people treated Indians worse than their dogs, regarding them as members of a subhuman race, quite a few members of the Theosophical Society, particularly the ladies of the English nobility, risked a great deal for the favor of a look, a touch, or a letter from the coming Messiah or his brother. They longed to serve them with all their mind, body, and soul regardless of their husbands' disapproval of this rechanneling of time, money, and affection away from their own families. Lady Emily Lutyens can serve as an example. She was a daughter of the first Earl of Lytton, who had been a viceroy of India. From their first meeting in 1911 until her death in 1964, Lady Emily and Krishnamurti had the warmest of relationships with each other—often arousing suspicion and jealousy, though in Krishnamurti's eyes she was like his dear mother.

However trapped Krishna and Nitya felt, their cages were certainly handsomely gilded. Fairly typical of the stay of Krishna and his brother in the West was the year 1919, a year of great political and social turmoil in India:

> Krishna and Nitya spent the summer partly at Old Lodge, Ashdown Forest, where they had stayed in 1912, and partly at West Side House, Wimbledon, which Miss Dodge shared with Lady De La Warr. In this large house with its beautiful garden, including two tennis courts, the boys were surrounded with every imaginable luxury, for Miss Dodge lived in great style.
>
> In July the boys went to stay with Lady De La Warr at a house she had taken by the sea in Scotland, at Gullane in East Lothian on the outskirts of the famous championship golf course at Muirfield; playing golf every day, Krishna became a scratch player. According to Mrs. Jean Bindley, National Representative of the Order of the Star in the East for Scotland, Krishna won a championship at Gullane which, he told her, was the proudest moment of his life.
>
> They wore pale grey spats, had their shoes made at Lobb's (their feet were far too narrow for ready-made shoes), their suits at Myers and Mortimer, their shirts at Beale and Inman, bought their ties at Liberty's, and had their hair cut at Trumper's. . . .[3]

It could not have been easy to lay aside the golden chains! These experiences had a very strong influence on the two brothers and shaped Krishnamurti's attitudes toward the repetitive, dull, and uncreative jobs ordinary people have to engage in to make ends meet.

Even their many upper-class connections, however, could not get the boys into Cambridge or Oxford. Neither university was willing to accept the Indian boy who had been proclaimed as the coming Messiah, nor was either willing to accept his brother, when both boys had been accused of homosexuality by their own father. Krishna and Nitya then took the entrance examination for the University of London. Nitya succeeded and went to study for the bar, but Krishna never managed to pass the examination, even after repeated attempts. He was finally advised to abandon that course. This outcome could hardly fail to deepen his dependence on the Theosophical circles, and also his wish for independence from them.

Nitya even went so far as to dabble in some money-making schemes; he longed so much to be his own man. Krishna was by nature more in harmony than Nitya with the ideal image of a pure and high spirit that the Theosophical Society projected on him, and was not at all drawn to base pursuits and pleasures. It is interesting to note, however, that when in 1926 a film company offered Krishna five thousand dollars a week to play the title role in scenes from the life of the Buddha, the offer gave him "the satisfactory feeling that he could always earn his own living if the need arose."[4] This feeling that he could make his own way financially must have helped him come to the decision to break away from the Theosophical Society a few years later. Before that period he seems to have vacillated for several years between a wish to free himself from the Theosophists and a wish to live up to their expectations. Periodically, he exhorted himself to be more serious, to work harder at meditation, or to develop a sound philosophy of life.

It is difficult to determine the exact nature of the training that Krishnamurti received in the Theosophical circles. Most of what he learned seems to have been a result of an atmosphere of holiness around the Theosophical Society. He was supposed to associate with the right people and to think lofty thoughts, to stay clear of the various sins and forbidden pleasures of sexuality, alcohol, and meat, and to be constantly receptive to the messages—received while in the astral body rather than in the physical—from Lord Maitreya or from the Masters and other members of the occult hierarchy. These influences left a lasting mark on Krishnamurti even after he had completely broken away from Theosophy and the associated occult hierarchy of the Masters and Apostles. It is ironic, for example, that Krishnamurti, who among the contemporary spiritual teachers was perhaps the most self-consciously antitraditional, should have been so thoroughly a traditional Hindu in his otherworldly attitude toward food, money, and sex.

While he was associated with the Theosophists, Krishna was exposed to the scriptures of many religions of the world. Among the Eastern religions, he seems to have been particularly struck by the life and teachings of the Buddha. In the early 1920s, for example, he read aloud to his Theosophical associates from *The Buddha's Way of Virtue.* At least one passage sufficiently impressed him that he copied it out for Lady Emily: "All conquering and all knowing am I, detached, untainted, untrammeled, wholly freed by destruction of desire. Whom shall I call Teacher? Myself found the way."[5] The style of the book also seems to have found its way into some of Krishnamurti's own later utterances. Among the various books of the Bible, his favorite was the Song of Songs, as he told me himself.[6] Krishnamurti was a poet and a lover at heart, especially receptive to nature's beauty and to spiritual truth. Somewhat in the fashion of St. John of the Cross, the great Spanish mystic of the sixteenth century, he regarded the soul as feminine in relation to God, her Beloved, and spoke of the Beloved with feminine sensitivity: "I have been united with my Beloved, and my Beloved and I will wander together the face of the earth. . . . It is no good asking me who is the Beloved. Of what use is explanation? For you will not understand the Beloved until you are able to see Him in every animal, in every blade of grass, in every person that is suffering, in every individual."[7]

Although later in life Krishnamurti often claimed never to have read the Gospels, this is highly unlikely, given the general religious orientation of the Theosophists who brought him up and the constant parallels drawn—especially by Annie Besant—between his life and that of Jesus Christ. He either completely forgot that he had read the Gospels, as he seems to have forgotten many other important details of his life prior to the powerful transformational processes that he underwent in the second half of the 1920s, or he had a very strong residual reaction against them, perhaps owing to the comparisons made earlier between his own life and that of Jesus.

The latter possibility can by no means be eliminated. One often had the impression of such reactions in Krishnamurti, with the accompanying violence, as if in his old age he was still fighting the battles of his youth, trying to free himself from the shrinking walls of the prison he had felt himself to be in. It is particularly noteworthy that in his conversations and talks he constantly—and often without any relevance to the topic at hand—returned to harangues against the Brahmins and the Christians, the only two religious groups with whom he had any prolonged contact during his Theosophical phase. It was quite difficult indeed to discover any compassion, charity, or love in him when he happened to mention either of these two groups. A similar and very deep reaction, with the same sort of emotional vehemence, existed in him against teachers, gurus, hierarchies, and spiritual paths—in fact, against any sort of discipline or process. It was as if he had two distinct parts. His deep spiritual essence could soar without effort like an angel in the clear skies of Truth. When he spoke from that part, it was as if the heavenly choir were singing. The listener felt blessed and in total accord. Then there was the relatively superficial personality, formed by his personal history and his struggles to be free of spiritual tyranny. This part was born of conditioning and not of insight. When it took over, it was like the discordant note introduced by the uninvited thirteenth fairy in the tale of Sleeping Beauty.[8]

The two important personal influences in Krishnamurti's life were his mother and his younger brother, Nitya. After his mother died, for the rest of his life, he sought and found women who would mother him, take care of his ordinary needs and give him protective affection. More than any other aspect of the eternal feminine—lover, daughter, sister—he was drawn to that of mother. During the various painful spiritual processes that he underwent, which caused him immense physical and psychological suffering, he always wanted women—especially youthful and pure virgins—to be near him and look after him. Often when he was in pain or in a trance, he would refer to them as mother. As he himself often said, the religious mind is an innocent mind, and the mark of innocence is its vulnerability. All who were close to Krishnamurti and cared for him recognized this vulnerability and tried to protect him. For the women around him, the only permissible public role seems to have been that of mother.

J. Krishnamurti

In his private life, matters seem to have been quite different. Several years after Krishnamurti's death, Radha Rajagopal Sloss published details of a long-lasting affair in the 1930s and 1940s between Krishnamurti and Rosalind Rajagopal, her mother.[9] These revelations of the enormous gulf between the public stance and private life of Krishnamurti have caused many of Krishnamurti's admirers and devotees considerable discomfort. Not unexpectedly, there have been shocks of recognition, denials of the scandal, and attempts to whitewash Krishnamurti as well as to vilify Ms. Sloss. The ethical problem posed by the behavior of Krishnamurti cannot be ignored. Anyone who lives in society and makes moral proclamations about it is obliged to be forthright and consistent in word and deed. But some understanding might emerge through the recognition of the deep-seated transformation in Krishnamurti. It is possible to say, with Plotinus, that "this man has now become another and is neither himself nor his own" (*Enneads* 4.9, 10).

This radical split in Krishnamurti, which has already been remarked on earlier in this article in a different context, may be a form of "sacred schizophrenia," which is not unknown in mystical literature. There was Krishnamurti, the vessel of revelation from on high, but also Krishnamurti the man subject to his personal conditioning, desires, and needs. These two parts were distinct and of entirely different orders of importance and significance. From the higher part, the lower, more personal aspects may not be given much importance. They may not even be recognized or remembered or identified as belonging to the self. There are phases in mystical life in which a sharp discontinuity is emphasized between the spirit and the body-mind, or between "heaven" and "earth." It can be said that the ability to separate the inner or higher Self from the lower self is a mark of spiritual development. But the ability to bring the two parts together intentionally and with freedom is a sign of divine wisdom and incarnation.

There is a story in one of the *purāṇas* about the God-incarnate Kṛṣṇa, who lived a long time ago, as he lives now, with his consort Rādhā. They live by a riverbank as householders. One day they receive a message from Durvasa, a sage well known for his spiritual austerities and for his short temper. He is on the other side of the river with a thousand of his followers and wishes to be fed. As proper householders, Kṛṣṇa and Rādhā undertake to do their part in the maintenance of *Dharma* (order) by preparing food for the mendicants. When Rādhā is ready to carry the food across to the other shore, she sees the river in full spate and wonders how she might get across. Kṛṣṇa says, "Go to the river and say 'If Kṛṣṇa is eternally celibate, O River, subside!'" Rādhā knows well the power of uttering the true word, but is this a word of truth? Of all people, she ought to know about the amorous delights of Kṛṣṇa! She smiles to herself, goes to the river, and asks her to subside if Kṛṣṇa is eternally celibate. Somewhat to her surprise, the river subsides. She goes across and takes the food to the sage Durhasa, who is well pleased and eats heartily along with his disciples. When it is time for Rādhā to return, she again sees the river in full spate and asks the sage for help. The sage says, "Go to the river and say, 'If Durvasa is eternally fasting O River subside.'" Rādhā has just seen the sage eat; she smiles to herself, goes to the river, and asks her to subside if Durvasa is eternally fasting. The river subsides and Rādhā returns home to Kṛṣṇa, there to continue the delightful play of *Prakṛti*.

It is then that she realizes the truth of what Kṛṣṇa teaches Arjuna, "All action is verily done by *Prakṛti* [Nature] and the Self is not the doer. . . . He who is above the *gunas* [constituents of Prakṛti] does not abhor illumination nor impulsion to action nor delusion when they occur, nor longs for them when they cease" (*Bhagavad Gītā* 13.29; 14.22). In the case of Krishnamurti, the difficulty is not in the fact that he cherished feminine companionship and love. That is quite natural—which is to say that his action is perfectly consonant with enjoying the play of *Prakṛti*. The problem lies more in the limited view of human wholeness that led him and his followers to a denial of what is and of parts of themselves rather than to a celebration of and a freedom from *Prakṛti*.

Krishnamurti's relationships with men were different from his relationships with women. Men who were close to him could try to place themselves in the role of his younger brother, Nitya, and an occasional person succeeded for a while. By all accounts, these two brothers had been very close to each other. They were discovered together; they traveled together and lived together most of the time until Nitya's death in 1925. Krishnamurti himself described his relationship with his brother:

> Silence was a special delight to both of us, as then it was so easy to understand each other's thoughts and feelings. Occasional irritation with each other was by no means forgotten but it never went very far as it passed off in a few minutes, we used to sing comic songs or chant together as the occasion demanded. We both often liked the same cloud, the same tree and the same music. We had great fun in life, though we were of different temperaments. We somehow understood each other without effort.[10]

In accordance with the explicit instructions of the Masters in the occult world, the Theosophists had regarded Nitya as absolutely essential to the mission for which Krishnamurti was being prepared. In November 1925, Nitya was very sick in Ojai, California. It was one of the very few occasions when Krishna traveled without him. He had an unquestioning faith that the Masters would prolong Nitya's life, since his brother was necessary for his own life mission. During the sea voyage—on his way to India to attend a Theosophical Society congress—he received the news of Nitya's death. According to the person who was sharing the cabin with Krishna on this voyage,

> [the news] broke him completely; it did more—his entire philosophy of life—the implicit faith in the future as outlined by Mrs. Besant and Mr. Leadbeater, Nitya's vital part in it, all appeared shattered at that moment. . . . At night he would sob and moan and cry out for Nitya, sometimes in his native Telugu which in his waking consciousness he could not speak. Day after day we watched him, heart-broken, disillusioned. Day after day he seemed to change, gripping himself together in an effort to face life—but without Nitya. He was going through an inner revolution, finding new strength.[11]

By the time the voyage ended, Krishnamurti had found a different inner stand. He had been strengthened by the suffering caused by his brother's death:

> An old dream is dead and a new one is being born, as a flower that pushes through the solid earth. A new vision is coming into being and a new consciousness is being unfolded. . . . A new thrill and a new throb of the same life is being felt. A new strength born of suffering is pulsating in the veins and a new sympathy and understanding is being born out of the past suffering. A greater desire to see others suffer less and if they must suffer to see that they bear it nobly and come out of it without too many scars. I have wept but I do not want others to weep but if they do I now know what it means. . . . I have seen my brother. . . . On the physical plane we could be separated and now we are inseparable. . . . For my brother and I are one. As Krishnamurti I now have greater zeal, greater faith, greater sympathy and greater love for there is also in me the body, the Being, of Nityananda. . . . I know how to weep still, but that is human. I know now, with greater certainty than ever before, that there is real beauty in life, real happiness that cannot be shattered by any physical happening, a great strength which cannot be weakened by passing events, and a great love which is permanent, imperishable and unconquerable.[12]

In August 1922, Krishnamurti underwent a series of experiences which radically changed his life and the lives of those who were near him at that time. His own description of these experiences is most illuminating from the point of view of the processes involved and their authenticity.[13] A particularly significant experience commenced on 17 August. The following excerpt is from a report given by Krishnamurti himself, written down within two days of the events described:

> Since August 3rd, I meditated regularly for about thirty minutes every morning. I could, to my astonishment, concentrate with considerable ease, and

within a few days I began to see clearly where I had failed and where I was failing. Immediately I set about, consciously, to annihilate the wrong accumulations of the past years. With the same deliberation I set about to find out ways and means to achieve my aim. First I realized that I had to harmonize all my other bodies with the Buddhic plane [the highest plane of consciousness] and to bring about this happy combination I had to find out what my ego [in the Theosophical language this is more or less equivalent to *soul*] wanted on the Buddhic plane. To harmonize the various bodies I had to keep them vibrating at the same rate as the Buddhic, and to do this I had to find out what was the vital interest of the Buddhic. With ease which rather astonished me I found the main interest on the high plane was to serve the Lord Maitreya and the Masters. With that idea clear in my mind I had to direct and control the other bodies to act and to think the same as on the noble and spiritual plane. During that period of less than three weeks, I concentrated to keep in mind the image of Lord Maitreya throughout the entire day, and I found no difficulty in doing this. I found that I was getting calmer and more serene. My whole outlook on life was changed.

Then on the 17th August, I felt acute pain at the nape of my neck and I had to cut down my meditation to fifteen minutes. The pain instead of getting better as I had hoped grew worse. The climax was reached on the 19th. I could not think, nor was I able to do anything, and I was forced by friends here to retire to bed. Then I became almost unconscious, though I was well aware of what was happening around me. I came to myself at about noon each day. On the first day while I was in that state and more conscious of the things around me, I had the first most extraordinary experience. There was a man mending the road; that man was myself; the pickaxe he held was myself; the very stone which he was breaking up was a part of me; the tender blade of grass was my very being, and the tree beside the man was myself. . . . I was in everything, or rather everything was in me, inanimate and animate, the mountain, the worm, and all breathing things. . . .

The morning of the next day . . . [m]y head was pretty bad and the top part felt as though many needles were being driven in. . . . When I had sat thus [cross-legged in the meditation posture] for some time, I felt myself going out of my body, I saw myself sitting down with the delicate tender leaves of the tree over me. I was facing the east. In front of me was my body and over my head I saw the Star, bright and clear. Then I could feel the vibrations of the Lord Buddha; I beheld Lord Maitreya and Master K. H. [Koot Hoomi], I was so happy, calm and at peace. I could still see my body and I was hovering near it. There was such profound calmness both in the air and within myself, the calmness of the bottom of a deep unfathomable lake. Like the lake, I felt my physical body, with its mind and emotions, could be ruffled on the surface but nothing, nay nothing, could disturb the calmness of my soul. The Presence of the mighty Beings were with me for some time and then They were gone. I was supremely happy, for I had seen. Nothing could ever be the same.

> I have drunk at the clear and pure waters at the source of the fountain of life and my thirst was appeased. Never more could I be thirsty, never more could I be in utter darkness. I have seen the Light. I have touched compassion which heals all sorrow and suffering; it is not for myself, but for the world. I have stood on the mountain top and gazed at the mighty Beings. . . . The fountain of truth has been revealed to me and the darkness has been dispersed. Love in all its glory has intoxicated my heart; my heart can never be closed. I have drunk at the fountain of Joy and eternal Beauty. I am God-intoxicated.[14]

Krishnamurti's experience was so powerful that even his biographer, writing more than fifty years later, decided that after this point in his life story she would refer to him simply as K, precisely as he did himself, referring to himself in the third person. (While addressing him, his friends and followers called him *Krishnaji*, the respectful suffix *-ji* being added in the traditional Indian manner.) Since that time in August 1922, when there began the explicit process of what can only be called the *alchemical transformation* of K's planetary body (including the emotions and the mind), he had many periods of intense physical pain and suffering, as his body seems to have been reconstituted, cell by cell, as it seems, by forces immeasurably higher than himself. He himself referred to this as "the process," and he experienced it off and on even into old age in a mild form, as is clear from the many entries in his *Notebook*, written in 1961–62.

Here is his own description of it, given in 1922: "All the time, I have a violent pain in my head & the nape of my neck & can't bear the touch of anyone. Also during that time, I become very sensitive, can't bear a sound, however small it may be. . . ."[15] His brother had concluded at that time that what K was experiencing was an awakening of *kuṇḍalinī*—which, according to the occultists, is coiled-up cosmic energy at the base of the spine that can, by proper practices and right living, be aroused and bring about a spiritual transformation of the human being. About two years later, this *process* came to a climax, which he described to Lady Emily:

> Last 10 days, it has been really strenuous, my spine & neck have been going very strong and day before yesterday, the 27th [February, 1922] I had an extraordinary evening. Whatever it is, the force or whatever one calls the bally thing, came up my spine, up to the nape of my neck, then it separated into two, one going to the right and the other to the left of my head till they met between the two eyes, just above my nose. There was a kind of flame and I saw the Lord & the Master. It was a tremendous night. Of course, the whole thing was painful, in the extreme.[16]

It is clear that K himself never doubted that all this pain was necessary and that all his experiences were genuine. It does not seem to have even occurred to him to consult a doctor or to take pain-relieving drugs. Some people who had known him for a very long time had no doubt that he was the *Sacrifice* who must relinquish any concern for himself or for his pleasure or pain, and that he had to respond to what was demanded of him, like the suffering servant.

As his experience deepened, and as he became more and more aware of the egotistic purposes to which the various stages of "initiation" and the various official positions within the Theosophical circles could be put, he became more and more disenchanted with the entire Theosophical structure and gradually with all forms that allow fear and temptation to corrupt the human heart. It was his very great respect for Annie Besant and his sense of gratitude that made him hesitate to debunk the Masters, the occult hierarchy, and the superstructure of the Theosophical Society publicly, but his skepticism became more and more evident to the people close to him, causing more and more pain to the leaders of the Society. Already in 1928, at one of the meetings in Holland, he had warned people against becoming his disciples:

> I say again that I have no disciples. Everyone of you is a disciple of the Truth if you understand the Truth and do not follow individuals. . . . The only manner of attaining Truth [is] to become disciples of the Truth itself without a mediator. . . . Truth does not give hope; it gives understanding. . . . I refuse to be your crutch. I am not going to be brought into a cage for your worship. . . . I am not concerned with societies, with religions, with dogmas, but I am concerned with life because I am Life.[17]

He could not for very long continue with the sort of double life he had been leading for the previous five years—progressively disillusioned with all forms, and in particular with those of the Theosophical Society—but he did not want to hurt anyone, especially Mrs. Besant, whom he always revered as his mother. Finally, on 2 August 1929, he dissolved the Order of the Star with the memorable speech in which he declared that "Truth is a pathless land . . . ," a part of which was quoted in the beginning of this essay.

Krishnamurti's words and actions shook the Theosophical Society to its core and caused a great split, from which it has not yet recovered. Many people, including Mrs. Besant, remained faithful to K, however hard they found it to understand and to accept him. Leadbeater declared that "the Coming has gone wrong," and went his own way. After the death of Mrs. Besant in September 1933, K's connection with the Theosophical Society was completely broken, until nearly fifty years later, when, in January 1983, on the invitation of Mrs. Radha Burnier, the president of the Society, K planted a tree in the compound of the Society headquarters in Adyar.

Krishnamurti's years of physical agony culminated in 1932 at Ojai, California. When he reached a new level of consciousness, he seems to have almost entirely lost a memory of his life before that period. It was almost physically like a *new birth* for him. Now this Brahmin boy was a *dvija, a twice born,* not only in hope and tradition but in fact. Having entered the Immensity (in Sanskrit, *Brahman*)—"I am that full flame which is the glory of life," as he said—he is neither a Brahmin nor anyone else in particular. For nearly the last sixty years of his life, he traveled all over the globe, constantly trying to express, with enormous passion and suffering, the same inexpressible Truth in different words. He suffered at the incomprehension of his hearers but went on teaching. As he himself said, a flower does not decide to give out perfume; it is in its very nature to do so. That is what makes it a flower! Just as a flower gives out fragrance, Krishnamurti taught. He could not help it.

He kept traveling and teaching, under an inner compulsion, until his death in February 1986. It was as if he was directed by some higher force and had no personal choice. Just ten days before his death, at the age of nearly ninety-one, he had a tape recording made of something he wanted to say:

> I was telling them this morning—for seventy years that super-energy—no—that immense energy, immense intelligence, has been using this body. I don't think people realize what tremendous energy and intelligence went through this body—there's a twelve-cylinder engine. And for seventy years—was a pretty long time—and now the body can't stand any more. Nobody, unless the body has been prepared, very carefully, protected and so on—nobody can understand what went through this body. Nobody. Don't anybody pretend. Nobody. I repeat this: nobody amongst us or the public, know what went on. I know they don't. And now after seventy years it has come to an end. Not that that intelligence and energy—it's somewhat here, every day, and especially at night. And after seventy years the body can't stand it—can't stand any more. It can't. The Indians have a lot of damned superstitions about this—that you will and the body goes—and all that kind of nonsense. You won't find another body like this, or that supreme intelligence, operating in a body for many hundred years. You won't see it again. When he goes, it goes. There is no consciousness left behind of *that* consciousness, of *that* state. They'll all pretend or try to imagine they can get into touch with that. Perhaps they will somewhat if they live the teachings. But nobody has done it. Nobody. And so that's that.[18]

What is K's teaching? It is a teaching that demands a mutation of the human being into another dimension, a dimension of being that is not of thought. This spiritual dimension is not created by the mind, nor is it an acquisition or an achievement of any sort. This dimension is manifested precisely when there is no center of ambition in the self which wishes possessions or struggles for achievement. It is the dimension of insight, a special sort of intelligence that can express itself through thought but has its origin beyond thought and is not conditioned by thought or brought about by it. Thought operates in time—in the past or in the future, in memory, or in anticipation. Within the dimension of time, thought can be good, orderly, coherent, and logical, or it can be incoherent and irrational. Rational and coherent thought can lead to knowledge that can be useful, as scientific and technological knowledge are useful. But however orderly this thought is, however vast the knowledge, it cannot offer the insight requisite for solving fundamental human problems. Only in the awakening of the intelligence which is beyond thought and beyond time can the knots of ignorance, compulsion, and repetition be dissolved.

It is extremely difficult to say anything about insight that exists in its fullness only as it comes into being. How can what is in flight be fixed in a picture, a poem, or some other description, unless the articulation made in a moment of insight triggers an internal reordering which permits a similarly intense and clear insight in the listener or the reader? The moment it is given expression, in speaking or in writing, it operates in the domain of thought, time, and knowledge. An insight that has been expressed is something that one knows of and thinks about, to which one reacts or around which one reasons. True action takes place only in the moment of the awakening of insight. Otherwise action is in fact a reaction to the memory of insight, whether it is one's own insight or someone else's.

The moment of insight is *in* time but it is not *of* time. It is a timeless moment, a point of intersection of eternity and time. Eternity is not merely an extension of time without end. It is a dimension of being altogether different from time. As Krishnamurti has said, "The eternal is not everlasting." The insight that arises from beyond thought carries with it a freshness and an innocence that are the chief characteristics of the religious mind. Listening to Krishnamurti from an external perspective, examining and analyzing his teaching, one might say that he had been saying the same thing for decades. It may even be true as far as the words and the formulations are concerned; one had heard them before. But for Krishnamurti speaking and teaching were acts of love. The accompanying words and actions may have been the same time after time, but each time there was a freshness of insight, an abundance of passion, and an urgency of expression. His timeless insight was poured out of him with love and compassion for those around him.

As he became exhausted with this outpouring, sometimes a great sadness came over him. Once, not long before his death, he said to me, with his eyes full of sorrow, "No one understands what I have been saying for the last sixty years. No one." This was not directed at anyone in particular, not even at me, though no doubt I too had added to K's sorrow by not understanding.

Soon his cup was filled again and he was ready to speak to anyone who would listen. He neither spoke because he liked to, nor could he stop because he would like to; he did what he had to do. In the choiceless awareness that he had, he saw that there was only one thing that he had to do, and he did it.

Freedom exists in that choiceless awareness and in the accompanying action: freedom from fear, from memory and anticipation, from time and all the things of time. This freedom is a freedom from the known, for it is the known that is the source of fear, not the unknown. What is truly unknown, and allowed to be unknown, cannot cause fear. It is the imagined continuation or termination of what is known that produces fear. It is the clinging to what one knows and to the center from which one knows that keeps one bound by time and by the ego. If one sees that these keep one in bondage and sorrow, then the need for a complete reorientation and a total revolution asserts itself. What is needed is a radical break from all that leads to bondage and suffering. What is required is freedom from the tyranny of one's own ego—from the tyranny of all that one has been taught, and the tyranny of one's own inclinations. What is necessary is freedom from authority—from external authority, of course, but also from the internal authority of oneself. Otherwise, future moments are always conditioned by what one knew or experienced in the past. Freedom from the grooves created by one's own past knowledge and experience is what can permit one to be fresh in the new moment and not always reacting through prejudice and conditioning.

For Krishnamurti *thought* leads to *fragmentation* and subsequently to fear and sorrow, just as for the Buddha *tanha* (selfish craving) leads to *dukkha* (sorrow), or for the Vedantist *ignorance* leads to *illusion*. In all of these teachings, *total attention* in the state of meditation is required to dissolve sorrow, fear, and illusion in the clear light of Intelligence and Truth. The meditative mind, open, whole, and quiet is the religious mind. This religious mind is natural, and ultimately this state of mind is reached by effortless being—just as an oak tree is the natural unfolding of an acorn. Patañjali's *Yoga Sūtra*, in the final chapter on Enlightenment puts it quite simply: "Any transformation into a new state of being is the result of fullness of Nature unfolding inherent potential" (4:2).

The difficulty comes with the need for the training of this total attention. It is for this that the Eightfold Path of the Buddha and the practices recommended in the earlier chapters of the *Yoga Sūtra* exist. Krishnamurti himself provided an excellent example of right living, right thinking, right posture, and other preliminary and necessary practices. He no doubt conveyed some of this to his followers, but he had a strange insistence about the futility and harmfulness of practices, disciplines, and teachings, and certainly of teachers and gurus. In his presence it was easy to forget that although consummate musicians do play without effort, as if the music plays itself through them, this ease is the fruit of long and hard struggle with the scales and exercises.

In a conversation in Madras in January 1983, Krishnamurti said to me that the Intelligence beyond thought is just there, like the air, and that it does not need to be created by discipline or effort. "All one needs to do is to open the window," he said. But if one sees that the windows are painted shut and need a lot of scraping before they can be opened, how does one scrape? When asked about the difficulty of sustaining attention, K replied that it is only inattention that fluctuates. That is true; but it still disturbs the mind. If weeds are choking a garden, no amount of water and sunshine will suffice to produce beautiful flowers. To quote the *Yoga Sūtra* again, "The apparent causes of a transformation do not in fact bring it about. They merely remove the obstacles to natural growth, as a farmer clears the ground for his crops" (4:3).

As time went on, even though there was a change in the phrases and words that K used, he always tried to bring us back to look at ourselves radically and totally. That look, that passionate insight, alone can bring about the transformation. Toward the end of his life, he did occasionally refer to his insights and ideas as "this teaching," and to himself as a "teacher." In a talk to some teachers in India he said "I am your teacher, not your guru."[19] This was quite a shift for him, although in his continued reaction against authority he forgot that *guru* is just a Sanskrit word for teacher. In any case, it can be said with certainty that anyone who met Krishnamurti with an open mind came away convinced that he had been in the presence of a very great man, a beacon of light. One could not help loving him and recognizing in him a free man. He was a distant and profound musician of the spirit to whom we need to listen:

> Silence has many qualities. . . . There is the silence between two noises, the silence between two notes, the widening silence between two thoughts. There is that peculiar quiet pervading silence that comes on an evening in the country, there is the silence through which you hear the bark of a dog in the distance or the whistle of a train as it comes up a steep grade; the silence of a house when everybody has gone to sleep, and the peculiar emphasis when you wake up in the middle of the night and listen to an owl hooting in the valley. . . . there is the silence of the mind which is never touched by any noise,

any thought or by the passing wind of experience. It is the silence which is innocent, and so endless. When there is silence of the mind, action springs from it, and this action does not cause confusion or misery. . . . The meditative mind flows in this silence, and love is the way of this mind. In this silence there is bliss and laughter.

Notes

1. Quoted in Mary Lutyens, *Krishnamurti: The Years of Awakening,* 272–75.

2. According to the Theosophists, Lord Maitreya, a World Teacher, had twice taken possession of a human body in order to bring a new teaching during a world crisis: once as Kṛṣṇa in the fourth century B.C.E. and then as Jesus Christ. They expected that he would come again in a human form to give a new teaching to the world. It should be noted that Maitreya is not the Buddha, who is a still higher spiritual entity in the Theosophical hierarchy; however, he is a Bodhisattva, which is to say a future Buddha.

3. Lutyens, *Krishnamurti: Awakening,* 104–7.

4. Ibid., 237.

5. Ibid., 120.

6. See Ravi Ravindra, "The Mill and the Mill-Pond: A Twenty-year Conversation with J. Krishnamurti," *The American Theosophist* 74 (1986) 298–303.

7. Quoted in Lutyens, *Krishnamurti: Awakening,* 250.

8. I was told in 1982 by Mrs. Dora Kunz, who was at that time the president of the Theosophical Society in America and who had known Krishnamurti since 1922 and who herself was a student of Leadbeater for a few years, that Krishnamurti felt chagrined with and betrayed by Leadbeater, who, it appeared to Krishnamurti, was refusing to see him while spending time with other, less important people. Krishnamurti seems to have been too occupied with his own deep searchings and the illness of his brother Nitya to realize that Leadbeater himself was very sick; he had had a few heart attacks and needed to save his energy by not exposing himself to Krishnamurti's rather violent rejection of anything told to him at that time. It is quite possible that the disappointment caused in Krishnamurti by his father's "betrayal" of him and later by what he perceived as this surrogate father's rejection of him, is the psychological cause of his deep reaction not only against Brahmins and Christians but also against all authority figures—teachers, gurus, Masters, and God.

9. See Radha Rajagopal Sloss, *Lives in the Shadow with J. Krishnamurti.*

10. Quoted in Lutyens, *Krishnamurti: Awakening,* 220.

11. Lutyens, *Krishnamurti: Awakening,* 220. It appears that with the death of Nitya also died that part of Krishnamurti which could be involved in a *personal* relationship with anyone.

12. Ibid., 220–21.

13. Full details of these experiences are given in Lutyens, *Krishnamurti: Awakening,* 152–88. The brief excerpts quoted here are taken from that book.

14. Lutyens, *Krishnamurti: Awakening,* 158–60.

15. Ibid., 165.

16. Ibid., 186.
17. Ibid., 261–62.
18. Quoted in M. Lutyens, *The Life and Death of Krishnamurti*, 206.
19. Pupul Jayakar and Sunanda Patwardhan, eds., *Within the Mind*, 148.

Bibliography

Sources

There are many books by and about J. Krishnamurti. His books are, in general, transcripts of the talks given by him at various places and to diverse groups. What follows is a representative selection of books about his life and thought. Many audio and video tapes of these talks are available from the Krishnamurti Foundation of America, Ojai, California.

Krishnamurti, Jiddu. *The Awakening of Intelligence.* New York: Harper & Row, 1973. This volume contains several talks of Krishnamurti, some small-group dialogues, and some individual conversations with him.

——. *Krishnamurti's Notebook.* New York: Harper & Row, 1976. A record of Krishnamurti's perceptions and states of consciousness for a period of six months, commencing on 18 June 1961.

——. *Krishnamurti to Himself—His Last Journal.* San Francisco: Harper & Row, 1987. This is the written record of Krishnamurti's last journal, which he himself dictated into a tape recorder, showing his concerns and very keen observation of nature.

——. *The Collected Works of J. Krishnamurti.* Dubuque, Ia.: Kendall/Hunt Publications, 1991–92. Many volumes are planned, at least seventeen have already been published containing his talks and discussions from 1933 to 1967.

Lutyens, Mary, ed. *The Penguin Krishnamurti Reader.* Harmondsworth, Middlesex, England: Penguin Books, 1970. A selection from three of Krishnamurti's books, namely, *The First and the Last Freedom, Life Ahead,* and *This Matter of Culture.*

Studies

Jayakar, Pupul. *Krishnamurti, A Biography.* New Delhi: Penguin Books, 1986. Written by a longtime devotee of Krishnamurti, this biography gives many details of Krishnamurti's visits in India, especially during 1947–49.

——, and Sunanda Patwardhan, eds. *Within the Mind: On J. Krishnamurti.* Madras: Krishnamurti Foundation of India, 1982. A collection of some articles about Krishnamurti's ideas, two of his talks, and some discussions with him. There is a "Letter to J. Krishnamurti" by the present author also in this collection.

Lutyens, Mary. *Krishnamurti: The Years of Awakening.* New York: Farrar, Straus & Giroux, 1975. This is a biography of Krishnamurti from his birth in 1895 to the year 1933, when he completely broke away from the Theosophical Society. The author's mother, Lady Emily Lutyens, was the chief confidante of Krishnamurti during most of this period, and many private letters by Krishnamurti to her are included in this volume.

——. *Krishnamurti: The Open Door.* New York: Farrar, Straus & Giroux, 1986. This is the last volume in the biography covering the period from 1980 to his death in February 1986.

——. *Krishnamurti: The Years of Fulfillment.* New York: Farrar, Straus & Giroux, 1983. This volume brings the story of Krishnamurti's life to 1980.

——. *The Life and Death of Krishnamurti.* London: John Murray Publishers, 1990. This volume is essentially a summary of all the biographical information about Krishnamurti contained in the above three books, with some additional material.

Ravindra, Ravi. "The Mill and the Mill-Pond: A Twenty-Year Conversation with J. Krishnamurti." *The American Theosophist* 74 (1986) 298–303. An affectionate and very brief personal recounting by the present author of a few of his meetings with Krishnamurti. This piece is included in R. Ravindra, *Krishnamurti: Two Birds on One Tree* (Wheaton, Ill.: Quest Books, 1995).

Sloss, Radha Rajagopal. *Lives in the Shadow with J. Krishnamurti.* London: Bloomsbury, 1991. This volume details a twenty-five year love affair between Krishnamurti and Rosalind Rajagopal, as witnessed, understood, and interpreted by Rosalind's daughter, who grew up with Krishnamurti very much a member of the household.

18

The Spiritual Descent of the Divine: The Life Story of Swāmi Sivānanda

DAVID M. MILLER

For whenever of righteousness
A languishing appears, son of Bharata,
A rising up of unrighteousness
Then I send myself forth.

For protection of the good,
And for destruction of evil-doers,
To make firm footing for righteousness
I come into being age after age.
(*Bhagavad Gītā* 4.7–8)

THE PRINCIPAL THEORETICAL TOOL for understanding medieval Hindu hagiographies, or for interpreting other Hindu hagiographies, including those written in recent times is the incarnation of the Divine (*avatāra*), a belief that is stated in its classical form in *Bhagavad Gītā* 4.7–8. The historical figures of Indian philosophical literature are turned into the folk heroes of Hindu hagiography. Each becomes a slightly altered version of the paradigm of the incarnation of the Divine, who takes on human form in order to destroy unrighteousness and evil and to restore righteousness and goodness. And, indeed, the myth of the incarnation or spiritual descent of the Divine, like the *samsaric* cosmos into which the incarnation is born, repeats itself into infinity.

For example, Śaṅkara (788–820), the founder of the Advaita Vedānta, is depicted as an incarnation of Śiva born to restore righteousness (*dharma*) over against the distortions of the true faith that had enveloped Hindu society under the Buddhists and under corrupt forms of Hinduism, such as the Kapālikas. I should note here that in Hindu literature the Buddha is viewed as an incarnation of Viṣṇu, born to lead astray the weak-hearted and the unfaithful. But the list of incarnations of the Divine is not limited to

Śaṅkara or the Buddha. As Phillis Granoff notes, the incarnation theory is "open-ended."[1] Rāmānuja (1017–1137), the historical founder of the Viśiṣṭādvaita Vedānta, is held to be as incarnation of Viṣṇu: Madhva (1199–1278), the key philosopher of the Dvaita Vedānta, is said, by his followers, to be an incarnation of the Vedic god Vāyu. Caitanya (1486–1535), who wrote only a few verses in Sanskrit, but whose religious innovations had a major impact on Hindu tradition in Bengal and Orissa, is believed to be an incarnation of the unity of Kṛṣṇa and Rādhā, Kṛṣṇa's human lover, who was an incarnation of the goddess Lakṣmi, the wife of Viṣṇu. And so the list goes on and on, in age after age: incarnations of the Divine take human form to reestablish true or eternal religion, *sanātana dharma*.

In the contemporary period, Rāmakrishna (1836–1886), who said on his deathbed that "He who was Rāma and Kṛṣṇa is now Rāmakrishna" and who had numerous visions of Hindu deities—more often the goddess Kālī—proclaimed that all religions were one in essence. Living for a time as a Christian, Rāmakrishna had a vision of Jesus, who "entered into" Rāmakrishna's body. Similarly, Rāmakrishna lived for a time as a Muslim and had a vision of Muhammad, who like Jesus entered into his body. Both experiences assert the oneness of all religions, at least at the mystical level. For the writers of Rāmakrishna's hagiography the foe to be defeated, therefore, was not just within India; rather, the foe was all religious dogmatism that asserted uniqueness, particularism, and hence the separation of religious traditions—a view, according to many Hindu writers, characteristic of much of Christianity and Islam.

Thus, anyone who reads Hindu hagiographical literature, whether it be Vidyāraṇya's *Śaṅkaradigvijaya* (1300) or Christopher Isherwood's *Rāmakrishna and his Disciples* (1959), encounters, in the first several pages or in the first chapter, the paradigm of the incarnation theory in narrative form, and the "life story" of the guru is retold from that basic premise of faith. So-called historical facts become problematic, at least for the scholarly reader of Hindu hagiography. But for the vast majority of readers who follow one guru or another, what we scholars label as "fiction" may to the majority be "fact" not to be doubted anymore than the average Christian doubts the incarnation of God as the man Jesus. I turn now to the life story of Swāmi Sivānanda Sarasvati (1887–1963) as an excellent example of the process of writing contemporary Hindu hagiography, the purpose of which is not only to spiritualize an extraordinary human life but to universalize that life story, providing a Hindu model of the spiritual life for all those who are "religious seekers" to emulate whether they live in the East or in the West.

Swāmi Sivānanda Sarasvati's teachings and his monastic/lay movement (The Divine Life Society) are known throughout India and in many parts of

North America, Europe, and Africa, although, after taking monastic vows (*sannyāsa*), Sivānanda remained, for the most part, at Rishikesh, a small village in northern India along the Ganges River. G. S. Ghurye notes that Swāmi Sivānanda was given the honorific title *Paramahaṃsa*, and he places him alongside Śaṅkara and Rāmakrishna, who also hold that title. Agehananda Bharati claims that Swāmi Sivānanda, as a "latter-day imitator" of Swāmi Vivekānanda, had a greater mass appeal in India than either Ramaṇa Maharishi or Śrī Aurobindo.[2]

Swāmi Sivānanda's fame has been spread in the West by his ascetic disciples whom he sent out of India several years before his death in 1963. A list of his most prominent disciples might include Swāmi Chidānanda and Swāmi Krishnānanda of the Rishikesh monastic center; Swāmi Chinmayananda (Bombay); Swāmi Satchidānanda (Buckingham, Virginia); Swāmi Jyotirmayānanda (Miami); Swāmi Vishnudevānanda (Montreal); Swāmi Venkatesānanda (Mauritius); Swāmi Sahajānanda (Durban, South Africa); and Swāmi Hridayānanda (Paris). In 1978, the headquarters at Rishikesh housed nearly three hundred people, of whom approximately eighty were ascetic-renouncers. In addition to religious duties, the residents ran a hospital with an extensive outpatient clinic, three small medical dispensaries, a publishing house and printing press, and an academy for the study of Indian philosophy, which included a first-rate library. The Divine Life Society, the missionary arm of the Sivānanda movement, has numerous branches throughout India and in the West, making it one of the largest Hindu religious institutions of its kind, second only to the Rāmakrishna monastery and mission.[3]

In the case of Swāmi Sivānanda Sarasvati, the historian of religion has abundant data on which to base a life history of Sivānanda after he had taken monastic vows and after he had been recognized as one of India's most renowned gurus. One hundred and twenty biographical works, of varying quality, have been written about him, but these "studies" of the life of Swāmi Sivānanda are dependent primarily on two books that serve as the basic sources for the life of Sivānanda: (1) *The Autobiography of Swāmi Sivānanda*, written by Sivānanda in 1958 only five years before his death; (2) *Gurudev Sivānanda*, published in 1960 by Swāmi Venkatesānanda, who was one of Sivānanda's closest disciples and, at times, his personal secretary.

Sivānanda's autobiography is a short, tightly written work of seventy-two pages, and, much to the frustration of his closest disciples, it adds little to what had been known about his early years from other sources. In his introduction to the *Autobiography*, Swāmi Sadānanda Sarasvati notes:

> When I received the manuscripts bearing the title: *The Autobiography of Swāmi Sivānanda*, I jumped with joy because I expected . . . that there was a

chance to know many of the details of Master's life, which in spite of my fairly long stay with him (running into many years) I was unable to learn either from him or any one else. But how great was my surprise—not to say disappointment—when I found I could not obtain even a glimpse of what my mind was curious to know. (i)

Swāmi Venkatesānanda's monumental tome, totaling 576 pages, beautifully paints the details of Sivānanda's early life, using the brush of a true devotee who holds his guru to be an incarnation of the Divine as announced in the *Bhagavad Gītā*. Characteristic of the universalistic thrust of modern Hinduism, Venkatesānanda places Sivānanda alongside the Buddha and Jesus Christ as an incarnation of the Godhead. Venkatesānanda declares:

> Gurdev's place in the history of the world is that of a Buddha or a Jesus. Historians will regard him as not only the greatest among modern religious leaders but also as an incarnate Divine Power that was able to work a miracle in the heart of Man. Buddha Himself was a King; so his religion soon earned royal patronage. Lord Jesus and His immediate followers won mass adherence to his religion by spectacular martyrdom. The twentieth century is an era of democracy. Gurudev's religion has to appeal to the heart of every individual, not merely the king, in order to spread far and wide. . . . Moreover, the twentieth century is an age of science, and people would not subscribe to a doctrine just because someone gave up his life for it—they have to be convinced that it is the Truth, that it is useful and that it is practical. . . . It is this superhuman factor that ranks Gurudev, in the mind of a seeker after Truth, with great incarnations of the Lord Himself, like Rama and Krishna (*Gurudev Sivānanda*, xxix–xi).

But Venkatesānanda's words are in opposition to Sivānanda's intended self-image. In his *Autobiography* Sivānanda angrily put down any attempt to identify him as an incarnation of the Godhead:

> I had no ambition to become world famous. . . . I never attempted to be Guru to anyone.
>
> I am not pleased when people call me "Sat Guru" or "avatar." I am dead against Gurudom. That is a great obstacle and has caused the downfall of great men in the spiritual path. Gurudom is a menace to society. . . . In 1933 the publishers in Madras wrote articles on my life and mentioned me as an "avatar." Immediately I gave a reply which explains the attitude I have always maintained: "Kindly remove all 'Krishna Avatar' and 'Bhagawan' business." (*Autobiography*, 30, 33)

Keeping in mind the tension between the "facts" of Sivānanda's life, as recorded in his autobiography, and the retelling of that story by one of his closest disciples, I shall juxtapose the two sources in order to illustrate the writing of a contemporary Hindu hagiography that seeks to appeal to the "modern" reader, whether he/she be of Hindu or of other religious background. This account will cover Sivānanda's life from his birth in 1887 to 1931. I shall first turn to Sivānanda's meager account of his ancestry, birth, and early childhood, and then add Venkatesānanda's richer, more detailed portrait of the same period.

The Divine Child

Sivānanda begins his life story by introducing a distant relative on his father's side, Śrī Appayya Dikshitar, a sixteenth-century Sanskrit scholar who, according to Sivānanada, was "one of the greatest names in the annals of South India." In fact, Sivānanda continues: "In almost all branches of Sanskrit literature—poetry, rhetoric, philosophy—he was peerless, not only among his contemporaries but even among scholars several decades before and after him" (*Autobiography*, 1–2). Indeed, Sivānanda claims that Appayya Dikshitar's fame was such that he "is considered to be an Avatara or incarnation of Lord Shiva" (ibid., 3).

Although Sivānanda gives the reader an enthusiastic account of the life of Appayya Dikshitar, he writes little about his father, P. S. Vengu Iyer, a revenue official (Tahsildar) for the Raja of a large estate near Pattamadai, Madras (Tamil Nadu), at the southern tip of India. He notes only that his father was "a virtuous and pure soul, a Shiva devotee and a Jnani," who "was worshipped by the Rajah Saheb of Ettiapuram and by the public at large . . . as a Mahatma, a Maha Purusha" (*Autobiography*, 4). Sivānanda provides no description of his mother, Pārvati Ammāl, and of his birth he states simply: "I was born to Śrīmati Pārvati Ammāl and P. S. Vengu Iyer their third son, on Thursday 8th September, 1887 at sunrise when the star Bharani was in ascendance" (ibid.). He was named Kuppuswāmy, a name that Venkatesānanda uses for Swāmi Sivānanda until he takes initiation into monastic orders at the age of thirty-six.

After recording this simple summary of the facts of his birth, Sivānanda jumps sixteen years to 1903, when he graduated from the Raja's high school on the Ettiapuram estate. The frustration expressed by Swāmi Sadānanda, noted above, must be shared by every reader of the *Autobiography*; we would like to know much more about the early childhood of a man whose fame as an adult has spread throughout India and the world. In Venkatesānanda's account of Sivānanda's birth and early childhood, however, a wholly different picture is revealed, which begins with the classic medieval paradigm of the incarnation of the Divine:

Sivānanda as a Young Ascetic
(Painting in the hospital out-patient clinic that he founded)

> The day of great rejoicing drew near, A divine delight filled the hearts of pious and Godly couple in Pattamadai. . . . They had supernatural experiences and visions. . . . For, to them had been allotted the good fortune of fathering and mothering a son who was soon to prove that he was an incarnation of God Himself with a prophetic mission. God-fearing as the Mother (Parvathy) already was, her devotion to God and His image in her own dear Lord, Sri Vengu Iyer, increased a thousand-fold the moment she realised that to her the Almighty had assigned the task of giving birth to a worthy son. She was anxious still more that during the period preceding the Day on which she would feast her eyes on the divine form, she should ensure that her thoughts were always holy and lofty. She would, therefore, pore over holy books during her leisure hours, and sing God's name with intense faith and devotion. . . . With unruffled mind, calm and peaceful, she would cheerfully go about her duties, always fervently praying that she should be blessed with a good son—Krishna was her ideal child. (*Gurudev Sivānanda,* 3–4)

Medieval as well as contemporary authors of Hindu hagiographies structure their birth stories around visions, dreams, and revelations of the pious couple whom God has chosen in his wisdom as the parents to whom He (or some saintly soul in his heavenly court) will be born. What is interesting is that Venkatesānanda gives these visions, in the main, to Sivānanda's mother Pārvati Ammāl, whose name Sivānanda records in his *Autobiography* without further comment. Equally interesting is that Venkatesānanda pictures this pious mother as a devotee of Kṛṣṇa, when elsewhere he holds Sivānanda to be an incarnation of Śiva, supporting Sivānanda's emphasis on the Śaiva lineage of his father, which he had traced back to Appayya Dikshitar. That a wife might select a different deity (*iṣṭadevata*) from that of her husband is, as I have observed in India, not uncommon in Hindu family life, and often this is the situation depicted in Hindu hagiographies.

Having set the stage for the birth of the divine child, Venkatesānanda describes the auspicious day on which Kuppuswāmy-Sivānanda was born. Again his account draws on hagiographical birth motifs found in other Indian hagiographies, perhaps going back to the birth stories of Gautama, the Buddha.

> The day that was to usher into the world this glorious child who was none other than the Lord himself, arrived. It was the 8th of September, 1887. The day was highly auspicious. There was a supernatural glow in the mother's face. Her heart was light. She and her husband had performed their daily worship of the Lord. Everyone rejoiced when the Lord was born. A learned neighbor well versed in the Shastras, read the almanac. "Bharani!" he exclaimed "He who is born in Bharani will rule the world."
>
> Many were the auspicious signs that foretold the greatness of what to them was but a most charming child. Nature was in her best form and glory. She

> had carpeted the whole earth with rich corn. Abundance was in evidence everywhere. It was nature's own prophecy, as it were. For, many close relatives of the family recall years later that this glorious son had brought plenty of food and wealth into the world even at his birth. On the very day of his birth Nature, the child's divine Mother, had given plenty of food and wealth to all; The child had imbibed this trait well, and throughout his life, giving food, giving service, giving knowledge, giving all that he had had become part of his nature. On the auspicious day of his birth, even the river Tamraparni was full, and reflected the joy of the Gods, as it were, at the birth of God on earth. Peace combined with supersensuous joy pervaded the very atmosphere of the village; everyone felt its influence. (*Gurudev Sivānanda,* 5–6)

Venkatesānanda now introduces P. S. Vengu Iyer, not as a *jñāni* or Sanskrit scholar in the tradition of the Appayya Dikshitar but as a god-intoxicated *bhakta*:

> Sri Narada says in his Bhakti Sutras that at the advent of a holy man, the forefathers rejoice; Devas dance in joy; and mother earth feels elated at the privilege of bearing on her bosom the footprints of divine being. How true are these sayings when we reflect for a moment on the events attending the birth of our Lord! The father—Vengu Iyer—did dance, not in mere joy, but in the pure bliss of ecstacy. The forefathers,—mortal eyes may not have been able to see them—could not have been any the less joyous. "Is not a son born in our family who will attain Divine Illumination and Final Liberation?" (*Gurudev Sivānanda,* 6)

And, with the loving words of someone spiritually close to Sivānanda, Venkatesānanda describes the newborn child:

> This child whom the parents fondly named Kuppuswami was a real delight to the eyes. Besides well-built limbs, he possessed a charming countenance; and a radiant smile always played on his full, colorful lips. He was the most beloved child of his parents. He compelled their love and held it. The parents delighted in dressing their child in a new fashion everyday, adorning his person with various kinds of jewels, and feasting their eyes on his gleeful face. The child grew up in the most congenial atmosphere. Love and love alone everywhere! The whole village adored the boy. (*Gurudev Sivānanda,* 13)

In his early childhood, according to Venkatesānanda, Kuppuswāmy was mischievous, like Kṛṣṇa and Caitanya, with whom Venkatesānanda compares Sivānanda:

> We have parallels in religious history. Lord Krishna, in His boyhood, was super-mischievous. Another Great One who was considered an Avatara and who bears very close resemblance to Gurudev in faith and ideals—Lord Gauranga—was equally mischievous in his early life. Every act of these noble Souls is pregnant with lofty significance. . . . Kuppuswami would break the

> chimney of a lantern and flourish it before his mother. She would laugh it away with a smiling admonition not to repeat it. But his own meaningful action was perhaps meant to convey his admonition: "Remember: what you consider very useful, nice and valuable, and so take particular care of, will come by this chimney's fate one day or another." (*Gurudev Sivānanda,* 14–15)

Venkatesānanda's point in drawing parallels with the childhood pranks of Kṛṣṇa and Caitanya is not to illustrate the miraculous yet mysterious powers of the divine child (as is the case with the childhood pranks of Kṛṣṇa) but rather to present Sivānanda as the child of wisdom and enlightenment, who knew from his infancy the Vedāntic teachings of the folly of *saṃsāra.*

As Kuppuswāmy grew, his interest in religious devotion and in religious life-styles manifested itself:

> He would bring flowers and bael (wood-apple) leaves for his father's Siva Puja. He was all attention to the chanting of the Mantras. Otherwise a mischievous boy, he proves to be much beyond his age in the matter of keeping attentive silence during worship. He would join his parents in their prayers and kirtan, and would listen attentively when Vengu Iyer read the Ramayana and Bhagavata. . . . His special attention even as a boy, was bestowed upon Sanyasins and wandering monks. He took the greatest delight in entertaining them. Beggars and decrepits, too, enjoyed special privileges at his hands. There was not a beggar who called at his house that did not make Kuppuswamy run to him with love, wherever he might be at that time. He transcended all conventions by inviting beggars inside his house and feeding them or giving them plenty of rice and other victuals. (*Gurudev Sivānanda,* 16–17)

Thus, with the creative pen of a man of faith, Venkatesānanda provides the reader with a detailed description of the young Sivānanda: a handsome, active, yet wise child, perhaps mischievous at times, but always centered in religious matters and with the philosophical insight of a born sage, an incarnation of the Divine. In creating his portrait of the child Sivānanda, Venkatesānanda used no sources except his own imagination, by which he rewrote hagiographic motifs taken from other Hindu hagiographies, contemporary as well as medieval. His purpose was to picture his Gurudeva, Swāmi Sivānanda, as the most recent incarnation of the Divine, a wonder child for the modern age, who, in the tradition of Swāmi Vivekānanda, would restore the *sanātana dharma* to its rightful place in India, which, in the eyes of many elite, was rapidly becoming westernized, materialistic, and secular.

In his *Autobiography,* Sivānanda provides no comment on what were perhaps the most formative years of his life. He leaves out completely the period of physical, emotional, and intellectual growth from his birth until he was sixteen. He covers the next two-year period with the simple statement that, after graduating from the Raja's high school on the Ettiappuram estate in 1903, he attended S.P.G. College at Tiruchi, from which he graduated in 1905, after having "passed the Madura Tamil Sangam examination creditably" (*Autobiography*, 5).

Once again the reader must turn to Venkatesānanda's account to fill in the missing pages of Sivānanda's life story. In his chapter 4, entitled "The Birth of Synthesis," Venkatesānanda paints a portrait of Sivānanda as the brilliant young scholar who always demanded practical results from his studies. Venkatesānanda seeks to integrate and to balance the traditional, devotionally oriented Hindu of Sivānanda's early childhood with the modernist Hindu intellectual who, as a spiritually motivated adult, perceived, as had Swāmi Vivekānanda, the need to serve humanity and to advance the lives of the poor, the sick, and the less fortunate masses.

Venkatesānanda begins chapter 4 with these words:

> The boy prodigy attained the school-going age. His father took him to the local school after initiating him into the mystery of letters and numbers (Aksharabhyasa), and admitted him in the first standard. The masters were struck by the genius that they detected in him. He had attractive physical features. Unlike other boys, he liked going to school. And, to their astonishment could already recite the alphabets and the numericals in proper order. . . .
>
> Kuppuswamy always stood first in his class. He won many prizes and medals, too. Goddess Sarawati appears to have chosen him as fit receptacle to pour her Grace into. . . . From the High School he passed into the S.P.G. College, Tiruchi. Very soon he attracted the attention of the Principal himself. The Principal and Professors loved Kuppuswamy. He was as humble and obedient as he was intelligent and studious. Besides, he was hard-working. Naturally, everyone who came into contact with him in those days was drawn towards him irresistibly. He got through every examination with distinction. He was especially proficient in Tamil literature. (*Gurudev Sivānanda*, 20–24).

One story that Venkatesānanda tells us of Kuppuswāmy's college days is important for our understanding of Sivānanda, the spiritually insightful adult. In this account Venkatesānanda copies Sivānanda's own words that were written for an article (undated) in *Bhavan's Journal*, entitled "How God came into My Life":

> I learnt fencing from a teacher who belonged to a low caste; he was a Harijan. I could go to him only for a few days before I was made to understand that it was unbecoming of a caste Brahmin to play student to an untouchable. I thought deeply over the matter. One moment I felt that the God whom we all worshipped in the image in my father's Puja room had jumped over to the heart of this untouchable. He was (my) guru all right. . . . I placed flowers at

his feet and prostrated myself before him. Thus did God come into my life to remove the veil of caste distinctions. How very valuable this step was I could realize very soon after this: for, I was to enter the medical profession and serve all, and the persistence of caste distinctions would have made that service a mockery. (*Gurudev Sivānanda,* 27)

In his later years Sivānanda did seek to break down caste distinctions and caste barriers, and low-caste sweepers and others had complete access to the Sivānanda Ashram.[4] This story, therefore, provides a symbol of Sivānanda, the Universal Guru, who "sees" all persons of high or low status as "One," in the Vedantic sense.

The Selfless Doctor

Returning to the *Autobiography,* we learn that in 1905, upon graduation from college, Sivānanda entered Tanjore Medical Institute, about which he writes:

I was a tremendously industrious boy in school. During my studies at the Tanjore Medical Institute, I never used to go home in holidays. I would spend the entire period in the hospital. I had free admission into the operation theatre. I would run about here and there and acquire knowledge of surgery—which only a senior student would possess. . . . I was first in all subjects. . . . with all humility I may mention that I possessed greater knowledge than many doctors with covetable degrees. In the first year of my study in the Medical school I could answer papers which the final year student could not. I topped the class in all subjects. (*Autobiography,* 5–6).

But something interrupted Sivānanda's study of medicine. N. Ananthanarayanan provides the following explanation: "When Kuppuswamy was halfway through his medical course, his father died. His mother too fell ill. And the family was thrown into straitened circumstances. Kuppuswamy was forced to leave the Tanjore Institute. His cherished career was brutally cut short."[5] Venkatesānanda, who no doubt was fully aware of the facts, glosses over Sivānanda's failure to finish medical school as he writes:

On emerging with brilliant colours from Medical College, Kuppuswamy looked out for a channel to direct his surging passion to be of some substantial service to humanity at large. He had acquired precious knowledge. Of what use is knowledge if it cannot be translated into practice? This thought which took deeper root in his later spiritual life, had shaped his conduct even in his early medical career. (*Gudurev Sivānanda,* 29)

From 1907 until 1913 Sivānanda lived in Madras City, where he published an English medical journal, entitled *Ambrosia*, and where he worked as a pharmaceutical assistant. In 1913, for reasons that are not made explicit by either Sivānanda or Venkatesānanda, he suddenly decided to leave India and move to Malaya in order to practice medicine. His decision met with the opposition of his mother and two brothers, who protested that the tradition forbade a high-caste Brahmin from "crossing the seas." Venkatesānanda comments that not all traditional rules apply to the present-day world and that in search of a field of service Sivānanda was right to ignore conventional codes of conduct: "after all, was not the call of the sick, the call of the Lord Himself?" (*Gurudev Sivānanda*, 40). Sivānanda traveled by boat to Malaya, and within a few days of landing he secured a job as medical practitioner for a large rubber plantation, near Seremban, which he held until 1920. From 1920 to 1923 he took a position at Jahore Medical Office, located near Singapore.

The years 1913-1923 must have represented for Sivānanda an important phase in his life; for the first time he provides an adequate description of this period. He writes:

> It was a bold and adventurous bid to throw myself on the high seas of uncertainty. I had no money to fall back upon in case of a reverse in my expectations. However, I had tremendous hopes and took a plunge to test the mettle of my destiny. Strength of will and a fiery determination played a big part in moulding my life and spiritual career. No easy going prospect was awaiting me in the distant swamps of Malaya, since I was altogether unknown and friendless, and had no financial safeguard whatsoever. I had to start from scratch. But later the events turned out much to my favour and my position became secure. . . . I quickly acquired a good knowledge of the hospital equipment and the stock of medicines, and found myself absorbed in the job. Here again hard work awaited me. There was not a single available English medical book at that time that I had not read and digested. Soon I became well known in Seremban and Johore Bahru. The bank manager would oblige me by honoring my cheques at any time, even on holidays. I became the friend of everybody through my sociable disposition and service. I got rapid promotions and with that my salary and private practice increased by leaps and bounds. All this was not achieved in a single day. It meant very hard work, unflagging tenacity, strenuous effort and indomitable faith in the principles of goodness and virtue and their application in daily life. (*Autobiography*, 7–9)

Venkatesānanda merely adds Sivānanda's five-page account to his own, exactly as Sivānanda had written it earlier. Then Venkatesānanda does something extraordinary to convince his readers that Sivānanda is the incarnation of the Divine for the modern world, the loving, caring, spiritually guided doctor born to rid humanity of its suffering. Venkatesānanda states that just as he was writing the chapters on Sivānanda's Malayan period, "Providence brought the noble Narasimha Iyer to the Sivanandashram (Rishekish). He was Dr. Kuppuswamy's cook in Malaya" (*Gurudev Sivānanda,* 50). Although Narasimha Iyer served Sivānanda as a cook for only six months out of the ten years that Sivānanda spent in Malaya, Venkatesānanda fills the next forty pages with stories and observations that were told to him by Narasimha Iyer, who is often referred to simply as "N". These stories are claimed to be "true," although Narasimha Iyer told them to Venkatesānanda some thirty years later. In any case two of these stories will illustrate Venkatesānanda's method. The first selection follows immediately after Venkatesānanda acknowledges Narasimha Iyer as "the main source of my information for Gurudev's life in Malaya":

> Dr. Kuppuswamy soon rose in the estimation of his fellow-doctors as well as that of his superiors in hospital—Dr. Parsons and Dr. Green—who loved, admired and respected him for his kindly nature, gentlemanly behaviour and spirit of selfless service. He was their "right hand"; and they soon found out that they could repose the fullest confidence in him. The entire management of the hospital thus gradually glided into his hands. . . . There was no such thing as "off duty" for him. He was perpetually "on duty"; and "excused himself" only a few minutes in the morning and at night for food and rest. This earned for him a fair name which spread like wild fire throughout Malaya. His sincerity, thoroughness of attention, Seva Bhav, and that "something" that always emanated from him, brought about almost miraculous cures in some of his patients who were suffering from diseases pronounced incurable by able doctors. This drew to the hospital many people suffering from dire physical maladies, mostly from the poorer sections of the community. All this to him meant the fulfillment of his desires: to serve, serve and serve till his physical frame withered away in service . . . . Gurudev today exalts selfless service of the sick as Sadhana as potent as Vedantic meditation. He speaks from his own experience. He has realised it himself in his own life. The inner transformation brought about by this service, and the joy and spiritual illumination he obtained from such selfless service of the sick in Malaya ought to have been so great as to inspire him to continue the service throughout the period of his Tapasya at Swarg Ashram and build it up into a great organisation in later years. (*Gurudev Sivānanda,* 50–53).

Here, through the eyes of Narasimha Iyer, Venkatesānanda depicts Sivānanda as the medical doctor who, as an incarnation of the Divine, is, like God, constantly giving of himself to others, especially to the poor and to the lower-caste masses. As Venkatesānanda notes, providing free medical treatment for the poor was one of the principal features of Sivānanda's ascetic life at Rishikesh, to which I shall refer later.

The second selection appears toward the end of Venkatesānanda's presentation of Sivānanda's life in Malaya.

> Let us turn to N. again. He had an agreeable shock of his life the first morning itself. As soon as coffee was ready the master himself poured out a cup for the cook and one for himself and insisted to the point of physical compulsion that he should take it along with him. This was quite a new experience to N. "What is the difference between you and me? You earn a little less and I earn a little more: that is all. Both of us take the same food; we both have to sleep; and in every other aspect of life we both have the same characteristics. Why then should you wait for me to take food? Are you not feeling hungry at the same time? Why should you stand before me? Your legs are as much subject to pain as mine. Why should you go about in dirty clothes? You have as much self-respect as I have, and the same principles of health and hygiene apply to both of us. Those are foolish ideas of superiority and inferiority entertained by some arrogant rich men. I know their habits. They will reserve spoilt food and stale plantain for their servants, I loathe even the thought. You shall be one of the members of my family. In future do not feel any reservations with me." This was the Doctor's first sermon to his cook, Sri N. (*Gurudev Sivānanda,* 80–81)

Again, as in the story of the low-caste fencing instructor, Sivānanda is pictured as the Universal Guru who early in his life broke caste rules and sought equality with his fellow humans, "seeing" all of humanity as One in the Vedāntic sense of oneness.

Sivānanda, however, in his *Autobiography* presents another side of his personality and life as a Malayan physician, one that is all but ignored by Venkatesānanda, who sought to present his Guru as a divinely inspired and divinely directed doctor. Sivānanda writes:

> In my youth I had a great liking for high-class dress, and kept collections of curios and fancy articles of gold, silver and sandalwood. Sometimes I used to purchase various kinds of gold, rings and necklaces and wear them all at a time. When I entered shops I never used to waste any time in selection. I gathered all that I saw. I did not like haggling and bargaining. I paid the shopkeepers' bills without scrutiny. Even now, whenever I enter a bookshop, I purchase a lot of books and add them to the Forest University library for the benefit of the students in the Ashram. I had many hats, but never wore them. Sometimes I used my felt cap and the silk turban, like that of a Rajput prince. (*Autobiography,* 10)

Here we are introduced to a man of the world, a man of affluence who enjoyed material things that gave him status—hardly the saintly, constantly giving, never taking doctor of Venkatesānanda's description. The self-expressed image of Sivānanda as a man with human desires and human failings contrasts sharply with the spiritualized portrait that Venkatesānanda seeks to create of the enlightened, selfless doctor, the incarnation of the Divine for modern times. Perhaps it was Sivānanda's inner despair of, rather than the doctor's joyous hopes for, the future of mankind that led Sivānanda to leave Malaya. In any case, sometime in 1923, toward the end of his stay at Jahore, Sivānanda began to have other thoughts. He reflects on his change in attitude toward worldly life as he writes:

> "Is there not a higher mission in life than the daily round of official duties, eating and drinking? Is there not any higher form of happiness than these transitory and illusory pleasures? How uncertain is life here! How insecure is existence on this earth plane, with various kinds of diseases, anxieties, worries, fear and disappointments! The world of names and forms is constantly changing. Time is fleeting. All hopes of happiness in this world terminate in pain, despair and sorrow."
>
> Such were the thoughts constantly arising in my mind. The medical profession gave me ample evidence of the sufferings of this world. For a man of compassion who has a sympathetic heart, the world is full of pain. True and lasting happiness cannot be found merely in gathering wealth. By purifying the heart through selfless service, I had a new vision. I was deeply convinced that there must be a place—a sweet home of pristine glory, purity and divine splendour—where absolute security, perfect peace and lasting happiness can be had through Self-realisation. (*Autobiography,* 14)

We are not told more about events that led to this change in attitude, but we do know that Sivānanda had begun to study the Upaniṣads and the *Bhagavad Gītā* during his last years in Malaya. He left Malaya as suddenly as he had come. At the age of thirty-six, Sivānanda sailed from Singapore, leaving behind him all of his earthly possessions; and, upon his reentry into India, he became a wandering mendicant. Venkatesānanda concludes this phase of Sivānanda's life story, again comparing his Gurudeva with Siddhartha Gautama, the Buddha:

> That is what we find in these two heroes: Lord Buddha and our Gurudev. They lodged themselves on the brink of the ocean of Samsara, smelt its captivating though deluding ozone, understood its deceptive essence and took to wings, thus mocking the very Maya and defeating her at her own game. Such was the pleasure-palace that Maya had built for him in Malaya, even as the King had built for Prince Siddhartha to prevent Him from renouncing the world. (*Gurudev Sivānanda,* 101)

The Austere Ascetic and Selfless Servant

Once in India, Sivānanda traveled north, visiting Banaras and arriving in Rishikesh, where he received initiation into ascetic orders from Visvānanda Sarasvati, about whom we learn little from Sivānanda: "From the sacred hands of Paramahansa Visvananda, I received Holy initiation on the banks of the Ganges on 1st June 1924. The religious rite of Varag Homa was done for me by Acharya Guru Sri Swāmi Vishnudevananda Maharaj at Kailas Ashram" (*Autobiography*, 16). Visvānanda Sarasvati gave Kuppuswāmy Iyer the name Sivānanda Sarasvati, thus continuing the tradition of his Advaitic monastic order, but his relationship to Sivānanda was more like that of John the Baptist to Jesus than the typical Hindu relationship of guru to disciple, for he spent only a few hours with his disciple before the two parted.

Venkatesānanda's description of the same event indicates that the two met at Charan Das Dharmasala, a place of temporary lodging for wandering ascetics. His account provides a depth of feeling that is lacking in Sivānanda's factual statement:

> His face was aglow with the Fire of Knowledge. It captivated Gurudev's heart, the moment he had the old Sannyasin's Darshan early in the morning. Gurudev fell at his feet and bathed them with his tears. Fondly, the saint Svami Visvanandaji raised him and embraced him with all love and affection. "My dear child! I see something on your forehead which tells me that you are going to be the fittest instrument in the hand of God for conveying his message to the world. . . . Am I right in assuming that you have renounced the world and desire to live the life of a monk?" "Most Holy Sire! Yes, you are right. Oh how fortunate I am to have the Darshan of a divine sage. . . . Shower your grace on this humble seeker. For it is only through thee I can obtain my goal." "Well said, my child! I should myself feel it the greatest privilege to initiate you into Sannyasa." (*Gurudev Sivānanda*, 123–24)

In a brief but lively account, entitled "How I Synthesized My Sadhana," Sivānanda describes his first year as a *sannyāsi*, a renunciate, living a solitary existence in Rishikesh:

> Service of the sick and the poor and of Mahatmas purifies the heart. . . . Mahatmas and the poor villagers who were sick did not have proper medical aid. Thousands of pilgrims to Badrinath and Kedarnath also needed medical help. Therefore, I started a dispensary, known as Satyasevashram, at Lakshmanjhula on the way to Badri-Kedar. I served the devotees with great love and devotion. I arranged special diet for the serious cases and provided milk and other requirements. Spiritual evolution is quicker through service done with proper Bhava or attitude. . . .
>
> With a view to devoting more time to prayer and meditation, I moved to Swarg Ashram. I lived in a small kutir, eight by ten feet, with a small verandah in front, and depended on the Kali Kambliwala Kshetra (almshouse) for my food. . . . For my Sadhana, I spent much of my time in meditation and in the practice of various kinds of yogas. I had set the goal of my life as Self-realisation, and determined to spend every bit of my energy and time in study, service and Sadhana.

Gradually people came to me in large numbers. That seriously affected my systematic work. With the permission of the Kshetra authorities, I fixed up a barbed-wire fence around my kutir and locked the gate. I kept a signboard at the entrance of my compound, which read: "Interviews—between 4 and 5 P.M.—only for five minutes at a time." During the winter the devotees were not many. . . . My joy was indescribable when I spent hours in the evenings on the sandbanks of the Ganges, sitting on fine rock and gazing at wonderful Nature. (*Autobiography,* 20–21)

The picture that Sivānanda presents of himself is one of a traditional *sannyāsi,* or renunciate, who, although he was willing to provide medical treatment for monastics and the poor of Rishikesh, clearly preferred the solitary life of the meditator and the yoga practitioner. After he had become known to the thousands of pilgrims who passed through Rishikesh on their way to Badrinath and Kedarnath, he began to isolate himself even more from the flock of humanity, in sharp contrast to Venkatesānanda's image of the "selfless doctor" who was tireless in the service of those in need.

Venkatesānanda, however, is unwilling to let his image of the synthesis of traditional and modern values, of austere asceticism and selfless service, be compromised by Sivānanda's own self-image, which stresses isolation, meditation, and austerities. He begins his lengthy account of Sivānanda's first year at Rishikesh by insisting on the synthesis of traditional and modern images:

What were the austerities that Gurudev put himself through in order to achieve the goal? We ought to remember all the time we dwell upon his illustrious life that at no stage, in regard to no aspect of spiritual practice—or even of life in general, for that matter—has Gurudev countenanced a lop-sided development. This extraordinary trait characterises the austerities that he imposed upon himself during his Swarg Ashram days. . . . Intense meditation, prolonged meditation, was without doubt primary concern. He was not satisfied with anything but an all-out attempt to dive deep and deeper into the innermost recesses of his heart in order to realise the Self, in the quickest possible time. But that takes us back again to the supreme Sadhana of selfless service whose personification Sri Gudurev is. Service and meditation, Sri Gurudev teaches us, should go hand in hand. One supplements and complements the other. Service purifies the heart and enables the Divine Light to descend; and meditation which receives the Light works out an inner transformation which enables the service to be rendered with the proper Bhav, "seeing God in all," and serving as an instrument in His Hands. (*Gurudev Sivānanda,* 140–43)

Venkatesānanda provides his readers with a colorful account of

Sivānanda's first year at Rishikesh, this time by speaking through the mouth of a Śaṅkara ascetic named Rāj Giri, who is not further identified. Rāj Giri is quoted as saying:

> In those days he was characterised by such extreme dispassion that he used to deny himself even the barest necessities of life. He did not spare himself even with regard to diet and covering. Rather than daily tolerate an interruption to his spiritual practices which the visit to Anna-Kshetra entailed, the Swāmi preferred to keep the body on stale bread. It was his wont to keep bread with him for several days on end, and drying it, he would dip it in the Ganges and eat that. It meant that sometimes he would subsist for one week on a ration of one day. Thus, day after day, using every moment of his precious time for meditation, Japa and Upasana, he made unsalted tasteless hard bread his main meal. We knew him to have only two pieces of clothing that he wore on his person. His room was severely bare of any other article except for a solitary water-pot and a blanket. (*Gurudev Sivānanda,* 151)

And again from Rāj Giri:

> To do Japa he used to be up very early in the closing watches of the night, plunging into the chill waters of the Ganges, he would stand waist-deep in the river and commence his rosary, continuing it until the sun rose up in the heavens. Only after invoking the deity through the sun and worshipping it would the Swāmi clamber up out of the cold waters. (*Gurudev Sivānanda,* 152).

These words describe a typical renunciate, whose world-rejectionist philosophy of austerity can be traced back to extremist ascetic movements that were contemporary with the Buddha and that the Buddha rejected in favor of his Middle Way. Venkatesānanda, however, is quick to reshape the traditional Hindu image of the austere ascetic by adding to it the modern version of the *sannyāsi* as one who renounced worldly attachments in order to commit himself/herself fully to the service of humanity—and, indeed, to all living beings. This is the modernist interpretation of *karmayoga* as the discipline of selfless service. Thus, just prior to his quotation from Rāj Giri, Venkatesānanda had cautioned: "Throughout the period of the most severe austerities, Gurudev has always shown the Middle Path to be infinitely superior to the Extremes. . . . Times without number he has warned Sadhaks against going to extremes, particularly in the matter of austerities" (*Gurudev Sivānanda,* 149). Immediately after the words quoted above from Rāj Giri, Venkatesānanda writes:

> This austere life was not one of dry self-centered life. It did not spring from any scorn of the world and humanity. On the contrary, its aim was the sublimation of the vision of the world and the children of the Lord. There was,

> therefore, the vigilant watch of the Lord. There was therefore the vigilant watch against a tendency to turn even this Tapas into a selfish endeavor. Service was part and parcel of an extraordinary type. It was utterly selfless, intense, dynamic and austere; it involved no small amount of personal discomfort and sacrifice. Gurudev used to keep in small packets, the simple, common drugs that Badri-pilgrims needed for use during the pilgrimage. . . . It happened on one occasion that a pilgrim had come to have his Darshan before proceeding on the pilgrimage. Before he took leave of Gurudev, the latter had presented him with the Yatra-medicine-set. The pilgrim had left. After a little while, it occurred to Gurudev that he should have included in the packet a small bottle of "Amrit Dhara." Early the next morning, long before dawn Gurudev took the bottle in his hand and proceeded along the road to Badrinath. The pilgrim had already left Lakshamjhula. Gudurev quickened his pace to a running speed in order to catch up with the advancing pilgrim. When even at Garud Chatti the pilgrim could not be found, the Great One was undaunted. He proceeded, running faster. After thus running for five miles, Gurudev at last caught up with the pilgrim and delivered the medicine he had brought. (*Gurudev Sivānanda*, 152–53)

At first reading this story might seem trivial, but it is one often cited by disciples of Swāmi Sivānanda as an excellent example of Sivānanda's total selflessness. Indeed, anyone who has walked the steep climb from Rishikesh to Badrinath would be impressed by the fact that Sivānanda ran up that road.

The Enlightened Guru

Sivānanda makes only the briefest notes describing his life between 1925 and 1930. He does write that in May 1926 he went on a pilgrimage to Kedarnath and Badrinath in the mountains north of Rishikesh and that he returned at the end of June. Venkatesānanda is equally silent in his description of this period, simply reworking Sivānanda's accounts. The years between 1926 and 1930, however, must have been crucial years in Sivānanda's life, for it was in this period that Sivānanda attained the enlightenment experience that he intensely sought. Nothing is said by Sivanānda of this experience, nor do Venkatesānanda or other biographers, such as Ananthanarayanan, add much to what must have been Sivānanda's key religious experience. Venkatesānanda concludes his section entitled "Peace, Power and Perfection" with these words:

> Yet, again, when he advanced further in the practice of meditation, he would deny himself all food, company and talk, and plunge in Dhyana for the better part of the day. Nothing except meditation and a few most important exercises. Living on dry bread and Ganges water, Gurudev plunged deeper and deeper into Samadhi and kept himself within closed doors for many days at a

> stretch. . . . Not a day's relaxation would he permit himself. Thus it went on from day to day, week after week and month after month for five long years: when on a blessed day Gurudev reached the goal of all Sadhana. It was sometime in 1929 or 1930. The date and nature of his realization Gurudev has kept to himself. (*Gurudev Sivānanda*, 188)

In my earlier studies of Hindu ascetics I found that the one experience that they did not readily talk about but that is central to a scholar's understanding and evaluation of their lives, was their enlightenment, or *samādhi*, experience, which they held to be essentially private and therefore best expressed by silence. This, of course, is the conclusion of Māṇḍukhya Upaniṣad on this matter. Christopher Isherwood's detailed description of Rāmakrishna's enlightenment experiences of *nirvikalpa* and *savikalpa samādhi* stand in marked contrast to the absolute silence of Sivānanda's biographers.

My guess is that Sivānanda, by willfully renouncing all contact with the outside world and by stripping away all elements of duality in the most severe meditation, realized what W. T. Stace labels as the Unitary Consciousness of the introvertive type of mystical experience. Stace defines Unitary Consciousness as that experience "from which all the multiplicity of sensuous or conceptual or other empirical content has been excluded so that there remains only a void and empty unity." This experience is also one that manifests "feelings of blessedness, joy, peace, happiness and a feeling that what is apprehended is holy, sacred, or divine."[6] Once Sivānanda had this experience of Unitary Consciousness or, more technically in Hindu terms, *nirvikalpa samādhi*, he was then able to "return" to the world, the world of duality, the world of I–other relationships and view it mystically as One in the Upaniṣadic sense. Ananthanarayan provides this oblique reference to Sivānanda's enlightenment experience:

> But somewhere around 1930, he was gripped by a burning desire to serve the world. Driven by this desire, Sivānanda came out of his seclusion in Swargashram and entered the cities and mingled with the masses. There was a sparkle in his eyes, a fire in his speech. The Sivānanda who cast a spell on the vast audiences in Sitapur and Lakhimpur, The Sankirtan Samrat who sang and danced his way into the hearts of tens of thousands in Rawalpindi and Lahore and threw them into high ecstacy, left no one in doubt about his being a realized soul. When and where he attained the Illumination, no one knew. It was a secret known only to Swamiji and God.[7]

The only descriptions that Sivānanda provides of his enlightenment experience (or experiences, as the case might be) are in a series of poems that he has appended to his *Autobiography*. Three of these poems were written after his period of intense meditation from 1925 to 1930 and hence reflect the wisdom of one who truly knows what it means to be enlightened to Absolute Truth—the Truth, in the Neo-Vedāntic sense, that everything is one and that all duality, however conceived, is false, an illusion, a product of ignorance.

> The Maya-made world has vanished now.
> Mind has totally perished,
> Names and forms have disappeared,
> All distinctions and differences have melted,
> The flood of Truth, wisdom and bliss
> Has entered everywhere in abundance:
> Brahman alone shines everywhere:
> I have become that; I have become that.
> Into Nirvikalpa Samadhi,
> Wherein there is neither the seer nor the seen,
> Wherein one sees nothing, hears nothing.
>
> (*Autobiography*, 133)

> I merged myself in great unending joy,
> I swam in the ocean of immortal bliss,
> Ego melted, thoughts subsided,
> Intellect ceased functioning,
> the Senses were absorbed
> I saw myself everywhere,
> There was neither within or without.
> There was neither "this" or "that,"
> There was neither he, you nor I nor she,
> There was neither time nor space,
> There was neither subject nor object,
> There was neither knower nor knowable,
> How can one describe this transcendental experience!
> Language is finite, words are impotent:
> Realize this yourself and be free.
>
> (*Autobiography*, 140)

In these poetic descriptions of his enlightenment experience Sivānanda uses the language of Advaita Vedānta, much in the tradition of his ascetic lineage. But characteristic of the Neo-Vedāntic or modernist position, Sivānanda often uses the poetic language of theism.

> O Mahadeva! O Kesava!
> By the sword of thy Grace
> I have cut off all my bonds,
> I am free, I am blissful;
> All desires have disappeared.

Now I aspire for nothing
But thy blessed feet;
I have lost all my thoughts
In thee, O Narayana!
I had Thy wondrous vision,
I was not lost in ecstacy,
I was at once transformed,
I was drowned
In the Divine Consciousness,
In the ocean of bliss.
Hail, hail, O Vishnu, my Lord!

Here Sivānanda's description reflects the theistic language of the *Bhagavad Gītā,* especially that of chapter 11, in which Arjuna had (in Stace's terms) an extrovertive theistic mystical experience. Again, writing sometime after 1950, Sivānanda used predominantly theistic language:

> God came to me in the form of all-consuming aspiration to realize Him as the Self of all. Meditation and service went on apace; and with them came various spiritual experiences. Till body, mind and intellect as the limiting adjuncts vanished and the whole universe shone in His light. God then came in the form of this Light in which everything assumed a divine shape; and pain and suffering that seemed to haunt everybody appeared to be a mirage, the illusion that ignorance creates.[8]

Whatever might be the case in 1930, after attaining enlightenment, Sivānanda initially expresses a reluctance to take on the task of gathering disciples and creating an institution that would put into practice the Neo-Vedāntic philosophy of nonduality, or Oneness, but that would drag him back into the world of human activity. He writes that it was "the Divine Will" that brought into being the Divine Life Society.

> I love seclusion. I have to hide myself at times. I do not crave for name and fame. . . . I was not pleased when people called me "Mahatma" or "Guru Maharaj." I never planned to have any institution to perpetuate my name. But the Divine Will was different. The whole world came to me with all divine glory and splendour. That may be due to the intense prayers of thousands of sincere seekers after Truth, coupled with my own inborn tendencies to share with others what I have and to serve the world on a large scale on the right lines for the attainment of light, peace and knowledge. I was induced to start the Divine Life Society when I found some facility and useful hands to carry on the work. (*Autobiography,* 42)

As might be expected, Venkatesānanda paints a more colorful picture of Sivānanda as the Enlightened Guru who was "afire with zeal and eagerness" to share wisdom with all:

> It was this fire of divine knowledge that emanated from his heart and consumed all ignorance from the hearts of all those who approached him, that confirms Sri Sivagyan's conviction that Gurudev had reached the goal of austerities and Sadhana sometime in 1930. It is further evident that Gurudev's utterances and writings, after this period, shone with special light and had air of the unmistakeable authority. There are further evidences of this attainment. Gurudev who, as a zealous Sadhaka, had maintained that he would not make any disciples but would spend his life in seclusion, singing the Lord's Names, manifests a sudden eagerness to runabout here and there distributing the pearls of wisdom that he had brought forth from the depths of the ocean of spiritual Sadhana. He had realised the very end and aim of all spiritual practices. He had no more need to practice austerities. . . . He was ever in communion with the Self, without any conscious effort. It was then that he had the inner urge to launch forth on an extensive campaign for the propagation of the spiritual science or Brahma Vidya. The people, too, knew their Savior. They flocked to him. . . . There was "that something" in his very Presence and his very Word that kept them spell-bound. (*Gurudev Sivānanda*, 210)

Venkatesānanda continues to create and to reinforce the image of his Gurudev as one who constantly follows the Middle Path and who, like the Buddha or, more importantly, like Swāmi Vivekānanda, sought to balance meditation and austerities with selfless service to suffering humanity.

The early part of Sivānanda's life story now comes to a close. The next period of incredible activity and manifold accomplishments began in 1931 after Swāmi Sivānanda returned to Rishikesh from travels that took him to the south. It is at this point in Sivānanda's life that the hagiographer has finished his task, and he allows the historian (or at least the "recorder" of historical data) to take his place. For the next 350 pages of the *Gurudev Sivānanda*, Swāmi Venkatesānanda assumes the additional role of the historical recorder, providing a variety of materials that could be checked and validated for historical accuracy from other sources.

Appendix: The Writing of Contemporary Hindu Hagiography

The Paradigm of Incarnation

This paradigm allows the contemporary Hindu hagiographer (and in this category I would include some Western, Hindu-sympathetic writers, such as Christopher Isherwood) to connect his/her guru with a major Hindu deity and then to provide that guru with a birth narrative that has all the elements of the birth narratives found in the hagiographies of medieval guru-saints. In fact, the incarnation paradigm enables the contemporary hagiographer to rank his/her guru with the great founders of medieval monastic/ascetic movements, such as Śaṅkara, Rāmānuja, or Caitanya, who were also held to be incarnations of the Divine. Further, contemporary hagiographical authors often "create" a family linkage between their gurus and one of the more famous medieval gurus. Thus, Vijaykrishna (1841–1899) is related to Advaita Acārya (1500), one of the closest disciples of Caitanya, and Rāma Tīrtha (1873–1906) is said to be descended from the family of Tulasidās (1531–1623). So also, Swāmi Sivānanda has blood linkage to the medieval Tamil scholar Appayya Dikshitar (1500), who also was held to be an incarnation of the Divine. In these ways, then, hagiographers give their gurus authenticity within classical Hindu tradition and attempt to invalidate any claim that "modernists" are not really part of the Hindu ascetic tradition and should not be considered as such.

Universalistic Missionary Thrust

Swāmi Vivekānanda's well-known and well-documented appearance in 1893 at the Parliament of Religions in Chicago introduced a universalistic missionary thrust into Hindu tradition that radically changed it or at least changed the attitudes of some of the intellectual elite, who then brought about innovations within the Hindu tradition. With the military-political dominance of India by the British and with the impact of Protestant Christianity upon the Hindu elite in Bengal, many Hindu intellectuals felt that Hindu "religion" was sadly inferior to Christianity, and they either rejected it or, as is the case of the Brahmo Samaj, they sought to reform it. Philosophically, Swāmi Vivekānanda, and later Śrī Aurobindo and Sarvepalli Radhadkrishman, made major attempts to reverse this situation. They argued that Hindu tradition, or at least the essential mystical core of that tradition (which had ancient roots), represented the model for religious experience and hence for religious commitment in the modern period. Hindu mysticism was universal spirituality *par excellence,* and other religious traditions, in particular Judaism, Christianity, Islam, and to some extent Buddhism, were particularistic and dogmatic, the religions of a specific people and therefore not models of religiosity for the modern world.

This new—indeed quite revolutionary—universalistic missionary thrust had a major effect on the writing of Hindu hagiography. Western scholars of international reputation, such as F. Max Muller and Romain Rolland, began to write biographies of Swāmi Vivekānanda and of his guru, Śrī Rāmakrishna. Rāmakrishna was compared to Jesus Christ and to the Buddha, while Vivekānanda was depicted as another St. Paul—or perhaps another Ānanda (of Buddhist tradition). Hindu apologists, the intellectual elite, were quick in adopting this approach. Swāmi Venkatesānanda's estimate of his guru, Swāmi Sivānanda, is perhaps the conclusion of this Hindu apologetic.

The hagiographer functions to place his guru not just within Hindu tradition as an incarnation of the Divine but, further, as an incarnation of the Divine who is equal to if not superior to Gautama the Buddha and Jesus the Christ. This claim, of course, makes the standard hagiography well worth reading, as it approximates sacred scripture in its importance for those of faith.

Modern Hindu Philosophy

The contemporary Hindu hagiographer performs another important function for those "devout seekers after truth" who must confront elements of "the modern world" whether they live in India or in the West. The hagiographer is a translator and communicator of his/her guru's philosophical position, worldview, and value system, and the hagiographer attempts to adapt his/her guru's life and teachings to a Hindu definition of modernity, which by Western scholarly standard is a "mix" of traditional and modern ways of thinking and acting. "Hindu modernity" may be defined as follows:

> an evaluation of a kind of Hindu thinking that adopts the language of Western science and technology as a model of communication and persuasion without renouncing traditional religious values. . . . To be a modern Hindu, then, is not only to engage in the rhetoric of the apologetic, but to carry out its pronouncements in religious action, and of those groups directing sociocultural change, the modernist sadhus are "at the helm of things."[9]

Let me briefly comment upon two hagiographies that exemplify this "mix" of traditional and modern ways of thinking and acting.

Śrī Rāmakrishna wrote nothing. The principal source for his life and teachings is *The Gospel of Sri Ramakrishna*, written by Mahendra Natha Gupta in the four-year period before Ramakrishna's death in 1886. Perhaps no other contemporary Hindu work, philosophical or otherwise, has been more widely read in India and the West than *The Gospel of Sri Ramakrishna*, first published in Bengali in 1897 and then in English in 1907. Although a critical analysis of this massive, 1,050-page tome surely would raise questions about the historical accuracy of what has been written, it would be most difficult to separate the "fact" from the "fiction." Mahendra Natha Gupta claims that he recorded verbatim the discussions between Rāmakrishna and the Bengali intellectual elite who came to visit him at Dakshineswar and elsewhere in the Calcutta area. Putting aside the question of historical accuracy, the picture that Gupta (known as "M") paints of Rāmakrishna is that of a traditional ascetic (although he was married and, for the most part, functioned as a priest). Furthermore, even in his lifetime Rāmakrishna was "seen" (here actually "seen") by his disciples as an incarnation of the Divine. Yet Rāmakrishna was an incarnation of the Divine and traditional ascetic whose views are distinctly "modern"—again, by a Hindu definition. In fact, his teachings provide the basis for the Hindu Apologetic that was interpreted and expounded later by Swāmi Vivekānanda, who is considered to be one of the Fathers of Modern India. He is also an interesting blend of traditional and modern Hindu ways of thinking and acting. Bharati adds further:

> All "modernities" overtly or covertly admire and venerate the "scientific," "modern" man who wears monastic robes: Swāmi Vivekānanda is an undisputed culture-hero not simply of all modern Bengali Hindus. . . . Modern Hindus derive their knowledge of Hinduism from Vivekānanda directly or indirectly. It was Vivekānanda and his latter day imitators, including the late Sivananda Sarasvati, who really created the diction and the style of the Apologetic.[10]

In *Gurudev Sivānanda* the images that Swāmi Venkatesānanda creates of his guru reflect this unique Hindu "mix" or synthesis of traditional and modern ways of thinking and acting. Swāmi Sivānanda was born an incarnation of the Divine equal to any previous incarnation of the Divine; here, of course, Venkatesānanda had in mind not only Rāma, Kṛṣṇa, the Buddha, and Jesus but also Rāmakrishna and, indeed, any other contemporary guru. Venkatesānanda briefly compares Sivānanda's infancy to that of the infant Kṛṣṇa, who was a naughty child but dearly loved for his mischief. He then quickly changes this traditional image: in his early youth Sivānanda was a highly intelligent, deeply motivated student who excelled not only in his schooling but also was a master of Hindu philosophical tradition. But Sivānanda was not just an intellectual. Like the young Vivekānanda, he was a superb athlete, a champion fencer. Yet he was equally good at performing and singing traditional devotional songs, *bhajans* and *kīrtans.* Finally, he was especially kind toward beggars, mendicants, and lower-caste peoples, who were often rejected or ignored by his high-caste peers. Upon completion of his college education Sivānanda, like Vivekānanda, began training in a modern, secular profession. Vivekānanda entered the study of law but did not complete his degree. So also, Sivānanda excelled as a young medical student, and, although he did not finish his degree, he did practice "modern" medicine in Malaya, where he became a successful and affluent doctor whom Venkatesānanda pictures as the model of selfless service. Again,

Venkatesānanda changes this modern image for a traditional one: at the age of thirty-six Sivānanda renounced worldly life, left Malaya for India, and took initiation into traditional Śaṅkara ascetic orders. He underwent extreme austerities, characteristic of world-rejecting ascetics, who often were attacked verbally by Vivekānanda and other exponents of the Hindu Apologetic. After a difficult struggle, Sivānanda attained enlightenment.

With the final stroke of his pen, Venkatesānanda balances this traditional image of world-rejection with the "modern" conception of the *sannyāsi* (the "renouncer") as one who has renounced worldly attachments in order to commit himself/herself fully to the service of all living beings, in the spirit of *karmayoga*, the discipline of selfless service. The traditional rendering of *karmayoga* as "the discipline of unattached or dispassionate action," which is one of the major themes of the *Bhagavad Gītā,* was radically changed by Swāmi Vivekānanda and "his latter-day imitators." The old *karmayoga* was an individualist moral code of nonattachment to the results of one's action, achieved by renouncing ego-involvement in results ("fruits") and by holding a mean between two extremes, between love and hate, joy and sorrow, pleasure and pain. The "new" *karmayoga* was a call to social action on behalf of others, a compassionate, ethical concern for the welfare of others, especially the poor, the sick, and the lower castes, a theory of action that was spiritually grounded in the Vedāntic concept of Oneness, which was experienced by Sivānanda in his enlightenment experience.

Swāmi Sivānanda, then, is pictured by Venkatesānanda as a divine embodiment of *karmayoga*, translated as "the discipline of selfless service," the "new" karma yoga. Thus, *tapas,* or meditational austerity, which is absolutely necessary in order to gain the mystical insight, the intuitive experience, that all beings are in Reality One, is balanced by *karmayoga*, selfless service on behalf of others, especially those others who are farthest from the enlightened vision of Oneness. Swāmi Sivānanda, therefore, as the Universal Guru for the present age, provides the ideal model for all "modernists," East or West, to emulate. The purpose for which the Divine had incarnated Himself as Swāmi Sivānanda was being accomplished.

Having read *Gurudev Sivānanda,* "the devout seeker after Truth" might be inclined to dismiss Sivānanda's own denouncement: "I had no ambition to become world famous. . . . I never attempted to be a Guru to anyone. I am not pleased when people call me 'Satguru' or 'Avatar.'" But here again Swāmi Sivānanda is placed alongside of Gautama the Buddha, Śaṅkara, and a host of other Indian gurus who in time, despite their pronouncements to the contrary, were held by the faithful to be incarnations of the Divine, born in human form to restore righteousness and goodness throughout the land. Indeed, the life story of Swāmi Sivānanda continues a spiritual tradition that, as it were, "comes into being age after age" and that provides a means by which Hindus integrate traditional and modern ways of thinking and acting as they encounter and adapt to a radically changing world.

Notes

1. Phillis Granoff, "Holy Warriors: A Preliminary Study of Some Biographies of Saints and Kings in the Classical Indian Tradition," *Journal of Indian Philosophy* 12 (1984) 291.
2. G. S. Ghurye, *Indian Sadhus,* 75; Swami Agehananda Bharati, The Hindu Renaissance and Its Apologetic Patterns," *Journal of Asian Studies* 29/1 (1970) 286.
3. See David M. Miller, "The Divine Life Society Movement."
4. Ibid.
5. N. Ananthanarayanan, *From Man to God-Man,* 5.
6. W. T. Stace, *Mysticism and Philosophy,* 110.
7. Ananthanarayanan, *From Man to God-Man,* 54.
8. Venkatesānanda, *Gurudev Sivānanda,* 468, quoting Sivānanda, "How God Came into My Life," *Bhavan's Journal* (undated).
9. Miller, "Divine Life Society Movement," 109–10.
10. Bharati, "Hindu Renaissance," 278.

Bibliography

Sources

Gupta, Mahendranath. *The Gospel of Sri Ramakrishna.* Translated by Swami Nikhilananda. Mylapore: Sri Ramakrishna Math, 1964.

Sivānanda, Swāmi. *Autobiography of Swāmi Sivānanda.* 1958. Reprint. Rishikesh: The Divine Life Society Press, 1983.

Venkatesānanda, Swāmi. *Gurudev Sivānanda.* Rishikesh: The Vedānta Forest Academy, 1960.

Studies

Ananthanarayanan, N. *From Man to God-Man: The Inspiring Life-Story of Swami Sivananda.* New Delhi: Indraprasha Press, 1976.

Bharati, Swami Agehananda. "The Hindu Renaissance and its Apologetic Patterns." *Journal of Asian Studies* 29/2 (1970) 267–88.

Dimock, Edward C. "Religious Biography in India: The 'Nectar of the Acts' of Caitanya." In *The Biographical Process,* edited by Frank Reynolds and Donald Capps. The Hague: Mouton, 1976.

Ghurye, G. S. *Indian Sadhus.* Bombay: Popular Prakashan, 1964.

Granoff, Phillis. "Holy Warriors: A Preliminary Study of Some Biographies of Saints and Kings in the Classical Indian Tradition." *Journal of Indian Philosophy* 12 (1984).

Isherwood, Christopher. *Ramakrishna and His Disciples.* New York: Simon & Schuster, 1965.

Lorenzen, David N. "The Life of Sankaracarya." In *The Biographical Process*, edited by Frank Reynolds and Donald Capps. The Hague: Mouton, 1976.
Madhava-Vidyaranya. *Sankara-Dig-Vijaya*. Translated by Swami Tapasyananda. Madras: Sri Ramakrishna Math, 1980.
Miller, David M. "The Divine Life Society Movement." In *Religion in Modern India*, edited by Robert D. Baird. Columbia: South Asia Publications, 1989.
———. "Swami Sivananda and the Bhagavad Gita." In *Modern Indian Interpreters of the Bhagavad Gita*, edited by Robert Minor. Albany: State University of New York Press, 1986.
Stace, W. T. *Mysticism and Philosophy*. Philadelphia: J. B. Lippincott Company, 1960.

19

Śrī Aurobindo: The Spirituality of the Future

Sisirkumar Ghose

When the fate of humankind hangs in the balance and prophets of doom are doing overtime, it is becoming rare to come across a thinker, in fact a visionary, who can fortify the grounds of a deeper faith and who can "justify our hope and aspiration by the very nature of the world and our cosmic antecedents and the inevitable future of our evolution."[1] A master of the triple times, creative not only of things as they are but, if he is right, as they are bound to be, Aurobindo (1872–1950) has identified spirituality as human beings' "most powerful means of self-fulfillment" (20:4), as the paraclete of an unimaged harmony, the fate and privilege of unborn humans. The plural is important. The thrust of Aurobindo's worldview is a collective breakthrough beyond the rational, religious, and revolutionary horizons. Commuting easily between Eastern wisdom and Western experience, and yoking yoga with evolution of consciousness, he has given history and the history of ideas a new subjective turn. Few have read, like him, the text of the without from within. A constant of human aspiration, spirituality has been glimpsed and voiced in every age by rare souls. But not many have defined, described, and developed its taxonomy or hinted at the plenitude of its possibility so constantly and confidently as this Indian sage, who has cast his dreams as a mold for coming things. But what a visionary foresees may take ages to fulfill.

I

From August to November 1918, Aurobindo wrote a series of four articles entitled *The Renaissance in India*, where, in the first and final chapters, he spelled out his spiritual ideas, which must have grown since his withdrawal from active politics. There would be further expositions and refinements in such works as *The Human Cycle*, *The Life Divine*, *The Synthesis of Yoga*, and *Essays on the Gita*. A certain bonding has been the essence of the Aurobindean "inview," his *Ansicht*; but its first foundations were laid in *Renaissance of India*. Welcoming new forms and expressions, Aurobindo was clear in his mind that "India will certainly keep her essential spirit, will keep her characteristic soul, but there is likely to be a great change of the body" (14:399).

For Aurobindo, not religion but spirituality is the master key of the Indian mind and society. But, Aurobindo is quick to add, spirituality did not, and will not, live in the void. What strikes an unprejudiced observer of the old Indian scene is its prolific creativeness, its vitality, and a strong mediating intellectuality, minute, massive, and curious. Unlike the exclusive and therefore dangerous reliance on reason, as in the secular modern West, "The work of the renaissance in India must be to make this spirit, the higher view of life, this sense of deeper potentiality once more a creative, perhaps a dominant power in the world" (14:409). But because its motives are little understood and less practiced, the renaissance in India has been more a matter of rhetoric than reality, more a hope than a fact. The more subtle and difficult the idea, the more difficult it is to embody.

True, in hours of decline a negative mood had taken hold of the Indian mind and society, a compromise with the status quo and a falling away, but it was never the whole tendency. As Aurobindo sees it:

> Spirituality is much wider than any particular religion, and in the larger ideas of it that are now coming on us, even the greatest religion becomes no more than a broad sect or branch of the one universal religion; by which we shall understand in the future man's seeking for the eternal, the divine, the greater self, the source of unity and his attempt to arrive at some equation, some increasing approximation of the values of human life with the eternal and the divine values. (14:427)

A higher verity of life, spirituality does not exclude any motive, problem, or function of the human being. "Spirit without mind, spirit without body is not the type of man, therefore a human spirituality must not belittle the mind, life, or body, or hold them of small account: it will rather hold them of high account, of immense importance, precisely because they are the conditions and instruments of the life of the spirit in man" (14:427). Spirituality "rejects no new light, no added means or materials of our human self-development" (14:432). Although it can be, it is not necessarily exclusive. In fact, in its fullness it must be all-inclusive, taking all human aims—art, science, politics, economics, society—and giving them a greater, a divine, or an ideal potentiality. Describing its workings, he tells us that spirituality will try to provide

> first, a framework of life within which man can seek for and grow into his real self and divinity; secondly, an increasing embodiment of the divine law of being in life; thirdly, a collective advance towards the light, power, peace, unity, harmony of the divine nature of humanity which the race is trying to evolve. This and nothing more but nothing less, this in all its potentialities, is what we mean by a spiritual culture and the application of spirituality to life. (14:430)

At the close of the series Aurobindo drops two more hints: first, "we should be, if possible, not less but more spiritual than our forefathers." Second, "what was dark to her before in its application, she can now, with a new light, illumine. . . ." Hopefully more creative, "she can, if she will, give a new and decisive turn to the problems over which all mankind is labouring and stumbling, for the clue to their solutions is there in her ancient knowledge" (14:433).

A closer, more detailed if somewhat repetitive exposition, seminal and original, will be found in another work of the same or the following period, *The Foundations of Indian Culture* (December 1918 to January 1921). Begun as a polemic against William Archer's ignorant and ill-natured attack on India, it turned out to be an in-depth defense of Indian values—in effect, the statement of a thesis that had become increasingly Sri Aurobindo's own. The five chapters on "Religion and Spirituality"—the "and" is indicative—suggest their closeness as well as the distinction, worked out in books such as *The Human Cycle* and *The Life Divine*.

What sets Indian civilization, "an immense religious effort of the human spirit," apart is precisely its two-in-one character, in which religion and spirituality play into each other. With his acute and balanced discriminations, Aurobindo has provided new canons and methods of understanding, a whole new dimension to human and social development. He starts by pointing out:

> A spiritual aspiration was the governing force of this culture, its core of thought, its ruling passion. Not only did it make spirituality the highest aim of life, but it even tried, as far as that could be done in the past conditions of the human race, to turn the whole of life towards spirituality. But since religion in the human mind is the first native, if imperfect form of the spiritual impulse, . . . [it] necessitated a casting of thought and action into the religious mould. . . . The highest spirituality indeed moves in a free and wide air far above. . . . But man does not arrive immediately at the highest inner elevation. . . . At first he needs lower supports and stages of ascent; he asks for some scaffolding of dogma, worship, image, sign, form, symbol, some indulgence and permission of mixed half-natural motive on which he can stand while he builds up in him the temple of the spirit. Only when the temple is completed can the supports be removed, the scaffolding disappear." (14:121–22)

The self-conscious institutions of Hinduism fulfilled this purpose fairly adequately, as much as the circumstances would permit. The point is missed by most Western observers, unless helped by a subtle philosophical training or a wide spiritual culture of one's own. The majority is struck by Hinduism's absence of dogmas, a fixed theology, a papal head or ecclesiastical authority. In fact, inspired critics have said that there is no such thing as a Hindu religion, but only a Hindu social system with a metaphysical whitewash. But, as Aurobindo insists, with all its social regulations, "the core of Hinduism is a spiritual, not a social discipline" (14:124–25). Indian culture had tried to make the spiritual ideal, variously realized, "the grand uplifting idea of life, the core of all thinking, the foundation of all religion, the secret sense and declared ultimate aim of human existence" (14:127). In this it displayed an unusual, simultaneous instinct for order and freedom, always a mark of maturity.

The plasticity of Indian religion or religions, more than creedal, more than polytheistic, is a sign of its truth and power, a tolerant synthesis. All paths lead to the same goal: "the Infinite full of many infinities." Through many names and forms, which are truths of the superphysical rather than mere symbols, one approaches, according to one's *svabhāva* and *adhikāra*, one's law of being and capacity, the Supreme Reality. To become aware of the divinity within us tnrough any and every opening is the basic credo, if any credo is needed, of the Indian experiment.

Aurobindo emphasizes over and again a more embracing, aspiring, and ambitious aim that hopes "not only to raise to inaccessible heights the few elect but to draw all men and all life and the whole human being upward, to spiritualize life and in the end to divinize human nature" (14:140). This, according to him, is the total thrust, the intrinsic aim of the Indian religion, the total movement of its spirituality.

Looking back, we can see how Indian religion kept close to two basic perceptions or propositions: (1) that for either the group or the individual the approach to the spirit cannot be sudden, simple, and immediate; (2) that there must be some kind of emphasis on the spiritual motive at all points. For the mass of the people this could only mean a religious influence. For the socialization of the spiritual impulse the ancient planners had provided three circles, which Aurobindo calls in a musical phrase the "triple quartet": *puruṣārtha*, *varṇāśrama*, and *caturāśrama*, the fourfold objects of life, the fourfold order of society, and the fourfold stages of life. These principles, beautiful even in ruins, are not incapable of resurrection, for the law of archetypes is hard to do away with.

Religion is the dynamics and structure of the ethos, which rested on the idea of the varying natural capacity of humans, *adhikāra*. The subtler sensitiveness of the Indian scheme made everyone, as and where one was, aware of something beyond the natural life, beyond the moment in time, beyond the individual ego, something beyond the needs and interests of the vital and physical nature. Here the *guṇa* classification into *sattvic*, *rajasic*, and *tamasic* personality types, or the Tantric classification of the animal, hero, and divine types comes to the mind. However, these "types" did not mean a permanent status or settlement, an unbridgeable division, since the actuality or potentiality of the three types coexist in all human beings and they may be overpassed.

The graded and complex system formed part of a total culture based on the well-ordered sciences, or *śāstras*. The knowledge of things went hand in hand with the knowledge of the Self, the whole of it constituting *dharma*, the right view of self-culture. Its catholicity did not ban the aesthetic or even the hedonistic side of humans. Nor, of course, were the political, economic, and social sides neglected. Each area of life had its own laws, but they were stamped with the idea of *dharma*. In the social order this led to a stereotype or ossification. From this the only escape route, if and when one opted for the religious life, was the life of a mendicant (*sannyāsi*). Then social rules did not apply. A rigid social law, a nobler discipline of the *dharma*, the wide freedom of the religious and spiritual life—these were the three props of the Hindu socioreligious ethos. In other words, each power or activity was made a gateway into his spiritual being. Thus came the Yoga of Works, Knowledge, and Love, each opening its own line toward self-exceeding.

The principles behind Indian religion, its intention and evolution, conceive of life as a movement of the Eternal in time, of the universal in the individual, of the Infinite in the finite, the divine in the human, principles that may be actualized through increasing self-knowledge. In the view of Aurobindo: "To have made this attempt is to have ennobled the life of the race; to have failed in it is better than if it had never at all been attempted; to have achieved even a partial success is a great contribution to the future possibilities of the human being" (14:173). According to Aurobindo, today the most vital movements of Indian thought and religion are tending toward the synthesis of spirituality which was the occult and self-conscious sense of the ancient Indian ideal. This is the leitmotif to which he bends his power of insight and persuasion.

In spite of what hostile critics might say, Aurobindo is convinced that "India has been as much a home of serious and solid realities, of a firm grappling with the problems of thought and life, of measured and wise organisation and great action as any other considerable center of civilisation" (14:184). The vividness and fullness of Indian culture, not only its art and literature but science and polity too, are too real to be ruled out. Its roll of leaders and saints, striking personalities, anything but "will-less dummies" (14:187) and "puppets," is long and continuous. Rajput and Maharashtrian heroism and the Sikh Khālsā show the livingness of the mainstream. Also in spite of various disabilities, the culture was widely and variously shared by the people, high and low. The religion, philosophy, poetry, and polity reached every strata, the entire community. The negative image of Indian culture in terms of the importance of human life, will, and activity is not true. Aurobindo points out: "The perfect man, the Siddha or the Buddha, becomes universal, embraces all being in sympathy and oneness, finds himself in others as in himself and by so doing draws into himself at the same time something of the infinite power of a universal energy" (14:195).

II

The intimate and invigorating exposé, in *The Foundations of Indian Culture*, of religion, society, and spirituality receives additional support from *The Human Cycle*. Published between August 1916 and July 1918 it is primarily a work on the psychology of social development (this was indeed its original title). A contribution to the history of ideas, the essays form an Aurobindean critique of reason and, his major theme, the possibility of a spiritual society. Taking his cue from Karl Lamprecht's clarification of the symbolic, typal-conventional, individualistic-rational, and subjective cycles of society, Aurobindo concentrates, for his purpose, on the last two.

The rigidities of a closed, conventional society finally bring in a spurt of protestant thinkers, the age of reason, with its cults of revolt, progress, and freedom. Limited in aim and method, the age of reason and individualism is seen to be a necessary passage to the next subjective period with its possibilities of a deeper self-discovery (15:10). Utilitarian, occidental, and scientific, the fulfillment of Individualism would also prove to be its end. Its gifts are not, however, to be ignored. According to Aurobindo, individualistic Europe has found out two important idea-forces: "the democratic conception of the right of all individuals as members of the society to the full life and full development of which they are individually capable" (15:20), and the deeper truth "that the individual is not merely a social unit" (15:20) but something in himself or herself. In the passage from the individual to the universal, which is bound to come, the modern mind relies exclusively on physical science and its universal laws of nature. Confined to the surface of things and a range of processes, after a point, the inadequacy of the scientific methodology betrays itself. To find the truth of things and one's relation to that truth humans must go deeper—to the subjective truth in oneself and things. "A momentous voyage of discovery," this has declared itself, among other things, in the collective self-consciousness of peoples.

This, "the right to be ourselves," is wholly right for nations. Yet, as the terrible Teutonic *faux pas* has proved, it can be wholly wrong. The root of the German error, a false subjectivism, a "bastard creed," lay in mistaking the life and body, the ego, for the Self. The true individuality of humanity and nations lies, on the contrary "in a Self one in difference which relates the good of each, on a footing of equality and not of strife and domination, to the good of the rest of the world" (15:47). Quick to draw the analogy with Indian archetypes, Aurobindo tells us: "It is the old Indian discovery that our real 'I' is a Supreme Being which is our true self and which it is our business to discover and consciously become and, secondly, that Being is one in all, expressed in the individual and in the collectivity. . ." (15.40).

The opposite ideals—individualism and collectivism—will have separate denouements accordingly as our approach is objective or subjective. Starting from the same data, objectivism inclines toward an external and mechanical view of things, while, proceeding from within, subjectivism finds a universal Being, Existence, or Self beyond the body, life, and mind. All three are seen as instrumental rather than as terminal values. And that makes a difference.

Subjectivism (Aurobindo does not use the word "subjectivity") has been more fruitful and creative than objectivism. The reason is that subjectivism makes clear not only what and how a human being has become in the past but what he/she might be in the future. Individuality is the mark of a human being; by this alone one understands the law of one's own being and development, in the end to go beyond oneself. Through him/her the One finds and manifests Itself in the many. But this ideal individual does not belong to humanity only; he/she also belongs to his/her race, type, class, temperament. And the community stands between oneself and humanity. Obviously the highest law for the individual would be to perfect his/her individuality by a free development from within and to respect and be aided by the same free development in others.

It is the same with the nation and the community. This is, no doubt, an ideal law that humankind has never perfected because it has understood the principle but imperfectly. Still, it is the business of a subjective age to hold it before the individual and self-conscious groups and to find out how it can become more and more the guiding principle of one's own individual and social existence.

The law of our true individuality and reciprocity helps us to see how and why self-realization is the sense, secret or overt, of our total development. A complete identification of the self with the physical, vital life, the sign of the Philistine, seems no longer possible. Science and education are there to prevent that. But science has led us to another kind of barbarism, which is characterized by an antihumanistic, commercial, military-industrial complex. Here the soul of humanity may linger for a while but cannot permanently rest. There is more to be done.

The mind turning upon life, matter, and itself marks a crucial stage of our psychosocial evolution. But this horizontal expansion of one's mental life, with an endless prospect of science and technology, is not the final point of human destiny. Aurobindo has put another rung or range—the spiritual—to humanity's possible existence. In this regard he speaks of two other values. According to him: "We must recognize both his need of integrality and his impulse of self-exceeding if we would fix rightly the meaning of his individual existence and the perfect aim and norm of his society" (15:76). A human being's complexities and contradictions are both one's glory and also misery, a point known to mature, nondogmatic observers. The preoccupation with the body and life, physical and economic factors, with little or no free play of the intelligence characterizes a low level of human existence. Today we have hordes of "civilized barbarians," masses of humans who outwardly live the civilized life but all the same are Philistines within. For a long time there have been educated classes and individuals, but the values of education, in the sense of right living, are still to be generalized. A cultured, educated humanity is a dream of the future.

After distinguishing the life of culture from its opposite, Aurobindo glances at the frequent quarrel between conduct and culture, between ethics and aesthetics, what Arnold called Hebraism and Hellenism. Of course, not Bohemia but Periclean Athens is the model of an aesthetic culture. Early Rome and Sparta provide examples of a strong and narrow ethical cast. Whatever their achievement, we are tempted to give the name of culture to those periods and civilizations which have encouraged a freely diverse human development. Yet, as with Athens and Renaissance Italy, we are bound to notice that without character, without some kind of high and strong discipline, there can be no enduring power of life. Neither the ethical nor the aesthetic is the whole person. The higher principle, capable of taking up both, will be found in the faculty of reason and intelligent will. On the human journey at a certain stage we cannot but turn to it. Indeed, whatever may be our final verdict, reason using the intelligent will for the ordering of one's inner and outer life has been for long the chief distinction of a human being. Now, however, we have become somewhat uncomfortable with such a situation and have come to feel that there is some greater godhead than reason, that there are degrees of knowledge, and that knowledge may not be the same as wisdom. It is seen that in spite of triumphant science still there are many problems that humans confront that cannot be solved by reason alone. At the heart of human existence there is something on which the unaided intellect can never lay a controlling hand; the human consciousness has to move beyond the limits of reason. Reason is but a link between what is beyond and beneath, between what Aurobindo calls the infrarational and the superrational.

The rational or the intellectual human is not the last and the highest ideal of humanhood. A rational society, or state, cannot be the ideal of our total development or perfection. Here, a happy factor, reason itself may and sometimes does help in its own surpassing. It has more than one field or station, higher echelons with laws and workings of their own. Even on its own level, reason's action is turned not only downward and outward but also upward and inward. We also notice that reason in humans has a kind of double working or motivation: disinterested as well as turned toward action and results. In the end, reason opens itself to higher realms of the Self, its gradual, harmonic unfolding in humanity and society.

By itself reason is an insufficient, often an inefficient, guide. Subjectivism points to an ancient or perennial truth, about superior ranges of being and cognition. Mediating between the infrarational and the suprarational, reason can but take two stances, both equally shallow, with regard to that which is beyond, expressed in religion. Reason either rejects or tries to "correct" religion, an arrogant attempt. And even when dealing with the infrarational aspects of religion, reason probably "pauperizes" more than it illumines. Still, as Sri Aurobindo's own example will show, the relation between reason and spirit need not be necessarily hostile. "What is impossible or absurd to the unaided reason, becomes real and right to the reason lifted beyond itself by the power of the spirit and irradiated by its light" (15:126).

The limitations of reason become equally clear in the two realms—the ethical and the aesthetic dimensions of human existence. Our sense of beauty has its infrarational elements, and reason is not the best guide here. Instead of recording responses, it tries to analyze and fix a grammar of techniques. As Aurobindo, aware at once of infrarational and suprarational beauty, puts it: "We find in the end the place of reason and the limits of its achievement are precisely of the same kind in regard to beauty as in regard to religion." "And for the same reason, because that which we are seeking through beauty is in the end that which we are seeking through religion, the Absolute, the Divine" (15:135).

As for ethics, the same rule holds. The utilitarian, hedonistic, and socialistic systems may deal with the lower levels of the ethical, but they are not enough for its higher reaches, what it points to. The value of utility cannot be denied, if only we knew what was humanity's final end or supreme good. Pleasure as a motive for virtue may explain its early forms. In the end it is or becomes a call of the being beyond the pleasure principle. As for society being the cause of human ethical growth, this again is only partially true. The core of the higher ethical demand may not agree with the social demand. "Therefore, it is with the cult of Good, as with the cult of Beauty and the cult of the spiritual. . . . it aims at an absolute satisfaction. . . . Rising from the infrarational beginnings through its intermediate dependence on reason, to a suprarational consummation, the ethical is like the aesthetic and the religious being of a man seeking after the Eternal" (15:144).

The presupposition is stated plainly: "In all the higher powers of his life man may be said to be seeking, blindly enough, for God" (15:145). The seeking has, it is true, the look of something remote to one's normal life, one's instincts, and one's activities. Normally one's life in society consists in three activities: the domestic and social; one's economic activity as a producer, wealth-getter, and consumer; and one's political status, a sphere of vital dynamism for which the Darwinian theory and Teutonic practice may seem adequate. The ancients were not innocent of these primary needs or activities, but they had the sagacity to admit also a higher goal. Individual or social, life cannot arrive at its secret ultimates by following its first infrarational motives. Neither can reason give it what it searches after. The ultimates of life, Aurobindo repeats, are spiritual, suprarational, and the first sign of the suprarational is the growth of absolute ideals.

"Since the infinite, the absolute and transcendent, the universal, the One is the secret summit of existence . . . and the Divine the ultimate goal and aim of our being and therefore of the whole development of the individual and the collectivity . . . reason cannot be the last and highest guide" (15:162). As the Asiatic mind has always suggested, religion is that light. On the other hand, with its faith in reason, the modern West seems to have rejected religion. But the root of the problem, and the difference, is not in religion itself but in what we have made of it. Religion has two sides: true religion, which is spiritual religion, and creedal religion, which emphasizes dogmas, forms, ceremonies, and some fixed or final religiopolitical or religiosocial system. The ambiguity is there because to the ordinary consciousness spirituality seems remote and hostile and is often associated with a life of suffering and mortification of the body, reflective of a "monastic attitude" toward life. For Aurobindo, it is not the *sannyāsi*, the religious recluse, that is a spokesperson of the spirit, but a *ṛṣi*. Aurobindo writes: "The spiritual man who can guide human life towards its perfection is typified in the ancient Indian idea of the Rishi, one who has lived fully the life of man and found the word of the supra-intellectual, supramental, spiritual truth" (15:169). Viewing all things from above and within, "he can guide the world humanly as God guides it divinely, because like the Divine he is in the life of the world and yet above it" (15:169).

In spirituality, our one hope for perfection lies not in the spirit that turns away from life but in one that accepts and fulfills it, be it for the individual or the community. Our evolution, we can see, moves necessarily through three stages: an infrarational, then toward a rational, and finally through a subjective turn toward a spiritual stage. But these stages are by no means exclusive. The infrarational need not be without its elements of beauty and power, its own rationality and even spirituality. Primitive cultures are not in every way inferior; in fact, in some ways they might be superior. These early dawns, however, as in India and during the age of the mysteries elsewhere, could not endure. Usually these cultures are destroyed by those outside the pale. Then comes the second stage, where one attempts to universalize the rule of reason in society by seeing reason as the highest developed human faculty.

The rational cycle of civilization has its typical course: a luminous, enthusiastic seed-time; next a partial victory; then disillusionment and a new beginning. The first of the cycles would be individualistic, increasingly democratic, with liberty for its principle; the second, socialistic and in the end "governmental Communism," with equality and the state for its principle; the third, if it ever gets beyond the stage of theory, anarchistic in the higher sense of the term, with "brotherhood" and not government for its principle.

In the individualistic cycle one tends to use reason somewhat less in order to come to an agreement with others, thus avoiding struggle and conflict. Among other things, democracy and education would be stressed. For want of deeper values, it has also unfortunately been plagued by plutocracy—control of the government by the wealthy.

In due course this cycle yields to democratic socialism. But because of the disadvantageous condition of its birth, in purely industrial and economic stress, the collective idea has violated both human nature and the original intention of its protagonists. In the process, both liberty and equality are sacrificed. In the Marxist no less than in the fascist regime the swing away from rationalism is too true to be good, but everything hangs in the balance. Will the subjective turn of the human mind have the time and the freedom to evolve and take up the spiral of social evolution where the curve of the age of reason ends and new vistas open up?

At first sight the rational collectivist idea has a powerful attraction. But between the idea and the facts of human nature falls the shadow, since, as Aurobindo emphasizes, "it ignores the soul of man and its supreme need of freedom" (15:196–97). The collective being is a fact, but this being is a soul and life, not merely a mind or a body to be ordered about by the all-powerful party or the state.

In the old infrarational societies, what ruled was not the state but the group-soul through customary regulations and institutions. If this entailed a subjection of the individual, this was not felt. The individualistic age was still not born and there was some latitude of social variation. Collectivism goes to the other extreme; standardizing and mechanizing, it spells the end of the age of reason and the hope of a rational society. With its fixed but opposite views, reason cannot provide the law of perfection. Reason or science has been victorious in the mechanic sphere precisely because it was mechanic. For vertical man, at once more and less than reason, reason may not be an ideal arbiter.

Will anarchistic thought be a better alternative? Its exaggerations apart, anarchism depends on the mixed action of enlightened reason and the principle of fraternity, undoubtedly the most neglected of the revolutionary slogans. No machinery invented by reason can produce the perfect human being or society. A spiritual or inner freedom, a yet unfounded law of love alone can be the sure foundation of a just society. Difficult? Aurobindo has no illusions. "This is not certain; but in any case, if this is not the solution, then there is no solution" (15:207). There is no harm in hoping. "After all there is no logical necessity for the conclusion that the change cannot begin at all because its perfection is not immediately possible" (15:207).

After a close look at how things are and have been, Aurobindo permits himself, in the last four essays, a number of speculations centering on the spiritual society. Both in its aim and in its method the spiritual society will differ from the normal society. The gregarious instinct modified by a possible antagonism of ego and interest—such is the image of society as we know it. It treats the human person as essentially a physical, vital, and mental being, for these are the three terms with which it has some competence to deal. In the end, however, society tends to fall by its own development, a sure sign that "there is some radical defect in its . . . method of development" (15:209). The modern idea of progress is not likely to escape the same fate. Irving Babbitt has spoken, uncharitably but perhaps not inaccurately, of progress toward the precipice.

What is the way out? Only in the turn toward the subjective, the discovery or re-discovery that the total truth of humanity is to be found in his soul and its energies, lies some hope. True, Aurobindo grants, the discovery was not unknown in the past. The religions knew this, but their "false socialization" (15:211) in favor of dogmas and a postmortem salvation took away the full potentiality. The discovery never became the law of social development; one evidence of this is that in order to find the soul one had to flee society. It was freedom from society rather than freedom in and for society. The spiritual aim in society will look upon humanity not solely as a mind, life, and body but, in spite of the difficulty of the task, accept the possibility of his whole being becoming divine.

Our normal living is a balance between the life-will and the modifying mind-will. One's uneasiness with life arises because one is unable to maintain this balance. The life of reason is often superimposed on the rest; certainly, domination is not transformation. We need to return to the ideal of the kingdom of God on earth. This calls for a change in the main power of our being, a dynamic transfer of our center of living to a higher consciousness. The spirit, not the mind, is the key to our existence and its transformation.

Subjectivity, be it vital, mental, or psychic, is not without its danger. If mankind is to be spiritualized, it must first cease to be material; the vital person should become the true "psychic" or "mental person." And while in this some will lead, the rest must be ready, able, and willing to receive what is being offered: the truths of God, freedom, and unity, three things that are really one. A society, even initially spiritualized, will make the revealing and finding of the divine Self, in the individual and in the group, the first and foremost aim of its activities. And, like its spiritual individuals, a spiritual society will not live in or by the ego; it will not be a collective ego but the collective soul. At no point will there be compulsion or the dissonance of disunity. One who sees God in all will not live either for oneself or for the state or society, but for God in oneself and the divine in the universe.

For a spiritual age to arrive, it is not enough that certain ideas, however utopian, gain common credence. Aurobindo is not unaware of the irony that the holding of an ideal often becomes an excellent excuse for not living according to the ideal. As will be the spirit and type of the individuals, so will be the realized power of the collectivity. "Therefore the individuals who will most help the future will be those who recognize a spiritual evolution as the destiny, and therefore the great need, of the human being" (15:250). Not held back by an a priori declaration of impossibility, and in spite of previous failures, they will hold on to their faith in the spiritual regeneration of humankind. The pioneers of the new life will take all life as their province. This will obviously be a difficult task for the individual. There is no end to the human journey, and there is perhaps more joy in the journey itself than in arriving at a destination. Aurobindo writes:

> if the number of individuals who seek to realize the possibility in themselves and in the world grows large and they get nearer the right way . . . the earthly evolution will have taken its great impetus upward and accomplished the

> revealing step in a divine progression of which the birth of thinking and aspiring man from the animal nature was only an obscure preparation and a far-off promise. (15:251)

III

From his original base in Hindu religion and society in *The Foundations of Indian Culture*, through a psychology of social development in *The Human Cycle*, Aurobindo moves toward their source in pure psychology. In *The Life Divine* he gives to the Vedāntic values a vast, evolving *élan vital*. Aurobindo's metapsychology, with a dash of evolution in a new key, finally goes beyond spirituality to the Supramental. Here is a discovery or recovery worthy of a *ṛṣi*.

The self-evident credo comes out often and early:

> We speak of the evolution of Life in Matter, the evolution of Mind in Matter . . . for there seems to be no reason why Life should evolve out of material elements or Mind out of living form, unless we accept the Vedantic solution that Life is already involved in Matter and Mind in Life because in essence Matter is a form of veiled Life, Life a form of veiled Consciousness. (18:3)

Again, for Aurobindo, the impulse toward "self-exceeding" exists more or less obscurely in Nature's different vessels; it "is gradually evolving and bound fully to evolve the necessary organs and faculties" (18:3). "The animal is a living laboratory in which Nature has, it is said, worked out man. Man himself may well be a thinking and living laboratory in whom and with whose conscious co-operation, she wills to work out the superman, the god" (18:3–4). The hypothesis calls forth another, both in effect veiled vision. "If it be true," he says, "that Spirit is involved in Matter and apparent Nature is secret God, then the manifestation of . . . God within and without are the highest and most legitimate aim possible to man upon earth" (18:4). The utopian thought is linked with the *Zeitgeist*, what the age demands. Cutting across the East–West conflict, and avoiding "the materialist denial" of the modern West and the "refusal of the ascetic" of the ancient East, Aurobindo points "towards a new and comprehensive affirmation in thought and in inner and outer experience and to its corollary, a new and rich self-fulfilment in an integral human existence for the individual and the race" (18:9).

Since truth of being must guide life, Aurobindo has throughout emphasized subjective factors. As above, so below, as within, so without—his works are an extended exposition of the occult law. As he puts it, "If in the Many we pursue insistently the One, it is to return with the benediction the revelation of the One confirming itself in the Many" (18:35). "Brahman is in the world to represent Itself in the values of Life. Life exists in the Brahman in order to discover Brahman in itself" (18:36). From this follows a revealing definition of the human being, and of his/her role and responsibility: "man's importance in the world is that he gives to it that development of consciousness in which its transfiguration by a perfect self-discovery becomes possible" (18:36). This is because Aurobindo is not tired of telling us: "Not to abandon the lower to itself, but to transform it in the light of the higher to which we have attained, is true divinity of nature" (18:36). Here is a method and a motive, a touchstone, another renaissance that transcends Western humanism, even if Pico della Mirandola might have prefigured it. Yet for all its futuristic bearing Aurobindo's thought is based on immemorial insights. As he himself confesses: "The Isha Upanishad insists on the unity and reality of all the manifestations of the Absolute; it refuses to confine truth to any one aspect. . . . It is this whole consciousness with its complete knowledge that builds the foundation of the Life Divine and makes its attainment possible" (18:636).[2]

Explaining alternative world hypotheses, Aurobindo speaks of

> four main theories, or categories of theory, with their corresponding mental attitudes and ideals in accordance with four different conceptions of truth of existence. These we may call the supracosmic, the cosmic and terrestrial, the supraterrestrial or otherworldly, and the integral or synthetic. . . . In this last category would fall our view of . . . a progressive manifestation, a spiritual evolution with the supracosmic for its source and support, the other-worldly for a condition and connecting link, and the cosmic or terrestrial for its field, and the human mind and life for its nodus and turning-point of release towards a higher and a highest perfection. (18:667)

In Aurobindean totality thinking, spiritual evolution becomes the bridge between life and spirit, "for it allows us to take into account the total nature of man and to recognize the legitimate place of his triple attraction, to earth, to heaven and to the supreme Reality" (18:677).

In this view: "Man is there to affirm himself in the universe, that is his first business, but also to evolve and finally to exceed himself" (18:684). "To become ourselves by exceeding ourselves" (18:685)—the knowledge includes three categories universally recognized: human being, God, and nature. Even if sometime one or all of these have been denied, there has been a constant pressure to unite the three in a supreme unified science, one's self-knowledge, world-knowledge, and God-knowledge. Here is a hope for the future rather than a present fact.

One notices in this a triple process: an evolution of forms of matter so as to admit the action of a growing consciousness; an upward evolutionary progress of consciousness itself from grade to higher grade, an ascent; a taking up of what has already been evolved, a transformation or integration more or less complete. Evolving in Matter, Mind and Life are themselves limited and modified by what they modify. This means that an entire transformation can come only by the emergence of a deeper occult Reality. To put it a little differently, "The past has been the history of a slow and difficult subconscious working with effects on the surface,—it has been an unconscious evolution; the present is a middle stage . . . an evolution slowly becoming conscious of itself; the future must be a more and more conscious evolution" (18:707). In taking up the lower parts, the human being looks not only downward but also upward and inward. This is the very field and justification of the occult and the subjective. One soon discovers worlds within worlds. Each level—physical, vital, mental—has endless sublevels, as it were. To go further, as we must, we have to bring in the mind itself the spiritual principle, the New Being. "The spiritual man is the sign of this new evolution" (18:722). But to leave it at that, with a few free ones and the many in bondage, is not enough: "it is only if the race advances that . . . the victories of the Spirit can be secure" (18:723).

Spirituality is a slow and difficult emergence, and Aurobindo is not unaware of its polarity or "dual tendency" (18:859): a drive toward the establishment of a spiritual consciousness even to the point of denouncing or renouncing earthly life, and a push toward its extension to our other parts and the whole of nature. Rejection is easier than transformation; still, as an ideal the latter is better. Eminently worth exploring, the fate of the human may depend on this. To make sense of the course of human evolution, of its ascent, we must consider it from two sides—first, the means used, and second, the actual results. Here Aurobindo fixes on "four main lines which Nature has followed in her attempt to open up the inner being—religion, occultism, spiritual thought and an inner spiritual realisation and experience: the three first are approaches, the last is the decisive avenue of entry" (18:860). All these have worked more or less in a connected fashion, whether simultaneously, independently, or exclusively, even in conflict with each other. Yet they fall into a pattern.

> Each of these means or approaches corresponds to something in our total being and therefore to something necessary to the total aim of her evolution. . . . [Man] must know himself and the world and discover and utilise all its potentialities. . . . This he can do only by knowing his inner mental, vital, physical and psychic being and its powers and movements and the universal laws and processes of the occult Mind and Life which stand behind the material front of the universe: that is the field of occultism. . . . He must know also the hidden Power or Powers that control the world . . . get into some kind of

> tune with the master Beings of the universe or with the universal Being and its universal Will or a supreme Being and his supreme will. . . . This approach is the aim of religion. . . . But this knowledge must be something more than a creed or a mystic revelation; his thinking mind must be able to accept it, to correlate it with principle of things and the observed truth of the universe . . . it can only be done by a spiritual philosophy. . . . But all knowledge and endeavor can reach its fruition only if it is turned into experience and has become a part of the consciousness and its established operations . . . this is the work of spiritual realisation and experience. (18:861–62)

If these have been the means for going "beyond oneself," the question forces itself: What has been their exact significance? The blatantly materialistic view dismisses the whole issue as an expedition into the unreal. The materialist mind feels confident that "the spiritual tendency in humanity has come to very little" (18:883), also that the otherworldly ascetic cannot help life, "has not solved the problem of life nor any of the problems with which humanity is at grips." True. But, as Aurobindo quietly qualifies, spirituality's "real work is not to solve human problems on the past or present mental basis, but to create a new foundation of our being and our life and knowledge" (18:883). As for the otherworldly tendency, this is "an extreme affirmation of his refusal to accept the limitations imposed by material Nature: for his very reason of being is to go beyond her; if he cannot transform her, he must leave her" (18:883). However self-defeating, the gesture is rational. "[I]f there has been no life-transformation, it is because man in the mass has always deflected the spiritual impulsion . . . and rejected the inward change" (18:884). Warning us against "any premature attempt at a large-scale collective spiritual life," Aurobindo underlines the fact that "Spirituality cannot be called upon to deal with life by a non-spiritual method or attempt to cure its ills by the panaceas, the political, social or other mechanical remedies which the mind is constantly attempting and which have always failed and will continue to fail to solve anything" (18:884). He also corrects a popular mistake that spiritual living will be dull and monotonous. As he puts it in a poetic phrase, it will not be a "single white monotone."

In a sense, spirituality is not the end. Not content with approximations, Aurobindo knows that "the spiritual man has evolved, but not the supramental being" (18:890). In Aurobindo's map of mutation, spirituality does not stand alone; it has a before and an after. For his purpose—since as he frankly says, "we have supposed a farther intention"—the aid of two other powers or processes is needed. To complete the picture he speaks of a triple transformation and explains:

> there must first be the psychic change, the conversion of our whole present nature into a soul-instrumentation; on that or along with that there must be a spiritual change . . . even into the lowest recesses . . . the darkness of our subconscience; last there must supervene the supramental transmutation . . . the ascent into the Supermind and the transforming descent of the supramental Consciousness into our entire being and nature. (18:891)

For the Aurobindean passion, the dream of a total transformation, the Supermind is a *sine qua non*.

At first the soul in Nature is entirely veiled; it evolves, passes through a slow development and formation, improves its communication with the within and intimations on the surface. The mind's clear perception of something that survives the death of the body helps in the process; but it may be varied and disturbed because, as "multi-personalities," a human being is rarely master in his/her divided house. To be centered or to find the center is not easy. Of itself the upward urge is drawn to the Good, the True, and the Beautiful. Working through the mind, it usually moves toward the formless and the impersonal. Another approach, more close and rapid, is through the heart center. There is still another well-known method, the separation of the conscious being from the formulated nature, of *puruṣa* from *prakṛti*, basic to the Indian yoga systems. All these methods have been followed and sometimes combined and have given rise to specialized yogas. Though these practices bring about a significant change in the individual, they are inadequate to bring about total transformation. For this to happen another power is needed, what Aurobindo calls the Supermind. Only the Supermind can descend without losing its full power of action, for its action is always intrinsic and automatic, the will and knowledge identical and the result commensurate. "Its nature is a self-achieving Truth-Consciousness and, if it limits itself or its working, it is by choice and intention, not by compulsion" (18:917).

Glimpsed and visited, the Supramental is yet to be mapped and domesticated. Here a helpful fact is that the process of evolution, of the higher principles, though greatly modified, is still essentially the same. A transition from Nature as we know it into Supernature is beyond the powers of Ignorance. Without the descent, or a pressure from above, a long evolution might give only a superior mentalization, fine flowers of the mind. "For a real transformation there must be a direct and unveiled intervention from above; there would be necessary, too, a total submission and surrender of the lower consciousness" (18:922), a principle of yoga that Aurobindo has elaborated elsewhere. A long, difficult stage of constant effort will be unavoidable, since a new decisive step can be taken only when the previous main steps have been sufficiently consolidated.

Rising through a series of sublimation of consciousness, each with its characteristic power and action—the Higher Mind, the Illumined Mind, Intuition and Overmind, and beyond, the Supermind—the aspirant arrives at the Apex, the source that is also the goal. Each of these levels—we cannot go into their nuances—is gnostic and dynamic and refers to the next higher principle; from thought to sight, to intuition, to the Overmind. But since the Overmind permits alternative possibilities, it is not the direct principle of transcendence, the transcendence that transfigures. The intricacy is so great that one might almost say that in this crucial change nothing is accomplished until all is accomplished. The adventure of the Absolute is as exacting as it is everlasting.

Essentially inner, a subjective spirituality may minimize or refuse commerce with the outer world; but this would be aloofness, not victory. The real difficulty in all this comes from the fact that the substance of our normal being and living is formed by the Inconscient and only the supramental force can wholly overcome this fundamental opposition. And since the logic of the Infinite is the magic of the finite, the mind cannot dictate or forecast how and what the supramental change will be. Yet, by way of analogy, one may assume, if not predict:

> As there has been established on earth a mental Consciousness and Power which shapes a race of mental beings and takes up into itself all of earth-nature that is ready for the change, so now there will be established on earth a gnostic Consciousness and Power which will shape a race of gnostic spiritual beings and take up into itself all of earthly nature that is ready for this new transformation. (18:967)

The supramental race is not going to be made according to a single stereotype. A manifold mystery, there will be diversity without difference. To use the words of *Savitri*, it will be a sweet difference of the Same. With his/her cosmic sympathy, the consummation of the spiritual person, the gnostic individual would be in the world but not of it. This individual's will, action, and knowledge at one with everything, will be a pure act of being, pure bliss of being, in each finite will be felt the Infinite. In brief, "As a consequence of the total change and reversal of consciousness establishing a new relation of Spirit with Mind and Life and Matter, and a new significance and perfection in the relation, there will be a reversal, a perfecting new significance also of the relations between the spirit and the body it inhabits" (18:985). Among its results will be immunity, serenity, and a merging of peace with ecstasy.

The manner in which Aurobindo relates the metapsychology to the modern crisis of the human being and civilization is more than a tour de force. What would have otherwise been but a dazzling display of antique doctrine shines forth as an existential challenge, a program, a remedy, a divine healing. The last chapter of *The Life Divine* is an ample summary of Aurobindo's essential worldview and the bearing of spirituality in actualizing human destiny, "a destiny that already exists in us as a necessity and a potentiality." If existence is indivisible, the not-self is in reality the self. The key idea here is: "a greater consciousness means a greater life" (18:1018). Also, as we have seen, "what is involved and emergent is not a Mind but a Spirit" (ibid.). And, as he has always held, the spiritual "must be not only an inner experience of the Divinity but a remolding of both the inner and outer existence . . . the appearance of a new order of beings and a new earth-life must be envisaged in our idea of the total consummation, the divine issue" (18:1018–19).

Aurobindo does not forget to refer to some of the likely alternative solutions and their inadequacy. First, the rational, scientific solution, with its partial ideas, the cult of the common person and the idealization of the state. An allied movement would be the better organization of the economic life of humankind, in which the interests of the individual are bound to be gradually sacrificed. Still another solution might be a new education policy persuading humans to accept a form of socialized living. There might also be a return to religion. But with its creedal tone and compromises with the lower nature of man, organized religion has not succeeded in changing human nature.

What then is the way out? For himself Aurobindo has little doubt: "A total spiritual direction given to the whole life and the whole nature can alone lift humanity beyond itself . . . for to hope for a change of human life without a change of human nature is an irrational and unspiritual proposition." The whole evolution has been a preparation for this change and every crisis brings it a little nearer. There will be problems of transition. "What is necessary is that there should be a turn in humanity felt by some or many towards the vision of this change, a feeling of its imperative need, the sense of its possibility and the will to make it possible in themselves and to find the way." Few have explored these possibilities, the way out, with such apocalyptic commitment and understanding as the yogi-thinker, Aurobindo.

This brings up the need for a creative gnostic change going far beyond the toy revolutions of today. The challenge of a deeper self-determination is unlikely to be met without inwardness. "[I]n our externalized surface existence, it is the world that seems to create us, but in the turn to the spiritual life, it is we who must create ourselves and our world" (18:1020). He draws the negative moral quite unambiguously: "A perfected human world cannot be created by men or composed of men who are themselves imperfect" (18:1022), a neat rapier thrust at mundane salvation *ab extra*.

To become ourselves is the one thing to be done. To become ourselves in being, in consciousness of being, in force of being, in delight of being, the being at once absolute, universal and individual, and to live in this integrated wholeness is the true sense of a divine life. It is only if our nature develops beyond itself that there can be a perfection of ourselves and our existence. "An evolution of innate and latent but as yet unevolved powers of consciousness is not considered admissible by the modern mind. . . . But there would be nothing supernatural or miraculous in such an evolution, except in so far as it would be a supranature or superior nature to ours just as human nature is a supernature or superior nature to that of animal or plant or material objects" (18:1041–42). There is nothing irrational or incredible about this, and the gnostic being would develop and use these powers even as humans develop and use the powers of their mental nature.

A civilization on trial faces us with a choice of destiny. Reason and science have built a civilization too big for the human person's limited mental and even more limited moral capacity, a dangerous servant of ego and its aggressive appetite. Perceptive thinkers painfully realize this and have warned us that our survival depends on finding the way. If history is to be something other than a "suicide club," there must be a change in motive and method. Here is a friend, philosopher, and guide to tomorrow.

In the struggle to liberate the visionary powers, through an equation of the evolution of consciousness with subjectivity and spirituality, Aurobindo has few equals. What others have seen through a glass darkly, he has seen clearly and consistently. He has made spirituality a new category of thought, behavior, and experience. From his base in the early Indian seminal insights and the psychology of social development and human becoming, he has built an architecture of trans-humanism that makes sense of the world and ourselves caught up in a worldwide crisis. Aurobindo is essentially a yogi, and his reading of the human situation is simply this: "The passage from the lower to the higher is the aim of yoga, and this passage may effect itself by the rejection of the lower and escape into the higher—the ordinary viewpoint—or by the transformation of the lower and its elevation to the higher nature. It is this, rather, that must be the aim of an integral yoga." The aim, he knows, may add to our struggle, but this cannot be avoided.

Choreographer of the coming and the inevitable—"I am vanquished by the beauty of the Unborn"—Aurobindo has given the world a task and a testament, his dreamed magnificence of things to be. Those who talk of the quality of life as of rising expectations may take a leaf out of his Book of Being and its "perpetual sacrament of spiritual experience."

Notes

1. Sri Aurobindo Birth Centenary Library, vol. 18, p. 150. All references in the body of the article refer to volume number and page numbers of this library.

2. His root experiences are no doubt part of "the central idea of the Vedic Rishis" (10:43). But see: "Why should the past be the limit of spiritual experience?" (26:134). "Truly, this shocked reverence for the past is a wonderful and fearful thing!" (22:93).

Bibliography

Sources

The following publications are from Sri Aurobindo Ashram, Pondicherry:

Sri Aurobindo. *Essays on the Gita*. 1942.
——. *The Foundations of Indian Culture*. 1959.
——. *The Future Poetry*. 1953.
——. *The Hour of God*. 1959.
——. *The Human Cycle*. 1949.
——. *Hymns to the Mystical Fire: Hymns to Agni from the Rig Veda*. 1952.
——. *The Ideal of Human Unity*. 1950.
——. *The Life Divine*. 1973.
——. *Glossary of Terms in Sri Aurobindo's Writings*. 1978.
——. *The Prophet of Life Divine*. Calcutta: Sri Aurobindo Path Mandir, 1951.

Studies

Choudhary, Haridas, ed. *The Integral Philosophy of Sri Aurobindo*. London: George Allen & Unwin, 1960.
Das, Adhar Chandra. *Sri Aurobindo and the Future of Mankind*. Calcutta: Calcutta University, 1934.
Maitra, S. *An Introduction to the Philosophy of Śrī Aurobindo*. 2nd ed. Benaras: Benaras Hindu University, 1945.
Purani, A. B. *Sri Aurobindo: Some Aspects of His Vision*. Bombay: Bharatiyavidya Bhavan, 1966.

20

The Spirituality of Ahiṁsā (Nonviolence): Traditional and Gandhian

John G. Arapura

> The man who raises himself above particular things, who sees through the individuation of the real . . . sees that the differences between him who inflicts suffering and who bears it is phenomenal only and not the thing in itself. The inflictor of suffering and the sufferer are one. If the eyes of both were opened, the inflictor of suffering would see that he lives in all that suffers pain.[1]

The Sanskrit word *ahiṁsā*, nowadays universally translated as "nonviolence," has a great depth of meaning that is not fully expressed by the English equivalent. Like many Sanskrit words of philosophical and ethical usage, it is polydimensional in its import, and "nonviolence," being rather one-dimensional, is hardly adequate as a translation. On the other hand, "nonviolence" is not without its own merits: because the English language was a witness to and a powerful medium of communication in one of the great epics of our time—that centered on the life and work of Mahatma Gandhi—this otherwise bland and pedestrian word has acquired nuances it never possessed in its own past, which were not derived from the Sanskrit. These nuances have been transmitted to the Sanskrit original itself, not least in the sociopolitical, activist, and revolutionary respects, which again have been the more effectively collected, transmuted, and expressed by the Gandhi-coined term *satyāgraha*, which quite evidently is terminologically unrelated, though most definitely related in import, to *ahiṁsā*.

Here I will probe, first, the traditional Indian spirituality of *ahiṁsā* and then the full bloom of it in Gandhi, in whom—to put it in another way—it was on fire in an unprecedented manner, marking a new phase of the world's spiritual history.

Traditional Indian Spirituality of *Ahiṁsā*

Both Hinduism and the other two world religions of ancient Indian origin, Buddhism and Jainism, attach the greatest importance to *ahiṁsā*. *Ahiṁsā* is the negative of *hiṁsā*, a noun formed from the verb *hiṁs*, which is itself derived from the root *han*. This verb has a wide range of meanings, including "injure," "harm," "kill," "destroy," as well as "commit an act of violence." In the Vedas the compound word *hiṁsā-karman* (*hiṁsā*-act) designates injury, harm, destruction, or death brought about by magical rites, which are condemned as sinful. But these rites too are of the generic nature of sacrifice (*yāga*) though antithetical to the good sacrifices for which the term *yajña* is exclusively reserved. The latter are calculated to promote earthly well-being (*abhyudaya*) as well as eternal felicity (*niḥśreyasa*). Śabara, the great commentator of the text of aphorisms bearing on Vedic rites, the *Mīmāṁsā-Sūtra*, distinguishes between the good sacrifices and the bad ones (1.1.2). The bad ones are called *śneya*, intended to do harm to one's enemies or other victims. The good ones are of the nature of *dharma*, being in accord with Supreme Reality and hence good, expressed by the term *artha*, bearing both senses. The *śneya* ones are opposite to *dharma* and to *artha*, and therefore called *anartha*, basically meaning "discordant with [Supreme] Reality."

Commenting on the above mentioned *Mīmāṁsā-Sūtra* 1.1.2, but harking back to the Vedas themselves, Śabara declares that the magical *śneya* sacrifice being *anartha* is *hiṁsā*, and *hiṁsā* is forbidden. And *śneya* is not to be performed, as it is a weapon only for those who wish to do harm.

The original meaning of *ahiṁsā* would then be the deliberate refusal to perform those (*śneya*) rites calculated to do harm to others, preceded of course by the renunciation of the very wish to injure—a resolution made doubly forceful by the fact that the power to do *hiṁsā* acts had been provided for in the Vedic system of knowledge like the tree with the forbidden fruit in the middle of the Garden of Eden—but so that one may not use it. The deliberate renunciation of it is the source of a new spiritual power that accords with the benign office of *yajña*, or true Vedic sacrifices, hence even supplementing it and augmenting its potency. This original meaning has inherently remained in the concept of *ahiṁsā* through history, often resurfacing in the literature, most notably in the *Bhagavad Gītā*.

However, while this original meaning has persisted in the background of the *ahiṁsā* concept as it developed in the Indian religion, a subtle shift is seen to have taken place in the crowning phase of the Vedic tradition, namely, in the Upaniṣads. That shift does not by any means amount to a replacement of the original meaning, as it is but the addition of a new, concrete though narrower meaning, namely, nontaking of life and noncausing of pain to any being. In this sense, it is recognized that even *yajñas*, by nature benign, might entail some *hiṁsā* if it includes the sacrifice of animal victims. No doubt this marks the advent of something very crucial, especially viewed from the ethical perspective. A significant testimony to this new slant in the concept of *ahiṁsā* is found in the great *Chāndogya Upaniṣad*, in explicit references where either the very word or some other with the same sense is used.

But before taking up the *Chāndogya* instances of the use of the explicit mention of *ahiṁsā*, we may consider one very important and well-known passage resorted to by even such a leading Western poet as T. S. Eliot—the *Bṛhadāraṇyaka Upaniṣad* 5.2.1–3, which employs three *da*-based expressions. There we may even see some light as to the transformation that resulted in the overly ethical meaning of *ahiṁsā*. The passage says that the god Prajāpati suddenly uttered the mysterious syllable *da*. Those who heard him took three different meanings from it: *dāmyata* (have self-control); *datta* (give); *dayadhvam* (have compassion). "This very thing heaven's thunderous voice repeats, *da, da, da* . . . one should practice this three-fold (thing)—self-control (*dāmam*), giving (*dānam*) and compassion (*dayā*)."

This furnishes a background—already becoming well established in the Vedic tradition—in which the Buddha, like Mahāvīra and others, enunciates his celebrated doctrine of compassion for all living creatures. Thus we read in the *Sāmanna-phala Suttam* (which is probably the earliest such reference in Buddhist literature): "A monk, refusing to harm any creature, moves about as a compassionate man, with sympathy for the well-being of all living beings" (2.5.45).[2] That the Upaniṣadic passage is much earlier than the Buddhist will not be contested. Hence we can gather that the Buddha did not teach *ahiṁsā* in a climate not already prepared for, and the doctrine was clearly not a new innovation.

Mahāvīra, the historical founder of Jainism, promulgated *ahiṁsā* with even greater rigor. With regard to Jainism, M. Hiriyanna correctly remarks: "Of the various virtues to be cultivated by the Jains, *ahiṁsā* occupies the foremost place. The doctrine of *ahiṁsā* is no doubt very old in India, but the way in which it is made to pervade the whole conduct is peculiarly Jain."[3]

We may briefly revert to the *Bṛhadāraṇayaka Upaniṣad* passage cited above in order to underline a remarkable point, though somewhat parenthetical in this context. The mystic syllable *da* revealed self-control to the gods, the spirit of giving to men, and compassion to the demons (*asuras*). Specifically speaking of the last, it is a demonic quality to hurt, and it is those persons possessed of the demonic character who need to be brought under compassion, fully expressed by *ahiṁsā*. But with that knowledge goes the belief of the Vedas that there is none so evil or so hardened as to have to remain outside *ahiṁsā's* boundless embrace: witness Mahatma Gandhi's unvanquishable faith, the source of which is ultimately rooted in Being itself rather than in human beings.

Now we will turn to the references to *ahiṁsā* by name in the *Chāndogya Upaniṣad.* In the first occurrence (3.17.4) we notice *ahiṁsā* placed within a cluster of associated virtues, along with penance (*tapas*), giving (*dānam*), uprightness (*ārjavam*), and truth speaking (*satya-vacanam*), and they are then described as the better kind of fees for the priests who perform sacrificial rites in order to bring benefits to the people. There is one other reference in this Upaniṣad, which is at all events the most striking anywhere. It occurs in its very last passage (8.15.1) and quite unmistakably, therefore, as its last great precept. The *Chāndogya Upaniṣad* has served as the very basis of what took shape as the Vedānta tradition, pulling in the substance of all other Upaniṣads as well. As the precept of *ahiṁsā* appears in the conclusion of the *Chāndogya,* it is clear that it has been given a place in the very heart of the tradition. Therefore it merits being discussed specifically as under the following head.

Ahiṁsā in Its Vedāntic-Philosophic Character

The passage runs as follows: "This Brahmā told to Prajāpati, Prajāpati to Manu, Manu to mankind. . . . He who has learned the Veda . . . who establishes all his senses in the *Ātman,* who conducts himself evenly, having attained the *Brahmā*-world [i.e., the plane of knowledge transitional to pure gnosis] *will not return higher*, yea he will not return."

It is evident that establishing one's senses in *Ātman* and comporting oneself *ahiṁsā*-wise toward all beings go hand in hand, the latter to be viewed as complementary to the former. The point of present interest to us is that *ahiṁsā*, along with establishment of one's senses in the *Ātman,* falls within the supreme objective of the Upaniṣads—that is, spiritual knowledge—or *ātma-vidyā*, which as Śaṅkara, the great Vedānta philosopher-commentator writes "is fully brought to light in the final three chapters—6 to 8"—of the *Chāndogya. Ahiṁsā* appears as a component in the very praxis of this spiritual knowledge, and hence as deep-rootedly Upaniṣadic, that is, Vedāntic. It governs the behavior towards all beings.

The words "all beings" (*sarva bhūtāni*) frequently occur in Indian scriptures, beginning with the celebrated *Puruṣa* hymn of the *Ṛg Veda* (10.90): "All beings" came out of the sacrificial dismemberment of the lowest quarter of *Puruṣa*. But in the *Chāndogya* passage under consideration we find something absolutely new and immensely significant: a docking of the concept of *ahiṁsā* with the concept "all beings." Hence, for the first time then, *ahiṁsā* is depicted as a mode of existence toward all beings. It is seen to be grounded in the mysticism of the oneness of all beings determined by the very origin of all things out of the sacrificed body of the primeval *Puruṣa*, and therefore it has nothing to do with some vague, hylozoistic notion, to which it is sometimes attributed. In the above Upaniṣad it is put forward as a teaching (*upadeśa, nirdeśa*), hence as an extension of the praxis of spiritual knowledge.

In one place in the *Commentary on the Brahma Sūtra* (2.3.44), Śaṅkara points out that "the very word 'being' [lower case *b*, as we should put it] signifies unmoving and moving creatures because of . . . the expression, 'to exist *ahiṁsā*-wise toward all beings.'"[4] This explanation by Śaṅkara follows on an exegesis he has given in the same context of the fuller scriptural meaning of "all beings." He cites in the same place another passage from the *Chāndogya Upaniṣad* (3.12.6), which itself is a citation from the *Puruṣa* hymn of the *Ṛg Veda*. Here Śaṅkara combines two aspects of *Puruṣa*, who is but *Brahman* called by another name, that is, "its filling (also comprehending) all beings, and its residence inside every being, thus each acting as a citadel." (However, we must not confuse this with the conventional transcendence–immanence notion, as it is better to see it as the unique idea that it is, with no parallel anywhere. For nowhere, as we know, has transcendence–immanence been loaded with *ahiṁsā*, except in the Vedic tradition and in its subsequent developments.)

So, according to Vedānta, *ahiṁsā* is the way one who lives in the ambience of spiritual knowledge (*gnosis*) and is devoted to its praxis experiences its *jīva* existence within the organic wholeness of the cosmos, while having simultaneously established one's senses in the *Ātman*.

Having said all this based on the concluding instruction of the *Chāndogya Upaniṣad*, now comes the crunch. We must cite the full text of the instruction, part of which we have held in abeyance until now. The complete clause provides an exception and it reads: "comporting oneself in *ahiṁsā*-fashion towards all beings except in the *tīrthas*." The question is, What is meant by *tīrtha*? It has more than one meaning. Ordinarily, it means a sacred spot (e.g., where sacrifice was conducted in Vedic times) or a place of pilgrimage (in modern times). But Śaṅkara offers the view that *tīrtha* means "a sacred rite enjoined by the Veda." So the exception implies that in principle the Veda reserves the right to overrule the application of *ahiṁsā* when it conflicts with the obligation to perform rites that may involve hurt to animals. However, it would seem that in fact there would have been in the Upaniṣadic view of religion no actual conflict, because that view did not include sacrificial rites literally, having already turned them into symbols for meditation like the one on the horse sacrifice with which the *Bṛhadāraṇyaka Upaniṣad* commences. But the Upaniṣads would not in principle set aside what the Vedas had enjoined. Therefore, the exception had to be included for the sake of the sacred form.

Even so, it seems to have troubled later Upaniṣadic circles, which is the reason a casuistic explanation was advanced by some members of these circles, as Śaṅkara himself reports: "These [he calls them "others"] say that the *tīrtha* exceptions (themselves) are in actuality only *ahiṁsā*. How could anything that proceeds from the Veda, even when it involves apparent hurt to animal victims, be other than *ahiṁsā*? The logic might be that the supremely holy cancels even the infraction upon any other holy—say the *ahiṁsā* conduct as here—and transmutes them.

Some others had recourse to the view that the twin instruction on establishing the senses on the *Ātman* and *ahiṁsā*—like its ground, the praxis of spiritual knowledge—is addressed to the monks and ascetics, and therefore the laity had an excuse for taking shelter under the exception. But the *Brahma Sūtra* would shatter such a plea, as it says (3.4.48), "This text which is the conclusion of the [*Chāndogya*] *Upaniṣad* is generally aimed at the layman inasmuch as he has to observe *all* injunctions." And Śaṅkara makes it even more clear that, like other injunctions, "*ahiṁsā* and sense-control apply to the layman." The position is further stengthened by the *Brahma Sūtra* aphorism that immediately follows (3.4.49): "these instructions are laid down for [the laity] as much as they are for monks."

There is a most interesting aside to all this which furnishes a reason for a profoundly human, and hence relaxed, approach to the whole question of *ahiṁsā*, which may otherwise burden an observant of the great precept, making one literalist and humorless. It comes from none other than Śaṅkara himself, who remarks concerning our very *Chāndogya* text that even an unworldly wandering monk cannot completely live up to the precept "for, in as much as he receives alms for his earthly wherewithal—food and raiment—meager as it is, he troubles (rather "hurts" and "persecutes") others." Thus Śaṅkara introduces a great relief into a situation that could otherwise become grim, by throwing in, in the deepest philosophical sense, an element of supreme irony which only one as great as he could do. Śaṅkara is no stranger to irony; he uses it on several occasions. A certain similarity with Socrates' irony, expressed especially in his discourses concerning virtue, is worth noting. Søren Kierkegaard speaks of irony as a seducer and as a guide, interpreting it as "mastered moment" that teaches us to actualize actuality rather than idealize it—and that approach seems to fit Śaṅkara's use of irony too.[5]

Finally, concerning the *ahiṁsā* precept in Vedānta, let it be said that while it is one of the discoveries of the Upaniṣads, to which they assigned an exalted position, neither it nor its psychic correlate—establishment of the senses in the *Ātman*—is a designated station for the posture of devout proximity to *Brahman* (which is what the word *upaniṣad* itself means) such as "that thou art," "I am *Brahman*," "all this is *Brahman*," and so on. But it does have a reflected glory within the Upaniṣads, which in any case are as a whole themselves the original postures of proximity to *Brahman*.[6] But all in all, like other ethical—or metaphysical—precepts, it can be extrapolated from its native home and grafted on to other religious systems—and it has been. In Vedānta itself its place is strictly as part of the praxis of spiritual knowledge, extended from the essential form of that praxis, that is, "study of the Upaniṣads" (*svādhyāya*).[7] However, it does indeed breathe an ethical life of its own as well, especially in our time, and has become universally valid as a fighting creed essential for human survival—so decreed by modern history itself, not by any thinker or system.

Later Evolution of Ahiṁsā to the Position of Supreme Dharma

That *ahiṁsā* was originally spawned in the Veda, more specifically making its decisive appearance in the Upaniṣads, is beyond doubt. Its advent was slow, methodical, and cosmologically conceived, with its roots going back to the primordial *Puruṣa* sacrifice, finally entering the stage as an item in the praxis of Vedāntic spiritual knowledge.

But it kept on evolving further through the post-Upaniṣadic, that is, epic and Purāṇic times. That evolution took place in concert with the significant Buddhist and Jaina contributions. It was rather a general movement in which the Vedic as well as non-Vedic religions took equal part, with a common cosmology and a common life philosophy behind them. There may, however, have been a difference in the degree of rigor in the application, especially pertaining to diet: extreme strictures on what to eat even within an emerging common vegetarian life-style, tying it, in a fundamentalist manner, to the question of salvation, clearly were a Jaina trait.

One area in which the Buddhists and the Jainas, especially the former, had creative input is that of inspiring the eventual abolition of the exception allowed in the *Chāndogya Upaniṣad*, so much so that the application of *ahiṁsā* became universal, brooking no violation. They had clearly protested against—and rejected—the rite so that they never needed to adapt their ethics to it.

On the other hand, the Vedic people were forced to adapt the rite—that is, bring it in line with the rigorous rule—even going to the extent of rejecting the theoretical provision for exception. The work had to be done beginning with the re-grasp of the foundational concept of *dharma* by extending its content. It is well known that the word *dharma* has a vast array of meaning. Of these, two, at two ends of a spectrum as it were, are of interest to us. Accordingly, on the one hand, with regard to the *Ṛg Vedic* text (90.16) where we come across a reference to *yajñas* as "the first of the *dharmas*" (*dharmāṇi prathamāni*), Śabara quotes this Vedic text in the context of his comment on *Pūrva Mīmāṁsā Sūtra* (1.1.2, earlier referred to) as his authority for defining *dharma* as *yajña*, leaving the question of *ahiṁsā* untouched. On the other hand, in the great epic *Mahābhārata*, amidst much discussion on *ahiṁsā* in a very large number of places, such statements occur as "*ahiṁsā* is the supreme *dharma*"; "*ahiṁsā* is the quintessence of all *dharmas*."[8] This characterization of it sometimes comes in combination with some subordinate proposition or injunction, such as "*ahiṁsā* is the supreme *dharma* to be chosen by all beings; therefore, one bound by *Brahman* (*brāhmaṇaḥ*) should never harm any being whatsoever" (*Ādi Parva* 11.11, 12); "*ahiṁsā* is the greatest *dharma*, while *hiṁsā* is *adharma*" (*Aśvamedha Parva* 43.19). Even a randomly selected portion of the text of the epic might contain some discussion on the theme. It is generally held that "*ahiṁsā* is the character of *dharma* on account of the primacy of the Vedic philosophy" (*Anuśāsana Parva* [13] 115.1). The great epic conveys the same idea also in many other places, for example, "*ahiṁsā* is the *dharma* of all beings, know it as the most excellent" (*Droṇa Parva* 192.38); "*ahiṁsā* excels the *dharmas* of all beings" (*Śānti Parva* 265.6).

The Purāṇas—belonging to an age later than the epics—repeat the same idea frequently. Thus, for example, the *Padma Purāṇa* states: "*ahiṁsā* is the supreme *dharma, ahiṁsā* is the supreme asceticism, always have the sages said that it is also the highest kind of giving."[9] "*Ahiṁsā* is the highest *dharma*; there is nothing that can make one more happy," says the *Kūrma Purāṇa* (II.11.13, 14; Kane, vol. 5/2, p. 946).[10] Descriptions of its excellence abound in several Purāṇas. It is called the doorway to *dharma* (*dharmasya dvāram, Brahmāṇḍa Purāṇa* II.31.35; Kane, vol. 5/2, p. 946) and is referred to by a number of similar epithets.

Further, it is of the greatest interest that a bold, explicit revaluation of the provisions of the Vedic sacrifices themselves, so as to bring them in line with the growing sentiment against injury to animals, is seen to have been in the making. Thus, in the *Matsya Purāṇa* in a dialogue that took place at the commencement of a sacrifice—hence appropriately called *Yajñārambhe devarṣi saṁvāda* (chap. 143)—the question was raised, and answered thus: "[Wherefore] the Vedic sages do not acclaim sacrifices involving injury [to animal victims]; (they prescribe oblations of) gathered roots, fruits and vegetables" (143.30–32).

As a side note—and significantly enough—such conduct is described as the foundation of what is called *sanātana dharma* (timeless *dharma*),[11] although it is not clear whether it has here the current meaning of "orthodox Hindu religion." But then this latter aspect must be viewed in light of the modern extension of the meaning of the word *dharma* itself, answering to "religion" even in its sociological definition.

Ahiṁsā in the Wider List of Virtues

In most of the Hindu sacred literatures *ahiṁsā* appears as an item in a group of virtues. Although the group varies from list to list, there are close similarities insofar as all the lists reflect the abiding principles of Indian moral philosophy, no doubt held together by an associative law intuitively formed, which itself is uniquely Indian. In most variations the difference consists only in the substitution of synonyms. The *ahiṁsā* concept is expressed by several other terms carrying the same meaning, among which figure most prominently *bhūtadayā* (kindness to beings) and *dayābhāva* (kindliness). *Ahiṁsā* or one of the other terms conveying its meaning occurs in a number of the lists of virtues. Thus, for instance, we read in the *Gautama Dharma Sūtra* of "kindness to all beings" (*dayā sarva bhuteṣu*), along with "serenity, goodwill, cleanliness, earnestness, graciousness, strength of mind and desirelessness" (VIII.24–25; Kane, vol. 5/2, p. 945) and in the *Matsya Purāṇa* of "kindliness" (*dayābhava*), followed by "serenity, celibacy, asceticism, purity, compassion, forbearance and courage" (143.33). The use of unmistakable synonyms is a pattern in evidence everywhere—in the Purāṇas, the epics, and the *dharma sūtras*.

In respect of ethical rules, a number of works, including *Yājñavalkya Smṛti*, *Vaikhānasa Smārta Sūtra*, and Manu's own *Dharma Sūtra*, have been seeking a rationale to divide them into two classes—inward and outward—calling them *yama* and *niyama* respectively. But the division is accomplished under a perfect rationale by the *Yoga Sūtra* of Patañjali. In that work *yama*, pertaining to one's outward conduct, that is, in relation to others and to the cosmos, and *niyama*, pertaining to one's inward conduct, that is, in relation to one's self (hence the one in purely ethical sense and the other in ethical-spiritual sense) are listed and expanded in chapter II, aphorism 30–45. They each consist of five principles. *Ahiṁsā* falls in the *yama* class, to make up five along with truth-speaking (*satya*), noncoveting (*asteya*), celibacy (*brahmacarya*), and nonowning (*aparigrahah*). (The five of the *niyama* class do not fall into our present purview.) The *Kūrma Purāṇa* follows the *Yoga Sūtra* faithfully and to the letter (in respect of the *yama* and also the *niyama* principles) (II.11.13–15; see Kane, vol. 5/2, p. 946). (The *Dharma Sūtra* of Manu while distinguishing the two—without listing their principles—insists that *yama* should be observed strictly while allowing for relaxation on *niyama* [IV.204].)

The five *yamas* are common across the board in Indian religions as a whole. In Jaina teachings they are called *vrata*, meaning "vow," a common word of great ethical-religious import in the whole Indian tradition. These vows, however, are vows made not to a god but to oneself, nor are they made for a time in order to meet a contingency but are permanent, character- and behavior-altering resolutions meant to be observed forever.

The *Yoga Sūtra* too uses the term *vrata* but gives it an even more intensified expression as *mahāvrata* (great vow, or "great course-of-conduct" as the classic translation of J. H. Woods puts it) to describe the five, beginning with *ahiṁsā* (II.31). Here the text also enunciates the *yama* principles in the sense of *mahāvrata* as what are unrestricted by considerations of caste, place, time, or circumstance, and hence as universally binding. It is most significant that the original commentator of the *Yoga Sūtra*, Vyāsa, dwells mostly on *ahiṁsā* in order to remove from its application any exceptions based on the above considerations. No exceptions whatsoever, he maintains. He repudiates the view of some that the rule means, for example, that no one except the fisherman (who lives by fishing) may kill fish and that no one may slay animals except in fulfillment of sacred rite, in sacred places and on sacred occasions. Pointedly referring to some people's understanding of the ostensible exception provided for in the *Chāndogya Upaniṣad*, he declares that while a yogi of course kills nothing at any time anywhere for any reason, he must further resolve, "I will not slay even for the sacred rite (*na tīrthe haniṣyāmi iti*)."

What we notice is increasing insistence on literal nonkilling/noninjury as the supreme virtue, stated so from the *Mahābhārata* down, but gradually removing from it any shade of doubt about its universal obligatoriness. This is unerringly echoed by the *Kūrma Purāṇa* when it declares: "The paramount sages have said that *ahiṁsā* is born of the woe-less condition" (II.11.15; Kane, vol. 5/2, p. 946).

Comparison with the Greek View of Virtues

How similar the Indian view of virtues is to the Greek is of some interest, especially insofar as *ahiṁsā* is called the supreme *dharma*. The Greek word *aretē* and the Sanskrit word *dharma* (among others) have much in common. In addition, there are in Sanskrit such other words as *satguṇa*, *yama*, and *niyama* in more narrow senses. The description of *ahiṁsā* as *supreme dharma* (*paramo dharma*) arouses images of the Greek "cardinal virtues." Sir M. Monier-Williams's *Sanskrit-English Dictionary* even calls *ahiṁsā* "a *cardinal* virtue of the Indians." But then we know better today and hence must reserve the term "cardinal" for what are specifically Greek *aretai*, that is, wisdom, courage, sobriety, and justice. Although these four are often called Platonic, as Hans-Georg Gadamer points out, Plato had actually inherited them from the Greek tradition but refined and "artfully stylized [them] in order to emphasize the element of knowledge they contain."[12] These so-called cardinal virtues are discussed by Plato in several places in his works, but most importantly in *The Republic*, IV.427ff. and VI.504ff.[13] In fact, it is with the Socratic-Platonic version of them that the Indian virtues can claim to hold affinity, that is, in the assertion that virtue is knowledge—in both cases self-knowledge, that is, *phronēsis* for the one and *ātma-jñāna* for the other. (Let us recall that in the conclusion of the *Chāndogya Upaniṣad*, *ahiṁsā*, singled out and set along with control of the senses, is an extension as well as an outcome and at the same time a means of the praxis of Self-knowledge.) The Socratic-Platonic identification of virtue with knowledge becomes even more palpable in the *Bhagavad Gītā* than in the Upaniṣads.

The great difference between Greek and Hindu thought lies in the sphere of application of the virtues. For the Greeks it is in the ideal state (*politeia*) of human beings that the cardinal virtues yield up their knowledge element at the altar, so to say, of the Good, in that way realizing their unity as well. On the other hand, for the Indians the sphere of application has always remained the unbounded world of all beings, where by means of virtue, especially of *ahiṁsā*, "the greatest good of all beings" (*hitatama sarva-bhūtānām*) is aimed at (see *Śānti Parva* 288.20; 330.13). In discussion on matters ethical the term "all beings" (mentioned previously) as beneficiary normally occurs, and it is not a pointless expression even though it may lack the bounded definiteness of the concept "state." There is, no doubt, an unmistakable cosmic character to Indian ethics, just as there is an inalienable ethical character to Indian views of the cosmos: this is important for *dharma*. Only in light of this inviolable relation between the moral life and the cosmos can such a high virtue as *ahiṁsā* be properly understood. The Indians never anchored their quest for the moral good in the realm that the Greeks defined and circumscribed as *politeia*, which may be considered either the strength or the weakness of each in turn, depending on the type of application sought. The greatest mistake is made when most scholars nowadays, including many Indians, try to understand *ahiṁsā* (and also *dharma*) essentially in terms of political action and social existence. In truth, an ethic that is also cosmic can only be a form of spirituality, and hence beyond, though including, the human element of politics. The principles of *dharma*, especially those called *yama*—the five—are but an integrated system of cosmo-ethical relations in which the individual stands and comports oneself. (It needs to be added that this cosmo-ethics is the real basis for the *karma* theory, which accordingly must be put beyond the pale of customary misunderstandings.)

That primacy of place must belong to *ahiṁsā* in the list of virtues—as viewed within a cosmo-ethical framework—has been the contention of the *Mahābhārata*, and later of the Purāṇas. That is what Vyāsa, the commentator of the *Yoga Sūtra*, also says in respect of the five *yamas*. "Of these (i.e., the *yamas*)" he writes, "*ahiṁsā* means the absence of malice towards all beings at all times and in all things. All other *yamas* as well as the (accompanying five) observances (namely, cleanliness, contentment, asceticism, study, and devotion to God) are rooted in it. By teaching them, the inculcation of *ahiṁsā* is aimed at so that it be attained" (commentary on II.30).

The objective of *dharma* as such, now clearly led by *ahiṁsā*, is twofold: (1) to educate humans in the art of the virtues; (2) to enable humans to take into their own hands the task of reducing the potentiality for evil in the world which is our home. In both respects, intuition is utilized to the maximum without yielding to the temptation to shift the burden to some theoretical probing and analysis of the nature and origin of evil. There is, thus, a wholesome directness in ethics that accords with the directness of reality itself.

Ahiṁsā in the Bhagavad Gītā

We are led to the *Bhagavad Gītā* in our inquiry into the spirituality of *ahiṁsā*, because it is the consummate text of Indian spiritual ethics. In the case of this scripture we break the customary chronological order and place it as the jumping-off point to modern times, especially to Gandhi, because it is the reigning scripture of modern Indian intelligentsia and most powerful in its contemporary influence. Its ethics too is ultimately cosmic, as are all Indian scriptures and systems—and none of them can be limited to the sphere of the human.

To the extent that we understand the essential cosmo-ethical character to be primary for *ahiṁsā*, it can be validly argued that the *Bhagavad Gītā* fully participates in it. As for the word *ahiṁsā*, it occurs in that scripture only in a cluster with similar terms, which, as we remarked earlier, are bound together by some associative law intuitively grasped by the Indian tradition. (And nowhere does it call *ahiṁsā* the supreme *dharma*—a matter of some interest.) The word occurs exactly four times within the seven hundred verses that constitute that scripture:

1. In 10.5: in a group, along with equanimity (*samatā*), contentment (*tuṣṭi*), austerity (*tapaḥ*), charity (*dānam*), and repute-disrepute (*yaśo 'yaśaḥ*), which are described as modalities of beings (*bhāva-bhūtānām*) that proceed from the Divine.

2. In 13.7–11: in a cluster that includes humility (*amānitvam*), integrity (*aḍambhitvam*), patience (*kṣānti*), and so on, ending with constancy in spiritual knowledge (*adhyātma-jñāna-nityatvam*) and—most interestingly—the vision of the meaning of philosophy (*tattva-jñānārtha-darśanam*). Then is added: "only this [perhaps, the entire block] is to be called wisdom (*jnānam*)." The word used here, *jñānam*, must in the context of the discourse be understood as wisdom, that is, life-wisdom rather than as pure gnosis, hence very much like *phronēsis*.

3. In 16.1–3: as a member of a community of virtues, along with fearlessness (*abhayam*), study (*svādhyāya*), fortitude (*dhṛti*), nonmalice (*adroha*), and so on.

4. In 17.14: as an item in a stock of virtues all together called austerity of the body (*śarīram tapaḥ*), beginning with worship of the gods, of the twice-born (i.e., those symbolically reborn by sacred knowledge), of the teachers and of the really wise (*devadvija-guru-prājña-pūjanam*). Other similar groups of virtues that constitute austerity of speech and austerity of mind are listed in the verses that follow (15 and 16). All these make up what is called good (*sāttvikam*), according to verse 17. There is no doubt that the virtue of *ahiṁsā* is given a high place in this scripture. Nevertheless, the vexed question as to its supremacy in this scripture's teaching will continue to be raised. There is no easy way to answer it. One may only begin by saying that the celebrated scripture is a dialogue in a dramatic setting. In a gradual, though highly involved, manner it describes the truth of things as a whole in response to a perplexed man's (Arjuna's) question in the critical field of battle put to Kṛṣṇa, his teacher: "What shall I do now, faced as I am with a quandary whether to fight and kill or resist not and be killed for the sake of promoting peace?" The truth of things as a whole is brought to bear by the teacher on Arjuna's immediate situation, clinching it with a mystical vision of the entire cosmic order as sparks from the Divine. A man's struggle for ethical wisdom has been brought in line with the paradigmatic unfolding of the truth of things as a whole, also subsuming within it the cycles of becoming and passing. But Arjuna must still come down from a vision thus vouchsafed, to the world of conflict, and Kṛṣṇa himself helps him down. The talk of war and Arjuna's obligation as a warrior-leader to fight it is resumed. The battle to the finish it is going to be now that the leader has

been prepared by profound metaphysical instructions crowned by an ecstatic vision. As to the net wisdom gained by it all, the scripture itself refrains from characterizing it by any privileged concept, including *ahiṁsā*. That is certain. Clearly, it is not a concept game. But concepts are human devices still to be used for approaching what is taught. It would appear that one way to come to grips with it is to relive the experience, not speculatively or by mere poetic imagination but by facing a call such as Arjuna himself faced—and by putting one's soul at stake. The only person known in modern history who did so relive it, though under uniquely different circumstances, is Mahatma Gandhi. He chose the name *satyāgraha* (truth-grasp/struggle) to describe the entire teaching and characterized it as *ahiṁsā*. Yet there is no reason to believe that others may not see it differently.

One thing is worthy of note: the scripture, at least arguably, exonerates the leader of the just war from blame and guilt if his action leads to death of his foes. But then it can equally be maintained that the enemies to be attacked and destroyed are internal within human beings, and the so-called human foes in the battlefield are only surrealistic personifications of these. That this view is not altogether fanciful is strongly supported by such verses as III.36–43. Desire (*kāma*) and wrath (*krodha*) are called the enemy (*vairi*), in verse 37. Hence, Arjuna is asked to "slay this sin-bearing destroyer of wisdom and discrimination" (v. 41), "to slay the enemy in the form of desire so difficult of access" (v. 43). One thing is certain: the option in interpretation is not decided by scholarship alone but by putting one's soul at stake as well. In any case, at the end, we must leave the matter pending, to be taken up for further discussion soon under the aegis of the Gandhian saga, where the most celebrated option, since the composition of the scripture, came to life. But now we turn to a medieval writer.

Ahiṁsā in Jñānadev's Commentary on the Bhagavad Gītā

It is a fact that no traditional commentator—or anyone else for the matter—saw fit to connect the Indian spirituality of *ahiṁsā* and the teaching of the *Bhagavad Gītā* in such a powerful fashion as did Gandhi. Among India's spiritual masters, one medieval figure, Jñānadev, gave much attention to the *ahiṁsā* principle as taught in that scripture. But he certainly did not bring *ahiṁsā* and this scripture together into that unique and absolute relation which is characterstic of Gandhi's interpretation.

Jñānadeva was a thirteenth-century *bhakti* poet-saint, from a village in the Maharastra country of India.[14] He is believed to have lived only twenty-one years (1275–1296); at the end of that short life he voluntarily entered final *samādhi*, from which to pass to death, having also previously arranged his own internment in the very spot in which he sat in *samādhi*. Jñānadev's commentary, called *Bhāvārthadīpikā* (later called *Jñāneśwarī*) on the *Bhagavad Gītā*, composed in the Marathi language, consists of about nine thousand stanzas, distributed as meditations on the eighteen chapters of the *Bhagavad Gītā*. (It is interesting that this huge work should date itself, in its own very last stanza, thus: "Jñanadeva composed this commentary during the *Śākha* year 1212, and Saccidānanda was his reverent scribe."—Śākha 1212 corresponding to 1290 C.E.)

But of this large number of stanzas, 103 (stanzas 216–318), apart from scattered stanzas, are a long continuous meditation on the precept of *ahiṁsā* as laid down in the *Bhagavad Gītā* 13.7 (verse 8 according to the *Jñāneśwarī* numbering).[15] It begins with a strong condemnation of Vedic rites and sacrifices which involves "the slaughter of animals," for "how can *ahiṁsā* be practised this way?" The irony of it is expressed by these similes: "As if one should break off the branches of a tree to form a fence around the trunk; cut off his arm and sell it in order to satisfy his hunger, or demolish a temple and then use the stone to build a wall around the god" (13.218, 219). Even the traditional Ayurvedic medicine is not spared from criticism inasmuch as it prescribes medicines that require the destruction of plant or even animal life in order to save human lives (13.224–29). A detailed, graphic picture of the man of *ahiṁsā* is painted: how he walks, talks, and looks. "Even before beginning to speak, love springs from him and compassion expresses itself before any word is uttered" (13.262). "In his speech there is no agitation or haste, no guile or false hope, doubt or deceit" (13.271). "His look is steady and his brow unruffled, for he holds that the universal spirit is in all beings and so usually he avoids looking at them lest this spirit be harmed. Should his inward kindliness impel him to look at another [his glance brings comfort] . . . the effect of his look on all creatures is such that even the tortoise does not know the depth of his tenderness" (13.272–76).

As is the case with the *Bhagavad Gītā* itself, Jñānadev's ideal virtue of *ahiṁsā* is linked with knowledge, or better "wisdom." But there is more in his thought than this equation, for, in true Indian fashion he looks to a man of *ahiṁsā* in its perfection who therefore, is an incarnation (*avatāra*) of wisdom. "When thou seest that a man has entirely renounced the doing of harm in speech, in thought or in outward action, know him to be an abundant storehouse of wisdom, indeed he is the very incarnation of wisdom. If thou dost desire to understand this harmlessness [*ahiṁsā*] which is heard, spoken or written of in books, we have only to look at such a man" (13.310–12). Clearly, the Indian ideals of the *jīvan-mukta* (as *avatāra* itself) is behind this thought. There again the *Bhagavad Gītā* is paradigmatic.

Ahiṁsā Reaching Full Bloom (in Association with Truth) in Mahatma Gandhi

Our discussion of the *Bhagavad Gītā* furnishes us with a logical bridge to *ahiṁsā* in Mahatma Gandhi, the reasons for which we shall soon see. Now the place of the Mahatma in the spirituality of *ahiṁsā* ought to be recognized as rather special; one may claim that *ahiṁsā* reached a state of full bloom in his life, his work, and his teachings and that it was on fire in him as perhaps never before in recent history.

Gandhi and the Bhagavad Gītā and Other Sources for Ahiṁsā

Gandhi himself often claimed the *Bhagavad Gītā* (the *Gītā*, for short, following the present-day custom that Gandhi too adopted) as the chief among his sources of inspiration—and, what is more, of philosophical vindication. Gandhi wrote *Exposition of the Gītā,* though not at the start of his career—and that fact is important.[16] Gandhi's *Exposition* is but a miniscule part of his literary output. Among his writings, his *Autobiography*, also called *The Story of My Experiments with Truth*, is undoubtedly the best known.[17] The extent of his writings is often not well known. His *Collected Works* have run into fully ninety large-sized volumes, amounting to many thousands of printed pages, making him one of the most prolific authors in all history.[18] Nevertheless, his writing (and speaking) was merely part of his epic activities. As for the nature of his writings, as the saying goes, "he that runs may read them"; moreover, it seems equally true that he—Gandhi—wrote them as he ran, so to speak.

Gandhi's *Exposition* is decidedly not a work of scholarship, nor does it pretend to be. His approach is mainly inspirational. He himself says that it was designed for a mass movement, in his own words, "for women, the commercial class, the so-called shudras and the like, who have little or no literary equipment." Gandhi informs us that it is a sequel to his *Autobiography*, both of which were originally published serially in his early journal, *Young India*, and fairly soon afterwards as books.

It is clear that he wrote the *Exposition* specifically to argue the case of *ahiṁsā* in action, and at the prodding of a co-worker, Swami Anand, who criticized Gandhi's attempted espousal of that great principle merely based on deductions made from "stray verses" from it. However, Gandhi leaves us in no doubt that he did write it in order to vindicate his faith in *ahiṁsā*. Even so, he is careful to point out that *ahiṁsā* is put forward not as some self-sufficient spirituality but as the ethical arm of a more comprehensive, and certainly more traditional, one—"self-realization." Thus he declares:

> Man is not at peace with himself till he has become like unto God. The endeavor to reach this state is the supreme, the only, ambition worth having. And this is self-realization. This self-realization is the subject of the *Gītā,* as it is of all scriptures. . . . The object of the *Gītā* appears to me to be that of showing the most excellent way to attain self-realization. (*Gītā Exposition,* p. 129)

Like other traditional writers, Jñānadev included, Gandhi, in the quest of how humans may become like God, resorts to the idea of incarnation (*avatāra*), as, for example, Kṛṣṇa, the teacher of *Gītā* was believed to be. It involves perfection. However, Gandhi takes the ideal of divine perfection in human form away from the mythological past and places it in the undetermined future of every person's possibility, that is, not as an object of worship but as an ideal goal for every one. He writes: "Krishna of the *Gītā* is perfection and right knowledge personified; but the picture is imaginary" (*Gītā Exposition,* p. 128). Further down, he adds, "This belief in incarnation is a testimony of man's lofty spiritual ambition."

Gandhi insists on the practical aspects of self-realization. By "practical," as in any genuine ethical thought, one means not "what it is possible to do" but what ought to be rendered into actual observance regardless of the difficulty in doing so. The realm where such rendering takes places is the intricate and ever-expanding system of life relations, beginning with one's immediate neighbors, extending to the outer limits of all existence (i.e., the age-old *sarva bhūtāni*). Accordingly, Gandhi reports: "It has been my endeavour, as also that of some companions, to reduce to practice the teaching of the *Gītā* as I have understood it." And so he adds, "The *Gītā* has become for us [i.e., for him and his associates], a spiritual reference book" (*Gītā Exposition,* p. 126). In the *Autobiography* he testifies, "to me the *Gītā* [at a given time] became an infallible guide of conduct. Just as I turned to the English Dictionary for the meanings of English words, I turned to this dictionary of conduct for a ready solution to all my troubles and trials" (p. 265).[19]

That the *Gītā* is a textbook for the complete and comprehensive spiritual life focused on self-realization, and that, further, it points one to practical (i.e., ethical) conduct in daily life as also in extraordinary contingencies like war will be generally agreed on by most scholars of this scripture. But the special character of Gandhi's standpoint is that the practical conduct taught by the *Gītā* is one marked by *ahiṁsā* and in no way by violence or bloodletting. In this he pulls against the current of opinion that has generally prevailed and been mostly taken for granted. That the *Gītā* is a guide to self-realization is accepted by most. That it entails action is accepted by a great many. But to say it teaches *ahiṁsā* as the essential character of the method of self-realization and action is a very different matter. In this Gandhi does not have much company.

Now, is Gandhi without justification? He would appear to be on solid ground only if it is acknowledged that his interpretation is the outcome of a special kind of existential understanding. Every existential understanding works like this: One who would understand is confronted head on by the scripture, which acts very much like a person who, waylaying one, hits one with rocks. Some of the words and concepts would feel like the rocks that hit one. Some peculiar correspondence and interaction take place between the impact of the "rocks" (i.e., the words and concepts) and the notions that may already have been taking shape in one, eventually leading to decisive insights and unshakable convictions. This account seems, in Gandhi's case, to be well borne out by his own report that when he read the *Gītā* "words like *aparigraha* (nonpossession) and *samabhāva* (equivability) gripped [one could substitute 'hit'] me" (*Autobiography*, 265). The notion of *ahiṁsā,* with the support of the even more fundamental notion of truth (cornerstone of his thought), which was already taking shape in his thought, furnished the interpretive criteria. Remarkably enough, *ahiṁsā* drew ever greater strength from truth and grew into the decisive—to use Gadamer's famous term—"prejudice" in Gandhi's understanding and interpretation of the *Gītā.* To this principle of prejudice, however, something else may be supplemented as a matter of great significance in dealing with Gandhi's approach to the *Gītā.* We may call it the principle of projectivity. By this we mean what will, on the basis of a certain configuration of the text, although seemingly "prejudiced" and ostensibly even ill-founded, be proven true in the future by actually living it out, naturally, in some existential fashion. In this manner one may reach out even beyond the *apparent* possibilities the book, or the author of the book, presents, but in terms of the text's own not yet apparent possibilities. In respect of this the following statement of Gandhi's is entirely telling: "Because a poet puts a particular truth before the world, it does not necessarily follow that he has known or worked out all its great consequences, or that having done so, he is able always to express them fully. In this perhaps lies the greatness of the poem and the poet. A poet's meaning is limitless. Like man the meaning of great writings suffers evolution. This is true of the *Gītā*" (*Gītā Exposition,* p. 133). We can see that even the most daring hermeneut cannot improve on this raw insight. Applied to the rule of *ahiṁsā*, here at issue, it means, for Gandhi, that "we are not required to probe the mind of the author of the *Gītā* as to his limitations of *ahiṁsā* and the like" (ibid.).

Now, while Gandhi maintains that the *Gītā* certainly teaches *ahiṁsā*, he does not think that it teaches it as though it were some new doctrine that needs to be established. That is why he observes: "And it may be freely admitted that the *Gītā* was not written to establish *ahiṁsā*" (*Gītā Exposition*, p. 133). But then he points to two other factors associated with this. First, that *ahiṁsā* is implicit in what he sees as the central teaching of the *Gītā*, that is, nonattachment to desire for fruits of one's work (meaning renunciation of fruit), what is called *niṣkāmakarma*. Gandhi spells out what is implicit: "I have felt that in trying to enforce in one's life the central teaching of the *Gītā* one is bound to follow Truth and *ahiṁsā*" (ibid., p. 132). Second, that it had been so universally accepted or taken for granted (as implicit in *niṣkāmakarma*) that, in people's mind, it simply coexisted even with its normal opposite, namely, the spirit of war and conflict, which is why the author of the *Gītā* could take "a warlike illustration." Hence Gandhi states: "When the *Gītā* was written, although people believed in *ahiṁsā*, wars were not only not taboo, but nobody observed the contradiction between them and *ahiṁsā*" (ibid., p. 133).

However, with regard to the above he believes that the noncontradiction is between *ahiṁsā* and the mental image of war, so that a poet could use a war imagery. He is convinced that the so-called war is no actual historical event, for the poet at least, but a pure symbol for the ever-real moral conflict within humanity so that the stronger that imagery, the deeper and the more urgent, it should be understood, is the need to fight the war within the soul. He goes so far as to take the radical step of rejecting the historical nature of the *Gītā* episode and also of its matrix, the epic *Mahābhārata*. In his words:

> Even in 1888–89 [that is, just touching twenty], when I first became acquainted with the *Gītā*, I felt that it was not an historical work, but that under the guise of physical warfare, it described the duel that perpetually went on in the hearts of mankind, and that physical warfare was brought in merely to make the description of the internal duel more alluring. The preliminary intuition became more confirmed on a closer study of religion and the *Gītā*. A study of the *Mahābhārata* gave it added confirmation. I do not regard the *Mahābhārata* as an historical work in the accepted sense. The *Ādiparva* contains powerful evidence in support of my opinion." (*Gītā Exposition*, p. 127)

Gandhi, rather cogently, adduces the presence of some surrealistic and highly stylized characters in the epic (being pictured as either superhuman or infrahuman) as powerful evidence in favor of his view, showing that the poet's intent was not so much to record actual events—despite some possible basis to it all—as to develop what may be called a symbolic morality play. Hence, he draws the conclusion: "The author of the *Mahābhārata* has not established the necessity of physical warfare; on the contrary he has proved its futility. He has made the victors shed tears of sorrow and repentance, and has left them nothing but a legacy of miseries" (*Gītā Exposition*, p. 128).

To round off this brief inquiry into Gandhi's relation to the *Bhagavad Gītā*, one thing must finally be said that has already been more than hinted at. That is the astounding fact that he had already discovered *ahiṁsā*, before he ever read or even saw that scripture (which was actually while a student in England) in a stanza of Shamal Bhatt's didactic poem (in Gujarati) quoted by him in the *Autobiography*, below (in translation):

> For a bowl of water give a goodly meal;
> For a kindly greeting bow thou down with zeal;
> For a simple penny pay them back with gold;
> If thy life be rescued, life do not withhold.
> Thus the words and actions the wise regard;
> Every little service tenfold they reward.
> But the truly noble know all men are one,
> And return with gladness good for evil done.
> (*Autobiography*, 35)

He was only seeking confirmation in the scriptures, among which the *Gītā* had a more dramatic impact on him than others. In it he rediscovered *ahiṁsā* and decisively discovered himself. This process went on via other scriptures too. Among these most worthy of mention is the New Testament, especially the Sermon on the Mount, about which he writes:

> [The Sermon on the Mount] went straight to my heart. I compared it with the *Gītā*. The verses, "But I say unto you, that ye resist not evil: but whosoever shall smite thee on thy right cheek, turn to him the other cheek also. And if any man take away thy coat let him have thy cloak also," delighted me beyond measure and put me in mind of Shamal Bhatt's "For a bowl of water give a goodly meal," etc. (*Autobiography*, 68–69)

Truth and Ahiṁsā in Gandhi

In the public mind Gandhi's philosophy has been primarily associated with nonviolence, especially because of the impact of his political action in India and South Africa as well as the inspiration some moral leaders like Martin Luther King, Jr., found in his example. This impression is entirely justified. Yet there is another side to Gandhi, as already indicated, that is, his even more fundamental stand on "Truth." In fact, the alternative title (which is actually the original title) of his *Autobiography* is *The Story of My Experi-*

ments with Truth. This fact gives good ground for a scholar of Gandhi's thought—T. K. Mahadevan—to say: "The core of Gandhian teaching consists of one concept and no other. It is Truth." "It is Truth that holds the Gandhian teaching together and gives meaning and significance to the meanest of his ideas."[20] Gandhi's teaching on truth has not received as much attention worldwide as his teaching on, and practice of, nonviolence. Among the studies that have attempted to concentrate on it, however, Erik Erikson's *Gandhi's Truth* stands as a distinguished contribution.[21] But the book, being a psychoanalytic study, by the very nature of the case, limits itself to that aspect of the matter as the opening sentence in the preface makes it clear: "This book describes a Westerner's and a psychoanalyst's search for the historical presence of Mahatma Gandhi and for the meaning of what he called Truth." On the other hand, the spiritual aspects of Gandhi's teaching on truth—as also of *ahiṁsā*—require that teaching to be placed in the stream of the Indian tradition first and foremost. To say this certainly is not to belittle the originality of Gandhi's own unique input into that stream itself. His originality seems to consist in the way truth and *ahiṁsā* were welded into one indivisible unit, making the product simultaneously serve (1) as a *sādhana*, attended by every kind of asceticism for self-realization, which is put forward as an individual's own and the world's essential goal; (2) as a militant instrument, in the shape of *satyāgraha*, for correcting every given unjust, or wrong, therefore "untrue," situation as well as for world reform, which are not goals divorced from the former. (The world's self-realization is very much the goal of the teaching of *Dharma*. The *Mahābhārata* declares: "*Dharma* has been taught so that all beings may advance towards their [common] goal" [*Śānti Parva* 110.10a].)

Behind Gandhi stands an enormous tradition that has exalted truth—*satya*—above all things. Every Indian child would become acquainted with some of its aspects, including the glorification of it to the highest, sometimes subjugating even the gods to its absolute majesty. Sacred literatures from the Upaniṣads on have extolled it, conveying every shade of meaning. There are graphic accounts of human characters who have embraced it as the absolute ground of their existence and have perfectly embodied it in their conduct even through unbelievable trials and tribulations. Gandhi tells us how a classic play (from the epic) called *Hariśchandra*, recounting the life of a person of this description undergoing untold trials, captured his imagination as a child, how it haunted him and how he acted it to himself "times without number," and how it could still move him (*Autobiography*, 7, 8). It is clear that he was captured by truth even before he was captured by *ahiṁsā*.

The Vedānta philosophy, following the teachings of the Upaniṣads, worked out the metaphysics of *satya*, formed from the base term *sat* (essence/being/reality/the good) both conceptually and etymologically in great depth.[22] While Gandhi, no academic philosopher, was essentially drawn to its existential and cosmo-ethical aspects rather than its metaphysics, he certainly was closely acquainted with the spirit of the metaphysical tradition, which, as is well known, drew the classic distinction between absolute truth (*paramārtha satya*) and relative truth (*vyavahāra satya*), assigning even existential and cosmo-ethical things to the latter. There are Gandhi scholars who are interested in his approach to these "two truths." Joan Bondurant in her excellent study of Gandhi—*Conquest of Violence*—says that "the effect" of his approach was "to transform the absolute truth of philosophical *Sat* to the relative truth of ethical principle,"[23] capable of being [existentially] tested. However, one doubts whether even Gandhi would meddle with absolute truth, that is, pure *Brahman*, in that manner. It would seem rather that he was existentially pushing to the utmost what he himself called "the relative truth as I have conceived it," but pushing it "to the death."[24]

Gandhi writes in his *Autobiography* that, while intensely studying the *Mahābhārata* in prison, light dawned on him that "morality is the basis of all things and truth is the basis of all morality" (*Gītā Exposition,* p. 34). (By "all morality" one gathers that virtues are intended.) It is significant that in this view even the *Yoga Sūtra* distinction between *yama* (relation to others and the world) and *niyama* (relation to oneself) seems to drop off. An underlying singleness of all morality breaks through, also no longer requiring any other intuition to bind together the various virtues, either conceptually or metaphysically (such as we saw earlier in this essay). This is truth as he understands it. It would seem that all other virtues, including *ahiṁsā,* follow truth, as the worker bees follow the queen bee. "All other observances," he instructed his disciples "take their rise from the quest for and worship of Truth."[25] In the *Autobiography* he writes:

> In the march towards Truth, anger, selfishness, hatred, etc., naturally give way, for otherwise Truth would be impossible to attain. A man swayed by passions may have good enough intentions, may be truthful in word, but he will never find the Truth. A successful search for Truth means complete deliverance from the dual throng such as of love and hate, happiness and misery. (p. 345)

Although truth comprehends all, it is the uniform pattern in all of Gandhi's writings to couple Truth and *ahiṁsā* as coordinates. A strong impression is formed in one's mind in reading his works that what he means by *ahiṁsā* is the entirety of truth's self-expression summing up all virtues save truth itself. He would find some powerful authority in the tradition for truth expressing itself through a galaxy of other virtues, though not to view *ahiṁsā* as comprehending all of them in essence. Here is a verse from the *Mahābhārata*:

> Truth expresses itself in thirteen principles—
> Equanimity, restraint, magnanimity,
> Forgiveness, humility, patience,
> Long-suffering, renunciation, meditation,
> Dignity, resoluteness, constancy and *ahiṁsā*.
> (*Śānti Parva* 156.8, 9)

There is an undeniable existential sense to Gandhi's experiment with truth and *ahiṁsā,* consisting of a three-pronged encounter with truth and *ahiṁsā* and with God too, both often in the encounter with people whom he would approach with some redemptive purpose or other in mind. Thus he records what took place in the village of Champaran, where he had gone to meet some peasants and hear about their problems. He writes: "It is no exaggeration, but the literal truth, to say that in this meeting with the peasants I was face to face with God, *Ahiṁsā* and Truth" (*Autobiography,* 345). The whole activity following it he describes as "a bold experiment with Truth and *Ahiṁsā*" (ibid., 416). Even the writing of the *Autobiography*—bearing testimony in public—is of a piece with that continuous encounter, which he puts in truly mystical language: "To describe truth, as it has appeared to me, and in the exact manner in which I have arrived at it, has been my ceaseless effort. The exercise has given me ineffable mental peace, because it has been my fond hope that it might bring faith in Truth and *Ahiṁsā* to waverers" (ibid., 503). The mystical element in this existential experience is most pronounced. He speaks of "the indescribable lustre of Truth, a million times more intense than that of the Sun" and of "what he has caught of it" as but "the faintest glimmer of that mighty effulgence" (ibid., 504).

The most important thing about Gandhi's unique brand of spirituality is the wholly dynamic relation between truth and *ahiṁsā,* which is what underlies his obverting the proposition "God is Truth," to the form "Truth is God." *Ahiṁsā* is "the loving service of all that lives," which is the way to reach truth, and that is what is implied in the formula God is Truth.[26] He declares with the finality of a personal testimony: "I can say with assurance, as a result of all my experiments that a perfect vision of Truth can only follow a complete vision of *Ahiṁsā*" (*Autobiography,* 504). It is at least in part due to the necessity of intensifying the place of *ahiṁsā* that he in later life obverted the formula to "Truth is God." Through *ahiṁsā,* one pushes relative truths to the utmost, even "to the death." That is why in a statement made in 1937 (as at other times) he declares: "I often described my religion as the religion of Truth. Of late instead of saying God is Truth, I have been saying Truth is God, in order to more fully define my religion."[27]

One can show that this observation is no cheap apologetic but a call to live in the highest imperative of truth and *ahiṁsā*, noting the need to face death, in an utterly inward (not necessarily martyr's) sense. So, "we shall have to die in the pursuit of truth. . . . One who desires to have a vision of God will have to transcend the body, to despise it, to court death."[28]

Ahiṁsā in the Indian tradition had great cosmo-ethical implications. But its sociopolitical possibilities were far from realized. The distinctiveness of Gandhi's epochal contribution has three sides to it: (1) that he experimentally discovered and applied the latter in concert with truth in a way never before quite so vividly demonstrated; (2) that he kept it in close touch with the former, without deviating from the path of the tradition; (3) that he brought forward what Erickson aptly calls "the realization of man in one all human species,"[29] to which we would add "with the keenest sense of cosmo-ethical responsibility, resulting in the care for all beings even here on earth, as it peculiarly rests on the shoulders of our species." "Look at Gautama's compassion," Gandhi said on one occasion, "it was not confined to mankind, it was extended to all living beings. Does not one's heart overflow with love to think of the lamb joyously perched on his shoulders?" (*Autobiography*, 160). "Mere non-killing is not enough" he said elsewhere, for "the active part of non-violence is love. The law of love requires equal consideration for all life from the tiniest insect to the highest man."[30]

Ahiṁsā can certainly be described as the highest principle that inculcates in one a cosmo-ethical attitude inasmuch as the life present in beings is the most concrete revelation of Being (*sat*), whereby one is made to realize that one's position in the cosmos is one of trusteeship, especially answerable to Being itself. That is how all life is considered sacred. Today, thanks to our having reached a high level of capability of destruction, humanity is being jolted into an awareness of the need to conserve nature and preserve life. It cannot but be some unacknowledged vindication of *ahiṁsā*, although, due to the limitation of the religious and philosophical resources on the basis of which it is worked out, it still moves in the horizon of mere ecological or "environmental" responsibility, centered on the human being, having not yet become cosmo-ethical in character with a sense of trusteeship for all life as in real *ahiṁsā*.

Related to the age-old Indian philosophy of the above kind, expressed through the concept of *dharma*, Gandhi advanced *ahiṁsā* as a mode of battle—truth's own battle, that is, *satyāgraha*—to right the wrongs in the social and political order in every concrete situation, but so as in each instance "one all human species" may be realized in humanity, which requires love, self-suffering, and refusal to violate the essence of the individuals and of the group with whom the contest occurs. The job of *satyāgraha* is *to* right the wrongs, which is possible because he believes that "right is truth" (*Gītā Exposition*, p. 196 [on 4.8]). Gandhi's writings are replete with the word "right." It is but a translation of the Sanskrit *saṁyak* (perfect) with a great history especially in Buddhism. Right, for him, has nothing to do with some logical or intellectual adequacy to things as they are or as stated to be, in the manner truth, *veritas*, often came to be regarded in medieval philosophy, or with what may be realized in the state, in the manner of the Hegelian philosophy (see Hegel's *Philosophy of Right*)—but a kind of what we may call moral adequacy of one's commitment and, action to human self-transcendence through the knowledge of "the immortality of the eternal *Ātman* [which is 'the highest truth'] and the fleeting nature of the physical body" (*Gītā Exposition*, p. 157). This adequacy is expressed by the manner in which "the highest truth and the performance of duty incidentally coincide with expediency [of whatever action is chosen for the performance of duty]" (ibid.). Gandhi knows that "right" belongs to the realm of ends as well as to the domain of means. Although in principle they may be distinguished, the rule of moral adequacy stipulates that the means too must be sought and striven for as an end, or as an essential, subordinate end, in every choice of the mode of action. Hence he writes, "Right means are themselves the things we want" (ibid., p. 130). Yet he recognizes that ultimately the realm of ends stands supreme, which is why he declares, "if the means and end are not identical they are *almost*[31] so," and within that logic he could further assert that "the extreme of means is salvation [i.e., end itself]" (*Gītā Exposition*, p. 130). The force of this statement is that the domain of means functions as a surrogate realm of ends. "Means" suggests more than one but all governed by the primordial duality of violence and nonviolence. But then one chooses only nonviolence and courses of action that are nonviolent. To drive home this point, Gandhi writes: "One rupee [Indian currency] can buy for us poison or nectar" (ibid.). The choice becomes existential, which too is a feature of "right," thereby adding something more to the traditional understanding of *saṁyak*.

One last thing that must be said of Gandhi's *ahiṁsā* (and truth) spirituality is its completely dynamic nature—of righting the wrongs in the world through militant action. (The subtitle of Erikson's *Gandhi's Truth*, i.e., "On the Origins of Militant Non-Violence," is entirely apt.) Gandhi envisages the *satyāgraha* warriors as a kind of church militant—he called Jesus the Prince of *satyāgrahis*. The militancy arises from the very dynamics of the negative particle in the key words, for example, *a-hiṁsā* (nonviolence).

From the negation springs militant *nonacquiescence* in wrong. And it is in no way passivity or pacificism but an activist, though entirely tranquil (peace-ful), spirituality that burns with care for the oppressed and is willing to live in the most dignified defiance of every circumstance and every wrong structure. Such spirituality of *ahiṁsā* (and truth) is in Gandhi's view the essence of the struggle for liberation. Thus: "Although [the *satyāgrahi*] must love the wrong-doer, he must never submit to his wrong or his injustice, but oppose it with all his might, and must patiently and without resentment suffer all the hardships to which the wrong-doer may subject him in punishment for his opposition."[32] Such spirituality of *ahiṁsā* (and truth), unremittingly carried out as *satyāgraha*, is for Gandhi the very essence of the struggle for liberation, that spirituality at work in the form of "service" (*sevā*), a term used countless times in his writings and utterances.

Notes

1. Schopenhauer, *The World as Will and Idea* (Eng. trans. R. B. Haldane and J. Kemp; London: Trench & Trübner, 1891), bk. 4, sec. 63.

2. *Pāṇātipātaṁ pahāya dayāpanno sabbapāna-bhūta-hitā anukampī viharati*, from the *Dighanikāya*, vol 1. (*Sīlakhaṇda vagga*) Nalanda Devanagari-Pali Series, published under the general editorship of Bhikku J. Kashyah (Bihar: Pali Publications Board [Bihar Government], 1958) 55.

3. M. Hiriyanna, *Outlines of Indian Philosophy* (London: Allen & Unwin, 1956) 67.

4. *atra bhūtaśabdena jīvapradhānāni sthāvara-jangamāni nirdiśati. ahimsā sarva bhūtāni . . . iti prayogāt.*

5. See Søren Kierkegaard, *The Concept of Irony*, trans. L. M. Chapel (New York: Harper & Row, 1965) 339.

6. See J. G. Arapure, "Spirit and Spiritual Knowledge in the Upanisads," *Hindu Spirituality*, vol. 1, ed. K. Sivaraman (New York: Crossroad, 1989).

7. Ibid., 80f.

8. E.g., *Ādi parva*, 11.11, 12; *Anuśāsana Parva*, 115.25. Quotations from the *Mahābhāratā*, unless otherwise mentioned, are from the critical edition published from the Bhandarkar Oriental Institute, Poona, 1977.

9. *Ahiṁsā paramo dharmaḥ, ahiṁsā param tapaḥ, ahimsā paramam dānam ityāhuḥ munaya sadā* (*Padma Purāṇa* I.31.26, 27, quoted from P. V. Kane, Poona, ed. *History of Dharma śāstra* [Poona: Bhandarkar Oriental Institute, 1977] vol. 5, pt. 2, p. 945).

10. *Ahiṁsā paro dharmaḥ nāsti ahiṁsāyā paraṁ sukham.*

11. *Sanātanasya dharmasya mūlam etat* (*Matsya Purāṇa* 143.30–32). The *Aśvamedha Parva* (91.32–34) of the *Mahābhāratā* mentions "gathered roots, fruit," etc., and *sanātana dharma*—evidence of older origin.

12. H. G. Gadamer, *The Idea of the Good in Platonic-Aristotelian Philosophy* (New Haven and London: Yale University Press, 1986) 64–65.

13. Plato, *The Collected Dialogues*, ed. Edith Hamilton and H. Cairns (Princeton, N.J.: Princeton University Press, 1980) 669–76, 739ff.

14. See *Bhāvārthadīpikā of Śri Jñānadeva*, translated from Marathi by R. K. Bhagat (1954; reprint, Madras: Samata Books, 1979) xi f. ("Life Sketch of Sri Jñanadev"). Also, *Preceptors of Advaita*, ed. T. M. P. Mahadevan (Secunderabad: Sri Kanehi Sankara Mandir, 1968).

15. See *Jñāniśwarī (Bhāvārthadīpikā)* translated from the Marathi by V. G. Pradhan, ed. H. M. Lambert (London: Allen & Unwin, 1969) vol. 2.

16. Mahadev Desai, *The Bhagavadgītā with Mahatma Gandhi's Exposition* (Ahmedabad: Navajivan Press, 1946); hereafter cited as *Gītā Exposition*.

17. Paperback edition, Boston: Beacon Press, 1957.

18. Published by the Publications Divisions, Ministry of Information and Broadcasting, New Delhi, 1958–1988.

19. The actual word in the *Gītā* cited as *aparigraha* is *aparigrahaḥ*, nominative singular of the masculine, meaning "nonpossessor" rather than "nonpossessions," as rendered here. But this is a trivial point, which does not affect the real import.

20. G. Ramachandran and T. K. Mahadevan, *The Quest for Gandhi* (New Delhi: Gandhi Peace Foundation, 1970).

21. Erik H. Erikson, *Gandhi's Truth* (New York: W. W. Norton, 1969).

22. J. G. Arapura, *Hermeneutical Essays in Vedantic Topics* (Delhi: Motilal Banarsidass, 1986) Essay No. 1.

23. Joan Bondurant, *Conquest of Violence* (Berkeley: University of California Press, 1965) 111.

24. See Erikson, *Gandhi's Truth*, 411.

25. "Instructions at Satyāgraha Ashram," 25 May 1915 (*Collected Works*, 36:399).

26. Mahatma Gandhi, *Collected Works*, vol. 36, in a message dated 27 April 1928 (see n. 18 above).

27. S. Radhakrishnan and J. H. Muirhead, *Contemporary Indian Philosophy* (London: Allen & Unwin, 1937) 21.

28. *Collected Works*, 36:165, in a speech to the disciples on 30 March 1928.

29. Erikson, *Gandhi's Truth*, 413.

30. *Collected Works*, 36:399.

31. My italics.

32. *Collected Works*, 36:399.

Part Five

CULTURAL EXPRESSIONS OF HINDU SPIRITUALITY

21

Hindu Temples and Festivals: Spirituality as Communal Participation

PREMA NANDAKUMAR

AT THE DAWN OF India's spiritual history, which is generally known as the Vedic age, people apparently felt that God was omnipresent and that therefore we can pray anywhere and worship any visible part of nature as God. After all, the One without a second cannot be comprehended easily by the human mind, which wants "something to hold on to" in this complex creation bound by decay and death:

> He through whom the heaven is strong
> and the earth firm,
> who has steadied the light
> and the sky's vault.
> and measured out the sphere
> of clouds in the mid air.
> Who is the Deity we shall worship with our offerings?[1]

"Who is the Deity we shall worship with our offerings?" was a question that was answered by an instinctive worship of all nature. It was thus that One was seen as Many for facilitating the worship of the Divine. The *Ṛg Veda*, for instance, speaks of the manifestation of devas in terms of *ṛa* and *satya.* This is the *vibhhuti yoga* of the Vedas, where the splendorous creation is worshiped as Uśas, Aśvins, Maruts, Sarasvatī, Indra, and Vāyu. Agni was considered the priest, the go-between bridging the mortal life with immortality.

> Thine, Agni, is the office of
> Invoker, of Purifyer,
> Priest and Leader. Thou art
> Kindler of the devout.
> Thine is the function of praiser.
> Thou art preparer of the rites

and Supervisor, and thou the Lord
of our homes.[2]

The sacrificial spot—*yajña vedi*—where people kindled a fire and worshiped the Gods by placing their offerings in the flames was perhaps the first idea of temple conceived by our ancestors. This was a common spot for worship by the lord of the household *(yajamāna)* and his family. According to Sri Aurobindo, the sacrificial ritual developed into rigid codes of obscurantist ritualism surrounding the *yajña vedi* and consequently the temple. Originally the choice of Agni was to inspire the student to be engaged in self-improvement. Sri Aurobindo considers the *agni sūkta* as of prime importance in this context:

> Agni first, for without him the sacrificial flame cannot burn on the altar of the soul. That flame of Agni is the seven tongued power of the Will, a Force of God instinct with knowledge. This conscious and forceful will is the immortal guest of our mortality, a pure priest and a divine worker, the mediator between earth and heaven. It carries what we offer to the higher powers and brings back in return their force and light and joy into our humanity.[3]

Sri Aurobindo considers Indra as the Divine Mind, Sūrya the Supreme Truth, Soma as Beatitude, Vāyu as Master of Life and so on:

> The soul of man is a world full of beings, a kingdom in which armies clash to help or hinder a supreme conquest, a house where the gods are our guests and which the demons strive to possess; the fullness of its energies and wideness of its being make a seat of sacrifice spread, arranged and purified for a celestial session.[4]

The worship of icons consecrated by the divine presence may perhaps be vaguely traced to the Vedas, says K. Bharadvaja:

> We read in the *Atharva-veda* that a sage, Atharva by name pays obeisance to a "prasthara" (stone) which belongs to sages and is sanctified by some Divinity. "Prasthara" is precursor of the colloquial "patthar," and it is thus clear that some sacred stone is referred to in the Vedic verse. Some would, however, like to interpret the word "prasthara" as a heap of *kuśa-grass,* but even then it remains obvious that the sage is offering his salutations to a material object wherein the Deity has been invoked.[5]

The *devasthāna,* or temple, may have begun in the erecting of a shed around the object of worship. In any case, the *purāṇas* held that the images of divinities have an important role in the spread of *bhakti,* and we do have temples of *purāṇic* cult that have been unearthed by archaeologists. The ruins of temples dedicated to Sankarashana and Vasudeva at Nagari near Chittoor are said to belong to 350–250 B.C.E.[6]

South Indian Temple

Icon of Viṣṇu

The Purāṇic age made good use of these principal images of the Vedic times for the sustenance of the temple idea. Though the Vedas do not speak of temple ritualism as such, it is obvious that people indeed felt they should pray in a place apart from their dwellings where the world did not intrude. If Agni was to be invoked as the Seer-Will, or Soma to be seen as the fosterer of Beauty within us, there was a very real need for meditating on that particular *deva*. This could best be done in privacy, and so the open-air fire sacrifices yielded to closed-door worship. People also retreated to mountains for such meditative loneliness and in the course of time found caves to be excellent homes for worship. If temples were built in these rocky mountains, these temples were for all time.

By the time of the epics, the *Rāmāyaṇa* and the *Mahābhārata*, temple worship had taken root. As we enter recorded history, there was virtually a race among Hindus, Jains, and Buddhists to build bigger, more artistic places of worship. In the course of this evolution, the sacred was entwined with the secular. Art and literature were drawn to the house of God as to a magnet. In the process, the secular shed much of its materialistic character as well. For example, Tamil Sangham poetics devoted to love and war was transformed to bridal mysticism, and the Deity was hailed as the King of kings.

Large structures that had housed the liege lord and his dependents (*ko-il*: the house of the king) became *kovil* (temple), and the entire paraphernalia associated with a king's court was transformed into temple rituals. Thus, we have victory processions, festivals to mark special incidents of valor, a full-fledged royal court, and even the lord's table in temple worship. Reports are presented to the Deity regarding the state of the nation on New Year's Day in the form of "reading the almanac" (*pañcāṅgam).* Accounts are delivered about the produce in the fields as well as the day's events. Honors are bestowed on chosen individuals. Music concerts and dance programs are held in the presence of the Deity. And of course every temple has a kitchen, where *bhog* is prepared for offering to the Deity before being distributed to the devotees. The kitchens of Lord Jagannāth at Puri and Śrī Venkateśvara at Tirupati are justly famous.

Absorbing the appurtenances of royalty meant the inclusion of royal sport for community participation. The idea of taking the Deity out of the sanctum on various mounts was born from the manner in which the king issued out of his palace. The creative imagination of the devotee added other unusual mounts later. These include the bull, the swan, the *kalpa-vṛkṣa* (the wish-yielding tree), and even a mythical beast called *Yāli*. The most sportive of these mounts is the horse. Scholars have traced the action-movement (*vaiyāli*) of the horse mount in the Sriangam temple to Hoysala influence in the thirteenth century. The *Manasollasa* speaks of the *vahyāli* (sports arena):

> In *Manasollasa* this sports arena, where runners, horses, elephants competed in a similar manner to the sports arenas of Rome and Greece, was called *Vahyali*. Certain of the royal pleasures were, in due course, converted into an activity that was performed in a subdued and pleasing form for the enjoyment of a temple deity, thereby bestowing as great an honour as that enjoyed by the kings. . . . Thus the *vaiyali* which is so popular in Srirangam, also known as *Parivettai* & *Vedu-pari*, on the 8th day of the festivities has a resplendent Ranganatha going forth, as if on a hunt, mounted on his horse *vahanam*. This is the *rajopachara*, i.e. transference of royal function to *utsava* deity, like the use of a *vahana* such as the horse, the bull, the elephant, to indicate the possession of a *chaturanga* army.[7]

After absorbing a full imitation of royalty, it was time to turn to the common person. It is interesting to note the several ways in which the temple attracted the attention of the common person and helped him or her receive a settled religious consciousness. Through word of mouth each temple—old and new—gained a legend that was often highly localized. The well-known Ratagiri temple is said to have originated from a king's killing of a brahmin in anger. Fortunately, the victim was Śiva in disguise, who forgave the king and stayed on the hill in an iconic form. In the same way Śiva in the Pallavan rock-cut temple at Tiruchi is said to have helped a motherless girl at her delivery time and is known as Tāyumānava (One who became a Mother). Goddess Garbharakshāmbikai of Tirukkarukāvur is also considered the guardian of the fetus. The very mud of the Śiva temple in Vaitheeswaran Koil is taken as medicine by the devout.

At the same time, these temples are also associated with Purāṇas, and most of the temples have a *sthala-purāṇa* of their own. The *sthalapurāṇa* literature of the Śiva temples in South India is a world by itself. Mythology and poetry help to further the human religious spirit by associating the temple with miraculous happenings in ancient times. When one of the planets is also brought into focus in this context, the temple gets an accession of sanctity for the common person. Arasavilli (Sun), Tirunallar (Saturn), and Tirunāgeswaram (Rāhu) may be mentioned in this connection. The interweaving of legends, real-life stories, and astronomy gave the worshipers a sense of belonging. The temples were made more integral to the people's life-style by giving importance to the gifts of nature. Each temple has its consecrated tree (*sthala-vṛkṣa*) and water source (*tīrtha*). Thus, the devotees were unconsciously made to live in tune with nature. In addition, most of the temples had special hymns for various rituals such as *suprabhātham* (dawn worship) and *pavvalimpu* (night rest). A properly consecrated temple had to have sculptures, and these were Purāṇa-oriented. Exposed to them from childhood, the Hindus absorbed meaningful legends such as *Gajendra-mokṣa*, *Narasimha-avatāra*, and others with ease.

The secular also was given a place among the sacred representations, and these sculptures and paintings executed down the centuries are now invaluable to historians. The temples were also repositories of sacred writings. That is how most of the musical compositions of Tallapakka Annamācārya survived the ravages of time. The *kritis* engraved on copper plates and kept in the vaults of the Tirupati temple were discovered in this century. The compositions show how, through music, the temple spread Vaiṣṇavism throughout Andhra Pradesh.

The most important of the temple's exterior religious ministry was the conduct of festivals. The *Brahmotsava* (Big Festival) apart, almost every month had special festival days. These days vary from temple to temple, but there was also a common calender like Mahāśivarātri (Śiva), Vaikuṇṭha Ekādaśi (Viṣṇu), and Devi Navarātri (Śakti), which were observed on the same dates.

The temples also developed into places of education because of the great teachers associated with them. Social service in the form of feeding pilgrims or the poor (*santarpana*) was made a part of the rituals. Hospitals were set up in temples, and we even know the names of some physicians. Tirumukkuḍal had Kodandarāman Asvatthāma-bhaṭṭan, and Kulottuṅgasola Mangalādhirājan Sirālan̲ was the chief physician of Kunrattur temple.[8] Garuḍavāhana Panḍithar of the Śrīraṅgam temple hospital is said to have set up the sanctuary of Dhanvantiri, the physician of the gods. The deity carries a pot of nectar in the right hand and a leech (to suck out infected blood) in the left hand, and is held in great veneration.

As we look back today, it becomes clear that one of the first leaps of the Hindu religion was the worship of the *arca* (icon). The idea caught on rapidly and by the tenth century the temple had become a focal part of the village and the town. It took within its fold secular activities for the good of the society. Temple funds were utilized to dig irrigation channels and provide food for people in times of drought. Thus, the temple, which began as a place of fire sacrifice, became a symbol of civilized, comfortable life in Indian society. The importance of the temple for society can be gauged from the familiar Tamil injunction, *kovil illā ooril kudiyirukka vendām* ("Do not live in a habitation that has no temple").

The temple culture that synthesized the sacred and the secular in an admirable manner reached perfection under the Cholas. While the Pallavas, the Pandyas, the Gangas, the Hoysalas, and other royal dynasties were no mean temple builders, it is Chola royalty that achieved marvels in the spread of temple culture. Āditya I (871–907 C.E.) was among the first Chola kings to build a series of temples to Śiva on the banks of the Kāveri. The temples at Tirupurambiyam and Tiruverumbūr were his early creations, and he decorated Chitrambalam in Chidambaram with gold plates. Most of the Chola kings, along with their wives, are associated with temple structures.

Sensing the powerful influence temple rituals and festivities had in disseminating religious feelings, the Cholas built ever-larger structures. The apex was reached when Rājarāja I (985–1014 C.E.) built the "Big Temple" at Tanjāvūr. Planned as a massive structure (793 feet in length and 397 feet in breadth), this temple to Śiva has a dome weighing eighty tons made of a single piece of granite placed at a height of 216 feet.[9] The Nandi facing the sanctum is a huge figure also carved out of a single block of granite. Certainly the temple was instrumental in exciting the religious instinct of the people. Though the days of grand festivals instituted by Cholan royalty are now a memory, the *anna-abhiṣeka* revived by the Śaṅkarācarya of Kāmakoṭi Pīṭha is a tremendous experience. Huge mounds of cooked rice are showered over the superb linga in the sanctum. The rice is then distributed to the thousands of devotees who throng the temple on that day.

A slightly smaller version of the big temple was built by Rājarāja's son, Rājendra I (1012–1044 C.E.) at Gangai Konda Cholapuram. Unfortunately, much of it has now fallen into decay. Even in their days of decline, the Cholas continued to show deep interest in their temples.[10] The Cholas had also systematically intertwined the sacred and the secular. Even the border stones for the fields of temples were marked with the trident or conch or the triple umbrella to indicate the ownership of Śiva, Viṣṇu, or Jīna temples. By being extremely generous when making endowments for temple servants, the day-to-day maintenance of the temple was assured. Priests, medicine men, dancers, expounders of epics, dance masters, drummers, accountants, actors, musicians, reciters of the Vedas and Tamil hymns were all given life tenures.

Many of the edicts of the Cholas were sculptured on stones and placed in temples, for the temples were the meeting place for the populace. Citizens knew what was happening because of these inscribed slabs. They learned of their rights as well as their duties. Thus, an edict in Varadarāja temple at Tirubhuvani (twelfth century) calls on priests, teacher, accountants, carpenters, masons, and others to do their assigned jobs within the village.[11] Should they try to go out and pursue their calling elsewhere, they would be considered transgressors of *dharma* and would be condemned as destroyers of the village.

Naturally, royal patronage inspired other communities to help the spread of religion by making endowments to temples, and the merchant community was in the forefront in the cause of serving religion through temples. They considered feeding pilgrims during festivals to be of prime importance. Freed from the worry of having to go in search of sustenance in strange places, people readily attended festivals and received the spiritual ambience.

Just when temple worship had become a settled way of life all over India, the Islamic onslaught on Hindu places of worship did incalculable damage to the finances, sculptural marvels and other activities associated with temple worship. Quite often, Hindu temples in North India were razed to the ground and mosques built over them. Not all Hindu communities could rally to the job of rebuilding temples as the devotees did in Somnath. This is why vital links in the history of temple worship in North India are missing today.

Fortunately for South India, the Nāyak rule reestablished several prime temples and encouraged new building activities. Thus, though architectural marvels in temples such as Simhāchalam have been defaced and disfigured, South India is still able to show a historical continuity in its temples. But there have been changes too. A good deal of its secular activities like education, medicine, human resources management, and social service have been taken over by the state. Literature and art have also lost their temple moorings. Sculpture alone appears to have still a stronghold in the precincts of the temple.[12]

So the temple, which began as a consecration of the sacred, has once again become a meeting place for the community to foster its religious and spiritual aspirations. Despite the overwhelming presence of materialism and the scientific temper today, temples and temple ritualism continue to be very popular with the masses. At the most primitive level, every village has its *grāma-devata* (village goddess), whose temple generally marks the entry to the human habitation. Here offerings such as cooked food and terra-cotta figures of men and animals are made in fulfillment of vows to mark the recovery from diseases. The goddess is worshiped also for granting the village good harvest.

However, temples that have come into existence under *āgamic* rules insist on their Vedic heritage. Suniti Kumar Chatterji feels that the Hindu ritual of worship is itself Dravidian, for the Vedic literature had only *homa*, also known as *paśu-karma* (the ritual with the animal):

> The word "pūja" and the ritual it denotes are both peculiar to India; they are not found among the kinsmen of the Indian Aryans outside India. The nature of the "pūja" is as follows: The whole universe is filled with the spirit of the Divinity. By a magical rite, the Supreme Spirit is invoked into some special

object—an image, a picture, a pot, a pebble or a piece of stone, a branch of tree, etc. When this ritual, known as *prāṇa-pratiṣta*, is performed, the image or the object becomes a sort of abode of the Divinity, temporary or permanent. The image or symbol is then treated as an honored guest. . . . In fact, in the deeper aspect of religion, this Dravidian or non-Aryan ritual of "pūja" conduces to a more intimate kinship with the Divine than can be postulated through the Aryan *homa*. The *homa* ritual is basically one of "take and give in return." In "pūja," we have an attendant spirit of abandon through devotion, which is absent in the *homa*. In later Hinduism, these two rituals were combined; and both "pūja" and *homa* have a place in Brahmanical Hinduism.[13]

Today the temple helps individual and communal worship in an excellent way. Whatever one's secular duties are, and even if it takes one away from one's town or country, he/she remains linked with his/her glorious past through temple culture. When an individual wants to make supplication or fulfill a vow, he/she can stand face to face with the Deity and place one's offerings in front of the image. Such worship often has an *arcana* (recitation of holy names) performed with the help of a priest. One can also retire to any corner of the temple (which usually has several corridors and halls) and sit in meditation after being inspired by the recitation of holy scriptures or by the consecrated Deity or by the temple music or by the paintings or by the sculptures or by the scented smoke within the temple precincts.

The achievements of India's great poets, philosophers, composers, and musicians are often traced to an incident in a temple with mystic connotations. Indeed, the lives of the Āḻvārs and Nāyanmārs are entwined with some great temples and Sekkiḻār's *Periya Purāṇam* speaks of several incidents in various temples made memorable by the presence of Śiva's devotees. This is how the temples praised by Āḻvārs (*maṅagala sāsanam*) and Nāyanmār's (*vaippu sthalam*) have acquired a special sacerdotal image in our religious imagination. In our own time, the mathematical genius Ramanujan is said to have been helped by Goddess Nāmagiri of the Nāmakkal Temple dedicated to Narasimha.

Though Hindu spirituality gave prime importance to personal effort for gaining realization, it recognized early the need for communal togetherness to reach one's ideal. Therefore the rituals in temple from dawn to night have been fashioned as a group worship. People also go to temples generally as a family group.

In Vedic times also the gain came through group living with spiritually inclined people in hermitages. Our mythology is, of course, full of such hermitages, and the twin epics of *Rāmāyaṇa* and *Mahābhārata* report on several great hermitages established by renowned spiritual luminaries like

Vasiṣṭha, Viśvāmitra, Gautama, Bharadhvāja, and Agasthya. *Sat-saṅgha,* or holy company, helped one tread fast the spiritual path. This point is effectively borne by the ritual of *Pāvai Nonbu,* which is common to both Vaiṣṇavas and Śaivas through the supernal poems of Āṇḍāl and Māṇikkavācakar.

An early Tamil anthology, *Paripāḍal,* gives particulars of the *vrata* (vow) undertaken by young girls (*pāvai*) in the month of *Mārgaḻi* (December–January). Virgins go to the river at dawn for their ceremonial bath (*thai neeradal*) and pray for abundant rains. They also express their single-minded desire to be united with the bridegroom of their choice.

By the eighth century, temple worship in the form of regular festivals had come to stay. Āṇḍāl's *Tiruppāvai* celebrates the ceremonial bath undertaken by groups as a vow for gaining the grace of Kṛṣṇa. Groups of young girls as well as devotees came to the temple singing hymns and worshiping the Deity, enacting the bridal mysticism that unites the individual soul with the Supreme. Incidentally, the original intention is also made clear in the opening verses of *Tiruppāvai.* The last verse of the poem makes it clear that this vow is best undertaken in terms of group participation (*saṅga-t-tamil*). In such a group situation, if one's attention wanders due to ignorance or excitement or sheer laziness, the others can always recall the aspirant to the *sādhana.* Goda Devi uses group images such as the *anaichattan* (Bharadhvaja) birds, the cowherds churning milk, the *sannyāsis* reciting the name of Hari, the attenders blowing the conch to mark the opening of the temple, the lotuses in the tank, the buffaloes grazing, to underline the need for communal worship to achieve speedy progress in spiritual life.

The communal singing of *Tiruppāvai* and listening to discourses on *Tiruppāvai* have now been conjoined with rituals in temples dedicated to Viṣṇu. There is a palpable aspirational atmosphere in these temples during the month of *Mārgaḻi* as the rituals begin in the hour before dawn. In fact, the month is devoted to the *Pagel Pathu-Raa Pathu* festival (Ten Days—Ten Nights), which draws enormous participatory crowds. In the premier Vaiṣṇavite temple of Śrīraṅgam, the day begins with pre-dawn rituals dedicated to *Tiruppāvai.* On the first day of the festival, the Deity is placed in a hall called the "Santhānu Mandapam" when Tirumañgai Āḻvār's *Tiru-nedunthandakam* is recited. On the following nine days, the Deity is placed in the "Arjuṇa Mandapam." Facing the Lord are the images of the Āḻvārs and *ācāryas.* The hereditary temple singers, *arayars,* recite the verses from *Nālāyira Divya Prabhandham.* On the tenth day, Lord Ranganatha is dressed as Mohini and on the eleventh is the most important festival of the year, the Vaikuntha Ekādaśi.

The "Ten Nights" opens from this day and takes place in the "Thousand-pillared Mandapam" where the Deity holds court with the Āḻvārs and *ācāryas* while the *arayars* recite the *Eedu,* which is a *maṇiprāvala* commentary upon Nammāḻvār's *Tiruvaimoḻi.* In the course of these twenty days, the *arayars* embellish their recitals with well-known Purāṇic stories.

These twenty days are a rare experience where a temple festival becomes instrumental in inculcating a spiritual view of life in the listeners. For centuries such community participation has been going on, and it is only in this century that this meaningful "Arayar Sevai" has fallen into disuse. But where it is still held, it is inspiring to see crowds listening or moving forward anxiously to get a glimpse of the Deity decked in special styles like the "Pearl Armor" or "Garnet Armor." This sight of the bedecked Deity gives a rare satisfaction to the devotees that verges on the ecstatic. For, in the context and the atmosphere, they are able to sense the transcendent Reality behind the apparent figure of bronze. The single converging point of the deity gives the mass a special camaraderie.

Certainly, to those listening to the recitation, the spiritual experience is of a different kind. This audience is drawn to the sacred poetry as well as to the Purāṇic tales, which are familiar yet ever new. The *maṇipravāla* commentaries provide charming glimpses of crystalline devotion in the Vaiṣṇava fold and the audience loves to hear episodes connected with Rāmānuja and Bhaṭṭar. People are once again brought close to the *pāsurams* of Nammāḻvar, which affirm the total self-surrender expected from a Vaiṣṇava:[14]

The food we eat, the water we drink,
The betal-leaves we munch—all these
She considers to be the Lord;
With wet eyes she wants to know
About His gracious home in this world;
And so my young daughter
Must have entered Tirukkolur.

Even as the majority of the people are thus effortlessly drawn into the spiritual ambience, the time for closing the divine court calls upon the appropriate mood of peace and tranquillity. The Lord returns to the sanctum escorted by the strains of the *Vīṇa* played by the hereditary musician of the temple. An indescribable peace touched by subdued joy becomes the portion of the devotees.

During this festival several individualized items help the audience remember its spiritual benefactor, Nammāḻvar. He is considered "the leader of aspirant souls," and hence when Nammāḻvar's image is elevated to come face to face with the Deity or Nammāḻvar is decked like a bride to symbolize the bridal mysticism of his poetry or Nammāḻvar's withdrawal from the physical is indicated by placing the image at the feet of the Deity, the audience gets the message in clear terms: "Remember Nammāḻvar and offer yourself!" Thus has the festival fostered spiritual aspirations down the centuries.

It may be pointed out here that both in the Viṣṇu and Śiva temples, special endowments have been created since the time of the Cholas and the Pandyas for the recitation of the Vedas, the epics, the Purāṇas, and the *Drāviḍa Veda* (the Tamil hymns of Āḻvārs and Nāyanmārs). Epigraphy assures us that even separate halls (*ambalam*) were set apart for such recitations and expositions in the temples.[15]

One of the important methods of disseminating religious and spiritual fervor in Hinduism has been the institution of the public appearance of the Deity. Though one's approach to the Deity in the sanctum, installed according to the *āgamic* rules, is subject to certain restrictions, perfect equality is assured to the citizens when enclosing rules are set aside and the Deity emerges out of the temple on various mounts. The car festival, in particular, is the community festival in which almost everyone takes part. Here caste-born differences are forgotten, class divisions hold no meaning. Everyone feels close to the Deity and all participants can touch the ropes and pull the chariot. Until the chariot returns to the temple after its safe circumambulation of the "car-streets," all those present hold themselves in anxious readiness.

During the day (or days) when the Deity enters the chariot, people are exposed to a variety of activities that help widen the devotional atmosphere. Bands of itinerant musicians gather and walk around singing hymns. Groups of villagers sing and dance their special folk songs that retell Purāṇic stories. Music programs and musical discourses are in great demand. Colorful fairs accompany the car festivals of Lord Jagannath at Puri and Ranchi. When a car festival is discontinued for some reason or other, there is general gloom. Often, natural calamities are attributed to such stoppages.

The South Indian temple cars made of wood are heavy. At one time there were thousands of them in villages and all of them displayed the artistic exuberance of master craftsmen. It is a pity that most of them have now been plundered and become extinct. This is because there has been a flight of youth from villages to cities in search of jobs. Once a temple chariot gets damaged by neglect or by floods, it cannot easily be repaired. Lacking the necessary means and resources to restore them, villagers have often left them to decay. Recently, however, there has been a new awareness among people about their valuable heritage. A few notable restorations have reestablished the unique experience of taking the image of the Deity in the chariot. For instance, the chariot of Tyāgarāja in the famous Śiva temple at Tiruvārūr has begun to move again on its annual peregrination.

Among other important festivals are the float and swing festivals, which are a common feature of Viṣṇu and Śiva temples. The float festival ensures the good upkeep of the water tank, which is often of vital importance to the village economy. There is a beauty and a majesty about the swing festivals when the Deity is placed in a swing and worshiped to the gentle tilt. The swing festival accompanied by the lullaby hymns sung by the *arayars* (in Viṣṇu temples) bedecked in their special attire awakens the delicate tints of humanity in the onlookers. The scene and the song bring the Divine to one's consciousness, as close to one's heart as the babe at home! The transcendent Divine's human manifestations as Rāmā or Kṛṣṇa is brought closer to our experience and love by inspired hymnologists like Periyāḻvār and Kulaśekhara Āḻvār. Thus sings Kulaśekhara:

> You were born to Kausalya
> Of ever increasing fame.
> You ordained the destruction
> Of the ten heads of Lanka's king
> My eye's pupil, resident of Kannapura,
> My sweet nectar
> Raghava! Come. Sleep.

Some of the temple traditions have been carefully planned to foster unity among people in a given area. For instance, the Vellalas (farming caste) have a special relationship with Suchīndram temple, as the Deity is said to have married a Vellala woman, Aramvalarthamman. The Vellalas from surrounding villages bring gifts to the goddess during the Tirumanral festival in the *Māsi* (February–March) month. Another example would be the right of worship granted to the forest tribe of Chenchus in the Brahminic Ahobilam temple. Here the presiding Deity is Narasimha, whose divine consort is said to have incarnated as a tribal girl, Chenchulakṣmi.

Hindu temples have also been repositories of communal and sectarian peace through upholding certain traditions that unite people in the hall of worship. The major division in Hindu religion today is between Vaiṣṇavism and Śaivism. Yet they are integrated in every way through temple worship. The temple of Sundareśvara (Śiva) in Madurai is closely aligned with that of Aḻakar (Viṣṇu). The wedding day of Sundareśvara and Mīnākṣi is as important in Madurai as Aḻakar crossing the river Vaigai to reach the wedding in time to give away his sister to Sundareśvara. Again, goddess Māriamman of Samayavaram (Śiva's creatrix power) is considered a sister of Lord Raṅganātha of Srīraṅgam.

There are also scores of Hindu temples that integrate the worship of Śiva and Viṣṇu. The sanctums of Śiva and Viṣṇu are close to each other in the famous temple at Chidambaram. Each sanctum follows its own rituals, but the devotional fervor of the aspirants is of a like kind. Watching with awe this two-in-one integration of the Śiva-Viṣṇu concept, the celebrated poet Gopalakrishna Bharatiyar sings:

I have had the vision
Of Śiva of Thillai
And Govindaraja.
Sustaining the worlds
And guarding the devotees from evil
They spread compassion.
Here garlands of *tumbai* blooms:
There the leaves of sacred basil.
Here the meditative truth of Chidambara:
There the love of the *Eight-Syllabled Name.*
Here offerings of millet and black-gram cakes:
There tamarind and curd rice.
Here dance to the tune of the drum:
There the calm of yogic sleep.
Here the recitation of *Thevāram, Tiruvācakam:*
There the ringing of *Tiruvāimoḷi.*
Here the *Five-Syllabled Name:*
There faith in Lord Nārāyaṇa.
We sing here, O supreme Śiva:
There We bow to the playful Kṛṣṇa.
Here the form that is beyond ken:
There the image of Ānanda Consciousness.[16]

The ancient temple of Uttamarkoil near Tiruchirapalli has sanctums dedicated to Śiva, Viṣṇu, and Brahmā within its complex. In fact, the priceless role of Hindu temples in eliminating communal differences may be seen in the great Raṅganātha temple at Śrīraṅgam. Here, next to the sanctum we find a niche to a Muslim princess who is spoken of as the daughter of a Sultan of Delhi. Tradition avers that when the icon of Raṅganātha was carried away by the Muslim Sultan who ravished Śrīraṅgam, his daughter fell in love with the icon, accompanied it back to Śrīraṅgam and merged in its effulgence. The Sultan made large endowments in her name to the temple. She is worshiped as "Thulukka Nāchiyār." Her niche contains only a portrait of the Princess and her horse, which carried her to Śrīraṅgam from Delhi. Even today offerings of wheat cakes and butter are made to the portrait and when Lord Raṅganātha's image is brought into the shrine, He is offered the *kaili* garment, which is used only by the Muslim community. In the same manner the Kapālīśvara (Śiva) temple tank is used by the Muslim community of Madras for one of their festivals.

Such is the unique temple culture that flourishes in India. This has been made possible because, though the Hindus come to the temple to worship the icon and receive the best of religious and spiritual impulsions of the atmosphere created by the very best in art and literature, they are quite aware (even if unconsciously) that there is a transcendent reality behind the construed image, that the whole of creation is charged with the grandeur of God, and that a temple is a definite gateway to God experience. As Sri Aurobindo says:

> An Indian temple, to whatever godhead it may be built, is in its inmost reality an altar raised to the divine Self, a house of the Cosmic Spirit, an appeal and aspiration to the Infinite.[17]

This is why the multiplicity of temples in the Hindu religion has not proved to be superfluous as they are part of India's everyday life. Temple renovations, temple building, and temple festivals continue to flourish. The Hindu temples have taught us the art of living together harmoniously as also living at peace with oneself. Entering a Hindu temple is, indeed, entering the life of the divine on earth. To conclude with the words of Sri Aurobindo:[18]

> The gods of Indian sculpture are cosmic beings, embodiments of some great spiritual power, spiritual idea and action, inmost psychic significance, the human form a vehicle of this soul meaning, its outward means of self expressions. . . . The divine self in us is its theme, the body made a form of the soul its idea and its secret.

Notes

1. *Yajurveda,* trans. A. C. Bose, in *Hymns from the Vedas* (Bombay: Asia Publishing House, 1966) 301.
2. Ibid., 281.
3. *Hymns to the Mystic Fire* (Pondicherry: Sri Aurobindo Ashram, Publication Department, 1985) 30.
4. Ibid., 34.
5. K. Bhavadvaja, *A Philosophical Study of the Concept of Viṣṇu in the Puranas* (New Delhi: Pitambar Publishing Company, 1981) 361–62.
6. Ibid., 363.
7. Chitra Biji in *South Indian Studies, II* (Madras: Society for Archaeological, Historical and Epigraphical Research, 1979) 174–75.
8. A. V. Jeyechandran, *South Indian Studies,* Dr. T. V. Mahalingham Commemoration Volume (Mysore: Geetha Book House, 1990) 317.

9. See T. V. Sadasiva Pandarather, *Pirkala Cholar Varalaru* (Annamalainagar: Annamalai University, 1974) 123–25.

10. Ibid., 466.

11. Ibid., 573.

12. See Jeyechandran, *South Indian Studies,* 321.

13. V. Raghavan, *The Cultural Heritage of India* (Calcutta: Ramakrishna Mission Institute of Culture, 1970) 1:82.

14. Translated by Prema Nandakumar.

15. See Raghavan, *Cultural Heritage of India,* 4:504–7.

16. Translated by Prema Nandakumar.

17. Sri Aurobindo, *Foundations of Indian Culture* (New York: Sri Aurobindo Library, 1953) 243.

18. Ibid., 261.

Bibliography

Studies

Kramrisch, Stella. *Hindu Temples.* Delhi: Motilal Banarsidass, 1976.

Michell, George. *Hindu Temple: An Introduction to Its Meanings and Forms.* Chicago: University of Chicago Press, 1988.

Ramachandra Rao, S. K. *The Indian Temple: Its Meaning.* Bangalore: IBH, 1977.

Soundararajan, K. V. *Indian Temple Styles: The Personality of Hindu Architecture.* New Delhi: Munshiram Manoharlal, 1972.

22

Spirituality and the Music of India

SUSHIL KUMAR SAXENA

CLASSICAL INDIAN MUSIC, in the main Hindustani (or North Indian), promotes human spiritual growth, through familiarity with the commonplace features of the ethico-religious heritage of Hinduism. The relation music bears to the good life is neither necessary nor easy to determine. It does not involve simply the free use of music at places of worship or the example of those great Indians of the past who are commonly believed to have realized life's ultimate end through the discipline of music. In the theory and *contemporary* practice of traditional Indian music itself there is ample room to perceive one's concern and involvement with the art such that it becomes a definite help to spiritual growth.

Involved in the sense of spirituality and in the treatment of music are the more important concepts of *svara*, *rāga*, *ālāpa*, *dhruvapad*, *laya*, and *tāla*.[1] With regard to the first of these tasks, the present writer must go essentially by what others say. Although the author is by no means insensible to the charm of the life that is spiritually nourishing, marked by the quality (*guṇa*) of goodness (*sattvika*), his own relation to it is rather fitful. He can perhaps claim to know what earnest prayer is. At times he has also experienced a quiet inner drip of the sense of His grace, and so felt steadied in surrender. But all this has been mostly determined by the flux of outer events. Spirituality as that quality of a formed character which issues from a steadfast inner commitment to the higher values of life is in the main but an object for thought.

Spiritualizing Sense Activity

One may wonder whether the emphasis on single-mindedness is not often allowed to bedim a very vital aspect of spiritual life: the living wakefulness that is here always at work, as a check on trespass and as a readiness to let in "intimations" from the most unsuspected sources, say, the "vernal wood" or brooks and stones. We must bear in mind the dynamics of spiritual life. Some impulses are here so subtle and so embracive of the many regions of life and experience—the sensuous and the practical, and the moral and the aesthetic—that it is difficult to seize them. One of these may be selected for comment, because of its possible relevance to music: *viveka* ("discrimination," or the capacity to separate the essential from what is merely a call to indulgence or possessiveness) is indispensable. Let us see how this impulse may work in the area of sense, for example, the simple act of eating. It satisfies hunger and nourishes the body. Any extra intake of food that ignores these essentials is a waste and often also an act of indulgence. Both the basic ends, it is clear, would be better served if one ate on keen appetite and the right kind of food. This exercise in rightness need not end here. Indeed, its much higher forms are seen in lives that are committed to goodness—say, where the person sips a little orange juice on the conclusion of a fast undertaken to wean his fellow beings from the way of violence, and kept up all along by prayer and surrender in faith. Here, the final intake of nourishment is nectar in its impact on the body; and, in relation to the person's inner being, it is that ineffable feeling of relief which wells up as a prayer of thanksgiving and therefore keeps one happy and free, insofar as it neither cloys nor generates conceit. What makes food *sattvik*,[2] says Vinoba, is in essence the quality of one's attitude when one sits down to eat. It must be one of prayerful acceptance; but this in turn demands that we care for the body in a particular way. The whole process of the godward tending of the body, *which distinguishes the spiritual life*, is at once a practice of economy in getting the utmost good from the little that falls to one's lot in the course of right living, and a watchful severance of sense activity from its natural proneness to enmesh us in sensuousness. Voluntary poverty or freedom from mere ornament is but a symptom of this inner motion of the spirit. Yet where we interpret spirituality as a matter of "finer perceptions" these may not be taken as all quite unrelated to sense.

But of course the nonsensuous content of spiritual life is of very great value. In fact and in substance, spirituality is one's abiding in and pursuit of the truths and riches of the spirit. To be spiritual is at once to be steadfast in goodness and to experience the bliss of self-control. Some clear marks here are nonattachment (not indifference) to all that is worldly and commitment to ultimate values, along with a yearning for, and a growing closeness to, a reality or experience of surpassing value. The spiritual among the orthodox Indians strive after liberation (*mokṣa*, or *mukti*), (*nirvāṇa*),[3] or a realization of God or the true Self. But the striving must run through life, and so, considered as a whole, spirituality may be taken to cover all "those attitudes, beliefs and practices which animate people's life and help them reach out toward the super-sensible realities."[4] In India, however, the recognized ways to the highest end are the different yogas.[5] Of these perhaps only the path of devotion (*bhaktiyoga*) may be said to make free use of music. Devotees in India even today use *kīrtana*—the singing of the glories of God and the good life—as a way to saturate themselves with religiousness evermore. In olden days a *bhakta* doing *kīrtana*—with the aid of *ektārā*[6] in hand—would often begin to dance out of sheer fervor.

This reminds one of the word Indian culture prefers to use in place of music—*sangīta*, by which is understood not merely music, both vocal and instrumental, but also dance. Dance in the Indian context is never quite disjointed from music. Nor is this relatedness baseless. There is a feature that dance and music share—*laya*. It is no mere passage of everyday time, but the pace of music (or dance) itself as it helps and is contemplated during the making of art. As such, it is rarely a mere flow except for very brief spells. It is generally the matrix of some accents, be they individual notes in music, beats (*mātrās*) in the fabric of rhythm, or gestures, mere syllables or footfalls in Indian classical dance. Even in (vocal) *ālāpa*, which prefaces a traditional *dhruvapada* and does not use language, some syllables are there. They convey no meaning, but only contribute effects by virtue of their very formal character. The important thing to note here is that diversities such as these not only lend shape, measure, and articulateness to the music but also help attunement. Where these are allowed only as much occupancy in music—of course, in addition to their formal correctness—as is essential for contemplative accord with the growing knitwork of art, they come to acquire a spiritual "look" because of the very leanness of manner. If we are only a little spiritual in life they can put an edge on our sense of the charm and possibility of so refining sense activity that it may directly make for, instead of inhibiting, ascent in the life of "goodness."

Reference may be made at this point to those *dhruvapad* songs which are called *ārādhanātmaka*. Here, along with a prayerful text the manner of singing must be all along inward-looking, so subdued; no *upaj* (improvisation) is allowed. The whole utterance gives one "the impression of a musical sign welling up from the depths of being or of incense borne aloft on the wings of devotion,"[7] emitting an aura of purity and quiet contemplation. Such songs are notable for their kind of beauty: it spellbinds us but is yet quite austere. The feeling is intense, but the manner is restrained, the different *svaras* appearing as mere accents of charm, projected with such poise that they lend a grip to attention without anywhere tending to ruffle it.

From Belief to Argument

There is a good deal of evidence to support the view that Indian music is spiritual. Its real aim, we are told, is the attainment of one's spiritual destiny, and not mere entertainment (*muktidāyakam na tu ranjakam*). Of all the forms of our classical (North Indian) vocal music, viz., *ālāpa-dhruvapad, khyāl,* and *tarānā,*[8] the first is commonly believed to be most suitable for attaining the ideal. I know of a *dhruvapad* song in *rāga bihag* which insists that the essence of *svara* (or of the euphonic aspect of music) can be seized only when one's very way of life becomes a pursuit of the spiritual goal.[9] It also indicates how the vital forces (*prāṇa*) can be so regulated and made to go through the six psychic centers that the passage through the uppermost of these may secure the individual's liberation. But this obviously highlights the way of yoga rather than anything in music itself. True, both Swāmi Haridās in the north and Saint Thyāgarāja in the south attained salvation through the worship of *Nāda Brahman* (or the Absolute as Sound). But there is no way to determine what helped them more in the ascent to the goal, the power of music or their own spiritual fervor.

So one must turn to see how the concepts and imagery and the euphonic and rhythmic substance of music itself provide for some progress toward the art's exalted end. One cannot directly affirm that the ideal is attainable—through a loving and worshipful communion with the mysteries of sound (*nādopāsna)* unless one personally witnesses it, in experience.

If it is granted that the concept of the Absolute as sound is true and that music is a possible way to the final Reality, it would follow that the musician must cultivate sound in all its aspects and infinite variety. Now every sound has its own perceptual character, determined in part by its extent in time. It may seem compressed or full-blown, gentle or insistent, wan or radiant, and sparkling or incurvate. The musician must see and cherish as many of these differences as he or she possibly can, and our dances and drummers build upon niceties of variety in the formal aspects of utterable syllables (*bols*). But a mere refinement of perceptual acuity is not enough. What is (in principle) aimed at, the ultimate end, is no mere fact but the highest value. The Absolute, when realized, satisfies our deepest needs. So the refinement of sensitiveness to sound and musical duration must somehow be made to assist the individual's yearning for and progress in cultivating the quality of goodness and spirituality. The linkage, I suggest, is provided by a kind of musical imagination, a working of the mind that can enable us to imbue the details of music—and so ourselves, because we here deal with melody and rhythm quite absorbedly—with a deepening affinity for ethical-religious values. But this must be brought out in relation to the more important elements of music. Let us consider them thus, one by one.

Svara

We speak of *svara,* or the musical note, as that which reigns in its own right: *svam eva rājate.* An important demand here is implicit. Every single note must seem effective in itself; configuration, though important, is by no means enough. The best of our singers may find it difficult to meet this requirement, but if they are only a little aware of our philosophical-religious language, the vocalists may feel, in the very course of singing, a measure of the same reverence for some individual notes—especially the key (*vādi*) ones—as is elicited by the thought of ultimate Reality. The concept of reigning-in-its-own-right is similar in meaning to *svaprakāsam* (self-luminous), an attribute that is commonly ascribed to God or *Brahman.*

In Indian vocal music, however, the traditional emphasis is not only on keeping the *svara* "naked" or free from needless outer ornament but on imaginative self-absorption in the utterance of a moveless note. Both are important for the purpose of this essay and are alike realizable in musical practice. A good Indian vocalist is freely seen to appear "lost" in the sweet and steadfast projection of a single *svara*, generally the upper tonic or the immediately preceding one. In some such cases, it appears that the note in question is indwelling and felt from within. One here "sees" contemplation within the very embrace of creation. This is quite a singular feature. In the areas of the other arts what one is able to observe is the mere *alteration* of creative and contemplative spells. But, even apart from this rarity, the absorption (*tādātmya*) that is often a visible feature of good Indian music is likely to turn the *svara* into a breath of sweeter and deeper attunement with the thought of the Ultimate, provided the singer is aware of the relation between It and the *svara.*

The ideal is to keep a *svara* quite unencumbered. If in the treatment of a *rāga* (a melodic type) the individual notes are kept pure, with minimal assistance from the grace of interlacement; they are kept tuneful; and, what is more, the manner of utterance is caressing rather than loud and assertive, the singing may seem to be an evocation in sound of spiritual repose and tranquillity.[10] The qualities are here not only seen in the fabric of song. The singer may be said to inhale them, as it were, because of one's inner orientation, provided this attitude is what we have assumed it to be, and the qualities in question issue from abstention from mere ornament, roughly in the same way as one's austerity may throw one's richness in spirit into bolder relief.

The way is now paved for a better understanding of the subject of this essay and of the Indian view that every *rāga* is good for a particular hour of the day. The classical musician never deals in mere notes, for they are always the constituent units of *rāga*. But in the estimation of the writer there is no point in relating a *rāga* to a particular part of the day unless the features or happenings of the hour—or the thoughts or feelings it may tend to generate—can be transfigured into or in some other way can help the substance of music itself. But is this achievable? There is a reason to say yes!

> Imagine a devotee hallowing the morn with *svara(s)* of the *bhairava* mode. Steadying himself with the basic *sā* (tonic), he sings to saturate himself with images and attitudes that suit the hour—the rising sun, yearning in prayer and chastening of self, pouring *arghya* (holy water) on the Deity, and nonattachment towards things of the world. A brief but sure touch at the tonic followed immediately by *komal re* (D flat) prolonged firmly and sweetly, at once blends the mind with the sunrise outside, by suggesting effulgence. The same note (D flat) touched while descending from *gā* (E) provides in a manner a clear euphonic transcript of the downward slant of pouring *arghya* on the idol. As attunement increases through aid of the *svara(s)*, detachment deepens, and the singer cooperates by possessing the *sā* (tonic) merely ideally and lingering repeatedly at the *re* (D flat), now *faintly*, though sweetly—the note suggesting transcendence. The *re* thus becomes a symbol of devotion and elevation of self.[11]

Such an imbuement of the note with devout feeling, however, depends on its adroit utterance. The purely technical question of how *svaras* are articulated is very important. In *ālāpa* of the traditional *dhruvapad* kind, a note may be made to twinkle like a star or to look like yearning for something far away. A small tuft of two or three adjacent notes in the upper regions, if it is sung in the *anuraṇātmaka* way (emitting a kind of nasal resonance) and is made to wax and wane in intensity, can evoke a delightful semblance of temple bells swaying to and fro. Effects of such as these are a clear help to those who are wedded to not music alone but to goodness in their daily life.

Rāga

Notes in Indian music, we have seen, are always the accents or elements of a *rāga* (a melody type). It is not a song but a melodic form within and according to which *any* number of songs can be composed. A *rāga* is always the unique organization of a fixed number of specific notes. When, however, it is actually sung, a true revelation of its nature may call for the use of *śrutis*, or microtones. Where this is properly done, the musician is able to work up the effect of pensiveness—by tracing the diversity implicit in a very narrow compass of seemingly unvarying sound. An allied device, which makes for the same effect, is the use of a gentle vocal glide across two closely adjacent *svaras* in such a seamless and tuneful way that their look of being separate or individual is quite transcended.[12] It is important to remember that in many little ways our music permits and invites acuteness of notice and intenseness of sympathy. This is no mean assistance to spiritual living, where, although reason may not be the final arbiter, mindfulness is all very necessary.

The morning *rāgas* are, as a rule, given great value in India because they are mostly meant for devotion. But all *rāgas* are alike in one respect. Each one of them is knit around the relation between two notes, one of which, the *vādi*, is more important than the other, called *samvādi.*[13] Where the nature of a *rāga* must be brought out in its fullness—say by means of *ālāpa*—the *vādi* note may not be touched straightway. The singer generally reaches it by means of *barhat,* which may be described as a kind of reverential access, as if with unshod feet, to the point where the *rāga* blooms in its distinctive hue. Here, by virtue of a leisurely, deliberate quality of singing, the vocalist is generally able to saturate himself or herself with the character of the *rāga* chosen; but where the *rāga* takes up a devotional one—and if in one's daily living one feels drawn toward "the other world"—*barhat* can serve to deepen the orientation.

Rāga-ālāpa: Its Dynamics

We believe that a *rāga*'s nature is brought out better in the (*dhruvapad*) *ālāpa* manner of singing than in other vocal forms, though classical forms seek to meet the *rāga*'s demands, both technical and aesthetic. But one can think of a better way to argue for the preeminence of *ālāpa,* or singing that uses neither language nor any set rhythm. Every *rāga* is suited (in principle) to evoke a particular feeling, *rasa,* taken generally. In practice, however, this evocation does not arise from the *rāga*'s grammatical structure alone. What the vocalist may put into the singing is also a vital determinant. To illustrate, the direct effect of *rāgas* like *jogiyā* and *sohni*, because of the very setting of the *svaras* that they use, is one of yearning. But the text of the songs is here, as a rule, amorous, and this ties the longing and our fancy to a *human* beloved. *Ālāpa* that keeps the notes "naked" or bereft of the raiment of language puts no such shackle in our way; and the singer and the listener are both left free to let the longing appear to look godward. Indeed, if we reflect on the singer's own experience and attitudes in the act of unfolding a *rāga*, as also on those of the *rasika*[14] as he or she follows the evocation, we may be struck by the following points of affinity with some details of the spiritual life.

Vigilance is necessary. The *rāga* chosen must be kept on its own rails, so to speak. Nowhere can one let it trespass into the idiom of a *rāga* that may be close to it generally. Two *rāgas* may comprise the same notes; but then they must highlight different *svaras*,[15] and this difference of emphasis must be kept all along. A subtle requirement in the case of some *rāgas* is that one of the notes that they build on should only be "touched." Here, even a little lingering at this *svara* may tend to blur the requisite difference between the *rāga* in hand and its melodic neighbor. At this point it is relevant to focus on a (prefixed) detail of *dhruvapad* singing, that is, on what is called *ābhog ki taan*. It has often appeared as an intentional exercise in vigilance. It is never easy to accomplish, and when it is properly sung it always impresses the *resika* with its, so to say, last-minute ability to avoid spilling into another *rāga*. It looks like regaining one's balance from the very brink of a slip and delights and disturbs us by virtue of what might be called its "wanton heed."[16]

But here, as in spiritual life, the mindfulness in question also works creatively, by availing one of chances to enrich and enlarge one's concern with the present endeavor. Thus, during the course of *ālāpa*, if an utterance of the syllable *nom* in the upper regions of the scale turns out to be unusually sweet, the singer may be impelled to commence, quite without forethought, a quick and iterative yet very soft singing of the same syllable at the *taar sā* (upper tonic) supported by some adjacent *svaras* in a way that appears to describe the embrace of two petals in a convex kind of utterance.

Even in the region of our instrumental music, where the constraints of rhythms are added to those of a right *rāga*-rendering, what I have called alertness as creative is seen to work variously. A delightful expression of it is what we admire as *jagah nilkanā*. It is the impromptu meandering of a pretty little phrase in a mere crevice in the fabric of melody.[17]

The Ethereal in Rāga-ālāpa

The buildup of vocal *ālāpa* is a slow, meticulous process. Its full-blown appearance, however, is not that of a large aggregate. It is rather one of an intense musical presence that seems to fill the auditorium and, in a measure, to suffuse both the *rasikas* and the singer with a feeling of peace and deep, elevating delight, so that what is contemplated is also somewhat esteemed. The singer finds himself dwarfed by what he has been able to evoke. It is true that what emerges in the end—the *rāga*-form of beauty and depth—is the result of his own earnest effort; but he can nowhere take liberties with the grammar of the *rāga*, and as he goes on eliciting its charms in ever-new ways he grows so impressed with its exhaustlessness that his final frame of mind is one of utter humility. At such consummate moments when the *rasikas* compliment the singer and wonder how he could produce such ethereal music, the answer is never a reflex of self-confidence but always a confession of passivity: it may be of just three words: *bas ho gaya* ("it just happened"). The confident and competent projection of predeterminate music is one thing; the watchful, even reverent, evocation of *rāga*-form—only the barest outline of which is foreknown to the singer—is quite another. The latter may be valued as a quite good analogue of a feature of the good life. Where the spirit soars heavenward one is just borne aloft in creaturely bliss. What is more, in case the *rāga* that a singer sets out to unfold in *ālāpa* is devotional, and if he is himself a little religious, the experience may put an edge on his will to shed worldliness.

The Aesthetic and the Spiritual

We may now turn to what is typical of Indian spirituality—insistence on the nearness of art experience to spiritual experience. In this regard one must bear in mind the account of *Brahmānubhava* in Indian philosophy (personal experience of *Brahman*, the Absolute Reality), our ancient view of *rasa* (aesthetic experience), and the actual "look" of good *rāga-ālāpa*.

If *rasa* is regarded, quite generally, as the delight that accrues to a competent listener (or onlooker/reader) from intense imaginative self-absorption in (or *tādātmya* with) the aesthetic object, listening to a good *ālāpa* may well be said to generate *rasa*. In Indian music, however, *rasa* is not taken as a merely secular experience. The text of some *dhruvapad* songs speaks of it as the locus of *Brahman* Itself,[18] and indeed if the various attributes used to explain *rasa*-experience are taken one by one, the closeness of *Brahmānubhava* to the experience of listening to *ālāpa* will appear quite impressive. Attributes of the experience include the following: it is undifferentiated (*niravicchinna*), transcendent of distinctions (*vitavighna)*, and *svātmaparāmarṣa*, *svātmavisrānti* (self-reverent, self-existent). Such words need no defense with reference to human beings' ultimate spiritual experience, for in this context they are commonly acknowledged. Only their relevance *to music* may seem unclear, but the writer does not for a moment doubt it. On the basis of his long experience as a devoted listener he believes that *ālāpa* can be marked by all that the attributes signify. If it is good and rightly followed, it can seem not only intense but very satisfying, so as to subdue all desire for the moment, except the one to inhale the present joy evermore. What is more uplifting is the sense of raising us above all differences, of self and the other, of time and space, and even beyond the plurality of constituent *svaras* considered as separate existences. Yet the two kinds of experience are by no means identical. Communion with good *ālāpa* surely is not merely interruptive. It enlivens sensibility and imagination alike and so helps our subsequent musical perceptions. But its direct impact on goodness is surely much feebler than that of prayer and the practice of faith.

Here a question may be put: Why do our ancient aestheticians appear oblivious to the fact that even after repeated art experience (of the exalted kind that is instanced) one may remain quite enmeshed in the world of sense? Because in India of the past our everyday life was not as indifferent to the truths of the spirit as it is today. The *rasikas* in those days could draw upon the impulse of their own general commitment to goodness, realize it then through the spiritual promise of art, and so minimize the hiatus between the spiritual and the merely aesthetic.

Rhythm and Spiritual Life

The only other concept of Indian music selected for analysis is rhythm, or *tāla*. Rhythm is musical duration (*laya*) as measured by means of beats (*mātrās*). It is to *laya* what a yard is to distance: the one is a measure of the other. Rhythm in Indian music, however, is no mere measure, but a form; and the form here is cyclic. In other words, the rhythm starts from and returns to the first beat, completing a cycle (*āvṛti*). The first (or central) beat, called the *sama*, is here preeminent not only technically but also aesthetically. Where the effort is made, failure to reach the *sama* with split-second accuracy is frowned upon as an index of technical incompetence. One single mistake of this kind is enough to render the music poor, even if the blemish appears after an hour of competent performance. On the other hand, the ability to gain access to the *sama* in ways of varying design is regarded as a welcome expression of creative ability. The basic rhythm as played on the drums is called *thekā;* and the latter—which is seen wheeling for most of the time where it figures as mere accompaniment—serves a moveless ground of many-sided value. It is continually registered by the main musician by instinct, and this enables him to keep and return to the chosen pace. What is more, it is partially in relation to this basic design that a good deal of the musician's creative work looks patterned, and no mere assortment. All this is, however, merely secular. How can it relate music to the good life?

In India we often clap to mark the rhythm. This little detail of practice, as it runs along with the ideal tuning induced by the "cyclic" flow, can enable a devotee to sing his *bhajans* more soulfully.[19] I may add that where the mind is absorbed in *quietly* contemplating a symmetrical and not too leisurely rhythm, the beats may be "seen" to peck the flow of *laya* in a way that appears very similar in manner to counting the beads of a rosary.

Our rhythm comprises not mere beats, but *bols*. A *bol* is a letter or a brief tuft of letters which are all meaningless but are roughly similar in sound to the details of drumming. These *bols* strike the ear quite variously. Examples include *tā*, *dhā*, *dhin*, *tirkit*, *tak*, *dhālang*, *ghinnan*, *tram*, *krhān*, *tharri*, *thungā*. Thus, if only indirectly, our rhythm may be said to be a way of *nādasādhana*.[20]

It is true that *mātrās* and *bols* of the cycle enable us to measure and articulate, and (so to say) enliven the *laya* flow. But even where they are numerous and close-banded they never quite exhaust the *laya*-flow continuum. As a symptom of creative abandon, our dancers and musicians delight in interjecting a *bol* or a mere emphatic nod *between* two adjacent beats[21] without losing their hold over the normal pace of the *thekā*. For one of spiritual bent, this may serve to refigure the thought that no number of distinctions, of name or form—no "manyness" of holy names—can really seize the one, unbroken Reality beyond.

A known subtlety of Hindustani rhythm is provided by patterns of *ateiet* and *anagat* variety. When they are played, the final beat (or *bol*) of the pattern is designedly made to occur just a little before or after the cycle's focal beat. Here if the basic rhythmic flow is not lost sight of, the intentional change in the usual order is felt as a moment of relish. This too may seem to echo a detail of good life. Those who live by faith cannot but cherish the truth of alternative designs, and if one is able to trust God's design, one will not be disturbed by upsets in one's own plans, because faith can work illatively and "see" some higher reason in the seeming wantonness.

The truth in question is better intimated by another subtlety of our experience of rhythm. After the mind of a musician or dancer (or of the *rasika*) has been saturated with the normal pace of the *thekā*, if an emphasis is put waywardly at a point that is not the set location of any beat, the musician will not only register the strain but, in place of getting upset over the oddity, will positively revel in his or her ability to hold onto the basic flow in the teeth of the vagary. Any *lahrā*-player[22] will vouch for the truth and uniqueness of the feeling when he has to keep the musical line unshaken against the willful disorder of a subtle rhythmic phrase or pattern. My own experience is that if we are equipped with even a little faith, this commonplace detail of our rhythmic practice can lend some credence to what otherwise bewilders us: that a spiritual person seems not only serene but even a little happy in unforeseen crisis.

Two Details of Glory

The following instance of a cognate idea from what the worker knew of the practice of *ālāpa* may, in conclusion, be cited. The note that is nearest to the tonic, *komal re*, can be so sung that it may seem not merely to follow but "to arise from within the *sa* (tonic)." Here one may be easily led to imagine that before this emergence the two notes were coincident, letting us see and be sure of only that *svara* which is our usual foothold, that is, the tonic. From this it is but a step to be quickened into a sense of the truth that, quite unlike our moments of achievement where God's sanction is at one with the impulse of our own efforts, their absolute failure at times shows God's will in its isolated majesty. It is surely not pointless to say that our dark days reflect the glory of God.

The music of India is no necessary push into the realm of the spirit, but its own character *and inner amplitude* are here certainly of help. Any number of songs can be composed in the same *rāga*. Every single segment of beat-measured *laya* admits of countless syllabic arrangements. This is an article of faith even with the illiterate dancers and musicians. Nor can one come to the end of the ways in which the *sama* of a cycle may be reached. This vision of infinity in a limited extent makes us revere the art; and insofar as the natural direction of reverence is at the personal, it seems only proper to let music inspire our longing for God.

Notes

1. *Svara* is any one of the seven notes of the gamut. A *rāga* is a distinct melodic form. *Ālāpa*, which precedes a *dhruvapad* song, is an attempt to sing effectively *without using language or rhythm*. *Dhruvapad* is the oldest living form of Northern Indian vocal music. A song in this form is also called a *dhruvapad*. This form is known for its "high seriousness." *Laya* is a musical duration, and *tāla* is *laya* as measured by means of beats.
2. *Sattvik* is the quality of being conducive to peace, purity, and patient endeavor. Vinoba Bhave has been a saint of modern India, known for his *bhūdān yajña*.
3. A concept of the highest religious ideal. Literally, "blowing out" of all desires; generally, release from the birth–death–rebirth cycle.
4. *A New Dictionary of Christian Theology*, ed. Alan Richardson and John Bowden (London: SCM, 1983) 549.
5. The more popular of these are the yogas of disinterested action (*karma*), knowledge (*jñāna*), and devotion (*bhakti*).
6. *Ektārā* is a musical instrument with but one string, symbolic of *undivided* dependence on God.
7. S. K. Saxena, "Essentials of Hindustani Music," *Diogene* No. 45 (1964) 19.
8. *Khyāl* is the more imaginative, freer, and popular form of classical North Indian

vocal music today. Unlike *khyāl*, where language is freely used, *tarānā* builds mainly on mnemonic syllables. Both *khyāl* and *tarānā* are set in a definite rhythm.

9. The opening words of this *dhruvapad* are *surtattva gyān tab pāve jab jeevan mukti ko roop sādhe.*. I owe this bit of knowledge to the late Usted Rahimuddin Khan Dagur, to whom I am indebted wherever in this essay I speak of *svara*, *ālāpa*, and *dhruvapad*.

10. I have in mind Ustad Rahimuddin Khan's exposition of *rāga gurjari todi* in the Radio Sangeet Sammelan of 1956 (New Delhi).

11. Saxena, "Essentials of Hindustani Music," 19.

12. This explains the distinctive charm of two *madhyams* (F and F sharp) in *rāgas*, *kedār*, and *lalit*, and of two *nishads* (B and B flat), in *rāga*, *miān kī malhār*.

13. The note that is concordant with and so helps the key note *vādi* in bringing out the *rāga*'s distinctive charm.

14. A *rasika* is one who is qualified to contemplate an art work, by virtue of his or her earlier training and experience.

15. *Rāgas*, *bhoopāli*, and *deṣkār* here provide good instances.

16. The reference here is to Milton's phrase: "wanton heed and giddy cunning."

17. This is specially true of our *sitār* players like Ustads Wilayat Khan and Abdul Halim Jaffer Khan.

18. There is, for instance, a *druvapad*, the text of which includes the following words: *Baiju ke prabhu rasa mein samāye brahma*.

19. I am here reminded of the words *Rāmanāmashoon tāli lāgi* in Gandhi's favorite bhajan: *vaiṣṇava jana to tene kahiye.*

20. Or, of cultivating the mysteries of sound.

21. This is called *jagah dikhānā* and is different from what I have earlier spoken of as *jagah nikalnā*.

22. *Lahrā* is a tune which is played repeatedly and without any major change, to keep the basic rhythm all along clear to the (solo) drummer or *Kathak* dancer.

Bibliography

Awasthi, S. S. *A Critique of Hindustani Music and Music Education*. Jullandar: Dhanpat Rai, 1963[?].

Desapande, Vamana Hari. *Between Two Tanpuras*. Translated by Ram Deshmukh and B. R. Dhekney. Bombay: Popular Prakashan, 1989.

Moutal, Patrick. *A Contemporary Study of Selected Hindustani Ragas: Based on Contemporary Practice*. New Delhi: Munshiram Manoharlal, 1991.

Ranade, Ashok D., *Keywords and Concepts: Hindustani Classical Music*. New Delhi: Promilla, 1991.

Saxena, Sushil Kumar. *Aesthetical Studies: Studies in Aesthetic Theory, Hindustani Music, and Kathak Dance*. Delhi: Chanakya Press, 1981.

——. *Winged Form: Aesthetical Essays on Hindustani Rhythm*. New Delhi: Sangeet Natak Akademi, 1979.

Srivasthava, Indurama. *Dhrupada: A Study of its Origin, Historical Development, and Present State*. Delhi: Motilal Banarsidass, 1980.

Sharman, Gopal. *Filigree in Sound: Form and Content in Indian Music*. Delhi: Vikas Publications, 1970.

23

The Spirituality of Carnatic Music

R. VENUGOPAL

MUSIC IN INDIA is as old as the country's ancient religious tradition, dating back to the times of the Vedas—the scriptures from which the religious principles of the majority of the Indians are drawn. The Vedas are chronologically placed sometime between 4000 B.C.E. and 2000 B.C.E.

The ancient Vedas give a call to sing to the Lord thus:

> Sing of Him (who is a refuge) like the strong castle,
> Now loudly let the gargara (a kind of violin) sound, Let the godha (a lute) send its resounding voice.
> Let the string send its tunes around
> To god is our hymn upraised. (*Ṛg Veda* 8.69.8–9)

In the Vedas, prayer means the musical outburst of a heart filled with love for the Creator.

Of the Vedas, the *Ṛg Veda* supplies the literary text; the *Yajur Veda* represents the ritual; and the *Sāma Veda* gives the musical representation. In the *Sāma Veda*, the text of the *Ṛg Veda* is altered to suit a musical way of chanting that originally employed only two notes. Certain vowels with no particular meaning were also introduced for chanting purposes. Later the number of notes employed in *Sāma Veda* increased to three, five, and seven.

All rituals in pursuit of spiritual ideals contained music as an essential part. The *Yajur Veda* mentions accompanying instruments such as the drum and *Vīṇa*, a stringed instrument: "For sound, the beater of the kettle drum. For sublimity the *Vīna* player."

"In the beginning was the Word and the Word was with God and the Word was God," says the Gospel of John. This statement will not strike a strange note to a Hindu especially as he/she looks at the Upaniṣads. The Word in ancient Indian religious thought was the *Aum*. *Taittrīya Upaniṣad* says: "Aum is Brahman, all this universe perceived and imagined is "Aum" (I.8). In other words *Aum* is the original sound from which all else has emerged. Again in the *Chāndogya Upaniṣad* we find the following statement: "He who having known this letter thus praised [this letter "Aum"] he enters into this very letter that is immortal and fearless. Having entered it he becomes immortal like the *Brahman*" (I.4.5). The *Chāndogya* goes on to say: "What is the support of Sama (the *Sāmagāna* or the *Sāma Veda*)? The musical scale, said he. What is the support of the musical scale? The vital force, he said. What is the support of the vital force? Food, he said. What is the support of food? Water, he said" (I.8.4). Thus, the musical form was considered to be the essence and sublimation of the grosser forms of creation.

After the Upaniṣads came the two great Hindu epics, *Rāmāyaṇa* and *Mahābhārata*. There are many references in these epics to music as part of everyday life. In the *Rāmāyaṇa* we find a range of musical instruments mentioned, and it even refers to the existence of *moorchanas*, that is, derived musical scales. In Hindu mythology, almost all important gods, goddesses, or celestial beings are associated with some form of music or dance. For example, Rāma is described as one well versed in music; Kṛṣṇa is stated to be a flute player; and Śiva and Pārvati are considered to be great dancers and masters of rhythm. The instrument associated with Śarasvati, Goddess of learning, is the *Vīṇa*. Sage Nārada is described as an expert on the *Vīṇa* and also as an expert vocalist.

The earliest treatise on music in India was the *Nātyaśāstra*, which is said to have been written by sage Bharata around 400 B.C.E. Although the main objective of this treatise was to define the form and grammar of *nātya* (dance), it also dealt in great detail with various aspects of music that were considered to be an integral part of dance, including not only vocal music but also specific musical instruments such as the *Vīṇa*, the flute, and a variety of drums.

Around this period, the role of music in the social fabric of Indian society grew substantially and generated several creative impulses in various parts of the country. Music was considered to be not only entertainment but also a source for one's spiritual growth and a means for raising one's consciousness from a merely mundane level to higher levels of contemplation. An ancient sage, Yājñavalkya, is quoted as saying "a person well versed in playing the instrument *Vīṇa*, having deep knowledge of the microtones and the rhythm, reaches the heavens without any effort!" (*Yajnavalkya Smrti* III.5 [N.S. Press edition, pp. 349–50]).

It has been said that it was from India that Pythagoras took the harmonic major, the Western musical scale. The spirit of the West being *rajasic*, vigorous, aggressive, and also enterprising, Western music developed on those lines covering and floating over any number of octaves with emphasis on instrumental and vocal virtuosity. Indian music, in consonance with its concept of music as a meek and humble prayer to God, adopted melody as its dominant motif.

As stated earlier, Indian music was derived from *Sāmagāna*, the ancient Vedic chants. The evolution of these chants from one to two, to three, to five, to seven notes, and ultimately to countless microtones, invested Indian music, more particularly the Carnatic music of South India, with a tremendous range of nuances and aesthetic values retaining the basic religious and spiritual core. In fact, at all times in the history of Carnatic music, if there was a secular form of music, it was not considered classical. Music employing lyrics of spiritual and religious contents alone was considered classical.

A great work entitled *Silappadikāram* in Tamil, mainly inspired by Bharata's *Nātyaśāstra*, appeared around the second century C.E. This treatise dealt with an array of musical instruments, the grammar of song and dance, and effectively reflected the cultural scene of that particular period.

We must pause here to take a look at a major revolution that was taking place on the religiophilosophic scene. The original Vedic philosophy had not only celebrated the harmony between the unseen, indeterminable spirit and gross, palpable matter but also had spoken of the identity of the two. Subsequently, however, its message was lost sight of, and ritual performance came to be overemphasized. Under these conditions, we see the emergence of Buddhism. Responding to the challenge faced by the popularity of Buddhism, Hinduism rediscovered and reasserted its roots in the eighth century of the Christian era through the efforts of Śaṅkara, who reinterpreted the Vedas and the Upaniṣads and established a philosophy of nondualism (Advaita Vedānta). This set in motion further waves in the ocean of Indian philosophic thought and brought into existence other Vedāntic schools, such as the Qualified Nondualism (Viśiṣṭadvaita Vedānta) of Rāmānuja and the Dualism (Dvaita Vedānta) of Madhva. But during all this period and afterward a sustaining influence of devotional approach to God remained strong. Devotion meant, of course, meditation, prayer, and contemplation of God's glories.

Around the seventh and eighth centuries South India saw also a great surge of devotionalism with the emergence of a number of devotee-poet-singers who expressed their deep devotion in thousands of metered verses set to classical music. These poet-singers were the Āḻvārs and the Nāyanmārs, who to a great extent constructed the foundation on which the edifice of the future Carnatic music was built.

Later there were many devotee-poet-musicians from both North and South India. While the northern region saw the great savants such as

Tulsīdās, Kabīr, Mīrā, Jayadeva, and others, the South witnessed the birth of great devotee-musicians such as Rāmadāsa, Purandaradāsa, Annamācārya, and Kśetrajña. The contributions of these great people culminated in the late eighteenth and early nineteenth century in a golden era of Carnatic music. Three great composers—Thyāgarāja, Muthuswāmy Dikshitar, and Shyāmaśāstri—dominated the scene, and Carnatic music reached a pinnacle in both its aesthetic and its technical aspects. The forerunner of this golden age was undoubtedly Purandaradāsa of the fifteenth–sixteenth century, who is said to be the father of present-day classical Carnatic music. He initiated a system of teaching Carnatic music and presented the initial scale of notes to be taught to a beginner. Purandaradāsa was a great devotee given to spending his whole life in meditation on God and singing His praises.

While to some extent North Indian music came to be an activity of the royal courts, particularly during Muslim rule, in the South music belonged more to temples and was practiced only by great devotees, who not only opted for a life of austerity and self-imposed indigence but also spurned the patronage of kings in any form. However, many of the kings of South India were themselves great devotees and did all they could to help promote classical Carnatic music in temples and other religious congregations.

The three great composers who lived in the eighteenth and nineteenth centuries were a product of their times, which witnessed a very high religious fervor coupled with cultural activity. These composers were naturally devotees in the first instance and only then musicians. They used their music as a form of worship; their lyrics pertained only to glories of the Lord; and their music, which flowed spontaneously and simultaneously with their lyrics, was majestic, suited to the theme of the lyrics, and emotional, suited to their devotion and total surrender to God. Each of these composers followed a highly individualistic style of music and lyrics, the common element being the devotional content. While Muthuswāmy Dīkshitar composed in Sanskrit, Shyāmāśāstri composed in Telugu and Tamil; and Thyāgarāja composed in Telugu and Sanskrit. Of the three, Muthuswāmy Dīkshitar was given less to emotion than the others; his compositions focused more on singing the glories of the Lord housed in various temples in South India. He visited numerous holy shrines and sang about each one of the deities. He was also a player of *Vina*, and his compositions reflected his progress and mastery of this stringed instrument. Another important aspect of his music was that his peregrinations included a visit to North India, where he interacted with musicians and adopted several of the North Indian scales in his compositions. He also exchanged notes with practitioners of Western music in South India, and the imprint of his absorption of the influence of the Western music can be seen on some of his compositions. However eclectic he might have been in his adoption of musical forms, spirituality was the basic content of his whole music.

Shyāmāśāstri was a more emotional composer but not as prolific as the other two. His lyrics were in a simple language showing a state of total surrender to the Supreme in the form of the Divine Mother. He did not propagate any high philosophic doctrines, but his songs reflect an unparalleled degree of emotion and devotion.

Thyāgarāja was unique among these three composers in that not only was he a prolific composer and a master of musicology but he also was one whose high philosophic contemplation was fused beautifully with his great music. Thyāgarāja thought considerably on music and widened its dimensions through his research and creativity. At the same time he believed in all earnestness that music was a form of the Divine. Being a great scholar in the ancient scriptures he drew enormously upon this knowledge for his lyrics. While his lyrics can be considered a treatise on Hindu philosophy, the musical form in which he clothed his lyrics rose to indescribably great heights of classicism and aesthetics. Thyāgarāja employed several moods in his music and lyrics. The lyrics were dialogues between him and God, on whom he constantly meditated; exercises in self-introspection; or discourses on God's glories and the impermanence of human existence and worldly possessions. He also narrated in his songs the spiritual experiences of other great devotees of God. He hardly ever touched on secular topics.

The Hindu epics include accounts of the various incarnations of Viṣṇu. Thyāgarāja's favorite incarnation was that of Rāmā, the hero of the epic *Rāmāyaṇa,* which describes how Rāmā, God incarnate, was born into the family of a king to destroy the evil demons and bring peace, tranquillity, and justice to the world.

Thyāgarāja sang of the great bliss that could come through constant meditation on God and in the chanting of His name. He considered devotion to God to be unequaled in the happiness it can offer. The bliss of such a state cannot be described in words but must be enjoyed by each for himself or herself. In the various states of trance in which he composed, he visualized his Lord Rāmā as standing before him, and some of his songs give an account of the dialogues he held "directly" with Rāmā.

Thyāgarāja sang several introspective songs in which he analyzed his own thoughts, feelings, strengths, and weaknesses and often wondered and worried how much he measured up to God's expectations of him and whether he would ever reach that state at all where the Lord would be pleased with him. Some of the songs signify a state of utter despair where he pleads with God that, however evil and unworthy he might be, the Lord has a duty to redeem the bad in the same manner that He protects the good.

All this self-castigation and self-pity may appear a bit lachrymose for a scholar and philosopher of the stature of Thyāgarāja, but Hindu philosophy does not prescribe any one way to reach God. In fact, it is even said that one can reach God through love or fear or hatred, by friendship or enmity! What is required, of course, is constant remembrance of God, a state of mind that could come even through enmity!

If the devotee believes that God exists, how is the devotee unable to experience His presence any more than the nonbeliever? But then who is a nonbeliever? A nonbeliever's major forte is reason and rationality, and so his nonbelief is not an irrational bigotry. At worst, the agnostic is only still looking for the proof of the existence of God. To Thyāgarāja, agnostics are just forgetful persons who do not remember that they themselves came from no source except God. They are like the bird that flies from the tree into the sky, flies higher and higher on the strength of its own wings and occasionally forgets the tree from which it took off in the first instance. This process can go on for some time and even for a long time but not for ever. The bird cannot be flying in the sky forever. It must return to the tree. Likewise, agnostics too, however intoxicated they may be with their own apparent rationality and denial of God, must return to a state of God-realization one day.

The faith of the believer is not always blind but is more often than not based on his or her own logic and rationality, and also on some kind of awareness that it is the right thing to do. In such a situation the believer, by not having any higher capacity to realize God than the nonbeliever, suffers a traumatic conflict in his or her mind. Thyāgarāja perceived this. He sings to his Rāmā: "You are far away from every one and at the same time you reside right in my own heart." But then, "Where do I look for you?" he asks in another song. The ancient scriptures come to Thyāgarāja's aid: He says "You are the sky, the air, the light, the water, the tree, the palpable and the impalpable." But all this is only a matter of "perception" for Thyāgarāja, and not one of "realization," which comes through knowing the presence of God within. Thyāgarāja says, therefore: "I wish to discover you in me and through such discovery achieve oneness with you." Such a discovery within, according to Thyāgarāja, is possible only through meditation. "There is no greater worship than meditation." This meditative process includes, for Thyāgarāja, chanting the names of the Lord. "Nothing is more blissful than chanting God's name," he says. In order to wholeheartedly meditate on God one needs to restrain one's mind from pursuit of worldly pleasures, to cleanse one's mind of all evil thoughts, and to get rid of the passions that cloud one's mind. There must be, he says further, a steadfast faith in Him under all conditions, whether fortune favors one or one is beset with misfortune.

Thyāgarāja says that good deeds are essential to purify one's mind, but they alone cannot take one to God. Good deeds can at best give one a better rebirth next time, but they cannot free us from the cycle of rebirths. According to the law of *karma*, a good person at best can look forward to an earthly reward for his or her good actions. But until one can love God without looking for a reward, one never can realize Him. Thyāgarāja tells himself in a song that "he does not want to be content with good deeds which would only give him a transient happiness in his next birth at the end of which he would be again back to where he was." He prays to God to give him that supreme state where one is free from births and rebirths.

The experience of God, according to Thyāgarāja, cannot be achieved through intellectual debates and discussions. What is needed is faith in God and constant remembrance of Him. "Realize there is only one God; do not swerve from the truth. Be a servant to the whole world." Also, "Do only good and dedicate all actions to Him." Addressing Rāmā, Thyāgarāja sings: "Whatever I see, whatever I speak, whomever I serve, whatever I worship, Oh God, may all that be you and nothing else. . . . Whatever my body does and even if I see what I should not, I consider all this as only you and remain happy in that thought."

But this state of mind is difficult to reach, since it is reached only through deepest devotion to God. Thyāgarāja says "there can be really no knowledge or no understanding to reach, it cannot come without the deepest devotion to God . . . there can be really no knowledge or no understanding of the Supreme if there is no such devotion in one's mind." Purity of thought, mental discipline, and nobility of actions are all essential in one's religious life. But above all one needs God's grace. For Thyāgarāja, true devotion is something given to us by God Himself. So he says to the Lord, "I beg you for alms, the alms of devotion to you." For him, devotion to God is its own reward; being deeply devoted to God is indeed salvation itself.

The above thoughts of Thyāgarāja reflect like a mirror the spiritual climate of the Vedas and the Upaniṣads and also the implied teachings of all Hindu epics and the *purāṇas*. But Thyāgarāja's songs express these thoughts with great directness and simplicity. Each one of Thyāgarāja's songs can be traced to a line or a verse in the ancient scriptures. The greatness of Thyāgarāja seems to lie in the fact that here was a man who lived so close to our times but still was able to realize and express the ancient spirituality of the Hindus to us in a form that we could understand easily and appreciate.

To Thyāgarāja one sure method of purging one's mind of all evil and of purifying the mind was through music, remembering God and reciting His glories. To him music was not just a source of sweet sounds; it was verily the path to God. Thyāgarāja says categorically that those who do not understand music do not qualify for salvation. He goes to the extent of saying that music itself is the form of God. Rāmā, the human incarnation of God, is none other than the personification of great and sublime music. He extends the same logic by saying that the seven notes of music are divine beings who should be worshiped as gods. Thyāgarāja then astounds us by saying that even the gods shone in resplendence because they practiced music. Of course, this is quite consistent with the teachings of the ancient scriptures according to which the primordial sound "*Aum*" is the origin of everything.

To sum up, in delineating spiritual values in his lyrics, in employing music as the means of worship, and ultimately in treating music itself as the form of the Supreme, Thyāgarāja was no different from other great composers of Carnatic music except that he was a lot more emphatic and categorical in his statements. He, more than the others, summed up effectively the evolution of spirituality in music over thousands of years of Indian cultural history and also established a shining example for posterity. He lived a life of austerity, spurning worldly acquisitions, focusing all his time on music and singing the glories of God. He died in a state of God-realization leaving an abiding influence on classical Carnatic music.

Thyāgarāja was more important to classical Carnatic music than the other composers because he encapsulated in his songs all the spiritual significance of music as well as the musical manifestation of the Spirit. He was as articulate as he was learned and as great a musician as he was a devotee. He summed up in his songs the age-old tradition of classical music and handed it down to posterity after enriching it with his own creativity. Even if his music were to disappear, his lyrics would stand sentinel to the rich spiritual heritage of Carnatic music.

In the post-Thyāgarāja period, several composers emerged on the scene, all in the world of Thyāgarāja. Not all of them were saints like Thyāgarāja but at least their approach to music was greatly influenced by Thyāgarāja's high ideals.

The holy character of Carnatic music has taken a beating in the modern days of secularism, but still when one listens to truly classical Carnatic music even in secular surroundings, its austere grandeur and its religious, spiritual tradition envelop the listener like a mist and take him to heights far above mere entertainment. The strength of this tradition is such that it has not allowed the chasm between the classical and commonplace music to close even up to this day.

Bibliography

Ayyanger, R. Rangaramanuja. *History of South Indian Carnatic Music From Vedic Times to the Present*. Madras: Padma Varadan, 1972.

——. *Sangetha Ratnakaram of Nissanka Sangradeva*. Bombay: Wilco Publishing House, 1978.

——. *Musings of a Musician: Recent Trends in Carnatic Music*. Bombay: Wilco Publishing House, 1977.

Jackson, William J. *Thyagaraja, Life and Lyrics*. Delhi: Oxford University Press, 1991.

Raghavan, V. *Thyagaraja*. New Delhi: Sahitya Academy, 1983.

——, and C. Ramanujachari. *The Spiritual Heritage of Thyagaraja*. Madras: Ramakrishna Mission Students Home, 1957.

24

The Spiritual Dimension of Indian Art

BETTINA BÄUMER

> Homage to Him who paints the picture of the Three Worlds, thereby displaying in full evidence His amazing genius (*pratibhā*), to Śambhu (Śiva) who is beautiful with the hundreds of appearances laid out by the brush of His own, unique, subtle and pure Energy (Śakti).[1]

ONE OF THE POSSIBLE APPROACHES to understanding the relationship between art and spirituality is the metaphysical idea that God is the greatest artist, and the world, His creation, is a marvelous picture or piece of art. This idea, which has been developed with all its implications in certain areas of Hindu religion, presupposes a very high estimation of the artist. The poet (*kavi*) has sometimes been called the creator (*Prajāpati*),[2] and in the theoretical treatises on art, which includes architecture, sculpture, painting, and the rest, called *Śilpaśāstra*, the artist is called the architect of the universe (*Viśvakarman*), or his earthly representative (see *Vāstusūtra Upaniṣad* I.1, 3; *Agni Purāṇa* 43, 26, etc.) because one can create a work of art worth the name only if one partakes in the divine creative power. What the *Śilpaśāstras* say of the visual arts has its roots in the Vedic conception of the poet as a seer (*ṛṣi*), who, as such, has "a share in the Divine Word" (*Ṛg Veda* 10.71). The divine word (*vāc*) (which is feminine in Sanskrit) has later been identified with Śakti, the creative female energy of God. Thus, the divine creative power, so to speak, descends from the Supreme to his Energy and thence to the human recipient, the poet or artist.[3]

This interrelationship is clearly expressed in the terminology of the texts. Thus, the term *pratibhā*, meaning "intuition," "imagination," or "insight," which occurs in the quotation at the beginning of this article, applies both to Śiva, the divine artist, as well as to the human artist in the sense of the creative intuition or vision which precedes any artistic creation. In his commentary on the *Nāṭyaśāstra*, Abhinavagupta says:

> Like the creator, the poet creates for himself a world according to his wish. Indeed, He is amply endowed with the power of creating manifold, extraordinary things, originating thanks to the favour of the Deity, the Supreme Word, called *pratibhā*, and continually shining within his heart. (*Abhinava Bhāratī* I.4)[4]

Elsewhere he defines *pratibhā* as consciousness *(prajñā)* which is able to create new extraordinary (*apūrva*) things (*Dhvanyāloka Locana*, 92).

Śiva is not only the painter or artist; he also enjoys his own art for He is the One:

> Whose consciousness is aroused by seeing the art (*kalā*) of his own play by his own Energy, of the various bodies of enjoyment and emotional states (*bhāva*). He alone paints the universe with the colour of his own being (*svabhāva*), becoming manifest he paints the universe, and the manifestation itself is nothing but his own nature (*svarūpa*, form or symbol).[5]

The metaphor of the artist befits the creator because the artist remains himself in his own creation. Moreover, it is, so to say, a part of himself, and he can enjoy himself reflected in it as in a mirror. Thus also: "The Lord himself enjoys the pleasure after drawing the picture of the universe on his own Self by means of the brush of his own Self and seeing it in himself" (*Parimala* on *Mahārthamañjari* v.48). The Śaiva conception of creation as a manifestation (*ābhāsa*) or reflection (*pratibimba*, *Abbild*) of an original image (*bimba*, *Urbild*) fits perfectly with the symbolism of God as the divine artist. It is this metaphysical vision that provides the background for a spiritual understanding of art in the Hindu tradition.

One may argue that art has to do with the senses and that the aim of spirituality is to transcend or interiorize sensual experience. Here again the Tantric tradition has a nondualistic approach to the experience of beauty:

> Sitting in the heart-lotus playfully,
> behind the veil of the eyes and other senses,
> O Goddess, you experience the honey (sweetness)
> of forms again and again.[6]

That is to say, in all conscious beings, it is only the Divine Energy which, "sitting behind" the senses, enjoys the beauty of forms from within. This verse also alludes to the traditional place of the Indian woman who sits behind a screen and from there can observe everything without herself being seen from outside. The senses are this screen strewn with the holes or openings of the body, as the *Kaṭha Upaniṣad* (IV.1) puts it, echoing the *Atharva Veda* (X.2.6).

It is the interpretation of the nature of the body and senses that marks the difference between classical yogic and Vedāntic spirituality, on the one hand, and Tantric spirituality, on the other. In the first case, where the body-consciousness and sensual experience are to be transcended, overcome, eliminated, or transformed, as the case may be, the senses are always seen as obstacles on the spiritual way. In the second case, that of Tantric spirituality, which pervades a large part of Hinduism, the senses themselves are the means of experiencing the Divine, provided that they are purified of egoistic attachment. The Tantric yogi can enjoy song and other artistic expressions which lead directly to divine bliss.

> When there is the sound of sweet songs and the touch of sandal wood, etc., the state of indifference disappears and the heart is invaded by a state of vibration. Such a state is precisely the so-called power of beatitude (*ānanda-śakti*) thanks to which man is "gifted with a heart" (*sahṛdaya*).[7]

This is also the purpose of the "aesthetic" dimension of ritual, where all the senses take part in worship (*pūjā*). For example, the eyes in the beauty of the image and decorations; the ears in the songs, music, bells, and so on; the nose in the offering of incense, flowers, and perfumes; the tongue in tasting the sweets and fruits blessed by the Deity (*prasāda*); the sense of touch by prostrating and touching the image, etc. Thus, the *pūjā*, or ritual itself, becomes a piece of art that does not negate but transforms all sensual experience in contact with the Divine.

There is a higher state of the *yogi*, when he can experience the joy of worshiping the Lord through all sense perceptions, as Utpaladeva sings in his mystical hymn:

> (O God) May I ever be intoxicated with your worship even while drinking continuously the nectar distilled in the bowls filled with all the objects experienced through the openings of the respective senses! (*Śivastotrāvalī* 13.8)

As the commentator Kṣemarāja says, the nectar that is distilled out of all sense experience is the unity of consciousness.

The Tantric conception of the body is expressed by Abhinavagupta by likening it to a temple.

> One's own body as well as that of another, no less than a jar and other objects, is His temple, full of the beautifully composed images and lattice windows (of the senses) and complete with all the thirty-six principles of existence (*tattva*). (*Paramārthasāra* v. 74)

The commentator Yogarāja elaborates on this simile by saying that the temple of stone with its divine images becomes the abode of God only by giving it life through the pervading action of consciousness of the guru in the ritual of installation.

> [For] otherwise both (the temple and the image) would be inert like a piece of sculptured stone—how could it lift up the devotees (spiritually), or how could it bring the dead near (to God)? Thus, the primary meaning of "body" (*śarīra*) is "abode of God" (*devagṛha*), because it is the support of consciousness. Residing in the body of all is the Self, who is God. In this way the body verily is the temple of God for the one who is fully enlightened.

Here a whole theology both of the temple and of the human body is contained in a nutshell, which we find in many texts on temple architecture in all its detailed implications. The temple in its elevation from "foot" to "head" is built in the image of Man, the divine Person.[8]

Puruṣa, the Original Model

The source of the analogy between the temple and the body is much more than an anthropomorphic model. It lies in the Vedic conception of the *Puruṣa*, Primal Person or the Cosmic Being whose body contains the entire universe and yet transcends it (*Ṛg Veda* 10.90). His body is sacrificed and divided up in order to give life to the creatures and to create order in all spheres of existence. *Puruṣa* becomes thus the archetype of every creation, which is always a creation born of sacrifice, and his cosmic body becomes the model of all art forms. Every art—the visual arts as well as music and poetry—must relate its own medium (stone, color, notes, words, etc.) in an ordered fashion to what is to be represented. In this act of creation or ordering, *Puruṣa* serves as the archetype, because in him the cosmic elements (*adhibhūta*), the human body and spirit (*adhyātman*), the divine (*adhidaiva*), and the creative power of the sacrifice (*yajña*) are contained in one single, powerful symbol. The same symbol becomes, in the Upaniṣads, the interior person, the spiritual person in the heart. How this apparently abstract conception is transformed into an image is shown in a text on sacred form in *Vāstusūtra Upaniṣad* IV.1. The commentary on the verse "From realization comes the symbol" reads as follows: "As the nature of the *Puruṣa* is conceived of the size of a thumb,[9] and in imagination the thumb means only light, so it is like the post of the *yūpa* (sacrificial post)." The subcommentary explains:

> Realization, symbol (*pratīka*), image (*pratimā*), in this order: these three are essential. When in the reflection of an aureole of light Brahman is realized, that is realization, like the *Puruṣa* consisting of consciousness, who is not seen

by the eye; but by whom the eye sees. That which manifests the experiences in the manner of the relationship between the resemblance and the things to be known, that is the symbol—*pratīka*), as for example, "the *Puruṣa* of the size of a thumb" and others. That which in worship bestows bliss, that is the image (*pratimā*).[10]

Here it is clear that it is *Puruṣa* who mediates between the spiritual experience and the external form and who is the principle of consciousness which assumes a body, being both transcendent and immanent.

For the spectators or worshipers, the seeing of the outward manifestation in temple and image leads them to the integration of their own self, body and spirit, and to the experience of the light within the heart, to the "inner person."[11]

Art as Sacrifice and Yoga

The earliest (and hence often quoted) reference to "art" (*śilpa*) in Vedic literature is found in the *Aitareya Brāhmaṇa* (VI.5, 1), which throws light on the early theory and practice of the plastic arts.

> It is imitation (*anukṛti*) of the divine works of art (*devaśilpāni*) that any work of art (*śilpa*) is accomplished here; for example, a clay elephant, a brazen object, a garment, a gold object, and a mule chariot are "works of art." A work of art (*śilpa*), indeed, is accomplished in him who comprehends this. For these divine works of art are an integration of the self (*ātmasaṁskṛti*); and by them the sacrificer likewise integrates himself (*ātmānam saṁskurute*) in the mode of rhythm (*chandomaya*).[12]

Three main ideas emerge from this Vedic view of art (it is clear here that there is no artificial distinction between fine and applied art): (1) Human art is a kind of imitation of the divine art—which is not to be interpreted in any naturalistic sense but rather as "conforming to the divine archetype." (2) Art is not only creation of external objects, but it is essentially "self-culture," *ātmasaṁskṛti*, "integration of the Self" (in Coomaraswamy's translation). It is a pervading feature of Indian culture that any external manifestation must ultimately be related to the Self, to the spiritual development of the human person. (3) This "integration" (*saṁskṛti*) is related to "rhythm," *chandas* (literally, hymn or meter), but can be applied to all the arts as the principle of order. What is meter in poetry and recitation becomes rhythm in music and dance. It can be principles of composition in the visual arts, measure and proportion in architecture. In N. Ray's interpretation: "The aim of such art-activity is to improve one's own Self by making life *chandomaya*, just as objects of art should be, the implication being that since art is *chandomaya*, through its making one is likely to imbibe *chanda* in life and thus improve one's own Self."[13]

If art activity is itself a means or a way of self-integration, it demands a preparation and a congenial state of mind. The spirit in which a piece of art is made obviously leaves its imprint on the material form—and it is here where the question of spiritual discipline (*sādhana*) for the artist or artisan arises. The creation of art—especially religious art, which is supposed to reflect an aspect of the Divine—presupposes a great purity of body and mind, self-control and one-pointed concentration (*ekāgratā*). In ritual and art manuals, the artist is instructed to observe fasting and silence before starting to work, and then to concentrate fully on the divinity or other subjects one will create. Thus, the *Āgamas* and iconographical texts give the *dhyānaśloka* (meditation verse) for each divinity or divine aspect, which projects an inner vision (*dhyāna)* of that which must become an outer image (*mūrti, pratimā*). Some texts advise the image maker to pray the night before starting the work to be granted a dream showing him the form he is to create and the way or method to proceed (starting from the selection of the material, wood or stone).[14] This again indicates that a deeper source of inspiration beyond the conscious mind and also beyond a mere imitation of the iconographical instructions given by tradition is necessary for representing a divine image.

A legend that has been recorded by the Chinese pilgrim Huian-tsang (seventh century C.E.) about the first image of the Buddha, another version of which is traditionally ascribed to the image of Jagannātha (Puri), reveals the mystery of the creation of an image.[15] The summary of the legend is this: A sculptor who resolved to create the image instructed everyone that he was closing himself in the workshop, observing silence and fasting, that nobody should dare to open the door before he came out, after completing the image. Many days passed and the people were getting anxious and curious what had happened to the artist. They opened the door before the time against his instructions. What they found was an incomplete image—but the artist had disappeared. He had given his life for making the image come alive, but the curiosity of the people was responsible for the fact that the image remained incomplete. If the principle of ritual worship is: "Becoming God one should worship God" (*devo bhūtvā devaṁ yajet*), here it means: creating the image of God (or of the Buddha) presupposes becoming it (or him), disappearing in him. For on the ultimate level there is no place for two (*Bṛhadāraṇyaka Upaniṣad* IV.5.15).[16]

We have already seen that the sacred art is intimately linked with the concept of sacrifice—either in the archetype of the *Puruṣa* or in the fact that its creation is itself a kind of ritual. In fact, the oldest treatise on all art forms, the *Nāṭyaśāstra*, calls art a sacrifice. All classes of beings, from the gods down to humans and demons, take part in this drama, and all human emotions are evoked in it, but to be transformed, for sacrifice is essentially a transformation from matter into spirit. Later, when the theory and practice of the Vedic sacrifice declined, art came to be regarded as yoga or spiritual practice (*sādhana*).[17]

It is said that art that is produced out of meditation (*dhyāna*) leads to the ultimate goal of life, liberation (*mokṣa*):

> From the knowledge of art arises divine knowledge, and such knowledge leads to liberation. . . . By *silpa* (art) images are produced. By images arises faith, from faith firm devotion. . . . from this comes knowledge which results in liberation. These are the five steps of Art (*vastu*, architecture). (*Vāstusūtra Upaniṣad* I.4–5)

The effect of seeing images (*darśana)* is again to bring about the mood of meditation (*dhyānabhāva*), which leads the devotee from the manifest, material form of the Deity to the Unmanifest, and hence ultimately to liberation from earthly bondage.

The Visual Testimony

Most of the principles and presuppositions mentioned above apply to practically all traditional arts in India, which are closely interrelated not only theoretically but even with regard to form and procedures.[18] But we must limit ourselves to the visual arts, and even this is too vast a topic, so that generalizations are unavoidable. We have so far given examples of sacred art, mainly temple and icon—and here the question may arise whether the spiritual element in India art is limited to religious subjects. This possible misunderstanding has to be clarified:

1. An art is not spiritual (or religious) only by representing a religious theme or serving a religious purpose. Unless its *form* itself is transparent to a spiritual reality and inspires or elevates the onlooker, without the intervention of a conscious thought or a preconceived label, it cannot be called spiritual. We will have to see at least in outline what characterizes such a form.[19]

2. All Hindu—as well as Buddhist or Jaina—art is basically religious (a statement of tautology indeed) for the distinction between sacred and profane came at a late stage and under foreign influence. Thus, even scenes that would be regarded as secular in other civilizations, such as natural beauty or human love, are here part of the spiritual universe. Apart from the so-called erotic sculpture on temples, which owes its inspiration to Tantric spiritual-

ity, even later miniature painting representing the love theme always equates the lovers with the divine couple (mostly Rādhā and Kṛṣṇa).[20] In this way the feelings of human love are elevated to the divine sphere; the individual human feelings are transformed into the universal and archetypal love.

Form

Regarding *form*, which is the ideal or congenial receptacle of spiritual truth, there are various aspects to be taken into account: (a) the purely formal structure, which we could equate with the underlying *yantra* or with the "principles of composition";[21] (b) the symbolic form language of myth and ritual, which is closely linked with the symbolism of the sacred texts; (c) the outer expression, which depends on the gift of the artist and on his spiritual state (as we have seen above).

The purely formal structure refers to "the perfect logic and harmony of design that prevails in the whole range of Indian sculptures,"[22] as well as in other art forms. Let us follow the understanding of Alice Boner:

> Particularly in the case of Hindu art, understanding of the language and suggestive meaning of form is indispensable, because the Hindu artist never uses form in an arbitrary or fanciful way, but always according to its primary fundamental significance. For him every form and line and every space-direction is pregnant with an inner sense. The vertical and the horizontal, the various inclinations, the angles and curves, the parallel, converging or diverging lines, all have their special implications and functions. Round and straight, expanding or tapering forms, single or aggregate forms, all have their own individual expression and significance. In the manifold play and interaction between all of these in the infinite variety of compositional patterns, the abstract form-elements always maintain their intrinsic, fundamental character.
>
> In its metaphysical essence, form constitutes a definite mode of cosmic operation. It arises from certain movements of the Life-force that animates all matter, and by a process of expansion and growth, or of condensation and contraction, causes it to crystallize into certain shapes. These, as its outer limiting circumscription, show the nature of its formation.
>
> Different movements, obeying different urges and impulses of the cosmic Life-force, create different forms. Thus lines, forms and colors are not accidental, but are direct manifestations of these inner forces, and therefore present a perfect analogy to spiritual reality, their ultimate Cause.[23]

The abstract geometrical line diagram that illustrates most clearly these formal structures is the *yantra*, which serves various purposes: as a means for concentration in meditation and ritual, as ground plan of a temple or as compositional diagram underlying a divine image. [24]

Form is determined not only by structure but also essentially by symbolism. It is the symbolic transparency of art that makes it a mediator of spiritual experience, for through the symbol (*rūpa, vyakta*) the symbolized (*arūpa, avyakta)* can be grasped or at least sensed. By symbol we do not mean conventional signs, though even these have mostly arisen from original symbols (e.g., the wheel, *cakra*, in the hands of Viṣṇu, a symbol of time and of cosmic law). As the Sanskrit word *pratīka* signifies, a symbol is the visible part of a reality, which is "turned towards us," the rest being invisible. If it is said of the original *Puruṣa* that "three fourths of him are in heaven" and one fourth is down on the earth (*Ṛg Veda* 10.90.4), it would be the one visible part which is the symbol of the three invisible fourths. A symbol never says everything; it alludes. Its allusion can be either universally understood, or else it requires some cultural background and knowledge to understand it (e.g., the many arms of Hindu gods which indicate their powerful nature and manifold activity). The symbol stands between two poles: on the one hand, it points to a transcendent reality; on the other, it appeals to the heart and mind of the one who beholds it. In short, it is never a "factual" or "objective" expression (though even facts can become symbols if seen in this perspective).

A symbol is inexhaustible, but never vague or confused. As A. K. Coomaraswamy puts it in a nutshell: "Symbolism and imagery (*pratīka, pratibimba*, etc.), the purest form of art, is the proper language of metaphysics."[25]

Let us quote as an example Coomaraswamy's interpretation of the figure of the dancing Śiva Naṭarāja:

> the arch . . . represents matter, nature, *Prakriti*; the contained splendour, Shiva dancing within and touching the arch with head, hands and feet, is the universal omnipresent Spirit (*Purusha*). Between these stands the individual soul. . . . Now to summarize the whole interpretation we find that the Essential Significance of Shiva's Dance is threefold: First, it is the image of his Rhythmic Play as the Source of all Movement within the Cosmos, which is Represented by the Arch: Secondly, the purpose of His Dance is to release the countless souls of men from the Snare of Illusion: Thirdly the Place of the Dance, Chidambaram, the Centre of the Universe, is within the Heart. . . .
>
> Every part of such an image as this is directly expressive. . . . In the night of Brahma, Nature is inert, and cannot dance until Shiva wills it: He rises from His rapture, and dancing sends through inert matter pulsing waves of awakening sound and lo! matter also dances appearing as a glory about Him. Dancing, He sustains its manifold phenomena. In the fullness of time, still dancing, he destroys all forms and names by fire and gives new rest.[26]

An image of God in a remnant of an ancient temple

The Religious Significance of Representations

The religious significance of all kinds of representations in Hindu art leads us to the important theme of the effect a work of art exercises on the spectator, and the inner transformation it produces. If a spiritual preparation is required from the artist, the spectator must also be prepared and must be endowed with the necessary sensibility to enjoy and understand the inner meaning of a work of art. This is contained in the concept of *sahṛdaya* ("possessed with a heart"), the sympathetic, receptive connoisseur. This word means both the predominance of the heart, that is, sensitivity, and the agreement with one's own heart,[27] also the "entering into identity with the heart of the poet."[28]

The "essence" which a *sahṛdaya* "tastes" in a work of art is *rasa*, the aesthetic flavor, taste, or the experience of the basic sentiment produced by a work of art. Though not many texts have applied this theory to the visual arts, it is meaningful beyond its original application to drama and poetry. The doctrine of *rasa* among other things answers the question regarding the spiritual meaning of images representing scenes of war, fighting, killing, love making, and so on. It is easy to see the spiritual significances of meditative and peaceful images which naturally lead the onlooker to contemplation, but what about the feelings evoked by frightful, cruel, or sorrowful images? In fact, all human emotions are represented in art and are evoked in the spectator—however not in their crude, everyday form but in a purified and universalized way. These emotional states—*bhāva* and their corresponding essences or basic experiences (*rasa*)—become a means for purifying human emotions.

Since the theory of *rasa* as expounded in the *Nāṭyaśāstra* is well known, and also its elaboration by Abhinavagupta, let us quote a less-known text which applies *rasa* or *bhāva* (the terminology here is not very precise) to sculpture. The *Vāstusūtra Upaniṣad* speaks on the "infusion of feeling" into the image (V,1) and gives reason for the various emotional states as the various fluctuations that arise in the mind and whose *rasa* (essence) is responsible for the creation of many different forms (V,3). Then it speaks about eight *rasas* and their application:

> The first *rasa* is love (*śṛṅgāra*)
> When there is a feeling of delight it takes the form of a love-image . . .
> . . . When desire is fulfilled the mind rejoices and bursts out in laughter. (V,5)
>
> Laughter (*hāsa*) is the second *rasa*.
> Images bestowing the mood of laughter give joy to the heart of men. . . .
> Where there is sorrow there is also happiness, that is the truth, (they are) like

night and day. Happiness changes into depression, and due to depression all the senses become slack. (V, 7)

Sorrow (compassion, *karuṇa*) is the third *rasa* or sentiment. Half closed eyes are its characteristic features. From affliction the mind becomes inactive. This is exhaustion. From exhaustion again results depression and from that arises anger. (V,9)

For *śilpakāras*, anger (*raudra*, the furious mood), is the fourth *rasa*.
The mouth is expanded, the eyes dilated, the hands hold fighting weapons, these are their features. (V,10)

The heroic sentiment (*vīrabhāva*) is the fifth. In these (figures) the body, the face and eyes are asymmetrical. . . . The lines (movement) of their feet are swift. . . . (V,12)

When the heroic sentiment becomes excessive it becomes terrifying (*bhayaṅkara*), this is the sixth *rasa*. . . .
Where these features are still heightened they turn into disgust (*bībhatsā*), creating ugly, exhausted figures whose limbs are in disarray.
When desires are given up a divine sentiment arises, this is the last means (of expression).
Due to realization one becomes detached. (V,13)

The sentiment of peace is the eighth *rasa* [normally the ninth].
In this way by the eight transformations of a living being the eight emotional states are produced. (V, 15)

The text is not fully explicit, but the meaning is clear: it is after and by passing through all the basic emotions that one becomes detached and hence finds peace. But, as Abhinavagupta says, in all *rasas* there is only one underlying ultimate experience or *rasa* (*eka eva paramārthato rasaḥ*),[29] which is bliss (*ānanda*). Through the emotional states it is only consciousness which is enjoyed and whose nature is bliss:

We think that what is enjoyed is consciousness itself, all full of bliss. What suspicion of pain may be here? The feelings of delight, sorrow, etc., deep within our spirit, have only one function, to create images, and the representation's function is to awake them.[30]

Though there is a clear distinction between the so-called aesthetic experience of *rasa* and the mystical experience, the first can very well lead on into the second, because "they spring from the same source."[31] And in all *rasas* the spiritual person experiences only peace, for he turns away from objects of the senses.[32] One of the important differences between the aesthetic and the mystical experience is that in the former the ego is temporarily merged in a single emotion, whereas in the latter, the ego merges permanently in the Divine.[33] As far as the distinction is valid, the former may be called an experience of immanence and the latter of transcendence.

Art and Indian Spirituality

It would lead us too far to trace a history of Hindu art in the light of spirituality, for that would require more than one book. Authors like A. K. Coomaraswamy, Stella Kramrisch, and others[34] have shown the relationship between the historical art forms and their spiritual meaning. Let us here take up only two points by way of example.

Hindu spirituality has its primary source in the Upaniṣads, but from the Vedic-Upaniṣadic time we have no "visual evidence." Temples and images were unknown in the Vedic period (leaving aside the Indus valley civilization, which did have artistic expressions). The symbols and images conceived by the Vedic seers were expressed in poetic language in the Vedic hymns and in symbolic language in the Upaniṣads. But most of these basic symbols and inner images became the seed of the later art forms. We have seen the example of the *Puruṣa*—and in fact perhaps the earliest type of anthropomorphic image or *mūrti* is the golden *Puruṣa*, who is inserted in the Vedic fire altar.[35] Other simple shapes like that of the *yūpa*, or sacrificial post, symbolizing the *skambha*, or pillar of the universe, were later developed in architecture and sculpture.

Even the Upaniṣadic conception of *prāṇa*, the life breath that permeates the whole body, being linked with its cosmic counterpart, the wind, and which is both physical and spiritual, has had its effect on the representation of the human body. It is the same *prāṇa* which has been developed as a spiritual discipline in Yoga, as a means for developing the subtle body. Stella Kramrisch writes about her impression of Indian sculpture:

> Indian art commands a set of visual signs in which the predominating figures are based on the shape of man. These figures, however, do not represent the physical but rather the subtle body of man. But to visualise the subtle body one must think of it as a combination of fluid, plastic shape and linear rhythm, a trans-substantiated form created by the Indian artist, and based on the shape of man. . . . Art divests it of the accidents of death, stagnation, labour and restlessness, and remakes it as a vessel that holds self-absorption in an unending flux of modelled form and gliding line.
>
> Yoga discipline is as much a pre-requisite for the Indian artist as was physical discipline for the Greek. It is as though in Indian art the image is embossed from within by the movement of breath, or circulation, through the vital centres of the living being, unimpeded by the gross matter of the actual physical body. A plastic quality results that is as though carried by the living breath

> with which the image is filled; conducted by the smooth channels of body and limbs. These smooth channels have a pristine glow and continuity of outline as though what they hold were an equivalent of the breath of God.[36]

This "subtle body" will have its effect on onlookers, and irrespective of their understanding they can feel the peace or power emanating from an Indian sculpture (the two aspects: *saumya*, gentle; and *ugra*, powerful, fierce). Heinrich Zimmer describes what distinguished this effect from the effect of, say, Greek or Roman art:

> The unforeseen and quite differently constituted spell cast upon us by the image of a Buddha or some other Indian divinity emanates from the immense, self-enveloping feeling of tranquility these images create. They do not compel our gaze by means of some essential nature they might manifest before us, for this they reveal not even to themselves; they are simply at rest within themselves. They are pure Being, undivided by self-knowledge; Being does not become an object in its own eyes, and therefore can dismiss us from Its presence without ever having wished to become, for us, an object.[37]

Zimmer here expresses a fundamental insight into Indian art: though we generally speak of "art objects," India's sacred art cannot be objectified (the "objects" are those which have been removed from their natural context, which is in most cases the temple).[38] It is a part of a totality, a cosmos of which we ourselves are a part (*adhibhūta*-aspect). It radiates a divine light that can be perceived only if the onlooker becomes absorbed in the same light (*adhidaiva*-aspect). It presents before our eyes the form of Man (the *Puruṣa*) as a reflection of the Divine, a mirror in which man can see himself (*adhyātma* -aspect).

The second example is again related to Upaniṣadic symbolism. One of the most powerful symbols in the Upaniṣads is the cave, *guhā*. The cave symbolizes the heart, the secret place of the *ātman* and of *Brahman* (see *Kaṭha Upaniṣad* I, 14; II, 12, 20; etc.). It is by retiring into one's own "cave of the heart" that one discovers the divine light within. Now one of the earliest manifestations of Indian art, both Buddhist and Hindu, as well as Jaina, is the so-called cave-temple (the earliest ones being Buddhist). In Ellora and Ajanta and elsewhere, the three religions had their caves side by side. What is important in our context is (a) that these caves were destined for monks and ascetics, for contemplation more than ritual, and (b) that they contain some of the best sculpture and paintings India has ever produced. These sculptures and paintings are hidden in half-darkness, almost as if they were to be seen by the "inner eye" more than by the outer. They were displaying before the contemplatives the great themes of Hindu mythology, the various manifestations of the Divine. Of course, the individual cells of the monks were bare, empty, and dark.

This is not all. For out of the same rock, complete temples were excavated, such as the famous Kailāsanātha in Ellora (eighth century). Here the process was one of "uncovering of the temple form out of the rock-mass. . . . The essential process, however, was one of recovering a form or idea latent in material inconscience or *avyakta*."[39] This again is an image of a spiritual process we could describe as removing the unnecessary weight of matter in order to bring out the inherent spiritual form. The Maharashtrian saint Jñānadeva (thirteenth century) uses this very image of the temple excavated from the rock in order to demonstrate that devotion to God is not useless though in reality there is nothing different from God:

> The idol of God, the temple and God's attendants, all of them are carved out of the same mountain-rock. So that in the same manner why should there not be the performance of the acts of devotion (though there is nothing but God everywhere)?[40]

There are some intermediate temple forms where half is in a rock cave and half (the *maṇḍapa*) is outside. But even when the temple is built separately, the idea of the mountain and the cave persists, the cave part being the *sanctum*, the *garbha-gṛha*, or "womb chamber." Here in the darkness without windows, where even the divine image is illumined only by oil lamps, the devotee returns to the womb, to the place of his or her origin, and enters into the cave of his or her own heart to be reborn divine.

These examples may suffice to show that the fundamental spiritual insights have created symbolic and artistic expressions in the Hindu world, and that sacred art in its turn has inspired the simple devotee as much as the mystics and philosophers and it will continue to do so as long as its formal and symbolic language is spontaneously understood.

Notes

1. Rāmakantha's *Vivṛti* on *Spandakārikā* (Srinagar: KSTS, 1913) p. 8, trans. Mark Dyczkowski.
2. Cf. Ānandavardhana, *Dhvanyāloka* III, 43; Abhinavagupta, *Abhinava Bhāratī* I, 4.
3. Abhinavagupta in his commentary on the *Nāṭyaśāstra* (*Abhinava Bhāratī* I, 291) calls the actor a mere "recipient" or vessel (*pātra*).
4. R. Gnoli, *The Aesthetic Experience according to Abhinavagupta*, XLVIII. Bhatta Tota defines *pratibhā* thus: "Intuition is a form of intuitive consciousness, *prajñā*, which is an inexhaustible source of new forms. It is by virtue of this intuition alone that one deserves the title of 'poet'" (ibid., LI).
5. *Mālinīvijayavārttika* by Abhinavagupta (Srinagar: KSTS, 1927) I, 276–77, p. 27.

6. *Śrīsaubhāgyahṛdaya Stotra*, quoted in Maheśvarānanda, *Mahārthamañjarī* with Parimala, p. 13.

7. Abhinavagupta, *Tantrāloka* 3.200 (see Gnoli, *Aesthetic Experience*, XLIV, note). See also *Vijñāna Bhairava*, v. 73ff. We will come back later to the concept of *sahṛdaya*.

8. See S. Kramrisch, "The Temple as *Puruṣa*," in *Studies in Indian Temple Architecture*, ed. Pramod Chandra (American Institute of Indian Studies, 1975) 40–46. See also *Śilparatnakośa*, v. 6ff. This applies to the *rekhā*-type of temple.

9. See the Upaniṣadic conception of *aṅguṣṭamātra puruṣa*. See my interpretation of this text in "Puruṣa and the Origin of Form," in *Rūpa Pratirūpa, Alice Boner Commemoration Volume* (New Delhi: Biblia Impex, 1982) 28ff.

10. Cf. Tippani n. VI, 19, *Vāstusūtra Upaniṣad*, pp. 92ff.

11. See Stella Kramrisch, *The Hindu Temple;* eadem, "Temple as *Puruṣa.*"

12. The translation follows A. K. Coomaraswamy in *Transformation of Nature in Art*, 8, with slight changes.

13. Niharranjan Ray, *An Approach to Indian Art*, 64.

14. See *Agni Purāṇa* 43, 12–25, quoted by A. K. Coomaraswamy, *The Dance of Shiva*, 26f.

15. See the interpretation by R. Panikkar, "Das erste Bild des Buddha," *Antaios* 6/4 (1964) 373–85.

16. See also the legends about great saints who are said to have merged in the image of their devotion, such as Caitanya and Mīrā.

17. For the idea of drama as a sacrifice, see C. Byrski, *Concept of Ancient Indian Theatre* (New Delhi: Munshiram, 1974). For art as yoga, see Heinrich Zimmer, *Artistic Form and Yoga in the Sacred Images of India.*

18. See Kapila Vatsyayan, *The Square and the Circle of the Indian Arts.*

19. See Titus Burckhardt, *Principes et methodes de l'art sacré* (Paris: Dervy Livres, 1976) 5ff.

20. See the *Gīta Govinda*, which, as a religious love poem, could be compared to the Song of Songs. Cf. several illustrated manuscripts of the *Gīta Govinda* which have been published and interpreted by Kapila Vatsyayan.

21. See Alice Boner, *Principles of Composition in Hindu Sculpture: Cave Temple Period.*

22. Ibid., 4.

23. Ibid., 11–12.

24. See Zimmer, *Artistic Form;* and A. Boner, S. R. Sarma, B. Bäumer, *Vāstusūtra Upaniṣad.*

25. A. K. Coomaraswamy, *A New Approach to the Vedas* (London: Luzac, 1933) 78. See also the interesting study by F. D. K. Bosch, *The Golden Germ: An Introduction to Indian Symbolism* (The Hague: Mouton, 1960).

26. Coomaraswamy, *Dance of Shiva*, 77–78.

27. Cf. *Dhvanyāloka Locana* by Abhinavagupta, p. 38, quoted in Gnoli, *Aesthetic Experience*, XLIII, n. 1.

28. *Abhinava Bhāratī* II, p. 339, quoted in Gnoli, *Aesthetic Experience*, XLIV, n. 1.

29. *Abhinava Bhāratī* I, p. 271.

30. Ibid., I, p. 292; cf. Gnoli, *Aesthetic Experience*, XXXVI.

31. Gnoli, *Aesthetic Experience*, XLI.

32. See *Abhinava Bhāratī* I, p. 340.

33. See Gnoli, *Aesthetic Experience*, XXXVIII ff.

34. Such as Heinrich Zimmer, Vasudeva S. Agrawala, Alice Boner, Kapila Vatsyayan, etc.

35. See *Agni, The Vedic Ritual of the Fire Altar*, ed F. Staal (Delhi: Motilal Banarsidass, 1983) 115, 242.

36. Kramrisch, *Exploring India's Sacred Art*, 4.

37. Zimmer, *Artistic Form*, 13.

38. In this view, orthodox brahmins are right in not allowing "outsiders" into their temples. The merely curious look at a piece of sacred art is itself desecrating (though on the other hand there is a belief in the purifying power of seeing a temple or divine image).

39. G. C. Pande, *Foundations of Indian Culture*, vol. 1, *Spiritual Vision and Symbolic Forms in Ancient India*, 312.

40. *Amṛtānubhava* 9, 42, trans. B. P. Bahirat.

Bibliography

Sources

Abhinavagupta. *Tantrāloka*, with Rājānaka Jayaratha's commentary, 12 vols. Srinagar and Bombay: KSTS, 1918–1938.

Ānandavardhana, Dhvanyāloka with Locana by Abhinavagupta. Edited by Pattabirama Sastri. Varanasi: Chowkhamba Sanskrit Series Office, 1940. Eng. trans. by D. H. H. Ingalls, J. M. Masson, and M. V. Patwardhan. Cambridge, Mass.: Harvard University Press, 1990.

Nāṭyaśāstra with Abhinava Bhāratī. Several editions.

Vāstusūtra Upaniṣad. Edited and translated by A. Boner, S. R. Sarma, B. Bäumer. Delhi: Motilal Banarsidass, 1982. 3rd rev. ed., 1997.

Studies

Boner, Alice. *Principles of Composition in Hindu Sculpture: Cave Temple Period.* Leiden: Brill, 1962. 2nd ed., Delhi: MLBD.

Coomaraswamy, A. K. *The Dance of Shiva*. New York: Noonday Press, 1957.

——. *The Transformation of Nature in Art.* Cambridge, Mass.: Harvard University Press, 1935.

Gnoli, R. *The Aesthetic Experience According to Abhinavagupta.* Varanasi: Chowkhamba Sanskrit Series Office, 1968.

Kramrisch, Stella. *The Hindu Temple*. Calcutta: University of Calcutta, 1946.

——. *Exploring India's Sacred Art, Selected Writings*, edited by B. Stoler Miller. Philadelphia: University of Pennsylvania Press, 1983.

Pande, G. C. *Foundations of Indian Culture, Spiritual Vision and Symbolic Forms in Ancient India*. New Delhi: Books & Books, 1984.

Ray, Niharrajan. *An Approach to Indian Art*. Chandigarh: Panjab University, 1974.

Vatsyayan, Kapila. *The Square and the Circle of the Indian Arts.* New Delhi: Roli Books International, 1983.

Zimmer, Heinrich. *Artistic Form and Yoga in the Sacred Images of India*. Delhi: Oxford University Press, 1984.

A contemporary Indian mendicant

Part Six

HINDU SPIRITUALITY IN DIALOGUE

25

Sant Kabīr: The Spirituality of Sahaja Sādhanā

K. Banerjee

Kabir and Indian Spirituality

One of the unique characteristics of Indian spirituality is that it manifests simultaneously in two forms, one conservative and the other liberal; and yet the two are virtually complementary to each other, the systole and diastole of the same heartbeat. There is a strange principle of vitality operating at its core, lending it the dual virtue of stability and dynamism. In its conservative manifestation, Indian spiritual tradition registers all its interesting developments and preserves age-old archives in an amazingly ever-fresh practical form, almost rejecting nothing. On the other hand, its liberal expression stands for expansion, assimilation, adaptation, revaluation, and rejuvenation. Through these two forces, the perennial tradition of Indian spirituality, atemporal in its essence, eloquently keeps pace with the march of historical time.

The conservative impulse has a sanction for all sincere endeavors for realization, all forms of worship and self-purification, but this sanction undergoes a scrutiny and a reassessment under liberating forces at each juncture of time when a new era is heralded. This chasm between two mighty waves of time, apparently presenting a crisis; is charged with immense possibilities. As evidenced by history, there always appears at this time the "Man of the Era," a prophet or a sage, who is destined to shape the new age. It is incumbent on him to fuse in just proportions the diverse trends that are the outcome of a commingling of horizons and subsequent branching out. Such a person was indeed Kabīr.

Convergence of Crossroads: Synthesis of Jñāna-Bhakti-Yoga

What is most striking about Kabīr's spirituality is the grand merger of all seeming opposites—singular in its wide range and easefulness. The century in which Kabīr was born saw the proliferation of cults and tenets to an unprecedented degree. The ritualistic and contemplative sides of Vedic spirituality, fundamentally related as two successive stages of spiritual development, had bifurcated in two almost opposite directions. Proper acquaintance with the scriptures was denied to the masses, and widely different ecumenical interpretations offered by pundits led only to divisions and subdivisions of schools and systems, held apart by virtue of external signs and symbols. The ritualists were more impatient to get their worldly petitions granted than concerned about enlightenment.

The contemplative side had flowered into the systems of Vedāntic philosophy, the oldest and most vigorous being the Advaita of Śaṅkara. But in spite of its exclusive stress on direct realization of Truth, later followers of Advaita, in the face of rival doctrines, were called upon to harness their scholarship and logical acumen in defense of their doctrine, more often than practice their faith in solitude, with the result that in the common person's estimation, Vedāntic nondualism (Advaita) started to appear as dry, intellectual exercise.

The qualified nondual Vedānta of Rāmānuja, Viśiṣṭādvaita, underscored the necessity for devotion and dedication of oneself to the Lord and proved more colorful and attractive on account of its emphasis on the love relationship between the individual self and *Brahman*, the Supreme Reality, whose beautiful and majestic form is manifested as Viṣṇu or Rāmā or Kṛṣṇa. Thus, Vaiṣṇavism as given shape by Rāmānuja's Vedānta spread rapidly from the South of India to the other parts of India. Rāmānanda brought the devotional (*bhakti*) movement to Varanasi (Benaras), the heart of spiritual life in Northern India. This great saint, who spread the worship of *Brahman* as Rāma throughout the northern part of India, is believed to be the guru of Kabīr.

In Rāmānanda, diverse crosscurrents of thought and practice met, and his liberal mind kept all doors open for free discourse and sharing of ideas. One of the distinguishing features of the *bhakti* movement has been its partial or absolute disregard for caste barriers, which are given maximum importance in brahmanical, Vedic Hinduism. This disregard for caste barriers is to be seen in the fact that a number of disciples of Rāmānanda were from low and the so-called untouchable castes. What reads like radicalism in Kabīr's songs has its moorings in the authenticated liberalism of *bhakti*.

Another mighty wave of spirituality as love of God, namely, Sufism, which had made its ingress in India toward the end of the twelfth century, had been sweeping across the subcontinent and intermingling with indigenous tenets. Some authorities suggest common Indo-Iranian roots of Sufism, a merger of Buddhist mysticism with Islam, and even a wider convergence of Aryan, Semitic and Hermetic trends traceable in neo-Platonism. Being sufficiently broad-based on the one hand, and on the other having all the appeal of a simple and ardent love-pursuit, the Sufi mysticism was readily mixed with the extant currents of mysticism in India. Both the Sufis and the *bhaktas* had one feature in common: they were gifted with musical sensibility, and many of them were inspired poets. They sang of their pangs of separation, their joys of union, and the ineffable wonders of God vision. Since the basic feeling was common, their dialects, thoughts, and metaphors took no time to intermingle. Kabīr's poems reflect this intermingling.

Another pervasive current of spirituality, Tantra, sent forth its waves on all sides and permeated the Indian spiritual scene. It was almost inevitable that Tantra should become an integral part of all philosophical and theological systems that grew out of the soil of India. Mahāyāna Buddhism as well as some of the Vedic schools had gradually absorbed Tantric tenets over the centuries. Moreover, the Śaiva and Śākta wings of āgama had already joined together in practice. The Buddhist Tantra and the Hindu Tantra interfused, and this grand fusion resulted in ramifications in the forms of *Vajrayāna* (the path of the Diamond) and *Sahjayāna* (the path of the innate). Followers of these occult lines were known as *siddhas* (adepts), and the tradition came to be known as *siddhamārga* (the path of the *siddhas*) or *siddhaparamparā* (the tradition of the *siddhas*). A parallel tradition arose, that of the *nāthas* (masters), which was an offspring of Śaivism. Different techniques of *layayoga* (merger in the Absolute) and *hathayoga* (awakening of psychophysical powers by controlling the energy currents of the body) were current among the *siddhas* and the *nāthas*. By the time of Kabīr's advent, they had already popularized the yogic concepts of *saṭcakrabheda* (penetration of the six nuclei of occult power in the body), the raising of *kuṇḍalinī*, *nāda sādhanā* (practice of the Unstruck Sound, *OM*), and so on. It is believed that Rāmānanda introduced his disciples to these concepts and taught them a very simplified form of their practice.

Kabīr's *sahaja sādhanā*, primarily anchored in devotion, absorbed salutary influences from all these sources. The term *sahaja* and the yogic nomenclature, such as *aṣṭakamala*, *haṁsa*, *śūnya*, *amṛta*, *suṣumnā*, *hīrā*, *nāda*, *bindu*, *ghaṭa*, and so on, he took from the āgamic tradition. From Vedānta he assimilated the concepts of *Brahman*, the unconditioned Absolute, *māyā*, *jīva*, and the basic unity of *Brahman* and *Ātman*. The boundless, formless Supreme Being he called "*Nirguṇa* Rāmā," whom he sought through devotion. Deep personal love for the impersonal Absolute was characteristic of the Sufis. Kabīr applied this Sufi trend to his own loving search for Rāma, not as an incarnation (*avatāra*) but as *Brahman*, the

Supreme Reality beyond descriptions, whom he called "Allah" after the Muslims, and *Alakh Nirañjana* (the Invisible Pure Being), after the *nātha* yogis.

As Evelyn Underhill observes:

> So thorough-going is Kabīr's eclecticism, that he seems by turns Vedantist and Vaishnavaite, Pantheist and Transcendentalist, Brahman and Sufi. . . . All are needed, if he is ever to suggest the character of that One whom the Upanishad called "the Sun-coloured Being who is beyond this Darkness": as all the colours of the spectrum are needed if we would demonstrate the simple richness of white light. In thus adapting traditional materials to his own use, he follows a method common amongst the mystics. . . . Thus we find that some of Kabīr's finest poems have as their subjects the commonplaces of Hindu philosophy and religion: the Lila or sport of God, the Ocean of Bliss, the Bird of the Soul, Maya, the Hundred-petalled Lotus, and the "Formless Form." Many, again, are soaked in Sufi imagery and feeling. Others use as their material the ordinary surroundings and incidents of Indian life: the temple bells, the ceremony of the lamps, marriage, suttee, pilgrimage, the characters of the seasons; all felt by him in their mystical aspect, as sacraments of the soul's relation with Brahma.[1]

The Simple Integrality of Sahaja Sādhanā

The line of spiritual pursuit followed and preached by Kabīr has come to be called *sahaja sādhanā* or *sabda-surati* yoga. Uninterrupted and impassioned contemplation of God the Beloved as Infinite Light enthroned within oneself, accompanied by mental repetition of the *mantra* or name received from one's guru, in keeping with the rhythm of inhalation and exhalation of breath is the crux of this practice. The ultimate goal is, of course, *samādhi*, or merger of the self in God—in the context of Kabīr's spirituality, it is *sahaja samādhi*.

The beauty of these words, *sahaja* and *surati*, lies in that they, being subtly ambiguous, are meaningful in all their ambiguities. *Surati*, as derived from *smṛti*, is recollection; it also suggests (as *su-rati*) deep love or love union. *Surati*, in brief, is continual remembrance as a means of union. The literal meaning of *sahaja* is innate; in common use, it means spontaneous, unforced, simple. In the Tantric tradition, *sahaja* is interpreted as born of the union of *sa* and *ha*, which respectively stand for exhalation and inhalation, and also the pair of vital currents, *idā* and *pinglā*, which are involved in the act of breathing. *Sahaja* here indicates a particular yogic discipline which advocates a special technique of *prāṇāyāma*, controlled breathing.

Sa and *ha* also constitute the individual self, characteristically called *haṁsa*, the swan. By practicing *sahaja* yoga, this "Swan-Self" is released from its cage of illusory individuation, gains levitation, and flies back to its home, *sahaja śūnya*, the original Void, actually a plenum of Bliss, where everything seems upside down from a mortal's point of view, and can be described best only in paradoxes. On reaching this plane, *haṁsa* is also reversed to *so-ham* (I am He)—now awakened to its identity as the very object of its pursuit.

Sahaja, then, connotes not only a mode or means of praxis but also the end. *Sahaja* is the origin of all Being, the first principle, *Brahman*. The act of creation entails forcing raw materials into shape: only that Being which is never created nor destroyed is *sahaja*.

Sahaja samādhi, in the first place, is the Self's reabsorption in infinite Being-Consciousness-Bliss. Second, it is distinguished from "ordinary" *samādhi* in that there is no stupefaction of the body, nor any *vyutthāna*, or return to worldly consciousness. In ordinary *samādhi*, one is apparently unconscious until one attains *vyutthāna*, that is, comes out from the depth of *samādhi* into consciousness of the world. But *sahaja samādhi* is a continuous state of enlightenment with normal consciousness and abilities intact. To be one's own self is the state of *sahaja*, the most easeful existence, free from all strain: being permanently established in this state is *sahaja samādhi*.

Kabīr himself defines *sahaja* and *sahaja samādhi* in the following words:

> *Sahaja*, *sahaja*, cry all, but none recognizes *sahaja*.
> Verily, the one who easily gives up
> sense objects is himself *sahaja*.
> He himself is *sahaja* who keeps his
> senses unperturbed even while
> in touch with their objects.
> By whatever means is the Lord easily
> available, that, indeed, is *sahaja*.
> (*Sākhī*, "Sahaja ko Aṅga," ds. 1, 2, 4)

> O Sadhu! the simple union is the best.
> Since the day when I met with my Lord,
> there has been no end to the sport of our love.
> I shut not my eyes, I close not my ears, I do
> not mortify my body;
> I see with eyes open and smile, and
> behold His beauty everywhere;
> I utter His name, and whatever I see,
> it reminds me of Him, whatever
> I do, it becomes His worship.
> The rising and setting are one to me;

all contradictions are solved.
Wherever I go, I move round Him,
All I achieve is His service:
When I lie down I lie prostrate at His feet.
(*Songs of Kabir* XLI)

Biographical Outlines

All that is known about Kabīr's life is a matrix of interwoven history and hearsay, except the three undisputed pieces of information gleaned from his works: that he lived at Varanasi (Benaras), was a weaver by family trade (*Sabad*, p. 231), and died at Maghar.

Varanasi is most widely believed to be Kabīr's birthplace. His biographers have suggested various dates for his birth and death. The general consensus is that he was born in 1399 C.E. and passed away in 1519 C.E., after covering a long life span of 120 years. Some legends hold that he was a brahmin by birth, but was adopted as a foundling by a Muslim couple.

According to his own confession (*Bījak, Sākhī* d. 187), Kabīr was illiterate; he gives credit to his guru for all his knowledge and wisdom (*Sākhī*, "Gurudeva ko Aṅga," d. 2). He must have been a very keen student to have mastered all the storehouse of ideologies just by listening to the wise and from practical experience.

Though endowed with the saintly qualities of nonattachment and renunciation, Kabīr stayed at home and worked at this loom without seeking mendicancy. Probably he had a family. Weaving was not just a profession to him: it was a source of poetic imagery to express his understanding of life and the world (*Bījak, Ramainī*, 28) and was symbolic of the inner weaving of threads of *surati* on the loom of his own body.

In the home is true union, in the home is
enjoyment of life: why should I forsake my home
and wander in the forest? If Brahma helps me
to realize truth, verily I will find both
bondage and deliverance in home. (*Songs* of Kabir XL)

O weaver, weave the name of the Lord,
whom all the world seek in meditation. (*Sabad*, p. 127)

Only two of his songs give testimony to the episode of his life when, enraptured by the love of God, he grew careless to weaving.

Kabīr has given up weaving at the loom,
He has imprinted the name of Rāma on his body.
(*Sabad*, p. 139)

I am so possessed by love,—who will weave "O mother!"
(*Kabir Granthavalī, Sabad*, p. 19)

There are stories of his persecution attempted in vain by orthodox Hindus and Muslims until they came to discover his saintliness and the truth of his teachings. His renown spread far and wide. He traveled from time to time, carrying his message to thirsting souls. There were celebrities like Raja Bir Singh and Nawab Bijli Khan among his disciples and devotees. Even the emperor Sikander Lodi, who first condemned him as a heretic, later recognized him as a saint and prophet of great eminence.

Toward the end of his life, he repaired to Maghar, where he chose to leave his body in proof of his conviction that an enlightened being merges in the Absolute wherever he may die. According to another belief, he was in exile from Varanasi during his last days. The Purāṇic tradition holds that liberation is granted to all who die within the precincts of Varanasi. Confident about his at-one-ment with the Lord, Kabīr says:

What is *Kāsī* (Varanasi), what, again is
barren Maghar, if there is Rāma in the heart?
(*Sabad*, p. 285)

Kabīr's devotees cherish the legend that his body was transformed into a heap of flowers so that both Hindus and Muslims could have the honor of performing the last rites of their beloved teacher. The two tombs of Kabīr at Maghar still stand witness to the saint's spiritual catholicity attracting alike both Hindus and Muslims.

Kabīr's Guru

While proclaiming the guru as indispensable on the spiritual path, Kabīr is nearly silent about the definite identity of his own guru. In Kabīr's songs, God and guru are often synonymous.

Kabīr is a child of *Allāh-Rāma*, He Himself
is my *Guru*, my *Pīr*. (*Sabad*, p. 23)

Guru is the same as *Govinda*: duality lies
only in form. (*Sākhī*, "Gurudev ko Aṅga," d. 26)

It is surmised, however, as stated before, that Kabīr was in close association with Rāmānanda. It is said that he had approached Rāmānanda for initiation. However, Rāmānanda seemed to have some expressed reluctance because of Kabīr's Muslim background. Thwarted but resolute, Kabīr resorted to a trick. Rāmānanda used to take his bath daily in the river Ganges in early morning. One day, in the twilight of the dawn, Kabīr lay on the steps of the riverbank. Rāmānanda inadvertently stepped on him. Surprised and embarrassed, he exclaimed, "Rāma, Rāma," which Kabīr accepted as the *mantra* of initiation. Rāmānanda gladly acknowledged the new disciple. There are a few references to Rāmānanda in Kabīr's poetry which seem to confirm this legend.

> Rāmānanda is intoxicated with the elixir of Rāma.
> (*Ramainī*, 77)

> I became suddenly revealed in Banaras and
> Rāmānanda illumined me. (*Songs of Kabir* XXIX)

Sheikh Takki of Manikpur is also mentioned as Kabīr's spiritual guide. It was a heyday of Sufism in India, and, in all likelihood, Sheikh Takki was a Sufi who introduced Kabīr to the Sufi doctrines. The name of Sheikh Takki occurs twice in Kabīr's verse (*Ramainī*, 48, 63), though nowhere is he openly acknowledged as Kabīr's guru.

It is also probable, as suggested by some scholars, that Kabīr did not take any formal initiation from anyone, but that he visited all whom he considered to be real spiritual personalities and profited by such encounters, and that his "True Guru" is none other than God Himself, who inspired him from within.

The Songs of Kabīr

Works and Compilations

Kabīr's spiritual journey, its culmination and experiences thereafter are recorded in the exquisite lyrics and couplets he left as his gospel to posterity. His works are classified broadly into three categories:

1. *Sākhī* comprises rhymed couplets set to the metrical form known as *dohā*. They are subdivided under fifty-nine aspects (*aṅga*) dealing with various themes of spirituality. The term *sākhī*, derived from *sākṣi* (witness), confers on Kabīr's poetry the significance of a book of revelation and calls for an anagogical approach ("*Sākhī* is the eye of wisdom" [*Bījak*, *Sākhī*, d. 353]).

2. *Śabda* or *Sabad* is a series of lyrics composed in the metrical form known as *pada*, traditionally adopted for songs. Etymologically meaning both "sound" and "word," *śabda* suggests mystical word power and sound vibrations of *mantra*.

3. *Ramainī* is lyrics composed in a particular meter (*caupāī*, sometimes concluded with a *dohā* dealing with the metaphysical theme of creation and the creatures' participation (*ramaṇa*) in the cosmic play. These lyrics are supposed to lead one to the enjoyment (*ramaṇa*) of spiritual bliss.

The following are the available compilations:

1. *Bījak*, which are regarded as the earliest compilation made by Kabīr's followers. The sacred text for the followers of Kabīr ("Kabīr Panth"), *Bījak* is the chart with cryptic indications for locating the hidden treasure trove *Bījak, Ramainī,* 2)—the knowledge of the Self. For centuries, *Bījak* was circulated only among the followers of Kabīr Panth. This practice kept this volume comparatively free from interpolations, and at the same time accounts for its belated popularity among lay scholars and readers. Apart from its own version of *Sākhī* and *Śabda*, it includes the whole series of *Ramainī*. The other verses in this volume are *Cautīsā, Vipra-matīsī, Kaharā, Basant, Belī (Beilī), Birhulī*, and *Hinḍolā*.

2. *Guru Granth Saheb* or *Ādi Granth*: The sacred book of the Sikh (from *siṣya*, disciple) followers of Guru Nānak, who as a junior contemporary, derived inspiration from Kabīr. Compiled about the year 1590 C.E. by Guru Arjun, the *Ādi Granth* incorporates a number of Kabīr's verses, besides the compositions of Guru Nānak and many other saints.

3. *Kabīr-Granthavalī* (Works of Kabīr): The most widely popular volume of Kabīr's verses, which has been compiled many times with revisions by various scholars.

Kabīr's Language

The first poet of the Hindi vernacular, Kabīr makes a bold use of the very idiom of the masses—the dialect spoken by the common person in the streets in northern India. Mainly derived from Sanskrit, this oldest form of Hindi was heavily laden with Urdu words and local phrases. He sang for the common folks, not for the gentry or scholars, and his language had the ring of authenticity to touch the hearer's heart. His language has the simplicity, vigor, and spontaneity characteristic of the *sahaja* approach to Reality.

The Ulaṭvāsi Style

The experiences of the spiritually illumined are so unlike common experiences that they cannot be described in words; they can at best be hinted at, just as a dumb person can only make gestures to express his joy of eating molasses (*Sabad*, pp. 1, 13). Moreover, spiritual experience is not just a modification of common experience but very often the reverse of it.

> . . . by a feast of reversal I have gained the bliss of *Sahaja samādhi*.
> (*Sabad*, p. 20)

Of such unique experiences he sings in a language of paradoxes and cryptic riddles known as *ulaṭvāsi*, the topsy-turvy language. The language of the mystic has always been marked by paradoxical expressions. With the Vedic seer, it was not a conscious practice. The *ṛṣi* who uttered the following line was more wonderstruck at the glimpse of *Brahman* than conscious of the style he was employing.

> Being seated, He walks a long distance;
> lying down, He goes everywhere.
> (*Katha Upaniṣad* II.21)

Later, speaking in riddles became a vogue among Tantric Buddhists, who called their cryptic language *sandhyā bhāṣā*, the twilight language, suggesting its ambiguousness. The *nāthas* and *siddhas* in later epochs cultivated this style in order to shroud the deeper import of their teachings from the profane glance. It seems that in Kabīr's time there were some such stock metaphors, mainly taken from Tantra, that all could freely apply with apt modifications, in fitting contexts. This is borne out by some resemblance between the symbols in Kabīr's poetry and those in the verses of Gorakhnath and his contemporary yogis. Here are a few examples from Kabīr:

> There is a well upside down in the sky and a
> damsel in the nether world, filling her jar;
> A Swan drinks of the water of that well—
> it is a rare soul who would understand this riddle.
> The lion makes his den in water, and the fish climbs
> the date tree. (*Sākhī*, "Parca ko Aṅga," d. 46)

> Without blossoming, a tree bears fruit, without a
> hand, the trumpet is being played;
> A woman fills her pitcher without water: this
> is how one realizes *Sahaja*. (*Sabad*, p. 13)

The Essentials of Kabīr's Sahaja Sādhanā

Sahaja is Being-in-Oneself, as one essentially and eternally is. *Sahaja* is the Absolute Reality and Its aspects, namely, *sat* (Being), *cit* (consciousness) and *ānanda* (Bliss). *Sahaja sādhanā* is striving to regain or recognize one's identity as *sahaja*, or union with *sahaja*. Kabīr's *sahaja sādhanā* is related to *layayoga*, a corpus of methodology based mainly on the Trantric conception of the body as a microcosm, containing the macrocosm, and its creator within itself.

> Within this earthen vessel are bowers and
> groves, and within it is the Creator:
> Within this vessel are the seven oceans and the
> unnumbered stars.
> The touchstone and the jewel-appraiser are within;
> And within this vessel the Eternal soundeth, and
> the spring well up.
> Kabīr says: "Listen to me, my friend! My beloved
> Lord is within." (*Songs of Kabir* VIII)

Layayoga means union through merger, dissolution, or reabsorption of the individual Self (*ātman*) in the Universal Self (*Paramātman* or *Brahman*). Of the various techniques of *layayoga*, Kabīr chooses the line of *nāda sādhanā* or practice of *mantra* to effect merger of the Self in the Infinite *Om*.

In order to realize the Lord within oneself, one must know the secrets of the body, *dehatattva*, and perform *kāyaśodhana*, or purification of the body. There are *hathayoga* methods, rather gross and forced, which Kabīr avoids; he prefers the subtle methodology of *sabda-surati-yoga*, the yoga of mentally repeating the "Word," which is simple as well as effective and can be practiced with devotion.

> O sadhu! purify the body in the simple way.
> As the seed is within the banyan tree, and
> within the seed are the flowers, the fruits
> and the shade:
> So the germ is within the body, and within
> that germ is the body again . . .
> Kabīr says: "Listen to the Word, the Truth,
> which is your essence. He speaks the Word to
> Himself: and He Himself is the Creator."
> (*Songs of Kabir* XLVI)

Sahaja is *madhi*, the Middle Point, of all existence. Just as each and every geographical form has a center, each and every creature has *sahaja* as its central point. Just as a circle may be conceived of as expanded out of its center, and it is possible to conceive of its being contracted back to the center, creation expands from and recedes back to this point of *sahaja*.

> All things are created by the Om;
>   the love-form is His body.
> He is without form, without quality, without decay:
>   Seek thou union with Him!
> But that formless God takes a thousand forms
>   in the eyes of His creatures . . . .
> He dances in rapture, and waves of form
>   arise from His dance. (*Songs of Kabir* XXVI)

Now, creation and dissolution are not physical but metaphysical events, enacted out on the stage of *citta*, the psychic plane. The Supreme Reality is the center in both the ontic parallels, the body and the universe. And the Center is all that is. The expansion and contraction are just playful assumptions accounted for in terms of *māyā*. *Māyā* is the Power or Free Will of *Brahman* manifesting on the material level through its three attributes (*guṇas*), or modes of function, namely, *sattva*, *rajas,* and *tamas*, which respectively represent light, clarity, stability, and joy; activity, restlessness, pain, and tension; and heaviness, inertia, darkness, and ignorance.

> Maya, I know, is the Super Swindler;
> She roams about with the noose of
> three strands in her hand, and
> utters honeyed words. (*Sabad,* p. 227)

Māyā projects forms and conceals *Brahman* as the One Reality: ". . . where *māyā* is not, there is *Brahma*." When the three *guṇas* of *māyā* suffer an imbalance, for the creation and sustenance of creaturehood, a centrifugal tendency is produced. Since balance is characteristic of *sattva*, it is subjugated by *rajas* and *tamas*, which, being disbalanced, set the pendulum of the cosmos in motion; the "Wheel of Time" (*kālacakra*) is set in motion. Space is introduced as a background to distances and measurements. Unity is hidden and diversity projected.

Because of agitation in the *guṇas*, consciousness is refracted, as it were; and, reflecting on the mirror-like *sattva*, projects ego, the individual "I" or *apa* as Kabīr calls it. Enwrapped in this ego, *ātman*, the Self, becomes *jīvātman*, or creature-self, subject to ignorance, bondage, suffering, and transmigration—which are all very *a-sahaja*, that is, contrary to his real nature. He feels a pull all the time toward his natural poise, *svabhāva*, but ignorant of the inner path leading to it, he seeks it in vain in sense objects.

Musk is hidden in the navel of the musk-deer;
ignorant, he seeks for it here and there
in the forest. (*Sākhī*, "Kasthūree Mṛga Aṅga," d. 1)

I laugh when I hear that the fish in the water is thirsty:
You do not see that the Real is in your home,
and you wander from forest to forest listlessly!
(*Songs of Kabir* XLIII)

The scriptures deal with this problem of nescience and suggest the manner of recovering one's *sahaja svabhāva*.

In the microcosm of the body, the above-mentioned *guṇas* operate through three *nādīs*, or nerve currents. The central current, *suṣumnā*, which corresponds to *sattva*, stretches through the spinal cord from its bottom to a point in the head. The current of *rajas*, *piṅgalā*, and the current of *tamas*, *idā*, rise from the bottom of the spinal cord, one to the right and the other to the left of *suṣumnā*, and, extending not through the spine but along either side of it, rise up to the meeting point of the two eyebrows in the forehead, called *trikutī*, where they both join *suṣumnā*, and do not rise further up. This is the point of the primal balance of the *guṇas*. The other extreme at the bottom of the spine is the locus of extreme disbalance. In the body of an ignorant *jīva*, the Serpent Power of creation, *kula kuṇḍalinī śakti*, lies asleep at this center. By *sādhanā*, She is awakened and made to rise toward the crest. This is also the rise of one's own consciousness. A seeker of *sahaja* must let consciousness travel all the way back to the point of primal balance and stay there as Pure Consciousness, enjoying the bliss of the Self.

Besides the three principal *nādīs*, there are many minor *nādīs*, which have woven the texture of the subtle body. The organization and control of these nerve currents depend on the six nerve centers called *cakra* (wheel) or *padma* (lotus). They are situated, one above the other, along the path of *suṣumnā*, so that *suṣumnā* passes through them. The *cakras* are like a series of lotus flowers blooming on a common stalk. They differ in pattern and structure, according to their functions. In Kabīr's mind, the *cakras* provoke the imagery of the spinning wheel spinning threads for the texture of the body.

In Kabīr's *sādhanā*, the sixth *cakra*, called *ājñā,* has received maximum attention. In a number of ways, the *sahaja* state pertains to *ājñā cakra*. The three nerve currents meet here. This point of perfect equilibrium is also known as *trikutī* (convergence of three peaks) and *trivenī* (confluence of three rivers). Here the mouth of *suṣumnā* opens toward the seventh *cakra,* called *sahasrāra*, which is termed by Kabīr as *sahaja śūnya* (the Void of *sahaja*). *Ātman* manifests here as *haṁsa*, the "Celestial Swan," since *ātman* is reunited with *Īśvara*, the Lord of creation.

> Even this morning, O Swan, awake, arise, follow me!
> There is a land where no doubt nor sorrow have rule:
> Where the terror of Death is no more.
> There the woods of Spring are abloom, and the
> fragrant scent "He is Me" is borne on the wind:
> There the bee of the heart is deeply immersed,
> and desires no other joy. (*Songs of Kabir* XII)

The *sahaja-śūnya* is also *Māna-sarovara*, the *Māna*-lake where the Swan, once liberated, disports himself forever. This is the highest altitude where all measurements (*māna*) end. From here above is the Immeasurable. Above this point is the transmental state, *unmanī daśā*. When this transmental state becomes "normal and natural" to an individual one is said to have attained the state of *sahaja samādhi*.

Ājñā cakra is the terminus for a "dualist," who, as a devotee, seeks proximity to the Lord, without aspiring for total merger with Him. Kabīr, a devotee in the line of Rāmānuja's Qualified Non-Dualism, seeks absolute union with the One in the seventh *cakra*, *sahasrāra*, but stays a *jīvanmukta* between the sixth and the seventh *cakra*, immersed in the bliss of *sahaja samādhi*.

Sahasrāra is the seat of Absolute Being-Consciousness-Bliss, the One Reality beyond the grasp of speech and mind. To Kabīr, He is *Parā Brahman*, *Alakh Nirañjan, Nirguṇa Rāmā, Sahaja*. He is also *spanda* (Vibration), *nāda* (Sound), *parā śakti* (Supreme Power), and *parā vāk* (Transcendental Speech).

The Supreme Reality being beyond space and time, His seat extends from the top of the head to infinity. It is beyond the wheel of temporality; the Supreme is Immortal, *amṛta*, nectar, and *avyakta*, unmanifest. This Boundless Being overflows with His freely vibrant bliss, which is described as *amṛta*, nectar, *somarasa*, the lunar juice, and as *anāhata nāda*, the "unstruck sound." *Parā vāk* (Transcendental Speech or Mystic Word), *spanda* (vibration), *ānanda* (bliss), *mahāsukha* (supreme joy), *anāhata nāda* (unstruck sound), *rasa* (juice) or *mahārasa* (supreme juice), and *amṛta* (nectar) are related terms, either as synonyms or as aspects of the same Reality. Plenum of Being is the Full Moon, complete and phaseless (*niṣkala*), and bliss, its ambrosia.

Nāda, caused by bliss for the sake of bliss, is "Bliss Itself." There is no exterior motivation. This uncaused springing forth of bliss is *anāhata nāda*, sound without percussion or friction. This flow of bliss or *nāda*, in its gesture of descent from the transcendental level, is the source of creation. Here *nāda* is coupled with Being resulting in *bindu*, the "metaphysical point" or the "drop of creative potency." *Om*, the symbolic form of *Brahman*, contains *nādabindu* in a state of equilibrium. For the cosmic disport of creation, the One *Brahman* appears as *nāda* and *bindu*, Śakti and Śiva, "Mother and Father" of the universe. These two aspects are also "*sa*" and "*ha*," which go into the making of *haṁsa*, the Self or *ātman*. Seen in this light, *sahaja* is that which is born of "*sa*" and "*ha*," the equilibrium of *nāda* and *bindu*.

On account of nescience, *nāda* and *bindu* are seen as *icchā*, personal desire, and *aham*, ego, respectively. A world of mock reality is projected in a reverse order. This is the upturned tree of *samsāra*, with its roots above and its branches spreading below (*Sabad*, p. 48). Within this reversed framework, *parā śakti* sleeps in *mūlādhāra*, the lowest *cakra*, as *kuṇḍalinī*. At this level, *nāda* is sex impulse, and *bindu* the creative potency.

Due to this topsy-turvy arrangement, *ātman* appears as *jīvātman*. *Jivātman* is concentrated in the lotus of the heart, *anāhata cakra*, which is also the seat of breath. Within the system of mutability, this *cakra* contains space, *ākāśa*, as a counterpart of the Infinite space of Consciousness, *cidākāśa*, above the *ājñā cakra*. There, with each breath, the *jīvātman* repeats the *ajapā mantra*—"I am He." It is thus a reminder, a plea for acknowledgment of Truth, a reiterated cancellation of duality. Ironically, this "Swan," although repeating "I am He" all the time, is in the slumber of self-forgetfulness, because of the prolonged sleep of *kuṇḍalinī*. The *jīva* is the "I" who craves fulfillment in worldly pursuits while in bondage, and it is also he who reaches the higher spiritual states with the help of the spiritual teacher, guru. It is said that the "unstruck sound" emanating from the *cakra*, with each breath activated by *prāna* (life force) provides a link, a thread, to "infinite consciousness" (*cidākāśa*) of *ājñā cakra*. A spiritual aspirant makes use of this thread to get out of the pit of *samsāra*.

By practicing *sahaja sādhanā, vāk, nāda, prāṇa, manas* (mind), *icchā* (desire), and *bindu* are gradually restored to *cidākāśa* and are dissolved in the light of *Brahman*. They are purified to become divine essence, and they circulate in the body only to keep it alive so that one's body could become an instrument in the hands of God and fulfill divine will. Different branches of yoga lay special emphasis on one or another of the five aspects listed above, the end results being more or less the same, "by realizing one, all is realized" (*Bījak, Sākhī*, d. 273).

Nāda or *śabda* is pivotal to Kabīr's praxis. Its three requirements are receiving the *mantra* or *śabda* from the guru; total self-surrender to love of God; and constant recitation of the *mantra* until one hears the spontaneous *anāhata nāda*, "unstruck sound," sees the Light of *Brahman*, tastes the nectar, *amṛta*, showered by the "Thousand-petaled Lotus," and is united forever with the Divine Spouse. At last, all practice ends, and the *sādhaka* becomes effortless *sahaja*. According to Kabīr, this practice, which is called *śabda sādhanā*, with full concentration and love, suffices to effect the rise of *kuṇḍalinī*, Her penetration of the six *cakras*, thus effecting the transformation of *jīvātman* into *ātman*. Meditation on light at the point of *trikutī* usually accompanies this practice. Kabīr mentions two other practices (e.g., *Sabad*, p. 29): (1) *khecarī mudrā*, which is stated to be "drinking of *rasa* through *bankanāli*," *bankanāli* here referring to the angular passage joining the nasal cavity through the throat. The practitioner of *khecarī mudrā* passes his tongue through it upward for the taste of nectar (*amṛta*). (2) *Mūlabandha*, which is the practice of *āsana* (posture) and *prāṇāyāma* (breathing exercises), resulting in the awakening of *kuṇḍalinī*.

Repudiation of Differentia: The Ethical Counterpart of Sahaja

All Kabīr's ethical preachings can be neatly summed up under two principal canons: truth and nonviolence—or, more precisely, truth and truth alone. For in committing violence, one not only outrages justice and sins against life on earth but also sins against himself by perverting the truth of his own being, which is not different from the one injured. Kabīr inveighs against all forms of falsehood: pedantry *sans* wisdom, rituals shorn of devotion, yogic practice that is mere physical exercise, vain shows of piousness, the saintly garb in which hypocrisy is dressed, the wearing of outlandish signalia which frighten rather than inspire reverence.

Interiorization of spiritual life is a major step toward the simplicity of *sahaja*. Temples and mosques, idols and sacraments, pilgrimage and holy bathing—all belong to the world of duality and multiplicity. One who has come out of the grip of *māyā* sees the Holy everywhere and encounters the Divine within himself.

Overemphasis on rituals alienates the Self from its own reality. Kabīr sensed this danger in the multisectarian medieval background of Indian spirituality. The two broad sectors, the Hindus and the Muslims, though sharing the same political-economic life, were alienated from each other, both socially and psychologically, and no spiritual dialogue seemed possible. The basic unity of spiritual life was refracted and threatened by exclusivism. Formal rites and ceremonies predominated; the common origin of faith was ignored; differences were more visible than similarities. Ostentatiousness and an extreme concern for minor details of ritualistic observances had laid a heavy encrustation upon the true visage of spirituality. Kabīr's lines, exposing the inanities of external cults, are sufficient to give him a place among the greatest satirists of the world.

> The yogi dyes his garments, instead of dyeing his mind
> in the colors of love:
> He sits within the temple of the Lord, leaving
> Brahma to worship a stone.
> He pierces holes in his ears, he has a great
> beard and matted locks, he looks like a goat.
> (*Songs of Kabir* LXVI)
>
> The Mullah cries aloud to Him: and why? Is your
> Lord deaf? The subtle anklets that ring on the
> feet of an insect when he moves are heard of Him.
> (*Songs of Kabir* LXVII)
>
> If God be within the mosque, then to whom
> does this world belong?
> If Ram be within the image which you find upon
> your pilgrimage, then who is there to know what
> happens without?
> Hari is in the East: Allah is in the West.
> Look within your heart, for there you will find
> both Karim and Ram;
> All the men and women of the world are His
> living forms.
> Kabīr is the child of Allah and of Ram: He is my
> Guru, He is my Pir. (*Songs of Kabir* LXIX)
>
> The Hindu says "Rāma is dear to me"; "It's Rahim,"
> cries the Turk.
> They perish fighting—neither knows the heart
> of Truth. (*Sabad*, p. 297)
>
> The Hindu and the Turk are equal in cruelty.
> The one kills goat, and the other cow.
> (*Bījak, Sabad*, p. 83)
>
> Qazi what Scriptures are you explaining?
> Day and night you drone and babble, but you've
> grasped not a single idea. (*Bījak, Sabad*, p. 84)
>
> What use is japa, penance, fast or worship, if one
> has the notion of duality in his heart? (*Sabad*, p. 101)

With their fingers passing on rosary beads, they
have their minds darting in all directions. . . .
(*Sākhī,* "Bheṣa ko Aṅga," d. 2)

The mind is *Mathurā,* the heart is *Dwārakā,*
and the body is *Kāsī:*
Discover the Divine Glow in the mansion with
ten portals! (*Sākhī,* "Bhrama Bidhansana ko Aṅga," d. 10)

They put on saintly uniforms, but their illusion
of creaturehood is not dispelled.
Until they meet the *Sat Guru*, the *Alakh* is
concealed in their heart, unnoticed.
(*Sākhī,* "Bheṣa ko Aṅga," d. 19)

Stages of Realization: Importance of Sat Guru and Initiation with Sabda

Encounter with a True guru is the first step toward enlightenment. A *Satguru* is also *Pārakh-guru*, endowed with spiritual insight to know the disciples' heart and duly cleanse it of ignorance. Initiation is an act of grace conferred on the earnest seeker who is unable to rest until he meets his destined Master.

I do not find anyone who can give me true instructions
And save me from drowning in the ocean of the world.
(*Sākhī,* "Gurusiṣya harā ko Aṅga," d. 1)

O brother, my heart yearns for that true Guru,
Who fills the cup of true love, and drinks of it
himself, and offers it then to me . . .
Kabīr says: "Verily he has no fear, who has such a
Guru to lead him to the shelter of safety!
(*Songs of Kabir* XXII)

Initiation with *śabda* does not imply any elaborate process; it is just divine grace which comes as a sudden flash of light.

Verily, by the grace of the Lord has my *Guru* appeared
before me. (*Sākhī,* "Gurudev ko Aṅga," d. 13)

The Guru came forward and handed me the lamp.
(*Sākhī,* "Gurudev ko Aṅga," d. 11)

There is none greater than the *Sat Guru*; He transforms a human into a god in no time, and opens the inner eye to see the Infinite. (*Sākhī*, "Gurudev ko Aṅga," d. 13)

Initiation is consummated with the shaft of the guru's *śabda* piercing the disciple's heart. *Om* being the *śabda par excellence*, it can also be associated with one's *iṣṭa mantra*, the chosen sacred name, the particular name of the Lord dearest to one's heart. In the case of Kabīr, the *mantra* is "Rāma," which he receives from his guru.

There is nothing that I can offer my Guru in
return for the name of Rāma. (*Sākhī*, "Gurudev ko Aṅga," d. 4)

The *mantra* received from the guru is so immense and powerful (*Bījak*, *Sākhī*, d. 125) that it effects a sea of change in the disciple's mode of existence. The first impact of the "Word" is stunning, bewildering, and painful. The ego is mortally wounded with the arrow of the "Word" and it writhes in pain.

The *Sat Guru*, an expert archer, struck me with His arrow;
To the ground I instantly fell, as it pierced my heart.
I've become dumb, mad, deaf and blind, crippled are
my legs,—the *Sat Guru* has hit me with His shaft.
(*Sākhī*, "Gurudev ko Aṅga," ds. 7, 10)

The Word of the guru dispels all his doubts, without leaving a trace, and sets his heart aflame with love of God (ds. 22, 33, 34).

Viraha and the New Life

The disciple dies to his former existence to be spiritually reborn.

When one becomes dead, even in this life, giving
up all worldly hopes,
God Himself takes his care, so that no trouble comes
to His devotee. (*Sākhī*, "Jīvat Mṛtak ko Aṅga," d. 7)

At first this abrupt inner transformation overwhelms him with an impatient longing for God. His mind becomes detached and purified in the flame of love as he experiences the pangs of separation (*viraha*) from the Beloved. In consonance with the Sufi and the Vaiṣṇava traditions, Kabīr describes himself as *virahinī*, a lady in absence of her lover or spouse.

The *virahinī* gets up and falls down, weak and distraught, for glimpse of yours, O Rāma!

What good would your coming do, if you come after her death?
(*Sākhī,* "Viraha ko Aṅga," d. 7)

When I am parted from my Beloved, my heart is full of
misery: I have no comfort in the day, I have no sleep
in the night. To whom shall I tell my sorrow?
The night is dark; the hours slip by. Because my Lord
is absent, I start up and tremble with fear.
Kabīr says: "Listen, my friend! There is no other
satisfaction, save in the encounter with the Beloved."
(*Songs of Kabir* LII)

But *viraha* is not altogether undesirable; sometimes it is most welcome, for it compels the mind to remember the Lord all the time with exclusive concentration. The sufferings which *viraha* inflicts on the devotee purify his soul and deepen his love—the more he suffers, the nearer he is to his goal.

Don't say *viraha* is bad—*viraha* is a King
The heart uninhabited by *viraha* is a funeral ground.
I am the damp fuel of *viraha*, slowly emitting smoke.
I would be rid of *viraha* the moment I am totally
consumed. (*Sākhī,* "Viraha ko Aṅga," ds. 21, 37)

Śabda Sādhanā as Love Pursuit and the Inner Wooing

Śabda sādhanā, at this stage of *viraha*, is the lover's impatient calling out from the agonized heart. The *virahinī* is gripped with the name of the Lord and it works wonder.

Bedimmed are my eyes, watching and watching Thy path,
My tongue has got blisters, uttering "*Rāma*" without a pause.
(*Sākhī,* "Viraha ko Aṅga," d. 22)

This loud utterance of the "Name" gradually fills his entire body with its vibrations.

All the nerves are strings, the body is lute, played
daily by *viraha*.
None else is able to listen, save the heart of the Lord.
(*Sākhī,* "Viraha ko Aṅga," d. 28)

Continual remembrance of the Lord is likened to spinning threads and making garlands for worship.

> The woman who is parted from her lover spins at the
> spinning wheel . . .
> Kabīr says, "I am weaving the garland of day and night.
> When my Lover comes and touches me with His feet, I shall
> shall offer him my tears. (*Songs of Kabir* XCII)

The *sadhaka* gradually reaches the second stage of *śabda sādhanā*, subtle and interiorized, with the help of the guru, who teaches him the *sahaja* way to discover the Beloved within himself. He learns to practice mental *japa* and subtle meditation, *sūsim surati*, or "Unstruck Sound" and the effulgence of *Brahman*, by which practice consciousness is levitated to the level of *Para Brahman* and *Para Vāk*, and both time and fate are conquered (*Sākhī*, "Suṣim Janam ko Aṅga," d. 1). The *sādhaka*, aware of the Divine in himself, experiences *jñāna viraha*, pangs of separation caused by the knowledge that the Spouse is close at hand, yet veiled off from sight. This spiritual love pursuit is subtle, and its sufferings are not shorn of joys.

> Subtle is the path of love!
> Therein there is no asking and no not-asking,
> There one loses one's self at His feet,
> There one is immersed in the joy of the seeking:
> plunged in the deeps of love as the fish in the water.
> (*Songs of Kabir* LV)

Even at this stage, one must attend to *śabda-sādhanā* with unfailing concentration.

> O weaver, weave the texture of the Lord's name!
> *Idā*, *piṅgalā* and *suṣumnā* provide the loom on which
> *surati* weaves the matrix of *Śabda*. (*Sabad*, p. 139)

> As soon as the thread breaks, join the two ends
> immediately!
> Your delay may render it irreparable . . . .
> Keep the breath quiet and the mind patient. (*Sabad*, p. 154)

Śabda-sādhanā is like the churning of cream out of curd: it separates the essential from the offal, the Real from the unreal. The body is the churning pot, mind the curd, *śabda* the churning rod, and the churning is done with the help of the three principal *nādīs*. The churning ends with the breaking of the pot (dissolution of erroneous identification of the Self with the body), and the inner light merging in the Universal Light (p. 330).

The effects of *śabda-sādhanā* in *jñāna-viraha* are described in a string of metaphors.

The ocean (mind) caught fire (*jñāna-viraha*), and
got burnt; the bird (*ātman*), the Swan (*Haṁsa*)
flew up and perched above (at *Tirukutī*).
The body (separate identity as *jīva*) once burnt,
is never revived (is never subjected to rebirth);
—such a fire was kindled by the *Sat Guru*.
(*Sākhī*, "Jñāna Viraha ko Aṅga," d. 6)

Idā and *piṅgalā*, metaphorically called moon and sun, Ganga and Yamuna, now gain equipoise through preponderance of *sattva*, an attribute of *suṣumnā*. The mind is cleansed of lust and greed, and it is desireless and calm. As a result, the dormant current of *prāṇa* in *suṣumnā* is electrified, as it were, and consciousness is dehypnotized. This is symbolically called the waking of *kuṇḍalinī*. With the transmutation of desire (*kāma*), *bindu* is restored to its purity as spiritual consciousness. The Self (*ātman*) feels the attraction of the Supreme Self, *Paramātmān*, and begins its journey back to the *sahaja* state. As *kuṇḍalinī* rushes through the canal of *suṣumnā*, piercing the six plexuses, toward the *ājñā-cakra*, new dimensions of Reality open up before the practitioner. The ineffable experiences at the summit of spiritual realization are lapped in riddles for only a kindred soul to comprehend.

The heart is astounded to look at the wonders,
Rare is he who would understand this song:
The earth reverts back to meet the sky;
Into an ant's mouth enters an elephant.
Without a storm a hundred rocks fly,
And all the creatures climb on the tree. (*Bījak, Sabad*, p. 101)

One who realizes the Lord in the *Sahaja* way,
In him flowers and fruits, the tree with leaves,
the sappling and the seed, all lie destroyed.
The *Guru*'s advice being followed, knowledge
blazes forth; the fire of *Brahman* is kindled.
The moon and the sun, far away from each other,
join together.
The air takes the opposite course, piercing the
six *chakras*,
It fills the spinal cord with sound.
The sky thunders, the mind is drowned in the Void,
the drum of *Anāhata* keeps resounding. (*Sabad*, p. 158)

There is a strange tree, which stands without roots
and bears fruits without blossoming;
It has no branches and no leaves, it is lotus all over.

Two birds sing there; one is the Guru and the other
the disciple.
The disciple chooses the manifold fruit of life and
tastes them, and the Guru beholds him in joy.
What Kabīr says is hard to understand:
"The bird is beyond seeking, yet it is most clearly
visible. The Formless is in the midst of all forms.
I sing glory of forms." (*Songs of Kabir* XLVII)

The Mystic Nuptials

In the language of the yoga of devotion (*bhaktiyoga*), the practitioner (*sādhaka*), at the first stage of enlightenment, is likened to a new bride, who, though happily wedded to her groom, has yet to know him fully. This is the phase of gradual acquaintance (*parcā* or *paricaya*) with the Lord. The exultation of the first sporadic glimpses of the Beloved is seasoned with the bride-soul's feeling of her personal worthlessness.

He whom I was searching for appeared before me;
But I the bride was soiled and he the dear
Spouse was luminous; so I could not fall at
His feet.
There is still a residue of duality.
I greet God with loving embrace, but my mind is
still impatient:
How can there be a total union, says Kabīr, while
there are two? (*Sākhī*, "Parcā ko Aṅga," d. 36)

Come into my eyes, let me receive you by closing them.
So that neither I see anyone else, nor allow you to
look at others. (*Sākhī*, "Nihkarmī Pativratā ko Aṅga," d. 2)

The individual self, as dedicated wife (*nihkarmī pativratā*), loves the Lord for His own sake, with complete self-surrender.

I am nothing in myself, whatever is there is Thine.
I am offering Thee what is already Thine, so,
what is my credit? (*Sākhī*, "Nihkarmī Pativratā ko Aṅga," d. 3)

The practitioner (*sādhaka*) soon forgets his tiny self, absorbed in the One All-pervading Supreme Self. The duality melts away at last.

When I was, *Hari* was not; and now as *Hari* is,
I am no more.

Too narrow is love's ally; it can't contain two.
(*Sākhī*, "Nihkarmī Pativratā ko Aṅga," d. 9)

Uttering "Thou," "Thou," I've become Thou—I'm no
longer in myself.
I've given myself up to Thee, now only Thou
appearest wherever I look. (*Sākhī*, "Sumiran ko Aṅga," d. 9)

Siddhahood—The Goal Attained

The practitioner is now a *siddha*, a realized soul. He becomes invulnerable, beyond all dangers, when all forms melt away into the Formless, "when *surati* merges in *nirati*, *japa* is lost in *ajapā*" (*Sākhī*, "Parcā ko Aṅga," d. 23). The meeting of *surati* and *nirati* is one of the signs of *sahaja-siddhi*; *surati* is an act of will even when the practitioner struggles to disengage himself from worldly attachments. But when his worldliness is totally destroyed with the dissolution of the ego, there is *nirati*, cessation of the mental flux, which implies cessation of all willed efforts. *Nirati* (*ni-rati*) is also cessation of attractions, since the object of attraction and the seeker are now one. In terms of *layayoga*, *nirati* is dissolution of the mind in "Sound," *nāda*. The yogi is called *ajapā-siddha*, since he no longer must perform *śabda-sādhanā* by meditating with effort on the "Unstruck Sound" (*anāhata nāda*). This sound is now audible to his inner ear all the time.

Surati merges in *nirati* and *nirati* stays supportless,
When *surati* and *nirati* meet, the portals of *Svayambhu*,
the Self-born, open ajar. (*Sākhī*, "Parcā ko Aṅga," d. 22)

In and out there is now nothing else but the Boundless Being. Now, without even the slightest effort, one has all the wealth of spiritual attainment at one's disposal. Nectar (*amṛta*) wells up of itself from the thousand-petaled Lotus and drenches one all over. Having settled on the banks of *Mānasarovara*, the *sahaja* yogi, like the Swan, eats the pearl of liberation. His consciousness is permanently crystallized into the Diamond of Divine Consciousness, as the nectar of "sound" (*nāda*) rains on him:

Amṛta showers forth, Diamond is produced, the bell
rings in the mint:
Kabīr the weaver reaches the Shore without fear.
(*Sākhī*, "Parcā ko Aṅga," d. 47)

Kabīr calls this blissful state of union as *Rāmarasa*, *Rāmarasāyana* and *Harirasa*, which from the devotee's point of view is also the joy experienced while taking the name of the Lord.

When at last you are come to the ocean of happiness,
do not go back thirsty.

Wake, foolish man! for Death stalks you. Here is pure
water before you; drink it at every breath.
Do not follow the mirage on foot, but thirst for the
nectar;
Dhruva, Prahlād, and Shukadeva have drunk of it,
and also Raidās has tested it:
The saints are drunk with love, their thirst is for love.
(*Songs of Kabir* LXI)

The guru, who distributes this *rasa*, demands the drinker's head (ego) for its price. There is no rejuvenating elixir as potent as *Rāmarasāyana*, which pervades the whole body in a moment and transmutes it into gold. The body of the *jīvanmukta* is absolutely subservient to the Divine Will, and it no longer gravitates the Self toward bondage (*samsāra*) (*Sākhī*, "Rasa ko Aṅga," ds. 1, 2, 4, 6, 8). Like the firebird (*analapakṣī*), he lives in space, in total detachment.

By the grace of the *Sat Guru*, I am away from both
heaven and hell;
Immersed in joy, I live for ever at the Lotus Feet
of the Lord. (*Sākhī,* "Madhi ko Aṅga," d. 6)

He need not shun the world nor seek it. All his acts are inspired and regulated by the Divine Will. In the world he discerns the play of *māyā* and has learned the secret of taking the essence and leaving out the trivia.

The name of *Hari* is milk, all else is water:
Rare is the saint, who, like a swan, takes only the
essence out of the mixture. (*Sākhī,* "Sāragrahī ko Aṅga," d. 1)

He has no worry, no anguish; God as *cintāmaṇi*, the Magic Jewel that materializes all thoughts, is treasured in his heart (*Sākhī*, "Besās ko Aṅga," d. 5). He has no fear, for fear cannot stay without the sense of duality (*Sabad*, p. 7).

In the Role of a Teacher

Attainment of the state of Swan, *haṁsa,* ordains one as a "Siddha Guru," an "Adept Teacher." Established in the voidness of *sahaja*, Kabīr, who refers to himself as "Haṁsa Kabīr," becomes a teacher of the *sahaja* Path. But since he has no personal will, he stays absorbed in the joy of *Brahman* and waits for seekers to come and seek enlightenment. One need not carry water from door to door; whoever is really thirsty will himself come impatient for a drink of water (*Sākhī*, "Birkataī ko Aṅga," d. 7).

Yet it is a festive moment when a true devotee approaches him for guidance.

I go on looking for a true lover of God, but find none:
If a lover of God meets such another, then
all poison becomes nectar.
(*Sākhī*, "Guru-Siṣ Herā ko Aṅga," d. 12)

At the summit of fulfillment, there is only silent bliss, except for the lyrical expressions of gratitude, wonder, and love.

I never did nor could I do anything,
nor is my body fit for any action;
All that is done is done by the Lord, and that has
made Kabīr what he is. (*Sākhī*, "Samrathai ko Aṅga," d. 1)

Petitioners must pray and keep vigil at the doors of ordinary people, but God is so kind that he wakens up the sleeping *jīva* to receive the gift of His grace (*Sākhī*, "Samrathai ko Aṅga," d. 4).

I have made friends with Him, says Kabīr,
who is free from the duality of joy and sorrow;
Now I shall always play with Him as my playmate,
and will never be separated from Him.
(*Sākhī*, "Abidhaḍ ko Aṅga," d. 1)

Conclusion

Saint Kabīr epitomizes India's spiritual gospel of harmony on the one hand and an uncompromising passion for truth-realization on the other. He embodies the spirit of synthesis and self-analysis, the two complementary aspects of Indian spirituality.

Originating in the Deccan, the devotional movement of Rāmānuja and the liberalism and syncretism of Rāmānanda underwent a glorious enrichment in Kabīr, and through him and his followers spread to the east, west, and north of India. In the western regions, Kabīr's influence has disseminated *nirguna bhakti*; and of the numerous *nirguṇa* devotees of the Western India, Guru Nānak, the founder of the Sikh order, has been the foremost in historical importance.

In the northern regions, especially at Varanasi and Maghar, as places related to his life, Kabīr's school of philosophy and spiritual practice, known as "Kabīr Panth," have been propagated by both Hindu *sādhus* and Muslim *fakirs*, who, however, have set up separate organizations. Today, Kabīr's influence is not confined only to Kabīr Panth; Kabīr has become part and parcel of Hindu spiritual culture. In Northern India, the strong tradition of worship of Rāma and the importance attached to the name of Rāma—which played a pivotal role in Gandhi's spiritual life—are traceable to Kabīr. The followers of Kabīr Panth, however, lay principal emphasis on the technique aspect of *sahaja* yoga, such as the raising of *kuṇḍalinī* by *ajapā japa*, and seeing the "luminous Point" in *ājñā cakra*.

In East India, the Bengali mystics, Bauls, and Sahajiyas, for instance, have a remote but definite link with Kabīr. Although these mystics have assimilated much directly from Hindu Tantra, Buddhist Tantra, and Sufism, they evince their acquaintance with Kabīr and their allegiance to the spiritual path trodden by Kabīr, in some of their mystical songs. Some of the ideologies they share with Kabīr are the supreme importance of the guru and total self-surrender to him; study of the body as the seat of the Divine; emphasis on devotion; raising *kuṇḍalinī* as a major and indispensable step toward realization; and repudiation of differences of caste and creed. Besides, they share with Kabīr the mystic language of paradoxes and the poetical and musical talents.

The Indian renaissance of the last century witnessed a renewal of interest in Kabīr, whose pungent verse satirizing and ridiculing thoughtlessness, hypocrisy, exclusivism, and fanaticism proved to be a mighty source of inspiration to the social, cultural, and religious reformers. Rabindranath Tagore, the first translator of Kabīr's verse in English, discovered a kindred soul in Kabīr as a poet and also as a mystic wooer of the Formless, All-Pervasive Being of the Upaniṣad, which was the focus of meditation for the members of the Brahmo Samaj, a religious order of reformist Hinduism, to which Tagore's family belonged. A devotee belonging to any caste, creed, or social status was called *harijan* ("devotee of God" or "favorite of God") by Kabīr and was given a place above all others (*Sākhī*, "Gurudeva ko Aṅga," d. 1). To this term, Mahatma Gandhi gave a countrywide sanction and popularity, and ever since then, the uplifting of Harijans, the neglected and ill-treated low castes, has been a powerful movement in India.

Through itinerant saints and village bards, the soul-stirring couplets and lyrics of Kabīr have enlivened the home and hearth of the common people of India for the last five centuries. To the spiritual seeker, they are a key to realization; to the lover of poetry, they are a treasure trove of profound delight; to the person in the street, struggling with the many adversities of his life, they are a source of wisdom and solace.

Notes

1. Cited in Rabindranath Tagore, *Songs of Kabir* (New York: Macmillan, 1915) 36–38.

Bibliography

Sources

The Bijak of Kabir. Translated by Linda Hess and Sukdev Singh. Berkeley: University of California Press, 1983.

Kabir. Introduction and translation by C. Vaudeville. Oxford: Clarendon Press, 1974.

Studies

Bose, Mahindra Mohan. *The Post-Caitanya Sahajiya Cult of Bengal.* Calcutta: Calcutta University, 1930.

Dimock, Edward C., Jr. *The Place of Hidden Moon: Erotic Mysticism in the Vaisnava-Sahajiya Cult of Bengal.* Chicago: University of Chicago Press, 1974.

Lorenzen, David. *Kabir Legends and Ananta-Das' Kabir Parachi.* Albany: State University of New York Press, 1991.

Machwe, P. B. *Kabir.* New Delhi: Sahitya Academy, 1968.

Tiwari, P. N. *Kabir.* Translated by J. P. Uniyal. New Delhi: National Book Trust, 1968.

Westcott, G. H. *Kabir and Kabir Panth.* Varanasi: Bharatiya Publishing House, 1974.

26

Indian Christian Spirituality

J. VALIAMANGALAM

THE MESSAGE OF CHRISTIANITY seems to have entered India already toward the middle of the first century of the Christian era. The missionary nature of Christianity must have been the main reason for its reaching India so early. Jewish presence there, trade routes to India, and the hospitable attitude of Indians would have facilitated the venture. Opinion varies as to whether Christianity first reached Northern or Southern India. In any case, Christians who claim their unbroken Christian tradition from the first century are centered now in the South, mostly in Kerala State. The Christian communities outside Kerala are of more recent origin, starting from the sixteenth century. There must have been Jewish converts to Christianity in India, but no separate Jewish Christian community exists; the assumption is that they merged into the Indian Christians.

Until recently, except for the ancient Christians of Kerala, the church in India has had very little national character, let alone any positive encounter with the Indian religions. The Kerala church had a very tolerant and cooperative attitude toward the Indian religions, probably a patrimony of their Hindu or Buddhist ancestry. Coming mostly from high castes, they entertained the caste mentality, though it did not fit in with Christianity.

Because of their close ties with the Middle Eastern churches, the ancient Indian Christians received and preserved the oriental Syriac liturgy. But both their openness to other religions and their oriental character were much damaged by the domination of the western Latin church over the oriental Indian Christians. This interference reached its climax at a synod popularly known as the Synod of Diamper in the year 1599.

The most encouraging recent development in the history of Christianity is the tolerance and appreciation the Christian churches have begun to show to other religions. This has opened a new chapter in the Christian presence in India. In this study, the term "Indian religion" refers generally to Hinduism. The other great Indian religions, Jainism and Buddhism, today constitute less than one percent of the total population of India, and Sikhism, although very vibrant, is also comparatively small.

History of Christianity in India

Thomas Christians

Christianity is believed to have reached India in the first century C.E. through the preaching of Thomas, of the apostles of Jesus. It is the strong and living tradition of the Indian Syrian Christians or those with the heritage of Syriac liturgy and rite, that they are the descendants of the converts of the apostle Thomas.[1] They are thus known as Thomas Christians. They live mostly in Kerala State (earlier, Malabar Coast) in the southwestern region of India. Some factors that strongly supported the early Christian mission in India were the commercial links that existed even before the Christian era between India and the ports of the Roman Empire; the Jewish presence in India from the very early Christian era; and the tomb of the apostle Thomas venerated at Mylapore in Tamil Nadu in Southern India.[2]

The Indian mission of the apostle Thomas is not believed to have been limited to the Malabar Coast, but his converts have survived only there. Little or no information is available today about the activities of this church or its personalities until after the coming of the Portuguese to India in the sixteenth century.[3] There is some knowledge about its close ties with the ancient Thomas Christian churches of Persia and Mesopotamia, traceable to some extent to the second century, and with certainty to the fourth century. The Malabar Christians probably inherited their Chaldean (Syriac) liturgy from these Middle Eastern churches.[4] Christian immigrants from these countries seem to have helped to strengthen the Thomas Christian community of Malabar. The Christians of today's Kottayam and Chingavanam dioceses, for example, believe that they are the descendants of a group that migrated to Kerala in the fourth century under the leadership of a certain Thomas of Canaan.[5]

Major and minor changes have taken place with regard to faith and worship among the Thomas Christians, especially during the last five hundred years, through divisions and separations. One of the major changes has been the alliance of the Thomas Christians with the Syrian Jacobites under the patriarchate of Antioch and the introduction of the Western Syriac liturgy of the same church by a group of Christians in Kerala. This came to be known as the *Jacobite* or *Orthodox* liturgy. This change resulted from the rift caused by efforts of the Portuguese to "romanize" the church. The turning point was a synod in the year 1599 at Diamper in Kerala, convened by the then archbishop of Goa, Dr. Menezes. He was quite dogmatic and biased against the Syrian Christians, and in this synod he brought about a complete latinization of the Syrian Christians of Kerala. He forced them to repudiate their longtime relations with the oriental churches of Persia and Mesopotamia. The dissatisfaction caused by this synod led to another event called the *Koonan Kurisu* (bent-Cross) oath in 1653, which was an open denouncement by Thomas Christians of Western domination.[6] All this led to divisions and separations. Diamper has therefore been described as "the most famous episode in the Indian Church history—famous not as a model of ecclesiastical assembly, but for the extraordinary nature of its decisions and their effect."[7]

The Protestant reformation in Europe and the Council of Trent may have contributed to the rigidity of Menezes. The Protestant influence on some of the Jacobites led to the formation of a group known as the *Mar Thoma* church. Among the Jacobites there emerged yet another division mainly due to a controversy about the ownership and administration of the church properties. One group expressed its allegiance to the patriarch of Antioch, and the other became practically an independent church. A section of the Jacobite church was reunited with Rome in 1930 and kept its identity in the *Syro-Malankara Rite* which it adopted from its earlier Jacobite Western Syrian tradition. The Thomas Christians of Kerala who had opted to stay with Rome even after the strain of the Portuguese-Latin domination have preserved their ancient Eastern Syrian heritage known today as the *Syro-Malabar Rite.* There exists in Kerala also a Nestorian Chaldean Syrian Christian community in the town of Trichur, which prefers to call itself the *Church of the East.*

It may be added here that the Jacobite and *Syro-Malankara* liturgies have a religious rhythm and spiritual function more congenial to the oriental Indian mind than the Latin and much latinized *Syro-Malabar* liturgies. However, all use Indian languages today and increasingly employ inspiring native classical recital tunes or *bhajans* and other native symbols.

Christian Expansion

In the rest of India outside Kerala, the Christian presence came much later, mainly because of a lack of emphasis on mission work on the part of the ancient Malabar Christians.[8] Christian expansion in India, in fact, coincided with the Portuguese, Dutch, and English traders and colonizers.

Latin Christians

With the great Jesuit missionary St. Francis Xavier, the real wind of European missionary zeal began to blow over India. He converted many thousands to Christianity along the west coast alone, in Goa and the then Travancore-Cochin (now Kerala). These converts belonged to the Roman Catholic Latin church and followed the Latin rite worship and other ecclesiastical disciplines. They were also adapting themselves more to the Western customs, as is especially evident today in Goa. The Goan church expanded to Mangalore and Bombay in the course of time. The Latin church of Kerala grew into a strong community, and for a time the Latin bishops of Goa and Kerala dominated and ruled over the ancient Syrian Christians. It was during this period that the Synod of Diamper was convened, which has been described by the oriental church historian E. Tisserant as "one of the darkest in the history of the relations between the Latins and Orientals."[9]

Protestant Missions

Another important period of Christian expansion in India opened with the Protestant missionary work that began at the dawn of the eighteenth century. Lutherans were the pioneers, of whom B. Ziegenbalg of the Royal Danish mission and C. F. Schwartz of the Society for Promoting Christian Knowledge (SPCK) deserve special mention. Translating the Bible into Tamil, one of the South Indian languages, and resisting the influence of the caste system among the Christians and converts were some of the main Christian activities they undertook. Tanjavoor (Tanjore) in Tamil Nadu was their most important mission center.

Baptists and Anglicans followed toward the end of the eighteenth century, opening their centers at Serampore in West Bengal and at Madras in Tamil Nadu. Of the various Baptist missionaries who worked in India, W. Carey was highly respected, and the Brahmo Samaj leaders such as Rammohan Roy kept in close contact with him and often sought his advice on important matters. The famous Serampore College, with its divinity faculty and a good many branches of science, as well as many other cultural activities in Calcutta are indebted to the initiative of the Baptists. The Bengali New Testament was published at the beginning of the nineteenth century. The Protestant missionary activities of the Church Missionary Society (CMS) and London Missionary Society (LMS) in Kerala and other parts of India also were begun at about this time. B. Bailey's translation of the Bible into Malayalam, the language spoken by the people of Kerala, was done in this period. (At present, Bible translations are available in almost all the Indian languages.)

The American Board of Foreign Missions entered the scene in the early years of the nineteenth century by sending Presbyterian, Methodist, Congregationalist, and Salvation Army missionaries to India. Introduction of the YMCA (Young Men's Christian Association) and YWCA (Young Women's Christian Association) centers in the latter part of the nineteenth century marked an important milestone in the history of Christian service in India. The Basel mission, which based itself in Mangalore, and A. Duff from the Church of Scotland, a leading pioneer missionary in the field of higher education in India, also belong to this period.

Other Expansions

By the middle of the nineteenth century, the Latin Catholic missionary movement, which was strong especially at the time of Francis Xavier, began to gather further momentum. Syrian Catholics of Kerala also joined force. The Syrian Catholics have expanded beyond the region of Kerala, and even today they are busy establishing new Syrian dioceses in many parts of India. At the same time they continue to contribute the highest number of priests and sisters to the Latin missionary dioceses and religious congregations.

Jacobite and Mar Thomite churches of Kerala also are establishing themselves in many places in the rest of India. Great numbers of Christian laity from Kerala who go out seeking jobs also add to the Christian presence throughout India.

Resistance to the Missions

There were not many converts from the educated or economically secure segments of Indian society. A famous Indian Jesuit missionary, Jerome D'Souza, remarked: "Converts choosing Christianity by personal preference from among the educated and high standing are few and almost negligible."[10] The converts have been mostly from the class of Harijans and the tribal aborigines, but mission work among these classes has suffered a setback because of growing consciousness of "Hindu identity" in India and the organized Hindu resistance to foreign and even indigenous missionaries. In fact, the government of India has in recent years placed some limitations on the entry of foreign missionaries into the country. Nevertheless, aid from abroad still provides the support and the financial resources for many missions in India.

Change in Missionary Attitude

Fortunately, Christians themselves have been changing their attitude regarding the missions, partly because of the resistance they face but more because of a change of outlook in their hitherto exclusive approach to religion. There is no doubt that the openness toward other religions that Christianity has begun to show is very much due to its encounter with the Indian religions at their depth, in terms of both their scriptural resources and the people who express their faith.

Swāmi Vivekānanda's humble yet bold and prophetic declaration about the teaching of Hinduism on its universal tolerance and acceptance of all religions, which he put before the Chicago Parliament of Religions in 1893, is bearing fruit. Other modern representatives of Hinduism and of the harmony of religions, such as Mahatma Gandhi, R. Tagore, Sri Aurobindo, S. Radhakrishnan, and others, and lovers of India, such as the clergyman C. F. Andrews and the theosophist Annie Besant, helped to open the eyes of Christians to the spiritual depth of other religions. Western scholars like Arthur Schopenhauer and Max Mueller have done a great deal to prepare the West for a fuller appreciation of the spiritual wisdom of Indian sacred scriptures, such as the Vedas and the Upaniṣads.

This change toward openness, however, is yet to grow fully in depth and breadth in order to become the general character of the Christian presence in India so that it can impress upon the Hindus that Christianity is increasingly in the process of dissociating itself from its proselytizing. This progression toward openness is difficult, given the traditional theological framework of Christianity, but the present change at least gives the hope that more progress will come.

Indian Christian Spirituality

To arrive at a general definition of spirituality and of Indian Christian spirituality in particular is not an easy task. We may look at "spirituality" in terms of a threefold relationship: to oneself, to God, and to other people (and even to other creatures). Christian spirituality, in short, derives these aspects from the model of Jesus. As far as his person was concerned, Jesus had denied himself to the extent of sacrificing his life for his religious convictions. He went around sharing God's love and mercy with all who suffered under life's burdens, and liberating those enslaved and oppressed by the legalism of the Jewish religion of his day. His relationship to God was one of unique intimacy as between a father and son. He considered all people to be children of the same Father and advised everyone to consider others in the same way and to be forgiving even to enemies. Jesus enjoyed unity with the Father through the Holy Spirit, giving rise to the Christian doctrine of the triune God, or Holy Trinity. Jesus was often found to be withdrawn in order to immerse himself in conversation with the Father, but he always returned to the midst of the people. Thus, Christian spirituality may be said to consist in the inner growth of a person toward the self-emptying that leads to opening oneself to God as to one's beloved father and to others as to one's own brethren.

Indian spirituality has many faces. In general, it recognized God's presence everywhere and in everything. One may even grow to the consciousness of total identity with the Absolute (*Brahman*), as we find in the Vedāntic school of Advaita. However, this thrust toward the realization of the identity with the Absolute can result in separation and isolation from the world, even to the assumption of the life of a mendicant, *sannyāsi*. There are also counter-religious movements in India to balance the thrust of this "otherworldly," *sannyāsa* spirituality, such as the *bhakti* traditions, which stress piety and devotion. Indian spirituality is rich with the notion of divine duality, God as both male and female, father and mother. Again, the concept of nonviolence, or *ahiṁsā,* becomes deep and profound when it takes into account the subhuman life also.

Christian spirituality, in order to be truly Indian, needs to have serious and sincere encounters with Indian spiritual traditions. Such encounters can indeed become mutually enriching and also mutually corrective, especially in the "spiritual dimensions" of the threefold relationship referred above, namely, to oneself, to God, and to other people.[11]

Indianized Christianity

In the whole of India, it is almost only in Kerala that Christianity has not been looked upon as a foreign religion. Several factors contributed to this. First of all, it seems that the major portion of the Thomas Christians came from the high castes in Indian society and were self-supporting. This must have greatly contributed to their survival in such a tiny corner of the world. Christian traders from the Middle Eastern and other Roman ports and other Christian immigrants surely increased the prestige of the Thomas Christians of Kerala before their rulers and other people. There is sufficient proof that they enjoyed many privileges from their kings and were treated with respect by the high-caste Hindus. They seem to have had also good military men who came to the aid of the rulers in times of need.

In addition, the Thomas Christians have been keeping their national identity intact. Most of the native customs have been preserved in their daily life. Many of the Hindu religious elements were kept in their church life as well. For example, church processions had all the external solemnity of the Hindu processions. Edible offerings brought by the devotees were distributed as *prasād* (food offered to the deity in a temple and shared among the people as symbol of divine benevolence and fellowship among themselves). In the Christian marriage ceremonies and in rites performed for the dead, many Hindu customs were observed.

One can gather from the prohibitory clauses of the Synod of Diamper that there was considerable cultural and religious contact between the Thomas Christians and the Hindus. For example, prohibition of the celebration of *Onam* (a harvest feast) by the Christians, of attendance at the temple feasts known as *utsavam*, and of invitations to Hindu musicians to play in the Christian churches. Items such as light (lamp and oil) and ornamental umbrellas for processions were passed on to the Hindu temples from the Christian churches and vice versa during the religious festivals. Instead of wine from grapes and bread from wheat, local rice cake and coconut sap or palm wine also seem to have been used for the Christian eucharistic service.

All this showed the attitude of openness and healthy religious tolerance of the ancient Indian Christians, probably a heritage from their ancestral Hindu religion. J. Placid Podipara, a great Thomas Christian church historian, says of the pre-Diamper church of Kerala: "Hindu in Culture, Christian in Religion and Oriental in Worship."[12]

The question of the extent to which the Thomas Christian church of Kerala was Indian and the extent to which the Christian faith was integrated with the Hindu religion *in depth* remains to be asked. That they kept the Syrian liturgy almost intact for worship and that it was in the Syriac language until recently raises a problem. Moreover, in the course of time the Thomas Christians became more and more alienated from the Hindu customs. They could even be externally distinguished as Christians because of their manner of dress. They began to view Hindu sanctuaries and worship as unholy and even devilish. The sight of Hindu *utsavam* was to be avoided by Christians as sinful. Although the Christian catechism had adopted a very indianized name, *Vedapatam*, the content does not seem to have been indianized at all. For example, Christianity is presented as the only true revelation or divine religion.

It is true that the Synod of Diamper was responsible for some of these extremes, but it is likely that Indian Christians, even the ancient Thomas Christians, kept the Hindu religious externals without seriously taking into account the deeper religious elements that produced them. A. M. Mundadan, a Thomas Christian scholar, observes: "The Thomas Christians were living as if in two worlds: the geographical, political and social world of the Malabar coast and the ecclesiastical world which was more or less Chaldean in character. . . . [This] prevented the Church of India from developing an Indian Christian culture, especially an Indian theology and Indian liturgy."[13] And Joseph Cardinal Parekkattil, a scholarly Thomas Christian bishop of recent time, has said that the tendency of his church has often been "to transplant a Syrian or European Church, instead of letting the seed . . . germinate, take roots and grow, drawing nourishment from the native soil."[14]

Neither the early meeting of Eastern Christianity with Hinduism in Malabar nor the later encounter of Western Christianity with Hinduism elsewhere in India produced any substantial and lasting fruitful integration in theology, philosophy, and spirituality. This might lead one to think that the early Indian Thomas Christians were not conscious of the depth of Christian theology and spiritual life. There is no record of any outstanding scholar from among the ancient Malabar Thomas Christians or any classical Christian treatise written by one of them. No Indian holy person from ancient days is commemorated in the Thomas Christian church services, nor is a single tomb or shrine of such a one venerated. This is even more surprising since in that time saints were canonized in local churches without the centralized scrutiny that exists today in the Catholic church. Still more mysterious is the fact that no lasting Christian monastic tradition developed in this country of contemplative spirituality.

Perhaps examples of conspicuous Christian maturity did not emerge in India because Christianity reached India not as an answer to a spiritual quest but as an institution. It still continues as an institution rather than as a spiritual adventure. Moreover, the depth of Hindu spirituality in theory and in practice is so great that no ordinary virtue could impress Hindus. Yet Hindus on spiritual quest, such as Gandhi, Ramohun Roy, Keshub Chunder Sen, or converts by inner urge, such as Sundar Singh and N. V. Tilak, seem to have profited more from Christ and Christianity than the traditional Christians themselves. Hinduism has an extraordinary magnanimity toward other religions and the power to absorb whatever is good in them. In the early stages Christianity in its own way also exhibited this attitude.

Another consideration is that the Middle Eastern church, to which the Indian church was closely related and on which it was dependent in ancient times, exerted such a domination over it that its indigenous leadership and growth could have been hampered. For example, for centuries the bishops who were sent to Malabar from the Middle East did not consecrate any Indian bishops. Later, the Indian church was dominated by the West, which resulted in a certain lack of originality and cultural consciousness of the Indian Christians. Although the Jacobities and Mar Thomites boldly separated themselves from Latin domination after Diamper, they became victims of other influences.

Today the Catholic Thomas Christians of Kerala are engaged in restoring their Eastern Syrian tradition to the pre-Diamper period. But they show very little consciousness of and enthusiasm for the deeper theological and spiritual riches of their tradition, and they have little interest in indigenization, which should be paramount. B. Griffiths has remarked: "Even if the Syrian Churches were to recover their Oriental tradition, it is doubtful whether this would be of such significance for India today. . . . The Church in India is now seeking for an Indian liturgy, an Indian theology and an Indian spirituality, which will embody the best traditions of Indian (including, of course, Hindu) cultures."[15] An indigenous liturgy may be a solution to the "rivalry of rites" among Christian churches in India, which causes great harm to Christian development.

It is consoling, however, to observe here that attention is being given to these problems today. Attempts are being made by Christians engaged in dialogue with the Indian religions to achieve a deeper meeting of East and West. Christianity has not overpowered India, and the Indian religions have a great role to play in the history of religion.

Christian Presence in India

Christian Influence on Hindu India

Despite the fact that until recently the Christian missions on the whole enjoyed exceptional freedom and material prosperity, the Christian population in India is small in comparison with the total population of India. According to the census of 1971, Christians constitute only about fourteen million people in India. Of these Christians, broadly speaking, half are Catholics and the other half are members of various Orthodox churches and Protestant denominations. Even though Christians are only 2.6 percent of the total population, they are the third largest religious group in India (Muslims are in second place, with 11.2 percent or about sixty million). Christians are more concentrated in the South, in Kerala, Tamil Nadu, and Goa, although their presence is strongly felt in almost all parts of India through their widely represented mission centers and charitable institutions.

The influence of Christianity on India as a whole is not to be judged by numbers alone, as Jerome D'Souza, a Jesuit missionary, has rightly observed. There is a general recognition of the valuable role that foreign missionaries and Indian Christians have played in the educational, medical, and social fields in India.[16]

Hindu India has been much influenced by the Christian West at both the individual and the collective level, especially with regard to the notion of equality of people belonging to various castes and classes, monogamy, individual liberty, and democracy, as well as rejection of certain "superstitions and taboos." Christian culture exerted no small influence on a segment of Hindu families in Kerala, especially among the Nair community, in establishing the dignity of the man as husband and father against the custom of giving the woman as mother more prominence. In India as a whole, however, Christianity was a liberating force for women.

For the vast majority of Hindus, the Christian presence in India had the appearance of colonial oppression, anti-Hinduism, and less spiritual greatness because the Christians ate meat and consumed alcohol. All the same, many educated Hindus drew much spiritual inspiration from Christ and Christianity. The nineteenth-century Hindu religio-cultural renaissance and reformist groups such as the Brahmo Samaj of Calcutta and *Prārthana Samāj* of Bombay drew cultural and spiritual inspiration from Christ, the Bible, and Christian life. Leaders such as Raja Rammohun Roy of the Brahmo Samaj fought against the custom of *sati* (in which widows were often forced to end their life by jumping into their husbands' funeral pyres) and resisted the worship of images of God; and Keshub Chunder Sen adopted the pattern of Christian prayer in the *New Dispensation.*

Such communities could be described as "Hindu-Christian," without a formal baptism. "His [Christ's] influences have woven round me for the last twenty years or more, and, outside the fold of Christianity as I am, have formed a new fold, wherein I find many besides myself," declared A. C. Mozoomdar.[17] Keshub Chunder Sen did not hesitate to celebrate an Indian Eucharist with a very inspiring sacramental prayer.[18] Rāmakrishna Paramahamsa, the spiritual master of Vivekānanda, was often aroused to the state of spiritual ecstasy by meditating on Jesus and Mary. The Ramakrishna Mission, formed by Vivekānanda, drew a great deal of inspiration from the Christian educational, social, and charitable organizations in defining its own mission and operations. Again, a Hindu leader such as Mahatma Gandhi acknowledged openly that Jesus' Sermon on the Mount influenced him a great deal in his formulation of the ideal of nonviolence.

The Spiritual Life of Christians

The number of devout families of strict Christian morals, of great religious piety, and of devotional practices was and is indeed large in India. Dedicated and charitable missionaries, men and women, native or otherwise, have been many. The close family ties that still exist between members of Indian families, the love and affection Indian children receive from their parents, and the care and support that the parents in their old age get from their children, impress many Westerners even today.

Dedicated service rendered by women, mostly mothers, and also men in some instances, often in the poor circumstances of the Indian families, is admirable. Of those who combine with it a life of silent prayer and heroic suffering in union with Jesus and Mary or other saints, it can surely be said that they indeed belong to the community of saints. Nevertheless, outstanding mystics or other heroic, spiritual champions are hard to find among the Indian Christians. Great political leaders with high spiritual and moral qualities like Mahatma Gandhi, *sannyāsis* like Śrī Aurobindo and Ramaṇa Mahariṣi, *ācāryas*/gurus like Rāmakrishna Paramahamsa and Vivekānanda in modern India were all basically products of Hinduism, although they drew much inspiration from the Christian sources.

However, Indian Christianity did produce *sādhus* (wandering holy men) like Sundar Singh of the Punjab, N. V. Tilak of Maharashtra, B. C. Sircar of Puri, Peter Reddy of Andhra-Tamil Nadu, and Mathaichan of Kerala, who were men of contemplation, heroic charity, and the spirit of self-sacrifice.[19] Ecumenical pioneers like P. D. Devanandan and indianizing forerunners and *sannyāsis* like B. Upadhyay were also men of deep spirituality and devotion. A few bishops, priests, and a couple of religious sisters of recent times are being esteemed after their death by more and more people for their spiritual achievements. The Indian church has also on record a few martyrs of faith.[20] The courage and dedication for the cause of the church and the country exhibited by clergymen like Mar Kariatty two centuries ago or Yuhanon Mar Thomas of recent time, and lay leaders like Thachil Mathu Tharakan or Kandathil Varghese Mapila from Kerala and the like from elsewhere in India require further study. Thus far, these men have received attention for their administrative expertise, literary qualities, and social involvements.

Christian spirituality in India in the past and present can be said to be distinguished by its charitable and social concerns. Although this spirituality might be seen as more outward-oriented than inward-looking, the spiritual quality of this outward service is not to be less valued. Love and service of the neighbor are next only to the love and worship of God or are even equal to it, according to the teachings of Christ (Matthew 22:39; 25:31–46). It is true, however, that, in the past especially, Christian charity was often motivated by missionary concerns, which diminished its spiritual quality. But this has changed today. In connection with the Christian presence of service in India, Mother Teresa of Calcutta deserves special mention. She lives a spirituality that is Christian and mystical, experiencing Christ himself in the poor and suffering. There are also other dedicated Christians serving orphans, leprosy patients, and others, even though they are not so well known.

Godly, useful, and necessary though the charitable activities are, they do not fully satisfy the Christian conscience of many today. Hence, *liberation theology* has begun to find favor in India also. M. M. Thomas, S. Kappen, Mar Ostathios, S. Rayan, and I. Puthiadom are among the leading Indian liberation theologians. On winning election to the Assembly of Karnataka State in 1983, Jacob, a Catholic priest, declared that it was the poor man's vote for justice and bread that made him win. A missionary priest in Andra Pradesh, F. Aureo, used to request that those who attended the service in his church bring with them rice and food items. He arranged for his parishioners to go to the homes of the sick and poor after the service, cook food there, and share it with them, thus celebrating the real *agapē*.

There are so many hard-working and dedicated people in India who live a life of faith and trust drawing inspiration and comfort in their toils and sufferings from the cross of Christ. This is certainly a living Christian spiritual presence in India. Many Christians and non-Christians alike have found the notion of the sufferings of Christ spiritually attractive. In the hands of some of the Indian theologians, Christ's *kenōsis,* or self-emptying, received a mystical explanation and a beautiful Indian insight. This self-emptying has often been interpreted as the abandoning of the divine glory by the Son while becoming incarnate. However, Keshub Chunder Sen and Chakkarai looked at the suffering of the "earthly Jesus" as his extreme self-denial and emptying of himself whereby a full in-dwelling by divinity became possible.

"Essentially, it [India] had sought only the emptiness and the fullness; and they are the same thing," an Indian Christian French priest and monk, J. Monchanin, observed.[21] Gandhi, perhaps the greatest unbaptized Indian Christian, saw Jesus on the cross as a perfect *satyāgrahi,* or example of heroic self-suffering. Suffering and forgiving as well as healing and liberating motifs from Jesus and the Bible have inspired many artists and literary people in India. Christian hymns such as "Wondrous Cross" were dear to Gandhi and other lovers of the cross in India; so also were hymns such as "Lead Kindly Light," which originated in the depth of the hearts of passionate seekers after truth.[22]

Christian interdenominational fellowship, fellowship between world religions, and the dialogue and cooperation springing from such ecumenism bear witness to a visible spiritual element of human culture today. India's contribution to ecumenism is not small. We have already noted the impact on Christianity of India's openness to other religions. It goes to the credit of Christianity in India that inspiration for unity of various Christian denominations first began in India and bore fruit in unions such as the Churches of South India (CSI) and the Churches of North India (CNI). A joint council for the further union of these two is also at work. Several modern ecumenical organizations and centers for Christian-Hindu ecumenical living, dialogue, training, research, and publications exist, of which the following are important: the Ecumenical Christian Centre, Whitefield, Bangalore; the Aikyalayam, Madras; World Religion Centre, Dharmaram College, Bangalore. The Catholic church has lately entered the ecumenical scene and has become very active, especially following the Second Vatican Council.

The Christian Ashram Movement

The Christian *Ashram* movement, a new, more visible chapter in the history of Christian spirituality in India, is still in its infancy. It is here that people on the spiritual quest may find some real challenge, and it is easier in the *ashram* to rise above the denominational and dogmatic barriers of traditional religions. For, "in the discovery of the Eternal beyond thought and feeling, there is no longer a division between classes and races and religions."[23] The observation that "the monk is not a 'converter,' he is a witness (through life)" is also significant.[24]

Christianity's new awareness regarding the truth of other religions has led many Indian Christians to take into account the spiritual depth of the Hindu theological and contemplative traditions, as well as India's various indigenous forms of worship. "Until recently the leaders of this movement were Christians from the West who had discovered the oriental tradition for themselves, but now more and more Indian Christians are beginning to discover their Indian heritage," writes Bede Griffiths, an English Benedictine monk who was in charge of the Indian Christian Ashram of Monchanin and Le Saux, near Tiruchirapalli in Tamil Nadu.[25]

Griffith's *ashram,* in fact, marks the latest phase of a positive Christian–Hindu encounter. The early phase was an experiment made by De Nobili and a few others in the seventeenth century at Madurai in Tamil Nadu, but it was conceived only as a change in the missionary method by the adoption of some Indian cultural elements and a few Hindu religious external symbols into the Christian lifestyle, together with some proficiency in Sanskrit. Nevertheless, it was a pioneering move; before that time, with the exception of the early Thomas Christians of Kerala, "conversion meant an undesirable break from the cultural and social traditions of India and adoption of an European way of life, which detached Christians from their social ambit."[26]

One might here also recall the great Brahmabandhab Upadhyay, a nineteenth-century Indian (Bengali) Christian convert, nationalist, social worker, editor, writer, and *sannyāsi*, who carried Hindu–Christian encounter beyond mere borrowing of externals, although he saw the Hindu philosophy as "hand-maid of Christianity" and Christ as the "fulfillment of Hinduism." Upadhyay found consolation in the contemplation of the Hindu concept of *Brahman* as *sat*, *cit*, and *ananda* as parallel to the Christian understanding of the Holy Trinity.

> The more we meditate on the cogitations of Hindu philosophy concerning the Supreme Being, on its marvellous but fruitless effort to penetrate into His inner nature . . . the more light is thrown upon the ever-mysterious Christian doctrine of the one God, one yet multiple, absolute yet related within himself, discovering in it a new fitness to appease the noblest cravings of man. . . . Indian soil . . . will make the ever-new Christian revelation put forth newer harmonies and newer beauties revealing more clearly the invincible integrity of the Universal Faith deposited in the Church by the Apostles of Jesus Christ.[27]

We should mention here Henri Le Saux, a Catholic priest, who is more commonly known by his Indian name, Abhishiktananda. The parallel between *Saccidananda* and the Trinity seems to have illumined Abhishiktananda in a different way from Upadhyay. It helped Abhishiktananda out of the disquieting problem regarding the *threeness* of Persons in the Trinity and the *oneness* of their Nature. For Abhishiktananda, the Christian contemplation of God as Trinity could become more inviting and absorbing in the light of the Hindu *advaitic* experience of the Absolute as the One without a second.

From among many parallels Abhishiktananda drew between Hindu and Christian traditions, his reflections relating *OM*, the supreme Hindu *mantra* (prayerful recital), representing the ineffable and unutterable *Ultimate*, to the most intimate Christian conception and invocation of God—*Abba*—is worth noting:

> *OM! ABBA!*
>
> The highest *mantra* among Hindus is OM. . . . More than any particular name of the Divinity, it conveys the ineffability and the depths of the divine mystery. It bears no special distinct meaning. . . . it is a kind of inarticulate exclamation uttered when man is confronted with the Presence in himself and around himself . . . uttered at the beginning and at the end of every scriptural recitation. . . . When the call to higher life is heard . . . they will abandon all

> prayers, all rites, all practices of devotion, but they will keep on whispering indefinitely the sacred OM. . . .
>
> St. Paul reminds us that the Spirit is constantly whispering in the depth of our hearts the sacred invocation, "Abba Father." "Abba Father" was, to be sure, the ceaseless prayer of Jesus also . . . he was at all times calling on the Father. "Abba" was his last prayer in Gethsemane (Mk. 14:36), his last word on the cross (Lk. 23:46).
>
> "Abba Father" is then a sacred *mantra* . . . makes the soul share in the most intimate life of God. . . . Could we not say that OM introduces man into the mystery of the Holy Spirit . . . who will reveal to the elect the mystery of the Son, and whispers in the sanctuary of the heart the eternal Abba?[28]

Vande Saccidānandam is a magnificent Hindu-Christian contemplative hymn of Upadhyay on *Saccidānanda*-Trinity, the Ultimate Reality conceived by the Hindu sages as *sat* (Being), *cit* (consciousness), and *ānanda* (bliss) related to the Christian Trinitarian notion of God or Father, Son, and the Holy Spirit.

Upadhyay had high hopes for Christian *ashrams* and had made all the arrangements to start one on the banks of Narmada at Jabalpur. But he had to give up the idea under ecclesiastical pressure—the Catholic hierarchy did not approve of his Hindu leanings. However, he both retained the saffron robe and remained a Catholic. At that time he had problems also with the British government in India because of his involvement in the freedom movement.

The Christukula *ashram* at Tirupattur, Tamil Nadu, was started in 1921 by two doctors, E. F. Paton and S. Jesudason. It may be said to have led all others in the history of the modern Christian *ashram* movement. A few other *ashrams* should be mentioned; some are more interdenominational, others more contemplative, and still others involved directly in the affairs of the people: Christa Prema Seva (CPSP) Ashram in Pune; Jeevan Dhara Ashram of Sr. Vandana in the Himalayas; Dhyan Ashram in Indore; Christavashram in Kerala (now consisting mostly of married people); Kurisumala Ashram in Kerala; Little Brothers of Jesus in Tamil Nadu; Anandasramam in Tamil Nadu; and Om Yesu Niketan Ashram in Goa. Of these the last serves also as a healing center for Western youth who have lost their orientation in the East through use of drugs and have been misled by "false gurus."[29]

Bede Griffith's approach to the Christian–Hindu encounter has probably evidenced greater openness to India and Hinduism than all his forerunners in the movement, and he was probably more detached than they regarding missionary motivations. The image he employed to explain his quest was more sublime than that of "grafting," conceived by Monchanin, and was also devoid of the sting in Upadyay's "handmaid" view. "Marriage" was the symbol Griffiths chose—marriage of his Western soul with the Eastern counterpart, which he wished to see extended also to the geographical and church dimensions. He wrote:

> For years I had been studying the Vedanta and had begun to realize its significance for the Church and the world. Now I was given the opportunity to go to the source of the tradition, to live in India and discover the secret of the wisdom of India. It was not merely a desire for new ideas which drew me to India, but the desire for a new way of life. I remember writing to a friend at the time: "I want to discover the other half of my soul." I had begun to find that there was something lacking not only in the Western world but in the Western Church. We were living from one half of our soul, from the conscious, rational level and we needed to discover the other half, the unconscious, intuitive dimension. I wanted to experience in my life the marriage of these two dimensions of human existence . . . . I wanted to find the way to the marriage of East and West.[30]

Withdrawal from the world is characteristic of Indian spirituality. Although contemplative spirituality is not unknown in the Christian tradition, a greater emphasis has been on service to the neighbor. The Indian Christian *ashram* movement on the whole cares for both the contemplative and service dimensions. While Hindus have been taking a "balancing lesson" from the Christian service orientation, Christians, who have lost their spiritual balance somewhat with overemphasis on material comforts and worldly involvement, and also because of the church's loss of its original faith experience as the result of its hardened institutionalization and dogmatism, fortunately have found a corrective in the contemplative and "liberal religiosity" of Eastern religions. The peace and enrichment that Abhishiktananda and Upadhyay derived from the Hindu understanding of the "Trinity," the Indian explanation of the *kenōsis* of Jesus, C. F. Andrews's experience of the universal Christ in the East, and the ecumenical dialogues that are taking place today are sufficient testimonies to the mutual benefits of spiritual encounters between the East and West.

Conclusion

A remarkable spiritual event of our time is, undoubtedly, Christianity's change of attitude regarding other religions. When one thinks of the earlier Christian teachings that Christianity alone was the divinely revealed, true, and perfect religion and that the non-Christian religions are false or even creations of the devil, the present change to openness is indeed a Copernican revolution, spiritually speaking. But it may still have to go further. For it is still at the stage of tolerance of others, whereas the ideal must be the equal partnership implied in Griffith's metaphor of marriage, as well as in Gandhi's call for equal respect for all religions. Such a stand would bring about a thorough reorientation of the missions, and preaching would be directed to discovering the richness of each religion for the others rather than aiming at converts. Eventually this will help all to realize that they are part of the other(s), for "if a man reaches the heart of his own religion, he has reached the heart of the others too."[31] Bede Griffiths did not hesitate to declare: "The Christian, to whatever Church he may belong, cannot claim to have the monopoly of Truth. We are all pilgrims in search of truth, of reality, of final fulfilment."[32] Further, the Indian Christian theologian P. Chenchiah states: "The Hindu will slowly and in different degrees come under the influence of the Spirit of Christ, without change of labels or nomenclature."[33]

Mahatma Gandhi is an outstanding advocate, as well as model, of the ecumenical principle in our time. However strange it might sound, Gandhi can be said to be one of the world's greatest examples of Christian spirituality, of love of God and love of neighbor or for the sacrifice of oneself in the service of others. Tagore had quite appropriately said that Gandhi had Christ's spirit. "Though I cannot claim to be a Christian in the sectarian sense," Gandhi writes, "the example of Jesus' suffering is a factor in the composition of my undying faith in non-violence which rules all my actions, worldly and temporal."[34] Although Gandhi labeled himself a Hindu, he declared to his coreligionists that "your life will be incomplete unless you reverently study the teachings of Jesus."[35] Gandhi's first biographer, Joseph Doke, well understood the character of Gandhi's faith, which went beyond the traditional boundaries of Hinduism. Doke wrote:

> I question whether any system of religion can absolutely hold him. His views are too closely allied to Christianity to be entirely Hindu; and too deeply saturated with Hinduism to be called Christian, while his sympathies are so wide and catholic, that one would imagine "he has reached a point where the formulae of sects are meaningless."[36]

What was most Christian or Christlike about Gandhi was his approach to suffering and nonviolence, his readiness to suffer to the last in the exercise of his creed of truth and nonviolence—truth through nonviolence. Truth, for Gandhi, is God, and the love of God and the love of neighbor are expressed through active nonviolence, *satyāgraha*. Gandhi gave a new dimension to nonviolence insofar as it did not stop with passive acceptance of suffering and death by individual saints, but actively and collectively resisted oppression and injustice in the world, using suffering as the weapon. Hatred had no place in this war without violence or war of love.

This meant love of enemies as well, and thus Jesus' Sermon on the Mount became so dear to Gandhi.

Gandhi's view of active nonviolence led him to involve himself in social problems and politics. Thus, Gandhi not only "mixed" religions by his principle of equal respect for all; he also mixed politics with religion.[37] In a sense, everything was a religious exercise for Gandhi, since he understood the main thrust of Hinduism to be nonviolence. At the same time, his view of the truth of all religions led him to be enriched by the insights of all other religions. In fact, he confesses: "It was the New Testament which really awakened me to the rightness and value of passive resistance." But he also adds: "The Bhagavad Gita deepened the impression."[38]

The claim of Christians, therefore, that Gandhi's nonviolence was a borrowing from the Bible cannot be substantiated. The ideal that was already there in his own tradition and upbringing from childhood received a push from the reading of the Sermon on the Mount. This can happen with other ideas and other religions. Sometimes a concept is lost sight of in one's own tradition because of distortion, repetition, or overemphasis of a particular aspect. For example, contemplative spirituality and simplicity in life are not alien to the Christian tradition. But they were distorted in the course of time by undue emphasis and concern for the material welfare of modern Western Christianity. The corrective was easier from the East, since the idea of contemplation was more alive there. One element may be stronger in one tradition than in the another, as it could be said of Indian religions concerning nonviolence and of Christianity concerning love of neighbor.

Finally, as Gandhi had advised Hindus to perfect themselves through the teachings of Jesus, his comments on Christian missionaries are worth noting:

> There is no doubt that among them [Christian missionaries] the spirit of tolerance is growing. Among individuals there is also a deeper study of Hinduism and other faiths and an appreciation of their beauties, and among some even an admission that the other great faiths of the world are not false. One is thankful for the growing liberal spirit but I have the conviction that much still remains to be done in that direction.[39]

This openness will be of mutual benefit, as Upadhyay has well testified:

> The negative plate of Jesus, developed in a solution of Hinduism, brings out hitherto unknown features of the portrait. . . . A Christian movement within Hinduism without its umbilical cord being cut is a decided advantage to the Hindu and the Christian.[40]

Many shrines and devotional centers help to maintain the popular piety of the ordinary believers at large but seem to preserve religion generally only on a superficial level. Many, especially in Kerala, have observed a regular evening family prayer, but it is falling out of use now. The new generation needs a deeper personal orientation of prayer. Among the methods of spiritual renewal today, the *charismatic movement* is creating a new wave. It has much in common with the Pentecostals, who have been active in many parts of India for a long time. The evangelical Christian meeting known as the *Maramon Convention* (organized by the Mar Thomite church) has been an important annual spiritual event in Kerala since 1896. Gandhi's *ashrams*, and particularly his public prayer meetings, may have had a better ecumenical character. A church without rigid institutional formalities is perhaps the best basis for a genuine Indian Christian spirituality, or even for a world religious culture.

Notes

1. There are also a few Latin rite St. Thomas Christians.

2. For detailed discussion regarding the apostle Thomas's Indian mission, see *The St. Thomas Christian Encyclopaedia of India*, ed. C. Menacherry (Trichur, 1973) vol. 1; C. B. Firth, *An Introduction to Indian Church History; History of Christianity in India, Source Materials,* compiled by M. K. Kuriakose; A. C. Perumalil, *The Apostles in India;* L. W. Brown, *The Indian Christians of St. Thomas;* P. J. Podipara, *The Thomas Christians;* J. N. Farquhar, "The Apostle Thomas in North India," *Bulletin of the John Rylands Library* 10 (1926) 80–111; idem, "The Apostle Thomas in South India," *Bulletin of the John Rylands Library* 11 (1927) 20–50; J. P. M. van der Ploeg, *The Christians of St. Thomas in South India and their Syriac Manuscripts* (Bangalore: G. Dharmaram Publications, 1983); G. Moraes, *A History of Christianity in India: From Early Times to Francis Xavier* (Bombay: Manaktalas, 1964).

3. Firth, *Introduction*, 18.

4. *Encyclopaedia*, ed. Menacherry, 1:6–7; 2:30–32; Firth, *Introduction*, 19–29; Padipara, *Thomas Christians*, 63–78; A. M. Mundadan, *Sixteenth Century Traditions of St. Thomas Christians* (Bangalore: Dharmaram College, 1970) 83–87; P. Thenayan, *The Missionary Consciousness of the St. Thomas Christians: A Historico-Pastoral Study* (Cochin: Vianai, 1982) 22–28.

5. *Encyclopaedia*, ed. Menacherry, 1:6–7; 2:74–75.

6. On Diamper, the Koonan Kurisu Oath, and their consequences, see Firth, *Introduction*, 89–108; E. Tisserant, *Eastern Christianity in India*, 27–68; J. Killaparambil, *The St. Thomas Christians' Revolution in 1653* (Kottayam: Catholic Bishop's House, 1981); *Christianity in India*, ed. H. C. Perumalil and E. R. Hambye (Alleppey: Prakasam Publications, 1973) 82–101; *History*, compiled by Kuriakose, 100–101.

7. Firth, *Introduction*, 89.

8. For some signs of missionary activity of ancient Thomas Christians, see Thenayan, *Missionary Consciousness;* for the opposite view, see J. A. Sharrock, *South Indian Missions Containing Glimpses into the Lives and Customs of the Tamil People* (Westminster: Society for Propagation of the Gospel in Foreign Parts, 1910) 295.

9. Tisserant, *Eastern Christianity*, 166.

10. Jerome D'Souza, "Christianity," in *The Gazeteer of India* (New Delhi, 1965) 1:498. See also Swami Vivekananda, "Address to the Parliament of Religions," in *History*, compiled by Kuriakose, 262.

11. The Benedictine monastery of Asirvanam at Bangalore, India, holds a yearly seminar on Hindu-Christian spirituality and publishes its papers.

12. *Encyclopaedia*, ed. Menacherry, 2:107; see also 4:107–11; Podipara, *Thomas Christians*, 80–85; Brown, *Indian Christians*, 167–74; *Christianity in India*, ed. Perumalil and Hambye, 35–37; Firth, *Introduction*, 88–93.

13. *Christianity in India*, ed. Perumalil and Hambye, 82.

14. *Encyclopaedia*, ed. Menacherry, 2:187.

15. B. Griffiths, "A Hindu Christianity," *The Tablet* (28 January, 1984) 93.

16. Jerome D'Souza, "Christianity," *The Tablet* (28 January, 1984) 93.

17. P. C. Mozoomdar, *The Oriental Christ* (Boston: Geo. H. Ellis, 1883) 13.

18. *History*, compiled by Kuriakose, 232. The Thomas Christians of Kerala observe an indianized Eucharist in their homes on Maundy Thursday night with homemade bread and a sweet drink make from the flesh of coconut fruit.

19. Sadhu Ittyavirah of Kerala has been until recently a wandering Christian holy man in the Indian style, meeting people of all classes and creeds and instructing them on the fatherhood of God and the brotherhood of people in Jesus, as has been well described by S. Rayan in *Modern Mission Dialogue* (Shannon, 1968) 29–45. Ittyavirah is now married and settled down, but has not apparently given up the sadhuhood. It may further be noted here that Indian tradition knows also married sadhus and *ṛṣis*. It is again noteworthy that married monkhood also is being approvingly discussed in some Christian (Catholic) circles; see R. Panikkar, *Blessed Simplicity: The Monk as Universal Archetype* (New York: Seabury Press, 1982) 113–34.

20. The martyrs are four Franciscan missionaries, Thomas, James, Peter, and Demetrius, mentioned in the letter of Friar Jordanus of Thana, Bombay, in 1321 (see *History*, compiled by Kuriakose, 16–17). The following are among the holy people whose esteem has been growing since their death: Fr. Jose Vaz, Goa; Fr. Angelo, Bombay; Sr. Alphonsa, Kerala; Fr. Kuriakose Elias, Kerala; Catholicos Mar Basilios, Kerala; St Mar Gregorios of Parumala, Kerala; Mar Ivanios, Kerala; Fr. Kunjachan, Kerala; Mariam Theresa, Kerala; and Br. Joseph Thamby of Andhra Pradesh.

21. *In Quest of the Absolute: The Life and Work of Jules Monchanin*, ed. and trans. J. G. Weber (Kalamazoo, Mich.: Cistercian Publications, 1977) 31.

22. It is the basic religious openness of Hindus that enables them to approve and appreciate the greatness of non-Hindu religions and saints. While many of them have written reverently on Christ and Christian themes, there is hardly any such writing on Hindu themes or saints from the Christian side until recently. Vallothal, a great Hindu Keralite poet, seems to have grasped Jesus' mind more deeply than Christians themselves as he sang about the encounter of Jesus and the penitent woman at the house of Simon thus: "Maiden, go without pining. . . . For your many sins, This your hearty repentance is enough penance." Have not the Christian clergy been breaking their heads for centuries at the confessional trying to prescribe a just or right penance for those who approach them with the confession of their sins!

23. B. Griffiths, *Marriage of East and West*, 167–68.

24. J. Monchanin and H. Le Saux, *A Benedictine Ashram* (rev. ed.; Douglas: Times Press, 1964) 33.

25. B. Griffiths in *Indian Spirituality in Action*, ed. Sr. Vandana (Bombay: Asia Publishing, 1973) 10.

26. D'Souza, "Christianity," in *Gazeteer* 1:489.

27. *History*, compiled by Kuriakose, 268.

28. Abhishiktananda, *Prayer* (New Delhi: ISPC, 1979) 70–75.

29. On Christian *ashrams*, see M. O'Toole, *Christian Ashram Communities in India* (Indore: Satprakashan, 1983); R. P. Saxena, *A Directory of Ashrams in India and Abroad* (Mathura: Ashram Publications, 1973); Vandana, *Gurus, Ashrams and Christians;* S. Jesudason, *Ashrams Ancient and Modern, Their Aims and Ideals;* Muz Murray, *Seeking the Master, A Guide to the Ashrams of India* (St. Helier, Eng.: Neville Spearman, 1980).

30. Griffiths, *Marriage*, 7–8.

31. M. K. Gandhi, *All Men Are Brothers* (Paris: UNESCO, 1959) 59.

32. Griffiths, *Marriage*, 203.

33. R. W. Taylor, *Religion and Society* (Madras: CLS, 1982) 273.

34. *Collected Works of Mahatma Gandhi* (New Delhi: Publications Division, Ministry of Information and Broadcasting, 1958) 68:278.

35. Gandhi, *All Men Are Brothers: Autobiographical Reflections*, ed. Krishna Kripalani (New York: Continuum, 1980) 60.

36. B. R. Nanda, *Gandhi and his Critics* (Delhi: Oxford University Press, 1985) 6.

37. Calvin Kytle, *Gandhi, Soldier of Nonviolence: His Effect on India and the World Today* (New York: Grosset & Dunlap, 1969) 3.

38. M. K. Gandhi, *The Science of Satyagraha*, ed. A. T. Hingorani (Bombay, 1962) 1.

39. *Collected Works of Mahatma Gandhi*, 30:71.

40. Robin H. S. Boyd, *An Introduction to Indian Christian Theology* (rev. ed.; Madras, 1975) 164.

Bibliography

Abhishiktananda. *Saccidananda, A Christian Approach to Advaitic Experience.* Delhi: ISPCK, 1974.

Amalorpavadass, D. S., ed. *Indian Christian Spirituality.* Bangalore: NBCLC, 1982.

Appasamy, A. J. *An Indian Interpretation of Christianity.* Madras: CLS, 1924.

Boyd, Robin H. S. *An Introduction to Indian Christian Theology.* Madras: CLS, 1975.

Brown, Leslie W. *The Indian Christians of St. Thomas: An Account of the Ancient Syrian Church of Malabar.* Cambridge: Cambridge University Press, 1956.

Chakkarai, V. *Jesus the Avatar.* Madras: CLS, 1932.

Devanandan, P. D. *Christian Concern in Hinduism.* Bangalore: CISRS, 1961.

Farquhar, J. N. "The Apostle Thomas in North India." *Bulletin of the John Rylands Library* 10 (1926) 80–111.

——. "The Apostle Thomas in South India." *Bulletin of the John Rylands Library* 11 (1927) 20–50.

Firth, C. B. *An Introduction to Indian Church History.* Reprint. Madras: CLS, 1968.

Griffiths, Bede. *The Marriage of East and West.* London: Collins, 1982.

Jesudason, S. *Ashrams Ancient and Modern, Their Aims and Ideals.* Vellore: S. R. Press, 1937.

Klostermaier, K. *Hindu and Christian in Vrindaban.* London: SCM, 1979.

——. *Christvidya: A Sketch of an Indian Christology.* Bangalore: CISRS, 1967.

Kuriakose, M. K., compiler. *History of Christianity in India: Source Materials.* Bangalore: Christian Literature Society, 1982.

Malancheruvil, C. *The Syro-Malankara Church.* Alwaye: Pontifical Institute of Theology and Philosophy, 1978.

Mattam, J. *Land of the Trinity: A Study of Modern Christian Approaches To Hinduism.* Bangalore: TPI, 1975.

Perumalil, A. C. *The Apostles in India: Fact or Fiction?* Patna: Catholic Book Crusades, 1952.

Podipara, P. J. *The Thomas Christians.* Bombay: St. Paul Publications, 1970.

Religious Hinduism. Edited by Jesuit Scholars. 2nd rev. ed. Allahabad: St. Paul Publication, 1964.

Thomas, M. M. *The Acknowledged Christ of Indian Renaissance.* Madras: CLS, 1970.

Tisserant, E. *Eastern Christianity in India.* London: Longmans, 1957.

Vandana, Sister. *Gurus, Ashrams and Christians.* London: Darton, Longman & Todd, 1978.

27

The Spiritual Experience in Sikhism

Nikky-Guninder Kaur Singh

Rather than "turning around from facing the world to face God," or a commitment to "worldlessness," the Sikh religious landscape is marked by a "turning fully into the world." The Sikh religion originated with the epiphanic experience of Gurū Nānak (1469–1539), and his unique inheritance was crystallized by his nine successors within a philosophically, religiously, and culturally rich milieu. Scholars of comparative religion can draw many exciting parallels between and among the vocabulary, concepts, and practices in Sikhism, Hinduism, Islam, and Buddhism, as they all interacted so closely and vibrantly on the North Indian soil. But unlike many of the other traditions, Sikhism has regarded the world as a positive space, inclusive of both divine creation and the secular sphere. "Turning fully into the world" therefore denotes a recognition of the Absolute significance of our natural and social context and an authentic existence in it. In the Sikh *Weltanshauung*, world and Ultimate Reality are not antithetically perceived; the temporal world is a part of the Infinite Reality and partakes of its characteristics. Here spirituality with the age-old human quest to seek liberation is oriented toward a vision of an all-pervasive singular transcendent Reality. The metaphysical experience in Sikhism is not apart or separate from the physical; rather, the deeper the awareness of the Transcendent, the more vibrant is the participation in the everyday world.

Gurū Nānak's *Jap*, the first hymn recorded in the *Gurū Granth*, the Sikh scripture, outlines a journey going through five spiritual spheres. The *Jap* opens with a theological assertion—the existence of a Singular Reality (*Ikk Oan Kār*); it closes with a spiritual journey toward That Reality. In thirty-eight stanzas, the *Jap* presents the quintessence of Sikh theology and spirituality. In this chapter we will focus on the spiritual journey which proceeds through the realms of *Dharam*, *Gyān*, *Saram*, *Karam* and culminates in the *Sach Khand*. A journey through these five realms remains the aspiration of devout Sikhs actively engaged in the world. Daily hectic schedules are prefaced in Sikh homes by a recitation of Gurū Nānak's hymn in the early part of the morning. Not asceticism or world renunciation but ethical engagement is the consequence of the metaphysical journey.

In fact, the theological and spiritual dimensions are so closely linked in Sikh life that even in the conception of Ultimate Reality, the individual experience is underscored. The *Jap* begins with *Ikk Oan Kār,* which is the quintessential statement of the Sikh faith. It remains central to their aural and visual world. Not only does *Ikk Oan Kār* form the very beginning of the *Gurū Granth,* but it is also repeated throughout the sacred text as a preface to many different sections. Similarly, it is ubiquitous in Sikh art and architecture, where we find it elaborately inscribed in silk, marble, steel, and gold. In his commentary on the *Jap*, the renowned Sikh scholar Bhai Vir Singh calls it *bīj mantra*—the root formula.[1] Although it is called a *mantra*, Sikhs do not regard it as a secret formula; on the contrary, it is for all a most apparent disclosure of the Transcendent. Indeed, it is a clear assertion and celebration of the One formless ontological ground of all that exists.

This essential Sikh theological statement is undergirded by an experiential dimension. It is no coincidence that from the rich variety of Sanskrit, Persian, and Arabic terms at his disposal, Gurū Nānak should have used *Oan* to articulate that One. *Oan* is the Punjabi equivalent of the Sanskrit word for being, *Aum* or *Oṃ*. *Aum* is expounded with much intellectual sophistication in Hindu scriptures. In the *Māṇḍūkya Upaniṣad*, it is explained as a four-tier psychological journey.[2] The fourfold *Māṇḍūkya* analysis begins with the first stage, "A", which is the realm of consciousness in which there is an awareness of the world existing out there. It is basically a stage in which the subject is contrasted with the objects, the self versus others. The second, "U", stage is the psychological state of the semi-conscious, where absolute categories start breaking down. The logical world begins to dissolve and there is an expansion of the self. One could, for instance, be in different places at the same time. The third stage, that of "M," is the deep sleep state, the state of utter unconsciousness, but here one does not experience anything. It is a state of utter oblivion. The final stage, the fourth one, in which the A and the U and the M are fused together, is the experience of totality. This is the unity that one is deeply aware of, a unity that one fully enjoys, a unity where the self is totally cognizant of its becoming Oneness Itself. Gurū Nānak's usage of *Oan* in the Sikh primal statement manifests the theological and spiritual nexus of the Sikh religion: the Ultimate is an inner, subjective experience of Infinity rather than an objective knowledge of a God out there. In turn, the five *Khands* enunciated in stanzas 34 through 37 at the close of the *Jap* reinforce the centrality of the Transcendent in the undertaking of the spiritual voyage.

Dharam Khand

The first is the *Dharam Khand*, the sphere of Duty.[3] Although the term *dharam* retains its Sanskrit meaning ("what holds together"), Gurū Nānak does not specify any duties in accordance with injunctions of the traditional *śāstras*. Gurū Nānak's usage has a very different meaning from that of the Hindu ideal, which regards the continuity of customary and conventional practices as *dharma*. In the *Bhagavad Gītā*, for example, Lord Kṛṣṇa instructs that Arjuna fight against the Kurus—in order to uphold his *dharma* as a Kṣatriya. Gurū Nānak's *Dharam Khand* does not prescribe the customary fourfold division of Hindu society into Brahmins, Kṣatriyas, Vaiśyas, and Śūdras, nor does it institute a division of the stages of life into that of *brahmacārin*, *grihastha*, *vānaprastha*, and *sannyāsin* (*varṇāśrama dharma*). In contrast to the fourfold societal hierarchy and its corresponding privileges, duties, and responsibilities, there is in this first spiritual stage an emphasis on equality. Everyone is equally impelled to perform one's ethical duty throughout one's entire life.

The universal and egalitarian structure of *Dharam Khand* is expressed in its very constitution:

> Amidst nights, seasons, solar and lunar days
> Amidst air, water, fire and netherworld
> The earth is placed, the place for righteous action. (*Gurū Granth* 7)

Clearly, *Dharam Khand* is described as a region made up of nights (*rātī*) and seasons (*rutī*) and dates (*thitī*) and days (*vār*). Time with its lunar and solar cycles remains its major factor. Then all the elements—air, water, fire, and earth—and all their compounds make it up. The physical universe in time and space and in form constitutes the *Dharam Khand*. On this neutral graph with the axes of time and space, the planet earth is located. *Vic dhartī thāpi rakhī dharamsāl*, "the earth is set within," goes Gurū Nānak's verse in the *Jap*. The Mother Earth (*dhartī*) forms the stage for all agents to become active participants. There is no need to limit oneself to a particular time and space. The whole world is open to perform actions in it. The earth as the *Dharamsāl* provides opportunities that are open to all equally. The *Gurū Granth* affirms that all the four castes possess one and the same Order: *khatri brāman sūd vais, updes cahu varṇā ko sājhā*, "be they Kṣatriyas, Brahmins, Śūdras, or Vaiśyas, the Message is shared by people of all complexions" (*Gurū Granth* 747). This is very important for our day and time because the four castes are based on complexion (*varṇa* literally means color or complexion), and although castes may seem of the past, color and race are vitally important issues that we still need to face. So the Message, according to Gurū Nānak, is shared not just by people of the four castes but by people of all complexions. The *Gurū Granth* declares that *Dharam* succeeds when the entire earth becomes equal, literally one color: "*sristī sabh ikk varan hoī*" (663).

Earth for Gurū Nānak is the link which not only brings all humans beings together but also the myriad species:

> Within this infinite matrix are myriads of species,
> Infinite are their names and forms. (*Gurū Granth* 7)

Here plurality and multiplicity depict a world that is colorful and vibrant. Without any monopolization or manipulation, the innumerable varieties of species remain interconnected, coexisting harmoniously with one another. There is no implication of any disjunctions or divisions of gender, race, and class in this organic Earth. The designation of earth as the *dharamsāl* (House of *dharam*) brings together her ontological and epistemological functions: she is the womb to which all beings owe their origin; she is the matrix where the infinite number of creatures can act ethically and purposefully. In *Dharam Khand*, the region of duty, everyone actually practices his or her way of life with its ethical standards. The earth as the stage for righteous action is reaffirmed by Gurū Arjan: *karma bhūmi mahi boahu nāmu*, "In the field (*bhūmi*) of actions (*karma*), sow the seed of devotion (*nām*)" (*Gurū Granth* 176). The earth, referred to as *dhartī* or *bhūmi*, provides us first with existence itself and then with the opportunity to engage in moral and ethical action. Earthly existence is not to be renounced but is to be lived fully and intensely. Without the earth, there is no being, and without her no meaningful or wise action. There is no inherent nature–culture split. She is necessary. The journey begins with her.

In Gurū Nānak's articulation of *Dharam Khand* we also discern an intrinsic bond between "earth" and "body." While earth is regarded as the *dharamsāl*, the body is regarded as *dharam* itself: *eh sariru sabhu dharam hai jis andari sace kī vici joti*, "This body entire is *dharam* for the divine spark remains within" (*Gurū Granth* 309). In this verse, Gurū Ram Das reiterates Gurū Nānak's perspective that the essential ingredient of *dharam* is the physical and the material. In *Rāg Māru*, Gurū Amar Das identifies the body with earth: *tanu dhartī hari bījīai*, "the body is the earth with the Divine as the seed" (ibid. 997). Gurū Amar Das also identifies the body with the earth: *ehu tanu dharatī sabadu bīji apāru*, "this body is the earth in which the infinite word is sown" (ibid. 1048). Just as earthly existence is not to be shunned, nor is the body, which sustains the infinite word. There is no Cartesian duality between body and mind in the Sikh world. The duality that not only splits one part of the self from the other but also has a built-in mechanism that degrades the one and exalts the other is negated by the Sikh Gurūs in their very articulation of the body as *dharam*. With *Dharam Khand* as the first stage, Body (*dharam*) and Earth (*dharamsāl*) are celebrated as the starting point of the spiritual odyssey.

Dharam Khand further maintains a fluid relationship between here and there, form and formless, finite and infinite. This entire "body" is *dharam* precisely because of the divine spark within it. It is after all the timeless, spaceless, genderless, causeless metaphysical spark (*joti*) that informs the myriad forms of this physical region. The *Gurū Granth* maintains that *joti* inheres within all humans equally. Similes of fire, which is within all vegetation, and of butter, which is within all kinds of milk, elaborate the point that all of creation is sustained by the divine light (617). In fact, the *Gurū* asserts, *e sarirā meriā hari tum mahi joti rakhī tā tu jag mahi āiā*, "everybody takes on material form only because of *joti*, the spiritual insertion by the Transcendent One" (921).

Throughout the *Gurū Granth* we find many interesting verses with a variety of nuances coming together to underscore the spiritual ingredient of our body:

> *naunidhi amrit prabh kā nāmu*
> *dehī mahi is kā bisrāmu*
> The ambrosial treasures of divine name rest within the body itself. (293)

> *jo brahmande soī pinde*
> Whatever lies in paradise beyond that in the body here can be found. (695)

> *kāiā harimandiru hari āpi savāre*
> Body is the home of the Divine One and by the Divine One is the body maintained. (1059)

> *kāiā andari āpe vasai alakhu na lakhiā jāī*
> Within the body the One dwells, but the ineffable One remains unfathomable. (754)

> *āsā manasā ehu sarir hai antari joti jagāe*
> Hope and desire are this body, illuminated by the inner light. (559)

sabhi ras dehī andari pāe/virale kau guru sabadu bujhāe
andaruru khoje sabadu salāhe bāhar kāhe jāhā he
The body contains all the treasures
but only one in a million recognizes.
Exalt the word within the self. Why stray outside? (1056)

merai kartai ikk banati banāī isu dehī vici sabh vathu pāī
My creator created a marvel: all treasures are deposited
in this very body. (1064)

We find many different terms used for the body, *tanu*, *deh*, *kāiā*, *pind*, but in each case it is maintained that the body houses the Divine Reality. Although the Infinite resides within the body, it is not a pantheistic notion, for the Infinite is never capsuled in the body as such. Infinite and Formless, the Sikh Ultimate is inherent within all and yet remains Transcendent. What is expressed throughout the *Gurū Granth* is the closeness of the spiritual goal: it is within the self. The overall result is a validation of the individual self, the affirmation of the material body, the celebration of all bodies irrespective of gender, race, class, and culture. Since the transcendent goal does not lie up high somewhere out there, we need not climb up anywhere. With its impulse toward the interior, we would be more correct in viewing the journey through Gurū Nānak's five *Khands* as a horizontally inward process rather than an "ascension," as it is usually categorized by scholars.[4] The spiritual journey in Sikhism is a retreat into the ground of our own selves—into the depths of our own being and existence. This entry into oneself brings to mind the recent revisioning of God by feminists in the West who have rejected the ideal notion of a white male God sitting out there and have instead re-visioned a spirit within.[5] This emphasis placed by contemporary writers on an inner experience of the Divine seems to emerge from the Sikh conception and perception of the Divine within the body.

However, the retreat within cannot be understood as renunciation of the social realm. Since the entire earth is *Dharamsāl*, there is no special spot demarcated for ethical duties. Morality is not fostered in some distant cave or faraway forest; rather it is practiced in the immediate world of here and now. Gurū Nānak repeatedly rejects a departure from the home and the world. This is such an important aspect of Gurū Nānak's teaching that when Bhai Gurdas, the first Sikh historian-theologian, wishes to narrate the beginnings of Sikhism, it is precisely this very theme that he focuses on. In one of his ballads he portrays a vivid scene in which the first Sikh Gurū meets with some *siddhas* on Mount Kailash. In the dialogue that ensues, Bhai Gurdas quotes Gurū Nānak denouncing the *siddhas*' retirement from the everyday world and their practicing of austerities on remote mountaintops.[6] Sikh spirituality is marked not by isolation but in relationships with others. We notice also that the body which is identified with *dharam* is metaphorically expressed as a home (*ghari*) (*Gurū Granth* 126); as a fort containing a bustling bazaar (*garh kāiā andari bahu hat bājārā*) (ibid. 1053); as gold (*kancanu*) (ibid. 585, 1064); as a smithy (*ehu tanu hātu sarāf ko*) (ibid. 636); and as a city within which resides the Ultimate One (*kāiā nagari nagari hari basio*) (ibid. 1336). This particular plurality of images presents a lively engagement in the social, economic, and political world. Discipline is not divorced from the home. Gold, bazaars, shops, smithies, and cities evoke a life lived within the usual hustle and bustle. Spiritual discipline is not against or in opposition to the home and the secular. Gurū Nānak's description of *Dharam Khand* implies an immersion into the particular and material and secular world.

What is stressed in Sikhism is the recognition of the Infinite One. The *Gurū* makes an appeal: *man tūn joti sarūpu hai, apnā mulu pachāni,* "recognize the spiritual treasure with which you are endowed."[7] There is something that prevents the individual from recognizing the Ultimate: it is *haumai,* which literally means "I-myself" (*hau-main*). It is investing oneself with pride and arrogance. By constantly centering on "I" and "me" and "mine," the self is circumscribed as a particular person, alienated from fellow beings, turned away from the universal source. Earlier in the *Jap* Gurū Nānak provides the image of a wall: just as a wall creates barriers, so does *haumai.* By building up the ego, the individual is divided from the One Reality. Duality comes into play. The ego sees itself in opposition to others, in opposition to the cosmos. The divine spark within remains obstructed. The singular harmony is broken. Such an existence is measured through competition, malice, ill-will toward others, and a craving for power. Blinded, the individual exists for himself/herself alone. In Sikh terminology, the self-willed person is called *manmukh* (turned toward oneself) in contrast with *gurmukh* (turned toward the Gurū) who remains in harmony with the divine word. Dominated by *haumai*, the person never experiences the joy and infinity of the Divine spark within. *Haumai* is a solid chain tightly binding humans into the cycle of death and life.

But *haumai* can be overcome. The walls of egotism can be shattered. A *manmukh* can become a *gurmukh*. Instead of being enmeshed in the selfish "I" one can become oriented toward the Divine Reality. Instead of being in bondage to the individual ego one can achieve the joy of Infinity. Gurū Nānak's answer lies in a simple maxim: *suniā*, *maniā*, *mani kītā bhāu*. He offers these three precepts in the *Jap* itself.

Suniā literally signifies hearing, and in the *Jap* it means hearkening to the divine word. It is the first step toward awakening to the Transcendent Core of the universe. Hearing is the sense that most directly connects the conscious and the unconscious realms. According to Gurū Nānak, by listening to the melodious Name, one fathoms the oceans of virtue. Stanzas 8 through 11 of the *Jap* explain the vital role of listening. Through listening one accomplishes the faculties of all the gods, one gains knowledge of all the continents, one acquires the import of all the ancient texts, one learns all the techniques of meditation, one masters the expertise of all the Hindu and Muslim sages, and through listening all suffering and distress are annulled. By hearing the Divine Name the ultimate objective is achieved: one becomes immortal and is freed from the finitude of death. The refrain in these stanzas acknowledges that the devotees who hear the Name of the True One remain in constant bliss.

Although the Transcendent Reality is beyond all human terminology, words are important for they give us an inkling of the Formless One. Gurū Nānak clearly maintains that the divine Names and the divine places are countless, and the countless worlds are inaccessible and unfathomable. Yet through words we name, through words we extol, through words we know, sing, and discuss. Through words all communication is conducted and expressed, and they are sanctioned by the Truth: "As the One utters, that is how the words are arranged." Hearing the divine word constitutes the first step for Gurū Nānak. Through sound one is initiated into an awareness of the Reality that permeates all space and time.

Maniā means paying heed. It is the second step, for it is only after something is heard that full trust and confidence can be placed in it. For Gurū Nānak this state is ineffable: Who is to describe it? In what words? On what paper? With what pen? Heeding the divine word is something that cannot be discussed or analyzed. However, Gurū Nānak also describes the state of faith in positive terms: through faith, mind and intellect become more conscious. It is the pathway to liberation, wide open to everybody. By believing in the Divine Word, one not only emancipates oneself from the constant bondage of birth and death but also assists in liberating one's family and friends. Implicit here is the Sikh ethical structure, one in which self and society are integrally related. The individual is interconnected with the community, the Ultimate One linking each and every one together harmoniously.

Mani kītā bhāu means to be full of love. This state of devotion is the third step, one that goes beyond hearing the Divine Name, and having faith in it. It is being drenched in love. Love is passionate and takes lovers to those depths of richness and fullness where there is freedom from all kinds of limitations and barriers. Gurū Nānak appropriates love as the highest form of action:

> Hearing, remembering, and loving the Name,
> Immerses us in the sacred fount within. (*Gurū Granth* 4–5)

Purgation through love and devotion is the starting point of Sikh life. Again and again in the *Gurū Granth*, love is applauded as the supreme virtue:

> They who worship the One with adoring love and
> thirst for Its True Love,
> They who beseechingly cry out discover peace,
> for in their heart lies love. (505)

The centrality of love distinguishes Gurū Nānak's triple formula from that which we find in the Upaniṣads. The Upaniṣads mention three preparatory stages to God-vison: *śravaṇa*, *manana*, and *nididhyāsana*, translated by Radhakrishnan as hearing, reflection, and contemplation.[8] There are indeed striking similarities between the first two processes in the Upaniṣads and *Jap*, but the substitution of *prema* (love) for *dhyāna* (contemplation) clearly sets the Sikh and Upanisadic approaches apart. *Dhyāna* requires a process of abstraction and isolation and a departure "to a field or a forest where the world and its noise are out of sight."[9] Such an approach is too narrow, excessively intellectual, and exclusive since it is applicable only to scholars sitting at the feet of a master. Gurū Nānak opens up this experience by setting love for the Transcendent within our world with its everyday sounds and sights. Emotion and passion take the place of *dhyāna*. By falling in love, freedom from all kinds of constraints is obtained. This powerful emotion dissolves the individual ego and opens avenues to experiencing the Other with an inexpressible intensity and richness.

Gurū Nānak and his successors explore the power of intimacy and passion in the human relationship with the Divine through the symbol of the bride who is forever seeking union with her Groom. They express the ardent love for the Ultimate Reality through the image and tone of a young woman. Sikh scripture is permeated with the longing for a vision of the Formless One: "Day and night, I thirst for a sight of the Groom." Following Gurū Nānak, the tenth Gurū, Gurū Gobind Singh, underscored the role of love and made it the pathway to the Infinite One. It is a central theme in his compositions: "Only they who love find the Ultimate Reality." For the Sikh Gurūs overall, love was to be the only path to ultimate liberation: "they who have love within their hearts alone are emancipated."[10]

Dharam Khand can be seen as the stage that provides intimations of the Transcendent, leading to reflections on and faith in It, and ultimately an urge to unite with It. It is in the *Dharam Khand* that senses, beliefs, intelligence, and emotions are awakened, and the spiritual itinerant discerns the Ultimate destination and begins to aspire to It. But this primal stage of the spiritual journey has a soteriological function as well, for Gurū Nānak says: *nadari karami pavai nīsānu*, "through *nadar* the actions (*karam*) are acknowledged (*pavai nīsānu*) by the One" (*Gurū Granth* 7). Besides the individual's own faculties, *nadar*, the benevolent glance of the Transcendent is also received here. Everyone in the *Dharam Khand* is provided with the opportunity to act ethically and purposefully. Earthly existence is not to be shunned but is to be lived fully and intensely. Actions are important, for whatever is done has an effect: as we sow, so do we reap. The sense of morality is developed in this region. The Truthful One is true; Its earth is also true. And by means of the benevolent glance, ethical conduct in the physical universe is rewarded, and the person can then launch on to the next stage of the spiritual journey.

Gyān Khand

Gurū Nānak's description of *Gyān Khand*, the Region of Knowledge, is prefaced by an indirect question. From a strictly grammatical point of view the term *ākhau* in the verse *giān khand kā ākhau karamu* ("tell us the actions of the realm of knowledge") is in the imperative form. The mode of searching and questioning is thus set up as the backdrop to this sphere of knowledge. That he would search for "actions" (*karamu*) in his introduction to the realm of knowledge further establishes the importance of conduct and performance for Gurū Nānak. Knowledge is not to be pursued for its own sake; it must have its practical manifestation. This principle forms the prelude to the *Gyān Khand*.

The opening of the *Gyān Khand* will appear curious until we realize that knowledge and social responsibility are not two separate paths. In the first line in stanza 35 of the *Jap*, which is really a description of the stage of knowledge, Gurū Nānak is still summing up the *Dharam Khand*. That ethical duty and intellectual enlightenment are close to each other is implied in his compositional technique. Actually, this pattern is repeated throughout the exposition of the five *Khands* because they are not cut apart from each other. The different stanzas of the *Jap* do not elaborate each of them separately; rather, one rhythmically flows into the other illustrating the intimacy of one with the other.

In this second stage, the individual becomes cognizant of the vastness of creation. The vastness of creation seems to be evidenced in several ways—through physical nature, through metaphysical deities, through languages, through political figureheads, and through devotees from different religious backgrounds. Innumerable varieties of atmosphere, water, and fire are acknowledged. The region is made up of millions of inhabited planets like our mother earth (*ketiā karam bhūmi*), countless mountains (*mer kete*), countless moons (*kete cand*), suns (*sūr*), and constellations (*mandal des*). In this widened horizon, terrestrial and celestial worlds are not split asunder and the earth is not put under the skies.

This sphere also contains innumerable gods and goddesses:

> . . . zillions of Kṛṣṇas and Śivas,
> How many Brahmās were created in millions of forms!
> Countless *siddhas, buddhas, nāthas*, and so many, many goddesses.
> (*Gurū Granth* 7)

Here the goddesses take equal place with the male gods. From Gurū Nānak's perspective, knowledge entails a perception of male and female figures from various Hindu, Buddhist, and Jaina schools. The expanded mind draws no inferences regarding gender or religion. Paradoxically, the countlessness of deities diminishes their significance in the Sikh view, enhancing at the same time the power of their maker, the Transcendent One. Gods and goddesses are a part of the created world. Many gods and goddesses are mentioned throughout the *Gurū Granth*, but they are understood differently from what they are in the Hindu point of view. In the Sikh world they are respected but they are not perceived as incarnations. The transcendent reality cannot be installed into any image or deity. Gurū Nānak and his successors were categorical in denouncing *avatārvād*. In the *Gyān Khand*, then, the individual's horizons are widened through seeing the vastness of nature and her innumerable gods and goddesses; this knowledge makes the individual stand fully in awe of the Invisible One, the Mysterium Tremendum. Gurū Nānak says, *aisā giān japahu man mere hovohu cākar sāce kere*, "Oh my mind meditate on that knowledge which would make me a slave of the Truthful One" (*Gurū Granth* 728).

Interestingly, in the *Gyān Khand* the spiritual voyager also discovers a diverse and plural world from a secular perspective:

> *ketīā khānī ketīā bānī kete pāt narind*
> *ketīā suratī sevak kete nānak ant na ant*
> How many species, how many languages
> and how many rulers and kings!
> How many revelations, how many devotees!
> says Nanak, There is no end to their end.

The diversity is reflected in an infinite number of species (*ketīā khānī*), including those born from the egg (*aṅdaj*), those born from the fetus (*jeraj*), those born from the sweat (*setaj*), and those born from the earth (*utbhuj*). It is reflected in the multiplicity of languages and cultures (*ketīā bānī*); it is reflected in the variety of political structures—the kings (*pāt*) and rulers (*narind*). Hierarchies and divisions have no place and no one species, language, culture, or country is put up higher than another. The panorama is a world without social discriminations, cultural dominations, and imperial oppressions. But in this stage of Gurū Nānak's spiritual journey, a simple encounter with diversity is not enough; it goes beyond mere tolerance and demands a response. The pluralism to which our modern society aspires underlies the *Gyān Khand*, for it is by truly responding to the Other that we become deeper in our own self.

As a response to infinity and diversity, the individual in this realm of "knowledge" experiences his/her own infinitesimalness. Knowledge in this sphere is not abstract; it is not an "idea." In Rudolph Otto's *Idea of the Holy*, mysticism is characterized by two distinctive notes: "We come upon the ideas, first of the annihilation of the self, and then, as its complement, of the transcendent as the sole and entire reality."[11] This is what happens in *Gyān Khand*. Realizing the infiniteness of the cosmos with its countless gods and goddesses, its myriad species, and its diverse cultures and systems, one experiences self-annihilation and recognizes the Transcendent as the sole and entire reality. In Otto's mystical world, however, it is ideas that constitute the realization; in *Gyān Khand* it is experience. This experience is described as follows:

> *gyān khand mahi gyānu parcandu*
> *tithai nād binod kod anandu*
> In the sphere of knowledge, knowledge blazes forth
> Here reign mystic melodies and myriad sports and joys.
> (*Gurū Granth* 7)

The "blazing of knowledge" immediately evokes the image of *joti* (light). A genuine response to diversity and a deep recognition of infinity burns off the walls of ego and leads to ineffable joy (*ānanda*). Knowledge has a sapiential quality, for it involves a joyful savoring. Knowledge is not a suppression of the senses nor an extinction of the self; rather, it is a celebration of the fullness surrounding the individual. It is really an ecstatic experience, one in which the individual goes beyond his/her finite self.

The experience of knowledge in this second region is delineated through feminine imagery which captures its beauty, radiance, power (the brilliant flame) and joy (music and dance are prevalent in this sphere). In a way, *joti*—the transcendental light, totally immaterial and insubstantial—appears at this stage shining forth palpably and physically. The mental illumination of the individual is the core of this sensuous experience, and it is appropriately expressed in such concrete imagery. Ironically, *Gyān Khand*, or the Realm of Knowledge in the Sikh *Weltanschauung*, does not parallel the concept of "Pure" Knowledge that we find for instance in Greek philosophy. In the writings of Plato and Aristotle, transcendent mind remains far above feelings and passions. Feminist thealogians have condemned this division, which has remained the basis of Western philosophy. Speaking of Aristotle's *Politics* and Plato's *Timaeus*, Rosemary Radford Ruether writes that Greek philosophy has subjugated matter or body to be ruled by or shunned by transcendent mind.[12] In the *Gyān Khand* of the *Jap*, experience—feelings and passions—are totally fused in with the mind and ideas! Mind and Body are not split apart.

Gurū Nānak's description of *Gyān Khand* is reminiscent of the path of knowledge put forth by Kṛṣṇa in the *Bhagavad Gītā*. The simile of the lamp is shared by both Lord Kṛṣṇa and Gurū Nānak. In the *Gītā* the path of knowledge is described poetically through the lamp on a windless night (6.19). The unfluctuating flame illustrates total self-control. Kṛṣṇa's usage of the simile of the tortoise withdrawing its limbs from all sides further establishes the importance of controlling the mind by divorcing it from the external world (2.58). In chapter 6 of the *Gītā* the path of knowledge is clearly enunciated: it begins with the disciplined person "abiding in a secret place, solitary, restraining his thoughts and soul. . . . In a clean place establishing a steady seat for himself . . . even body, head and neck holding motionless, steady, gazing at the tip of his own nose and not looking in any direction."[13] In contrast to the unflickering lamp in a windless night, knowledge in the Sikh context is imaged as blazing forth (*giān khand mahi giānu parcandu*). In *Rāg Sūhī* it is repeated: *giānu pracandu baliā*—"the flame of knowledge was set ablaze" (*Gurū Granth* 774). Such "flaring" and "blazing" imagery denotes a gusty and passionate attitude. As the individual views the myriad species, planets, cultures, and divinities, there is not a tortoiselike recoiling but rather an ecstatic leaping.

Yogic techniques do not find any place in Gurū Nānak's *Gyān Khand*. We find no mention of a secret place or solitariness or the practice of meditation. Steadiness of mind or intellectual refinement is not brought through physical techniques. Actually, by medieval times, yoga with its varied schools had proliferated throughout Northern India. Hatha Yoga along with Rāja Yoga, Śaktism, and *Kuṇḍalinī*, emphasizing *āsana* (bodily postures) and *prāṇāyāma* (breath control) and other bodily exertions to induce levitation and exalted states of consciousness were prevalent.[14] But Gurū

Nānak and his successors continually rejected all prescribed texts, bodily exercises, and ritualistic techniques to induce higher states of consciousness. In *Rāg Mārū* Gurū Nānak says clearly:

> Some wander about naked and hungry,
> Others force themselves to death by undergoing austerities (*hatha*)
> Some go on pilgrimages, fast, and starve themselves,
> Others burn away their bodies before blazing fires;
> But without the Divine Name, there is no liberation.
> Without the Divine Name, how to cross this ocean?
> (*Gurū Granth* 1043)

He repeated his disapproval of yogic techniques in *Vār Rāmkalī*:

> Through practice of *hatha* (yoga) the body is emaciated,
> Through fasting and penances the mind is not absorbed
> in the love of the One. (*Gurū Granth* 905)

Again, in *Rāg Mārū*:

> Ritual cleansing of the intestines and igniting the furnace of
> *bhuiangam*,
> The inhaling, exhaling, and controlling of breath,
> All these are but outward shows of religion and do not
> lead to true love for the One . . . (*Gurū Granth* 1043)

Throughout the *Gurū Granth,* the Sikh Gurūs reject enfeebling the body, fasting and starving (*bhūkeh bhave* or *anu nā khāvehi*), and practicing austerities (*hathu kari*); they reject kindling the power of the hidden serpent in one's body known as *bhuiaṅgam* or *kuṇḍalinī;* they reject the technique of breath control (*recak*, exhaling; *pūrak*, inhaling; and *kuṁbhak*, keeping the breath in); and they reject physical pain such as withstanding the heat of burning flames (*agani jalāvehi*). Knowledge cannot be acquired through rigorous physical and mental techniques.

Instead, the various metaphors for *giān* in the *Gurū Granth* are more in tune with the everyday life. The term *anjani* (mascara) is often used for *giān*:

> *giān anjanu jākī netrī pariā tākau sarab prakāsā*
> Those who have their eyes lined with knowledge,
> for them everything becomes illuminated.

In contrast to the arduous path of yogis and ascetics, Sikh scripture presents a delectable way. By bedecking the eyes with knowledge, the entire cosmos comes to shine. Made up with mascara and eyeliner, eyes become striking; these in turn can see through the material and glimpse into the transcendent dimension. As the eyeliner of knowledge is gently put, the pitch heavy darkness of ignorance disappears (293, 573). The equation between eyesight and insight, physical eye and mental eye, seeing and knowledge, has been arrestingly brought out in Sikh scripture. When the dark veil of duality is lifted, the intrinsic, transcendent core of the infinite universe becomes brilliantly elucidated. In the Sikh world, dressing up in fineries is not rejected. There are some lovely verses in the *Gurū Granth* that describe the very positive and powerful consequences of physical makeup. Bodily adornment is representative of mental purification; cosmetics not only enhance physical appearance but also contribute to intellectual strength. In fact, cosmetics like the mascara or eye liner acquire a transcendent value, disclosing the infinite in this very world. Similarly, all external rituals and pilgrimages are rejected, giving primacy to the font of knowledge within:

> The pilgrimage spot is knowledge
> and the true Gurū shows its location inside the very self.
> (*Gurū Granth* 587)

In Sikhism, the efficacy of paying homage at sacred spots is attributed to knowledge, which remains within the person. For the person undertaking Gurū Nānak's spiritual journey all external visits are useless. Baths and purifications and paying homage take place inwardly. In *Rāg Dhanāsarī*, Gurū Nānak reiterates that pilgrimage constitutes contemplation of the divine word and an inner knowledge (*Gurū Granth* 687). Sikhism maintains the Socratic view that each individual is pregnant with knowledge, but Socrates perceived himself as the midwife who through his dialectic could bring forth knowledge. In the Sikh instance it is not discursive reasoning with the help of a "midwife" that brings about an epistemological disclosure but the sheer experience of multiplicity and infinity on a purely personal level.

Knowledge is also perceived as a sword. The infirmities of the psyche, such as ego, deceit, and desire, are obstacles that eclipse the vision of the Singular Being. The dark and opaque obstacles to luminosity are cut through by the sparkling and sharp sword of knowledge (*giān kharag*). The five brute obstacles to recognizing the inner transcendent source—*kāma*, *krodha*, *lobha*, *moha* and *ahankār*—are destroyed by swordlike knowledge (*Gurū Granth* 1022).

The lotus symbol central to the *Bhagavad Gītā* is used in Sikh literature, but again with a marked difference. In the *Gītā* the lotus is used to exemplify detachment: it represents the person of action, performing action in inaction. Existing within the murky waters of the world, the person remains—like the lotus—totally unattached to the fruits of the world. But in the *Gurū Granth*, the lotus carries an epistemological emphasis: the blossoming lotus represents the illuminated mind. While the ignorant person remains closed and stifled and knotted with all kinds of phobias and prejudices, true knowledge makes one bloom joyously like the lotus.

Knowledge as expressed in the *Gyān Khand* entails both knowing and seeing the diversity and infinity, whether of nature, deities, languages, or rulers. This combination of knowledge and seeing can be traced to the Indo-European root *vid*, which is found in Sanskrit *vidyā*, Latin *videre*, Greek *oida*, and English "wit." According to Franklin Edgerton, the belief of the early Vedic thinkers (one that was retained by Hindus of classical time) was to control the most fundamental and universal powers by knowing them. He points out that the Sanskrit word *vidyā* (knowledge) also means magic. "Whatever you know you control, directly, and by virtue of your knowledge. The primitive magician gets his neighbors, animal, human, or supernatural into his power, by acquiring knowledge of them."[15] Gurū Nānak, however, does not subscribe to such a notion about knowledge, because for him knowledge should not result in a domination and mastery over others. Furthermore, knowledge in Gurū Nānak's *Weltanschauung* consists not in magic or mastery over any traditional language, grammar, scripture, philosophy, or logical expertise. External and formal knowledge of ancient Hindu and Islamic texts, including the four Vedas and the Qur'an, is disregarded. Traditional scholars are even criticized for empty and loud preaching (*Gurū Granth* 86, 728). The *Gurū Granth* respects sacred scriptures from different traditions, but it is critical of their claims to an absolute and exclusive knowledge of reality.

Knowledge for Gurū Nānak is simply an opening for the individual: it is a re-cognition of infinity, which paradoxically leads to the experience of the infinitesimalness of the person. The littleness of the self is experienced in contrast with the infinitude of the cosmos. Any kind of intellectual arrogance dissolves. The individual ego is shattered. The subject does not view the world as an object out there but begins to experience an immediate relationship with its infinite inhabitants. The selfish manipulation of others gives way to an all-embracing sorority. According to Gurū Arjan, the truly enlightened person is inspired to do good to others (*Sukhmanī*). The *Gurū Granth* regards knowledge as an avenue for helping fellow beings (356). True knowledge destroys all kinds of limitations and prejudices and creates an all-accepting and welcoming attitude.

Saram Khand

The third stage is the *Saram Khand*. Most expositions of this *Khand* begin by stating how "unclear," "cryptic," or "disputed" the term *saram* is. Indeed, there are three possible origins for the word: the Sanskrit *śrama*, meaning "effort"; the Sanskrit *śarman*, meaning "joy" or "bliss"; and the Persian *śharm*, meaning "shame" with connotations of humility and surrender. We have thus three choices: this third stage could be the realm of effort; it could be the realm of joy; and it could be the realm of humility. I do not wish to argue for any of these. Instead, I would like to focus on the definition of the stage itself which is: *saram khand kī bānī rūpu*, "The form of *Saram Khand* is beauty itself" (*Gurū Granth* 7). The artistic form (*bānī* here does not mean "word" but is derived from the term *banāvat*, meaning "creation," "formation," or "art") of this region is beauty itself (*rūp*)! *Saram Khand* can be inferred as the realm of art where things are chiseled and beautified. Their exquisiteness is beyond description:

> Its praise cannot be put into words,
> Whosoever tries must regret [the inadequacy].
> (*Gurū Granth* 8)

Although nothing of this region of beauty itself can be described in words, several human faculties are mentioned which get sharpened here:

> *tithai gharīai surati mati mani buddhi*
> Here are sharpened consciousness, wisdom,
> mind, and discrimination. (*Gurū Granth* 8)

Saram Khand is understood as a dynamic realm in which a lot of activity takes place. Here wisdom (*mati*) along with consciousness (*surati*), mind (*man*), and the power of discrimination (*buddhi*) is refined. *Ghariai*, from the infinitive *gharnā*, literally means to sharpen or chisel. In this sphere then any blunt mental, psychological, intellectual, and reasoning faculties are keenly chiseled. The chiseling, refining, and sharpening lead to such wondrous forms that any attempt to portray them would be futile.

In Sikh spirituality, aesthetic refinement is crucial. Without this sensitivity, the goal remains unapprehended. As Gurū Nānak says, "one who can appreciate fragrance will alone know the flower" (*Gurū Granth* 725). The individual has to have refined physical senses to appreciate the marvelous presence of the Metaphysical Reality everywhere in the world. Only then may one begin to know that Reality Itself. Knowledge is fruitful only when it is appreciated, unfolding Gurū Nānak's emphasis on the experiential dimension. Opposite of anaesthetics, which has the effect of deadening, aesthetics is a means of heightening the individual sensibilities. In Sikhism, heightened aesthetic joy and the perception of absolute Truth remain closely connected. Some years ago, Samuel Laeuchli in his provocative book *Art and Religion in Conflict* showed that there is an antithesis between aesthetic appreciation and religious belief.[16] Philosophy in the West has created many splits and hierarchies between the dimensions of religion and aesthetics. We may recall how Kierkegaard degrades aesthetics to the bottom rung, way below the realm of ethics and religion. In Sikhism, however, aesthetics coexists with religion itself: the aesthetic experience becomes the route to the Transcendent One and route it remains. "Religion is a means and not the end. If we make it the end in itself we become idolatrous," stated Radhakrishnan so accurately.[17] Consequently, Sikh sacred literature and architecture become essential vehicles for Sikh spirituality. Indeed, the origins of Sikhism are traced to the aesthetic experience of Gurū Nānak's drinking of the cup of Name-Adoration recorded in the *Purātan Janamsākhī*. As he is ushered into the Divine Presence, Nānak has a profound insight into the existence as well as into the nature of the Transcendent Reality. He is given a cup full of nectar and is asked to recite the Divine Name. Gurū Nānak does not see the Divine in any form; he only hears Its voice and drinks from the ambrosial cup of Its Name. The hearing of the command, the holding of the cup, the savoring of the nectar of Its Name—these together constitute the fullness of his vision of the Infinite One. Drinking the ambrosia signifies the sapiential quality of knowledge received from the Divine. It is an utterly simple yet a most viable and highly penetrating portrayal of Gurū Nānak's encounter with the Transcendent Reality. He does not see any being at all and yet acquires insight into the very ground of Being. After receiving the Divine calling, Gurū Nānak sings a hymn of exultation and celebration. Divinely inspired, he recited many more. This poetic mode was to be the starting point of the Sikh scripture, the *Gurū Granth*. The *Gurū Granth* evolved from the sacred verse of Gurū Nānak.

As Gurū Nānak fervently longed for the Infinite, as he marveled at the grandeur and vastness of creation, as he sympathized with his fellow beings in their suppression and bondage, beautiful poetry burst forth in a variety of moods. Gurū Nānak's range of experience from utmost exaltation to deepest grief, in fact his entire message, is expressed artistically in his poetry. He reveled in calling himself a poet: "to you belong my breath, to you my flesh; says the poet Nānak, you the True One are my Beloved" (*Gurū Granth* 660). The source of Gurū Nānak's artistic outpourings was the Ultimate Reality. He himself said to his companion Lalo that he had no control over himself: "As comes to me the Lord's Word, that is how I deliver it, O'Lalo" (ibid. 772). Thus, whatever he said and however he said it, Gurū Nānak acknowledged it to be divinely inspired.

Crystallizing Gurū Nānak's message, Gurū Angad affirmed that the divine word had an aesthetic as well as an epistemological value: "It is ambrosia, it is the essence of all, it emerges from deep knowledge and intense concentration" (*Gurū Granth* 1243). Thus, while heightening and refining the senses, poetry also reveals the essence of existence itself. Gurū Angad added his poetry to that of Gurū Nānak's collection and signed it too with the name "Nānak." It was Gurū Angad who developed the *Gurmukhi* script in which the *Gurū Granth* was to be written.

Overall, the Sikh sacred text contains no historical narratives. There are no biographical details. There is no dogma. There is no code of specific social behavior prescribed in it. There are no obligatory acts enumerated. The Sikh Holy Book is spiritually exalted poetry carrying only intimations. The theme running throughout is that of the individual's longing for the Ultimate Reality, which is molded into poetic symbolism of great aesthetic delicacy and beauty.

The *Gurū Granth* ends with the seal put by its compiler and editor, Gurū Arjan. It is called the *Mundavani*. In it Gurū Arjan suggests the artistic efficacy of the Holy Volume:

> On the platter lie arranged three delicacies:
> Truth, contentment, and contemplation . . .
> All who eat them, all who savor them
> Obtain liberation.

The sacred scripture is therefore seen as a sumptuous platter full of delicacies, namely, Truth, Contentment, and Contemplation. According to Gurū Arjan, then, the *Gurū Granth* offers the food of knowledge: the fundamental essence of the universe is perceived through it. It offers the food of contentment: the dissatisfied appetite, the hunger for more and more is fulfilled by it. It offers the food of contemplation: the flickering psyche is harmoniously anchored by hearing and reflecting on its verses.

But the "food" is not merely to be partaken of; rather, as Gurū Arjan says, it should also be savored. Not through elaborate conceptualizing but through a full and rich relishing of the sacred poetry does the individual obtain liberation from all finite confinements and from the ever-continuing cycle of birth and death. Just as the aesthetic experience forms the heart of Gurū Nānak's epiphany as recorded in the *Purātan Janamsākhī*, the artistic aspect of poetry is reinforced by the fact that Gurū Arjan put most of the *Gurū Granth* into musical measures. The poetry of love and devotion is to be approached with reverent wonder; it cannot be pried into with mere intellect. The words of the *Gurū Granth* come with their own speedy meter and cadence. As the Gurūs said, they had no control over the flow of their utterances. From the very outset, they regarded their communication as divinely inspired. Full and sensuous to begin with, the words were further energized by the musical measures. The poetic dynamism of the Sikh sacred literature comes from the presence of alliteration, assonance, consonance, constant repetition, symmetry, and rhythm, which create a momentum so that the readers, hearers, and singers go beyond themselves and are launched on to intuiting the Unintuitable One. How can one separate the realms of religion and art? The two here are fused together. Divine poetry coming from the Beyond is empowered by the artistic devices and musical measures; in turn, it becomes the channel to stimulating the senses and mind into experiencing the Ultimate One that Gurū Nānak experienced in the River Bein. The revealed Word here is art *par excellence*. It has the power to awaken the mind to Ultimate Reality, to the love of the Transcendent, to the quest for Its vision. Religion and aesthetics are not two separate dimensions. The beauty of the text launches the imagination of both male and female itinerants—individually or collectively—on a spiritual journey toward the Beyond.

Similarly, Sikh architecture is a medium toward evoking the spiritual feelings. A Sikh shrine is called a Gurūdwara, literally, a door (*dwara*) to ultimate enlightenment (*gurū*). They are beautifully designed, and this appeal to the senses entices the worshipers to intuit the Transcendent Reality. The architectural design of the Gurūdwaras includes large expanses of open space so that the mind and senses are not confined. The traditional Gurūdwaras can be recognized by their white domes and minarets leading the eyes toward the infinite skies. They have large courtyards, which provide an immediate feeling of expansiveness. There is a pond attached, and the combination of the transparent waters extending horizontally and the diaphanous designs in marble going vertically creates a holistic effect in the visitor. A walkway goes around the pool, and devotees are seen bathing in the water, sitting on the edge saying prayers, and circumambulating in a contemplative mood. The Gurūdwaras have four doors, which is an architectural statement that they welcome people from the four castes. There is no hidden womblike chamber or altar to which only the chosen are admitted. There are no sculptures or icons that incarnate deity in any form. The congregation can gather inside or outside; it does not really matter. There are no chairs, and all sit on large mats spread on the floors. The center, of course, is the *Gurū Granth*. With its metaphysical poetry in sensuous imagery leading the self to the Ultimate Reality Beyond, it is readily present to all people from the four directions.

Just as the words of the *Gurū Granth* are not static, neither are the geometric designs on the Gurūdwara floors nor the floral designs on its walls of marble and stone. Denaturalization, symmetry, rhythm, and repetition are distinct characteristics of the architecture of Sikh sacred space. Denaturalized patterns enable a spiritual passage into the Transcendent, toward a dimension that the senses are not ordinarily used to. Symmetric designs serenely emerging from a multiplicity of intricate details create a surging sentiment of tranquillity. The black and white marble slabs on which one walks are repeated rhythmically. So are the stylized flowers and birds and arabesques and latticework on the walls and sides. The structure itself repeats its arches, domes, pillars, kiosks, windows, and storeys. Among the unending repetitions on which one walks, which one touches on the sides and sees on the building, the melodious words are heard. The rhythmic repetitions create a dynamic movement for the senses and imagination. Together they are impelled onwards. Any feeling of uneasiness gives way to harmony; sentimental knots and discords start to wither away; doubts and dualities begin to dissolve; the ignorant psyche is inspired to discover its essential spark. Through its finite structures the Gurūdwara creates an energetic movement toward the Infinite Transcendent.

Indeed, the aesthetic experience is an essential element of Sikh spirituality. Since the Sikh worldview does not distinguish between physical, mental, or spiritual sensibilities, they together constitute the person and together they are developed in this realm of art and beauty. From this stage, the person moves on to *Karam Khand*. This transition from the realm of art finds a remarkable parallel in the thought of twentieth-century Western artist Wassily Kandinsky. In *Concerning the Spiritual in Art*, Kandinsky states that "art is not vague production, transitory and isolated, but a power which must be directed to the improvement and refinement of the human soul—to, in fact, the raising of the spiritual triangle."[18] Refinement and cultivation of the aesthetic faculties open the way to *Karam Khand*.

Karam Khand

The next two stages are that of *Karam Khand* and *Sach Khand*, and they are both described in stanza 37 of Gurū Nānak's *Jap*. Their presence within one single stanza is a stylistic indication of their close interrelationship.

The fourth stage, *Karam Khand*, is the Region of Grace. Again, exegetes have differed on the meaning of the term *karam*. M. A. Macauliffe, Teja Singh, and Khushwant Singh have taken *karam* to be the equivalent of the Sanskrit *karma* and have translated *Karam Khand* as the Domain of Action.[19] W. H. McLeod argues against this view. According to him, if

Saram Khand is to be regarded as the Realm of Effort and *Karam Khand* as the Realm of Action, there is scarcely any difference between the third and the fourth stages. Instead, he translates *Karam Khand* as the Realm of Fulfillment, wherein *karam* still retains the Sanskrit meaning of *karma* but with an emphasis on fulfillment, the reaping of the rewards of previous action. As I have said in my earlier work, I agree with McLeod in not accepting *Karam Khand* as the Domain of Action (though not for the reason he provides), but I do not agree with its translation as the "Realm of Fulfillment." Fulfillment of action will not come at this later stage. The action performed and its reward belonged to the first stage, the *Dharam Khand*, where in the True One's Truthful Court the good and the bad are judged. It was this fulfillment that led to the second stage of the widening of horizons, which then led to the aesthetic plane, the *Saram Khand*.

Karam, it seems, retains its Persian meaning, and *Karam Khand* is more aptly rendered as the Realm of Grace. Bhai Jodh Singh, Gopal Singh, Narain Singh, and Bhai Vir Singh subscribe to this interpretation.[20] McLeod very insightfully states that grace occupies a position of primary importance in the thought of Gurū Nānak and that it extends over the whole process.[21] Grace should be relevant to the first realm as well, for without divine grace one would not take to this path at all. *Nadar*, the benevolent female aspect of the Transcendent, sustains the seeker throughout her/his spiritual quest. But it is of crucial importance at this fourth stage, for from here will begin the last stage of the journey to the omega point, the *Sach Khand*. That *nadar* or grace lies so close to the ultimate, Realm of Truth enhances its relevance.

Gurū Nānak describes *Karam Khand* as the abode of those who cherish none other than the Transcendent One. "Here live warriors and heroes of mighty power," *tithai jodh mahā bal sūr* (*Gurū Granth* 8). His very vocabulary and imagery express a region brimming with might and strength. We find here the genesis of the spirit of "Singh," or "lion-hearted," which was formally formulated by Gurū Gobind Singh, Nānak X. In light of the pervasive imagery of valiance in the fourth *Khand*, we cannot interpret Gurū Gobind Singh's encouragement of the martial spirit and his formulation of the Khālsāhood in 1699 as a deviation from Gurū Nānak's vision. Clearly, the Tenth Gurū's ideal of heroism and the martial temper of his poetry finds its precedence in Gurū Nānak's *Jap*. From Gurū Nānak to Gurū Gobind Singh, the Sikh Gurūs recognized valor as an essential element of spirituality because the way to the Transcendent is paved by battling against the lower passions and destroying the wall of obstruction and ignorance. Who in fact are the warriors and heroes? Gurū Nānak provides the definition in a verse in the measure *Srī:*

> *nānak so sūrā variām jini vichhu dustu ahankaranu māriā*
> The true hero, says Nānak, is one who kills the evil of egoity within. (*Gurū Granth* 86)

The real might and strength lie in one's conquering her/his own self. Herculean muscle and power are not the ideal. *Mani jītai jagu jītu*, "by conquering oneself, one conquers the world" (*Gurū Granth* 6). Inner strength leads to true victory, whereby one neither rules over others nor turns away from them, but exists peacefully with fellow beings. Power over the self is not an oppression of oneself, nor is it a power over others; rather, self-empowerment ensures an inner confidence and a harmonious coexistence with others. Gurū Nānak's portrayal of the fourth spiritual realm reiterates his orientation toward life with others: in the *Karam Khand* many heroes and heroines from a variety of traditions are acknowledged as dwelling harmoniously together. Here dwell many devotees from various worlds as well: *tithai bhakta vasahi ke lo*. Without a hierarchy, without a division, without a leader, and without any religious or cultural exclusions, a vast array of heroes and heroines and devotees are presented as abiding in peace and harmony.

Gurū Nānak's *Karam Khand* also highlights the presence of women: heroines are given equal importance with the male heroes. What requires special notice is that Sītā in all her beauty receives pride of place in the *Karam Khand*:

> Here abide many heroines like Sītā of surpassing praise,
> Their beauty beyond words. (*Gurū Granth* 8)

Gurbachan Singh Talib comments: "It would be superfluous to dilate on the symbolic character of Sita as representative of all that is noblest and purest in human nature."[22] But for women, the presence in *Karam Khand* of "heroines" along with "heroes" is very significant. Indeed, it is a striking instance of Gurū Nānak's validation of the female spiritual experience.

Among the heroines and heroes, Sītā alone is mentioned by name. We need to address ourselves to the question why she receives so much importance. Sītā's power includes fertility (*sītā* literally means "furrow"), and she is related to plants and animals. Her character as portrayed in the *Rāmāyana* is very familiar: a princess and the designated future queen, she renounced all her material comforts and security to accompany her husband Rāma into exile. Rāma renounced his throne for the younger half-brother Bharata and went into exile to protect his father's honor. During the hardships of exile, Sītā was a constant source of strength and joy to Rāma. When abducted by the demon Rāvaṇa, who tried to tempt her in various ways, Sītā remained steadfast. She went through many trials and ordeals but stuck to her love and faith.[23] Cornelia Dimmitt has also shown

Sītā as the source of Rāma's political power: as *śakti*, the female energy, Sītā inspires King Rāma to action.[24] It is for her virtues of inner power, devotion, and love that hers is the most popular, most revered name in Indian classical tradition. Actually it is not so much the historical Hindu wife Sītā that is evoked in the Sikh scriptural passage: here, in fact, that role is transcended by the use of the name in the plural—*Sīto-Sītā*, that is, Sītā-s. She is presented here as the ideal to be emulated by men and women. That she and other women like her are mentioned as the denizens of *Karam Khand* is not without meaning. Women like Sītā are the models and archetypes for heroism. Women are represented as paradigmatic figures; Sītā and women like her are chosen to depict the intense and heightened spiritual awareness experienced in *Karam Khand*. In contrast to the remark made by Judith Baskin that "in Rabbinic Judaism no woman is deemed capable of any direct experience with the divine,"[25] the close, deep, and indeed direct experience with the Divine is expressed by Gurū Nānak through both males and females. The patriarchal messages women across ages and across cultures have received—that they are limited and cannot comprehend the deeply spiritual or intellectual aspects of life[26]—have been reversed in Gurū Nānak's worldview. His usage of "Sītās" in the plural, further, takes away the distant "goddess" stature of Lord Rāma's wife and makes her more accessible, as one who could be more easily emulated. Many feminists have observed that the goddess often represents a dehumanization of women rather than their genuine exaltation. Simone de Beauvoir, for example, had serious misgivings about the goddess, and she speculated upon the urge to metamorphosize women into such idols, which she felt was largely a male urge: "Man wishes her to be carnal, but he would also have her smooth, hard, changeless as a pebble."[27] In India itself, the chasm between goddess and woman and its tragic consequences are readily apparent. There are innumerable powerful female deities such as Durgā, Lakṣmī, Kālī, and yet women in the everyday life are far from being invested with the goddesses' attributes. By presenting Sītā in the plural, Gurū Nānak takes her off the deified pedestal and makes her a significant but realistic role model for people in his society.

Heroines and heroes in *Karam Khand* are exempt from the cycle of birth and death. "They do not die and they are beyond all allurement" (*Gurū Granth* 8). Gurū Nānak's spiritual journey is a liberating process, and we get the sense that one can attain freedom from the migratory cycle of life and death in this very life. However, what happens after death or upon obtaining that deathless state is not an elaborated theory in Sikh philosophy, as it is, for example, in the *Bhagavad Gītā* and the Upaniṣads. In the *Gītā*, Kṛṣṇa expounds the two paths that the individual soul takes after death.

They are *devayāna* and *pitṛyāna*. Through the former, the soul travels through light and reaches *Brahman* with which it exists eternally thereafter; through the *pitṛyāna*, the soul travels through darkness and returns into the bodily form again. These two paths are also central to the eschatology of the Upaniṣads and are delineated in the *Bṛhadāraṇyaka* (VI.2) and *Chāndogya* (V.10) Upaniṣads. Such speculations are absent in the *Gurū Granth*, and that may be because of the Sikh emphasis on an authentic existence in this world. The embarkment of the spiritual journey with its continuous refinement of the physical, mental, moral, and divine faculties here and now takes precedence over what happens after death.[28] The *Gurū Granth* upholds that paradise is simply a spot where the divine hymns are recited: "that itself is paradise (*baikunth*) where the holy music (*kīrtan*) resounds."

That the heroes and heroines in *Karam Khand* cannot be beguiled or enticed indicates that they are approaching Reality, the Truth. "They are rejoicing for that True One is close to their hearts" (*Guru Granth* 8). Experience of joy (*anandu*) which we first encountered in the second stage of Knowledge is reiterated. The person undertaking the spiritual journey is not extinguished or dissolved, but becomes fully cognizant of deep enjoyment. The enjoyment at this stage is of course a recognition of the Transcendent Self. In *Rāg Rāmkalī*, Gurū Amar Das clearly establishes the identity between bliss and knowledge: "everyone talks about *ānanda* but *ānanda* is known only through the Gurū" (ibid. 917). The joyous experience of bliss, according to the Sikh Gurūs, is an intellectual one! A popular passage from Gurū Amar Das which is recited during Sikh ceremonies further shatters the Cartesian mind–body dualism and illustrates intense joy celebrated by the mind: "Joy pervades me, my mother, for I have found my True Gurū; serenely have I found the True Gurū and my mind rejoices with joy supreme" (ibid.). With the sight of the True One, Gurū Amar Das's mind resonates with celebrations. His feeling of joy is combined with the sense of vision, an intellectual apprehension of the Formless One, and the sense of sound, for the celebrations ring aurally in his mind (*mani vajīā vadhāiā*). The denizens of *Karam Khand* seem to rejoice in a similar way; they are so closely located to the Realm of Truth that they can see into it. The Sikh spiritual journey is almost complete.

Sach Khand

Sach Khand (The realm of Truth) is the fifth and final stage. According to Gurū Nānak:

> *sach khand vasai nirankāru*
> *kari kari vehkhai nadari nīhāl*

In *Sach Khand* [the Sphere of Eternity],
dwells the Transcendent [*Niraṅkār*, *Nir*, "without," and *kār*, "form"],
Who having created watches over Its creation
with a benevolent eye. (*Gurū Granth* 8)

As another common name for the Transcendent One, "Truth" occupies a vital presence in the Sikh scripture. Once again, we discern Gurū Nānak using an important Upaniṣadic term—*sat*. The opening of the *Gurū Granth* named the *Ikk Oan Kār* as "Truth" (*sat nām*), and the first stanza of the *Jap* articulates the identity: "Truth it has been from timeless eternity, Truth it has been within circles of temporality, Truth it is in the present, and Truth it shall be forever" (*ādi sacu jugadi sacu hai bhī sacu nānak hosī bhī sacu*). Sikhism fully celebrates the existence of the Transcendent as Truth. Gurū Nānak and his successors do not raise Descartian doubts. No ontological, epistemological, moral, or teleological proofs are required about the immutability of the Singular Truth, and the Sikh spiritual destination is essentially an immediate and exhaustive experience of That Truth.

Sach Khand is the sphere of the Timeless One, the abode of the Formless Reality. As one enters into it, one is in the home of Ultimate Reality, one is at home with Ultimate Reality: there is a total union between the human and the Divine Reality. The benevolent glance of the Divine One upon the seekers and their joyful vision of That One come together in this realm. Here in the sphere of Eternity, unity that is achieved with the Formless One is not a physical merging of one into the other but a two-way meeting of "vision." Gurū Nānak reaffirms that in this realm dwells the *Niraṅkār*, the Formless One. Truth is not manifested in any physical form; it cannot be installed into any shape, and so the union cannot take on any external mode. Grounded within his or her own world, the individual undertakes an inward journey; the benevolent glance—*nadar*—comes from the Transcendent. The union is the crux of the equation of eyesight with insight: the individual yearns to see the Transcendent One, and something from the Divine—Its *nadar*—reaches out to the individual.

The destination of the spiritual journey—the ultimate experience in Sikhism is a sense of infinity:

tithai khand mandal varbhand
je ko kathai ta aṅt na aṅt
Here are continents, constellations, and universes,
Their counting never ending, never . . . (*Gurū Granth* 8)

The individual thus comes face to face with Infinity Itself. Countless in Gurū Nānak's *Sach Khand* are the continents (*khand*), constellations (*man-*

dal), and universes (*varbhand*). An entry into the Realm of Truth reveals diverse and infinite forms. The goal of the Sikh spiritual journey is not a knowledge of or communication with the figure of a majestic Theos or a God somewhere out there. Indeed, the Reality is One, but it is not imaged or reified in any form, anywhere, whatsoever; it is simply an experience of ultimate infinity and unity. The focus in the *Sach Khand* turns from the individual to the Transcendent; the infinite panorama steers one from the microcosmic self to the Macrocosmic Self. The One, says the verse, "watches over [the creation] ever in bliss, in contemplation—*vekhai vigsai kari vīcāru*" (*Gurū Granth* 8). Interestingly, the process of watching over is depicted through the feminine power, *nadar*, of the Transcendent. In the *Sach Khand*, the self and the One have become a unity, an ineffable juncture wherein the seeing by the individual becomes the seeing by the Transcendent! The spiritual journey culminates in the metaphysical vision of the Infinite One and yet returns to Its magnificent and vast creation. Through the integral insight the individual sees the essential oneness after which the myriad forms of matter are recognized as possessing a singular force, a singular progenitor. The subject does not view the transcendent object; the subject–object duality dissolves and the individual partakes of the Infinite. At this point of the spiritual journey, the origin and destination have become one.

Gurū Nānak fully accepts the ineffability of this experience. The ultimate unity is hard to describe—"as hard as iron" is the simile employed by him. Gurū Nānak's inarticulation also implies an acceptance for a variety of ways in reaching the Truth. No particular method is propounded by him; no singular way is specified; no one technique is identified. The fact that to describe unity is "as hard as iron" opens the spiritual experience for everyone, and the omega point of Gurū Nānak's spiritual journey ends up acquiring universal import. Throughout his life, Gurū Nānak never asked anyone to renounce their religious affiliation; to the contrary he asked them to fully acknowledge and be who they were. Of the Hindus he asked that they be authentic Hindus; of the Muslims that they be authentic Muslims. Truth is common to people from all different faiths and cultures. Gurū Arjan, the fifth Gurū, reiterated Gurū Nānak's vision and declared that the essence is the same: "Some call it Rāma, some call it Khudā; some worship it as Visnu, some as Allah" (*Gurū Granth* 885). By manifesting the intrinsic similarity of the two Ideals from the Hindu and Islamic traditions (represented respectively by Rāma and Khudā), Sikh Gurūs tried to usher in a message of peace and harmony to their divided society. According to them, differences were only superficial. Once one went beyond formalities and externalities, there was just the singular Truth. That the goal of the spiritual journey would be the same for all people—Hindu, Muslim, Christian, or Sikh—is summed up in Gurū Gobind Singh's statement:

> . . . Hindus and Muslims are one!
> The same Reality is the creator and preserver of all;
> Know no distinctions between them.
> The monastery and the mosque are the same;
> So are the Hindu form of worship (*pūjā*) and the
> Muslim prayer (*namaz*)
> Humans are all one!

This same idea is perfectly embodied in a moving public prayer recited by Mahatma Gandhi. According to Radhakrishnan, Mahatma Gandhi got it from Gurū Gobind Singh:

> *Īśvara allā tere nāma*
> *mandira masdija tere dhāma*
> *sabko san-mati de bhagavān*[29]

Gurū Nānak's ecumenical vision, which was crystallized by his successors, obviously touched a chord in the twentieth-century leader. By not propounding the ultimate experience in any specific way, he leaves it open to a wide variety of personal interpretations. And his use of the everyday simile "hard like iron," shows that Gurū Nānak is embracing an inclusive approach to this ineffable spiritual destination. The final stage enunciated by Gurū Nānak is one of universal affirmation which finds meaningful affinities with the Upaniṣadic goal of Truth (*sat*) and the Sufi goal of *baqā*. We can also find fascinating parallels with Plato's "Aletheia," Buber's "I-Thou" relationship, and St.Teresa's "Divine Marriage." In fact, there is a striking similarity among these journeys through the cultures and across the centuries. It would be quite wrong, therefore, to limit this similarity to the Indian context alone, and even more so to claim that Gurū Nānak was merely reworking or reinterpreting any existing schools of thought. This is in effect what McLeod does when he argues that "the pattern of salvation enunciated in Yoga-Vāsiṣṭha" contributed to Gurū Nānak's five *Khands*.[30] Such a genetic thrust reduces and undermines the originality and uniqueness of a sacred text, and its application in this particular instance is especially inappropriate. If we look more closely at the journey through Gurū Nānak's five *Khands* and the seven stages set out in the Yoga-Vāsiṣṭha, it becomes quite obvious that these spiritual processes are in fact diametrically opposed. Gurū Nānak's goal is not one of universal negation (*sarvāpahnava*), which is the ultimate state described in Yoga-Vāsiṣṭha. There can be no real affinity between Gurū Nānak's *Sach Khand*, with its full and intense experience of infinity, and the *sarvāpahnava* of Yoga-Vāsiṣṭha, a state of utter feelinglessness "like that of a stone" (*pāsānavat-samam*).[31] The intense feelings that inspire Gurū Nānak's vision are much more in harmony with the affirmative and celebratory spirituality that can be found in so many of the other religious traditions.

Clearly, the realm of Truth in the Sikh spiritual journey is not an objective category but an existential mode of life. Immediately after articulating *Ikk Oan Kār* as Truth, and stating the immutability and eternity of Truth, the first question raised at the outset of *Jap* involves becoming true: *kiv saciārā hoīai kiv kūre tutai pāl*—"How to live a Truthful life? How to break the barriers of falsity?" The transition from Truth to True living is immediate and spontaneous, underscoring the experiential dimension of Reality. We find this pattern repeated toward the end of the *Jap* as well: the articulation of the infinite and ineffable experience of *Sach Khand* is immediately followed by a scene in a smithy. With its anvil, bellows, and hammers, the thirty-eighth and final stanza of the *Jap* quickly shifts to the phenomenal world:

> Let smithy be the continence, patience the goldsmith;
> Let anvil be wisdom, knowledge the hammer;
> Let bellows be divine fear and fire be inner control and heat;
> On the crucible of divine love, let the ambrosial gold flow;
> In this True mint forge the transcendent word.
> Such fulfillment comes to those blessed with the Gaze;
> Says Nānak, happy are those who are gazed upon by the Divine.

This brief passage constitutes a wonderful intersection of all five *Khands*. Through the simple metaphor of the smithy, Gurū Nānak alludes to the complex stages of the spiritual journey: performing action with patience and love (*Dharam*); using knowledge and wisdom (*Gyān*); refining artistic sensibilities, for after all it is the goldlike Divine Name that is being forged (*Saram*); receiving the benevolent glance (*Nadar*); and enjoying the fulfillment (*Sach*). Far from being reified states, the *Khands* represent dynamic processes of spiritual travel. The juxtaposition of stanza 37, with its description of the *Sach Khand*, and stanza 38, with its common, everyday working scene, illustrates the importance of living out the Truth. And yet, the very familiar and ordinary workshop is a metaphor for the spiritual mode of existence, a smithy in which the goldsmith forges the Divine Name on the crucible of love. This motion (*phora*) across (*meta*) the physical and the metaphysical, noumenon and the phenomena, spiritual and the practical, is the quintessence of Sikh religion. "Truth is higher than all, but higher still is true living" says Gurū Nānak. In the *Sach Khand* the individual finally lives out true living! It is the ultimate end and purpose of human existence.

The Sikh spiritual journey begins and ends in love for fellow beings, an immersion into our particular and material and secular world, and an insight into beauty and intimate relationships here and now. The vision of the Metaphysical Reality finds a full concretization in Sikh life, and the institutions of *langar*, *seva*, *sangat*, and the *khālsā* serve as a means of providing a practical outlet for the insight into infinity and unity. The recognition of the Singular Creator is manifested in acts of love toward all fellow beings. Since all are equally the progeny of the Infinite One, they have to be treated as kinsfolk. The response of love is vital to Sikhism.

To conclude, Sikh spirituality is not a journey away from our world; rather it is grounded in and of this earth. It is here in our everyday existence that we develop our moral, intellectual, aesthetic, and spiritual capacities and experience the Ultimate Reality. The more deeply we enter into the five realms of *Dharam*, *Gyān*, *Saram*, *Karam* and *Sach*, the more intensely we experience our life here and now. Sikh spirituality involves experiencing That One within this life; it seeks the Eternal One within our day-to-day existence. The journey through Gurū Nānak's five *Khands* is not an ascension into some higher regions beyond our lives and our world; rather, with its maps and charts drafted totally on the longitudes and latitudes of our planet earth, Sikh spirituality is based on drawing the Ultimate Reality into the human situation. Thus we live in the truest sense, living as life would be in *Sach Khand*, the Realm of Truth.

Notes

1. Bhai Vir Singh, *Japujī Sāhib Santhyā* (Amritsar: Khālsā Samācār, 1981) 10.
2. S. Radhakrishnan, *The Principal Upanisads* (London: George Allen & Unwin, 1953) 695–705.
3. For a full discussion of the feminine imagery pervading the five *Khands*, see my *Feminine Principle of the Sikh Vision of the Transcendendent* (Cambridge: Cambridge University Press, 1993) 81–89.
4. See W. H. McLeod, *Gurū Nanak and the Sikh Religion.* I myself adhered to this view in my earlier writings.
5. See Alice Walker, *The Color Purple* (New York: Harcourt Brace Jovanovich, 1982); and Sallie McFague, *Models of God: Theology for an Ecological, Nuclear Age* (Philadelphia: Fortress, 1987).

6 The Ballads of Bhāī Gurdās I.29, also 40–44, in *Vārān Bhāī Gurdās*, ed. Giani Hazara Singh and Bhai Vir Singh (1911; Amritsar: Khālsā Samācār, 1977) 25–39.

7 Gurū Nānak's term "*man*" itself brings together the range of thought, emotion, and spiritual being that are ordinarily distinguished as "mind," "heart," and "soul." See W. H. McLeod, *Who is a Sikh?* (Oxford: Clarendon, 1989) 9.

8. Radhakrishnan, *Principal Upanisads*, 133.
9. Ibid., 135.

10. For Gurū Gobind Singh's verse, see *Śabdārath: Dasam Granth Sāhib* (Patiala: Punjabi University, 1973) vol. 1.

11. Rudolph Otto, *The Idea of the Holy* (New York: Galaxy, 1958) 21.

12. Rosemary Radford Ruether, *Sexism and God-Talk: Toward a Feminist Theology* (Boston: Beacon, 1983) 79.

13. Franklin Edgerton, trans., *Bagavad-Gītā* (Cambridge, Mass.: Harvard Paperback, 1972) 6.10–13.

14. G. S. Talib, *Gurū Nānak: His Personality and Vision* (New Delhi: Gurdas Kapur & Sons, 1969) 186–226; see also Mircea Eliade, *Yoga: Immortality and Freedom* (Princeton: Bollingen, 1969) 47–100.

15. Edgerton, trans., *Bhagavad-Gītā*, 109–10.

16. See Samuel Laeuchli, *Religion and Art in Conflict* (Philadelphia: Fortresss, 1980).

17. S. Radhakrishnan, "Gurū Nānak: An Introduction," in *Guru Nanak: His Life, Time and Teachings*, ed. Gurmukh Nihal Singh (Delhi: Guru Nanak Foundation, 1969) 2.

18. Wassily Kandinsky, *Concerning the Spiritual in Art* (New York: Dover, 1977) 54.

19. Introduced by W. H. McLeod, *Gurū Nānak and the Sikh Religion*, 222–23. See also Max Arthur Macauliffe, *The Sikh Religion*, 1:216; Teja Singh, *The Japjī* (Lahore, 1930) 14, 40; Khushwant Singh, *Jupjī: The Sikh Prayer* (London) 22.

20. Bhai Jodh Singh, *The Japjī* (Amritsar, 1956) 55; Gopal Singh, *The Song of Gurū Nānak, English Translation of the Japji* (London, 1955) 11; Narain Singh, *Tīkā, Japujī Sāhib* (Amritsar) 225–26; Bhai Vir Singh, *Santhya Srī Gurū Granth Sāhib* (Amritsar: 1958) 1:167.

21. McLeod, *Gurū Nānak and the Sikh Religion*, 223.

22. G. S. Talib, *Japujī: The Immortal Prayer-Chant* (New Delhi: Munshiram Manoharlal, 1977) 135.

23. Kana Mitra, "Woman in Hinduism," *Journal of Ecumencial Studies* 20 (1983) 588.

24. Cornelia Dimmitt, "Sītā: Mother Goddess and Śaktī," in *The Divine Consort: Rādhā and the Goddesses of India*, ed. Jack Hawley and Donna Wulff (Boston: Beacon, 1986) 210–23.

25. Judith Baskin, "The Separation of Women in Rabbinic Judaism," in *Women, Religion and Social Change*, ed. Yvonne Yazbeck Haddad and Ellison Banks Findly (New York: State University of New York, 1985) 3.

26. Charlene Spretnak, ed., *The Politics of Women's Spirituality* (NewYork: Anchor/ Doubleday, 1982) 247.

27. Simone de Beauvoir, "Myths: Dreams, Fears, Idols," in *The Second Sex: The Classic Manifesto of the Liberated Woman* (New York: Vintage, 1952) 179.

28. Interestingly enough, the word "garment" for body is shared by both Gurū Nānak and Lord Kṛṣṇā. In the *Jap*, Gurū Nānak says, "*karmī āvai kaprā nadarī mokhu dūāru*—through actions (*karmī*) one achieves the body, but, through *nadar*, liberation from the cycle of birth and death." His point is that actions bring one into this world but liberation depends upon *nadar*, the benvolent glance of the Transcendent Reality. Lord Kṛṣṇa tells Arjuna that "bodies are cast like worn out garments . . ." (*Bhagavad Gītā* 2.22).

29. Radhakrishnan, *Principal Upanisads*, 139.

30. McLeod, *Gurū Nānak and the Sikh Religion*, 221.

31. Explaining the goal of Yoga-vasistha, Dasgupta writes, "the destruction of *citta*

by cessation of knowledge—a state of neither pain nor pleasure nor any intermediate state, a state as feelingless as that of the stone (*pāsānavat-samam*)—is the ultimate state aimed at." See S. Dasgupta, *A History of Indian Philosophy* (Cambridge: Cambridge University Press, 1932) 2:265–66.

Bibliography

Sources

Singh, Gopal, trans. *Sri Guru Granth Sahib*. Vols. 1–4. Chandigarh: World Sikh University Press, 1978.

Singh, Nikky-Guninder Kaur. *The Name of My Beloved: Verses of the Sikh Gurus*. San Francisco: HarperCollins, 1995.

Studies

Cole, Owen W., and Piara Singh Sambi. *The Sikhs: Their Religious Beliefs And Practices*. New Delhi: Vikas Publishing House, 1978.

Macauliffe, Max Arthur. *The Sikh Religion: Its Gurus, Sacred Writing and Authors*. 6 vols. Oxford: Clarendon, 1909.

McLeod, W. H. *Guru Nanak and the Sikh Religion*. Oxford: Clarendon, 1968.

———. *The Sikhs: History, Religion and Society*. New York: Columbia University Press, 1989.

Singh, Harbans. *Guru Nanak and Origins of the Sikh Faith*. Bombay: Asia Publishing House, 1969.

———, ed. *Perspectives On Guru Nanak*. Patiala: Punjabi University, 1975.

Singh, Nikky-Guninder Kaur. *The Feminine Principle in the Sikh Vision of the Transcendent*. Cambridge: Cambridge University Press, 1993.

Singh, Sher. *The Philosophy of Sikhism*. Amritsar: Shiromani Gurdwara Parbanhak Committee, 1980.

Talib, Gurbachan Singh. *Japiji: The Immortal Prayer-Chant*. Delhi: Munshiram Manoharlal, 1977.

Glossary

abhiṣeka. Consecration, anointing, inaugurating by sprinkling of water, coronation, installation (of kings or religious heads), religious bathing.

abhyāsa. Repeated practice or exercise, continued use.

Ācārya. Teacher or preceptor, spiritual guide, holy teacher who instructs the pupil in the Vedas; when affixed to proper names, learned venerable (doctor).

adharma. Unrighteousness, wickedness, sinful injustice, an unjust act, a quality pertaining to the soul or mind imperceptible but inferred from reasoning and from transmigration.

Advaita. Non-duality, identity, denial of otherness, unitive life; indivisibleness of the web of life and existence, communion of the soul with God.

adyāropa/adhyāsa. Superimposition, the initial phase of identification as a heuristic device prior to the subsequent recession or de-identification.

Āgama. Scripture, testimony from the most reliable source, the Vedas, special scriptures that are foundational texts to specific traditions of Hinduism such as Śaivism.

ahiṁsā. Nonviolence, nonkilling as a practice or vow; a spiritual ideal of regard for life and absence of malice; either meaning a total repudiation of force or employing force in an ethical spirit in the line of vindication of "own duty."

ākāsa. "Space," sky, ether; one of the five elements of Hindu cosmology.

āḻvār(s). Tamil word used as proper name to refer to the Tamil saints, twelve in number and belonging to the period between the second and the eighth century of the Common Era. They are God-intoxicated mystics, "divers" immersed in the ocean of ecstatic love for God in his beauteous extraterrestrial form as Narayana pervading all beings and things and communicating the joy of their communion with him to humanity; their hymns collected under the label "four thousand sacred lyrics" are venerated as "revelation" by the Sri-Vaiṣṇava community.

ānanda. Supreme bliss, felicity, plenteousness, name of Viṣṇu, of Śiva.

antaryāmin. Inner ruler; inner self of all beings; Brahman immanent in the self.

anugraha. "Favor"; ritual request of the deity's presence at worship.

anubhava. Experience either of the normal, mediated kind, i.e., sensory and even rational, or some direct experience which becomes realized through a special cognitive process; sometimes refers to aesthetic experience (*rasanubhava*), also unmediated as in the case of spiritual experience; used also interchangeably with the content of experience (*rasanubhava*), also unmediated as in the case of spiritual experience; used also interchangeably with the content of experience (*anubhuti*).

anuṣtāna. Commencing or undertaking a course of action; practice of religious rites or ceremonies.

apara. (As a pronoun) another, more, matchless, different; inferior or lower; nonextensive.

aprākṛta. Not ordinary, extraordinary; special.

apūrva. Not preceded, new, unknown, not first; the remote consequence of an act, like going to heaven as the result of good acts; virtue and vice as the external cause of future happiness or misery.

arcāvatāra. Material image (*arca*) into which the Deity "descends" (*avatāra*) as disclosing his accessible grace to enable worship and communion.

arpaṇa. Placing or putting upon or in offering, resigning; giving back.

arūpa. Formless; being devoid of visible form (*rūpa*).

āsana. Firm posture as a condition that renders possible fixing of one's mind on any object that one chooses; the particular postures of body, hands, and feet prescribed for all spiritual exercises and described in yoga texts.

āśrama. The differentiated stages of a man's lifetime according to the Hindu *dharma.* The four of them are (1) that of the student who submits to learning, (2) that of the householder marking the period of man's maturity and enactment of his due rule in the world, (3) the stage of retirement to the forest for meditation, and (4) the mendicant wandering stage.

Ātman. The individual soul or life-monad; that which makes the universe animate, a living organism, by circulating through its [the universe's] limbs and spheres; the life monads contained within and constituting the very substance of corporeal body, ascending and descending through various stages of being, now human, now divine, now animal, now lower, those enjoying the highest states of being possessing five sense faculties as well as the faculties of thinking and speech; self or oneself, in which sense it is used reflexively for all three persons and in the singular number, masculine gender, or number of the noun to which it refers (indicated by the non-capitalized use of *ātman*); Supreme Soul, Brahman; essence, nature (*ātman*); Supreme Soul, Brahman; essence, nature (*ātmaka*); the person of the whole body; mind, intellect; the understanding; reason; form; care, efforts, or endeavors (non-capitalized *ātman*).

AUM, om, aum. The name for addressing Supreme Spirit, the declaratory name Brahman itself expressed in an address form and hence enjoined to be meditated on by the old, sacred chant which symbolizes it; as a symbol for meditation of Brahman, it is also called *pranava,* as preeminent prayer; by extension, it refers to all the Vedas, hence chanted before commencing and after ending recitation of any part of the Veda.

āvāhana. "Invitation"; ritual request of the deity's presence at worship.

avatāra. Divine descent or incarnation, combining history and mythology, characteristic of the Hindu epics and the Puraṇas; represents according to tradition the concrete manifestations of divine grace and its periodic incursion into all species and into the history of humanity, when evil triumphs over goodness.

bhakti, bhakta. Devotion, attachment, loyalty, faithfulness, reverence, service, worship, homage; a worshiper, devotee, adorer, attendant.

bhakti-mārga. The way of devotion to God regarded as the way to the attainment of final emancipation and eternal bliss.

bhakti yoga. A yogic scheme of God-realization as the completion of moral and spiritual disciplines; a disciplinary process involving different stages, all of which are dominated by the single aim of seeing God face to face.

bhara-samarpaṇa. Renunciation of the sense of responsibility involved in the saving act; casting oneself on the saving power of grace by which the weight of world-weariness is lifted and a state of being without fear (*nirbhaya*) is accomplished.

bhāva. The internal aspect of action pertaining to motive or intention of one who acts, the purity of which makes the act intrinsically good; positive nature; being, on which depends negation; what generates the cognition "it is."

bīja. Seed, a germ element, origin, cause; the seed or germ of the plot of a play; the mystical letter forming the essential part of the mantra(s) of a deity.

Brahman. The mystic power pervading the universe; the utterances founded upon the manifestations of the brahman.

brahman. The priestly class and the priestly functionary.

cakra. Wheel, disk; center in the subtle body, six in number, through which the cosmic energy lying dormant at the base of the spine uncoils and ascends to the apex of *brahmarandra.*

cidambaram. The expanse of Spirit as Light; name of a sacred temple and shrine of South India in the sanctum of which is called the Hall of Ethereal Consciousness (*cid sabhā*), wherein resides the Deity imaged as the Sovereign Dancer (*naṭarāja*).

cit. Intelligence, consciousness.

dayā. Compassion, tenderness, sympathy; sentiment of heroic compassion.

devi. Goddess; a female deity; a crowned queen who has undergone consecration along with her husband; a respectful title applied to a lady of the first rank.

dharma. Righteousness; goodness; merit; justice, a just act; a quality of the mind or soul imperceptible but inferred from reasoning; the whole context of religious and moral duties; the doctrine of the duties and rights of each in the ideal society and as such the law of all action.

dharmaśāstra. Books of the Law attributed to mystical personages like Manu ("forefather of man") and eminent brahmin saints and teachers of antiquity;

earlier works filled with social, ritual, and religious prescriptions intended for one or other of the Vedic schools; the later law books expanded to cover the whole context of orthodox Hindu life.

dhvani. Letter sounds; noise in general; tune, note, tone; the sound of musical instrument; the suggested sense, as different from the expressed, of a passage.

dhyāna. Meditation by deep concentration; one of the accessories—"internal disciplines"—of yoga, marked by the constant repetition of what the mind seeks to fix on.

dīkṣā. Consecration for a religious ceremony; initiation in general; a ceremony preliminary to a sacrifice; investiture with the sacred thread.

Divya Prabandham. Name for the collection of the Tamil utterances of the Āḻvār(s) totalling four thousand hymns held as divine and authoritative for the tradition of Śrīvaiṣṇavism.

Gāyatri mantra. Famous vedic *mantra* used in prayer and worship; Gāyatri is personified as a Goddess.

guṇa. Strand, quality; the three strands of primordial matter (*prakṛti*), called *sattva* (being, virtue, goodness), *rajas* (excitement, intense activity), and *tamas* (darkness, dullness).

guru. Teacher; preceptor; any venerable or respectable person, an elderly personage or relative, the elders; a religious teacher, spiritual preceptor; one who performs the purificatory ceremonies for someone and instructs him in the Vedas.

hlādinī. "Enjoyment."

hatha-yoga. A particular mode of yoga so-called because it is difficult, involving constant practices of elaborate nervous exercise; it is also associated with healing and other supernatural powers; influenced the development of Tantra.

himsā. The intent to kill; injury inflicting harm on any creature.

homa. Offering oblations to gods by pouring anything fit to be offered, like melted butter, into the consecrated fire; one of the fire daily "sacrifices" to be performed by a *brahman.*

icca. Wish, desire; according to wish or inclination.

Īśa, Īśvara. The supreme Lord, owning master; name of Siva; powerful, able; a king, ruler.

iṣṭa devata. A desired or cherished deity; the worshiper's special tutelary divinity.

japa. "Muttering," whispering; repetition of the names of God or of a sacred verse (*mantra*).

jāti. Class, caste, the classic role into which one has been brought by birth; the collective.

jyotiṣa. From "light," the science of light; Vedic science of astronomy and astrology.

jīva. Life-monad, uncreated and imperishable, intrinsically alike but "tainted" in its perfection through the influx of the non-self (*ajiva*) constituents of the universe; individual life-monad subject to transmigration but with a transcendent affinity or oneness with God.

jīvan mukta, jīvan mukti. One who becomes spiritually free while continuing in the embodied life; the state of spiritual freedom attained while yet in the body.

jñāna. Knowledge; wisdom, cognition; intellectual intuition; knowledge of details in contrast to knowledge of things without their details.

jñāna mārga. The path of knowledge in contrast to the paths of ritual action or devotion.

jñāna yoga. Knowing of self as finding its true fulfillment in the knowledge of God; the yoga by which is actualized self-knowledge through the knowing of God, the reality of realities; the spiritual apprehension of the real (to be contrasted with the intellectual pathway to perfection) in the non-dual enstasis of immediacy.

kaiṅkarya. Service consecrated to that in whom one takes refuge.

kāma. Pleasure and love; desire incarnate, the god of love who sends desire quivering to the heart; one of the human ends making its imperious demands on life.

karma. Action, work, rite, performance (from the root *kr*, "to make"); the fruits of action reaped or yet to be reaped, here and in the other world; the connecting link between desire and rebirth; a kind of subtle matter produced through the actions of body, speech, and mind, which sticks to the soul (Jainism); three stratifications or kinds of karma: the seeds of destiny stored as a result of former actions but which have not yet begun to germinate, not yet begun to sprout, mature and transform themselves into the harvest of a life; the seeds that would normally collect and be stored if one were to continue in the path of ignorance basic to the present biography; seeds collected and stored in the past that have actually begun to grow, i.e., the karma bearing fruit in the shape of actual events.

karmayoga. The discipline of selfless action proclaimed in *Bhagavad Gītā;* shedding of selfishness and giving up of the false notion taking the form "I am the doer" and "the world is mine."

kriyā. "Activity"; also refers to religious rites and ceremonies.

krodha. "Anger."

kṛpa. "Favor" or grace.

kula. Family, home, lineage.

kuṇḍalinī yoga. The yoga of arousing of the *kuṇḍalinī*, "that which is coiled up," i.e., the great store of potential energy at the base of the spine that is normally all but unused or aroused save for going into sex drives and other physical appetites; when fully aroused by the practice of meditation and other spiritual disciplines, it is said to travel up the spine through the middle passage in the spine called *suṣumnā*, traversing six centers of consciousness, until it reaches the seventh, the center of the brain. The rise of *kuṇḍalinī* to the higher centers of the navel, heart, throat, etc., all located within the *suṣumnā* itself, provides various degrees of enlightenment.

kuśa. A kind of grass required for Vedic sacrifice.

līlā. Play or sport, used as the descriptive model for explaining divine work or cosmic and soteriological activities; indicative of the indistinction of play and work on the higher level of reference, where activity is not compelled by conditions not of one's own choosing.

lokasaṅgraha. Universal welfare.

mahātmā. One who has identified completely with One self (*mahat ātman*); applied to any holy person in the sense of a great soul.

manas. The thinking faculty; a constituent of the "inner sensorium" (*antah karaṇa*); what works through the senses, the latter not giving rise to knowledge unless *manas* be in touch with them; source of two movements—indeterminate sensing and conceiving prior to the rise of definitive understanding; coordinates the indeterminate sense materials into determinate conceptual forms as class notions with particular characteristics.

mantra. Sacred formula, word sounds, representing the form of the Deity, to be recited and repeated as part of "meditative thinking"; oral repetition of a word or phrase evoking the referent of the word and the spiritual power attached thereto; Vedic hymn or sacred prayer addressed to any deity; earliest Vedic literature; an incantation; consultation, deliberation, secret.

mārga. Spiritual pathway.

māyā. From the root *mā*, "to measure," "to form," the word denotes the power of a god or demon to produce illusory effect, to appear under deceptive masks ("magic" derives from this sense); the illusion superimposed upon reality as an effect of ignorance; the entire visible cosmos is *māyā* as superimposed upon true being by one's deceitful senses and unillumined mind; also a positive cosmological sense as what gives forth the world, the whence and the whither of the evolution of the cosmos.

moha. Infatuation, affective insensibility; spiritually at the opposite pole of happiness (*sukha*); blinding feeling through ignorance; confusion.

mokṣa, mukti. Spiritual freedom, the fourth of the four aims or human ends of life; the final human good often set over against the first three, namely, *artha*, *kāma*, and even *dharma*; from the root *muc*, "to loose," "set free," the word imparts rescue, deliverance, emancipation, in the negative but also in the positive sense, described as realizing the sameness of nature with god or identity with the higher self.

mudrā. Seal, the mystic hand postures playing an important role in Indian ritual and art; fried paddy and the like as are chewed; one of the items in the sacramental fare in certain Tantric rites.

mūlādhāra. The deep place at the root of the spine at which place lies coiled away like a sleeping serpent the divine power asleep; the seat of the "earth" pictured on a crimson lotus of four petals.

mūrti. Material form, embodiment, image; an icon used in worship.

nātya. Dance; dramatic representation; refers to India's classical dance, especially to Bharatanatya.

nivṛti. Abstinence; withdrawal from action.

parā. The supreme word; identified with *sabda brahman* as the source from which the word as well as the meaning derives.

parā-bhakti. Highest *bhakti* prior to the perceptual awareness of God.

paramā-bhakti. The *bhakti* generated by the direct vision of God; sometimes also spoken of as *bhakti* descriptive of spiritual realization (*sādhya bhakti*).

paramātma. The Supreme Soul, truly free from attachment and aversion; it has conquered all passions and thus may be said to realize its potentialities of infinite knowledge, perceptions, bliss, and power; the highest liberated self; experienced as either what comes about by actual climbing upward to the spiritual apex or meditatively contacted by one on the way to siddhahood when he "perceives" a soul in that formless, unfettered state which he is destined someday to reach.

piṇḍa. Lumb, ball; small ball of rice ritually offered to ancestors.

piṅgalā/iḍā. Psychic currents flowing along the spine.

prāṇa. Vital energy or life principle; literally, vital air.

prāṇayama. Breath control; a yogic technique to master vital energy or life force.

prasāda. Divine grace.

prīti. Affection, love, kindly feeling; fondness for.

puruṣārtha. (Four) aims of life.

Puruṣottama. "Supreme person."

pūjā. Offering of worship with flowers (*pū*, a Tamil word for flower).

rasa. Juice; sentiment.

ṛṣi. The Vedic seer, the sage, who with his mind's eye directly perceives Truth unfolding through layers of reality, cosmic harmony unfolding within his being.

rūpa. Color, appearance, form, shape.

sādhana. Means for the attainment of the goal (*sādhya*); means of fitting the mind for instruction of knowledge; two main paths of *sādhana*, discrimination and devotion.

samādhi. Absorption, total perceptual attention, which has two forms: with a consciousness of the duality of the perceiver and the perceived and without it, i.e., a non-dual absorption beyond even the exquisite consciousness of the union of the two. While the former is a fully conscious state of absorption founded on an ecstatic identification of two entities that are yet felt to be distinct, the latter is a merging of the mental activity, the oscillating vitality (*citta vṛtti)* of consciousness in the self to such a degree that the distinction becomes dissolved. The first deepens into the second where the two terms of the vision deliquesce in each other, now truly one-without-a-second.

sampradāya. "To give," to grant, to hand down by tradition; religious order.

sannyāsa. Renunciation of household life, abandoning ceremonial observances including the worship of the sacred fires; the spirit of renunciation is also said to consist in "renouncing and yet working," i.e., without coveting its fruits.

śānta. Composed, calm; sentiment of peacefulness.

sarīra. Body, corporeality which includes the gross, cellular body subject to constant destruction and creation but also the inner world of forms and experiences—the notions, ideas, thoughts, emotions, visions, fantasies, of the "subtle body."

sat, satya. Being which was declared to be "in the beginning," "one only without a second"; "that being" (*tat*) also declared as the true or truth (*satyam*).

satya yuga. The first "age" in the cosmic cycle.

seva. Service; wait on, serve, to honor.

siṣya. "He who is to be taught" by the guru.

śrāddha. Last rites for the deceased performed each year.

sṛṅgāra. Feeling of erotic love.

sthūla. Gross, coarse, physical (body).

svabhāva. Own manner of being; innate disposition or nature.

svarūpa. "Own form"; essence that is identical with and does not merely belong to something; what is intrinsic.

tapas. Penance, religious austerity, mortification; warmth, fire; pain, suffering; meditation connected with practice of personal self-denial or bodily mortification.

treta yuga. Second "age" in the cosmic cycle following *satya yuga*.

upāsanā. Service, attendance, waiting upon, engaging in; being intent on; worship; adoration; religious meditation.

vairāgya. Aversion, dispassion; indifference to the world.

vātsalya. Tenderness, affection; love toward a child.

vidyā. Knowledge, learning, science.

viśiṣṭādvaita. The doctrine according to which the relation between the supreme being and the particular things is that of *viśeṣya*, "the substance that is qualified," and *viśeṣana*, "the attribute that qualifies," the relation between substance and attribute, soul and its body, the whole and its parts.

vrata. Vowed observance; a religious act of devotion or austerity; a vow in general.

yāga/yajña. Sacrifice; form of sacrifice in the Vedic religion.

yuga dharma. Code of conduct appropriate to the "ages" in the cosmic cycle. These ages are *satya*, *treta*, *dvapara*, and *kali*.

Contributors

K. R. SUNDARARAJAN, an editor of this volume, is Professor and Chairman, Department of Theology, St. Bonaventure University, New York; he has published numerous articles on such subjects as Incarnation according to Hinduism and Christianity, and Limits of Hindu-Christian Dialogue, in journals in the United States and India.

BITHIKA MUKERJI, an editor of this volume, is retired Reader of Philosophy, Benaras Hindu University, and is the author of *Neo-Vedanta and Modernity* and a monograph on Hinduism published in German and English; also member, Board of Editors and Advisors, World Spirituality.

JOHN G. ARAPURA is Professor Emeritus of Religious Studies, McMaster University, Canada. He is the author of *Radhakrishnan and Integral Experience*; *Religion as Anxiety and Tranquility*; *Gnosis and Question of Thought in Vedanta*; and numerous articles. His article "Spirit and Spiritual Knowledge in the Upaniṣads" appeared in the first volume of *Hindu Spirituality.*

KRISHNA BANERJEE is Reader in English, Women's College, Benaras Hindu University, India. She has an M.A. in English, an M.A. in Philosophy, and a Ph.D. from Benaras Hindu University. Banerjee's writings include a book in Spanish, *Shri Shri Anandamayi Ma Su vida y sus palabras*, and many articles in Indian journals.

BETTINA BÄUMER is Dr. Phil. (Ph.D.) from the University of Munich, Germany. Presently she is the Research Director, Alice Boner Foundation for Research on Fundamental Principles in India Art, Honorary Coordinator, Indra Gandhi National Centre for the Arts, and Visiting Professor, University of Vienna. Bäumer has published extensively and has authored several books, including, *Schöpfung als Spiel: Der Begriff lila im Hinduismus, seine philosophische und theologische Bedeutung; Upanishadein: Befreiung zum Sein;* and *Abhinavagupta, Wege ins Licht*. She has been the coauthor of *The Vedic Experience, Mantramañjari* (with R. Panikkar), and *Vāstusūtra Upanisad: The Essence of Form in Sacred Art* (with Alice Boner and S. R. Sárma).

S. N. BHAVASAR is Professor and Practitioner of Ayurvedic Studies in the University of Poona, India, and is author of several articles in Marathi and English. His article "Spirituality and Health (Āyurveda)" (with Gertrud Kiem) appeared in the first volume of *Hindu Spirituality.*

GIORGIO BONAZZOLI is currently teaching at Sacred Heart Seminary in Kokopo, New Guinea. He has been the editor of the journal *Purana*, published in Benaras, India, for many years. He is a respected scholar of Hindu Purāṇas and has published many articles, including "Composition, Transmission and Recitation of the Puranas" and "Kumbhamela: A Way to Moksa," which appeared in *Purana*.

HÉLÈNE BRUNNER taught Mathematics and Physics in French Establishments in France and abroad, most recently at Pondicherry, India, where she studied Sanskrit. She was a member of the French Centre National de la Recherche Scientifique section of the Oriental Studies. After retiring, she continued her work in Agamic Saivism. Her publications include an edition and French translation of *Samaśambhupaddhati* and a French translation of *Mṛgendrāgama* and *Caryāpāda*.

SITANSU S. CHAKRAVARTI is Visiting Professor in Philosophy at Visva-Bharati, Santiniketan, India. He has a Ph.D. in philosophy from Syracuse University, New York, having worked in the area of Modal Logic. He studied Sanskrit and Indian Philosophy in Government Sanskrit College, Calcutta, and in Indian Academy of Philosophy, Jadhavpur, India. He is the author of a book and several articles in scholarly journals in India and abroad. Besides his book *Hinduism—A Way of Life*, his articles have appeared in *Journal of Indian Philosophy* (Holland) and in *Notre Dame Journal of Formal Logic*, and *Journal of the Indian Council of Philosophical Research*. In his writings, Chakravarti has attempted to combine the philosophical perspectives of the East and the West.

HEMENDRA NATH CHAKRAVARTY is the Chief Pandit in the Kalakosha project of Indra Gandhi National Centre of Arts, Varanasi, India. He has published and edited many books, including *Granthapanji* and *Mahamohopadhyaya Mahamanishi Gopinath Kaviraj*, both in Bengali; and *Naradiya Purana*, English translation with annotation. He has also translated *Tantrasara of Abhinavagupta* into Hindi. He has edited *Amarvani Bengali with the commentary of M.M. Kaviraj* and *Arca Smriti, A Souvenir of M.M.G.N. Kaviraja*.

V. A. DEVASENAPATHI is the former Director of the Centre of Advanced Study in Philosophy, University of Madras, India. He received his Ph.D. from the University of Madras and taught in Pachaiyappa's College, Madras, before joining the Philosophy Department at the University of Madras, and later in the Centre of Advanced Study in Philosophy. A specialist in Saiva Siddhanta, Devasenapathi has published several books and many articles in journals in India and abroad. His books include *Saiva Siddhanta as Expounded in Sivajñāna Siddhiyār and Its Commentaries*; *On Human Bondage and Divine Grace*; *Towards the Conquest of Time*; *The Ethics of Tirukkural*; and *The Mysticism of Nammalvar*.

T. N. GANAPATHY, formally Post-Graduate Professor and Head of the Department of Philosophy at Vivekananda College, Madras, has served as Visiting Professor at Sri Sathya Sai Institute of Higher Learning in Prasanthi Nilayam, India. He has published books and many articles in India and abroad, including *An Invitation to Logic*; *Mahavakyas*; *Bertrand Russell's Philosophy of Sense-data*; and *The Philosophy of Tamil Siddhas*. His article "The Twilight Language of the Siddhas" was published in *Indian Philosophical Annual*, University of Madras, India.

SISIRKUMAR GHOSE was Professor of English in the Department of English and Other Modern European Languages in Visva-Bharati, Santiniketan, India, for over three decades. He lectured at the universities of Annamalai (India), Bangalore (India), Kathmandu (Nepal), and at the University of California at Berkeley and at Yale University in the United States. Some of his works include *Aldus Huxley: A Cynical Salvationist*; *The Late Poems of*

Tagore; *Metaesthetics and Other Essays*. He contributed the core article on mysticism to the *Encyclopedia Britannica*.

S. GOPALAN retired after teaching in the department of Philosophy at Singapore National University. Earlier he had taught at the Centre of Advanced Study in Philosophy, University of Madras. He has a Ph.D. and a D.Lit. from the University of Madras, and a Ph.D. from McMaster University, Canada. He has written several books and published articles in scholarly journals in India and abroad. His books include *Hindu Philosophy of Social Reconstruction*; *Outlines of Jainism*; *Social Philosophy of Tirukkural*; *Studies in Social Philosophy*; and *Jainism as Metaphilosophy*.

DAVID M. MILLER is Associate Professor of Religion, Concordia University, Montreal, Canada. He received his Ph.D. from Harvard University. His publications include *Hindu Monastic Life: The Monks and Monasteries of Bhubaneswar* (with Dorothy Wertz) and chapters in the following collections: *Swami Sivananda and the Bhagavat Gita* (ed. Robert Minor); *Karma, Rebirth, and Contemporary Guru* (ed. Ronald W. Neufeldt); *Swami Sivananda and the Divine Life Society Movement* (ed. Robert Baird); and *Religious Institutions and Political Elites in Bhubaneshwar* (ed. Susan Seymour).

NAGENDRA is Professor and Head of the Department of Hindi, Delhi University, India. He is one of the best known scholars in the area of Hindi literature and linguistics. He has published several books in Hindi and English and edited several works. His works in English include *Emotive Basis of Literature and Other Essays*; *Surdasa: A Revaluation*; *Surdasa, His Mind and Art*; *Tulsidasa: His Mind and Art*; and *Literary Criticism in India*.

PREMA NANDAKUMAR is Visiting Professor at Mahatma Gandhi University of Kottayam, India. Her publications include *A Study of Savitri*, *Dante and Sri Aurobindo*. She has translated the Tamil epic *Manimekalai* into English. Twenty-eight of her writings were collected and included in *The Glory and the Good* (1995). Nandakumar is recipient of the "For the Sake of Honour Award in Writing English" by the Booksellers and Publishers of South India at Madras in 1995.

WALTER G. NEEVEL, JR., is Associate Professor of Philosophy and Religious Studies at the University of Wisconsin-Milwaukee. In addition to holding an appointment in the Department of Philosophy, he is a founding member of the interdepartmental Comparative Study of Religion Program at the University. His previous publications have primarily focused on Sri Ramakrishna and on the philosophical works of Yamuna and the Sri Vaishnavas, while his current research involves a comparative study of Hindu and Buddhist saviors. His publications include *Yamuna's Vedanta and Pancatantra: Integrating the Classical and the Popular*.

ANANTANAND RAMBACHAN is Associate Professor of Religion and Asian Studies at Saint Olaf College in Minnesota. He has been working in recent years on epistemology and on the interplay between scripture and personal experience as sources of valid knowledge in Hinduism. Among his books are *Accomplishing the Accomplishing: The Veda as a Valid Source of Knowledge in Sankara*; *The Limits of Scripture: Vivekananda's Reinterpretation of the Authority of the Vedas*. His writings have also appeared in numerous scholarly journals. Rambachan has a special interest in interreligious dialogue and has been a participant in meetings sponsored by the World Council of Churches.

RAVI RAVINDRA is Professor and Chair of Comparative Religion and Adjunct Professor of Physics in Dalhousie University, Halifax, Canada. He is the author of many papers in Physics and Philosophy of Religion. His books include *Whispers from the Other Shore*; *Theory of Seismic Head Waves*; *The Yoga of the Christ*; *Science and Spirit*; and *Krishnamurthi: Two Birds on the Tree*. His article "Yoga: The Royal Path to Freedom" appeared in the first volume of *Hindu Spirituality*.

S. K. SAXENA teaches Philosophy of Religion and Philosophy of Art at the University of Delhi, India. He is one of India's leading authorities on Indian art and Western aesthetics. His publications include *Studies in the Metaphysics of Bradley*; *Aesthetical Essays: Studies in Aesthetic Theory, Hindustani Music and Kathak Dance*; *The Winged Form: Aesthetical Essays on Hindustani Music*; *Swinging Syllables: Aesthetics of Kathak Dance*; and *Ever unto God: Essays on Gandhi*.

NIKKY-GUNINDER KAUR SINGH is Associate Professor in the Department of Religious Studies at Colby College in Maine. She has published widely in the field of Indian religions. Her recent books include *The Feminine Principle in the Sikh Vision of the Transcendent* and *The Name of My Beloved: Translation of Verses of the Sikh Gurus*.

BRAJ M. SINHA is Professor and Head of the Department of Religious Studies, University of Saskatchewan, Canada. He received his Ph.D. from McMaster University, Canada, and a D.Litt. in Philosophy from Patna University, India. He has traveled extensively and lectured in India, Europe, Mexico, the United States, and Canada. He has authored and published scholarly works in the area of Hindu-Buddhist studies. The books he has edited include *Contemporary Essays on the Bhagavadgita* and *South India Horizons: Essays and Observations on India and Pakistan* (with S. Parvez Wakil). He is the author of *Time and Temporality in Sankhya-Yoga and Abhidharma Buddhism*.

P. T. SAROJA SUNDARARAJAN is Research Scientist in Humanities and Social Sciences, currently working at the University of Madras. She has a Ph.D. from the University of Poona, India. Sundararajan has been very active professionally and has authored two books, *Models and Conceptual Frame Works in the Philosophy of Social Sciences* and *Four Ways of Being a Woman* (with R. Sundara Rajan). Her articles have appeared in *Indian Philosophical Quarterly* and in the *Journal of Indian Council of Philosophical Research*. Sundararajan has published a monograph entitled *An Essay in the Tiruppavai*.

J. VALIAMANGALAM received a B.A. from Kerala University, an M.A. from Dharwar, an M.Phil. in Peace Studies from Gujarath Vidyapith, India, and a doctorate in Theology from Gregorian University, Rome. He was Professor of Bible at Thomas Seminary, Kottayam, India. He authored many books in Malayalam. Presently Valliamangalam is working in a village in Kerala.

R. VENUGOPAL studied at Loyola College, Madras, India, and received his bachelors degree and law degree from the University of Madras. He retired from Spencer and Company as its Vice-Chairman and Managing Director. Venugopal is a well-known musicologist and music composer in the tradition of carnatic music.

Photographic Credits

THE EDITOR AND PUBLISHER thank the custodians of the works of art for supplying photographs and granting permission to use them.

Page	
50	Bharat Kala Bhavan
89	French Institute of Pondicherry
89	French Institute of Pondicherry
163	Archaeological Survey of India
163	D. G. Archaeology in India
179	American Institute of Indian Studies
197	Archaeological Survey of India
197	Kyosuke Ito
215	American Institute of Indian Studies
286	Vedanta Society of St. Louis
305	Vedanta Society of St. Louis
327	Karish, Ottawa
346	David Miller
423	American Institute of Indian Studies
423	American Institute of Indian Studies
468	American Institute of Indian Studies
476	Kyosuke Ito

Index

Abhinavagupta, 4-19, 470
Abhishiktananda, 521
ādhāras, doctrine of the six, 242-43
adhyatma, xvi
Ādinātha, 235
advaita (nondualism), in Kashmir Śaivism, 3, 5
Advaita Vedānta, 452, 480
Āgamas. *See Śaivāgamas*
Agastya, the Sage, 235-36, 239
Agni, 421-22
ahiṁsā (nonviolence), Gandhian, xxx, 392, 407-17
  scriptural basis for, 407-11
  teachings on truth and, 411-17
ahiṁsā (nonviolence), traditional Indian, xxv, 392-406
  as a Hindu virtue, 400-401
  animal sacrifices and, 396-97, 406
  in the *Bhagavad Gītā*, 403-6
  compared with Greek virtues, 401-3
  and the concept of a just war, 404-5
  etymology of, 393-95
  as supreme *dharma*, 398-400
  Vedantic philosophy of, 395-98
ājā cakra, 491-92
Alcyone, 323
āḻvār, 97
Āḻvārs, xxi, 97, 129, 429, 452
Amar Das, Gurū, 533
āṇava, 12-13
Āṇḍāl, xxi-xxii, 97
  spiritual quest of, 127-38
Andrews, C. F., 512
anupāya, 17-19
  art, xxxiii, 459-73
  as a means of self-integration, 463-64
  as a means to liberation, 465
  the distinction between secular and religious, 465-66
  form, 466-67
  Indian spirituality and, 471-73
  the religious significance of representations, 469-71
  as sacrifice and yoga, 463-65
  and the theory of *rasa*, 469-70
Arutprakāsa Vaḷḷalār. See Rāmaliṅgar, Saint
asceticism, in Bengal Vaiṣṇavism, 58-59
Ashram movement of Christianity in India, 520-23
ātman, 30
Aurobindo, Śrī (Aurobindo Gohsay, 1872-1950), xxix-xxx, 370-91, 422, 512, 518